JEFFERSON DAVIS

JEFFERSON DAVIS

EX-PRESIDENT OF THE CONFEDERATE STATES
OF AMERICA

A MEMOIR

BY

HIS WIFE
VARINA DAVIS

VOL. II

The Nautical & Aviation Publishing Company of America

Baltimore, Maryland

Library of Congress Catalog Card Number: 90-6596

Printed in the United States of America

Photos on front and back of book: Courtesy of The Museum of the
Confederacy, Richmond, Virginia

Library of Congress Cataloging in Publication Data
Davis, Varina, 1826-1906.
    Jefferson Davis: ex-president of the Confederate States of
America: a memoir by his wife/Varina Davis; introduction by
Craig L. Symonds.
        p. cm.
    Originally published: New York: Belford Co., 1890.
    ISBN 1-877853-03-8 (pb: v. 1). — ISBN 1-877853-04-6 (pb: v.2).
— ISBN 1-877853-08-9 (pb: set). — ISBN 1-877853-06-2 (hb: v.1).
— ISBN 1-877853-07-0 (hb: v.2). — ISBN 1-877853-05-4 (hb: set)
    1. Davis, Jefferson, 1808-1889. 2. Presidents—Confederate
States of America—Biography. 3. Statesmen—United States—
Biography.
    4. Davis, Varina, 1826-1906. I. Title.
E467.1.D26D3   1990
973.7'13'092—dc20

                                                    90-6596
                                                    CIP

CONTENTS OF VOLUME II.

CHAPTER XXXVI.

CHAPTER XXXVII.

CHAPTER XXXVIII.

CHAPTER LIV.

CHAPTER LXXIV.

CHAPTER LXXV.

CHAPTER LXXVI.

CHAPTER LXXVII.

CHAPTER LXXVIII.

JEFFERSON DAVIS.

CHAPTER I.

FROM WASHINGTON TO MISSISSIPPI.

THE task of relating my husband's life in the Confederacy is approached with anxious diffidence, but it must be fairly set forth for his justification. I am unwilling needlessly to antagonize any part of the country, but love my own with devotion proportionate to the great sacrifices made in its behalf. The memories of the Confederacy, its triumphs, its decadence, and fall, are proud, and very bitter. If in dwelling upon the splendid gallantry of our soldiers, the cheerful endurance and unwonted labor of all classes of our women, or the barbarities practised upon us, both before and after the subjugation of our country, I speak plainly, it is because my memory furnishes data which the deliberate judgment of my old age does not contradict, and the anguish is a living pain which years have done little to soothe, and from which the desire for recrimination, or even for revenge, is totally absent.

One of the most patriotic, humane, and benevolent of men has been portrayed as a monster of ambition and cruelty, and the mistaken policy of silence under these accusations has fixed upon the minds of right and fair-minded opponents their belief in the truth of the allegations.   Here, before a jury of his peers and the world, I would present his case as he stated it, and with it contemporary testimony. This proof impartially weighed will show him to have honorably and religiously lived, and fearlessly died.   His services to his country were many and brilliant; to it he sacrificed his ambitions, his prosperity, his time, health, and happiness.   He gave his all—and since he enjoyed the love and confidence of eight millions of our own people, " verily great was his reward."

" During the interval," wrote Mr. Davis, " between the announcement by telegraph of the secession of Mississippi and the receipt of the official notification which enabled me to withdraw from the Senate, rumors were in circulation of a purpose, on the part of the United States Government, to arrest members of Congress preparing to leave Washington on account of the secession of the States which they represented. This threat received little attention from those most concerned. Indeed, it was thought that it might not be an undesirable mode of testing the question of the right of a State to withdraw from the Union." *

"No attempt was made, however, to arrest any of the retiring members ; and, after a delay of a few days, spent in necessary preparations, I left Washington for Mississippi, passing through Southwestern Virginia, East Tennessee, a small part of Georgia, and North Alabama. A deep interest in the events which had recently occurred was exhibited by the people of these States, and much anxiety was indicated as to the future. Many years of agitation had made them familiar with the ideas of separation. Nearly two generations had risen to manhood since it had begun to be

---

* Mr. Davis remained a week in Washington, hoping that he might be the person arrested. A part of this time he was ill and confined to his bed. To him came Commodore Shubrick, Captain Semmes, General Floyd, Colonel Chesnut, Senator Wigfall, C. C. Clay, and others too numerous to mention, as Southern men anxious about the fate of their country. I did not hear the conversations or know the purport of them from my husband, but was pained to see the deep depression under which he labored. The only time he ever seemed cheerful was when he spoke of his hope that the moderation of the President and his advisers would restrain the ardor of the anti-slavery men. "If they will give me time," he said, "all is not lost ; violence on one side and extreme measures of wrong on the other now, will dissolve the Union." And by telegrams and letters to every Southern State he endeavored to postpone their action.

discussed as a possible alternative. Few, very few, of the Southern people had ever regarded it as a desirable event, or otherwise than as a last resort for escape from evils more in- tolerable. It was a calamity which, however threatened, they still hoped might be averted, or indefinitely postponed, and they had re- garded with contempt, rather than anger, the ravings of a party in the North, which de- nounced the Constitution and the Union, and persistently defamed their brethren of the South.

" Now, however, as well in Virginia and Tennessee, neither of which had yet se- ceded, as in the more southern States which had already taken that step, the danger so often prophesied was perceived to be at the door, and eager inquiries were made as to what would happen next, especially as to the probability of war between the States.

" The course which events were likely to take was shrouded in the greatest uncertainty. In the minds of many there was not the un- reasonable hope (which had been expressed by the Commissioner sent from Mississippi to Maryland) that the secession of six Southern States—certainly soon to be followed by that of others, would so arouse the sober thought and better feeling of the Northern people as to compel their representatives to agree to a Convention of the States, and that such guarantees would be given as would secure to the South the domestic tranquillity and equality in the Union which were rights assured under the Federal compact. There were others, and they the most numerous class, ·who considered that the separation would be final, but peaceful. For my part, while believing that secession was a right, and, properly, a peaceable remedy, I had never believed that it would be permitted to be peaceably exercised. Very few in the South, at that time, agreed with me, and my answers to queries on the subject were, therefore, as unexpected as they were unwelcome."

To wrench oneself from the ties of fifteen years is a most distressing effort. Our friends had entered into our joys and sorrows with unfailing sympathy. We had shared their anxieties and seen their children grow from infancy to adolescence. To bid them farewell, perhaps to meet in the near future with a " great gulf between us," was, " death in life." Mr. Davis was resigning an office which, of all others, was the most congenial to his taste, and conducive to the increase of his reputation. He anticipated a long and exhausting war, and knew that his property in cotton planting would be utterly destroyed in

the course of the impending conflict. Deeply
depressed and supremely anxious, he made
his preparations to go home.

We left Washington " exceeding sorrowful," and took our three little children with
us. As we came into the Southern States the
people surrounded the train at every little
hamlet, and called Mr. Davis out. Wherever
we stayed long enough, he told them to prepare for a long and bloody war, and tried to
impress them with the gravity of the occasion. After many short speeches, he became
very much exhausted from the constant exertion. When the conductor noticed it he said,
" Never mind, when we stop at the next two
or three stations I will blow off steam at
' My friends and fellow-citizens,' and go off
at once ; " and so he did, much to the disgust
of the crowd.

We proceeded without accident until we
reached the Crutchfield House, at Chattanooga. There a crowd was gathered, among
whom was the cordial proprietor, the elder
Crutchfield. While the supper was being
prepared, a speech was called for. Mr.
Crutchfield's brother was a Union man, and
had been drinking. He began a violent tirade against Mr. Davis. He had twelve or
thirteen people with him who seemed to be
his companions in jollity, but who did not par-

take of his irritation. He offered to resent
personally anything Mr. Davis might say.
The excitement became intense. The office
was in one corner of a large, unfurnished
room. News of the disturbance was brought
to me, and I went into the room. The excitement was at its highest pitch. A rough
man sitting on a barrel said to a negro near
him, " Tell that lady she need not be uneasy,
Jeff Davis ain't afraid. He will make his
speech." Mr. Davis proceeded at once to
make the address for which the crowd called,
and his audience closed around him with expressions of affectionate respect. The dis-
turber of the peace was " hustled out." The
interruption lasted about ten minutes. Much
has been made of this scene, but it was merely the vagary of a drunken man, for which his
brother apologized.

As soon as we reached Mississippi, man
after man boarded the train and accompanied
us to Jackson, until nearly a brigade was on
the cars. The Governor and the State authorities met Mr. Davis informally, and went
with him to a boarding-house kept by an old
lady of wonderful acumen, named Dixon,
whose husband had been a member of Congress. She knew intimately every man of
prominence in the State, and had no little
political influence. We were rendered very

anxious by the accounts she gave of the state
of excitement pervading everyone; there was
no rest anywhere.

At Jackson, Mr. Davis found his commission from Governor I. I. Pettus, as Major-
General of the forces of Mississippi, dated
January 25, 1861. Then began the business
of making provisions for arms, and for the organization and discipline of the forces of Mississippi. Governor Pettus came to Mr. Davis
to consult about the purchase of arms. He
thought 75,000 stand would be sufficient.
Again Mr. Davis was very emphatic, saying, " The limit of our purchases should be
our power to pay. We shall need all and
many more than we can get, I fear." Governor Pettus, once or more during the conference, remarked, " General, you overrate
the risk."

There were hundreds coming to and fro
during the week of our stay, and on nearly
every occasion a warning was given to prepare, by rigid economy and by the establishment of such small factories as were practicable, to supply the domestic needs of those
who remained at home, and to take every
other means of making the South independent; for a great war was impending over
the country, "of which no man could foresee
the end."

Mr. Davis wrote thus of his arrival in Jackson :

" On my arrival at Jackson, the capital of Mississippi, I found that the Convention of the State had made provision for a State army, and had appointed me to the command, with the rank of Major-General. Four brigadier-generals, appointed in like manner by the Convention, were awaiting my arrival for assignment to duty. After the preparation of the necessary rules and regulations, the division of the State into districts, the apportionment among them of the troops to be raised, and the appointment of officers of the general staff, as authorized by the ordinance of the Convention, such measures as were practicable were taken to obtain necessary arms. The State had few serviceable weapons, and no establishment for their manufacture or repair. This fact (which is as true of other Southern States as of Mississippi) is a clear proof of the absence of any desire or expectation of war. If the purpose of the Northern States to make war upon us because of secession had been foreseen, preparations to meet the consequences would have been contemporaneous with the adoption of a resort to that remedy—a remedy the possibility of which had for many years been contemplated. Had the Southern States possessed

arsenals and collected in them the requisite
supplies of arms and ammunition, such preparations would not only have placed them
more nearly on an equality with the North in
the beginning of the war, but might, perhaps,
have been the best conservator of peace.

"Let us, the survivors, however, not fail to
do credit to the generous credulity which
could not understand how, in violation of the
compact of Union, a war could be waged
against the States, or why they should be invaded because their people had deemed it
necessary to withdraw from an association
which had failed to fulfil the ends for which
they had entered into it, and which, having
been broken to their injury by the other parties, had ceased to be binding upon them."

He was deeply distressed by the temper of
the people. Time and again, when visitors
left the room, Mr. Davis ejaculated, "God
help us, war is a dreadful calamity even when
it is made against aliens and strangers. They
know not what they do."

At the end of the week we returned to
Briarfield, and then my husband began to
make provisions for a long absence.

He advised with the older negroes about
the care of their families, urged them to look
after the old and helpless, and interrogated
old Bob, the oldest man on the place, as to

the comforts he thought he might need. I remember his study of the best rocking-chairs for Bob and his wife Rhinah. Mr. Davis bought him cochineal flannel for his rheumatism, and furnished an extraordinary number of blankets for the old couple.*

In one of his conversations with the more dependable of the men, he said : " You may have to defend your mistress and her children, and I feel I may trust you."

Mr. Davis was so careworn and unhappy that when we were alone it was piteous to see him. He never gave up the hope of an adjustment and a peaceful reunion with the North until the first blood was spilled. He slept little and talked nearly all night. In one of these conversations I asked the question, how he thought the contending sections could be pacified. He said " a guarantee of our equal rights would bring the whole country back to-morrow." He then spoke of a dual presidency, but did not think the scheme practicable. He said, " In any case, I think our slave property will be lost eventually," and then went on to speak of the cordon of custom-houses which would be needful, if a com-

---

* When the Federal soldiers took his furniture, flannel, and other comforts at the sacking of our plantation, they said, in answer to Bob's remonstrance, that they did not believe he had received so many things from us, he must have stolen them.

mercial treaty of free trade could not be made,
and of the immense standing army that would
necessarily deplete the resources of the country if the slaves were still to be kept in bond-
age. He went on to say that our swamp
lands, he feared, could not be cultivated by
white men. They were the most fertile lands
in the country, but they must, he feared, lie fal-
low. That rivers were bad boundaries, and
must necessarily constitute ours. He wound
up, generally, by saying, " Let us pray for
that peace on earth and good-will to men that
is needful for prosperity and happiness." This
expression is copied from one of his letters at
this time, and I heard the invocation many
times during and before the war.

We both congratulated ourselves that he
was to be in the field. I thought his genius
was military, but that, as a party manager, he
would not succeed. He did not know the
arts of the politician, and would not practise
them if understood, and he did know those
of war.

CHAPTER II.

THE Convention of the seceding States was held at Montgomery, Alabama, on February 4, 1861. It was composed of delegates legally appointed. Their first work was to prepare a provisional Constitution for the new Confederacy, to be formed of the States which had withdrawn from the Union, for which the style "Confederate States of America" was adopted. The powers conferred upon them were adequate for the performance of this duty, the immediate necessity for which was obvious and urgent. This Constitution was adopted on February 8th, to continue in force for one year, unless superseded at an earlier date by a permanent organization. It was modelled on the Constitution of the United States.

The Constitution was copied from the one the Confederates had just relinquished, to those who neither respected nor held its provisions sacred. Guided by experience, some stronger and more explicit clauses were interpolated. Instead of " We, the People of the

United States," etc., " We, the People of the
Confederate States, each State acting in its
sovereign and independent character, in order
to form a permanent Federal Government,"
was substituted. The old Constitution provided that " the Congress may at any time, by
law, make or alter such regulations," etc. ; but
the words which preceded this clause in the
Confederate Constitution are, " subject to the
provisions of this Constitution." Another
clause was added to the prohibition against
" Senators and Representatives holding any
other office until the term of their official position should have expired." But Congress
may, by law, grant to the principal officer in
each of the executive departments a seat
upon the floor of either House, with the privilege of discussing any measures appertaining to his Department." This provision was
intended, as in the case of the English houses
of Parliament, to bring the heads of departments in direct personal relations with the
Congress—and in their phrase, to " go to the
country " upon their policy, by resignation of
their offices.

A prohibition against a protective tariff was
enacted, by granting the power to levy duties " necessary for revenue." . . . " Nor
shall any duties or taxes on importations from
foreign nations be laid to promote or foster

any branch of industry; and all duties, im-
posts, and excises, shall be uniform throughout the Confederate States." Again, in the
clause regulating the commerce, discrimination between the States or Sections is provided against by the prohibition against internal improvements by the General Government. The two-thirds rule was insisted upon
in the appropriations of money. The African
Slave Trade was forbidden, and the introduction of slaves from without the Confederacy
was forbidden, except in the case of those
States which held slaves, and which were expected very soon to formally become members of the new Government, their citizens in
numbers having been already enrolled in the
Confederate army. They of course would
have the right to bring with them every species of property. The right of property in
negro slaves was reaffirmed, ·and provision
made against interference with it. Taxes
discriminating against any State must not be
laid, " except by a vote of two-thirds of both
houses."

The most careful precautions were taken
against the expenditure of public money except by the two-thirds rule, or by estimates
from the Executive branch approved by the
legislative branch of the Government, and the
claims against the Confederate States must

be heard and granted by a special tribunal created for the purpose by Congress.

No extra compensation was to be granted to any public contractor after the service rendered. No resolution or law should be voted upon in any other manner than separately and on its own merits.

" No State shall, without the consent of Congress, levy duties except on sea-going vessels, for the improvement of its rivers and harbors navigated by the said vessels; but such duties shall not conflict with any treaties of the Confederate States with foreign nations." The surplus revenue from these was to be " paid into the common treasury."

Rivers flowing between the boundaries of States were to be improved by mutual compacts.

The terms of President and Vice-president were limited to one term, and extended to election for six years.

The principal officers in the Executive Departments might be removed at the President's pleasure, as well as all other civil officers, but the reasons must be presented to the Senate and subject to their approval. No person rejected by the Senate shall be reappointed during the ensuing recess to the same office.

The rights of all the citizens of all the States were secured in any new territory to be acquired by the Confederate States by an express guarantee.

Any three States legally assembled could call a Constitutional Convention, and the Amendments to the Constitution should be concurred in by two-thirds of all the States voting by their legislatures.

The slave trade was "*hereby forbidden,*" positively and unconditionally, from the beginning. Neither the Confederate Government nor that of any of the States could permit it, and the Congress was expressly "required to enforce the prohibition." The only discretion in the matter entrusted to the Congress was whether or not to permit the introduction of slaves "from any of the United States or their Territories."

Mr. Davis regarded the Confederate Constitution as "a model of wise, temperate, and liberal statesmanship." He wrote :

"On the next day (February 9th) an election was held for the chief executive officers, resulting, as I afterward learned, in my election to the Presidency, with the Hon. Alexander H. Stephens, of Georgia, as Vice-President. Mr. Stephens was a delegate from Georgia to the Congress.

"While these events were occurring, having completed the most urgent of my duties at the capital of Mississippi, I had gone to my home,

Briarfield, in Warren County, and had begun, in the homely but expressive language of Mr. Clay, " to repair my fences." While thus engaged, notice was received of my election to the Presidency of the Confederate States, with an urgent request to proceed immediately to Montgomery for inauguration.

" As this had been suggested as a probable event, and what appeared to me adequate precautions had been taken to prevent it, I was surprised, and, still more, disappointed. For reasons which it is not now necessary to state, I had not believed myself as well suited to the office as some others. I thought myself better adapted to command in the field, and Mississippi had given me the position which I preferred to any other—the highest rank in her army. It was, therefore, that I afterward said, in an address delivered in the Capitol before the Legislature of the State, with reference to my election to the Presidency of the Confederacy, that the duty to which I was thus called was temporary, and that I expected soon to be with the Army of Mississippi again."

The messenger with the notification that Mr. Davis had been elected President, and Alexander H. Stephens Vice-president, of the Confederate States, found him in our garden assisting to make rose-cuttings ; when reading the telegram he looked so grieved that I feared some evil had befallen our family. After a few minutes' painful silence he told me, as a man might speak of a sentence of death. As he neither desired nor expected the position, he was more deeply depressed than before. He assembled his negroes and made them an affectionate farewell speech, to which they responded with expressions of devotion, and he left home next day for Montgomery.

CHAPTER III.

MR. DAVIS CONTINUES HIS NARRATIVE.

"WHILE on my way to Montgomery, and waiting in Jackson, Miss., for the railroad train, I met the Honorable William L. Sharkey, who had filled with great distinction the office of Chief-Justice of the State. He said he was looking for me to make an inquiry. He desired to know if it was true, as he had just learned, that I believed that there would be war. My opinion was freely given, that there would be war, long and bloody, and that it behooved everyone to put his house in order. He expressed much surprise, and said that he had not believed the report attributing this opinion to me. He asked how I supposed war could result from the peaceable withdrawal of a sovereign State. The answer was, that it was not my opinion that war should be occasioned by the exercise of that right, but that it would be.

"Judge Sharkey and I had not belonged to the same political party, he being a Whig, but we fully agreed with regard to the question of the sovereignty of the States. He had been an advocate of nullification, a doctrine to which I never assented, and which had at one time been the main issue in Mississippi politics. He had presided over the well-remembered Nashville Convention in 1849, and had possessed much influence in the State, not only as an eminent jurist, but as a citizen who had grown up with it, and held many offices of honor and trust.

"On my way to Montgomery, brief addresses were made at various places at which there were temporary stoppages of the train, in response to the calls from the crowds assembled at such points. Some of these addresses were grossly misrepresented in sensational reports, made by irresponsible parties, which were published in Northern newspapers, and were not considered worthy of correction under the pressure of the momentous duties then devolving upon me. These false reports, which represented me as invoking war and threatening devastation of the North, have since been adopted by partisan writers as authentic history. It is sufficient answer to these accusations to refer to my farewell address to the Senate, already given, as reported for the press at the time, and in connection therewith, to my inaugural address at Montgomery, on assuming the office of President of the Confederate States, February the 18th.

These two addresses, delivered at the interval of a month, during which no material change in circumstances had occurred, being one before and the other after the date of the sensational reports referred to, are sufficient to stamp them as utterly untrue. The inaugural was deliberately prepared and uttered as written, and, in connection with the farewell speech to the Senate, presents a clear and authentic statement of the principles and purposes which actuated me on assuming the duties of the high office to which I had been called."

An eye-witness wrote: " I have been honored with the friendship of the late President Davis since early in 1861. Of the voluntary escort which met him near the Georgia line and went with him to Montgomery when he first assumed the Chief Magistracy of the Confederacy, then consisting of seven States, I can recall but three who are now living—Alexander Walker, Thomas C. Howard, and myself.

" In those days there were no sleepers, and we secured a car which had been roughly fitted up for the use of Dr. Lewis, and which contained a comfortable bed. Soon after an introduction, we were at Ringgold about ten P.M., where bonfires were blazing and where he made a ringing speech, of which I remem-

ber the opening phrase: 'Countrymen, fellow-citizens, Georgians! I give your proud-
est title last,' etc. He went to sleep at once
without undressing, but at every station as
we came down the line he insisted upon responding to the greetings of the assembled
crowds, and always in fresh, eloquent language. In the morning, from the balcony of
the Trout House, he made a stirring address
to a crowd of some five thousand citizens,
which manifested an enthusiasm that I have
never seen equalled; and so all the way to
and in Montgomery similar scenes were repeated."

The President was met with acclamations
by the throng collected at Montgomery,
which, as will appear in a letter subjoined, only
depressed, while their enthusiasm gratified,
him, and in two days thereafter he was inaugurated, and delivered his address at the
Capitol at one o'clock on Monday, February
18, 1861.

*Inaugural Address of President Davis.**

" GENTLEMEN OF THE CONGRESS OF THE
CONFEDERATE STATES OF AMERICA—FRIENDS
AND FELLOW-CITIZENS : Called to the difficult
and responsible station of Chief Executive of

---

* Delivered at the Capitol, Montgomery, Ala., Monday, February
18, 1861, at 1 P.M.

the Provisional Government which you have
instituted, I approach the discharge of the
duties assigned to me with an humble distrust
of my abilities, but with a sustaining confidence in the wisdom of those who are to guide
and to aid me in the administration of public
affairs, and an abiding faith in the virtue and
patriotism of the people.

"Looking forward to the speedy establishment of a permanent Government to take the
place of this, and which by its greater moral
and physical power will be better able to combat with the many difficulties which arise
from the conflicting interests of separate nations, I enter upon the duties of the office, for
which I have been chosen, with the hope that
the beginning of our career, as a Confederacy,
may not be obstructed by hostile opposition
to our enjoyment of the separate existence
and independence which we have asserted,
and, with the blessing of Providence, intend to
maintain.

"Our present condition, achieved in a manner unprecedented in the history of nations, illustrates the American idea that governments
rest upon the consent of the governed, and
that it is the right of the people to alter or
abolish governments whenever they become
destructive to the ends for which they were
established.

" The declared purpose of the compact of
Union from which we have withdrawn was
' to establish justice, insure domestic tranquillity, provide for the common defence, promote the general welfare, and secure the
blessings of liberty to ourselves and posterity ; ' and when, in the judgment of the sovereign States now composing this Confederacy,
it had been perverted from the purposes for
which it was ordained, and had ceased to
answer the ends for which it was established,
a peaceful appeal to the ballot-box declared
that, so far as they were concerned, the government created by that compact should
cease to exist. In this they merely asserted
a right which the Declaration of Independence of 1776 had defined to be inalienable.
Of the time and occasion for this exercise
they, as sovereigns, were the final judges,
each for itself.

" The impartial and enlightened verdict of
mankind will vindicate the rectitude of our
conduct, and He who knows the hearts of
men will judge of the sincerity with which we
labored to preserve the government of our
fathers in its spirit. The right solemnly proclaimed at the birth of the States, and which
has been affirmed and reaffirmed in the Bills
of Rights of States subsequently admitted
into the Union of 1789, undeniably recog-

nizes in the people the power to resume the authority delegated for the purposes of government. Thus, the sovereign States, here represented, proceeded to form this Confederacy, and it is abuse of language that their act has been denominated a revolution. They formed a new alliance, but, within each State, its government has remained, and the rights of person and property have not been disturbed. The agent through whom they communicated with foreign nations is changed, but this does not necessarily interrupt their international relations.

" Sustained by the consciousness that the transition from the former Union to the present Confederacy has not proceeded from a disregard on our part of just obligations, or of any failure to perform any constitutional duty, moved by no interest or passion to invade the rights of others, anxious to cultivate peace and commerce with all nations, if we may not hope to avoid war we may at least expect that posterity will acquit us of having needlessly engaged in it. Doubly justified by the absence of wrong on our part, and by wanton aggression on the part of others, there can be no cause to doubt that the courage and patriotism of the people of the Confederate States will be found equal to any measure of defence which honor and security may require.

"An agricultural people—whose chief interest is the export of a commodity required in every manufacturing country, our true policy is peace, and the freest trade which our necessities will permit. It is alike our interest, and that of all those to whom we would sell, and from whom we would buy, that there should be the fewest practicable restrictions upon the interchange of commodities. There can be but little rivalry between ours and any manufacturing or navigating community, such as the Northeastern States of the American Union. It must follow, therefore, that a mutual interest would invite good and kind offices. If, however, passion or the lust of dominion should cloud the judgment or inflame the ambition of those States, we must prepare to meet the emergency and to maintain, by the final arbitrament of the sword, the position we have assumed among the nations of the earth. We have entered upon the career of independence, and it must be inflexibly pursued. Through many years of controversy with our late associates, the Northern States, we have vainly endeavored to secure tranquillity, and to obtain respect for the rights to which we are entitled. As a necessity, not a choice, we have resorted to

the remedy of separation; and henceforth
our energies must be directed to the conduct
our own affairs, and the perpetuity of the
Confederacy which we have formed. If a
just perception of mutual interest shall permit us, peaceably, to pursue our separate political career, my most earnest desire will
have been fulfilled. But if this be denied to
us, and the integrity of our territory and jurisdiction be assailed, it will but remain for us,
with firm resolve, to appeal to arms and invoke the blessings of Providence on a just
cause.

"As a consequence of our new condition,
and with a view to meet anticipated wants, it
will be necessary to provide for the speedy
and efficient organization of branches of the
Executive Department having special charge
of foreign intercourse, finance, military affairs,
and the postal service.

"For purposes of defence the Confederate
States may, under ordinary circumstances, rely mainly upon their militia ; but it is deemed
advisable, in the present condition of affairs,
that there should be a well-instructed and
disciplined army, more numerous than would
usually be required on a peace establishment.
I also suggest that for the protection of our
harbors and commerce on the high seas a
navy adapted to those objects will be re-

quired. These necessities have doubtless engaged the attention of Congress.

"With a Constitution differing only from
that of our fathers in so far as it is explana-
tory of their well-known intent, freed from
the sectional conflicts which have interfered
with the pursuit of the general welfare, it is
not unreasonable to expect that States from
which we have parted may seek to unite
their fortunes with ours under the Government which we have instituted. For this
your Constitution makes adequate provision ;
but beyond this, if I mistake not the judgment and will of the people, a reunion with
the States from which we have separated is
neither practicable nor desirable. To increase the power, develop the resources, and
promote the happiness of a Confederacy, it is
requisite that there should be so much of
homogeneity that the welfare of every portion should be the aim of the whole. Where
this does not exist antagonisms are engendered which must and should result in separation.

"Actuated solely by the desire to preserve
our own rights and promote our own welfare
the separation of the Confederate States has
been marked by no aggression upon others,
and followed by no domestic convulsion. Our
industrial pursuits have received no check,

the cultivation of our fields has progressed as heretofore, and even should we be involved in war, there would be no considerable diminution of the production of the staples which have constituted our exports, and in which the commercial world has an interest scarcely less than our own. This common interest of the producer and consumer can only be interrupted by an exterior force which would obstruct its transmission to foreign markets, a course of conduct which would be as unjust toward us as it would be detrimental to the manufacturing and commercial interests abroad. Should reason guide the action of the Government from which we have separated, a policy so detrimental to the civilized world, the Northern States included, could not be dictated by even the strongest desire to inflict injury upon us ; but, if otherwise, a terrible responsibility will rest upon it, and the sufferings of millions will bear testimony to the folly and wickedness of our aggressors. In the meantime there will remain to us, besides the ordinary means before suggested, the well-known resources for retaliation upon the resources of an enemy.

"Experience in public stations, of subordinate grade to this which your kindness has conferred, has taught me that care and toil and disappointment are the price of official elevation. You will see many errors to forgive, many deficiencies to tolerate, but you shall not find in me either a want of zeal or fidelity to the cause that is to me highest in hope and of most enduring affection. Your generosity has bestowed upon me an undeserved distinction, one which I neither sought nor desired. Upon the continuance of the sentiment, and upon your wisdom and patriotism, I rely to direct and support me in the performance of the duty required at my hands.

" We have changed the constituent parts, but not the system of our government. The Constitution formed by our fathers is that of these Confederate States, in their exposition of it; and in the judicial construction it has received we have a light which reveals its true meaning.

" Thus instructed as to the just interpretation of the instrument, and ever remembering that all offices are but trusts held for the people, and that delegated powers are to be strictly construed, I will hope, by due diligence in the performance of my duties, though I may disappoint your expectations, yet to retain, when retiring, something of the good-will and confidence which will welcome my entrance into office.

" It is joyous in the midst of perilous times

to look around upon a people united in heart;
where one purpose of high resolve animates
and actuates the whole ; where the sacrifices
to be made are not weighed in the balance
against honor, and right, and liberty, and
equality. Obstacles may retard, they cannot
long prevent, the progress of a movement
sanctified by its justice, and sustained by a
virtuous people. Reverently let us invoke the
God of our fathers to guide and protect us in
our efforts to perpetuate the principles, which
by his blessing they were able to vindicate,
establish, and transmit to their posterity, and
with a continuance of His favor, ever gratefully acknowledged, we may hopefully look
forward to success, to peace, and to prosperity."

The letter to me given below was the first
written from Montgomery, and shows none
of the elation of an ambitious, triumphant
conspirator, but rather bears the imprint of a
patriot's weight of care and sorrow.

"Montgomery, Ala., February 20, 1861.

"   .   .   .   I have been so crowded and
pressed that the first wish to write to you has
been thus long deferred.

"I was inaugurated on Monday, having
reached here on Saturday night. The au-

dience was large and brilliant. Upon my weary heart was showered smiles, plaudits, and flowers; but, beyond them, I saw troubles and thorns innumerable.

"We are without machinery, without means, and threatened by a powerful opposition; but I do not despond, and will not shrink from the task imposed upon me.

"All along the route, except when in Tennessee, the people at every station manifested good-will and approbation by bonfires at night, firing by day; shouts and salutations in both.

"I thought it would have gratified you to have witnessed it, and have been a memory to our children.

"Thus I constantly wish to have you all with me. . . . Here I was interrupted by the Secretary of the Congress, who brought me two bills to be approved. This is a gay and handsome town of some eight thousand inhabitants, and will not be an unpleasant residence. As soon as an hour is my own, I will look for a house and write to you more fully. . . ."

CHAPTER IV

GOING TO MONTGOMERY.—APPOINTMENT OF THE
CABINET.

IT was necessary to close up our home and
abandon all we had watched over for years,
before going to Montgomery; our library,
which was very large and consisted of fine
and well-chosen English books, was the
hardest to relinquish of all our possessions.
After all was secured, in the best manner
practicable, I went to New Orleans en route
to Montgomery, and remained a few days at
my father's house. While there, Captain
Dreux, at the head of his battalion, came to
serenade me, but I could not command my
voice to speak to him. when he came on the
balcony; his cheery words and the enthusiasm
of his men depressed me dreadfully. Vio-
lets were in season, and the captain and his
company brought several immense bouquets.
The color seemed ominous. Perhaps Mr.
Davis's depression had communicated itself
to me, and I could not rally or be buoyed up
by the cheerfulness of those who were to do
battle for us. The *morituri te salutant* always
greeted me as our men entered the arena.

Captain Dreux was of the French type of soldier, not quite of the average size, with flashing eyes, and an exceedingly pleasant address. His blood was the first spilled on the Peninsula, near Yorktown. In the ardor of his attack he exposed himself too soon and fell mortally wounded. His body was brought back to Richmond, and I looked upon his face a second time, calm in death ; for him all problems were solved and the smile of his first youth had settled upon the rigid features. If a soldier must fall in battle, it is not the worst fate to be the first to seal his faith with his blood, his comrades have time to miss and deplore him. My journey up the Alabama River to join Mr. Davis in Montgomery was a very sad one, sharing his apprehensions, and knowing our needs to be so many, with so little hope of supplying them.

The young men who came to tell me of the " general's sash " they hoped to win ; the old men who spoke of the " soldiering," as an unlooked for circumstance, depressed me still more. No one was bitter, but each thought he had a perfect right to secede and " did not mind Mr. Davis being a *little slow.*" A secession man said, " We see that he thinks we ought to assert our rights, but we began to fear that he had stayed too long up there with the Yankees." A Mississippi man an-

swered this remark with flushing face by saying, " Remember Mexico, sir, remember Mexico ; " which silenced the joker.

When we reached the hotel where the
President was temporarily lodged, the Provisional Congress had assembled, he had
been inaugurated, and the day of my arrival
the Confederate flag had been hoisted by the
daughter of Colonel Robert Tyler, and the
grand-daughter of the ex-President. The
family were at that time living in Montgomery. Mr. Davis was very averse to re-
linquishing the old flag, and insisted that a
different battle-flag would make distinction
enough between the combatants ; but he was
overruled and a new one substituted, with a
blue union containing the stars in white at
equal distances ; the flag had one broad white
and two red stripes the same width. Under
it we won our victories, and the memory of
its glory will never fade. It is enshrined
with the extinct Confederation in our hearts
forever.

The town swarmed with men desiring and
receiving commissions. Statesmen, lawyers,
congressmen, planters, merchants pressed
forward ardently to fulfil their part in the
struggle. The Hon. William C. Rives, of
Virginia, Pierce Butler, T. Butler King,
William L. Yancey, James M. Mason, R. M.

T. Hunter, John S. Preston, of Virginia, William Preston, of Kentucky, F. S. Bartow, of Georgia, J. P. Mallory and Steven Mallory, the Hon. James Chesnut, of South Carolina, and thousands of others. Dr. Russell, a very storm-bird of battles, the correspondent of the London *Times*, came to see and report.

Very few battled for rank ; they were there for service ; and the majority simply gave their names ; if they had previously held rank in the army or navy they mentioned the grade, and left the authorities to define their position in the Confederate army.

The house chosen for us was a gentleman's residence, roomy enough for our purposes, on the corner of a street and looking toward the State Capitol. There were many charming people there, who were all intent on kind services to us ; our memory of Montgomery was one of affectionate welcome, and if we should have judged from the hampers of blossoms poured out before us, it was a flowery kingdom.

The members of the Cabinet were chosen not from the intimate friends of the President, but from the men preferred by the States they represented ; but it would have been difficult to find more honest, capable, fearless men than they were. They established themselves as best they could in boarding-houses and hotels, until more leisure would enable them to choose fitting habitations.

Mr. Davis wrote of the formation of his Cabinet thus:

"Unencumbered by any other considera· tion than the public welfare, having no friends to reward or enemies to punish, it resulted that not one of those who formed my first Cabinet had borne to me the relation of close personal friendship, or had political claims upon me; indeed, with two of them I had no previous acquaintance."

Mr. Davis wished very much to appoint the Honorable Robert Barnwell to be Secretary of State, on account of the great confidence he felt in him and of his affection for him; but Mr. Memminger, of South Carolina, was pressed for Secretary of the Treasury. Mr. Barnwell therefore declined the portfolio of State.   Mr. Memminger's portfolio had been intended for Mr. Toombs, of Georgia. Mr. Mallory had been chairman of the Naval Committee in the Senate, and was urged for Secretary of the Navy.

Mr. Benjamin's legal attainments caused him to be invited to be Attorney-General. Mr. Reagan was appointed Postmaster-General because of his sturdy honesty, his capacity for labor, and his acquaintance with the territory of the Southern States.   Mr. Leroy

R. TOOMBS.

J.P.BENJAMIN.

T. BRAGG.

J.H. REAGAN.

T.H.WATTS.

G. TRENHOLM.

C.C. MEMMINGER.

CABINET OF THE CONFEDERACY.

Pope Walker's name was the only one urged by Alabama for the War Department.

The Confederate Congress declared that the laws of the United States in force and use in the Confederate States of America on November 1st were continued, until repealed by Congress. The collectors and assistant treasurers were also continued in their offices.

The Provisional Government recommended that immediate steps be taken to adjust the claims of the United States Government on the public property, to apportion the assumption of the common debt and all other disputed points " upon principles of right, justice, equity, and good faith."

They passed a resolution on February 15th, before the President's arrival at Montgomery, that a commission of three persons should be appointed by him as early as possible to be sent to the Government of the United States, for the purpose of negotiating friendly relations between the two governments.

The known courage, inflexible principle, self-denial, and devotion to duty of the President had been personally observed by the men of the Provisional Congress in the body from which they had just seceded, where the majority of its members had served with him in the United States Congress for years. With many of them he held relations of per-

sonal friendship, and the Executive and Legislative branches of the Government were in
that close accord which seemed to promise
the utmost efficiency for each.

Mr. Davis went to his office before nine
o'clock and came home at six, exhausted and
silent, but he was so gentle and patient that
Pierce Butler, who was our guest at this time,
asked me jestingly, if he was always a "combination of angel and seer like that." He
slept little and ate less, but seemed to derive
great comfort from the certainty that the Provisional Congress had a thorough co-intelligence with him, and would heartily co-operate with the Executive in all essentials.

Now began in earnest the business of per-
petuating the old Government under which
the rights of the minority had been for fifty
years fully protected, but against which a revolution had prevailed. Every change in the
Constitution was jealously avoided. New
and more express guarantees for the old liberty were sought to be enacted, so that no
future majority could have color of pretext for
overriding another minority, which might be
evolved in the future out of the divergent interests of the Confederate States.

MADISON HOUSE.

CHAPTER V.

THE OFFICE WAS NOT SOUGHT.

ONE of the most popular political maxims of the country, a maxim more honored in the breach than the observance, is that "the office should seek the man, not the man the office." This maxim was rigidly observed by my husband from the beginning to the end of his long public career. He never intrigued for any of the public positions he held, either in person or by authorized representatives. An active and zealous participant in all political contests, he never made a canvass for himself, excepting during one Presidential campaign, when a candidate on the list of Presidential electors—a vote for which was a vote not for the men on the ticket but for Mr. Polk, the Democratic candidate for President of the United States.

After defeat had settled on our cause, some malcontents stated publicly that Mr. Davis had been a candidate for the Presidency of the Confederate States, and that his election to that position was the result of a misunderstanding or of accidental complications ; that

he held " extreme views," and had, at that
period, "an inadequate conception of the
magnitude of the war probably to be waged."

These expressions called out prompt contradiction from several eminent Confederates
who had personal knowledge of the facts.
As some of these misrepresentations have
found their way into books that may be quoted
as authorities when the present survivors of
the war are no longer here to refute them, I
deem it proper to refer to this evidence, volunteered at a time when the events were fresh
in the memories of their contemporaries.
The Honorable J. A. P. Campbell, of Mississippi, afterward Justice of the Supreme
Court of that State, wrote in 1870:

" If there was a delegate from Mississippi,
or any other State, who was opposed to the
election of Jefferson Davis as President of
the Confederate States, I never heard of the
fact.   No other man was spoken of for President in my hearing.   It is within my personal knowledge that the statement ' that
Mr. Davis did not have a just appreciation of
the serious character of the contest between
the seceding States and the Union ' is wholly
untrue.   Mr. Davis, more than any man I
ever heard talk on the subject, had a correct
apprehension of the consequences of secession, and of the magnitude of the war to be

waged to coerce the seceding States. While at Montgomery, he expressed the belief that heavy fighting must occur, and that Virginia was to be the chief battle-ground. Years prior to secession, in his address before the Legislature and people of Mississippi, Mr. Davis had earnestly advised extensive preparation for the possible contingency of secession.

"After the formation of the Confederate States, he was far in advance of the Constitutional Convention and the Provisional Congress, and, as I believe, of any man in it, in his views of the gravity of the situation and the probable extent and duration of the war, and of the provision that should be made for the defence of the seceding States. Before secession, Mr. Davis thought war would result from it; and after secession he expressed the view that the war then commenced would be an extensive one.

"The idea that Mr. Davis was so 'extreme' in his views, is a new one. He was extremely conservative on the subject of secession.

"The suggestion that Mississippi would have preferred General Toombs or Mr. Cobb for President has no foundation in fact. My opinion is that no man could have obtained a single vote in the Mississippi delegation

against Mr. Davis, who was then, as he is
now, the most eminent and popular of all the
citizens of Mississippi."

" The late Duncan F. Kenner, of Louisiana,
formerly a member both of the Federal and
Confederate Congress, wrote : " My recollections of what transpired at the time are
very vivid and positive.

" Who should be President? was the absorbing question of the day. It engaged the
attention of all present, and elicited many letters from our respective constituencies. The
general inclination was strongly in favor of
Mr. Davis—in fact no other name was so prom-
inently or so generally mentioned. Next to
Mr. Davis the name of Mr. Rhett, of South
Carolina, was probably more frequently mentioned than that of any other person.

" The rule adopted at our election was that
each State should have one vote, to be delivered in open session, *viva voce*, by one of
the delegates as spokesman for his colleagues.
The delegates of the different States met in
secret session to select their candidate and
spokesman.

" Of what occurred in these various meetings I cannot speak authoritatively as to
other States, as their proceedings were considered secret. I can speak positively, however, of what took place at a meeting of the

delegates from Louisiana. We, the Louisiana delegates, without hesitation, and unan-
imously, after a very short session, decided in
favor of Mr. Davis. No other name was
mentioned. The claims of no one else were
considered, or even alluded to. There was
not the slighest opposition to Mr. Davis on
the part of any of our delegation; certainly
none was expressed; all appeared enthusiastic
in his favor; and, I have no reason to doubt,
felt so. Nor was the feeling induced by any
solicitation on the part of Mr. Davis or his
friends. Mr. Davis was not in or near Montgomery at the time. He was never heard
from on the subject, as far as I knew. He was
never announced as a candidate. We were
seeking the best man to fill the position, and
the conviction at the time, in the minds of a
large majority of the delegates, that Mr. Davis
was the best qualified, both from his civil and
military knowledge and experience, induced
many to look upon him as the best selection
that could be made.

" This conviction, coupled with his well-re-
cognized conservative views—for in no sense
did we consider Mr. Davis extreme in either
his views or purposes—was the deciding consideration which controlled the votes of the
Louisiana delegation."

The Honorable James Chesnut, of South

Carolina wrote: "Mr. Davis, then conspicuous for his ability, had long experience in the United States Senate in civil service, was reputed a most successful organizer and administrator of the military department of the United States when he was Secretary of War, and came out of the Mexican War with much *éclat* as a soldier. Possessing a combination of these high and needful qualities, he was regarded by nearly the whole South as the fittest man for the position. I certainly so regarded him."

Honorable W. Porcher Miles, of Virginia, formerly of South Carolina, and a member of the Provisional Congress of 1861, wrote: "To the best of my recollection there was entire unanimity in the South Carolina delegation at Montgomery on the subject of the choice of a President. I think there was no question that Mr. Davis was the choice of our delegation and of the whole people of South Carolina."

Thus Mr. Davis came to be the commander-in-chief of a country not yet torn loose from the clinging memories of a common glory, and which he would gladly, had it been in his power, have merged in the United States, even on the day of his election, could he have offered any guarantee to the Southern people for the exercise of their unalienable rights and the security of their lives and property.

He approached the task of creating a nation with a longing beyond expression to have his extended hand of fellowship grasped by that of the North before blood had been spilled, and with many humble petitions to Almighty God for guidance and support.

CHAPTER VI.

PEACE PROPOSITIONS.

THE Provisional Congress, before the arrival of Mr. Davis, passed a law that the Government should immediately take steps to settle everything appertaining to the common property, debts, and common obligations of the late Union upon " principles of right, justice, equity, and good faith." On February 15th Congress also advised and ordained that three persons be appointed as early as the President conveniently could, and sent to the Government of the United States, to " negotiate friendly relations."

As the minds of the Western people had been much excited about the free navigation of the Mississippi River and its tributaries, on February 25, 1861, an act was passed " to declare and establish free navigation of the Mississippi River without any duty or hinderance except light-money, pilotage, and other like charges."

"All laws imposing discriminating duties on foreign vessels or goods imported in them were rejected." The hope cherished by the

Congress that peace would be maintained inclined them rather to overstep the bounds of duty to their own country, and grant privileges greater than those considered due to any other nation. The President hoped for reunion, with guarantees against aggression by the stronger section of the much-beloved Union.

Within a week after his inauguration, on February 25, 1861, Peace Commissioners were appointed, and on the same day Messrs. A. B. Roman, of Louisiana, Martin J. Crawford, of Georgia, and John B. Forsyth, of Alabama, were confirmed by Congress. The politics of these Commissioners represented strangely the three phases of opinion which most generally prevailed in the United States when the difference arose between the States. Judge Roman had been a Whig, Mr. Crawford a States Rights Democrat, and Mr. Forsyth a zealous Douglas man. No secret instructions were given. Their own convictions and honest and peaceful purpose were to be their guide.

In the meanwhile Virginia, through the General Assembly, on January 19, 1861, adopted a series of resolutions deprecating disunion and inviting all States that were moved by a like desire to appoint Commissioners to unite with her. Ex-President John

Tyler, Messrs. William C. Rives, John W.
Brockenbrugh, George W. Summers, and
James A. Seddon, "five of the most distinguished citizens of the State, were appointed
to represent Virginia in the proposed conference." If any agreement could be made
they were to report to the Confederate Congress for ratification by each State severally.

The border States acceded and others followed. Twenty-one States were represented. They met, debated, made propositions
and counter-propositions, and adjourned February 27th. Texas and Arkansas were not
of the number, because they were at that
time passing ordinances of secession. Michigan, Wisconsin, Minnesota, and the two Pacific States — Oregon and California — held
aloof. The two senators from Michigan opposed the Peace Convention, as was afterward
learned from a correspondence read in the
Senate on February 27th, because it would
be "a step toward obtaining that concession
which the imperious slave power so insolently
demands."* Finally the writer changed his
policy and recommended that "true, unflinch-
ing men" be sent, who would be "in favor of
the Constitution as it is," or, in other phrase,

---

* See letter of S. K. Bingham to Governor Blair of Michigan,
Congressional Globe, Second Session, 36th Congress, Part II., page
1147.

oppose any effort at pacification of the contending parties. The other Senator wanted
" stiff-backed " delegates, and added that
" without a little blood-letting " the Union
would not be " worth a rush."

Mr. Z. Chandler wrote that Governor
Bingham telegraphed him, at the request of
Massachusetts and New York, to send " delegates to the Peace or Compromise Congress.
Ohio, Indiana, and Rhode Island are coming
in, and there is danger of Illinois ; and now
they beg us, for God's sake, to come to their
rescue, and save the Republican party from
rupture." *

A plan was finally agreed upon by the majority of the States present. Its provisions
were nearly like the resolutions of Mr. Crittenden, which were still under consideration
in the Senate, though rather less favorable to
the South. But the extreme Radicals objected even to considering it ; they failed to
prevent its being debated, but, both Mr.
Crittenden's resolutions and the plan of the
Peace Conference, were defeated on a vote,
and so these efforts at pacification came to
naught, except that the fierce pulse-beat of
the aggressive North was felt.

Mr. Lincoln came into office, elected by a

---

* See the Congressional Globe, *ut supra.*

sectional party ; very soon after he took the
oath to administer impartial justice. There
were not wanting men of all parties in the
North who boldly adhered to the provisions
of the Constitution, notably the New York
Tribune, the Albany *Argus*, the New York
Herald, and others.

A great meeting was held in New York,
January 31, 1861, where Governor Seymour
asked the pertinent question, "If successful
coercion by the North is less revolutionary
than successful secession by the South?"
The *Detroit Free Press* suggested that a fire
would be opened on the rear of troops raised
to coerce a State. The *Union* of Bangor,
Me., spoke much to the same effect, and even
Mr. Lincoln did not care to advocate coercion in his inaugural. "Something new and
strange" was making its home among us,
and freemen had not yet learned its name or
determined to bid it welcome. Mr. Lincoln
deemed it better to forego filling the offices
in the South, because it would be "irritating,
and so nearly impracticable withal."

Thus far the conservative men of the North,
who, though they differed from the Confederates, mingled no fanaticism with the di-
vergence of policies, were making strenuous
efforts to stay the ill-advised policy of coercion. In the United States Senate Stephen

A. Douglas offered a resolution recommending the "withdrawal of the garrisons from all forts within the limits of the States which had seceded, except those at Key West and the Dry Tortugas, needful to the United States for coaling stations." He said unless we intended to reduce the seceding States to subjection, that Sumter must revert to the power that should hold Charleston. Pensacola was entitled to Fort Pickens. "I proclaim boldly," said the eloquent Senator, "the policy of those with whom I act. We are for peace."

Mr. Douglas knew that the occupation of the fort was a standing menace and provocation to the people of the South.

The Southern people had never as yet given up the hope that the better feelings of the masses at the North would assert themselves, and constantly the expression was heard, "Secession was a last resort; would to God it could yet be prevented." The Southern people did not believe that the rank and file of the North desired to oppress them, or forcibly seize their property and destroy their prosperity. But the Republicans, excited by the sound of their own threats, became more and more intolerant and overbearing. Mr. Clarke, of New Hampshire, announced in his place that amendments to

the Constitution were not needful—what was
required was obedience to its provisions, not
amendments to it, and advised a rigorous en-
forcement of the law.

His resolutions passed both houses of Congress without demurrers from the Southern
members. The Republicans refused all suggestions for compromise, and ignored the
right of the South to property in slaves, or
their rights in the Territories.

The most notable of these projects for
pacification was the series of resolutions offered by Mr. Crittenden, of Kentucky, which
soon came to be known as the " Crittenden
Compromise."

" They proposed to amend the Constitution
by introducing articles declaring that south of
a given latitude neither Congress nor any
electoral legislature should have power to
abolish, modify, nor interfere with slavery in
the Territories ; that Congress should have
no power to abolish slavery in the District
of Columbia, or wherever else the Federal
Government had exclusive jurisdiction ; and,
finally, by an amendment providing that in
case of failure, from violence to the officer of
the law, to arrest any fugitive from labor,
the community where such failure took place
should be compelled to pay the value of such
alleged fugitive to the owner thereof, and may

be prosecuted for that purpose or to that effect." " The adoption of this compromise in the existing state of affairs was the last hope of saving the Union ; but the North rejected it, and even refused to entertain a series of propositions still less favorable to the South that were offered by Mr. Etheridge."

The Confederate Commissioners had been sent to Washington. Mr. Crawford left Montgomery on February 27th, and reached there two or three days before the expiration of Mr. Buchanan's term. He bore a letter to the President from Mr. Davis. Mr. Buchanan had sent an intimation that he would be happy to receive Commissioners from the Confederate States, and would refer their communications to the Senate. Mr. Crawford found Washington in a state of great excitement, and an army of office-seekers blocking the pavement in order to interview the President-elect — Mr. Lincoln. Care and foreboding sat upon every brow in Congress. Mr. Buchanan " was in a state of most thorough alarm, not only for his home at Wheatland, but for his personal safety." He had previously expressed to Mr. Davis his fear of his homeward route being lighted by burning effigies of himself. Actuated by this dread, he refused to receive the Commissioners or send any message to the Senate.

Eight days after the inauguration of Mr. Lincoln the Commissioners announced their presence and object.

The most concise account is found in a message of the Confederate President, sent April 29, 1861.

" . . . Scarce had you assembled in February last, when, prior even to the inauguration of the Chief Magistrate, you had elected, you expressed your desire for the appointment of Commissioners, and for the settlement of all questions of disagreement between the two Governments upon principles of right, equity, and good faith.

" It was my pleasure, as well as my duty, to co-operate with you in this work of peace. Indeed, in my address to you, on taking the oath of office before receiving from you the communication of this resolution, I had said that, as a necessity, not as a choice, we have resorted to the remedy of separating, and henceforth our energies must be directed to the conduct of our own affairs, and the perpetuity of the Confederacy which we have formed. If a just perception of mutual interest shall permit us to peaceably pursue our separate political career, my most earnest desire will then have been fulfilled.

" It was in furtherance of these accordant views of the Congress and the Executive that I made choice of three discreet, able, and distinguished citizens, who repaired to Washington. Aided by their cordial co-operation and that of the Secretary of State, every effort compatible with self-respect and the dignity of the Confederacy was exhausted, before I allowed myself to yield to the conviction that the Government of the United States was determined to attempt the conquest of this people, and that our cherished hopes of peace were unobtainable.

" On the arrival of our Commissioners in Washington, on March 5th, they postponed, at the suggestion of a friendly intermediator, doing more than giving informal notice of their arrival. This was done with a view to afford time to the President of the United States, who had just been inaugurated, for the discharge of other pressing official duties in the organization of his administration, before engaging his attention to the object of their mission.

" It was not until the twelfth of the month that they officially addressed the Secretary of State, informing him of the purpose of their arrival, and stating, in the language of their instructions, their wish to make to the Government of the United States overtures for the opening of negotiations, assuring the Government of the United States that the

President, Congress, and people of the Confederate States desired a peaceful solution of
these great questions; that it was neither
their interest nor their wish to make any demand which was not founded on the strictest
principles of justice, nor to do any act to injure their late confederates.

" To this communication no formal reply
was received until April 8th. During the interval the Commissioners had consented to
waive all questions of form, with the firm resolve to avoid war, if possible. They went
so far even as to hold, during that long period,
unofficial intercourse through an intermediary,
whose high position and character inspired
the hope of success, and through whom constant assurances were received from the Government of the United States of its peaceful
intentions, of its determination to evacuate
Fort Sumter; and, further, that no measure
would be introduced, changing the existing
status, prejudicial to the Confederate States;
that, in event of any change in regard to Fort
Pickens, notice would be given to the Commissioners.

" The crooked path of diplomacy can
scarcely furnish an example so wanting in
courtesy, in candor, and directness as was
the course of the United States Government
toward our Commissioners in Washington.

For proof of this I refer to the annexed documents, taken in connection with further facts, which I now proceed to relate.

"Early in April the attention of the whole country was attracted to extraordinary preparations, in New York and other Northern ports, for an extensive military and naval expedition. These preparations were commenced in secrecy for an expedition whose destination was concealed, and only became known when nearly completed; and on the 5th, 6th, and 7th of April, transports and vessels of war, with troops, munitions, and military supplies, sailed from Northern ports, bound southward.

"Alarmed by so extraordinary a demonstration, the Commissioners requested the delivery of an answer to their official communication of March 12th, and the reply, dated on the 15th of the previous month was obtained, from which it appears that, during the whole interval, while the Commissioners were receiving assurances calculated to inspire hope of the success of their mission, the Secretary of State and the President of the United States had already determined to hold no intercourse with them whatever, to refuse even to listen to any proposals they had to make; and had profited by the delay created by their own assurances, in order to prepare secretly the means for effective hostile operations."

About this time a letter was written by Major Anderson as noble as it was unselfish.

"FORT SUMTER, S. C., April 8, 1861.

" To COLONEL L. THOMAS, Adjutant-General, United States Army.

" COLONEL : I have the honor to report that the resumption of work yesterday (Sunday) at various points on Morris Island, and the vigorous prosecution of it this morning, apparently strengthening all the batteries which are under the fire of our guns, shows that they either have just received some news from Washington which has put them on the *qui vive*, or that they have received orders from Montgomery to commence operations here. I am preparing, by the side of my barbette guns, protection for our men from the shells which will be almost continually bursting over or in our works.

" I had the honor to receive by yesterday's mail the letter of the Honorable Secretary of War, dated April 4th, and confess that what he there states surprises me greatly— following, as it does, and contradicting so positively, the assurance Mr. Crawford telegraphed he was 'authorized' to make. I

trust that this matter will be at once put in a
correct light, as a movement made now, when
the South has been informed that none such
would be attempted, would produce most
disastrous results throughout our country.
It is, of course, now too late for me to give
any advice in reference to the proposed
scheme of Captain Fox. I fear that its result cannot fail to be disastrous to all concerned. Even with his boat at our walls, the
loss of life (as I think I mentioned to Mr.
Fox) in unloading her will more than pay for
the good to be accomplished by the expedition, which keeps us, if I can maintain possession of this work, out of position, surrounded by strong works which must be
carried to make this fort of the least value to
the United States Government.

"We have not oil enough to keep a light
in the lantern for one night. The boats will
have to, therefore, rely at night entirely upon
other marks. I ought to have been informed
that this expedition was to come. Colonel
Lamon's remark convinced me that the idea,
merely hinted at to me by Colonel Fox, would
not be carried out.

"We shall strive to do our duty, though I
frankly say that my heart is not in this war,
which I see is to be thus commenced. That
God will still avert it, and cause us to resort

to pacific means to maintain our rights, is my ardent prayer.

"I am, Colonel, very respectfully,
"Your obedient servant,
"ROBERT ANDERSON,
"*Major, First Artillery,* commanding."

The Count of Paris libels the memory of Major Anderson, and perverts the truth of history in this, as he has done in other particulars, by saying, with reference to the visit of Captain Fox to the Fort, that, "having visited Anderson at Fort Sumter, a plan had been agreed upon between them for revictualling the garrison" ("Civil War in America," authorized translation, vol. I., p. 137). Fox himself says, in his published letter, "I made no arrangements with Major Anderson for supplying the fort, nor did I inform him of my plan;" and Major Anderson, in the letter above, says the idea had been "merely hinted at" by Captain Fox, and that Colonel Lamon had led him to believe that it had been abandoned.

When General Beauregard discovered that Major Anderson was endeavoring to strengthen, in place of evacuating, Fort Sumter, the Commissioners wrote an interrogatory note to discover the facts, and were assured by Mr. Seward that the Government had not receded from his promise. On April 7th, Mr. Seward sent the message, "Faith as to Sumter fully kept; wait and see." On that day the Federal fleet with a large force sailed for Sumter, and the Commissioners left Washington, hopeless of accomplishing anything.

"That these assurances were given has been virtually confessed by the Government of the United States, by its act of sending a messenger to Charleston to give notice of its purpose to use force, if opposed, in its intention of supplying Fort Sumter."*

"No more striking proof of the absence of good faith in the conduct of the Government of the United States toward the Confederacy can be required than is contained in the circumstances which accompanied this notice.

"According to the usual course of navigation, the vessels composing the expedition, and designed for the relief of Fort Sumter, might be looked for in Charleston harbor on April 9th. Yet our Commissioners in Washington were detained under assurances that notice should be given of any military movement. The notice was not addressed to them, but a messenger was sent to Charleston to give notice to the Governor of South

---

*See Rise and Fall of the Confederacy, Appendix L, p. 675, vol. i.

Carolina, and the notice was so given at a late hour on April 8th, the eve of the very day on which the fleet might be expected to arrive.

" That this manœuvre failed in its purpose was not the fault of those who controlled it. A heavy tempest delayed the arrival of the expedition and gave time to the commander of our forces at Charleston to ask and receive instructions of the Government." . . .

CHAPTER VII.

PREPARATIONS FOR WAR.

THE troops received were tendered by independent organizations, " or who may volunteer by consent of their State " for twelve months, unless sooner discharged. There was a strong disinclination to a longer term being prescribed. The arms and munitions within the limits of the States were their property, they were received with their State organization, and officered by the State, and on March 16th, the States were recommended to cede the forts, arsenals, navy and dock yards, and all other public establishments to the Confederate States. May 6, 1861, the army of the Confederate States was lawfully established in contra-distinction to the Provisional army.

The relative rank of the officers of the Confederate States was regulated by the position that they had previously held in the United States army, or to which they had been elected or appointed in their State. The right of the States to confer the grade of colonel was secured ; a higher grade might be by selection.

The three highest officers of the Confederate army, " whose fame stands unchallenged either for efficiency or zeal," were all so indifferent to any question of personal interest that they had received their appointment before they were aware it was to be conferred. The order of their rank was : General Samuel Cooper, Albert Sidney Johnston, and Robert E. Lee. When General A. S. Johnston was assigned to the West, he for the first time asked and learned what relative position he would serve. General Lee, in like manner, when he was assigned to duty beyond the limits of Virginia, learned for the first time his increased rank. Brevet Lieutenant-Colonel A. C. Meyers was appointed Quartermaster-General ; Captain L. B. Northrop was appointed to command the Subsistence Department. He made no memoir of his service, and Mr. Davis could not notice it *in extenso*. Surgeon-General Moore, from the Materia Medica of the South, supplemented the lack of drugs made contraband of war, and by the aid of his own ingenuity and that of his corps, supplied the surgical instruments, which were unfortunately scarce and especially needful for the hospitals in the field.

General Gorgas was appointed Chief of Ordnance, and if space were permitted to particularize the incalculable service he rendered, the offering would be gladly made to the memory of one who was as unpretending as he was useful and devoted to the cause.

Captain Semmes was sent to the North to buy guns and all the available arms in the market, and also to get machinery and artisans for Government arsenals and shops; he ably performed the service, but the intervention of the civil authorities prevented the delivery of the arms and machinery. He was also directed to buy vessels suitable for defensive and offensive use, but unfortunately could find none. Major Huse was sent to Europe, on the *third day after Mr. Davis's inauguration*, to buy arms there. He found few serviceable arms on the market, but made such extensive contracts that, to bring them through the blockade, was after this the only difficulty encountered.

In the shop of the Government gun repairers was a musket from the Tower of London, made in 1762; it might have been fired in the Revolutionary war of 1776, taken part in the Indian wars, in the war of 1812, in the Indian wars of 1836 and 1837, in the Mexican war of 1845, and last in the war between the States.

The appropriations for the Navy had for years been mainly spent upon the Northern navy-yards, notwithstanding that much of the timber used had been from the South. We had not the accessories for building vessels with the necessary celerity; we had no powder depots, and no store of it on hand, no saltpetre, and only the store of sulphur needful for clarifying the cane-sugar crop.

General G. W. Rains was appointed to establish a manufactory of ammunition, and he brought to the work experience and zeal which achieved a triumph that will be long remembered. The powder of the Confederate mills, under all the disadvantages that surrounded him, was recognized to be the best in the world.

On April 19, 1861, President Lincoln proclaimed a blockade, not as the effort to embarrass and destroy the commerce of a separate nation, but to subdue insurrection.

Mr. Davis wrote of the false presentation of the case to foreign governments made by Mr. Seward:

"As late as April 22, 1861, Mr. Seward, the United States Secretary of State, in a despatch to Mr. Dayton, Minister to France, since made public, expressed the views and purposes of the United States Government in the premises as follows. It may be proper to explain that, by what he is pleased to term 'the Revolution,' Mr. Seward means the withdrawal of the Southern States; and that the words italicized are, perhaps, not so distinguished in the original." He wrote: "The Territories will remain in all respects the same, whether the revolution shall succeed or fail."

"There is not even a pretext for the complaint that the disaffected States are to be conquered by the United States if the revolution fails ; for the rights of the States and *the condition of every being in them* will remain subject to exactly the same laws and forms of administration, whether the revolution shall succeed or whether it shall fail. In one case the States would be federally connected with the new Confederacy ; in the other they would, as now, be members of the United States ; but their Constitutions, laws, customs, habits, and institutions, in either case, will remain the same."

Mr. Lincoln said in his inaugural address : "I have no purpose directly or indirectly to interfere with the institution of slavery in the States where it exists ; I believe I have no lawful right to do so, and I have no inclination to do so."

The President of the Confederacy called the Congress together April 29th, and set before them the fact that the President of the United States had called out seventy-five thousand men, who were first to capture our forts. A blockade had been proclaimed to destroy our commerce and intercept the necessary supplies. This he declared was in effect a declaration of war. He closed his message with these words : " We protest solemnly in the face of mankind, that we desire peace at any sacrifice save that of honor."

No one who scrutinizes impartially the history of this stirring period of Mr. Davis's life can fail to observe the activity with which he pressed every available resource into service, how large was the discretion allowed to the government agents, and how prompt and far-reaching were his provisions. His previous service in the United States War Department had rendered him familiar with all the sources of supply, and all that man could accomplish he did to equip our army and navy to meet the heavy odds with which they were confronted.

Nitre beds were established, manufactories of arms and powder were erected with marvellous celerity, old arms were altered, men were drilled and initiated in the arts of war ; in fact, his activity was unceasing and his success abnormal.

That large and learned, if not useful, class who after the event see lost opportunities, criminal negligence, and a supine disregard of the interest of the people, demonstrated by the leaders of a cause for which they have staked their all, have not been silent at the Confederate President's failure to buy every-thing needful everywhere. The fame of an unsuccessful leader is like the picture in the fable. Each hypercritical spectator picks out an error and obliterates the trait, until, were there not true artists with high aims and God-given talents and enthusiasm, there would re-main to us no presentation of the noble fig-ure of a heroic ruler.

If Moses found, in the theocratic govern-ment he served, a golden calf lifted on high under the blaze of the " pillar of fire by night," one cannot wonder at my husband's fate.

Detraction is the easiest form of criticism or eloquence, but just, discriminating praise requires the presence in the commentators of many of those qualities which are commend-ed in the subject. It is probable that Junius would have made a sorry figure in the place of either Lords Mansfield or Chatham.

Before going further into the record of the invasion of the seceded slave-holding States, and the subjugation of those that still re-mained in the Union, it seems proper to glance briefly at the relative resources of the two powers that were so soon to be arrayed against each other in deadly conflict *à l'ou-trance.*

In 1860 the United States had a popula-

tion exceeding thirty-one millions in the free
States and eight millions in the South.

But the disparity between the two sections
was more pronounced in the material resources of war than in the population. The
Missouri was connected with the sea-board
by the best system of railways in the world,
having a total mileage of over thirty thousand, and an annual tonnage estimated at
thirty-six millions. The annual revenue of
this tonnage was valued at four thousand millions of dollars. The manufactures of the
North represented an annual product of two
thousand millions.

The North had all the manufacturing establishments necessary to produce all the
matériel of war. She had an uninterrupted
commerce with the outside world. Altogether, her manufacturing resources were about
five hundred to one compared with those of
the South. She had in addition to this the
inestimable advantage of having all the work-
shops of the world open to her.

Nor did Europe furnish her with the matériel of war only ; but the vast immigration
that flocked from the Old World and landed
in Northern ports brought an unfailing supply of recruits to her armies whenever the
emergencies of the war made a fresh levy nec
essary to refill the depleted armies in the field.

The fury of the North was met by a cyclone of patriotic enthusiasm that swept up from the South. Tens of thousands of men of both sections who had hesitated, and who still hoped for an amicable adjustment of the troubles between the sections, were converted by the guns of Sumter to the belief that the time for compromise had passed, and that duty to their country demanded that they should join in patriotic efforts to repel the invader. When this "ground swell" moved the masses at the North, the Confederate Congress was still in session; Mr. Davis, who had never underestimated our peril, issued a proclamation calling on the States for volunteers, and also inviting applications for privateers to sail the high seas under Confederate letters of marque and reprisal.

Agents were despatched to foreign countries to buy small-arms, guns, and ships with their armaments. No limit was placed upon the amount to be purchased, or the price. The Confederate credit was good, and their President was willing to strain it to the utmost. Prompt, general, and enthusiastic was the popular response to the appeal of the President. Railway and transportation companies offered the free use of their lines and resources for the conveyance of troops and matériel of war. The railways not only vol-

untarily reduced the charges hitherto demanded for the postal service, but offered to
receive their pay at the reduced rates tendered in the bonds of the Confederacy.

The number of volunteers far exceeded the
demand or *the possibility* of arming them.
It was shown that if the Government had
possessed arms enough for the entire adult
white population of the Confederacy, they
could have been enrolled at this time. Notwithstanding that men have railed long and
loudly over volunteers having been refused,
they knew at the time that, having no weapons with which to arm them, to accept their
services was but to cripple the industries of
the country without increasing the ranks of
our defenders.

On May 20, 1861, the Congress resolved
that the seat of Government of the Confederate States should be transferred from Montgomery to Richmond, and that it should ad-
journ to meet there on July 20th. It had
already become evident that Virginia would
be the battle-ground of the coming struggle,
and it was desirable, therefore, that the Confederate Government should have its headquarters in that State.

Anxiety and unremitting labor had prostrated President Davis; and, when he left
Montgomery, it was upon his bed. His mails

were heavy with warnings of an attempt at assassination; therefore it was a source of relief to us to know he had gone to Virginia. A few days before he had seen a man heavily armed peering into his room at our residence; he accosted him, but the man jumped over a fence and ran out of sight. He went on, accompanied only by his cabinet and staff, and in advance of the rest of the family. He was quite ill on the road and obliged to keep his bed. The crowd that gathered at each station would walk quietly down and look in on his sleeping face with the greatest tenderness; one or two said—"If he can only pull through the war!"

Within a week, the family followed by the ordinary train. The country was alive with soldiers—men in butternut trousers with gray homespun coats and epaulets of yellow cotton fringe. Several companies of soldiers waiting for transportation gave us very sweet serenades at the different stations. We reached Richmond in the morning, and the President met us in a carriage and four, sent down for our use by the citizens until our own carriage and horses came. This equipage was a trial to us, and as soon as possible we reduced our establishment to a carriage and pair. We were conducted to the Spottswood Hotel as guests of the city, until the house intended

for the residence of the Chief Executive
should be finished.   In the hotel we were
domiciled with the cabinet and the aids, besides a number of ladies and gentlemen.

CHAPTER VIII.

THE BOMBARDMENT OF SUMTER.

On March 3d, President Davis appointed General Beauregard to the command of all the Confederate forces in and around Charleston.

On arriving there, General Beauregard, after examining the fortifications, proceeded to erect formidable batteries of cannon and mortars bearing on the fort.

On April 7th, Lieutenant Talbot, an agent of the Federal Government, conveyed a message to Governor Pickens from President Lincoln, announcing that an attempt would be made to supply Fort Sumter " with provisions only," and that if the attempt be not resisted no effort to throw in men, arms, or ammunition would be made without further notice, or in case of an attack upon the fort.

" The 'relief squadron,' as with unconscious irony it was termed, was already under way for Charleston, consisting, according to their own statement, of eight vessels carrying twenty-six guns, and about fourteen hundred

men, including the troops sent for reinforcement of the garrison."

Upon the receipt of General Beauregard's
telegram, that provisions would be sent to
Fort Sumter, forcibly if need be, he was directed by the Secretary of War to demand its
surrender at twelve o'clock, on April 11th.
The demand was accordingly made in a note
borne by Colonel James Chesnut and Captain Lee, with the offer of permission for Major Anderson to salute the flag he had upheld
with so much fortitude." Major Anderson
made answer on the same day, that he regretted that his sense of honor and of obligation to his government would not permit him
to accede to the demand of General Beauregard.

Next day at 4.30 A.M. the signal was given
from Fort Johnston; the fire was gradually
followed by shots from Moultrie, Cummings'
Point, and the floating battery.

Fort Sumter did not reply until seven
o'clock. The firing continued all day. During the bombardment a portion of the Federal
fleet rendezvoused off Charleston, but took no
part in the fight.

Early on the morning of the 13th the Confederate batteries renewed the bombardment,
concentrating their fire on Fort Sumter, which
directed a vigorous fire on Fort Moultrie.

About eight o'clock in the morning, smoke was seen issuing from Fort Sumter. The fire of the Confederate batteries was thereupon increased and concentrated on the fort, whose flag still floated. After this time, although Fort Sumter continued to fire from time to time, the shots came at irregular periods, amid thick smoke and bursting shells. The Confederate soldiers, at every discharge from the fort, jumped on the different batteries and cheered the garrison for its gallant defence, while they hooted the fleet that lay alongside the bar, an idle spectator of the fight.

At half-past one a shot struck the flag-staff of Sumter and brought down the ensign. By this time the condition of the fort and its defences had become desperate ; the parapet had been so badly damaged that few of the guns were in position ; the smoke in the casemates rendered it impossible for the men to work the guns ; and the incessant toil and excitement had utterly exhausted the garrison.

When the flag went down General Beauregard sent offers of assistance, as the conflagration was apparently on the increase.

Before the General's aids reached the fort the flag was again displayed, but it was soon hauled down and a white flag substituted. Fort Sumter had surrendered.

As an honorable testimony to the gallantry
of the garrison, Major Anderson was allowed
on leaving the fort to salute his flag with
fifty guns.

Notwithstanding the heavy and long cannonading not a man was killed or wounded
on either side; a mule was the only thing
slain. But, in firing the parting salute, a
cannon exploded. Four of the garrison were
mortally wounded by this accident.

The victory was celebrated in Charleston
by the firing of cannon and the pealing of
bells, and by every form of popular demonstration of delight.

When the news reached the President of
the Confederacy his first expression was of
thankfulness that no blood had been shed;
he said " Separation is not yet of necessity
final—there has been no blood spilled more
precious than that of a mule." He then
spoke of his old friend "Bob Anderson," of
his splendid gallantry, and of his sorrow at
being separated from him.

In the North, the news produced a simul-
taneous burst of execration and excitement.
For the first time the people of that section
realized that the South was in deadly earnest.
The Federal administration promptly availed
themselves of the frenzy of the people to
arouse fresh hatred of the South, and to incite

the young men to enlist in the armies of invasion. Two days after Sumter surrendered President Lincoln issued a proclamation calling for 75,000 troops.

The first effect of this proclamation in the South was the secession of Virginia—an example which was promptly followed by the States of North Carolina, Tennessee, and Arkansas.

That the real object of Lincoln's renewed calls for troops was the unconditional subjugation of the South, was soon made manifest; for, by repeated levies, there were soon 200,-000 men under arms in the Northern States.

Maryland was overrun with troops; a garrison of 12,000 men was established at Fortress Monroe; in Maryland and Missouri, the citizens were disarmed, the habeas corpus was denied them, and civil liberty was throttled by the mailed hand of military power.

Maryland, at the inception of secession, resolved, for purposes of pacification and other reasons, to remain neutral. The authorities refused the right of United States troops to pass through her domain with hostile intent toward the South, announced her determination not to send her troops to the soil of any other State, and Governor Hicks officially demanded new guarantees for her rights, and proclaimed her sympathy with the Southern

people.   On April 19, 1861, a body of troops
was brought to the railway depôt, and the
citizens, being unarmed, assailed them with
stones.   The soldiers fired upon them, and
killed a few and wounded many.   A few
troops passed through the town, and the
others were sent back.

The Legislature of Maryland appointed
commissioners to the two Governments.   The
Confederate President, on April 21st, in an
answer to those sent to him, expressed his desire for " peace, peace, with all nations and
people."   The President of the United States
alleged the protection of Washington as his
only object for concentrating troops, and protested that none of the troops brought through
Maryland were "intended for any purposes
hostile to the State, or aggressive against
other States."

The sequence to these pledges was, that,
on May 5th, the Relay House, at the junction
of the Washington and Baltimore railways,
was occupied by Federal troops, and General
Butler, on the 13th instant, moved to Baltimore and occupied with the United States
troops, Federal Hill.   Reinforcements were
received the next day, and the General proclaimed his right to discriminate between
" well-disposed citizens " and those who did
not agree with him, they who he opprobri-

ously characterized. Then followed a demand for the surrender of arms.

" The mayor, Charles Howard, and police
commissioners, W. H. Gatchell, and J. W.
Davis," met and protested against the suspension of their functions by the appointment
of a provost-marshal, but resolved to do
nothing to obstruct General Banks in his arrangements for the preservation of the peace
of the city.

The provost-marshal at once commenced
a series of domiciliary visits, ostensibly in
search of arms and munitions. On July 1st,
the before-named citizens were arrested. Of
the mayor, Mr. Davis said, " He was of an
old Maryland family honored for their public
services, and himself adorned by every social
virtue."

A provost-marshal was sent to Frederick,
where the Legislature was in session. A
cordon of pickets were drawn around the
town, out of which no one could go without a
permission from General Banks or his staff.
Twelve or thirteen members and some officers
of the Legislature were arrested. The quo-
rum was destroyed. S. T. Willis, whose report in defence of the constitutional rights of
his fellow-citizens was considered cause for
imprisonment, and Henry May, a member of
Congress, were arrested.

Governor Hicks found himself convinced by these strenuous measures, and came out in sympathy with the successful party.

Mr. Davis said : " Last in order, but first in cordiality, were the tender ministrations of Maryland's noble daughters to the sick and wounded prisoners who were carried through the streets of Baltimore, and it is with shame we remember that brutal guards, on several occasions, inflicted wounds upon gentlewomen who approached these suffering prisoners to offer them the relief of which they stood so ardently in need." One dear and much honored young friend ruined her eyes painting photographs for sale, after having used to the fullest extent all her own available means to aid the Southern soldiers. Union ladies who had held close relations with those of Confederate sympathies, forced an entrance into the houses of their quondam friends to make a report of disloyalty upon them. In the worst days of the French Revolution there was no more insecurity for the exercise of free opinions than that which prevailed in Baltimore.

The citizens were conveyed to Fortress Monroe and eventually to Fort Lafayette, and turned into a battery-room occupied by twenty - four others, chiefly Marylanders. The Government furnished an iron bed, a pallet of straw, and a thin blanket; but five bags of straw could be found, and the rest of the prisoners slept on the floor in their clothes. The room was sixty-six by twenty-two feet, with a brick floor, occupied by thirty-eight people. It contained also five thirty-two-pound cannon with their cumbersome carriages, occupying fully half the space in the room.

Several of the sick were on the floor without either blankets or pillows. No light was allowed. It is weary work recalling these dreadful experiences, but the deep feeling of hostility it aroused is seen in the appeal of General Bradley T. Johnson in the autumn of the next year:

" Rise at once. Remember the cells of Fort McHenry. Remember the dungeons of Fort Lafayette and Fort Warren ; the insults to your wives and daughters ; the arrests ; the midnight searches of your houses.

" Remember these your wrongs, and rise at once in arms and strike for Liberty and Right."

CHAPTER IX.

THE PRESIDENT ARRIVES IN RICHMOND.

RICHMOND was one great camp—men hurried to and fro with and without uniforms and arms, with that fixed look upon their faces that they acquire when confronted with danger and the necessity for supreme effort. A long war debases a nation, but individuals rise higher then and develop more quickly than in piping times of peace.

Upon the President's arrival in Richmond he found General R. E. Lee in command of the army of Virginia, with the rank of Major-General.

Many troops had been sent from other States of the Confederacy to the aid of Virginia, and the forces there assembled were divided into three armies, at the most important positions threatened: one, under command of General J. E. Johnston, at Harper's Ferry, covering the valley of the Shenandoah; another under General G. T. Beauregard, at Manassas, covering the direct approach from Washington to Richmond; and the third, under Generals Huger and Magruder, at Norfolk

CONFEDERATE CAPITOL AT RICHMOND.

and in the Peninsula between the James and York Rivers, covering the approach from the seaboard. The armies of Johnston and Beauregard, though separated by the Blue Ridge, had such practicable communication with each other as to render their junction possible when the necessity should be foreseen.

Each of the three were confronted by forces greatly superior to their own, and it was doubtful which would first be the object of attack.

The temporary occupation of Harper's Ferry was especially needful for the removal of the valuable machinery and material located there.

The demonstrations of General Patterson, commanding the Federal army in that region, caused General Johnston earnestly to insist upon being allowed to retire to a position nearer Winchester. Under the circumstances an official letter was addressed to him, from which the following is an extract:

"ADJUTANT AND INSPECTOR-GENERAL'S OFFICE,
"RICHMOND, June 13, 1861.

" To GENERAL J. E. JOHNSTON, commanding Harper's Ferry, Virginia.

" SIR : You have been heretofore instructed to exercise your discretion as to retiring from your position at Harper's Ferry, and taking the field to check the advance of the enemy.

. . . The effective portion of your command, together with the baggage and whatever else would impede your operations in the field, it would be well to send, without delay, to the Manassas road. . . . For these reasons it has been with reluctance that any attempt was made to give you specific instructions, and you will accept the assurance of the readiness with which the freest exercise of discretion on your part will be sustained.

"Very respectfully, your obedient servant,

"S. COOPER."

The two first encounters of the Northern and Southern troops occurred about this time. On June 11, 1861, at Bethel Church, and on June 18th Colonel Vaughan met the enemy at the twenty-first bridge on the Baltimore & Ohio Railroad, charged upon his camp, captured and brought off two pieces of artillery and the enemy's flag.

While General Johnston was keeping the army under Patterson in check in the Valley, a disaster to the Confederate arms occurred in West Virginia. General Garnett was defeated at Rich Mountain by McClellan and Rosecrans and forced to retreat. General Garnett was killed.

The enemy in front of General Johnston were reinforced, and he, anticipating an attack by a superior force wrote, July 9, 1861, to General Cooper, a letter of which the following extract is the last paragraph:

" If it is proposed to strengthen us against the attack I suggest as soon to be made, it seems to me that General Beauregard might, with *great expedition*, furnish five or six thousand men for a few days.   J. E. J."

The enemy did not attack General Johnston, but the Federal army in front of Washington, under General McDowell, advanced to attack the army of General Beauregard at Manassas, and a few hours before they took up their line of march, a lady gave notice of the fact to the Confederates, and a telegram was sent to General Johnston:

"RICHMOND, July 17, 1861.

" To GENERAL J. E. JOHNSTON,
          " Winchester, Va.

" General Beauregard is attacked. To strike the enemy a decisive blow, a junction of all your effective force will be needed. If practicable, make the movement, sending your sick and baggage to Culpepper Court-House, either by railroad or by Warrenton.

" In all the arrangements exercise your discretion.

          (Signed)   " S. COOPER,
               " *Adjutant and Inspector-General.*"

To this telegram General Johnston replied:

"HEADQUARTERS, WINCHESTER, VA., July 18, 1861.

"GENERAL: I have had the honor to receive your telegram of yesterday.

"General Patterson, who had been at Bunker Hill since Monday, seems to have moved yesterday to Charleston, twenty-three miles east of Winchester.

"Unless he prevents it, we shall move toward General Beauregard to-day.

"JOSEPH E. JOHNSTON."

After Johnston moved to join Beauregard, he telegraphed an inquiry to Mr. Davis, regarding his relative rank to Beauregard, and the following answer was returned:

"RICHMOND, July 20, 1861.

"GENERAL J. E. JOHNSTON,
    "Manassas, Va.

"You are a General in the Confederate Army, possessed of the power attached to that rank. You will know how to make the exact knowledge of Brigadier-General Beauregard, as well of the ground as of the troops and preparation, avail for the success of the object in which you co-operate.

"The zeal of both assures me of harmonious action.

"JEFFERSON DAVIS."

CABINET OF THE CONFEDERACY.

Though the date of General Johnston's commission gave him precedence, to avoid a misunderstanding between these generals, whose cordial co-operation was necessary to the welfare of their country, Mr. Davis decided at the earliest moment to go in person to the army.

CHAPTER X.

ENGAGEMENT AT BULL RUN, AND BATTLE OF MANASSAS.

THE Federal Army under the command of General McDowell reached the vicinity of Fairfax Court-House on July 17th, and General Bonham, commanding that advanced post with a brigade of South Carolina troops, fell back and took position behind Bull Run, where, in line along that stream, were located the different regiments, batteries, and brigades of General Beauregard's army. The line extended a distance of eight miles from Union Mills on the right, to the stone bridge over Bull Run on the left, where it is crossed by the Warrenton and Alexandria turnpike.

McDowell, arriving at Centreville, threw forward, on the 18th, a division under General Tyler, to "feel" General Beauregard's line, but "not to bring on an engagement." But General Tyler, brought forward a battery of the Washington Artillery and opened fire upon the Confederates. After a sharp fight his forces were withdrawn with loss.

This affair, being one almost exclusively of

artillery, was a notable event, and gave assurance that our volunteer artillery could successfully cope with the regular batteries of
the United States.*

This battalion of veterans formed the guard
of honor which followed my husband's remains twenty-eight years afterward, when he
was laid to rest in the Tomb of the Army of
Northern Virginia, at New Orleans.

General Johnston arrived at General Beauregard's headquarters on July 20th. While
on the march, Beauregard sent him a suggestion to march by Aldie and attack the rear of
the Federal right at Centreville, while his
troops from Bull Run assailed that army in
front. Johnston did not agree with this plan,
he considered it impracticable to direct the
movements of troops so distant from each
other, by roads so far separated, in such a
manner as to combine their action on a field
of battle.

Early on July 21st, a cannonade was
opened by the enemy from the opposite bank
of Bull Run, and it was evident that he was
marching against the left of the Confederate
line of battle, at and beyond the stone bridge.

---

* General Beauregard, in his official report of the engagement,
says : " The guns engaged in this singular conflict on our side were
three 6-pounder rifled pieces and four ordinary 6-pounders, all of
Walton's Battalion, the Washington Artillery, of New Orleans."

The troops there stationed met the advance with great steadiness, but were outnumbered, and fell back to the plateau around the Henry House.

The battle raged with varied success upon the Henry plateau until after four o'clock, when the Federal army yielded to a flank attack of Generals Kirby Smith, with Elzey, and later Early, and were routed.

Around the house of Mrs. Henry the fight raged the fiercest, and here were stationed the Federal batteries. Mrs. Henry, old and bed-ridden, was caught between the cross fire of the artillery and was killed in her bed.

The details of the great battles of the war I will not attempt to describe, leaving that duty to the participants, and refer my readers to the many able historians who have depicted them, and to official reports now being published by the Government.

Where Mr. Davis was present, I will record his connection therewith. He thus wrote of this battle:

" After the delivery of the message to Congress, on Saturday, July 20th, I intended to leave in the afternoon for Manassas, but was detained until the next morning, when I left by rail, accompanied by my aide-de-camp, Colonel J. R. Davis, to confer with the generals on the field. As we approached Manassas Railroad junction, a cloud of dust was visible a short distance to the west of the railroad. It resembled one raised by a body of marching troops, and recalled to my remembrance the design of General Beauregard to make the Rappahannock his second line of defence. It was, however, subsequently learned that the dust was raised by a number of wagons which had been sent to the rear for greater security against the contingencies of the battle. The sound of the firing had now become very distinct, so much so as to leave no doubt that a general engagement had commenced. Though that event had been anticipated as being near at hand after the action of the 18th, it was both hoped and desired that it would not occur quite so soon, the more as it was not known whether the troops from the valley had yet arrived.

" On reaching the railroad junction, I found a large number of men, bearing the usual evidence of those who leave the field of battle under a panic. They crowded around the train with fearful stories of a defeat of our army. The railroad conductor announced his decision that the railroad train should proceed no farther. Looking among those who were about us for one whose demeanor gave reason to expect from him a collected answer,

I selected one whose gray beard and calm face gave best assurance. He, however, could furnish no encouragement. Our line, he said, was broken, all was confusion, the army routed, and the battle lost. I asked for Generals Johnston and Beauregard ; he said they were on the field when he left it. I returned to the conductor and told him that I must go on ; that the railroad was the only means by which I could proceed, and that, until I reached the headquarters, I could not get a horse to ride to the field where the battle was raging. He finally consented to detach the locomotive from the train, and, for my accommodation, to run it as far as the army headquarters. In this manner Colonel Davis, aide-de-camp, and myself proceeded.

" At the headquarters we found the Quarter-master-General, W. L. Caball, and the Adjutant-General, Jordan, of General Beauregard's staff, who courteously agreed to furnish us horses, and also to show us the route. While the horses were being prepared, Colonel Jordan took occasion to advise my aide-de-camp, Colonel Davis, of the hazard of going to the field, and the impropriety of such exposure on my part. The horses were after a time reported ready, and we started to the field. The stragglers soon became numerous, and warnings as to the fate which awaited us if we advanced were not only frequent, but evidently sincere.

"There were, however, many who turned back, and the wounded generally cheered upon meeting us. I well remember one, a mere stripling, who, supported on the shoulders of a man, who was bearing him to the rear, took off his cap and waved it with a cheer, that showed within that slender form beat the heart of a hero—breathed a spirit that would dare the labors of Hercules.

"As we advanced, the storm of the battle was rolling westward, and its fury became faint. When I met General Johnston, who was upon a hill which commanded a general view of the field of the afternoon's operations, and inquired of him as to the state of affairs, he replied that we had won the battle. I left him there and rode still farther to the west. Several of the volunteers on General Beauregard's staff joined me, and a command of cavalry, the gallant leader of which, Captain John F. Lay, insisted that I was too near the enemy to be without an escort. We, however, only saw one column near to us that created a doubt as to which side it belonged; and, as we were riding toward it, it was suggested that we should halt until it could be examined with a field-glass. Colonel Chesnut dismounted so as the better to use his

glass, and at that moment the column formed
into line, by which the wind struck the flag so
as to extend it, and it was plainly revealed to
be that of the United States.

"Our cavalry, though there was present
but the squadron previously mentioned, and
specified in a statement of the commander
from which I will make some extracts, dashed
boldly forward to charge. The demonstration was followed by the immediate retreat of
what was, I believe, the last, thereabout, of
the enemy's forces maintaining their organization, and showing a disposition to dispute the
possession of the field of battle. In riding
over the ground, it seemed quite possible to
mark the line of a fugitive's flight. Here was
a musket, there a cartridge-box, there a
blanket or overcoat, a haversack, etc., as if
the runner had stripped himself, as he went,
of all impediments to speed.

"As we approached toward the left of our
line, the signs of an utter rout of the enemy
were unmistakable, and justified the conclusion that the watchword of 'On to Richmond' had been changed to 'Off for Washington.'

"On the extreme left of our field of operations, I found the troops whose opportune
arrival had averted the impending disaster,
and so materially contributed to our victory.

Some of them had, after arriving at the
Manassas railroad junction, hastened to our
left; their brigadier-general, E. K. Smith,
was wounded soon after going into action,
and the command of the brigade devolved
upon Elzey, by whom it was gallantly and
skilfully led to the close of the battle; others,
under the command of General (then Colonel)
Early, made a rapid march, under the pressing necessity, from the extreme right of our
line to and beyond our left, so as to attack
the enemy in flank, thus inflicting on him the
discomfiture his oblique movement was designed to inflict upon us. All these troops
and the others near to them had hastened
into action without supplies or camp-equipage; weary, hungry, and without shelter,
night closed around them where they stood,
the blood-stained victors on a hard-fought
field.

"It was reported to me that some of the
troops had been so long without food as to
be suffering severe hunger, and that no supplies could be got where they were. I made
several addresses to them, all to the effect
that their position was that best adapted to a
pursuit of the enemy, and that they should
therefore remain there; adding that I would
go to the headquarters and direct that supplies should be sent to them promptly.

" General (then Colonel) Early, commanding a brigade, informed me of some wounded
who required attention; one, Colonel Gardner, was, he said, at a house not far from
where we were. I rode to see him, found him
in severe pain, and, from the twitching visible
and frequent, seemed to be threatened with
tetanus. A man sat beside him whose uniform was that of the enemy; but he was gentle, and appeared to be solicitously attentive. He said that he had no morphine, and
did not know where to get any. I found in
a short time a surgeon who went with me to
Colonel Gardner, having the articles necessary
in the case. Before leaving Colonel Gardner,
he told me that the man who was attending
to him might, without hindrance, have retreated with his comrades, but had kindly remained with him, and he therefore asked my
protection for the man. I took the name and
the State of the supposed Good Samaritan,
and at army headquarters directed that he
should not be treated as a prisoner. The sequel will be told hereafter.

" It was late, and we rode back in the
night, say seven miles, to the army headquarters. I had not seen General Beauregard on the field, and did not find him at
his quarters when we returned; the promise
made to the troops was therefore communi-

cated to a staff-officer, who said he would have the supplies sent.   At a later hour, when I met General Beauregard and informed him of what had occurred, he stated that, because of a false alarm which had reached him, he had ordered the troops referred to from the left to the right of our line, so as to be in position to repel the reported movement of the enemy against that flank.   That such an alarm should have been credited, and a night march ordered on account of it, shows how little the completeness of the victory was realized."

The army under McDowell numbered, present for duty, 34,127.

The Confederate force present at the battle and engaged, was 13,000.

When the first telegram came to Richmond announcing the victory, the President said: "Several cannon were captured."   A less reliable report said two, but I felt sure, with his habitually cautious habit of under-statement, he would have said two, if there were not more, and so it proved to be.   He was the only person I have ever known, who, in moments of triumph, or while moved by personal distaste, or violent anger, habitually understated what was achieved, or the provocation offered.

CHAPTER XI.

CONFERENCES AFTER THE BATTLE OF MANASSAS.

Mr. Davis thus continued the narrative:

"At a late hour of the night, I had a conference with Generals Johnston and Beauregard; the Adjutant - General of the latter, Colonel Jordan, was present, and sat opposite to me at the table.

"When, after some preliminary conversation, I asked whether any troops had been sent in pursuit of the enemy, I was answered in the negative. Upon further inquiry as to what troops were in the best position for pursuit, and had been least fatigued during the day, General Bonham's brigade was mentioned. I then suggested that he should be ordered in pursuit; a pause ensued, until Colonel Jordan asked me if I would dictate the order. I at once dictated an order for immediate pursuit. Some conversation followed, the result of which was a modification of the order by myself, so that, instead of immediate pursuit, it should be commenced at early dawn. Colonel Jordan spoke across the table to me, saying, 'If you will send the order as you first dictated it, the enemy won't stop till he gets into the Potomac.' I believe I remember the words very nearly, and am quite sure that I do remember them substan- tially. On March 25, 1878, I wrote to Gen- eral Beauregard as follows :

" 'DEAR SIR : Permit me to ask you to re- call the conference held between General Johnston, yourself, and myself, on the night after the close of the battle of Manassas ; and to give me, if you can, a copy of the order which I dictated, and which your Adjutant- General, T. J. Jordan, wrote at my dictation, directing Brigadier-General Bonham to fol- low the retreating enemy. If you cannot fur- nish a copy of the order, please give me your recollection of its substance.

" 'Yours respectfully,
" 'JEFFERSON DAVIS.'

" To this letter General Beauregard cour- teously replied that his order-book was in New York, in the hands of a friend, to whom he would write for a copy of the order de- sired if it be in said book, and that he would also write to his adjutant, General Jordan, for his recollection of the order, if it had not been inscribed in the order-book.

" On April 29th, General Beauregard forwarded to me the answer to his inquiries in my behalf, as follows :

"'NEW YORK, 63 BROADWAY, April 18, 1878.

"'MY DEAR GENERAL: In answer to your note, I hasten to say that, properly, Mr. Davis is not to be held accountable for our failure to pursue McDowell from the field of Manassas on the night of July 21, 1861.

"'As to the order, to which I presume Mr. Davis refers in his note to you, I recollect the incident very distinctly.

"'The night of the battle, as I was about to ascend to your quarters over my office, Captain E. P. Alexander, of your staff, informed me that Captain ——, attached to General Johnston's army of the Shenandoah, reported that he had been as far forward as Centreville, where he had seen the Federal army completely routed, and in full flight toward Washington.

"'This statement I at once repeated to Mr. Davis, General Johnston, and yourself, whom I found seated around your table—Mr. Davis at the moment writing a despatch to General Cooper.

"'As soon as I made my report, Mr. Davis, with much animation, asserted the necessity for an urgent pursuit that night by Bonham, who, with his own brigade and that of Longstreet, was in close proximity to Centreville at the moment. So I took my seat at the same table with you, and wrote the order for pursuit, substantially at the dictation of Mr. Davis. But while writing, either I happened to remember, or Captain Alexander himself—as I am inclined to believe—called me aside to remind me, that his informant was known among us of the old army as —— —— because of eccentricities, and in contradistinction with others of the same name. When I repeated this reminder, Mr. Davis recalled the sobriquet, as he had a precise personal knowledge of the officers of the old army. He laughed heartily, as did all present.

" ' The question of throwing General Bonham forward that night, upon the unverified report of Captain ——, was now briefly discussed, with a unanimous decision against it; therefore, the order was not despatched.

" ' It is proper to add in this connection that, so far as I am aware—and I had the opportunity of knowing what occurred—this was the only instance during Mr. Davis's stay at Manassas in which he exercised any voice as to the movement of the troops. Profoundly pleased by the junction of the two Confederate armies upon the very field of battle, his bearing toward the generals who commanded them was eminently proper, as I have testi-

fied on a former occasion ; and, I repeat, he
certainly expressed or manifested no opposition to a forward movement, nor did he display the least disposition to interfere by
opinion or authority touching what the Confederate forces should or should not do.

" ' You having, at the close of the day, surrendered the command, which had been left
in your hands, over both Confederate armies
during the engagement, *General Johnston
was that night in chief command.* He was
decidedly averse to an immediate offensive,
and emphatically discountenanced it as impracticable.

"' Very truly your friend,
"' THOMAS JORDAN.
"'To GENERAL P. G. T. BEAUREGARD,
New Orleans, La.' "

" General Beauregard, in his letter forwarding the above, wrote : ' The account given
herewith by General Jordan of what occurred
there respecting further pursuit that night,
agrees with my own recollection.'

" It was a matter of importance, as I regarded it, to follow closely on the retreating
enemy, but it was of no consequence then or
now as to who issued the order for pursuit,
and, unless requested, I should not have dictated one, preferring that the generals to

whom the operations were confided would issue all orders to the troops. I supposed the
order, as modified by myself, had been sent.
I have found, however, since the close of the
war, that it was not, but that an order to the
same effect was sent on the night of July 21st,
for a copy of which I am indebted to the
kindness of that chivalrous gentleman, soldier,
and patriot, General Bonham. It is as follows :

"'HEADQUARTERS OF THE ARMY OF THE POTOMAC,
MANASSAS, July 21, 1861.

" ' (Special order, No. 140.)

" ' I. General Bonham will send, as early as
practicable in the morning, a command of two
of his regiments of infantry, a strong force of
cavalry, and one field battery, to scour the
country and roads to his front, toward Centreville. He will carry with him abundant
means of transportation for the collection of
our wounded, all the arms, ammunition, and
abandoned hospital stores, subsistence, and
baggage, which will be sent immediately to
these headquarters.

" ' General Bonham will advance with caution, throwing out an advanced guard and
skirmishers on his right and left, and the utmost caution must be taken to prevent firing
into our own men.

" ' Should it appear, while this command is occupied as directed, that it is insufficient for the purposes indicated, General Bonham will call on the nearest brigade commander for support.

" ' II. Colonel P. St. George Cooke, commanding, will despatch at the same time, for similar purposes, a command of the same size and proportions of infantry, artillery, and cavalry, on the road via Stone Bridge ; and another command of two companies of infantry and one of cavalry on the road by which the enemy retreated, toward and via Sudley's Mills.

" ' By command of Brigadier-General Beauregard.

" ' THOMAS JORDAN,
" ' *A. A. Adjutant-General.*'
" ' To BRIGADIER BONHAM.' "

" Impressed with the belief that the enemy was very superior to us, both in numbers and appointments, I had felt apprehension that, unless pressed, he would recover from the panic under which he fled from the field, rally on his reserves, and renew the contest. Therefore it was that I immediately felt the necessity for a pursuit of the fugitives, and insisted that the troops on the extreme left should retain their position during the night

of the 21st, as has been heretofore stated.
In conference with the generals that night,
this subject was considered, and I dictated an
order for a movement on the rear of the
enemy at early dawn, which, on account of
the late hour at which it was given, differed
very little from one for an immediate movement. A rainfall, extraordinary for its violence and duration, occurred on the morning
of the succeeding day, so that, over places
where during the battle one could scarcely get
a drink of water, rolled torrents which, in the
afternoon of the 22d, it was difficult to cross.

" From these and other causes, the troops
were scattered to such an extent, that but few
commands could have been assembled for immediate service. It was well for us that the
enemy, instead of retiring in order so as to be
rallied and again brought to the attack, left
hope behind, and fled in dismay to seek for
safety beyond the Potomac.

" Each hour of the day following the battle added to the evidence of a thorough rout
of the enemy. Abandoned wagons, stores,
guns, caissons, small-arms, and ammunition,
proved his complete demoralization. As far
as our cavalry went, no hostile force was met,
and all the indications favored the conclusion
that the purpose of invasion had for the time
been abandoned.

" The victory, though decisive and important, both in its moral and physical effect, had been dearly bought by the sacrifice of the lives of many of our bravest and best, who at the first call of their country had rushed to its defence.

" When riding to the front, I met an ambulance bearing General Barnard Bee from the field, where he had been mortally wounded, after his patriotism had been illustrated by conspicuous exhibitions of skill, daring, and fortitude. Soon after, I learned that my friend, Colonel Bartow, had heroically sealed with his life-blood his faith in the sanctity of our cause. He had been the chairman of the Committee on Military Affairs in the Provisional Congress, and after the laws were enacted to provide for the public defence, he went to the field to maintain them. It is to such virtuous and devoted citizens that a country is indebted for its prosperity and honor, as well in peace as in war.

" Reference has been made to the dispersion of our troops after the battle, and in this connection the following facts are mentioned : In the afternoon of the 22d, with a guide supposed to be cognizant of the positions at which the different commands would be found, I went to visit the wounded, and among them a youth of my family, who, it was reported to me, was rapidly sinking.

After driving many miles, and witnessing very painful scenes, but seldom finding the troops in the position where my guide supposed them to be, and always disappointed in discovering him I particularly sought, I was, at the approach of night, about to abandon the search, when, accidentally meeting an officer of the command to which the youth belonged, I was directed to the temporary hospital to which the wounded of that command had been removed. It was too late; the soul of the young soldier had just left the body; the corpse lay before me.* Around him were many gentle boys, suffering in different degrees from the wounds they had received. One bright, refined-looking youth from South Carolina, severely, if not fatally, wounded, responded to my expression of sympathy by the heroic declaration that it was ' sweet to die for such a cause.' †

"Many kindred spirits ascended to the Father from that field of their glory. The roll need not be recorded here; it has a more enduring depository than the pen can make —the traditions of a grateful people.

---

* While in the agonies of pain, and parched by thirst, some of the ambulance corps came to take private Edward Anderson to the hospital, but he pointed to a wounded man near him, saying, "Take him, he may recover, I cannot."

† These two incidents were never mentioned by my husband without glistening eyes and faltering voice.

" On the night of the 22d, I held a second conference with Generals Johnston and Beauregard. All the revelations of the day were of the most satisfactory character, as to the completeness of our victory. The large amount gained of fine artillery, small-arms, and ammunition, all of which were much needed by us, was not the least gratifying consequence of our success. The generals, like myself, were all content with what had been done.

" I propounded to them the inquiry as to what it was practicable to do. They concurred as to their inability to cross the Potomac, and to the further inquiry as to an advance to the south side of the Potomac, General Beauregard promptly stated that there were strong fortifications there, occupied by garrisons which had not been in the battle, and were therefore not affected by the panic which had seized the defeated army. He described these fortifications as having wide, deep ditches, with palisades which would prevent the escalade of the works. Turning to General Johnston, he said, ' They have spared no expense.' It was further stated in explanation that we had no sappers and miners, nor even the tools requisite to make regular approaches. If we had possessed both, the time required for

such operations would have more than suf-
ficed for General Patterson's army and other
forces to have been brought to that locality,
in such numbers as must have rendered the
attempt, with our present means, futile.

" This view of the matter rests on the supposition that the fortifications and garrisons
described did actually exist, of which there
seemed then to be no doubt.   If the reports
which have since reached us be true, that
there was at that time neither fortifications
nor troops stationed on the south bank of the
Potomac ; that all the enemy's forces fled to
the north side of the river, and even beyond ;
that the panic of the routed army infected the
whole population of Washington City ; and
that no preparation was made, or even contemplated, for the destruction of the bridge
across the Potomac—then it may have been,
as many have asserted, that our army, following close upon the flying enemy, could
have entered and taken possession of the
United States capital.   These reports, however, present a condition of affairs altogether
at variance with the information on which we
had to act.   Thus it was, and, so far as I
knew, for the reasons above stated, that an
advance to the south bank of the Potomac
was not contemplated as the immediate sequence of the victory at Manassas."

CHAPTER XII.

REFLECTIONS ON THE VICTORY.

MR. DAVIS continued: "The victory of Manassas was certainly extraordinary, not only on account of the disparity of our numbers and the inferiority of our arms, but also because of many other disadvantages under which we labored. We had no disciplined troops, and, though our citizens were generally skilled in the use of small-arms, which, with their high pride and courage, might compensate for the want of training while in position, these inadequately substituted military instruction when manœuvres had to be performed under fire, and could not make the old-fashioned musket equal to the long-range, new-model muskets with which the enemy was supplied. The disparity in artillery was still greater, both in the number and kinds of guns; but, thanks to the skill and cool courage of the Rev. Captain W. N. Pendleton, his battery of light, smooth-bore guns, manned principally by the youths whose rector he had been, proved more effective in battle than the long-range rifle-guns of the enemy. The character of the ground brought the forces into close contact, and the ricochet of the round balls carried havoc into the columns of the enemy, while the bolts of their rifle-guns, if they missed their object, penetrated harmlessly into the ground.

" The field was very extensive, broken, and wooded. The senior general had so recently arrived that he had no opportunity minutely to learn the ground, and the troops he brought were both unacquainted with the field and with those with whom they had to co-operate. To all this must be added the disturbing fact that the plan of battle, as originally designed, was entirely changed by the movement of the enemy on our extreme left, instead of right and centre, as anticipated. The operations, therefore, had to be conducted against the plan of the enemy, instead of on that which our generals had prepared and explained to their subordinate commanders. The promptitude with which the troops moved, and the readiness with which our generals modified their preconceived plans to meet the necessities as they were developed, entitled them to the commendation so liberally bestowed at the time by their countrymen at large.

" General Johnston had been previously promoted to the highest grade in our army, and I deemed it but a fitting reward for the services rendered by General Beauregard that he should be promoted to the same grade, to which accordingly I promoted him at once."

"I have related how, in riding over the field of Manassas, I encountered a Federal soldier of whom it was said that, although he might have retreated in safety with the Federal army, he had remained within our lines to nurse a wounded Confederate officer, and that I ordered that in consideration of his humanity he should not be treated as a prisoner of war. After the conference of the 22d, and because of it, I decided to return to Richmond and employ all the power of my office to increase the strength of the army, so as the better to enable it to meet the public need, whether in offensive - defensive or purely defensive operations, as opportunity should offer for the one, or the renewal of invasion require for the other.

"A short time subsequent to my return, a message was brought to me, from the prison, to the effect that a non-commissioned officer, captured at Manassas, claimed to have a promise of protection from me. The name given was Hulbert, of Connecticut. I had forgotten the name he gave when I saw him; but, believing that I would recognize the person who had attended to Colonel Gardner, and to whom only such a promise had been given, the officer in charge was directed to send him to me. When he came I had no doubt of his identity, and explained to him that I had directed that he should not be treated as a prisoner, but that, in the multi-tude of those wearing the same uniform as his, some neglect or mistake had arisen, for which I was very sorry, and that he should be immediately released and sent down the river to the neighborhood of Fortress Monroe, where he would be among his own people. He then told me that he had a sister residing a few miles in the country, whom he would be very glad to visit. Permission was given him to do so, and a time fixed at which he was to report for transportation ; and so he left, with manifestations of thankfulness for the kind-ness with which he had been treated. In due time a newspaper was received, containing an account of his escape, and how he lingered about the suburbs of Richmond and made drawings of the surrounding fortifications. The treachery was as great as if his drawings had been valuable, which they could not have been, as we had only then commenced the detached works which were designed as a system of defences for Richmond."

The following letter, written by a Virginia soldier, illustrates the kindness of manner which characterized Mr. Davis toward all subordinates. He was approachable by all, even to the lowest in rank. The latter is given in illustration.

"On Monday, July 22, 1861, the day after the first battle of Manassas, it was raining very hard ; President Davis, Beauregard, and Johnston were holding a council of war in a tent. A young Mr. Fauntleroy, of my company, asked me to go with him on a little matter of business, not telling me what it was. He took me in the direction of the Moss mansion, and upon reaching the arched gateway we were confronted by a sentinel who promptly halted us. Fauntleroy remonstrated, telling the sentinel that he must see President Davis ; the sentinel refused, as President Davis was holding a council of war. Directly President Davis came out of the tent, Fauntleroy and myself were then allowed to pass. We reached there almost simultaneously with the President—he was half-way up the steps: Fauntleroy hailed him, with, ' Is that President Davis ? ' and he, in his inimitably bland way replied : ' Yes, sir,' and added, ' walk up, gentlemen, out of the rain.' We declined with thanks, and Fauntleroy then told him that he was T. K. Fauntleroy, of Clarke County, Virginia, and wanted a commission in the regular Confederate army. President Davis asked him if he was any relation to Colonel Fauntleroy of the United States army ; he replied that he was his uncle.

"The President told him he was really glad to meet him, and that if he lived to go back to Richmond, he would send him a commission ; to which Fauntleroy replied : '*Can I rely upon you, Mr. President?*' I was dumfounded, but the President was equal to the occasion, and in a manner that no man on earth could imitate or use, quietly and gently said, '*You can.*' I can never forget it.

"A month afterward, when we were in camp near Fairfax Court-House, one morning, a courier came up to where we were, bearing a commission to T. Kinloch Fauntleroy, as lieutenant in the regular Confederate army ; and I need not add that he was the happiest man I ever saw. . . .

"JOSEPH H. SHEPARD."

CHAPTER XIII.

RESPONSIBILITY FOR THE FAILURE TO PURSUE.

I CONTINUE my husband's review of the causes and responsibility for the failure of the Confederate army to pursue the Federals after the victory of Manassas, for those who loved him could scarcely give the just and impersonal account that he has, of the misrepresentations which fell thick as hail from his detractors upon him.

" When the smoke of battle had lifted from the field of Manassas, and the rejoicing over the victory had spread over the land and spent its exuberance, some who, like Job's war-horse 'sniffed the battle from afar,' but in whom the likeness there ceased, censoriously asked why the fruits of the victory had not been gathered by the capture of Washington City. Then some indiscreet friends of the generals commanding in that battle, instead of the easier task of justification chose the harder one of exculpation for the imputed failure. Their ill-advised zeal, combined, perhaps, with malice against me, induced the allegation that the President had prevented the generals from making an immediate and vigorous pursuit of the routed enemy.

" This, as the other stories had been, was left to the correction which time, it was hoped, would bring ; the sooner, because it was expected to be refuted by the reports of the commanding generals with whom I had conferred on that subject immediately after the battle.

" After considerable time had elapsed it was reported to me that a member of Congress, who had served on that occasion as a volunteer aid to General Beauregard, had stated in the House of Representatives that I had prevented the pursuit of the enemy after his defeat at Manassas.

" This gave to the rumor such official character and dignity as seemed to me to entitle it to notice not hitherto given. Wherefore I addressed to General Johnston the following inquiry, which, though restricted in its terms to the allegation, was of such tenor as left it to his option to state all the facts connected with the slander, if he should choose to do me that justice, or should see the public interest involved in the correction, which, as stated in my letter to him, was that which gave it, in my estimation, its claim to consideration and had caused me to address him on the subject :

" ' RICHMOND, VA., November 3, 1861.

" ' GENERAL J. E. JOHNSTON, Commanding Department of the Potomac.

" ' SIR : Reports have been and are being widely circulated to the effect that I prevented General Beauregard from pursuing the enemy after the battle of Manassas, and had subsequently restrained him from advancing upon Washington City. Though such statements may have been made merely for my injury, and in that view might be postponed to a more convenient season, they have acquired importance from the fact that they have served to create distrust, to excite disappointment, and must embarrass the administration in its further efforts to reinforce the armies of the Potomac, and generally to provide for the public defence.   For these public considerations I call upon you, as the commanding general, and as a party to all the conferences held by me on July 21st and 22d, to say whether I obstructed the pursuit of the enemy after the victory of Manassas, or have ever objected to an advance or other active operation which it was feasible for the army to undertake.

" ' Very respectfully yours, etc.,

" JEFFERSON DAVIS.'

" ' To His Excellency the President.

" ' Sir : I have had the honor to receive
your letter of the 3d instant, in which you call
upon me " as the commanding general, and as
a party to all the conferences held by you on
July 21st and 22d, to say whether you obstructed the pursuit after the victory of Manassas, or have ever objected to an advance
or other active operation which it was feasible for the army to undertake ? "

" ' To the first question I reply, No ; the
pursuit was " obstructed " by the enemy's
troops at Centreville, as I have stated in my
official report.   In that report I have also
said why no advance was made upon the
enemy's capital for reasons as follows :

" ' The apparent freshness of the United
States troops at Centreville, which checked
our pursuit, the strong forces occupying the
works near Georgetown, Arlington, and Alexandria ; the certainty, too, that General Patterson, if needed, would reach Washington
with his army of more than thirty thousand
sooner than we could ; and the condition and
inadequate means of the army in ammunition,
provisions, and transportation, prevented any
serious thought of advancing upon the Capitol.

" ' To the second question I reply that it has never been feasible for the army to advance farther than it has done — to the line of Fairfax Court - House, with its advanced posts at Upton's, Munson's, and Mason's Hill. After a conference at Fairfax Court-House with the three senior general officers, you announced it to be impracticable to give this army the strength which those officers considered necessary to enable it to assume the offensive. Upon which I drew it back to its present position. Most respectfully, your obedient servant,

" 'J. E. JOHNSTON.' "

" This answer to my inquiry was conclusive as to the charge which had been industriously circulated, that I had prevented the immediate pursuit of the enemy and had obstructed active operations after the battle of Manassas, and thus had caused the failure to reap the proper fruits of the victory.

" No specific inquiry was made by me as to the part I took in the conferences of July 21st and 22d, but a general reference was made to them. The entire silence of General Johnston in regard to those conferences is noticeable from the fact that, while his answer was strictly measured by the terms of my inquiry as to pursuit, he added a statement about a conference at Fairfax Court-House, which occurred in the autumn, say October, and could have had no relation to the question of pursuit of the enemy after the victory of Manassas, or other active operations therewith connected. The reasons stated in my letter for making an inquiry, naturally pointed to the conferences of July 21st and 22d, but surely not to a conference held months subsequent to the battle, and on a question quite different from that of hot pursuit. In regard to the matter of this subsequent conference I shall have more to say hereafter.

"I left the field of Manassas proud of the heroism of our troops in battle, and of the conduct of the officers who led them. Anxious to recognize the claim of the army on the gratitude of the country, it was my pleasing duty to bear testimony to their merit in every available form.

"With all the information possessed at the time by the commanding generals, the propriety of maintaining our position while seeking objects more easily obtained than the capture of the United States capital, seemed to me so demonstrable as to require no other justification than the statements to which I have referred, in connection with the conference of July 22d. It would have seemed to me then, as it does now,* to be less than was due to the energy and fortitude of our troops, to plead a want of transportation and supplies for a march of about twenty miles through a country which had not been denuded by the ravages of war.

"Under these impressions and with such feelings, I wrote to General Beauregard as follows:

"'RICHMOND, VA., August 4, 1861.

"'GENERAL BEAUREGARD, Manassas, Va.

"'MY DEAR SIR: I think you are unjust to yourself in putting your failure to pursue the enemy to Washington to the account of short supplies of subsistence and transportation. Under the circumstances of our army, and in the absence of the knowledge since acquired, if indeed the statements be true, it would have been extremely hazardous to have done more than was performed. You will not fail to remember that, so far from knowing that the enemy was routed, a large part of our forces were moved by you, in the night of the 21st, to repel a supposed attack upon our right, and that the next day's operations did not fully reveal what has since been reported of the enemy's panic. Enough was done for glory, and the measure of duty was full. Let us rather show the untaught that their desires

---

* This was written after deliberation in 1887.

are unreasonable, than, by dwelling on the possibilities recently developed, give form and substance to the criticisms always easy to those who judge after the event.

"'With sincere esteem, I am your friend,
"'JEFFERSON DAVIS.'"

"I had declared myself content and gratified with the conduct of the troops and the officers, and supposed the generals, in recognition of my efforts to aid them by increasing their forces and munitions, as well as by my abstinence from all interference with them upon the field, would have had neither cause nor motive to reflect upon me in their reports, and it was with equal surprise and regret that in this I found myself mistaken.

"General Johnston, in his report, represented an order to him to make a junction with General Beauregard as a movement left to his discretion, with the condition that, if made, he should first send his sick and baggage to Culpepper Court-House. I felt constrained to put upon his report, when it was received, the following endorsement:

"The telegram referred to by General Johnston in this report, as received by him at about one o'clock on the morning of July 18th, is inaccurately reported; the following is a copy:

"'Richmond, July 17, 1861.

"'General J. E. Johnston, Winchester, Va.

"'General Beauregard is attacked. To strike the enemy a decided blow a junction of all your effective force will be needed. If practicable make the movement, sending your sick and baggage to Culpepper Court-House, either by railroad or by Warrenton. In all the arrangements exercise your discretion.

"'S. Cooper,

"'*Adjutant and Inspector-General.*'

"The word 'after' is not found in the despatch before the words 'sending your sick,' as is stated in the report; so that the argument based on it requires no comment. The order to move 'if practicable,' had reference to General Johnston's letters of July 12th and 15th, representing the relative strength and positions of the enemy under Patterson, and of his own forces, to be such as to make it doubtful whether General Johnston had the power to effect the movement.

"Upon the receipt of General Beauregard's report of the battle of Manassas, I found that it contained matter which seemed to me out of place, and therefore addressed to him the following letter:

" 'RICHMOND, VA., October 30, 1861.

" ' GENERAL BEAUREGARD, Manassas, Va.

" ' SIR : Yesterday my attention was called
to various newspaper publications, purporting
to have been sent from Manassas, and to be
a synopsis of your report of the battle of July
21st, last, and in which it is represented that
you have been overruled by me in your plan
for a battle with the enemy, south of the Potomac, for the capture of Baltimore and
Washington, and the liberation of Maryland.

" ' I inquired for your long-expected report,
and it has been to-day submitted for my inspection. It appears, by official endorsement,
to have been received by the Adjutant-General on October 18th, though it is dated August 26, 1861.

" ' With much surprise I found that the
newspaper statements were sustained by the
text of your report. I was surprised, because if we did differ in opinion as to the
measure and purposes of contemplated campaigns, such facts could have no appropriate
place in the report of a battle; further, because it seemed to be an attempt to exalt
yourself at my expense ; and, especially, because no such plan as that described was
submitted to me. It is true that, some time
before it was ordered, you expressed a desire for the junction of General Johnston's

VOL. II.—9

army with your own. The movement was
postponed until the operations of the enemy
rendered it necessary, and until it became
thereby practicable to make it with safety to
the Valley of Virginia. Hence I believe was
secured the success by which it was attended.

" ' If you have retained a copy of the plan of
campaign which you say was submitted to me
through Colonel Chesnut, allow me to request that you will furnish me with a duplicate of it.

" ' Very respectfully yours, etc.

" ' JEFFERSON DAVIS.'

" As General Beauregard did not think it
proper to omit that portion of his report to
which objection was made, it necessitated,
when the entire report was transmitted to
Congress, the placing of an endorsement upon
it reviewing that part of the report which I
considered objectionable. The Congress in
its discretion, ordered the publication of the
report, except that part to which the endorsement referred, thereby judiciously suppress-
ing both the endorsement and the portion of
the report to which it related. In this case
and *every other* official report ever submitted
to me, I made neither alteration nor eras-
ure.

" That portion of the report which was sup-

pressed by the Congress has, since the war, found its way into the press, but the endorsement that belongs to it has not been published. As part of the history of the time, I here present both in their proper connection :

" ' GENERAL S. COOPER, *Adjutant and Inspector-General*, Richmond, Va.

" ' Before entering upon a narration of the general military operations in the presence of the enemy on July 21st, I propose, I hope not unreasonably, first to recite certain events which belong to the strategy of the campaign, and consequently form an essential part of the history of the battle.

" ' Having become satisfied that the advance of the enemy with a decidedly superior force, both as to numbers and war equipage, to attack or to turn my position in this quarter, was immediately impending, I despatched on July 13th one of my staff, Colonel James Chesnut, of South Carolina, to submit, for the consideration of the President, a plan of operations substantially as follows :

" ' I proposed that General Johnston should unite, as soon as possible, the bulk of the army of the Shenandoah with that of the Potomac, then under my command, leaving only sufficient force to garrison his strong works at Winchester, and to guard the five defensive

passes of the Blue Ridge, and thus hold Patterson in check.   At the same time Brigadier-
General Holmes was to march hither with all
his command not essential for the defence of
the position at Acquia Creek.   These junctions
having been effected at Manassas, an immediate impetuous attack of our combined armies
upon General McDowell was to follow, as
soon as he approached my advanced position
at and around Fairfax Court-House, with the
inevitable result, as I submitted, of his complete defeat and the destruction or capture of
his army.   This accomplished, the army of
the Shenandoah, under General Johnston,
increased with a part of my forces and rejoined, as he returned, by the detachment left
to hold the mountain-passes, was to march
back rapidly into the Valley, fall upon and
crush Patterson with a superior force, where-
soever he might be found.   This, I confidently estimated, could be achieved within fifteen
days after General Johnston should march
from Winchester for Manassas.

" ' Meanwhile, I was to occupy the enemy's
works on this side of the Potomac, if, as I
anticipated, he had been so routed as to enable me to enter them with him ; or if not, to
retire again for a time within the lines of Bull
Run with my main force.   Patterson having
been virtually destroyed, then General John-

ston would reinforce General Garnett sufficiently to make him superior to his opponent
(General McClellan), and able to defeat that
officer.   This done, General Garnett was to
form an immediate junction with General
Johnston, who was forthwith to cross the
Potomac into Maryland with his whole force,
arouse the people as he advanced to the recovery of their political rights and the defence of their homes and families from an
offensive invader, and then march to the investment of Washington, in the rear, while I
resumed the offensive in front.   This plan of
operations, you are aware, was not acceptable at the time, from considerations which
appeared so weighty as to more than coun-
terbalance its proposed advantages.   Informed of these views and of the decision of
the War Department, I then made my preparations for the stoutest practicable defence of
the line of Bull Run, the enemy having developed his purpose, by the advance on, and
occupation of, Fairfax Court-House, from
which my advance brigade had been withdrawn.

" ' The War Department having been informed by me, by telegraph, on July 17th, of
the movement of General McDowell, General
Johnston was immediately ordered to form a
junction of his army corps with mine, should

the movement in his judgment be deemed
advisable.   General Holmes was also directed
to push forward, with two regiments, a battery, and one company of cavalry.' "

" The order issued by the War Department
to General Johnston was not, as herein reported, to form a junction ' should the movement in his judgment be deemed advisable.'
The following is an accurate copy of the
order :

" ' General Beauregard is attacked.   To
strike the enemy a decisive blow, a junction
of all your effective force will be needed.   If
practicable make the movement, sending your
sick and baggage to Culpepper Court-House,
either by railroad or by Warrenton.   In all of
the arrangements exercise your discretion.' "

" The words ' if practicable ' had reference
to letters of General Johnston of July 12th
and 15th, which made it extremely doubtful if
he had the power to make the movement, in
view of the relative strength and position of
Patterson's forces as compared with his own.

" The plan of campaign reported to have
been submitted, but not accepted, and to have
led to a decision of the War Department,
cannot be found among its files, nor any reference to any decision made upon it ; and it
was not known that the army had advanced
beyond the line of Bull Run, the position pre-

viously selected by General Lee, and which was supposed to have continued to be the defensive line occupied by the main body of our forces. Inquiry has developed the fact that a message, to be verbally delivered, was sent by the Honorable Mr. Chesnut. If the conjectures recited in the report were entertained, they rested on the accomplishment of one great condition, namely, that a junction of the forces of General Johnston and Holmes should be made with the army of General Beauregard and should gain a victory. The junction was made, the victory was won ; but the consequences that were predicted did not result. The reasons why no such consequences could result are given in the closing passages of the reports of both the commanding generals, and the responsibility cannot be transferred to the Government at Richmond, which certainly would have united in any feasible plan to accomplish such desirable results.

" If the plan of the campaign mentioned in the report had been presented in a written communication, and in sufficient detail to permit proper investigation, it must have been pronounced to be impossible at that time, and its proposal could only have been accounted for by the want of information of the forces and positions of the armies in the field. The facts which rendered it impossible are the following :

" I. It was based, as related from memory by Colonel Chesnut, on the supposition of drawing a force of about 25,000 men from the command of General Johnston. The letters of General Johnston show his effective force to have been only 11,000, with an enemy 30,000 strong in his front, ready to take possession of the Valley of Virginia on his withdrawal.

" II. It proposed to continue operations by effecting a junction of a part of the victorious forces with the army of General Garnett, in Western Virginia. General Garnett's forces amounted only to 3 or 4,000 men, then known to be in rapid retreat before vastly superior forces under McClellan, and the news that he was himself killed and his army scattered arrived within forty-eight hours of Colonel Chesnut's arrival in Richmond.

" III. The plan was based on the improbable and inadmissible supposition that the enemy was to wait everywhere, isolated and motionless, until our forces could effect junctions to attack them in detail.

" IV. It could not be expected that any success obtainable on the battle-field would enable our forces to carry the fortifications on the Potomac, garrisoned, and within supporting distance of fresh troops ; nor, after the actual battle and victory, did the generals on the field propose an advance on the Capitol ; nor does it appear that they since have believed themselves in a condition to attempt such a movement.

" It is proper also to observe that there is no communication on file in the War Department, as recited at the close of the report, showing what were the causes which prevented the advance of our forces and a prolonged, vigorous pursuit of the enemy to and beyond the Potomac."

I reproduce these evidences of the injustice of the slanders that attributed to my husband the failure to follow the victory at Manassas, because they have been reproduced in book form, and may be regarded in foreign lands as Confederate authorities. I learn the refutations have not been seen by writers who otherwise would have been impartial historians of the war between the States, and have far from exhausted the proof of the absolute verity of my husband's refutation ; but I have quoted enough to enable the reader to see the gross injustice of the accusation that he was responsible for the non-action of our armies.

CHAPTER XIV.

AFTER the battle of Manassas the Confederate army settled down in camp at and around Centreville.

Although after combining the armies of Generals Johnston and Beauregard at Manassas the command of the whole would unquestionably devolve upon General Johnston, matters did not apparently run smoothly between the two generals, and conflicts of authority occurred, as will appear by the following letters and telegrams.*

In fact, General Johnston brooked no interference with his command, even by his superiors in the government at Richmond.

On July 24, 1861, General J. E. Johnston wrote to General Cooper, the Adjutant-General, as follows :

" GENERAL : Lieutenant-Colonel Maury reported to me this morning as A. A. G., being assigned to that place by General Lee. I had already selected Major Rhett for the po-

---

* Published for the first time.

sition in question, who had entered upon its duties, *and can admit the power of no officer of the Army to annul my order on the subject;* nor can I admit the claim of any officer to *the command of 'the forces,' being myself the ranking General of the Confederate Army.**

"Let me add that I have a high opinion of Lieutenant-Colonel Maury as an officer, and warm personal regard for him.

"Most respectfully,

"Your obedient servant,

"JOSEPH E. JOHNSTON,

"*General C. S. A.*"

Upon this letter President Davis endorsed the word, "insubordinate."

On July 29, 1861, General Johnston wrote again to General Cooper:

"HEADQUARTERS, MANASSAS, July 29, 1861.

"GENERAL: I had the honor to write to you on the 24th instant on the subject of my rank compared with that of other officers of the Confederate Army. Since then I have received daily orders purporting to come from the '*Head Quarters of the forces,*' some of them in relation to the internal affairs of this army.

---

* The italics are the author's.

"Such orders I *cannot regard, because they are illegal.*

"Permit me to suggest that orders should come from your office.

"Most respectfully,
"Your obedient servant,
"J. E. JOHNSTON,
"*General C. S. A.*"

Upon this letter President Davis also endorsed the word "insubordinate."

On August 1, 1861, President Davis wrote to General Johnston at Manassas as follows:

"We are anxiously looking for official reports of the battle of Manassas, and have present need to know what supplies and wagons were captured. I wish you would have prepared a statement of your wants in transportation and supplies of all kinds, to put your army on a proper footing for active operations. . . .

"I am as ever your friend,
(Signed)   "JEFFERSON DAVIS."

General Johnston apparently becoming more and more impatient and irritated at affairs at Centreville and at Richmond, wrote to the President under date of September 10th, as follows:

"MANASSAS, September 10, 1861.

" HIS EXCELLENCY, THE PRESIDENT.

" SIR : It was said that during the past summer I have been censured by the two persons in Richmond highest in military rank, for not having assumed command of this army, and that they complain of the inconvenience to the service which had been produced thereby.

" Permit me to say that this accusation is untrue. I am, and have been, in command of the army. Have felt the responsibility of that command, and understood that, even if so disposed, I could not put it aside.

" The fact that I treat General Beauregard in the manner due to the commander of a corps d'armée, not in the manner usual from a United States colonel to his next in rank, must have produced this impression. Let me remind you, too, that in an army which has been almost stationary, there are few orders necessary to the commander of an army corps.

" Having heard no specification of inconveniences, I shall not attempt specific defence, but will venture to say that the inconveniences perceived in the army have been thought by it to have been produced in Richmond.

" I have taken the liberty, more than once,

to suggest to you to assume the military functions of the Presidency, and to command on
this northern frontier. I thought my meaning was very plainly expressed. I find I was
mistaken, and that you regard one of the
last expressions of this idea as not applicable
to yourself. I may have written carelessly
because, being by our laws *next in military
place to yourself*, it did not occur to me that
anyone else could be supposed to be thought
of. In offering this suggestion, I was prompted by the idea that such a course on your
part would prevent any political agitation in
the country.

" Most respectfully,
" Your obedient servant,
" J. E. JOHNSTON, *General.*"

" I could not doubt from your letters to
me that you considered me as commanding
this army.   " J. E. JOHNSTON."

"RICHMOND, VA., September 13, 1861.

" GENERAL J. E. JOHNSTON, Manassas, Va.
" MY DEAR GENERAL : Yours of the 10th
instant is before me, and I can only suppose
that you have been deceived by someone
of that class in whose absence 'the strife
ceaseth.' While you were in the Valley of
Virginia, your army and that of General

Beauregard were independent commands; when you marched to Manassas, the forces joined and did duty together. I trust the two officers highest in military rank in Richmond were too well informed to have doubted in either case as to your power and duty.

"Persons have talked here of the command of yourself and Beauregard as separate armies, and complaints have been uttered to the effect that you took the reinforcements and guns for your own army; but to educated soldiers this could only seem the muttering of the un-instructed, the rivalry of those who did not comprehend that unity was a necessity, a law of existence.

"Not having heard the accusations, I am like yourself ignorant of the specifications, and will add that I do not believe any disposition has existed on the part of the gentlemen to whom you refer to criticise, still less to de-tract from, you. If they believed that you did not exercise command over the whole it was, I doubt not, ascribed to delicacy.

"You are not mistaken in your construc-tion of my letters having been written to you as the Commanding General. I have, how-ever, sometimes had to repel the idea that there was a want of co-operation between yourself and the second in command, or a want of recognition of your position as the senior and commanding general of all the forces serving at or near the field of your late brilliant achievements.

" While writing, it occurs to me that statements have been made, and official applications received, in relation to staff officers which suggested a contingence of separation rather than unity in the ' army of the Potomac.'

" I did not understand your suggestion as to a commander-in-chief for your army. The laws of the Confederacy in relation to generals have provisions which are new and unsettled by decisions, their provisions special, and as the attention of Congress was called to what might be regarded as a conflict of laws, their action was confined to the fixing of dates for the generals of the Confederate States Army.   " Your friend,
            " JEFFERSON DAVIS."

Before the receipt of the foregoing letter of the President, General Johnston addressed him as follows :

" HEADQUARTERS, MANASSAS, September 12, 1861.

" SIR : I have had the honor to receive through the War Department a copy of the proceedings of Congress on August 31, 1861, confirming the nominations made by the President of the Confederate States of five Generals of the Confederate Army and fixing their relative rank.

" I will not affect to disguise the surprise and mortification produced in my mind by the action taken in this matter by the President and by Congress. I beg to state further, with the most profound respect for both branches of the Government, that these proceedings are in violation of my rights as an officer, of the plighted faith of the Confederacy, and of the Constitution and laws of the land. Such being my views, lest my silence should be deemed significant of acquiescence, it is a duty as well as a right on my part, at once to enter my earnest protest against the wrong which I conceive has been done me. I now and here declare my claim that, notwithstanding the nominations made by the President, and their confirmation by Congress, I still rightfully hold the rank of first General in the armies of the Southern Confederacy. I will proceed briefly to state the grounds upon which I rest this claim.

" The act of the Confederate Congress of March 6, 1861, section 8, amended by that of March 14, 1861, section 2, creates the .grade of Brigadier-General as the highest rank in their service, and provides that there shall be five officers of that grade. The fifth

section of the last-named act enacts ' That in
all cases of officers who have resigned, or who
may within six months tender their resignation from the army of the United States, and
who have been or may be appointed to original vacancies in the army of the Confederate
States, the commissions issued shall have
been one and the same date, so that the relative rank of officers shall be determined by
their former commissions in the United States
Army held anterior to the secession of the
Confederate States from the United States.'

" Under these laws, on May 13, 1861, R.
E. Lee and myself were nominated as Brigadier-Generals in the Confederate States Army.
Samuel Cooper had been nominated to the
same grade and confirmed a few weeks previously.

" The nominations of myself and R. E. Lee
were confirmed by Congress promptly. Each
of the three had resigned his commission in
the United States Army in accordance with
the terms of the law. The other two had resigned colonelcies, but the commission which
I had resigned was that of a Brigadier-General. It is plain, then, that under these laws
I was the officer first in rank in the Confederate Army. Two or three days afterward,
on May 16th, Congress, by the second section
of its act of that date, enacted, ' That the five

general officers provided by existing laws for the Confederate States shall have the rank and denomination of " General " instead of " Brigadier-General," which shall be the highest military grade known to the Confederate States. They shall be assigned to such commands and duties as the President may specially direct, and shall be entitled to the same pay,' etc.

" I conceive, and I submit to the careful consideration of the Government, that this section of the act last cited operated in two ways : 1. It abolished the grade of Brigadier-General in the Confederate Army. 2. It at once, by the mere force of law, raised the three officers already named to the rank and denomination of ' General' in the army of the Confederate States. The right, therefore, which I claim to my rank is founded on this act. Congress by its act, the President by his approval of it, at once made us Generals. It is clear that such likewise was the construction of both branches of the Government, else why were not nominations made then ? It was a time of flagrant war. Either we were Generals, or the army and country were left without such officers. Our former grade had been abolished. We were not Brigadier-Generals, we were nothing, and could perform no military duty, exercise no command. I think it

clear that I was a General by the plain terms
of the law. It is plain from the action of the
President and Congress that such was their
construction, as I was at once ordered to Harper's Ferry to take command in the valley of
Virginia, and the President soon after placed
three Brigadier - Generals under my orders.
In hurrying to assume the command in the
valley of Virginia, I did not wait for my commission to be sent to me. I did not doubt
that it would be made out, for I was persuaded that it was my right, and had no idea
that there was any purpose of withholding it.
I remained two months in the valley, too earnestly engaged in the public service to busy
myself particularly in my personal interests.
But when the emergencies of the campaign
required me to march to Manassas, and to act
with another general officer, I appreciated
the importance and the indispensable necessity of not leaving the question of rank open
or doubtful between us. With this view I
transmitted a telegraphic despatch to the
President on July 20th, inquiring, in the sim-
plest and most direct terms, what my rank
was. He replied that I was a General. The
battle of Manassas ensued on the next day.
The President came in person to participate
in it, but reached the scene of action soon after the close of the struggle. The morning

after the battle he announced his purpose to elevate General Beauregard to the rank of General. He returned to Richmond the ensuing day. The nomination was made immediately on his return, and was promptly confirmed by Congress. General Beauregard then became a General and ranked me unless I was such by virtue of the act of Congress on May 16th, already referred to. Yet from the time of General Beauregard's appointment to the day of the renewed nominations I continued to act as the commanding General of the 'Army of the Potomac,' under the authority of the President and of the Department of War. Thus it appears that I have the sanction of the President to my claim of rank under the act of Congress. In addition to this, my rank was expressly recognized by Congress also in the resolutions adopted by that body returning the thanks of Congress to General Johnston, to General Beauregard, and to the officers and soldiers of the army for the victory of Manassas.

" Thus stood matters when the recent nominations were made. But one additional name was offered—that of A. S. Johnston. His commission in the army of the United States had been that of Colonel. I as resigning the higher rank in that army, was, by the provisions of the act of Congress of March 14, 1861,

and the plighted faith of the Government of
the Confederate States, the General first in
rank in their armies. By that act and that of
May 16, 1861, the rank would stand thus : J.
E. Johnston, S. Cooper, A. S. Johnston, R. E.
Lee, G. T. Beauregard.*

"I held, and claim to hold, my rank as General under the act of May 16, 1861. I was a
General thenceforth or never. I had the full
authority of the constitutional Government of
the Confederate States to sustain me. Heretofore those who disputed my authority as
General have done so because they denied
the existence of the Government whose officer
I claimed to be. Now that Government joins
the hostile power in denying my authority.
When I sent back the missives of the Gov-

---

* In a letter from the President, in answer to one of mine regretting
that General Johnston should feel annoyed, as he was a friend and
his wife was very dear to me, I find this remark : " General Johnston
does not remember that he did not leave the United States Army
to enter the Confederate States Army, but that he entered the Army
of Virginia, and when Virginia joined the Confederacy he came to
the Confederate States ; also that in the Virginia Army he was the
subordinate of Lee, and that they were nominated to our Provisional
Congress at the same time and with the same relative rank they had
in Virginia. The Quartermaster-General had only assimilated or
protective rank, and from it derived no right to command, but by law
was prohibited from exercising command of troops." General Johnston's promotion under the old Government to be Quartermaster-
General was violently opposed in the Senate, and Mr. Davis, then a
Senator, spoke for the greater part of two hours to carry the point,
and did so, and received General Johnston's acknowledgments for
the service.

ernment of the United States, because they ignored the Government which I served and acknowledged, I little thought that one of the
acts of that Government would be to ignore me
as its officer, by trampling upon its own solemn
legislative and executive action. The nomination seeks to annul the irrevocable part, and to
make me such only from the 4th day of July.
The present, and so far as human legislation
may operate, the future, may be controlled by
Congress. Human power cannot affect the
past. Congress may vacate my commission
and reduce me to the ranks. It cannot make
it true that I was not a General before July
4, 1861.

" The effect of the course pursued is this :
It transfers me from the position first in rank
to that of fourth. The relative rank of the
others among themselves is unaltered. It
is plain that this is a blow aimed at me only.
It reduces my rank in the grade I hold. This
has never been done heretofore in the regular service in America but by the sentence of
a court-martial as a punishment and as a disgrace for some military offence. It seeks to
tarnish my fair fame as a soldier and as a man,
earned by more than thirty years of laborious
and perilous service. I had but this—the
scars of many wounds, all honestly taken in my
front and in the front of battle, and my father's

revolutionary sword. It was delivered to me
from his venerable hand without a stain of dis-
honor. Its blade is still unblemished as when
it passed from his hand to mine. I drew it
in the war, not for rank or fame, but to defend
the sacred soil, the homes and hearths, the
women and children, ay, and the men of my
mother, Virginia—my native South. It may
hereafter be the sword of a general leading
armies, or of a private volunteer. But while I
live and have an arm to wield it, it shall never
be sheathed until the freedom, independence,
and full rights of the South are achieved.
When that is done, it may well be a matter of
small concern to the Government, to Congress,
or to the country, what my rank or lot may be.

"I shall be satisfied if my country stands
among the powers of the world free, powerful, and victorious, and that I as a general, a
lieutenant, or a volunteer soldier, have borne
my part in the glorious strife, and contributed
to the final blessed consummation.

"What has the aspect of a studied indignity is offered me. My noble associate with
me in the battle has his preferment connected
with the victory won by our common trials
and dangers. His commission bears the date
of July 21, 1861, but care seems to be taken
to exclude the idea that I had any part in
winning our triumph.

" My commission is made to bear such a date that my once inferiors in the service of the United States and of the Confederate States shall be above me. But it must not be dated as of July 21st, nor be suggestive of the victory of Manassas.

" I return to my first position. I repeat that my rank as General is established by the acts of Congress of March 14, 1861, and May 16, 1861. To deprive me of that rank it was necessary for Congress to repeal these laws. That could be done by express legislative act alone. It was not done, it could not be done by a mere vote in secret session upon a list of nominations.

" If the action against which I have protested is legal, it is not for me to question the expediency of degrading one who has served laboriously from the commencement of the war on this frontier, and borne a prominent part in the only great event of that war, for the benefit of persons neither of whom has yet struck a blow for this Confederacy.

" These views and the freedom with which they are presented may be unusual, so likewise is the occasion which calls them forth.

" I have the honor to be, most respectfully,
" Your obedient servant,
" J. E. JOHNSTON, *General*."

To which letter Mr. Davis briefly replied as follows :

"RICHMOND, VA., September 14, 1861.

"GENERAL J. E. JOHNSTON :

"SIR : I have just received and read your letter of the 12th instant. Its language is, as you say, unusual ; its arguments and statements utterly one-sided, and its insinuations as unfounded as they are unbecoming.

"I am, etc.,

"JEFFERSON DAVIS."

General Johnston in his "Narrative" respecting the foregoing letter says :

"I wrote the President such a statement as the preceding (referring to his rank in the army of the United States), and also expressed my sense of the wrong done me.

"But in order that the sense of injury might not betray me into the use of language improper for an officer to the President, I laid aside the letter for two days, and then examined it dispassionately. I believe, and was confident that what it contained was not improper to be said to the President, nor improperly said. The letter was therefore despatched.

"It is said to have irritated him, and that his irritation was freely expressed."

Those who have read the telegrams and letters from the President sent to General Johnston up to the date of the above-mentioned letter, will observe the kind, courteous and friendly tone in which the President always addressed him, and it is not to be wondered at that it produced the "irritation" (if nothing more) that General Johnston mentions. That it did not interfere, however, with their "official" relations will be observed in their later correspondence.

General Johnston's remark that the President's irritation was freely expressed shows either a desire to justify himself for constant strictures upon the President, or that he ignored the President's reticent temper. In the whole period of his official relation to General Johnston, in the confidence of family intercourse, I never heard him utter a word in derogation of General Johnston, though he often differed from him in his views of military strategy.

Of camp gossip one would suppose that a man so eminent as General Johnston would take no cognizance, still less repeat it as the substance of a charge against another.

In connection with the foregoing letter of General Johnston, it may be as well to give here the roster of the "Generals" of the

Confederate army in 1861–62.   They were as
follows :

Samuel Cooper, to rank May 16, 1861.

Albert Sidney Johnston, to rank May 30,
1861.

Robert E. Lee, to rank June 14, 1861.

J. E. Johnston, to rank July 4, 1861.

G. T. Beauregard, to rank July 21, 1861.

Braxton Bragg, to rank April 12, 1862.

To explain even more fully the position
taken by Mr. Davis in assigning the above-
named officers to their relative rank, the
following extract is taken from " Destruction
and Reconstruction " by General Richard
Taylor.   He writes :

"Near the close of President Buchanan's
administration, in 1860, died General Jessup,
Quartermaster-General of the United States
Army ; and J. E. Johnston, then Lieutenant-
Colonel of Cavalry, was appointed to the
vacancy.

"Now the Quartermaster-General had the
rank, pay, and emoluments of a Brigadier-
General ; but the rank was staff, and by law
this officer could not exercise command over
the troops unless by special assignment.
When, in the spring of 1861, the officers in
question entered the service of the Confederacy, Cooper had been Adjutant-General of
the United States Army, with the rank of

Colonel; Albert Sidney Johnston, Colonel, and Brigadier-General by brevet, and on duty as such; Lee, Lieutenant-Colonel of Cavalry, senior to J. E. Johnston in the line before the latter's appointment above mentioned; Beauregard, Major of Engineers.

" General Beauregard, who about this time was transferred to the Army of the West, commanded by Albert Sidney Johnston, was also known to have grievances. . . . Indiscreet persons at Richmond, claiming the privilege and discharging the duty of friendship, gave tongue to loud and frequent plaints, and increased the confusion of the hour."

In a letter to Honorable James Lyons, of Richmond, Va., dated August 30, 1878, Mr. Davis says:

" In relation to the complaint of my giving General Lee the higher rank, I have only to say that it seems to me quite absurd. Of the two, General Lee had the higher rank as a cadet; came out of Mexico with a higher brevet; had the higher rank in the cavalry of the United States; had the higher rank in the Army of Virginia, from which they both came to join the Confederate Army, and was named first when both were nominated to the Congress for commissions as Brigadier-Generals of the Confederacy. It is true General Johnston, as Quartermaster-General of the

United States, had the staff commission as
Brigadier-General.   It is equally true that he
was prohibited by virtue of that commission
from assuming command of troops.

"I suppose he knew that when he was
nominated to be Quartermaster-General.   I
was chairman of the Committee on Military
Affairs, reported the nomination with the recommendation that he be confirmed ; that it
met serious opposition, and that all my power
and influence were required to prevent its
rejection.

"In that contest I had no aid from the
Senators of Virginia, perhaps because of their
want of confidence in Mr. Floyd.

"If Mason were living, he could tell more
of this than I am disposed to say."

An officer of the War Department at Washington, when sending Mr. Davis, in September, 1880, copies of General Johnston's letters
of March, 1862, said : "The official records
when published will not add to, but greatly
detract from, General Johnston's reputation."
He adds : "I can hardly conceive how you
(Mr. Davis) could so long have borne with
the 'snarly tone' of his letters, which he
wrote at all times and on all pretexts."

CHAPTER XV.

THE OPPOSITION OF CONGRESS TO THE PRESIDENT.

THE term of the Provisional Congress was now rapidly drawing to a close. The newly elected senators and members were to be sworn in, and the President's co-laborers in the formative period of the Government were to go out of office. Many of them were valued friends, and had a co-intelligence with him born of esteem and long observation of his habits of thought and his methods in the United States Senate. He was loth to part from them, and felt that their experience would render them more useful to the Government than new men could be, even though these might possess more ability; so that the year opened with an anxious sense of something being out of tune.

The paramount questions of the hour were, of course, to arm men for the contest, to procure ships and equip them for the destruction of the merchant marine of the United States, and to form an effective financial policy. On this last point there were many

opinions, and there had been many efforts
made by members of both houses to convince
the President of the expediency of selling
cotton to the enemy ; a larger party advocated the exportation of all the cotton grown
in the country to England.   Where the ships
were to come from for this immense exportation they did not point out ; carriers would
not be swift enough to run the blockade, and
the cotton would be captured, and serve to
supply the manufacturers of New England.
The men whose families were in need, and at
whose gin-houses the means of relief lay piled
in bulky plenty, of course leaned toward the
malcontents.   When all this cumbrous and un-
available wealth was burned by the Government, the dissatisfaction of some gave tongue.
The President and his advisers looked to the
stringency of the English cotton market, and
the suspension of the manufactories, to send
up a ground-swell from the English operatives
that would compel recognition, and grudged
every pound of cotton exported.   Now for
the first time there appeared to be an organized party in opposition to the Administration.   This might have been weakened by
daily social intercourse, and habituated as we
were to giving numerous entertainments of
an official character, we should gladly have
kept up the custom ; but during every enter-

tainment, without exception, either the death
of a relation was announced to a guest, or
a disaster to the Confederacy was telegraphed to the President. He was a nervous dyspeptic by habit, and if he was forced
to eat under any excitement, was ill after it
for days. He said he could do either one
duty or the other—give entertainments or
administer the Government—and he fancied
he was expected to perform the latter service
in preference ; and so we ceased to entertain,
except at formal receptions or informal dinners and breakfasts given to as many as Mr.
Davis's health permitted us to invite. In the
evening he was too exhausted to receive informal visitors. The *Examiner* sent forth a
wail of regret over the " parsimony of the
Administration." It touched feelingly upon
the deprivation to the young people of Richmond of not being received in the evening,
the assumption of " superior dignity by the
satraps," etc. This became a fierce growl,
as it contemplated the awful contingency of
the " President getting rich on his savings."

It would have been much better if the
President could have met the Congress, and
the State officials as well as the citizens,
socially and often, for the magnetism of his
personality would have greatly mollified their
resentments ; but for years his physician had

forbidden him to go at all into society in Washington, and he found this disability greater in Richmond, proportionately to the burden he bore.

One or two of the generals had their little cliques who sympathized with them. Some disappointed politicians felt that they had been overlooked, or their claims disregarded. Some thought they knew that their names had been preferred for the office which had been conferred upon Mr. Davis ; others felt sure that everyone except the President had preferred them for the portfolios unworthily held by others. In fact, it was the " Spectator's " allegory of the man who, dissatisfied with his short face, was allowed to lay it down, and yet could find none other to suit him. To these malcontents, always noncombatants, the blighter's hand was the President's.

Congressional committees made earnest and honest recommendations to him to do this or that, ignorant of what had transpired since they formulated their projects—which were perhaps well conceived when formed, but had become impracticable from the change of circumstances ; a politician would have flattered and appeared to confide in them without communicating anything, but Mr. Davis was too sincere for this policy. To have explained these difficulties would often have exposed the army or navy to danger; he therefore had to take refuge in silence; this was interpreted to mean contempt or a stubborn desire to dictate to the co-ordinate branch of government, and increased the discontent.

He was abnormally sensitive to disapprobation: even a child's disapproval discomposed him. He felt how much he was misunderstood, and the sense of mortification and injustice gave him a repellent manner. It was because of his supersensitive temperament and the acute suffering it caused him to be misunderstood, I had deprecated his assuming the civil administration.

He was always inclined to sacrifice himself rather than betray the trust even of an enemy. Once, when an officer he loved had been censured by one of the generals in a letter marked " private," and was indicated as one whose removal was required, the officer remonstrated warmly with the President, and, with the freedom of old friendship, said, " You know me, how could I ever hold my head up under implied censure, from you, my old friend?" The President, who could not explain that he found no fault in him, to cover his discomposure said, curtly, " You have, I believe, received your orders; I can suggest nothing but obedience."

His old friend left him wounded to the quick, and Mr. Davis came home and went, without eating, to his room and slept little. As soon as he could speak quietly of it, he said : " I would not secretly censure a man and ask another to take the responsibility, but, as the letter was confidential, all I could do was to make the poor fellow too mad with me to ask an explanation." So, little by little the Congress became alienated, or at least a large portion of them with a few of the military men. The President let the conviction gnaw at his vitals in silence. He used to say with a sigh, " If we succeed, we shall hear nothing of these malcontents ; if we do not, then I shall be held accountable by the majority of friends as well as foes. I will do my best, and God will give me strength to bear whatever comes to me."

CHAPTER XVI.

BEAUREGARD'S LETTER.

THE victory at Manassas was followed by a period of inactivity and of fancied security, so sure did many feel that this battle would end the war. This was shown by the decrease of enlistments; but President Davis did not coincide with this view. Foreign recognition was looked forward to as an assured fact, and the politicians began at once to speculate upon the future recipients of the most prominent offices in the new Confederacy.

Mr. Hunter, of Virginia, about this time left the Cabinet, in order, his enemies said, that his identification with the Administration should not damage his chances as Mr. Davis's successor to the Presidency. Mr. Davis was attached to him and thought he did not care to share the responsibility of a possible failure.

General Beauregard was also named in some quarters as the next Confederate President, the popular nominee of an honor to be conferred six years hence. Before the puta-

tive nomination he wrote the following discouraging letter to the Richmond *Whig.*

"CENTREVILLE, VA. (Within hearing of the enemy's guns.)
November 3, 1861.

"To the Editors of the Richmond *Whig.*

"GENTLEMEN : My attention had just been
called to an unfortunate controversy now going on, relative to the publication of the synopsis of my report of the battle of Manassas.
None can regret more than I do this publication, which was made without my knowledge
or authority.

"The President is the sole judge of when,
and what parts of, the reports of a commanding officer should be made public. I, individually, do not object to delaying its publication as long as the War Department shall
think it necessary and proper for the success
of our cause.

"Meanwhile I entreat my friends not to
trouble themselves about refuting the slanders and calumnies aimed at me. Alcibiades,
on a certain occasion, resorted to a singular
method to occupy the minds of his traducers ;
let, then, "that synopsis" answer the same
purpose for me in this instance. If certain
minds cannot understand the difference between *patriotism,* the highest civic virtue,
and *office-seeking,* the lowest civic occupa-

tion, I pity them from the bottom of my
heart.   Suffice it to say that I prefer the respect and esteem of my countrymen, to the
admiration and envy of the world.   I hope,
for the sake of our cause and country, to be
able, with the assistance of a kind Providence,
to answer my calumniators with new victories over our national enemies; but I have
nothing to ask of the country, the government, or my friends, except to afford me all
the aid they can in the great struggle we
are now engaged upon.

"I am not, and *never* expect or desire to be,
a candidate for any civic office in the gift of
the people or the Executive.

"The *acme* of my ambition is, after having
cast my *mite* in the defence of our sacred
cause, and assisted to the best of my ability
in securing our rights and independence as a
nation, to retire into private life (my means
then permitting), never again to leave my
home, unless to fight anew the battles of my
country.

"Respectfully, your most obedient servant,
(Signed)   "G. T. BEAUREGARD."
"A true copy,
"S.W. FERGUSON, *Aide-de-Camp*."

Prior to the date of the above letter, in
which General Beauregard entreats his

friends "not to trouble themselves about refuting the slanders and calumnies aimed at
him" (in consequence of the publication of
the synopsis of his report of the battle of
Manassas), his relations with the Confederate
officials, "except Colonel Northrop, the Commissary-General," "had been those of un-
studied friendship." *

Having occasion to recommend the appointment of an officer as Chief of Ordnance
of the "First Corps," in the place of Captain
E. P. Alexander, an accomplished officer who
had been transferred to General Johnston, he
received from a "subordinate" † in the War
Department the brief reply that "the President did not approve the division of the army into two corps, and preferred that there
should be but one chief of ordnance to the army of the Potomac." At this General Beauregard took umbrage, esteeming himself a
better judge of such matters than the President. This circumstance led to an estrange-
ment between General Beauregard and the
authorities at Richmond, which apparently
widened as the war progressed.

The widely published synopsis of General
Beauregard's report of the battle of Man-

---

* Military Operations of General Beauregard, page 157.
† Colonel Alfred T. Bledsoe, Assistant Secretary of War.

assas, wherein it was stated that the rejection of his so-called plan of campaign, *verbally* presented by Colonel Chesnut to the
President, in the presence of Generals Lee
and Cooper, prevented the Federal army
from being destroyed before July 21st.
The President addressed a letter to those
officers, asking them to give him their opinions and recollections of the interview in
question.

The letter is dated November 4th, the day
after the publication of General Beauregard's
letter, written " *within hearing of the enemy's
guns.*" The reply of General R. E. Lee
should render any further discussion of the
vexed and profitless question unnecessary.

"RICHMOND, VA., November 4, 1861.

" GENERALS COOPER AND. LEE, Confederate
States Army.

" GENTLEMEN : The injurious effect produced by statements widely published to
show that the army of the Potomac had been
needlessly doomed to inactivity by my rejection of plans for vigorous movements against
the enemy, which were presented to me by
General Beauregard, induces me to ask you
to state what was the communication made
by that officer, through the Honorable Mr.

Chesnut, on the subject of his position at Manassas in July last, and what were the propositions and requests then conveyed to me.

" You are invited to refer to the introduction of General Beauregard's report of the battle of Manassas, that you may see how far the statement made therein agrees with the communication made to me by the Honorable Mr. Chesnut, in the interview at which you were present.

" I have requested General Beauregard to furnish me with a plan of battle and campaign, which he says in his report was submitted to me, but have not received an answer.

" Very respectfully yours, etc.,

" JEFFERSON DAVIS."

" COOSAWHATCHIE, S. C., November 24, 1861.

"HIS EXCELLENCY, The President of the Confederate States :

"My absence on an examination of the coast of South Carolina and Georgia has prevented until now my reply to your note of the 4th instant, asking what communication was made by General Beauregard to you through the Honorable Mr. Chesnut, on the subject of his position at Manassas in July last, and what were the propositions and requests conveyed by him.

"I have not seen the report of General Beauregard of the battle of Manassas, and am unable to refer to his introductory statement to which you call my attention. I cannot therefore say how far it agrees with the communication of Mr. Chesnut. I recollect, however, that at the interview at which I was present Mr. Chesnut urged, on the part of General Beauregard, the importance of reinforcing the army of the Potomac to enable it to oppose the Federal forces accumulating in its front. As a means of accomplishing this end, he suggested that a portion of the army in the Shenandoah Valley, under General Johnston, be ordered to join it. With the aid thus afforded, General Beauregard thought he could successfully resist an attack of the enemy. Should he succeed in repulsing him, he could in turn reinforce General Johnston. Should General Johnston succeed in driving back General Patterson, then in his front, he could reinforce the army in Northwestern Virginia. The advantages of the union of the armies on the Potomac had been more than once the subject of consideration by you, and I do not recollect that at the interview in question they were less apparent. The difficulty of timing the march of the troops so as to benefit one army without jeopardizing the object of the other, was therefore mainly con-

sidered, and you decided that the movements
of the enemy in and about Alexandria were
not sufficiently demonstrative as to warrant
the withdrawal of any of the forces from the
Shenandoah Valley. A few days afterward,
however, I think three or four, the reports
from General Beauregard showed so clearly
the enemy's purpose, that you ordered General Johnston with his effective force to march
at once to the support of General Beauregard,
and directed General Holmes, with such
troops as could be spared from the defence
of the approaches of Fredericksburg to move
upon Manassas.

" The successful combination of the armies
was made, and the glorious victory of July
21st followed.

" I have the honor, etc.,

" R. E. LEE."

About this time a controversy arose between General Beauregard and the Secretary
of War, Mr. Benjamin, caused by the organization of a rocket battery for the Army of the
Potomac. Mr. Davis wrote as follows :

" RICHMOND, VA., October 25, 1861.

" GENERAL BEAUREGARD, Manassas, Va.

" MY DEAR GENERAL : Your letters of October 20th and 21st have just been referred

to me, and I hasten to reply without consulting the Secretary of War. This enables me to say, without connecting his expressions of feeling with the present case, that you have alike his admiration and high personal regard, evinced by so many signs that it cannot be to me a matter of doubt. As the essence of offence is the motive with which words are spoken, I have thus, it is hoped, removed the gravest part of the transaction.

"You were unquestionably wrong in the order to recruit a company for the Provisional Army. The Congress, with jealous care, reserved to men of such companies the power of selecting their own officers. The Executive could not recruit a company except for the regular army, and as provided by law; to that extent he could delegate his power to Generals in the field, but he could not do more. I presume the objection was not, that it was to be a rocket battery, but was to the recruiting of a company for special service, the commander having been selected not by the men but by the Confederate authority.

"More than half of the controversies between men arise from difference of education and habits of thought. The letter in relation to the law of organization was written like a lawyer, and had it been addressed to one of that profession would not probably have wounded his sensibilities, except in so far as to provoke debate upon the accuracy of his position; but it was addressed to a soldier, sensitive as to the propriety of his motive, and careless about the point which I am sure the Secretary intended alone to present—inattention to, or misconstruction of the laws governing the case. He desired that your position should be entirely satisfactory to you, and that the freest scope should be given for the exercise of your genius and gallantry in the further maintenance of the cause, which amid the smoke and blaze of battle, you have three times illustrated. Prompted by that desire, he anticipated my purpose, which had been communicated to him, to place you in the immediate command of the Army of the Potomac, by referring to an order which would soon be issued, and which he hoped would be satisfactory to you.

"Now, my dear sir, let me entreat you to dismiss this small matter from your mind; in the hostile masses before you, you have a subject more worthy of your contemplation. The country needs all your mind and your heart; you have given cause to expect all which man can do, and your fame and her interests require that your energies should have a single object. My prayers always attend you, and with confidence I turn to you in the hour of peril.

"Very truly your friend,

(Signed) " JEFFERSON DAVIS."

"P.S.—The Secretary has not seen your letter, and I will not inform him as to the correspondence.

"J. D."

The Secretary, writing upon this subject to General Beaurega d, expressed his "no small surprise" that he should have committed an act " without warrant of law," and excused him only on account of his motives and his defect of judgment. This letter of Mr. Benjamin "staggered" General Beauregard, and he, overlooking Mr. Benjamin, referred the letter to the President. The President replied to the General, under date of November 10, 1861, and below his letter is given entire:

" RICHMOND, VA., November 10, 1861.

" GENERAL BEAUREGARD, Manassas, Va.

" SIR : When I addressed you in relation to your complaint because of the letters written to you by Mr. Benjamin, Acting Secretary of War, it was hoped that you would see that you had misinterpreted his expressions, and would be content. But while in yours of the

6th instant you accept the assurance given
that Mr. Benjamin could not have intended
to give you offence, you serve notice that
your 'motives must not be called into question,' and that when your 'errors are pointed
out it must be done in proper tone and style,'
and express the fear that Mr. Benjamin 'will,
under all circumstances, view only the *legal*
aspect of things, and that insensibly this
army and myself (yourself) will be put into
the straight-jackets of the law,' etc. I do
not feel competent to instruct Mr. Benjamin
in the matter of style. There are few whom
the public would probably believe fit for that
task. But the other point quoted from your
letter presents matter for graver considerations, and it is that which induces me to
reply. It cannot be peculiar to Mr. Benjamin to look at every exercise of official
power in its legal aspects, and you surely did
not intend to inform me that your army and
yourself are outside of the limits of the law.

"It is my duty to see that the laws are
faithfully executed, and I cannot recognize
the pretension of anyone that their restraint
is too narrow for him.

"The Congress carefully reserved to all
volunteers the selection of their company
officers, and provided various modes for recruiting them into service as organized

bodies. When you disregarded that right, and the case was brought to the notice of the Secretary of War, it could but create surprise; and the most mild and considerate course which could have been adopted was to check further progress under your order and inform you of the errors committed.

"Very respectfully yours, etc.,
(Signed) "JEFFERSON DAVIS."

The President was in this instance, as in every other, watching over the strict construction of the laws and the individual rights of the people of each State. He looked with anxious care to the elective rights of the men in the army, and it is very apparent by his first letter how anxious he was to conciliate General Beauregard and while impressing restrictions upon him, to avoid giving him pain. The first letter shows his animus, the second vindicates the law and protects the dignity of the Secretary of War.

VOL. II.—12

CHAPTER XVII.

ROANOKE ISLAND.—MR. DAVIS'S INAUGURATION.

THE year 1862 was destined to be a noted one in the annals of the country, and the military campaigns in the Confederate States opened early, to end only with the expiration of the year.

Early in the year, Mr. Walker having resigned his portfolio, a general reorganization of the cabinet was arranged, and, on March 17th, the Senate made the following confirmations :

Secretary of State—J. P. BENJAMIN.
Treasury—C. G. MEMMINGER.
Secretary of War—J. P. BENJAMIN.
Secretary of Navy—S. R. MALLORY.
Postmaster-General—J. H. REAGAN.
Attorney-General—THOMAS H. WATTS.

The dissolution of his cabinet disquieted the President greatly, and about this time the organized opposition party began to be felt. The enemy also manifested unusual activity.

Their first move was the capture of Roanoke Island, on the low coast-line of North Carolina, for it was an important outpost of

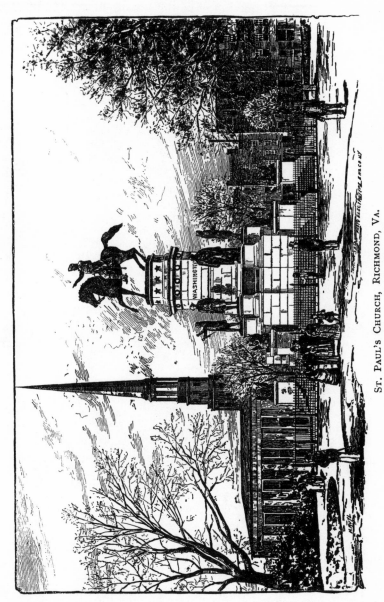

St. Paul's Church, Richmond, Va.

Where Mr. Davis worshiped—Washington Monument in the foreground

the Confederates. Its possession by the enemy would give them access to the country from which Norfolk drew its supplies.

On January 22, 1862, General Henry A. Wise was placed in command.

The defence of this island consisted of six land batteries, and after manning the guns there were not one thousand effective men for duty. Seven gunboats were in the Sound to aid in its defence.

On February 8th General Burnside attacked the defences of the island, and with overwhelming numbers outflanked them, and captured almost the entire force.

In this action Captain O. Jennings Wise, of the Richmond Blues, was killed. When he fell on the field, with a mortal wound, one of his men inquired if he was much hurt. His answer was, " Never mind me ; fight on, men, fight on, and keep cool." As he was being borne from the field a random shot struck and killed him. Nothing could have been more pathetic than the moan of his old father, " Oh, my brave boy, you have died for me ; you have died for me."

CHAPTER XVIII.

THE INAUGURATION.

THE Provisional Government had expired. The beginning of the new term of the Executive and the opening of the newly elected Congress drew nigh.

A contemporary account of the inaugural ceremonies is quoted, as it is, perhaps, a better description than could now be given. The sky lowered until 10 o'clock, and then a hard rain poured steadily down for four hours, and Mr. Davis came in from an early visit to his office and went into his room, where I found him, an hour afterward on his knees in earnest prayer "for the divine support I need so sorely."

"RICHMOND, February 22, 1862.

"The inauguration took place at 12 o'clock to-day, in accordance with the published programme. The two houses of Congress met in their respective halls at 11.30 o'clock, and soon thereafter repaired to the hall of the House of Representatives of Virginia. The President and Vice-President-elect were conducted to the hall by the Joint Committee of

Arrangements, the President arriving a few minutes after 12 o'clock, and were received by the assembly standing. The Honorable R. M. T. Hunter, of Virginia, the President of the Senate, occupied the seat on the right of the President-elect ; the Vice-President-elect that of the left on the President, and the Speaker of the House that on the left of the Vice-President.

"Invitations to the hall, and to join in the procession from thence to the bronze equestrian statue of Washington, at the foot of which the inaugural ceremony would take place, had been extended to members of the cabinet; the Governor of Virginia and his staff; the Governors of any other of the Confederate States who might be in Richmond, and ex-Governor Lowe, of Maryland; the Senate and the House of Delegates of Virginia, and their respective officers ; the Judges of the Supreme Court, and of any of the Confederate District Court at Richmond ; the members of the late Provincial Congress ; the officers of the army and navy who might be in the city ; the members of the Press ; the mayor and the corporate authorities of the city ; the reverend clergy and masonic and other benevolent societies.

" These assembled, at the hour indicated, and the procession, accompanied by an immense crowd, moved from the hall by the eastern door of the Capitol to the statue of Washington on the public square.

" A temporary platform and awning had been erected at the monument, which is a bronze equestrian statue of great size, surrounded by statues of Jefferson, Henry, and Mason. It was fortunate that an awning had been provided, since it commenced to rain early in the day, and has not yet stopped. An immense crowd had assembled around the monument, and bravely stood it out to the last, notwithstanding the rain.*

" The President and Vice-President were received with hearty and prolonged cheers. Upon the restoration of order an eloquent prayer was offered up by the Right Reverend Bishop Johns.

" The President-elect then delivered his inaugural address. It was characterized by great dignity, united with much feeling and grace, especially the closing sentence. Throwing up his eyes and hands to heaven he said, ' With humble gratitude and adoration, acknowledging the Providence which has so visibly protected the Confederacy during its brief, but eventful career, to Thee,

---

* It was a panorama of umbrellas, and a wag who took the census of them found there were twelve blacks to one brown, eight blacks to one green, and the blues hid their diminished heads.

O God, I trustingly commit myself, and prayerfully invoke Thy blessing on my country and its cause.'" Thus Mr. Davis entered on his martyrdom. As he stood pale and emaciated, dedicating himself to the service of the Confederacy, evidently forgetful of everything but his sacred oath, he seemed to me a willing victim going to his funeral pyre, and the idea so affected me that making some excuse I regained my carriage and went home.

" The oath to support the Constitution of the Confederate States was then administered by Judge Haliburton, of the Confederate District Court for this District, a nephew of Mrs. Washington. Mr. Hunter, President of the Senate, proclaimed Jefferson Davis to be President of the Confederate States of America for the term of six years from this day. The announcement was received with immense cheering.

" Mr. Hunter next administered the oath to the Vice-President, and then made proclamation that Alexander H. Stephens was the Vice-President of the Confederate States for a similar term of six years. This announcement was made amid great applause. There was an effort to induce Mr. Stephens to say something ; but as such a thing was not expected, or perhaps proper, he simply made a profound bow to the audience and returned to his seat.

CHAPTER XIX.

EFFORT TO EFFECT EXCHANGE OF PRISONERS—
EVACUATION OF MANASSAS—VISIT TO FREDER-
ICKSBURG.

ABOUT the end of January, 1862, the Confederate Government endeavored to procure
the exchange of prisoners taken by the armies of the belligerents, and an officer was sent
by General Johnston to General McClellan.

The proposition was not entertained by
the Federal Government, and our efforts to
shorten the imprisonment of the captives in
our hands met no encouragement from their
own friends.

Thus early in the war the Confederate Government displayed its desire to secure a free
exchange of prisoners, which, had it been
carried out in good faith by the Federals,
would have saved from unavoidable suffering
and death, thousands of both armies.

In view of the near approach of the spring
campaign, President Davis issued the following proclamation :

" By virtue of the power vested in me by
law, to declare the suspension of the privilege

of the writ of habeas corpus in cities threatened with invasion ;

"I, Jefferson Davis, President of the Confederate States of America, do proclaim that martial law is hereby extended over the city of Richmond and the adjoining country to the distance of ten miles.   And I do proclaim the suspension of all civil jurisdiction with the exception of the Mayor of the city, and the suspension of the privilege of the writ of habeas corpus within the said city and surrounding country to the distance aforesaid.

"In faith whereof I have hereunto signed my name and set my seal, at the city of Richmond, on the first day of March, in the year one thousand eight hundred and sixty-two.

(Seal.)   "JEFFERSON DAVIS."

On February 2d General Beauregard took leave of the Army of the Potomac, having been transferred to the army in West Tennessee, commanded by Albert Sidney Johnston.

The Federal forces then organizing in front of Washington, under General George B. McClellan, and estimated to number one hundred thousand men, gave indication of active operations.   General Johnston, in a personal interview in Richmond, gave notice that he considered his position as unsafe, and a withdrawal of the army from Centreville was

necessary before McClellan's invasion; the
latter accordingly addressed to him the following letter :

"RICHMOND, VA., February 28, 1862.

"GENERAL J. E. JOHNSTON : Your opinion
that your position may be turned whenever
the enemy chooses to advance, and that he
will be ready to take the field before yourself,
clearly indicates prompt effort to disencumber
yourself of everything which would interfere
with your rapid movement when necessary,
and such thorough examination of the country
in your rear as would give you exact knowledge of its roads and general topography, and
enable you to select a line of greater natural
advantages than that now occupied by your
forces.

" The heavy guns at Manassas and Evans-
port, needed elsewhere, and reported to be
useless in their present position, would necessarily be abandoned in a hasty retreat. I regret that you find it impossible to move them.

" The subsistence stores should, when removed, be placed in positions to answer
your future wants. Those cannot be determined until you have furnished definite information as to your plans, especially the line to
which you would remove in the contingency
of retiring. The Commissary-General had
previously stopped further shipments to your

army, and given satisfactory reasons for the establishment at Thoroughfare.* . . ."

" I need not urge on your consideration the value to our country of arms and munitions of war; you know the difficulty with which we have obtained our small supply; that to furnish heavy artillery to the advanced posts we have exhausted the supplies here which were designed for the armament of the city defences. Whatever can be, should be done to avoid the loss of these guns. . . .

" As has been my custom, I have only sought to present general purposes and views. I rely upon your special knowledge and high ability to effect whatever is practicable in this our hour of need. Recent disasters have depressed the weak, and are depriving us of the aid of the wavering. Traitors show the tendencies heretofore concealed, and the selfish grow clamorous for local and personal interests. At such an hour the wisdom of the trained and the steadiness of the brave possess a double value. The military paradox that impossibilities must be rendered possible, had never better occasion for its application.

" The engineers for whom you asked have been ordered to report to you, and further additions will be made to your list of briga-

---

* Thoroughfare Gap was the point at which the Commissary-General had placed a meat-packing establishment.

dier-generals.   Let me hear from you often and fully.

"Very truly and respectfully yours,

"JEFFERSON DAVIS."

The President again wrote as follows :

"RICHMOND, VA., March 6, 1862.

"GENERAL J. E. JOHNSTON : Notwithstanding the threatening position of the enemy, I infer from your account of the roads and streams that his active operations must be for some time delayed, and thus I am permitted to hope that you will be able to mobilize your army by the removal of your heavy ordnance and such stores as are not required for active operations, so that, whenever you are required to move, it may be without public loss and without impediment to celerity.   I was fully impressed with the difficulties which you presented when discussing the subject of a change of position.   To preserve the efficiency of your army, you will, of course, avoid all needless exposure ; and, when your army has been relieved of all useless encumbrance, you can have no occasion to move it while the roads and weather are such as would involve serious suffering, because the same reasons must restrain the operations of the enemy.   .   .   .

"Very respectfully yours,

"JEFFERSON DAVIS."

General Johnston began his retreat on March 7th, but such was the confusion incident upon moving the troops out of their winter quarters, that it was not until the evening of the 9th that order was restored to the retreating column. The troops moved out on the 8th, passed the succeeding twenty-four hours on the roadside, and suffered much from the inclement weather and excessive cold.

The retreat continued to the south bank of the Rappahannock, where a halt was called, and the troops encamped.

In the undue haste to retire from the front of McClellan, who did not follow, nor even interfere with General Johnston's rear-guard, stores, arms, clothing, etc., were abandoned and burned, notwithstanding the urgent warning of Mr. Davis in his letters of February 28th and of March 6th.

General Early, in stating the amount of unnecessary loss at Manassas, wrote as follows :

" A very large amount of stores and provisions had been abandoned for want of transportation, and among the stores was a very large quantity of clothing, blankets, etc., which had been provided by the States south of Virginia for their own troops. The pile of trunks along the railroad was appalling to behold. All these stores, clothing, trunks, etc., were consigned to the flames by a portion of our cavalry left to carry out the work of their destruction. The loss of stores at this point, and at White Plains, on the Manassas Gap Railroad, where a large amount of meat had been salted and stored, was a very serious one to us, and embarrassed us for the remainder of the war, as it put us at once on a running stock."

The same officer subsequently wrote, in regard to the loss of supplies :

" I believe that all might have been carried off from Manassas if the railroads had been energetically operated."

On March 10th the President, not then informed of General Johnston's retrograde movement, telegraphed him as follows :

" Further assurances given me this day that you shall be promptly reinforced, so as to enable you to maintain your position and resume first policy when the roads will permit." The first policy was to carry the war beyond our own border.

On March 15th the President received notice that the army was in retreat, and replied :

"RICHMOND, VA., March 15, 1862.

" GENERAL J. E. JOHNSTON,

" Headquarters Army of the Potomac.

" GENERAL : I have received your letter of the 13th instant, giving the first official ac-

count I have received of the retrograde movement of your army.

"Your letter would lead me to infer that
others had been sent to apprise me of your
plans and movements. If so, they have not
reached me ; and before the receipt of yours
of the 13th I was as much in the dark as to
your purposes, condition, and necessities, as
at the time of our conversation on the subject
about a month since.

"It is true I have had many and alarming
reports of great destruction of ammunition,
camp equipage, and provisions, indicating
precipitate retreat; but having heard of no
cause for such a sudden movement I was at
a loss to believe it.

"I have not the requisite topographical
knowledge for the selection of your position.
I had intended that you should determine
that question ; and for this purpose a corps
of engineers was furnished to make a careful
examination of the country to aid you in your
decision.

"The question of throwing troops into
Richmond is contingent upon reverses in the
West and Southeast. The immediate neces-
sity for such a movement is not anticipated.

"Very respectfully yours,
"JEFFERSON DAVIS."

On the same day the President sent the following telegram :

"RICHMOND, VA., March 15, 1862.

"GENERAL J. E. JOHNSTON,

"Culpepper Court-House, Va.

"Your letter of the 13th received this day, being the first information of your retrograde movement. I have no report of your reconnaissance, and can suggest nothing as to the position you should take, except it should be as far in advance as consistent with your safety.

"JEFFERSON DAVIS."

The President immediately went to General Johnston's headquarters, and found him on the south bank of the Rappahannock River, to which he had retired, in a position possessing great natural advantages.

Upon inquiring whether the south bank of the river continued to command the other side down to Fredericksburg, General Johnston replied he did not know, that he had not been there for many years.

The President and General Johnston proceeded to Fredericksburg, and a reconnaissance soon manifested that the hills on the opposite bank commanded the town, and therefore Fredericksburg could only be defended by an army occupying the opposite

Mrs. Henry's House, near the center of the battlefield of Manassas, in which the wounded were nursed by Bishop Wilmer of Ala — as it appeared after the battle.

hills, for which the Confederate force was inadequate.

While in Fredericksburg the President and General Johnston were the guests of J. Temple Doswell, and at his house met a large number of ladies and gentlemen, among whom were the Honorable W. S. Barton, R. W. Adams, F. T. Forbes, J. L. Marye, and the venerable T. B. Barton. In answer to the question as to the result of the reconnaissance, the President replied to Mr. Doswell, during their ride, that Fredericksburg was " right in the wrong place " for military defence.

Upon learning that the town was not to be defended, young and old, with self-sacrificing patriotism, answered, " If the good of our cause requires the defence of the town to be abandoned, let it be done."

The President returned to Richmond to await the further development of the enemy's plans.

General Johnston, in an article in the *Century* of May, 1885, entitled " Manassas to Seven Pines," seems to have entirely forgotten that Mr. Davis visited him at his headquarters in the field after he had retreated to the south bank of the Rappahannock, and that together they went to Fredericksburg.

He uses these words :

" Mr. Davis's narrative that follows is disposed of by the proof that after the army
left Manassas the President did not visit it
until about May 14. . . . That he did
not make such a visit is proved by Major J.
B. Washington, aide-de-camp, Dr. Fauntleroy, surgeon, and Colonel E. J. Harvie, staff
officers, who testify that they have no recollection whatever of such a visit at such a time."

While it may not be of any great importance
to history whether Mr. Davis and General
Johnston did or did not visit Fredericksburg
together, still positive proof is presented that
such a visit was made, and that General
Johnston's memory has failed him.

In the Rebellion Records, published by the
War Department at Washington, volume xi.,
part 3, page 392, will be found the following
order, issued to General Johnston by the
President, while at Fredericksburg, May 22,
1862.

"FREDERICKSBURG, VA., March 22, 1862.

" GENERAL JOSEPH H. JOHNSTON,

"SIR : I. You will relieve Major-General
Holmes of his command, and direct him to
report at Richmond for further orders.

" II. You will detach two brigades of infantry and two companies of artillery, with
orders to report to Major-General Holmes with

the least delay at his headquarters in the field.

"III. The troops when passing through Richmond will be reported to the Adjutant-General for any instructions which it may be needful to give them at that point.

"Very respectfully yours,

"JEFFERSON DAVIS."

"HEADQUARTERS, DEPARTMENT OF NORTHERN VIRGINIA,
"RAPIDAN, March 23, 1862.

"Special Orders, No. 83.

"Under orders of the President:

"I. Major-General T. H. Holmes, commanding Acquia District, is relieved from the command of that district, and assigned to duty temporarily with General Lee, and will report to the Adjutant and Inspector-General, Richmond, Va., for further orders.

.   .   .   .   .

"By command of General Johnston.

"A. P. MASON."

The following letters, written by residents of Fredericksburg, are also appended to prove conclusively that Mr. Davis, and not General Johnston, is right:

"FREDERICKSBURG, VA., August 10, 1885.

"JUDGE WILLIAM S. BARTON.

"MY DEAR SIR: In reply to your inquiry whether I knew that President Davis visi-

ted Fredericksburg in March, 1862, I beg to
say that I know he did. At what time of
the month it was, I cannot now state positively, but my impression is, it was between
the 15th and the 20th.

"On my return from Richmond, about 9 or
10 A.M., I found President Davis, General
Johnston, and General Holmes at my house.
Very soon after General Holmes ordered me
(I was his aide) to go with the President
and General Johnston across the river, to
make a reconnoissance of the country, etc.

"On the return from the reconnoissance
across the river, I well remember, in coming
through the little town of Falmouth, the
President, at whose side I was riding at the
time, made this remark to me: 'To use a
slang phrase, your town of Fredericksburg is
right in the wrong place,' to which I replied
I was well aware of the fact so far as its ca-
pability for being defended against an invading force was concerned.

"Yours truly,
"J. T. DOSWELL."

"FREDERICKSBURG, August 17, 1885.

"In March, 1862, President Davis and General J. E. Johnston visited Fredericksburg,
and were guests of my friend and connection,
Mr. J. T. Doswell. The morning after their

arrival, they crossed to the north side of the Rappahannock River, and were absent some hours examining the country. On their return to Mr. Doswell's house, many citizens called to pay their respects to the President.

"The result of their examination of the locality was understood here to be unfavorable to the defence of the town itself against an attack from the opposite bank of the river. I am unable to give the exact date of that visit. But some matters, personal to myself and distinctly remembered, enable me to state positively that it was before the arrival here of any of General Johnston's troops on their movement toward Yorktown, and before any of General McClellan's transports had passed down the Potomac River.

"W. S. BARTON."

CHAPTER XX.

THE EXECUTIVE MANSION—THE HOSPITALS.

IN July we moved to the " old Brocken-brugh house," and began to feel somewhat more at home when walking through the old-fashioned terraced garden or the large airy rooms in the seclusion of family life.

The mansion stands on the brow of a steep and very high hill, that is sharply defined against the plain at its foot through which runs the Danville railway that leads to the heart of Virginia.*

---

* On this plain, where the working class lived exclusively, the "Butcher cats" laid in wait for, and were sworn to eternal enmity against, the Hill cats. These high contending parties had a heredi-tary hate which had impelled them for nearly a hundred years to fight whenever close enough for either stones or fists to strike. They were the children of the poor against the gentlemen's sons. "I was," said a very steady painter's apprentice to me, "a Butcher cat before I moved up on Main Street." Allegiance seemed to change with the domicile. Woe betide the boy who stood at certain hours on the hill alone ; a shower of stones and bricks were thrown by the sturdy little lowlanders. The Hill cats gathered to the sound of a shrill whistle and sallied down with hands full of like weapons, to flee again to their hill-top as soon as they had discharged them. There were also set battles, in which, though the Hill cats had the advantage of position, the Butcher cats most often came out victors. A little orphan free negro boy whom we had rescued from one of his own color, who had beaten him terribly, lived from that time

The house is very large, but the rooms are comparatively few, as some of them are over forty feet square. The ceilings are high, the windows wide, and the well-staircases turn in easy curves toward the airy rooms above. The Carrara marble mantels were the delight of our children. One was a special favorite with them, on which the whole pilaster was covered by two lovely figures of Hebe and Diana, one on either side in bold relief, which, with commendatory taste, were not caryatides. The little boys, Jefferson and Joe, climbed up to the lips of these "pretty ladies" and showered kisses on them. The entablature was Apollo in his chariot, in basso relievo. Another was a charming conception of Cupid and Psyche, with Guido's Aurora

---

with us. Mr. Davis, notwithstanding his absorbing cares, went to the Mayor's office and had his free papers registered to insure Jim against getting into the power of the oppressor again. Jim Limber, which he said was his name in his every-day clothes, who became Jeems Henry Brooks in his best suit on Sunday, was a fearless ally of the Hill cats. Once he came in with the blood pouring over his face from a scalp wound made by a stone.

Mr. Davis was much troubled, for we were fond of the little boy. He descended the hill and, relying on his popularity with children, he made a little speech to the Butcher cats, in which he addressed them as the future rulers of their country. They listened attentively, nudging their approval to each other, but when he concluded, the tallest boy said, "President, we like you, we didn't want to hurt any of your boys, but we ain't *never* goin' to be friends with them Hill cats." So the President, like many another self-appointed peace-maker, came back without having accomplished anything except an exhausting walk.

for the entablature. A lady more in love
with art than learned in pronouncing gazet-
teers, said, with pleasure shining through her
eyes, "I do so love Cupid and Pish, sometimes I forget anyone is talking to me in
gazing at them."

The tastes, and to some extent the occupations and habits, of the master of a house, if
he, as in this case, assisted the architect in his
design, are built in the brick and mortar, and
like the maiden's blood in the great bell, they
proclaim aloud sympathy or war with those
whom it shelters.   One felt here the pleasant
sense of being in the home of a cultivated,
liberal, fine gentleman, and that he had dwelt
there in peaceful interchange of kind offices
with his neighbors.   The garden, planted in
cherry, apple, and pear trees, sloped in steep
terraces down the hill to join the plain below.
To this garden or pleasance came always in
my mind's eye a lovely woman, seen only by
the eye of faith, as she walked there in
"maiden meditation."

Every old Virginia gentleman of good social position who came to see us, looked pen-
sively out on the grounds and said, with a tone
of tender regret, something like this: " This
house was perfect when lovely Mary Brockenbrugh used to walk there, singing among
the flowers ; " and then came a description

of her light step, her dignified mien, her sweet voice, and the other graces which take hold of our hearts with a gentle touch, and hold them with a grip of steel. At first it seemed odd, and we regretted our visitor's disappointment, but after a while Mary came to us, too, and remained the tutelar goddess of the garden. Her name became a household word. "Whether Mary would approve," was a question my husband playfully asked, when he liked the arrangement of the drawing-rooms.

Mrs. James Grant lived in another fine old house next door to us, and with her we formed a lasting friendship, which was testified on her part by every neighborly attention that kind consideration could suggest. If Mr. Davis came riding up the street with General Lee, and their staff officers clattering after them, Mrs. Grant heard them and sent some dainty which her housewifely care had prepared, or fruit from her farm on the outskirts of Richmond. If our children were ill, she came full of hope and kind offices to cheer us by her good sense and womanly tenderness. The very sight of her handsome face brought comfort to our hearts. She fed the hungry, visited the sick, clothed the naked, showed mercy to the wicked, and her goodness, like the city set upon the hill, " could not be hid." Her brothers, the Crenshaws, had great flouring mills near Richmond, and made a noble use of their surplus in their unostentatious Quaker fashion. When flour became scarce and so high-priced as to prohibit the use of it to the poor, they dispensed it with glad alacrity to all who were in need. There were numbers who received it gratuitously and daily in small quantities from the mills. When a great fire consumed everything about them, the mills were untouched, and we, who believed in a special Providence, thought they were saved through the righteousness of their owners.

On my first introduction to the ladies of Richmond, I was impressed by the simplicity and sincerity of their manners, their beauty, and the absence of the gloze acquired by association in the merely " fashionable society." They felt the dignity attached to personally conducting their households in the best and most economical manner, cared little for fashionable small-talk, but were full of enthusiasm for their own people, and considered wisely and answered clearly any practical question which would tend to promote the good of their families or their country.

I was impressed by a certain offishness in their manner toward strangers ; they seemed to feel that an inundation of people perhaps of doubtful standards, and, at best, of different methods, had poured over the city, and they reserved their judgment and confidence, while they proffered a large hospitality. It was the manner usually found in English society toward strangers, no matter how well introduced, a wary welcome. In the more southern and less thickly settled part of our country, we had frontier hospitality because it was a necessity of the case. In Virginia, where the distances were not so great, and the candidates for entertainment were more numerous, it was of necessity more restricted.

We were fortunate in finding several old friends in Richmond. The Harrisons, of Brandon, and the handsome daughters of Mr. Ritchie, who had been for many years dear and valued friends. During our stay there we made other friends, who, if I never have the good fortune to meet them again, will remain to me a blessed memory. As I revert to the heroic, sincere, Christian women of that self-sacrificing community, it is impossible to specify those who excelled in all that makes a woman's children praise her in the gates and rise up and call her blessed, and this tribute is paid to them out of a heart full of tender reminiscences of the years we dwelt with them in mutual labor, sympathy, confidence, and affection. They clothed and cared for

their own households, sewed for the soldiers,
made our battle-flags, and sent their dearest
and only bread-winners to give their lives for
them. They fed the hungry, cared for the
orphans, deprived themselves of every wonted
luxury to give it to the soldiers, and were
amid their deprivations so cheerful, as to ani-
mate even the men with hope. When all
was lost, they awaited their fate with as much
silent courage as was evinced by the men.
The exception was a woman who did not
nurse at some hospital. I did not, because
Mr. Davis felt it was best for me not to expose the men to the restraint my presence
might have imposed, and in lieu of nursing I
issued provisions which had been sent to me
from the Governor of Virginia, and other
persons charitably inclined toward the families of soldiers.

Among those who labored in the hospitals,
I recall now with great clearness Mrs. Lucy
Webb, Miss Emily V. Mason, Mrs. Phœbe
Pember, and as well, Mrs. James Alfred
Jones's beautiful young face, in a tobacco
warehouse which had been converted into a
hospital ward for desperately wounded men.
She came forward with a bowl of water and a
sponge with which she had been wetting the
stump of a suffering soldier's arm. The atmosphere was fetid with the festering wounds,

and must have oppressed her greatly, for she
was as fragile as she was beautiful ; the tears
brimmed over her lovely eyes as she exclaimed, " Oh, Mrs. Davis, there has been a
case of pyæmia here, can nothing be done?"
We took counsel together for a moment, and
then I went to my husband, who had the
wounded men camped out, and fortunately
only one died.

Here I saw a remarkable instance of the
position our private soldiers occupied at home.
Some money had been sent to me from
Vicksburg to relieve the "boys from Warren
County." Hearing that there were several
at this hospital, I walked from one end to the
other and tried in vain to find a man who desired pecuniary aid. One fair - haired boy,
with emaciated face and armless sleeve, looked
up and whispered, " There is a poor fellow
on the other side who I think will take a little,
I am afraid he has no money ; my father gives
me all I want." I crossed the room and
asked the sufferer, who had neither hand, if I
could not get him something he craved. He
flushed and said, " I thank you, madam, for
your visit, but I do better than that poor fellow over there ; he has lost his leg and suffers
dreadfully." And so on to the end of the
ward.

Mr. James Lyons and his handsome wife

dispensed a large and graceful hospitality at
Laburnum, their country home in the suburbs,
and a finer example of a high-bred Virginia
household could not have been found.   The
Haxalls, McFarlands, Allens, Archers, An-
dersons, Stewarts, Warwicks, Stanards, and
others well and admiringly remembered, kept
pace with them, and bravely they bore aloft
the old standard of Virginia hospitality.

My husband's health was at this time very
precarious, and he was too weak to ride to
headquarters.   General Lee came up from
camp one day evidently worn out and worried,
to find Mr. Davis lying quite ill on a divan, in a
little morning-room in which we received only
our intimate friends.   General Lee, with a bow
and excuse for coming in on the white carpet
with his splashed boots, sat down and plunged
at once into army matters ; the outlook was
not encouraging, and the two friends talked
in a circle until both were worn out.   There
was a little silver saucepan on the hearth,
and the General stopped abruptly and said,
" That is a comfortable and pretty little thing,
what do you use it for ? "   And then what a
delight it gave me to heat steaming hot the
café au lait it contained and hand it to him
in a little Sèvres cup.   When I attempted to
ring for a servant to bring luncheon, he said,
" This drink is exquisite, but I cannot eat ; do

not call a servant, it is very cozy just so ; "
then looking at the cup, he remarked, with a
twinkle in his eye, " my cups in camp are
thicker, but this is thinner than the coffee."
Behind the playful speech I saw the intense
realization he had of the coarse ways and uncomfortable concomitants of a camp, and that
he missed as keenly the refinements of life to
which he had been accustomed after four
years, as he did at first.

In the last part of the war no one had delicacies, invitations very common among intimate friends were, " Do come to dinner or
tea, we succeeded in running the blockade this
week." This meant coffee after dinner, preserved fruits, loaf-sugar, good tea, or sometimes that which was always very acceptable
to Mr. Benjamin's palate, anchovy paste. He
used to say, with bread made of Crenshaw's
flour spread with the paste, English walnuts
from an immense tree in the grounds, and a
glass of the McHenry sherry, of which we had
a small store, "a man s patriotism became
rampant." Once, when he was invited to par-
take of a beefsteak pie, of which he was very
fond, he wrote : " I have never eaten them in
perfection except in the Cunard steamers (my
cook had been chef on one), and I shall enjoy
the scream of the sea-birds, the lashing of the
sea, and see ' the blue above and the blue

below,' while I eat it; so you may expect me."

The close relations that fellowship in danger brings about are sweet memories, and are harder to relinquish than those of courtly ceremony or triumph. Our women knitted like Penelope, from daylight until dark. They did it, however, not as a subterfuge, but to clothe their families and the soldiers—socks, gloves, mufflers, under-clothing, everything that could be worn of this fabric, was made and admirably shaped.

Mr. W. C. Rives was an exceedingly neat, well-dressed man always, and the careful attention he gave to his attire made him appear much younger than his long and distinguished service proved him to be. He came by invitation to our house one morning to breakfast, wearing such a beautifully fitted suit of gray clothes, with gaiters of the same, and they became him so well, that some of the young men remarked upon it and suggested that Mr. Rives must have "run the blockade;" he overheard them and whispered to me, "Look at me, my wife knitted every stitch of these clothes herself, and had the yarn spun and dyed first. She even knitted covering for the buttons." It required very close inspection by young eyes to see that they were knitted, and the dainty, soigné old gentleman looked his best in them.

Mrs. Robert E. Lee and her daughters, all honor to them, furnished one hundred and ninety-six socks and gloves to Posey's Brigade, and this when Mrs. Lee was confined to her chair, a hopeless victim of rheumatism, and her daughters' time was consumed by nursing in the hospitals.

Mrs. Mary Arnold, wife of W. T. Arnold, of Coweta, Ga., made in the year 1863 one thousand and twenty-eight yards of cloth, besides knitting gratis socks and gloves for the soldiers.

The ladies made themselves natty little gloves embroidered beautifully. Mrs. Pemberton sent me an admirable pattern, which with increase or decrease served our whole family. They covered their worn-out shoes with pieces of silk and satin, drawn from old boxes long unused; old scraps of silk were cut in strips, picked to pieces, carded and spun into fine yarn, and silk stockings knitted from it. The most beautiful hats were plaited from palmetto, dried and bleached, as well as from straw. The feathers from domestic fowls were so treated that they were very decorative to their bonnets, and if one sometimes regretted that millinery should be a matter of private judgment, still, in their pretty homespun dresses they would have passed favorably in review with any ladies.

All their accomplishments were pressed into the service of the soldiers. I remember going to one of the hospitals, to carry delicacies to the sick. Miss Emily V. Mason sat by one bed reading the prayers of the church to a man *in extremis*, while her gentle sister, Mrs. Roland, sat in another ward singing old-fashioned songs to her guitar as the dying boy would call for them, her eyes full of unshed tears, and her voice of melody. She was going blind and could not work, so she gave what she could.

We had no artificial appliances at the beginning of the war to supplement the loss of any member of the body. There had been, happily, little need for such aids before the war, and these few had been bought at the North; but very soon the most perfect artificial limbs were made in Charleston, as good, one maimed general told me, as those to be had anywhere.

It is a proud memory that the people of our country rose in their might, and met every emergency with industry, ingenuity, self-sacrifice, and reckless daring, worthy of their noble cause.

CHAPTER XXI.

EMANCIPATION PROCLAMATION.

THE Executive usurpation of unconstitu-
tional powers became conspicuous in 1862.
One after another barrier had been passed
without shocking the people. The session of
the Maryland State Legislature had virtually
been prorogued, some of its members arrested and imprisoned under circumstances of
great outrage.

Men had been arrested at long distances
from the seat of government, by *lettres de
cachet.* The Secretary of State's bell called
the emissary, and his signature was the only
warrant. Drum-head courts-martial condemned civilians to death by the verdicts of
military commanders. Domiciliary visits were
made at all hours for unspoken suspicions.
In fact, all civil rights were for the time suspended.

President Lincoln, reasoning by analogy,
thought that the immense property in slaves
possessed by the South might be the animat-
ing cause of the ardor and unanimity of the
Confederates, and conceived the project of

liberating all the slaves by a proclamation of gradual emancipation. He hoped to compass the voluntary relinquishment by each State of the right to hold them, by the manner of their manumission. His plan was to make it subject to the decision of each State, and the compensation for the loss was to be decided upon by the State with the co-operation of the United States Government. He said : " The leaders of the existing rebellion entertain the hope that this government will ultimately be forced to acknowledge the independence of some part of the disaffected region, and that all the slave States north of such part will then say, ' The Union for which we struggled being already gone, we now choose to go with the Southern section.' To deprive them of this hope substantially ends the rebellion, and the initiation of emancipation will deprive them, and all States including it."

President Lincoln hoped the love of gain would distract the counsels and alienate the rank and file of the Confederates, but feared that when slavery was abolished the Western States would find no further objection to a union with the Southern States, their natural allies, their neighbors and congeners in manners and tastes, and the Union would not be completely restored. The philanthropists and agitators, however, very soon saw, after a general computation, that if the proposition should be accepted by the States, the Government could not assume the payment of four hundred billions for the manumitted slaves, even though this might be an inadequate compensation to their owners. So the project of legally emancipating the slaves by the consent of their owners, and by offering compensation for them was abandoned.

Of the Act of Confiscation, issued July 25, 1862, Mr. Lincoln wrote, July 17, 1862 :

" It also provides that the slaves of persons confiscated under these sections shall be free. I think there is an unfortunate form of expressing, rather than a substantial objection to this. It is startling to say the Congress can free a slave without a State, and yet, were it said that the ownership of the slave had first been transferred to the nation, and that Congress had then liberated him, the difficulty would vanish, and this is the real case. The traitor against the general Government forfeits his slave, at least as justly as he does any other property, and he forfeits both to the Government against which he offends.*

---

* " How," said Mr. Davis, " can a people who glory in a Declaration of Independence which broke the slumbers of a world, declare that men united in defence of liberty, property, and the pursuit of happiness are ' traitors ? ' Is it henceforth to be a dictum of hu-

The Government, so far as there can be ownership, owns the forfeited slaves; and the question to Congress, in regard to them, is: Shall they be made free or sold to new masters? I see no objection to Congress deciding in advance that they shall be free."

On September 15th, Mr. Lincoln, to a deputation who urged him to issue the emancipation proclamation without compensation or restrictions, answered, with one of his pithy antitheses, " Such a proclamation would have no more effect than the Pope's tirade against the comet."

When our army suffered defeat, he conciliated the Radicals; when we were victorious, he took counsel with the more conservative men. We were just at that time in the ascendant, but after Sharpsburg Mr. Lincoln felt that he was in position to issue his first proclamation, in which he declared slavery abolished in all States after the 1st of January succeeding, except in such States as had submitted to Federal authority. After a hundred days he issued his second proclamation, to take effect at once.

---

manity that man may no more take up arms in defence of rights, liberty, and property? . . . Is the highwayman henceforth to be lord of the highway, and the poor, plundered traveller to have no property which he may defend at the risk of the life of the high-wayman?"

Then was consummated the series of aggressions of the anti-slavery party of the North, extending over thirty years, which now sought at a single dash of the pen to annihilate four hundred billions of our property, to disrupt the whole social structure of the South, and to pour over the country a flood of evils many times greater than the loss of property.

The effect of the Emancipation Proclamation on the people of the South was unmistakable. It roused them to a determination to resist to the uttermost a power that respected neither the rights of property nor constitutional guarantees.

The authority under which this usurpation was to be accomplished was alleged to be derived first from a " military necessity," and second, from the clause which gave to the Federal Government the right " to provide for the general welfare."

The verdict rendered by the people in their next elections was, therefore, a protest not only against interference with slavery in the Confederate States, but against the suspension of the writ of habeas corpus, and the other usurpations of Mr. Lincoln's Administration.

The Confederates were willing to have peace, but not to yield their rights under the Constitution, and the projects for reconstruc-

tion discussed by the North; none of them
guaranteed our equality in the Union. The
fatal policy of compromise was still adhered
to by our enemies, and the South was in Mr.
Webster's words on another occasion, to
"get just what the North yielded, nothing."
Meanwhile, almost every family in the South
had lost some dear defender of their honor,
who had died for liberty's sake, and the
bonds of the old loving Union had been
wrenched asunder. Our people were unwilling to yield an inch to the aggressions of the
North, for they no longer loved the Union as
it had been distorted by our enemies, and as
sincerely detested it as the abolitionists had
before secession, though even then our people did not characterize it as "a compact
with h——." The time had passed when a
compromise of our rights would have been
willingly made, that we might fight under the
banner our fathers so manfully aided to make
the ensign of freedom to all nations.

President Davis said: "The proclamation
will have a salutary effect in calming the fears
of those who have constantly evinced the apprehension that this war might end by some
reconstruction of the old Union, or some renewal of close political relations with the
United States. These fears have never been
shared by me, nor have I been able to perceive

on what basis they could rest. But the proclamation affords the fullest guarantee of the impossibility of such a result. It has established a state of things which can lead to but
one of three consequences—the extermination
of the slaves, the exile of the whole white
population of the Confederacy, or absolute
and total separation of these States from the
United States."

Now the North bent its energies to the
effort of subjugating the South, cast the
Constitution to the winds, and kept their
" powder dry." But though the majority of
the Confederates knew that, without a miracle, they must submit to the forces of the
world arrayed against them, they felt,"

Si cadere necessi est, occurrendum discrimini.

The condition of our servants began to be
unsettled, and it was said that there were clubs
of disaffected colored men in Richmond, generally presided over by a white man, who were
furnished with two thousand dollars for each
servant who ran off from our service; however,
as we lost but two in that way, it was hoped the
negroes did not sympathize with their abduc-
tors.

One young woman, who was an object of
much affectionate solicitude to me, followed

her husband off, but systematically arranged
her flight, made a good fire in the nursery,
and came to warn me that the baby would be
alone, as she was going out for a while. We
never saw her afterward, and the following
article copied in a Washington paper filled us
with grave apprehensions for the poor creature's safety.

"October 7, 1862.

" There are thousands of contrabands in
Alexandria, and such another set of miserable beings I have never seen in this country.
Some entire houses are set apart for them,
and into these the abandoned flock in droves.
Others live in tents, and others in the open
commons of the town.

" There is already great mortality among
them, and an Alexandria physician told me
that the small-pox had already broken out,
and would undoubtedly make great ravages
in their midst as soon as the cold weather
sets in. There is little or no occupation for
these contrabands. They are, in nine cases
out of ten, lazy, good-for-nothing vagabonds,
who seem impressed with the idea that it is
the duty of the Government to provide for
them. It is certain that Cuffee finds small
favor in the eyes of the troops who are now
there, particularly since the issue of the emancipation decree. Every day negroes are un-

mercifully beaten by white soldiers, and consider themselves lucky to get off with whole
bones. Well-dressed darkies are the special
aversion of the volunteers, and woe be unto
them if they show themselves in fine feathers
on King Street." (Alexandria, Va.)

CHAPTER XXII.

MISSOURI, MONITOR, AND VIRGINIA (MERRIMAC).

THE Confederate hopes were not easily daunted. After each disaster victory again crowned our army, and our confidence kept pace with our pride and admiration.

While the fight was going on in Missouri, the most dramatic contest of the war was in progress on the waters—a fight that not only ended in a great victory for the Confederacy, but revolutionized the art of naval warfare.

It was the fight between the *Virginia* (formerly the United States frigate *Merri-mac*) and the Federal fleet, including the new iron-clad the *Monitor*, at Hampton Roads, in which the *Virginia* sunk the *Congress*, and disabled and sunk several smaller vessels, besides silencing all the guns at Newport News but one.

The evacuation of Norfolk necessitated the destruction of the ram *Virginia*, as she could not be brought up the James river. The consternation was great when her loss was known—coming as it did so fast upon the heels of her triumph over the Federal fleet. The flag captured by her was brought to the Executive mansion for the President to see. It was borne by Colonel John Taylor Wood, a gallant participant in the fight, and was a bunting flag of very fine quality and large size. I took hold of it and found it damp with blood, and retired to my room sick of war and sorrowful over the dead and dying of both sections.

CHAPTER XXIII.

SHILOH, 1862.—CORINTH.

On February 4th General Beauregard arrived at Bowling Green and reported to his superior officer, General Albert Sidney Johnston. On the 6th Fort Henry surrendered after a soldierly defence.

February 11th the evacuation of Bowling Green was begun and ended on the 13th, and General Beauregard left for Columbus, Ky.

On the 16th Fort Donelson fell.

The loss of Forts Henry and Donelson opened the river routes to Nashville and North Alabama, and thus turned the positions both at Bowling Green and Columbus, and subjected General Johnston to severe criticism. The President was appealed to, to remove him; but his confidence in General Johnston remained unimpaired. In a letter to the President, dated March 18, 1862, General Johnston himself writes : " The test of merit in my profession, with the people, is success. It is a hard rule, but I think it right."

In reply to the letter from which the above

is an extract, the President wrote him as follows :

"RICHMOND, VA., March 26, 1862.

"MY DEAR GENERAL: Yours of the 18th instant was this day delivered by your aid, Mr. Jack. I have read it with much satisfaction. So far as the past is concerned, it but confirms the conclusions at which I had already arrived. My confidence in you has never wavered, and I hope the public will soon give me credit for judgment, rather than continue to arraign me for obstinacy.

" You have done wonderfully well, and now I breathe easier in the assurance that you will be able to make a *junction of your two armies.*

" If you can meet the division of the enemy moving from the Tennessee *before it can make a junction with that advancing from Nashville*, the future will be brighter. If this cannot be done, our only hope is that the people of the Southwest will rally *en masse* with their private arms, and thus enable you to oppose the vast army which will threaten the destruction of our country.

" I have hoped to be able to leave here for a short time, and would be much gratified to confer with you, and share your responsibilities. I might aid you in obtaining troops; no one could hope to do more unless he underrated your military capacity. I write in great haste, and feel that it would be worse than useless to point out to you how much depends on you.

" May God bless you, is the sincere prayer of your friend,   JEFFERSON DAVIS."

General Beauregard left Nashville on February 14th, to take charge in West Tennessee, and made his headquarters at Jackson, on February 17th.

He was somewhat prostrated with sickness, which partially disabled him through the campaign. The two grand divisions of his army were commanded by the able Generals Bragg and Polk. On March 26th he removed to Corinth.

The enemy commenced moving up the Tennessee River March 10th, with the design to mass the forces of Grant and Buell against the Confederate forces under Johnston and Beauregard at Corinth. General Grant assembled his army at Pittsburg Landing on March 17th.

The Confederate force at Corinth numbered about forty thousand, divided into four corps commanded respectively by Major-Generals Polk, Bragg, and Hardee, and Brigadier-General Breckinridge. General Beauregard was second in command under General Johnston.

The orders for the march and battle of the Confederate army were issued on the afternoon of April 3d, and the movement began with the intention of striking the enemy at Pittsburg Landing on the 5th, but delays, caused by confusion and intermingling of corps upon the road, were so great that the line of battle was not formed in front of the enemy's outposts until late in the evening of that day.*

General Bragg, in a monograph on the battle of Shiloh, says : " During the afternoon of the 5th, as the last of our troops were taking position, a casual and partly accidental meeting of general officers occurred just in rear of our second line, near the bivouac of General Bragg. The Commander-in-Chief, General Beauregard, Generals Polk, Bragg, and Breckinridge, are remembered as present. In a discussion of the causes of the delay and its incidents, it was mentioned that some of the troops, now in their third day only, were entirely out of food, though having marched with five days' rations. General

---

* *Telegram from the President.*

"RICHMOND, VA., April 5, 1862.
"To GENERAL A. S. JOHNSTON, Corinth, Miss.

"Your despatch of yesterday received. I hope you will be able to close with the enemy before his *two columns unite.* I anticipate victory.

"JEFFERSON DAVIS,"

Beauregard, confident our movement had been discovered by the enemy, urged its abandonment, a return to our camps for supplies, and a general change of programme. In this opinion no other seemed fully to concur; and when it was suggested that the enemy's supplies were much nearer, and could be had for the taking, General Johnston quietly remarked, 'Gentlemen, we shall attack at daylight to-morrow.' The meeting then dispersed, upon an invitation of the commanding general to meet at his tent that evening." That meeting did not change their determination. "The next morning, about dawn of day, the 6th, as the troops were being put in motion, several generals again met at the camp-fire of the general-in-chief. The discussion was renewed, General Beauregard again expressing his dissent; when rapid firing in the front indicating that the attack had commenced, General Johnston closed the discussion by remarking: 'The battle has opened, gentlemen; it is too late to change our dispositions.' He prepared to move to the front, and his subordinates promptly joined their respective commands, inspired by his coolness, confidence, and determination. Few men have equalled him in the possession and display, at the proper time, of these great qualities of the soldier."

The results of the first day of this famous
battle are summarily presented in the following brief report of General Beauregard :

" At 5 A.M., on the 6th instant, a reconnoi-
tring party of the enemy having become engaged with our advanced pickets, the commander of the forces gave orders to begin the
movement and attack as determined upon,
except that Trabue's brigade of Breckinridge's division was detached and advanced
to support the left of Bragg's corps and line
of battle, then menaced by the enemy; and
the other two brigades were directed to advance by the road to Hamburg to support
Bragg's right ; and at the same time Maney's
regiment of Polk's corps was advanced by the
same road to reinforce the regiment of cavalry and battery of four pieces, already thrown
forward to watch and guard Grier's, Tanner's,
and Borland's Fords of Lick Creek.

" Thirty minutes after 5 A.M. our lines and
columns were in motion, all animated evidently by a promising spirit. The front line
was engaged at once, but advanced steadily,
followed in due order, with equal resolution
and steadiness, by the other lines, which were
brought successively into action with rare
skill, judgment, and gallantry by the several
corps commanders, as the enemy made a
stand with his masses rallied for the struggle

for his encampments. Like an Alpine avalanche our troops moved forward, despite the
determined resistance of the enemy, until after
6 P.M., when we were in possession of all his
encampments between the Owl and Lick
Creeks but one; nearly all of his field-artil-
lery, about thirty flags, colors, and standards,
over three thousand prisoners, including a
division commander (General Prentiss) and
several brigade commanders, thousands of
small-arms, an immense supply of subsistence, forage, and munitions of war, and a
large amount of means of transportation, all
the substantial fruits of a most complete victory—such, indeed, as rarely have followed
the most successful battles, for never was an
army so well provided as that of our enemy.

" The remnant of his army had been driven
in utter disorder to the immediate vicinity of
Pittsburg, under the shelter of the heavy guns
of his iron-clad gunboats, and we remained
undisputed masters of his well-selected, admirably provided cantonments, after twelve
hours of obstinate conflict with his forces,
who had been beaten from them and the contiguous covert, but only by the sustained on-
set of all the men we could bring into action."

There are two words in this report which,
if they could have been truthfully omitted, it
would have been worth to us the surrender of

all "the substantial fruits of a most complete
victory." It says: " Our troops moved forward despite, the determined resistance of the
enemy, until after 6 P.M., when we were in
possession of all his encampments between
the Owl and Lick Creeks, *but one.*" It was
that "one" encampment that furnished a foot-
hold for all the subsequent reinforcements
sent by Buell, and gave occasion for the final
withdrawal of our forces ; whereas, if that
had been captured, and the " waters of the
Tennessee" reached, as General Johnston
intended, it was not too much to expect that
Grant's army would have surrendered ; that
Buell's forces would not have crossed the
Tennessee.

General Johnston fell at 2.30 P.M., while his
victorious army was pushing the enemy before him and in the full tide of glorious victory.

" The mortal wound was from a Minié-ball,
which tore the popliteal artery of the right
leg. He did not live more than ten or fifteen
minutes after receiving it. It was not necessarily fatal. General Johnston's own knowledge of surgery was adequate for its control
by an extemporized tourniquet, had he been
aware or regardful of its nature.

" Dr. D. W. Yandell, his surgeon, had attended his person during most of the morning,
but finding a large number of wounded men,

including many Federals, at one point, General Johnston ordered Yandell to stop there,
establish a hospital, and give them his services. He said to Yandell, ' These men
were our enemies a moment ago, that are
prisoners now ; take care of them.' Yandell
remonstrated against leaving him, but he was
peremptory, and the doctor began his work.
He saw General Johnston no more. Had
Yandell remained with him, he would have
had little difficulty with the wound. It was
this act of unselfish charity which cost him
his life." *

When rumors began to be circulated in
Richmond that a battle had been fought and
won at Corinth, the President endured the keen-
est anxiety; when remonstrance was made
against his depression he said, " I know Johnston, and if he is alive either good or bad news
would have been communicated at once."
When at last the dreadful certainty settled
upon him that General Johnston was no more,
he said the cause could have spared a whole
State better than that great soldier. He
wrote of him in the " Rise and Fall: "

" Sidney Johnston fell in the sight of victory ; the hour he had waited for, the event
he had planned for, had arrived. His fame

* Life of A. S. Johnston, by his son.

was vindicated, but far dearer than this to
his patriotic spirit was it with his dying eyes
to behold his country's flag, so lately drooping in disaster, triumphantly advancing. In
his fall the great pillar of the Southern Confederacy was crushed, and beneath its frag-
ments the best hope of the Southwest lay
buried. A highly educated and richly endowed soldier, his varied experience embraced
also civil affairs, and his intimate knowledge
of the country and people of the Southwest
so highly qualified him for that special command, that it was not possible to fill the place
made vacant by his death. Not for the first
time did the fate of an army depend upon a
single man, and the fortunes of a country
hang, as in a balance, on the achievements
of a single army. To take an example far
from us, in time and place, when Turenne
had, after months of successful manœuvring,
finally forced his enemy into a position which
gave assurance of victory, and had marshalled
his forces for a decisive battle, he was, when
making a preliminary reconnoissance, killed
by a chance shot ; then his successor, instead
of attacking, retreated, and all which the one
had gained for France, the other lost."

   .   .   .   .   .

The extracts which have been given
sufficiently prove that, when General John-

ston fell, the Confederate army was so fully
victorious that, had the attack been vigorously
pressed, General Grant and his army would
before the setting of the sun have been fugitives or prisoners.

The command then devolved upon General
Beauregard, who checked the advance all too
soon. An hour more and the enemy would
have surrendered or perished in the Tennessee. That this is not a reckless statement,
let us hear what the actors in the battle have
to say.

General Hardee, who commanded the first
line, says in his report:

" Upon the death of General Johnston, the
command having devolved upon General
Beauregard, the conflict was continued until
sunset, and the advance divisions were within
a few hundred· yards of Pittsburg, where the
enemy were huddled in confusion, *when the
order to withdraw was received.*"

General Polk in his report says:

" We had one hour or more of daylight
still left, were within one hundred and fifty to
four hundred yards of the enemy's position,
and nothing seemed wanting to complete the
most brilliant victory of the war but to press
forward and make a vigorous assault on the
demoralized remnant of his forces."

Statement of Colonel C. H. LeBaron.

" About 2 o'clock P.M., the first day's fight, when the enemy held a stubborn front to us, I was near General Bragg. He ordered me to go to General Johnston to ask for reinforcements. I obeyed his command and went to look for General Johnston. Some distance in the rear of the line of battle, I met Major Thomas Jordan, one of General Beauregard's staff. I was acquainted with him, and asked where I could find General Johnston. His reply was, 'General Johnston has been killed, General Beauregard is now in command; say nothing of General Johnston's death, the army must not know it. You will find General Beauregard back there, tell him Major Jordan requests him to come nearer to the front.' I went on my errand and asked for reinforcements, but said nothing about Major Jordan's request about coming nearer to the front.

" I returned to General Bragg and informed him of the death of General Johnston. The Confederates continued to drive the Federals from one stand to another, until about five o'clock P.M., when the latter ceased fighting and got under the river bank. At this time all was quiet, except an occasional shell from

the gunboats, which went high over our
heads; the Confederates coming up to the
front and resting. At this time, I saw at a
short distance off the Twenty-first Alabama
Regiment. Having two nephews and a cousin
in it, with numerous friends from Mobile, I
asked General Bragg's permission to go to
that regiment, which he granted. I found
them all in high spirits, feeling as if the work
had been done completely. Major Stewart, in
command, requested me to ask General Bragg
for orders. I went back to General Bragg,
and he ordered the Twenty-first Alabama to
advance and drive the enemy into the river,
and ordered me to carry the order along the
line. I left Major Stewart and was about to
carry out General Bragg's orders, when I
met one of General Beauregard's staff, who
inquired for General Bragg. I rode back to
General Bragg with this officer, who said to
General Bragg, 'General Beauregard orders
you to cease fighting and to rest your men to-
night;' to which General Bragg replied,
'Have you promulgated this order to the
command?' The officer replied, 'I have.'
General Bragg said: 'If you had not, I would
not obey it; the battle is lost.'"

Statement of Colonel William H. McCardle.

" As A. A. General of the First Division of the First Corps (Polk's), I had occasion to see General Beauregard twice during Sunday, April 6th. The first time I saw him was between ten and eleven o'clock A.M.; and the second time was between the hours of two and three o'clock P.M. Each time I saw him at his headquarters, some two miles in the rear, a distance that was constantly being lengthened by the advance of our troops and the retirement of the enemy. On each occasion he was eagerly anxious for news in regard to the progress of the fight. While retracing my steps to the front (with Howell Hinds) in the afternoon, I was met by Colonel Mumford, of the staff of General Johnston, who informed me of the death of General Johnston, and that he was hastening to General Beauregard to announce to him the sad news, and that the command devolved upon him. Of course it amounts to nothing when I say that I did not see General Beauregard on the field until after the fall of Johnston, but the conclusion is irresistible that he was *not* present until after that disastrous event. . . . I have nothing to say of the blunders of Beauregard after the death of Johnston, for they are sufficiently manifest to every one. . . ."

As the condition of affairs on the Confederate side has been plainly shown, what was
that of the enemy, and what would have been
the result of a further advance of the Confederates?

Colonel Geddes, of the Eighth Iowa Volunteers, says as follows:

"About three P.M., all communications with
the river (landing) ceased, and it became evident to me that the enemy was turning the
right and left flanks of our army. . . .

"About two o'clock the whole Union right,
comprising the Forty-sixth Ohio, which had
held that flank two hours or more, was driven
back in disorder, and the Confederate forces
cut the centre off from the landing soon after
General Johnston's fall."

When General Beauregard sent the order
for the battle to cease, Nelson's division of
Buell's army had just arrived on the opposite
bank of the river at Pittsburg, and was preparing to cross and go to the rescue of a
beaten and demoralized army. The junction
of the two Federal armies that General Johnston had tried to anticipate had been made.

In the "History of the Sixth Ohio Regiment," by E. Hannaford, the arrival of Nelson is thus described:

"On reaching the river opposite the battle-
field, General Nelson looked in vain for the

promised boats. The two or three stern-
wheel steamers that were lying under the
eastern bank, had come over simply to avoid
the rush of the mob on the farther shore, not,
however, until after some scores of the scared
wretches had succeeded in getting on board.

" Nelson had almost to force the captains
of these boats to take his foremost regiment,
the Thirty-sixth Indiana, across; and, having given orders to Colonel Ammen to get
his brigade over as quickly as possible and
then to follow in person, crossed to Pittsburg
Landing. He was the first to ride off the
boat, Dr. Bradford being the second. General Buell met him on the bank, and ordered
the men formed rapidly into line as they
should arrive, and moved to the front. 'You
have had the advance throughout the march,'
said Buell, 'and here, General, is your opportunity. There is still one hour left in
which to decide this fight.' At this time
the roar of battle sounded appallingly near;
everything was in confusion; thousands of
panic-stricken fugitives were cowering under
the bluff, filling the air with their cries and
lamentations; and hundreds of teams, with
all the débris of a beaten army, were com-
mingled in the utmost disorder, and covered
the landing down to the·water's edge. It
was a sickening sight—one that has never

been adequately described, and never can be. Finding that words were thrown away upon the rabble around him, General Nelson afterward asked permission to open fire upon them. 'Get out of the way, you d——d cowards,' he exclaimed, furiously, as a rush was made toward one of the boats whence a detachment of the Sixth Ohio was disembarking ; "get out of the way !   If you won't fight yourselves let these men off that will.   Sixth Ohio, follow me !'

"Upon the bluff overlooking the landing, General Grant was met, moody and silent, and at that moment on foot.   Colonel Ammen, having meanwhile transmitted to Colonels Bruce and Hazen the order to hurry the men across, reported to Nelson upon the bluff.   The Thirty-sixth Indiana was over. Companies A, F, and D, of the Sixth Ohio were landing, and the Twenty-fourth, and the remaining companies of the Sixth Ohio, were either in the stream or in the act of disembarking.   Grant told Ammen that he wanted him to support ' that battery on the left there,' pointing, as he spoke, to Captain Stone's battery ; whereupon Colonel Ammen hastened to form such of his troops as had already arrived.   While affairs were in this posture, a cannon-ball came whistling between the trees, took the head of one of Grant's orderlies off,

shot away the saddle from under Lieutenant
Graves, one of Nelson's aids, and went plung-
ing over the bluff into the river below, producing consternation indescribable among the
thousands herded about the landing. 'Don't
stop to form, Colonel, don't stop to form,' implored a staff officer, hurrying toward Colonel
Ammen; 'we shall all be massacred if you
do! There isn't a man out yonder, on the
left, between us and the rebels. For God's
sake, Colonel, hurry your men forward.'
. . . As soon as the Thirty-sixth Indiana
could be formed, and, without waiting for the
remainder of the brigade, Colonel Ammen
moved it forward; General Buell, who had
previously examined the ground, showing
him where to post it. The position assigned
it was only about two hundred yards from the
bluff, on the extreme left of the Union line, if
line it might have been called, and behind the
crest of the hill that rises above the ravine
before described. Companies A, F, and D,
of the Sixth Ohio, formed on its left and a
little in the rear, but the rebel attack was too
far to their right to permit them to get into
action that night. In this quarter the artillery had been left absolutely without any organized infantry support, and the handful of
troops that still remained, chiefly cannoneers,
were in extreme disorder. Had Bragg been

able to renew his assault upon this portion of the Union lines before the opportune arrival of Ammen's brigade—in all human probability he would have forced the position."

Says a staff officer of the Tenth Brigade, U. S. A.:

"I doubt whether, on any battle-field during the war, any set of men ever formed under just such circumstances as the Sixth Ohio at Shiloh. I shall never forget the scene. More than half of our artillery was gone, our entire force driven into twelve or fifteen acres of ground, a thousand wagons and nearly all of the tents were captured, the enemy pressing forward almost in sight; batteries and musketry in front, and a cross-fire of cannon from above, and ten thousand panic-stricken men of our own fled out of the fight, hailing the troops just arriving with such cries as, 'We're whipped!' 'The fight is lost!' 'We're cut to pieces!' 'It's no use to form!' 'They're driving us into the river,' etc. In this terrible extremity the regiment fell quickly and orderly into line, and at the word moved gallantly forward. I could not resist the temptation of riding my iron-gray close up to the lines, and crying out, 'Bully for the Sixth Ohio!' The regiment was halted a short distance in the rear of the Thirty-sixth Indiana, the firing having materially slackened;

in a few minutes it ceased entirely. Within the next half-hour the deepening darkness, setting at rest the question of further fighting for that day, had decided the issue of the struggle : 'Night and Blucher had both come.'"

Mr. Davis, in reply to a letter from a friend, says : "There was no need to say more than you have said about Shiloh, concerning which, notwithstanding his report, where little was said of Sidney Johnston except the fact that he was killed, Beauregard has but two sustained claims. One to have prepared the order of march, which resulted in failure to bring the troops on the ground at the time and manner required; and the other, to have withdrawn the army at the moment of victory, and thus to have sacrificed all which the skill and heroism of Johnston had achieved."

On the morning of the 7th, the enemy, now reinforced by Wallace's division and the army of Buell, advanced about six o'clock and opened a heavy fire of musketry and artillery.

The Confederates fought these new enemies with their accustomed valor and spirit, but after the junction of Buell and Grant had been effected, and General Johnston's plan for fighting them in detail miscarried by the delays incident upon getting the troops upon the field, a retreat to Corinth became a necessity.

The field return of the army of Mississippi before the battle of Shiloh, showed a total of 40,335. The effective force of Grant's army was 49,314; reinforcements of Buell, 21,579; total, 70,893. The casualties were as follows : Confederates killed, wounded, and missing, 10,699; Grant's army, April 6th, 11,220, leaving for duty on the 7th, 59,673.

"About 9 P.M. on the evening that we crossed the river," says Dr. Stephens, surgeon of the Sixth Ohio, " Lieutenant-Colonel Anderson ordered me to take charge of the old log-house on the top of the bluff (the same building, as it would appear, that General Grant had occupied during the day as headquarters), and there organize our regimental hospital, which was accordingly done, and the place made as comfortable as its bare walls and our scanty supplies would permit. About eleven o'clock our attention was called to some general and a staff officer seated close together on the top of two empty barrels that stood in the middle of one of the rooms. I thought it a strange place for them, and was still more surprised a few minutes afterward to hear the staff officer address his companion as General Grant. Both officers appeared to be much dejected (as was my impression

at the time), very little conversation, however, being carried on between them. Several times during the night, guns and pistols
were fired close around the building by some
of the demoralized troops at the landing.
This appeared to annoy the General greatly,
and once or twice he left his seat on the barrel, and, going to the door, cried, at the top
of his voice, ' Stop that firing ! ' Once, on returning to his companion, he said, ' The
cowards ! if they were to get their deserts,
the first thing to be done in the morning
would be to take a cannon and shell them out
from there.' The pair occupied their positions on the top of the barrels, 'grand, gloomy,
and peculiar,' until daylight of Monday morning, when they disappeared as mysteriously
as they came." *

On April 9th, General H. W. Halleck left
St. Louis and proceeded to assume command
of the Federal force at Pittsburg Landing.
A reorganization was made in which General
Grant's divisions formed the right wing ; those
of General Buell the centre ; and those of General Pope the left wing ; and an advance on
Corinth was commenced on April 28th, with a
force exceeding 85,000 effectives. On May
2d he had reached within eight miles of Co-

---

* Story of a Regiment (Sixth Ohio).

rinth, and on the 21st his batteries were within three miles. His movements were very
slow, and at night his army was protected by
an intrenched camp; by day he was assailed
by the Confederate skirmishers. At 9 A.M.
of the 29th, Halleck's works were substantially done and the siege train brought forward.

The force of Beauregard was less than 45,-
000 men. He estimated that of the enemy
between 85,000 to 91,000.

General Beauregard being unable to hold
Corinth, commenced the removal of his sick
preparatory to an evacuation on May 26th, and
on the next day arrangements were made
for falling back on the 29th. The evacuation
was complete, not only the army but every
piece of ordnance was withdrawn. The retreat was continued to Tupelo, the enemy not
interfering.

On June 14th orders were sent to General
Bragg from Richmond to proceed to Jackson,
Miss., and temporarily to assume command
of the department then under the command
of General Lovell. The order concluded as
follows :

" After General Magruder joins, your further services there may be dispensed with.
The necessity is urgent and absolute.

" JEFFERSON DAVIS."

On application to General Beauregard for the necessary orders, he replied :

" You cannot possibly go. My health does not permit me to remain in charge alone here. This evening my two physicians were insisting that I should go away for one or two weeks, furnishing me with another certificate for that purpose, and I have concluded to go, intending to see you to-morrow on the subject ; and I leave you in command."

The certificate of the surgeons was as follows :

" We certify that, after attendance on General Beauregard for the past four months, and treatment of his case, in our professional opinion he is incapacitated physically for the arduous duties of his present command, and we earnestly recommend rest and recuperation.

(Signed)   " R. L. BRODIE, P.A.F.S.
" SAM. CHOPPIN."

These facts were telegraphed to the President at once by General Bragg. Soon after Mr. Davis sent him another telegram, renewing the order, and expressing his surprise that he should have hesitated to obey, when the original order stated " *the necessity is urgent and absolute.*" Before this second telegram was received by General Bragg, General Beauregard had transferred the command of the army to him, and had departed for Bladen Springs. General Bragg thus describes the subsequent proceedings:

"Prepared to move, I telegraphed back to the President that the altered conditions induced me to await orders. In reply to this I was immediately notified by telegraph of my assignment to 'permanent command of the army.'

The telegram read as follows:

"RICHMOND, June 20, 1862.

"GENERAL BRAXTON BRAGG, Tupelo, Miss.

"Your despatch informing me that General Beauregard had turned over the command to you and left for Mobile on surgeons' certificate was duly received.

"You are assigned permanently to the command of the department, as will be more formally notified to you by the Secretary of War.

"You will correspond directly and receive orders and instructions from the Government in relation to your future operations.

"JEFFERSON DAVIS."

As the telegrams sent to Secretary of War Stanton, after the evacuation of Corinth, are of such a remarkable character, and evincing so little regard for the truth that they are amusing, I cannot refrain from adding the following as specimens:

"HALLECK'S HEADQUARTERS, June 4th.

"General Pope with 40,000 is thirty miles south of Corinth, pushing enemy hard. He already reports 10,000 prisoners and deserters from the enemy, and 15,000 *stand of arms* captured. *Thousands of the enemy are throwing away their arms.* A farmer says that when Beauregard had learned that Colonel Elliott had cut the railroad on his line of retreat, he *became frantic and told his men to save themselves as best they could.* . . .

"H. W. HALLECK,

"*Major-General* (Commanding).

"To E. M. STANTON, *Secretary of War.*"

"CORINTH, June 9, 1862.

"The enemy has fallen back to Saltillo (Tupelo?), fifty miles by rail and near seventy by wagon road. General Pope estimates rebel loss from casualties, prisoners, and desertions at *over* 20,000, and General Buell at between 20,000 and 30,000. An Englishman employed in the Confederate Commissary Department says they had 120,000 *men in Corinth*, and that they cannot muster much over 80,000. *Some fresh graves on the road have been opened and found filled with arms* (?).

"H. W. HALLECK, *Major-General.*"

"CORINTH, July 3, 1862.

". . . I am not responsible for the *truth* of the statements thus communicated. . . .

"In regard to the number of prisoners and arms taken,* I telegraphed the *exact language of General Pope.* If it was erroneous the responsibility is his, not mine.

"H. W. HALLECK, *Major-General.*"

CHAPTER XXIV.

NEW ORLEANS.

ALTHOUGH depressed by the loss of the victory virtually won by General Johnston at Shiloh, because "someone had blundered" after his death, the people were still far from being hopeless of final success. They knew that we were still masters of the river south of Fort Pillow, and they believed that we should be able still to retain the rich valley of the lower Mississippi.

But general disappointment and a temporary feeling of alarm suddenly arose from an event unexpected, and never hitherto feared : the fall of New Orleans, which had been regarded as strong enough to repel the attacking force. Such also had been the belief of General Lovell, the military commander there, as late as December 5, 1861. Chains were stretched across the approaches to New Orleans, and obstructions sunk in the river at the narrowest points; the forts had been all strengthened ; but all these were passed. Our new ram, the *Mississippi*, was destroyed by our forces, and all the machinery and ma-

teriel of war was lost, and the key to the
Mississippi was in the enemy's hands.

The loss of New Orleans was a terrible
disaster. But deeply as its capture was de-
plored by the Confederates, the spirit of the
people did not become despondent, and a
series of Confederate victories soon revived
their most ardent hopes of achieving national
independence.

General Butler was soon inaugurated as
the autocratic ruler of the city.

His course in hanging Mumford upon the
charge of hauling down the United States
flag from the Mint, of which act he was innocent, and in issuing " Order No. 28," excited strong resentment not only in the South,
but in the North and abroad, but does not
properly come within the scope of a biography
of the President of the Confederacy. The
moral effect of his infamous " Order No. 28 "
was great, and reconciled whomsoever might
have differed from the policy of the Confederate leaders within our borders.*

---

* *General Butler's Order* 28.

"HEAD QUARTERS DEPARTMENT OF GULF,
"NEW ORLEANS, May 15, 1862.

"As officers and soldiers of the United States have been subject
to repeated insults from women calling themselves ladies of New
Orleans, in return for the most scrupulous non-interference and courtesy on our part, it is ordered hereafter, when any female shall, by
mere gesture or movement, insult or show contempt for any officers

Butler's government in New Orleans, and his assaults upon the helpless women and non-combatants, filled our army with horror and indignation.

Upon the receipt of a copy of this infamous order, President Davis issued his proclamation as follows :

After reciting that General Halleck had put General Lee off by delay, to avoid either avowal or disavowal of General Butler's cruel course in the execution of an innocent non-combatant, the President said :

" And whereas, the silence of the Government of the United States and its maintaining of said Butler in high office under its authority for many months after his commission of an act that can be viewed in no other light than as a deliberate murder, as well as of numerous other outrages and atrocities hereafter to be mentioned, afford evidence only too conclusive that the said Government sanctions the conduct of said Butler, and is determined that he shall remain unpunished for his crimes ;

" Now, therefore, I, Jefferson Davis, Presi-

---

or soldiers of the United States, she shall be regarded and held liable to be treated as a woman about town plying her avocation.

"By command of

" MAJOR-GENERAL BUTLER.

" GEORGE C. STRONG, A. A. G."

dent of the Confederate States of America,
and in their name, do pronounce and declare
the said Benjamin F. Butler to be a felon, deserving of capital punishment. I do- order
that he be no longer considered or treated
simply as a public enemy of the Confederate
States of America, but as an outlaw and common enemy of mankind ; and that in event of
his capture, the officer in command of the
capturing force do cause him to be immediately executed by hanging ; and I do further
order that no commissioned officer of the
United States taken captive shall be released
on parole before exchange until the said Butler shall have met with due punishment for
his crimes.

" And whereas the hostilities waged against
this Confederacy by the forces of the United
States under the command of said Benjamin
F. Butler have borne no resemblance to such
warfare as is alone permissible by the rules
of international law or the usages of civilization, but have been characterized by repeated
atrocities and outrages, among the large number of which the following may be cited as
examples :

" Peaceful and aged citizens, unresisting
captives and non-combatants, have been confined at hard labor, with balls and chains attached to their limbs, and are still so held, in

dungeons and fortresses. Others have been subjected to a like degrading punishment for selling medicines to the sick soldiers of the Confederacy.

"The soldiers of the United States have been invited and encouraged by general orders to insult and outrage the wives, the mothers, and the sisters of our citizens.

"Helpless women have been torn from their homes and subjected to solitary confinement, some in fortresses and prisons, and one especially on an island of barren sand under a tropical sun; have been fed with loathsome rations that had been condemned as unfit for soldiers, and have been exposed to the vilest insults.

"Prisoners of war, who surrendered to the naval forces of the United States on agreement that they should be released on parole, have been seized and kept in close confinement.

"Repeated pretexts have been sought or invented for plundering the inhabitants of the captured city by fines, levied and exacted under threat of imprisoning recusants at hard labor with ball and chain.

"The entire population of the city of New Orleans have been forced to elect between starvation, by the confiscation of their property, and taking oath against conscience to bear allegiance to the invaders of their country.

"Egress from the city has been refused to those whose fortitude withstood the test, even to lone and aged women and to helpless children ; and after being ejected from their homes and robbed of their property, they have been left to starve in the streets or subsist on charity.

"The slaves have been driven from the plantations in the neighborhood of New Orleans till owners would consent to share the crops with the commanding general, his brother, Andrew J. Butler, and other officers ; and when such consent had been extorted, the slaves have been restored to the plantations, and there compelled to work under the bayonets of guards of United States soldiers.

"Where this partnership was refused, armed expeditions have been sent to the plantations to rob them of everything that was susceptible of removal, and even slaves too aged or infirm for work have, in spite of their entreaties, been forced from the homes provided by the owners and driven to wander helpless on the highway.

"By a recent order (No. 91), the entire property in that part of Louisiana lying west of the Mississippi River has been sequestrated for confiscation, and officers have been assigned to duty, with orders to 'gather up and collect the personal property, and turn over to the proper officers, upon their receipts, such of said property as may be required for the use of the United States Army; to collect together all the other personal property and bring the same to New Orleans, and cause it to be sold at public auction to the highest bidders'—an order which, if executed, condemns to punishment by starvation at least a quarter of a million of human beings of all ages, sexes, and conditions; and of which the execution, although forbidden to military officers by the orders of President Lincoln, is in accordance with the confiscation law of our enemies, which he has directed to be enforced through the agency of civil officials. And, finally, the African slaves have not only been excited to insurrection by every license and encouragement, but numbers of them have actually been armed for a servile war—a war in its nature far exceeding in horrors the most merciless atrocities of the savages.

"And whereas the officers under the command of the said Butler have been in many instances active and zealous agents in the commission of these crimes, and no instance is known of the refusal of any one of them to participate in the outrages above narrated;

"And whereas the President of the United States has, by public and official declaration, signified not only his approval of the effort to excite the servile war within the Confederacy, but his intention to give aid and encouragement thereto if these independent States shall continue to refuse submission to a foreign power after the first day of January next, and has thus made known that all appeals to the laws of nations, the dictates of reason, and the instincts of humanity would be addressed in vain to our enemies, and that they can be deterred from the commission of these crimes only by the terms of just retribution ;

"Now, therefore, I, Jefferson Davis, President of the Confederate States of America, and acting by their authority, appealing to the Divine Judge in attestation that their conduct is not guided by the passion of revenge, but that they reluctantly yield to the solemn duty of repressing, by necessary severity, crimes of which their citizens are the victims, do issue this my proclamation, and by virtue of my authority as Commander-in-chief of the Armies of the Confederate States, do order :

"First. That all commissioned officers in the command of said Benjamin F. Butler be declared not entitled to be considered as soldiers engaged in honorable warfare, but as robbers and criminals, deserving death ; and that they and each of them be, whenever captured, reserved for execution.

" Second. That the private soldiers and non-commissioned officers in the army of said Butler be considered as only the instruments used for the commission of the crimes perpetrated by his orders, and not as free agents ; that they therefore be treated, when captured, as prisoners of war, with kindness and humanity, and be sent home on the usual parole that they will in no manner aid or serve the United States in any capacity during the continuance of this war, unless duly discharged.

" Third. That all negro slaves captured in arms be at once delivered over to the executive authorities of the respective States to which they belong, to be dealt with according to the laws of the said States.

" Fourth. That the like orders be executed in all cases with respect to all commissioned officers of the United States, when found serving in company with armed slaves in insurrection against the authorities of the different States of this Confederacy.

" In testimony whereof I have signed these presents and caused the seal of the Confederate States of America to be affixed thereto, at the city of Richmond, on this 23d

day of December, in the year of our Lord
one thousand eight hundred and sixty-two.
                              " JEFFERSON DAVIS."

In the House of Lords, on the 13th, Lord
Carnarvon called attention to General Butler's proclamation relative to the ladies of
New Orleans, and condemned it in severe
terms as without precedent in the annals of
war. He asked if the Government had information of its authenticity, and if it had protested against it. He also asked if there was
any truth in the rumors of the mediation of
France and England. The success of such
mediation would depend greatly upon the
manner in which, and the time when, it was
offered, but he trusted the Government was
in position to give the subject favorable consideration.

Earl Russell said that, from Lord Lyons's
despatches, the Government believed the proclamation to be authentic, but with respect to
any action of the United States Government,
in the way of approval or disapproval, they
had no information. Lord Lyons had made
no representation to the American Government upon the subject, and he did not appear
to have any information respecting the proclamation upon which he could do so. For his
own part, he (Russell) hoped the American

Government would, for its own sake, refuse its sanction to and disapprove the proclamation. It was important to the whole world that the usages of war should not be aggravated by proclamations of this kind. He then gave the explanation of the treatment the proclamation referred to, but thought such proclamation, addressed to forces which had just captured a hostile town, was likely to lead to great brutality. He therefore thought this explanation was no defence for the proclamation, and sincerely hoped the American Government would disavow it.

With respect to the rumors of mediation, Earl Russell was glad the question had been put, for the rumors were likely to lead to much mischief. Her Majesty's Government had made no proposal to France, and the French Government had made no proposal to England; and therefore upon this subject there had been no communications of any kind between the two Governments. Without, however, giving any opinion as to the propriety of offering mediation at some future time, if circumstances should prove favorable, he must say that at the present time such mediation appeared to him to be the most inopportune. He conceived that in the embittered state of feeling in America, it would not only lead to no good, but would retard the time for such offer being favorably made.

Mr. Hopwood asked if there was any truth in the mediation rumors.

Lord Palmerston said that no communication had been received from the French Government on the subject; and as to the British Government, they had no intention at present to offer mediation.

CHAPTER XXV.

YORKTOWN AND WILLIAMSBURG.

On February 27, 1862, with the approval of the President, the office of Commanding-General of the Confederate forces was created by the House of Representatives.

When General McClellan heard of the retreat of the Confederate Army from Manassas, he ordered a reconnoissance and ascertained that our troops had crossed the Rapidan.

General McClellan's account of this movement was given in a report to the Secretary of War, dated Fairfax Court-House, March 11, 1862, 8.30 P.M. From it I make a short extract:

" I have just returned from a ride of more than forty miles. Have examined Centreville, Union Mills, Blackburn's Ford, etc. The works at Centreville are formidable; more so than at Manassas. Except the turnpike, the roads are horrible. The country entirely stripped of forage and provisions. Having fully consulted with General McDowell, I propose occupying Manassas with a portion of

Banks's command, and then at once throwing all the forces I can concentrate upon the line agreed upon last week."

The " formidable fortifications " at Centreville consisted of nine small earthworks containing thirty-one wooden guns, known at that time as " Quakers." They were made of pine logs, charred black, and were in some cases mounted on wagon wheels ; where they were not, leaves and brush were laid over the embrasures.

This armament was indeed formidable, in appearance at least, and had the effect of producing the impression desired upon General McClellan. " Intelligent contrabands " made frequent reports to him of the strong position of the Confederates at Centreville.

The Federal army was transferred to the Peninsula early in April, and General McClellan landed about one hundred thousand men at Fortress Monroe. At this time General Magruder occupied the lower Peninsula with seven or eight thousand men.

General Magruder was then reinforced until his army numbered about 20,000 men.

As soon as it was definitely ascertained that General McClellan, with his main army, was on the Peninsula, General J. E. Johnston was assigned to the command of that department. After spending a day on Magruder's

lines, he returned to Richmond, recommended the abandonment of the Peninsula, and
that a position nearer Richmond should be
taken.

The recommendation was held for consideration, and the President proposed to invite
to the conference the Secretary of War,
George Randolph, and General Lee, then
stationed in Richmond.

General Johnston asked that he might invite General Longstreet and General G. W.
Smith to be present, which was assented to.

After hearing the views expressed by the
several officers named, the President decided
to resist the enemy on the Peninsula, and,
with the aid of the navy, to hold Norfolk and
keep command of the James River.

The Confederates numbered, when General
Johnston took command, over 50,000 men.

On April 16th, an assault was made upon
the Confederate lines at Warwick, but was repulsed with heavy loss.

The month of April was cold and rainy,
and our men were poorly provided with shelter and with only the plainest rations, but labored steadily to perfect the defences.

By the following telegram, sent by the President to General Johnston, the contents of
that which he had received from him will be
readily inferred.

"RICHMOND, VA., May 1, 1862.

"GENERAL J. E. JOHNSTON, Yorktown, Va.

"Accepting your conclusion that you must soon retire, arrangements are commenced for the abandonment of the Navy Yard and removal of public property both from Norfolk and the Peninsula.

"Your announcement to-day that you would withdraw to-morrow night, takes us by surprise, and must involve enormous losses, including unfinished gunboats. Will the safety of your army allow more time?

"JEFFERSON DAVIS."

General Johnston withdrew his army from the line of the Warwick River on the night of April 3d. Heavy cannonading both on the night of the 2d and 3d, concealed his intention, and the evacuation was made so successfully that the enemy was surprised the next morning to find the lines unoccupied.

The loss of public property was, as anticipated by Mr. Davis, very great.

General Johnston, after an engagement at Williamsburg, in which the Fifth North Carolina was annihilated, and the Twenty-Fourth Virginia suffered terribly in officers and men, and General Early was wounded, retired from the Peninsula, and halted his army in the vicinity of Richmond.

As soon as Norfolk was evacuated, a very severe course was adopted toward the citizens. In consequence of some fancied offence to the wife of General Viele, the ladies were forbidden to speak while crossing on the ferry-boat, and every species of indignity was inflicted upon the townspeople. Mr. Davis's anxieties were greatly increased by the evacuation of the Peninsula, and the consequent losses that he saw no speedy means to repair.

He thought it could have been held, and yet had much faith in General Johnston's military opinions, and more in his patriotism.

Our supplies of every useful implement were beginning to require replenishing. We had lost large numbers of entrenching tools on the retreat, and many heavy guns, including some recently received and not yet mounted.

General Beauregard appealed for bells to be melted into cannon, March 20, 1862. These bells were contributed, and captured by the enemy in New Orleans, and sold in Boston at Lombard's North Wharf, East Boston, and averaged thirty cents a pound ; the sum for which they were sold amounted to over $30,000. Thus resulted the sacrifice so gladly made by individuals in the Confederacy.

In this year the Church and the world sustained a great loss in the death of Bishop Meade. He had been General Lee's preceptor, and when the General went to see him, he called him in the old simple way: "Robert, come near that I may bless you."

He left a message for the Confederate people. "Tell your people to be more determined than ever. This is the most unjust and iniquitous war that was ever waged." He was buried from St. Paul's Church, and followed by a multitude of sincere mourners.

In these days of self-sacrifice and dumb suffering many things were endured which should exalt the name of Confederates.

The burning of all the cotton in the country was a stupendous sacrifice, and there is probably no man who remembers it now well enough to state the facts. Generally it was burned by the owner, but in a few cases the Government agent was charged with the duty. The following is the form of certificate given for cotton burned June 10, 1862:

"This is to certify that —— bales of cotton, belonging to ——, was burned on his plantation this day.

"————,

"*Provost-Marshal,*

"—— Parish, La."

The issues for which we were battling fortunately rendered us indifferent to the personal losses we were everywhere sustaining.

Mr. Davis, after hearing of the loss of our property, the sacking of our house on Brier-field, the destruction of our fine library, the loss of all the blooded stock on the place, and the demoralization of the negroes, and their forcible deportation, wrote to me a long letter about the army, etc., and in a paragraph said:

" You will have seen a notice of the destruction of our home. If our cause succeeds we shall not mourn over any personal deprivation ; if it should not, why, "the deluge." I hope I shall be able to provide for the comfort of the old negroes."

It is hard, in recalling the memory of all our heroes who fought and fell, to individualize their separate acts, heroism, or self-abnegation, but here is one culled from an old newspaper.

" The officers of the Second Louisiana Regiment, Stafford's Brigade, Johnson's Division, Army of Northern Virginia, went into the ranks as privates, not being near enough home to recruit." No word of approval is appended to the announcement — the act elicited no expression of surprise.

These men came of people who act rather than write, and now they have no historians ; but their names are affectionately recalled by our firesides, and their deeds here, like the righteousness of the Hebrew warriors, exalted their nation.

CHAPTER XXVI.

THE GUN-BOATS IN THE JAMES RIVER—BATTLE OF SEVEN PINES.

ABOUT May 9th Mr. Davis insisted that we should leave Richmond, and relieve him from unnecessary anxiety. On the eve of the 9th there was a reception, and we were to go in three days. A courier came to the President with despatches, and as he passed me on his return to the drawing-room I looked a question and he responded, in a whisper, "The enemy's gun-boats are ascending the river." Our guests remained quite late, and there was no opportunity for further conversation.

As soon as they were gone my husband told me he hoped the obstructions would prevent the gun-boats reaching the river, but that he preferred we should go the next morning. Always averse to flight, I entreated him to grant a little delay, but he was firm, and I communicated the news to the family. Dr. William M. Gwin and his daughter were visiting us, and a friend from the next corner had tarried beyond the rest. As soon as our dear little neighbor was told the news, she dropped on her knees and raising her hands to heaven, ejaculated, " Lord Jesus, save and help me." Notwithstanding the crucial period through which we were passing, we all laughed heartily, except our friend. She was a woman of rare attainments and keen wit, and had written a journal which extended over a long period of intercourse with the greatest men of their day at home and abroad. Such a record of the passing show would have been almost as valuable an addition to the history of the time as Madame Junot's or Madame de Rémusat's diaries, but she burnt it at once for fear of its being taken from her by the enemy.

We left for Raleigh, N. C., on the morning of May 10th ; the panic began some days later, and it was pitiable to see our friends coming in without anything except the clothes they had on, and mourning the loss of their trunks in a piteous jumble of pain and worriment.

The Sunday before our departure, Mr. Davis was baptized at home by Mr. Minnegerode, in the presence of the Right Rev. Bishop Johns, and a peace which passed understanding seemed to settle in his heart, after the ceremony. His religious convictions had long occupied his thoughts, and the joy of being received into the Church seemed to pervade his soul.

Now the campaign began in dreadful earnest. Soon after General Johnston took position on the north side of the Chickahominy; accompanied by General Lee, my husband rode out to his headquarters in the field, in order to establish a more thorough co-intelligence with him. General Johnston came in after they arrived, saying he had been riding around his lines to see how his position could be improved. A long conversation followed, which was so inconclusive that it lasted until late at night, so late that they remained until the next morning, when Mr. Davis sent me the following letter:

"RICHMOND, May 13, 1862.

" Yesterday afternoon I went to the headquarters of General Johnston's army, about twenty-two or three miles from here. He was out when we reached there, and the distance was so great that after consultation it was decided to remain, and I rode in this morning.

" The army is reported in fine spirits and condition. If the withdrawal from the Peninsula and Norfolk had been with due preparation and a desirable deliberation, I should be more sanguine of a successful defence of this city. Various causes have delayed the obstructions and the armament of the covering fort, while the hasty evacuation of the defences below and the destruction of the *Virginia*

hastens the coming of the enemy's gun-
boats.

"I know not what to expect when so many
failures are to be remembered, yet will try to
make a successful resistance, and if it were
the first attempt, would expect to sink the
enemy's boats."

On May 15th, the enemy's fleet of five
ships of war, among them the *Monitor*,
steamed up the James River, and took position within range of the fort at Drewry's
Bluff, and opened fire between eight and
nine o'clock. The little *Patrick Henry* was
lying above the obstructions, and co-operated
with the fort in its defence. General Lee
had also some light batteries in position on
the banks of the river to sweep the ships'
decks with cannister.

The *Monitor* and *Galena* steamed up to
within six hundred yards of the fort, the
smaller vessels were kept at long range.

When it was known in Richmond that
General Johnston's army had fallen back to
the vicinity of the city, and that the enemy's
gun-boats were ascending the James, a panic
became imminent. Many were apprehensive
that Richmond would be abandoned by the
Confederate forces.

During the engagement which ensued with
the fort the flag-ship *Galena* was badly in-

jured by its guns, and her crew driven below by the light pieces on the banks, with
many casualties.   The *Monitor* was struck
repeatedly, but the shot did little damage,
save denting some of her plates.

At eleven o'clock the enemy drew off, out
of range, and moved down the river.   The
attempt was not renewed.

Richmond breathed freer, when it was
known the danger had passed.   On the
16th, my husband rode out to see the works
and obstructions in the James River, and
upon his return wrote to me as follows :

". . . I returned this evening from a
long ride through rain and mud, having gone
down the James River to see the works
and obstructions on which we rely to stop
the gun-boats.   The attack of yesterday has
given an impulse to the public, and our working parties have been increased so much that
a few days will now enable us to effect more
than has been done in weeks past.   I reached
the fort yesterday, arriving after the firing had
ceased, and found the garrison quite elated
at their success, and each one prompt to tell
that the gun-boats were clear gone.   David
was under fire and eloquent in relation to
the nervousness of the raw troops, he and
the marines being the veterans. . . .
The panic here has subsided, and with in-

creasing confidence there has arisen a desire
to see the city destroyed rather than surren·
dered. 'They lightly talk of scars who
never felt a wound,' and these talkers have
little idea of what scenes would follow the
battering of rows of brick houses. I have
told them that the enemy might be beaten
before Richmond, or on either flank, and we
would try to do it, but that I could not allow
the army to be penned up in a city. The
boats, we ought to be, and I hope are, able
to stop. Their army, when reduced to small-
arms and field pieces, I think we can defeat,
and then a vigorous pursuit will bring results
long wished for, but not given to the wind.
. . . Be of good cheer and continue to
hope that God will in due time deliver us
from the hands of our enemies and 'sanctify
to us our deepest distress.' As the clouds
grow darker, and when one after another of
those who are trusted are detected in secret
hostility, I feel like mustering clans were in
me, and that cramping fetters had fallen from
my limbs. The great temporal object is to
secure our independence, and they who engage in strife for personal or party aggran-
dizement deserve contemptuous forgetfulness. I have no political wish beyond the
success of our cause, no personal desire but
to be relieved from further connection with

office; opposition in any form can only disturb me insomuch as it may endanger the public welfare. . . . Maggie is a wise child. I wish I could learn to let people alone who snap at me, in forbearance and charity to turn away as well from the cats as the snakes. Dear little Joey may well attract admiration, and the people who think him like me must have formed complimentary ideas of my appearance. . . . Our church was not fully attended to-day, the families have to a great extent left town, and the excitement, no doubt, kept away many men. Mr. Minnegerode was sick, Bishop Johns preached extemporaneously, and his address was fervent and appropriate. I thought him more eloquent than on any former occasion. The resemblance to Mr. Clay is probably accidental."

. . . .

Not receiving a definite reply to a letter sent to General Johnston by his aide-de-camp, Colonel G. W. C. Lee, Mr. Davis rode out to visit him at his headquarters, and was surprised, in the surburbs of Richmond, the other side of Gillis's Creek, to meet a portion of the light artillery, and to learn that the whole army had crossed the Chickahominy.

General Johnston explained that he thought the water of the Chickahominy would prove

injurious to his troops, and had therefore directed them to cross, and to halt at the first
good water.

General McClellan following up Johnston's movement, drew his lines nearer to the
Confederate capital. His army at this time
numbered, present and absent, 156,838; effectives present 105,825. The army under
Johnston, 62,696 effectives.

On May 19th, my husband again wrote to
me as follows :

". . . I have but a moment to say that
I am well as usual, and busier than heretofore. General Johnston has brought his
army back to the suburbs of Richmond, and
I have been waiting all day for him to communicate his plans."

" The enemy have pushed out their pickets, and have found out his movements while
concealing their own."

" We are uncertain of everything, except
that a battle must be near at hand."

Under date of May 28th Mr. Davis wrote
me as follows :

". . . We are steadily developing for
a great battle, and under God's favor I trust
for a decisive victory. The enemy are preparing to concentrate in advance by regular
approaches ; we must attack him in motion,
and trust to the valor of our troops for suc-

cess. It saddens me to feel how many a
mother, wife, and child will be made to grieve
in bitterness, but what is there worse than
submission to such brutal tyranny as now
holds sway over New Orleans. . . ."

Continuing Mr. Davis's narrative in reference to the operations around Richmond at
this time, he said :

" Seeing no preparation to keep the enemy
at a distance, and kept in ignorance of any
plan for such purpose, I sent for General R.
E. Lee, then at Richmond, in general charge
of army operations, and told him why and how
I was dissatisfied with the condition of affairs.

" He asked me what I thought it was
proper to do. Recurring to a conversation
held about the time we had together visited
General Johnston, I answered that McClellan
should be attacked on the other side of the
Chickahominy before he matured his preparations for a siege of Richmond. To this he
promptly assented, as I anticipated he would,
for I knew it had been his own opinion. He
then said : ' General Johnston should of
course advise you of what he expects or proposes to do. Let me go and see him, and
defer this discussion until I return.'

". . . When General Lee came back,
he told me that General Johnston proposed,
on the next Thursday, to move against the

enemy as follows : General A. P. Hill was to move down on the right flank and rear of the enemy. General G. W. Smith, as soon as Hill's guns opened, was to cross the Chickahominy at the Meadow Bridge, attack the enemy in flank, and by the conjunction of the two it was expected to double him up. Then Longstreet was to come on the Mechanicsville Bridge and attack him in front. From this plan the best results were hoped by both of us.

" On the morning of the day proposed, I hastily despatched my office business and rode out toward the Meadow Bridge to see the action commence. On the road I found Smith's division halted and the men dispersed in the woods. Looking for someone from whom I could get information, I finally saw General Hood, and asked him the meaning of what I saw. He told me he did not know anything more than that they had been halted. I asked him where General Smith was ; he said he believed he had gone to a farm-house in the rear, adding that he thought he was ill.

" Riding on the bluff which overlooks the Meadow Bridge, I asked Colonel Anderson, posted there in observation, whether he had seen anything of the enemy in his front. He said that he had seen only two mounted men across the bridge, and a small party of infan-

try on the other side of the river, some distance below, both of whom, he said, he could
show me if I would go with him into the
garden back of the house.   There, by the use
of a powerful glass, were distinctly visible two
cavalry videttes at the further end of the
bridge, and a squad of infantry lower down
the river, who had covered themselves with a
screen of green boughs.   The Colonel informed me that he had not heard Hill's guns ;
it was, therefore, supposed he had not advanced.   I then rode down the bank of the
river, followed by a cavalcade of sight-seers,
who I supposed had been attracted by the
expectation of a battle.   The little squad of
infantry, about fifteen in number, as we approached, fled over the bridge, and were lost
to sight.

"Near to the Mechanicsville Bridge I
found General Howell Cobb, commanding the
support of a battery of artillery.   He pointed
out to me on the opposite side of the river the
only enemy he had seen, and which was
evidently a light battery.   Riding on to the
main road which led to the Mechanicsville
Bridge, I found General Longstreet, walking
to and fro in an impatient, it might be said
fretful, manner.   Before speaking to him, he
said his division had been under arms all day
waiting for orders to advance, and that the

day was now so far spent that he did not know what was the matter. I afterward learned from General Smith that he had received information from a citizen that the " Beaver-dam Creek presented an impassable barrier, and that he had thus fortunately been saved from a disaster." Thus ended the offensive-defensive programme from which Lee expected much, and of which I was hopeful."

On the morning of May 31st my husband wrote me as follows :

". . . I packed some valuable books and the sword I wore for many years, together with the pistols used at Monterey and Buena Vista, and my old dressing-case. These articles will have a value to the boys in after-time, and to you now. . . . They will probably go forward to-day.

"Thank you for congratulations on success of Jackson. Had the movement been made when I first proposed it, the effect would have been more important.

"In that night's long conference it was regarded impossible. We have not made any balloon discoveries. The only case in which much is to be expected from such means will be when large masses of troops are in motion.*

---

* A balloon called "the Intrepid," containing two people, ascended from Richmond and hung over McClellan's camp for two hours, about the end of July, 1862.

"Yesterday morning I thought we would engage the enemy, reported to be in large force on the Upper Chickahominy. The report was incorrect, as I verified in the afternoon by a long ride in that locality.

"I saw nothing more than occasional cavalry videttes, and some pickets with field artillery.

"General Lee rises to the occasion . . . and seems to be equal to the conception. I hope others will develop capacity in execution. . . . If we fight and are victorious, we can all soon meet again. If the enemy retreat to protect Washington, of which there are vague reports, I can probably visit you."

In the meantime the enemy moved up, and finding the crossing at Bottom Bridge undefended, on the 25th threw a corps across the Chickahominy.

He afterward added another corps, and commenced fortifying a line to Seven Pines.

Mr. Davis continued his narration in "The Rise and Fall" of the Confederacy:

"In the forenoon of May 31st, riding out on the New Bridge road, I heard firing in the direction of Seven Pines. As I drew nearer, I saw General Whiting, with part of General Smith's division, file into the road in front of me; at the same time I saw General Johnston ride across the field from a house before

which General Lee's horse was standing. I
turned down to the house, and asked General Lee what the musketry firing meant. He
replied by asking whether I had heard it, and
was answered in the affirmative; he said he
had been under that impression himself, but
*General Johnston had assured him that it
could be nothing more than an artillery duel.
It is scarcely necessary to add that neither of
us had been advised of a design to attack the
enemy that day.*

"We then walked out to the rear of the
house to listen, and were satisfied that an action, or at least a severe skirmish, must be
going on.

" *General Johnston states in his report that
the condition of the air was peculiarly unfavorable to the transmission of sound.*

" General Lee and myself then rode to the
field of battle, which may be briefly described
as follows :

"The Chickahominy flowing in front, is a
deep, sluggish, and narrow river, bordered by
marshes and covered with tangled wood.
The line of battle extended along the Nine-
mile road, across the York River railroad,
and Williamsburg stage-road. The enemy
had constructed redoubts, with long lines of
rifle-pits covered by abatis, from below Bottom Bridge to within less than two miles of

New Bridge, and had constructed bridges to
connect his forces on the north and south
sides of the Chickahominy. The left of his
forces, on the south side, was thrown forward
from the river ; the right was on its bank, and
covered by its slope. Our main force was on
the right flank of our position, extending on
both sides of the Williamsburg road, near to
its intersection with the Nine-mile road. The
wing consisted of Hill's, Huger's, and Longstreet's divisions, with light batteries, and a
small force of cavalry ; the division of General
G. W. Smith, less Hood's brigade ordered to
the right, formed the left wing, and its position was on the Nine-mile road. There were
small tracts of cleared land, but most of the
ground was wooded, and much of it so covered with water as to seriously embarrass the
movements of troops.

"When General Lee and I, riding down
the Nine-mile road, reached the left of our
line, we found the troops hotly engaged.
Our men had driven the enemy from his advanced encampment, and he had fallen back
behind an open field to the bank of the river,
where, in a dense wood, was concealed an infantry line, with artillery in position. Soon
after our arrival, General Johnston, who had
gone farther to the right, where the conflict
was expected, and whither reinforcement

from the left was marching, was brought back severely wounded, and, as soon as an ambulance could be obtained, was removed from the field.

"Our troops on the left made vigorous assaults under most disadvantageous circumstances. They made several gallant attempts to carry the enemy's position, but were each time repulsed with heavy loss.

"After a personal reconnoissance on the left of the open in our front, I sent one, then another, and another courier to General Magruder, directing him to send a force down by the wooded path, just under the bluff, to attack the enemy in flank and reverse. Impatient of delay, I had started to see General Magruder, when I met the third courier, who said he had not found General Magruder, but had delivered the message to Brigadier-General Griffith, who was moving by the path designated to make the attack.

"On returning to the field, I found that the attack in front had ceased ; it was, therefore, too late for a single brigade to effect anything against the large force of the enemy, and messengers were sent through the woods to direct General Griffith to go back.

"The heavy rain during the night of the 30th had swollen the Chickahominy; it was rising when the battle of Seven Pines was fought; but had not reached such height as to prevent the enemy from using his bridges; consequently, General Sumner, during the engagement, brought over his corps as a reinforcement. He was on the north side of the river, had built two bridges to connect with the south side, and, though their coverings were loosened by the upward pressure of the rising water, they were not yet impassable. With the true instinct of the soldier to march upon fire, when the sound of the battle reached him, he formed his corps and stood under arms waiting for an order to advance. He came too soon for us, and, but for his forethought and promptitude, he would have arrived too late for his friends. It may be granted that his presence saved the left wing of the Federal army from defeat.

"As we had permitted the enemy to fortify before our attack, it would have been better to have waited another day, until the bridges would have been rendered impassable by the rise of the river.

"General Lee at nightfall gave instructions to General Smith, the senior officer on that part of the battle-field, and left with me to return to Richmond."

Mr. Davis had a personal observation of the left of the line of battle only. For the operations on the right he referred to the report of General Longstreet, who was in chief command. From this report, published by the War Department at Washington, the following extract is taken :

"Agreeably to verbal instructions from the Commanding General, the division of Major-General D. H. Hill was, on the morning of the 31st ultimo formed at an early hour on the Williamsburg road, as the column of attack upon the enemy's front on that road. . . . . The division of Major-General Huger was intended to make a strong flank movement around the left of the enemy's position, and attack him in the rear of that flank. . . . After waiting some six hours for these troops to get into position, I determined to move forward without regard to them, and gave orders to that effect to Major-General D. H. Hill. The forward movement began about two o'clock, and our skirmishers soon became engaged with those of the enemy. The entire division of General Hill became engaged about three o'clock, and drove the enemy back, gaining possession of his abatis and part of his intrenched camp, General Rodes, by a movement to the right, driving in the enemy's left. The only reinforcements on the field, in hand, were my own brigades, of which Anderson's, Wilcox's, and Kemper's were put in by the front on the Williamsburg road, and Colston's and Pryor's by my right flank. At the same time the decided and gallant attack made by the other brigades gained entire possession of the enemy's position, with his artillery, camp-equipage, etc. Anderson's brigade, under Colonel Jenkins, pressing forward rapidly, continued to drive the enemy till nightfall. . . . The conduct of the attack was left entirely to Major-General Hill. The entire success of the affair is sufficient evidence of his ability, courage, and skill."

In reference to the failure of General Huger to make the attack expected of him, Mr. Davis said : " Some explanation should be given of an apparent dilatoriness on the part of that veteran soldier, who, after long and faithful service, now fills an honored grave.

" It will be remembered that General Huger was to move by the Charles City road, so as to turn the left of the enemy and attack him in flank. The extraordinary rain of the previous night had swollen every rivulet to the dimensions of a stream, and the route prescribed to General Huger was one especially affected by that heavy rain, as it led to the head of the White-Oak swamp. The bridge over the stream flowing into that swamp had been carried away, and the alternatives presented to him was to rebuild the bridge or leave his artillery. He chose the former, which involved the delay that has subjected him to criticism. If any should think an excuse necessary to justify this decision, they are remanded to the accepted military maxim, that the march must never be so hurried as to arrive unfit for service ; and, also, that they may be reminded that Huger's specialty was artillery, he being the officer who commanded the siege-guns with which General Scott marched from Vera Cruz to the City of Mexico."

General Rodes, alluding to the difficulty he had with his infantry in getting on the field, said: " The progress of the brigade was delayed by the washing away of the bridge, which forced the men to wade in water waist-deep, and a large number were entirely submerged. . . . The ground was covered with thick undergrowth, and the soil very marshy. It was with great difficulty that either horses or men could get over it— guided as they were only by the firing in front. Only five companies of the Fifth Alabama emerged from the woods under a heavy fire of artillery and musketry."

General Huger's line of march was nearer to the swamp, and the impediments consequently greater than where General Rodes found the route so difficult as to be dangerous even to infantry.

On the next day, June 1st, the enemy endeavored to retake the works Hill's division had captured the day before.

General Longstreet was ordered to attack on the morning of the 31st. The division of General D. H. Hill drove the enemy steadily back until nightfall. Our troops on the left did not co-operate with General Hill. *If the battle was preconceived*, why did they not come to his aid? Why were they so far removed as not to hear the first guns?

General G. W. Smith seems not to have been informed of the Federal works in his front, as he says in his report:

" The enemy was driven, but they were reinforced and held a strong position—*either fortified* or *naturally strong.* . . . Fire came from a *low bank of an old ditch, either drain or foundation of a fence very near the surface of the ground.*"

General Smith continued: " After leaving the wood, I heard for the first time that General Johnston had been severely wounded, and compelled to leave the field. This unfortunate casualty placed me in command of the Army of Northern Virginia. . . . The next morning I was compelled by illness to leave the field."

Mr. Davis wrote:

"On the morning of June 1st, I rode out toward the position where General Smith had been left on the previous night, and where I learned from General Lee that he would remain. After turning into the Nine-mile road, and before reaching that position, I was hailed by General Whiting, who saw me at a distance, and ran toward the road to stop me. He told me I was riding into the position of the enemy, who had advanced on the withdrawal of our troops, and there, pointing, he said, 'is a battery which I am surprised has not fired on you.' I asked where our troops were. He said his was the advance, and the others behind him. He also told me that General Smith was at the house which had been his (Whiting's) headquarters, and I rode there to see him. To relieve both him and General Lee from any embarrassment, I preferred to make the announcement of General Lee's assignment to command previous to his arrival.

"After General Lee arrived, I took leave, and being subsequently joined by him, we rode together to the Williamsburg road, where we found General Longstreet, his command being in front, and then engaged with the enemy on the field of the previous day's combat.

VOL. II.—19

" On the morning of June 1st, the army was withdrawn to its old position in front of Richmond.

" By official reports our loss, ' killed wounded, and missing," was 6,804 ; of which 4,851 were in Longstreet's command on the right, and 1,233 in Smith's command on the left. On the right we captured 10 pieces of artillery, 4 flags, a large amount of camp-equipage, and more than 1,000 prisoners.

" Our aggregate of both wings was about 40,500. The enemy's 37,936, until Sumner's corps crossed the Chickahominy, when the enemy's aggregate in excess of ours was in round numbers 16,000.

" General R. E. Lee was now in immediate command, and thenceforward directed the movements of the army in front of Richmond. Laborious and exact in details, as he was vigilant and comprehensive in grand strategy, a power, with which the public had not credited him, soon became manifest in all that makes an army a rapid, accurate, compact machine, with responsive motion in all its parts. I extract the following sentence from a letter from the late Colonel R. H. Chilton, Adjutant and Inspector-General of the Army of the Confederacy, because of his special knowledge of the subject :

" ' I consider General Lee's exhibition of

grand and administrative talents and indomitable energy, in bringing up that army in so short a time to that state of discipline which maintained aggregation through those terrible seven days fights around Richmond, as probably his grandest achievement.' "

On June 2d * and 3d my husband wrote me the following letters :

" . . . On Saturday we had a severe battle and suffered severely in attacking the enemy's intrenchments, of which our Generals were poorly informed. Some of them, and those most formidable, were found by receiving their fire. Our troops behaved most gallantly, drove the enemy out of their encampments, captured their batteries, carried their advanced redoubts, and marched forward under fire more heavy than I had ever previously witnessed. Our loss was heavy, that of the enemy unknown. General J. E. Johnston is severely wounded. The poor

---

* June 2, 1862, the President addressed a letter of thanks "To the Army of Richmond."

"At a part of your operations it was my fortune to be present. On no other occasion have I witnessed more of calmness and good order than you exhibited while advancing into the very jaws of death, and nothing could exceed the prowess with which you closed upon the enemy when a sheet of fire was blazing in your faces. . . . You are fighting for all that is dearest to men ; and though opposed to a foe who disregards many of the usages of civilized war, your humanity to the wounded and the prisoners was the fit and crowning glory to your valor."

fellow bore his suffering most heroically.
When he was about to be put into the ambulance to be removed from the field, I dismounted to speak to him; he opened his
eyes, smiled, and gave me his hand, said he
did not know how seriously he was hurt, but
feared a fragment of shell had injured his
spine. It was probably a shell loaded with
musket-balls, as there appears to be a wound
of a ball in his shoulder ranging down toward
the lungs. I saw him yesterday evening; his
breathing was labored, but he was free from
fever and seemed unshaken in his nervous system. Mrs. Johnston is deeply distressed and
very watchful. They are at Mr. Crenshaw's
house, on Church Hill. I offered to share
our house with them, but his staff obtained a
whole house and seemed to desire such arrangement. General Lee is in the field, commanding. General G. W. Smith has come in
this morning, sick—his old disease, it is said.

" Yesterday we had some heavy skirmishing, and increased our stock of prisoners, but
no important result was gained. Unaccountable delays in bringing some of our troops into action prevented us from gaining a decisive
victory on Saturday. The opportunity being
lost, we must try to find another. The same
point and manner of attack would not succeed
if again attempted.

" God will, I trust, give us wisdom to see, and valor to execute, the measures necessary to vindicate the just cause."

" RICHMOND, VA., June 3, 1862.

" . . . I cannot telegraph to you of our military operations without attracting attention and exciting speculation which it is desirable to avoid. The events of the last few days have not varied our condition in any decisive manner, and you have seen enough of rumor to teach you to reject babbling.

" General Johnston is improving, and though his confinement must be long, it is confidently believed that his wounds will not prove fatal. General Smith is sick, a return of his former disease, superinduced, it is said, by loss of sleep.

" The movements of the enemy are slow and well concealed; our scouts will, I hope, succeed better hereafter, than heretofore, in obtaining intelligence.

" *The Yankees had been eight or ten days fortifying the position in which we attacked them on Saturday, and the first intimation I had of their having slept on this side of the Chickahominy, was after I had gone into an encampment from which they had been driven.*

" *The ignorance of their works caused much of the loss we suffered.* . . .

"If the Mississippi troops, lying in camp when not retreating under Beauregard, were at home, they would probably keep a section of the river free for our use, and closed against Yankee transports.

"It is hard to see incompetence losing opportunity and wasting hard-gotten means, but harder still to bear is the knowledge that there is no available remedy. I cultivate hope and patience, and trust to the blunders of our enemy and the gallantry of our troops for ultimate success.

"Tell Helen that Captain Keary has been in the column most distinguished of late. . . . Jackson is probably now marching toward this side of the Blue Ridge."

CHAPTER XXVII.

JACKSON IN THE VALLEY.

ON May 8th, General Jackson formed a junction in the valley with General Edward Johnston.

On May 25th Generals Jackson, Edward Johnston, and Ewell, drove the enemy across the Potomac into Maryland. Two thousand prisoners were taken. General Banks, the commander-in-chief, said, "there never were more grateful hearts in the same number of men than when, at midday on the 26th, we stood on the opposite shore."

General Geary moved to Manassas Junction, burned his tents and destroyed a quantity of arms, and General Duryea telegraphed to Washington for aid. A panic ensued in Washington, and the Secretary of War issued a call to the Governors of the "loyal" States "for militia to defend the city."

Jackson pressed eagerly on to disperse the garrisons at Charlestown and Harper's Ferry.

General Winder's brigade drove the ene-

my in disorder from Charlestown toward the
Potomac.

When in the vicinity of Harper's Ferry,
General Jackson, with an effective force of
about fifteen thousand men, much less than
either of the two armies under Shields and
Frémont that were marching to intercept
him, by a forced march, arrived on the night
of May 31st at Strasburg, and learned that
General Frémont's advance was in the immediate vicinity.

General Ewell held Frémont in check with
so little difficulty that General Taylor described it as "offering a temptation to make
a serious attack upon Frémont's whole army."

Ashby, vigilant and enterprising, soon perceived this, and pointing it out to Ewell, asked
for infantry to attack the pursuing party so as
to destroy them before their supports could
get up. This force was given to him, and
just in the dusk of the evening Ashby came
upon them intrenched behind a fence. In a
moment Ashby's horse was shot dead, but
jumping to his feet he cried, "Virginians,
forward!" and in the instant fell dead. As he
fell Colonel Johnson with the First Maryland
charged and swept the fence clear, and killed
and wounded most of the routed enemy;
they proved to be the Pennsylvania Bucktails, a crack battalion under Lieutenant-

Colonel Kane, who was wounded and captured.

Colonel Johnson's horse was killed, shot in three places. His color-sergeant and three corporals were shot down in instantaneous succession at the colors, but Corporal Shanks seized them and bore them to the end.

Two days afterward, June 8th, as the First Maryland was moving into the battle of Cross Keys they passed General Ewell. He said to the commanding officer, " Colonel Johnson, you ought to affix a bucktail to your colors as a trophy." Whereupon Colonel Johnson took a bucktail from the cap of one of the men in ranks and tied it to the color lance above the colors, where it was carried in pride and triumph in all the battles of the regiment. After the battle of Port Republic, General Ewell issued the following order:

"HEADQUARTERS THIRD DIVISION, June 12, 1862.

" General Order, No. 30.

" In commemoration of the gallant conduct of the First Maryland Regiment on June 6th, instant, when led by Colonel Bradley T. Johnson, they drove back with loss the Pennsylvania Bucktail Rifles, in the engagement near Harrisonburgh, Buckingham County, Virginia, authority is given to have one of the captured bucktails (the insignium of the Federal Regiment) appended to the color staff of the First Maryland Regiment.

"By order of

"Major-General Ewell.

"James Barbour, A. A. G."

At Crosskeys, on June 8th, Jackson defeated Frémont, and on the 9th, General Shields at Port Republic. With such eagle-like swoop he had descended upon each army of the enemy, that his name had come to inspire terror. It was believed that he was about to come down, like an avalanche, upon Washington, with a vast army.

The magnificently equipped armies of Milroy, Banks, Shields, and Frémont, had all melted away before the resistless charges of Jackson's hard-fighting, hard-marching, ragged "foot-cavalry," and the Valley of the Shenandoah was our own again.

Jackson went into camp near Port Republic, where the valley was well wooded, and thus closed his famous valley campaign of 1862.

A description of the personal appearance of the now famous "Stonewall" Jackson may prove of interest to my readers. I will therefore insert the interesting account given by General Dick Taylor, of their first meeting.

"The mounted officer who had been sent

out in advance, pointed out a figure perched on the topmost rail of a fence overlooking the road and field, and said it was Jackson. Approaching, I saluted and declared my name and rank, and waited for a response. Before this came I had time to see a pair of cavalry boots covering feet of immense size, a mangy cap with vizor drawn low, a heavy, dark beard, and weary eyes—eyes I afterward saw filled with intense but never brilliant light. A low, gentle voice inquired the road and distance marched that day, 'Keazle-town road, six and twenty miles.' 'You seem to have no stragglers.' 'Never allow stragglers.' 'You must teach my people, they straggle badly.' A bow in reply. Just then my Creoles started their band and a waltz. After a contemplative suck of a lemon, 'Thoughtless fellows for serious work,' came forth. I expressed the hope that the work would be not less well done on account of the gayety. A return to the lemon gave me an opportunity to retire. Where Jackson got his lemons 'no fellow could find out,' but he was rarely without one."

He adds :

" Ere the war closed the valley of Virginia was ravaged with a cruelty surpassing that inflicted on the Palatinate two hundred years ago. That foul deed smirched the fame of

Louvois and Turenne, and public opinion, in
what has been deemed a ruder age, forced an
apology from the ' Grand Monarque.' Yet
we have seen the official report of a Federal
General wherein are recounted the many
barns, mills, and other buildings destroyed;
concluding with the assertion that ' A crow
flying over the Valley must carry his own rations.' In the opinion of the admirers of the
officer making this report, the achievement,
on which it is based, ranks with Marengo.
Moreover, this same officer, many years after
the close of the war, denounced several hundred thousands of his fellow-citizens as ' ban-
ditti,' and solicited permission to deal with
them as such. May we not well ask whether
religion, education, science, and art combined
have lessened the brutality of men since Wal-
lenstein and Tilly ? "

CHAPTER XXVIII.

MR. DAVIS'S LITERARY PREFERENCES.

In one of the most disheartening periods of the War, when Norfolk had been evacuated and the *Virginia* destroyed, he came home, about seven o'clock, from his office, staggered up to a sofa in his little private office, and laid down. He declined dinner, and I remained by his side, anxious and afraid to ask what was the trouble which so oppressed him. In an hour or two he told me that the weight of responsibility oppressed him so, that he felt he would give all his limbs to have someone with whom he could share it. I found that nothing comforted him, and at last picked up Lawrence's "Guy Livingstone." Knowing that he had not read it, I thought it might distract his mind. The descriptions of the horses and the beau sabreur Guy interested him at first, in a vague kind of way, but gradually he became absorbed, and I read on until the sky became gray and then pink. He was so wrapped in the story that he took no notice of time. When Guy's back was broken, and when Cyril Brandon in the interview that fol-

lowed, struck him, my husband rose up, in the
highest state of excitement, and called out,
" I should like to have been there to punish
the scoundrel who would strike a helpless
man when he was down."

The stream of light literature which was
then just gathering into a flood, had flowed
by him, with very few exceptions, from 1845
until 1861, and he had read none of it, being
too busy with the severer studies of state-
craft to attach any importance to it.

The first book bearing upon anything except governmental problems that he read with
eagerness, was the introduction to Buckle's
" History of Civilization." We read this together, and he seemed to greatly enjoy the
stately fragment.

Novels were to him only a means of driving
out thoughts of more serious things. For
many years he did not read them at all, and
preferred essays, history, biography, or governmental treatises ; though he remembered
with astonishing clearness Walter Scott's
poems and novels, Cooper's novels, " The
Children of the Abbey," " The Scottish
Chiefs," Theodore Hook's, and even Miss
Edgeworth's books. There was one sporting
novel, which came out in short instalments in
the old *Spirit of the Times*, called " The
Handley Cross Hounds," in which he took

great delight, and so frequently quoted from it that his brother declared he would cease to take the paper if the story was continued. One special jest in it was Jorax's statement that " he called his horse Zerxes and his little groom's horse Arterzerxes, 'cause Bengy rode arter him."

His love for poetry was continuous throughout his life. In his youth he memorized a large part of Moore's " Lalla Rookh," Byron's " Childe Harold," " The Giaour," " Lara," " English Bards and Scotch Reviewers," and especially the storm in " Don Juan," and the " Lady of the Lake." I have often seen him sitting at night, and, in a half-whisper, repeating :

> "Time rolls its course,
> The race of yore that danced our infancy upon its knee ;
> How are they blotted from the things that be ? "

His voice was musical in the extreme, and added charm to the numberless verses he had unconsciously committed to memory from his favorite poets.

The fight at Coilantogle's Ford was another great favorite of his. Fitz-James's interview with Blanche of Devon before her death, and Douglas's contempt of the fickle crowd who deserted him, were two others. His recitation of " I saw Duncanon's Widow stand,

her husband's dirk gleamed in her hand,"
gave new force to the verse. He was so familiar with Burns, that at almost any part of
his poems he could, when given a line, go on
to repeat those contiguous to it, especially
" The Cotter's Saturday Night," and the
" Advice to a Young Friend."

In after-years Clough's " Poems of Patriotism " were great favorites with him, and the
edition we have is marked all through with
passages which he admired. Milton to him
was a dreadful bore, while he was very familiar with Virgil, and loved to quote from him.
He read parts of Tennyson, and a little of
Browning, but had little sympathy with the
latter. Of heroic songs, he had memorized
a great number, and quoted them in intimate
intercourse with his friends with apposite-
ness. I never saw anyone who could resist
the charm of these recitations, when he was
in the mood. He had a lovely, high baritone
voice in song, no musical culture, but a fine
ear; and if he heard a song rendered accurately and well, sang it afterward very
sweetly. One of his favorites was Moore's
" Had I the leisure to sigh and mourn, Fan-
nie dearest, I'd mourn for thee." Another
was, " Has sorrow thy young days shaded;"
and those he liked the best were, " The harp
that once in Tara's halls," and " The Minstrel

Boy." These were the fashionable songs
of his day, and his retentive memory kept
them intact as long as he lived. His voice
never lost its sweetness, or its upper notes,
and, when feeling very well, it was common
for him to sing in his room while arranging
his papers. There was an Indian song
which calmed our children whenever they
were obstreperous :
" Cora wankee shangmonee, sheereerra
notty hiee, notty hiee."
The translation he gave—of so much as I
remember — was, " Friends, a man walks
through your village."
He was at one time able to speak several
Indian languages rather fluently, and knew a
great deal of the Indian traditions and customs, and was a more than ordinarily good
French scholar, but had learned the language
simply to read military books, and pronounced it as though it were English. He
was also a very good Spanish scholar, and
was fond of reading Spanish literature in his
younger days. He was also a fair classical
scholar, and never forgot his Greek and
Latin.

CHAPTER XXIX.

SEVEN DAYS' BATTLES AROUND RICHMOND.

MR. DAVIS wrote substantially the following account, which is condensed. For the full text see "The Rise and Fall of the Confederate Government."

"When riding from the field of battle (Seven Pines) with General Robert E. Lee, on the previous day, I informed him that he would be assigned to the command of the army, *vice* General Johnston, wounded. On the next morning he proceeded to the field and took command of the troops. During the night our forces on the left had fallen back, but those on the right remained in the position they had gained, and some combats occurred there between the opposing forces.

"Our army was in line in front of Richmond, but without intrenchments. General Lee immediately constructed earthworks. They were necessarily feeble because of our deficiency in tools. It seemed to be the intention of the enemy to assail Richmond by regular approaches, which our numerical inferiority and want of proper utensils made

OFFICERS OF THE CONFEDERATE ARMY AND NAVY.

it improbable that we should be able to resist.

"The day after General Lee assumed command, I was riding out to the army, and I found him in a house in consultation with a number of his general officers. Their tone was despondent, and one, especially, pointed out the inevitable consequence of the enemy's advance by throwing out *boyaux*, and constructing successive parallels. I expressed my disappointment at their views, and General Lee remarked that he had, before I came in, said very much the same thing.* I soon withdrew and rode to the front, where General Lee joined me, and entered into conversation as to what, under the circumstances, I thought it most advisable to do. I answered, substantially, that I knew nothing better than the plan he had previously explained to me, which was to have been executed by General Johnston, but was not carried out; that the change of circumstances would make one modification necessary—it would be necessary to bring the stronger force of General T. J. Jack-

---

* "Mr. Davis told me at the time that some generals of high rank had urged in council that we should not maintain a line of defence north of James River, and that General Lee answered, with considerable feeling, that such a course of argument, pursued to its legitimate results, would leave us nothing, except gradually to fall back to the Gulf of Mexico."—COLONEL WILLIAM PRESTON JOHNSTON, Belford's Magazine for June, 1890.

son from the Valley of the Shenandoah. So far as we were then informed, General Jackson was hotly engaged with a force superior to his own, and, before he could be withdrawn, it was necessary to drive the enemy out of the Valley. For this purpose, and to mask our design to make a junction of Jackson's forces with those of Lee, a strong division under General Whiting was detached to go by rail to join General Jackson, and, by a vigorous assault, drive the enemy across the Potomac. As soon as he commenced a retreat which unmistakably showed that his flight would not stop within the limits of Virginia, General Jackson was, with his whole force, to move rapidly on the right flank of the enemy, north of the Chickahominy. The manner in which the division was detached to reinforce General Jackson was so open, that it was not doubted General McClellan would soon be apprised of it, and would probably attribute it to any other than the real motive, and would confirm him in his exaggerated estimate of our strength.

" As evidence of the daring and unfaltering fortitude of General Lee, I will here recite an impressive conversation which occurred between us in regard to this movement. His plan was to throw forward his left across the Meadow Bridge, drive back the enemy's right flank, then, crossing by the Mechanicsville

Bridge with another column, to attack in
front. I pointed out to him that our force and
intrenched line between that left flank and
Richmond was too weak for a protracted resistance, and, if McClellan was the man I took
him for when I nominated him for promotion
in a new regiment of cavalry, and subsequently selected him for one of the military commission sent to Europe during the War of the
Crimea, as soon as he found that the bulk of
our army was on the north side of the Chickahominy, he would not stop to try conclusions, but would immediately move upon
his objective point, the city of Richmond.
If, on the other hand, he should behave like
an engineer officer, and deem it his first duty
to protect his line of communication, I thought
the plan proposed was not only the best, but
would be a success. Something of his old
esprit de corps manifested itself in General
Lee's first response, that he did not know *engineer officers* were more likely than others to
make such mistakes ; but, immediately passing
to the main subject, he added: " If you will
hold him as long as you can at the intrenchment, and then fall back on the detached
works around the city, I will be upon the
enemy's heels before he gets there." *

---

* " The chief danger was that, while Lee with his main body was
assailing and turning McClellan's right on the north side of the

From President Davis to Mrs. Davis.

"CONFEDERATE STATES OF AMERICA,
"EXECUTIVE DEPARTMENT, June 11, 1862.

". . . I am in usual health, though the weather has been very inclement. The roads to the different positions of the army could not be worse and remain passable.

"The enemy is intrenching and bringing up heavy guns on the York River railroad, *which not being useful to our army nor paid for by our treasury, was of course not destroyed.* His policy is to advance by regular approaches covered by successive lines of earth - works, that reviled policy of West Pointism and spades, which is sure to succeed against those who do not employ like means to counteract it.

"Politicians, newspapers, and uneducated officers have created such a prejudice in our army against labor, that it will be difficult, until taught by sad experience, to induce our troops to work efficiently. The greatest generals of ancient and modern times have

Chickahominy, McClellan might make a show of resistance there, and with his superior forces cross the Chickahominy with his main body, and, breaking through our centre, go right into Richmond.

"The understanding with General Lee was, that President Davis should stay with our centre, and if McClellan made that attempt he should hold the centre as long as he could."—COLONEL WILLIAM PRESTON JOHNSTON, Belford's Magazine, June, 1890.

won their renown by labor. Victories were
the results. Cæsar, who revolutionized the
military system of his age, never slept in a
camp without intrenching it. France, Spain,
and Great Britain retain to this day memorials
of Roman invasion in the massive works constructed by the Roman armies.

"I will endeavor, by movements which are
not without great hazard, to countervail the
enemy's policy. If we succeed in rendering
his works useless to him, and compel him to
meet us on the field, I have much confidence
in our ability to give him a complete defeat,
and then it may be possible to teach him the
pain of invasion, and to feed our army on his
territory. The issues of campaigns can never
be safely foretold ; it is for us to do all which
can be done, and trustingly to leave our fate
to Him who rules the universe."

Our infant son, William Howell, lay at the
point of death, and Mr. Davis, who could not
come, wrote.

"RICHMOND, June 13, 1862.

". . . My heart sunk within me at
the news of the suffering of my angel baby.
Your telegram of the 12th gives assurance
of the subsidence of disease. But the look
of pain and exhaustion, the gentle complaint,
'I am tired,' which has for so many years
oppressed me, seems to have been revived ;

and unless God spares me another such trial,
what is to become of me, I don't know. Dr.
Garnett will, I hope, reach you this morning.
He carried with him what he regarded as a
specific remedy. . . . My ease, my health,
my property, my life I can give to the cause
of my country. The heroism which could lay
my wife and children on any sacrificial altar
is not mine. Spare us, good Lord.

"I was out until late last night on the lines
of the army. The anticipated demonstration
was not made, and reconnoissance convinces
me that the reported movement of the enemy was unfounded. He keeps close under
cover, is probably waiting for reinforcements,
or resolved to fight only behind his own
intrenchment. We must find, if possible,
the means to get at him without putting
the breasts of our men in antagonism to his
heaps of earth. Beauregard claims by telegram to have made a "brilliant and successful" retreat, and pleads his constant occupation as the cause of his delay to reply to the
inquiry made through the Adjutant-General,
as to reason for his retreat and abandonment
of the Memphis and Charleston Railroad.
There are those who can only walk along
when it is near to the ground, and I fear he
has been placed too high for his mental
strength, as he does not exhibit the ability

manifested in smaller fields. The news from the Valley of Virginia confirms the report of the flight of the enemy, and the danger to our troops has been mainly passed. We have sent reinforcements who, as fresh troops, will move in front of the old command. . . . I saw a little boy yesterday in the street, he had his trousers rolled up and was wading in the gutter; he looked something like Jeff, and when I persuaded him to get out of the water, he raised his sunny face and laughed, but denied my conclusion. Mrs. Greenhow is here. Madam looks much changed, and has the air of one whose nerves are shaken by mental torture. General Lee's wife has arrived, her servants left her, and she found it uncomfortable to live without them."

From the President to Mrs. Davis.

"RICHMOND, VA., June 21, 1862.

". . . We are preparing and taking position for the struggle which must be at hand. The stake is too high to permit the pulse to keep its even beat, but our troops are in improved condition, and as confident as I am hopeful of success. A total defeat of McClellan will relieve the Confederacy of its embarrassments in the East, and then we must make a desperate effort to regain what Beauregard has abandoned in the West."

From the President to Mrs. Davis.

"Richmond, Va., June 23, 1862.

" You will no doubt hear many rumors, as even here the air is full of them. Be not dis turbed, we are better prepared now than we were on the first of the month, and with God's blessing will beat the enemy as soon as we can get at him. . . . I am nearly well again. The heat and dust are very oppressive. The wagon-trains move along in a cloud which quite conceals everything except the leading team ; this, of course, refers to the roads around our main encampments."

" General G. W. Smith, after the manner of Beauregard, has taken a surgeon's certificate, and is about to retire for a season to recruit his health. General J. E. Johnston is steadily and rapidly improving. I wish he were able to take the field. Despite the critics who know military affairs by instinct, he is a good soldier, never brags of what he did do, and could at this time render most valuable service."

From the President to Mrs. Davis.

"Richmond, Va., June 25, 1862.

" . . . Skirmishing yesterday and to-day, but not of a character to reveal the purpose of the enemy, and designed to conceal our own. Van Dorn is at Vicksburg, and preparing to make a desperate defence. Bragg may effect something, since Halleck has divided his force, and I hope will try, but there is reason to fear that his army has been woefully demoralized. Butler, properly surnamed the 'beast,' has added to his claim for infamous notoriety by his recent orders, and report charges him with wholesale peculations, and daily selling licenses for private gain.

" For instance, two respectable gentlemen assured me that he sold permits for the export of salt, at the rate of five dollars per sack. How much better it would have been had the city been left a pile of ashes ! "

The offensive-defensive campaign which resulted so gloriously to our arms was thus inaugurated, and turned from the capital of the Confederacy a danger so momentous that, looking at it so retrospectively, it is evident that a policy less daring or less firmly pursued would not have saved the capital from capture. The President wrote substantially as follows :

" General J. E. B. Stuart was sent with a cavalry force, on June 8th, to observe the enemy, mask the approach of General Jackson, and to cover the route by which he was to march, and to ascertain whether the enemy had any defensive works or troops to interfere with the advance of those forces. He reported favorably on both these points. On June 26th, General Stuart received confidential instructions from General Lee, the execution of which is so interwoven with the seven days' battles as to be more appropriately noticed in connection with them.

" According to the published reports, General McClellan's position was regarded at this time as extremely critical.

" During the night I visited the several commands along the intrenchment on the south side of the Chickahominy.

" In one of these engagements our loss was small in numbers, but great in value. Among others who could ill be spared, here fell the gallant soldier Brigadier-General Richard Griffith. He had served with distinction in foreign war, and when the South was invaded was among the first to take up arms in defence of our rights.*

" Our troops slept upon their arms. The enemy retreated during the night, and by the time thus gained, he was enabled to cross the White Oak Creek and destroy the bridge.

" It is an extraordinary fact that, though the capital had been threatened by an attack from the sea-board on the right, though our

---

* Mr. Davis leaned over him and said, " My dear boy, I hope you are not seriously hurt." The General grasped his hand and said, "Yes, I think fatally ; farewell, Colonel."

army had retreated from Yorktown up to the Chickahominy, and, after encamping there for a time, had crossed the river and moved up to Richmond ; yet, when at the close of the battles around Richmond McClellan retreated and was pursued toward the James River, *we had no maps of the country in which we were operating ; our generals were ignorant of the roads, and their guides knew little more than the way from their homes to Richmond. It was this fatal defect in preparation, and the erroneous answers of the guides, that caused* General Lee first to post Holmes and Wise, when they came down the River road, at New Market, where, he was told, was the route that McClellan must pursue in his retreat to the James. Subsequently he learned that there was another road, by the Willis church, which would better serve the purpose of the retreating foe."

The President was on the field every day during the seven days' fight, and slept on it every night, and in the sixth day's fight he had taken his position in a house near the field and received a message from General Lee to leave it, as the enemy's guns were bearing upon it. Within a few minutes after Mr. Davis left it, the house was riddled.

Even thus early the presence of foreigners in the army of the North began to be noticed,

and the ranks of the Federal Army were filled
up from this year forth with foreigners of all
sorts and conditions of men, July 18, 1862.
Of 237 dead Union soldiers who had served
in these battles under the command of Colonel Woodbury, of Michigan, it was said there
was but one who was American born.

These men sacked and burned without
the sympathy a common language would have
necessarily created.

"When McClellan's army was in retreat, to
the fatigue of hard marches and successive
battles, enough to have disqualified our troops
from rapid pursuit, was added the discomfort
of being thoroughly wet and chilled by the
rain. I sent to the neighboring houses to
buy, if it could be had, at any price, enough
whiskey to give each of the men a single gill,
but it could not be found.

"The foe had silently withdrawn in the
night by a route which had been unknown to
us, but which was the most direct road to
Harrison's Landing, and he had so many
hours the start that, among the general officers who expressed their opinion to me,
only one thought it possible to pursue effect-
ively. That was General T. J. Jackson, who
quietly said, 'They have not all got away, if
we go immediately after them.'

". . . General Lee was not given to

indecision, and they have mistaken his character who suppose caution was his vice. He was prone to attack, and not slow to press an advantage when he gained it. He ordered Longstreet and Jackson to advance, but a violent storm which prevailed throughout the day greatly retarded their progress. The enemy, harassed and closely followed by the cavalry, succeeded in gaining Westover, on the James River, and the protection of his gun-boats. His position was one of great natural and artificial strength, after the heights were occupied and intrenched. It was flanked on each side by guns of his shipping, as well as by those mounted in his intrenchments. Under these circumstances it was inexpedient to attack him; and our troops, who had been marching and fighting almost incessantly for seven days, under the most trying circumstances, were withdrawn in order to afford them the repose of which they stood so much in need.

" Several days were spent in collecting arms and other property abandoned by the enemy, and, in the meantime, some artillery and cavalry were sent below Westover to annoy his transports. On July 8th, our army returned to the vicinity of Richmond.

" The siege of Richmond was raised, and the object of a campaign which had been prosecuted after months of preparation, at an enormous expenditure of men and money, was completely frustrated.

General Lee was now gaining fast the confidence of all classes; he had possessed that of the President always. The Richmond *Dispatch* of July 19, 1862, said, "The rise which this officer has suddenly taken in the public confidence is without a precedent. At the commencement of the war he enjoyed the highest reputation of any officer on the continent.

"The operations of General Lee in the short campaign which is just over were certainly those of a master. No captain that ever lived could have planned or executed a better campaign. It was perfect in all its parts, and will be set down hereafter as among the models which the military student will be required to study."

The army under General Johnston on May 31st, from official reports, showed an effective strength of 62,696.

Deduct the losses sustained in the battle of Seven Pines, as shown by the official reports of casualties, say, 6,084 and we have 56,612 as the number of effectives when General Lee took command of the Army of Northern Virginia.

Before the seven days' battles around

Richmond, reinforcements to the number of
24,150 were brought to the army, so that at
the beginning of the contest with McClellan,
Lee had 80,762 effectives for battle.

If we adopt as correct the Confederate loss
as given by Swinton, say 19,000, then it would
appear that when McClellan reached the
James River with " 85,000 to 90,000 men,
he was being pursued by Lee with but
62,000." *

When the news of our great victory over
such long odds came to Raleigh, everyone
was breathless with excitement. The telegraph office was separated by a narrow alley
from my room in the hotel. As I walked my
ill baby to and fro by the window, a voice
came from the street, " Tell us what you
know, please." Just then a crowd filled the
alley and another voice cried, " Boys, I can
take it off as it passes." Another one said to
me, " Do tell us it is a victory ;" and as a telegram from the President to me was recorded,
every word was shouted to the crowd. At the
end of the message someone said, " Don't
hurrah, you will scare the sick baby." The
crowd could not keep silent long, and after
they reached the middle of the street they
shouted themselves hoarse. One old man

* Colonel Taylor : Four Years with Lee.

stopped in the alley and called up—" I say, madam, we will pray for your poor baby; don't be down-hearted."

From the President to Mrs. Davis.

After the siege of Richmond was raised, the President wrote to me as follows:

"RICHMOND, July 6, 1862.

". . . Had all the orders been well and promptly executed, there would have been a general dispersion of McClellan's army, and the remnant which might have been held together could have only reached the James River by first crossing the Chickahominy. Our success has been so remarkable that we should be grateful, and believe that even our disappointments were ordered for our gain. McClellan certainly showed capacity in his retreat, but there is little cause to laud a general who is driven out of his intrenchments by a smaller and worse armed force than his own, and compelled to abandon a campaign in the preparation of which he had spent many months and many millions of dollars, and seek safety by flying to other troops for cover, burning his depots of provisions, and marking his route by scattered arms, ammunition, and wagons. The reinforcements sent to him may advance. His army would never have fought us again if we had been left to an even-handed settlement of the issue which he made and we joined.

"It is reported that all their forces now available are to be sent to the James River, and one great effort is to be made to defeat us here. Our army is greatly reduced, but I hope recruits will be promptly sent forward from most of the States, and there are many causes which will interfere with the execution of the enemy's plans, and some things they have not dreamed which we may do. If our ranks were full we could end the war in a few weeks. There is reason to believe that the Yankees have gained from England and France as the last extension, this month, and expect foreign intervention if we hold them at bay on the first of August. My great grief at the loss of the *Virginia* is renewed and redoubled by our want of her now in the James River. The timber for the completion of the *Richmond* was burned at Norfolk, and the work on her has been thus greatly delayed; it is uncertain when she will be finished. The batteries on the river, eight miles below here, will stop the gun-boats, and we must intercept and defeat any land force which attempts to take them from the land side. Our troubles, you perceive, have not ended, but our chances have improved, so I repeat, be of good cheer."

I went to Richmond for a short visit immediately after the seven days' fight, and the odors of the battle-field were distinctly perceptible all over the city. The ladies during the battles had spent the greater part of their time on the roofs of their houses, watching the course of the smoke and gleam of battle, and as the lurid light drifted down to the Peninsula they rejoiced and thanked God ; when it shone nearer to the city they prayed for help from above. The President slept upon the field every night, and was exposed to fire all day.

About this time Mr. Davis gave me news of the *Sumter.*

From President Davis to Mrs. Davis.

"CONFEDERATE STATES OF AMERICA,
"EXECUTIVE DEPARTMENT, July 7, 1862.

". . . The *Sumter* was found to be unseaworthy, and as she could not be prepared at Gibraltar, she was laid up there, the crew discharged, and the officers ordered to go home. Becket sailed from Hamburg, and reached Nassau about the middle of June on his way home. Captain Semmes sailed from England, and reached the same port a few days thereafter, and finding orders which assigned him to a new vessel * now under construction, returned from Nassau to England to superintend the building of his vessel, and took Becket with him. . . . Nothing important from the army to-day ; the enemy are still sending off demoralized troops, and are said to be still receiving reinforcements. If, as is reported, they are leaving the Southern Coast and the Tennessee line, we may expect another great effort in this region, and will be able to bring up some troops to aid us."

The Confederate women looked on at the struggle with ever-increasing interest ; they offered their jewels, their plate, and everything of value they possessed which would be useful to their country. One of these devoted patriots said to me, "I tried, and could not make up my mind to part with my wedding-ring, and it was so thin from wear ; else I think I could have given it up."

There were some quaint appeals made to Mr. Davis, and his sympathy and sense of humor brought him into correspondence with the writers, or induced him to make as quaint endorsements on their letters.

One girl, whose sweetheart was a gallant soldier in the Fifth South Carolina Regiment,

---

* The 290, or the Alabama.

and who had fought bravely all through the seven days' battles, made the following earnest request :

"Dear Mr. President : I want you to let Jeems C., of company oneth, 5th South Carolina Regiment, come home and get married. Jeems is willin', I is willin', his mammy says she is willin', but Jeems's capt'in, he ain't willin'. Now when we are all willin' 'ceptin' Jeems' captain, I think you might let up and let Jeems come. I'll make him go straight back when he's done got married and fight just as hard as ever.

"Your affectionate friend, etc."

Mr. Davis wrote on the letter, "Let Jeems go," and Jeems went home, married the affectionate correspondent of Mr. Davis, returned to his regiment, and did fight as well as ever.

CONFEDERATE GENERALS.

CHAPTER XXX.

MR. MASON was appointed our Representative in London, Mr. Slidell in Paris, Mr. Rost in Spain, and Mr. Mann in Belgium. I hope Mr. Mann's memoirs, which are very full and written from diaries, will be published, and these will shed much light upon the diplomatic service of the Confederacy.

The Confederate States having dissolved their connection with the United States, whose relations were securely and long established with Foreign Governments, it devolved upon the Confederate States formally to declare to these Governments her separation from the United States. This the Provisional Congress did, but the United States antecedently had claimed sovereignty over the Confederate States, and the Governments of Europe announced that they could not assume to judge of the rights of the combatants. These Governments had fallen into the error, now commonly prevailing, that our

separate sovereignty had been merged into
one supreme Federal authority, and they
therefore announced their neutrality, and
merely recognized the existence of a state of
war. This decision was in effect hostile to
our rights, for if we were, like the United
States, belligerents, why refuse us the same
privileges of international intercourse accorded to the United States? Under this view
European powers recognized for a year a¡
" paper blockade," forgetful that " blockades
to be binding must be effective." *

The Government of the Confederate States
remonstrated against this injustice, and was
answered by silence.

However, Her Majesty's foreign office published a despatch dated February 11, 1862, in-
terpolating into the agreement of the Paris
Congress, that if the blockading ships " created an evident danger of entering or leaving" the ports blockaded, that " should be
considered a blockade."

Soon after the right of neutral ships to
trade with English ships was abandoned by
England. The duty to recognize a belligerent was postponed, and all the recognized
neutral rights by which we might have been
benefited were alternately waived or asserted,

---

* The language of the five great powers of Europe in the Congress
at Paris, 1856.

as they might prove of service to the United States.

The commerce of the United States was not protected by its Government, but reclamation for all the loss resultant from the enterprise of the Confederate cruisers was claimed from, and partially accorded by Great Britain, because our vessels were built in her ports. Thus, though the armies of the United States were recruited from the whole world, protection was claimed for her commerce from the same source. Had the English Government not leaned to the side of the United States, the fact that the ballot-boxes used at elections were those of the States, and that the vote for their secession had been unanimous, would have been conclusive against characterizing the war as an " insurrection."

On October 3, 1862, the French minister of foreign affairs, Monsieur Drouyn de L'Huys, addressed a note to the ambassadors at London and St. Petersburg, proposing that these great powers should arrange an armistice for six months, in view of the blood shed and the equal success of the combatants. The English Government answered that their offer might be declined by the United States Government. The Russian Government answered that their interposition might cause the opposite to the desired effect. For want of co-operation, the effort was not made by France. In May, 1861, Her Britannic Majesty assured our enemies that "the sympathies of this country were rather with the North than with the South," and on June 1, 1861, she interdicted the use of her ports to armed ships and privateers, though the United States claimed this right for themselves. On June 12, 1861, the United States reproved Great Britain for holding intercourse with the Commissioners of the Confederate States, "so-called," and received assurances that it would not occur again.

On June 14, 1862, Mr. Seward justified himself for obstructing Charleston Harbor and other commercial inlets, by saying that three thousand miles were more than could be successfully blockaded. He could stop up the "large holes" by his ships, but could not stop up all "the small ones." Her Majesty's minister for foreign affairs, May 6, 1862, said, "this blockade kept up irregularly has injured thousands. Yet Her Majesty's Government have never sought to take advantage of the obvious imperfections of this blockade in order to declare it inoperative."

Her Majesty's Government interposed no objection to the purchase of arms for the United States, but in May, 1861, Earl Russell entertained the complaint that the Confederate Government was buying arms at Nassau, contraband of war, and the Confederate States vessel was ineffectually seized, because it touched at Nassau, at the instance of the United States, and was made subject to a prosecution, when simultaneously cargoes and munitions of war were openly shipped to the United States to be used in our destruction.

An example of the diplomatic blockade enforced by the United States against our Commissioners is given in a correspondence between Earl Russell and Mr. Mason, and will give some idea of how Mr. Mason and other envoys were met at every turn by rebuffs under Mr. Seward's promptings — sometimes with evasion, but more often with the absurd assumption that our organized government, large and efficient army, and united population were rebels, not belligerents.

The Honorable James T. Mason had been unavailingly trying to procure from Europe the acknowledgment of our rights as belligerents before the nations of the world, and had been from time to time met with diplomatic evasions. The astute and watchful ambassador from the United States, Charles Francis Adams, had thus far forestalled every effort to this end by presenting Mr. Seward's exparte statements of the causes, conduct, and prospect of an early termination of the war.

Mr. Seward predicted the war would end in thirty days. The English overestimated the readiness of the United States for war, and knew that the affair of the *Trent* had left on their minds toward Great Britain a bitter sense of injury. The only measure by which Mr. Seward governed his presentation of the condition and conduct of either section of the States, was how much Her Majesty's Government would believe. Our Commissioners were, through his misrepresentation, refused interviews with her ministers, and our assured success seemed to be the only avenue to their intercourse with them. Under these circumstances, the following correspondence took place between Mr. Mason and Lord John Russell:

"No. 54 Devonshire Street, Portland Place,
"London, July 17, 1862.

"My Lord: In late proceedings of Parliament, and in reply to inquiries made in each House as to the intention of Her Majesty's Government to tender offices of mediation to the contending powers in North America, it was replied in substance, by Lord Palmerston and your Lordship, that Her Majesty's Government had no such intention at present, because, although this Government would be ever ready to offer such mediation whenever it might be considered that such interposition would avail, it was believed by the Government that, in the present inflamed or irritated temper of the belligerents, any such offer might be misinterpreted, and might have an effect contrary to what was intended.

" I will not undertake, of course, to express any opinion of the correctness of this view so far as it may apply to the Government or the people of the United States, but as the terms would seem to have been applied equally to the Government or people of the Confederate States of America, I feel warranted in the declaration that, while it is the unalterable purpose of that Government and people to maintain the independence they have gained; while under no circumstances or contingencies will they ever again come under a common Government with those now constituting the United States; and although they do not in any form invite such interposition; yet they can see nothing in their position which could make either offensive or irritating a tender of such offices on the part of Her Majesty's Government, as might lead to a termination of the war—a war hopelessly carried on against them, and which is attended by a wanton waste of human life at which humanity shudders. On the contrary, I can entertain no doubt that such offer would be received by the Government of the Confederate States of America with that high consideration and respect due to the benign purpose in which it would have its origin.   " I am, etc.,

"J. M. Mason.

"To Lord John Russell."

"Foreign Office, July 24, 1862.

"Sir: I have the honor to acknowledge the receipt of your letter of the 17th instant, respecting the intention expressed by Her Majesty's Government to refrain from any present mediation between the contending parties in America, and I have to state to you, in reply, that in the opinion of Her Majesty's Government, any proposal to the United States to recognize the Confederacy would irritate the United States, and any proposal to the Southern States to return to the Union would irritate the Confederates.

" This was the meaning of my declaration in Parliament on the subject.

"I am, etc.,

" Russell.

"To James M. Mason."

"No. 54 Devonshire Street, Portland Place,
"London, July 24, 1862.

" My Lord : In the interview I had the honor to have with your Lordship in Febru-

ary last, I laid before your Lordship, under
instructions from the Government of the Confederate States, the views entertained by that
Government, leading to the belief that it was,
of right, entitled to be recognized as a separate
and independent power, and to be received
as an equal in the great family of nations.

" I then represented to your Lordship that
the dissolution of the Union of the States of
North America, by the withdrawal therefrom
of certain of the Confederate States, was not
to be considered as a revolution in the ordinary acceptation of that term ; far less was
it to be considered as an act of insurrection
or rebellion; that it was, both in form and
in fact, but the termination of a confederacy
which during a long course of years had
violated the terms of the Federal compact by
the exercise of unwarranted powers, oppress-
ing and degrading the minority section.
That the seceding parties had so withdrawn
as organized political communities, and had
formed a new Confederacy, comprising then,
as now, thirteen separate and sovereign
States, embracing an area of 870,616 square
miles, and with a population of 12,000,000.
This new Confederacy has now been in
complete and successful operation for a period
of nearly eighteen months, has proved itself
capable of successful defence against every

attempt to subdue or destroy it, and in a war, conducted by its late confederates on a scale to tax their utmost power, has presented everywhere a united people determined at every cost to maintain the independence they had affirmed.

"Since that interview more than five months have elapsed, and during that period events have but more fully confirmed the views I then had the honor to present to your Lordship. The resources, strength, and power of the Confederate States developed by these events, I think, authorize me to assume, as the judgment of the intelligence of all Europe, that the separation of the States of North America is final; that under no possible circumstances can the late Federal Union be restored ; that the new Confederacy has evinced both the capacity and the determination to maintain its independence ; and, therefore, with other powers the question of recognizing that independence is simply a question of time.

"The Confederate States ask no aid from, or intervention by, foreign powers. They are entirely content that the strict neutrality which has been proclaimed between the belligerents shall be adhered to, however unequally it may operate, because of fortuitous circumstances, upon them.

"But if the principles and morals of the public law be, when a nation has established before the world both its capacity and its ability to maintain the government it has ordained, that a duty devolves on other nations to recognize such fact, then I submit that the Government of the Confederate States of America, having sustained itself unimpaired, through trials greater than most nations have been called to endure, and far greater than any it has yet to meet, has furnished to the world sufficient proof of stability, strength, and resources to entitle it to a place among the independent nations of the earth.   I have, etc.,

"J. M. MASON."

To this letter no answer was returned, and after waiting a reasonable time Mr. Mason addressed another letter to the minister:

Mr. Mason to Earl Russell.

"No. 54 DEVONSHIRE STREET, PORTLAND PLACE,
"LONDON, July 24, 1862.

"Mr. Mason presents his compliments to Earl Russell, and if agreeable to his Lordship, Mr. Mason would be obliged if Earl Russell would allow him the honor of an interview, at such time as may be convenient to his Lordship.

" Mr. Mason desires to submit to Earl Russell some views connected with the subject of the letter he has the honor to transmit herewith, which he thinks may be better imparted in a brief conversation."

Earl Russell to Mr. Mason.

"FOREIGN OFFICE, July 31, 1862.

" Lord Russell presents his compliments to Mr. Mason. He begs to assure Mr. Mason that it is from no want of respect to him that Lord Russell has delayed sending an answer to his letter of the 24th instant.

" Lord Russell has postponed sending that answer in order that he might submit a draft of it to the cabinet on Saturday next. It will be forwarded on Monday to Mr. Mason.

" Lord Russell does not think any advantage would arise from the personal interview which Mr. Mason proposes, and must therefore decline it."

"No. 54 DEVONSHIRE STREET, PORTLAND PLACE,
"August 1, 1862.

" My LORD : In the interview I had the honor to propose in my last note, I had intended briefly to submit the following views, which I thought might not be without weight in the consideration to be given by Her Majesty's Government to the request for recognition of the Confederate States, submitted in my letter of July 24th ultimo. I ask leave now to present them as supplemental to that letter.

"If it be true, as there assumed, that in the settled judgment of England the separation of the States is final, then the failure of so great a power to recognize the fact in a formal manner imparts an opposite belief, and must operate as an incentive to the United States to protract the contest.

"In a war such as that pending in America, where a party in possession of the government is striving to subdue those who, for reasons sufficient to themselves, have withdrawn from it, the contest will be carried on in the heat of blood and of popular excitement long after its object has become hopeless in the eyes of the disinterested public.

"The Government itself may feel that its power is inadequate to bring back the recusant States, and yet be unable at once to control the fierce elements which surround it while the war wages. Such, it is confidently believed, is the actual condition of affairs.

"It is impossible, in the experience of eighteen months of no ordinary trial, in the small results attained, and in the manifest exhaustion of its resources, that any hope remains with the Government of the United States either of bringing about a restoration of the dissevered Union, or of subjugating those who have renounced it. And yet the failure of foreign powers formally to recognize this condition of things disables those in authority from conceding that fact at home.

" Again, it is known that there is a large and increasing sentiment in the United States in accordance with these views ; a sentiment which has its origin in the hard teachings of the war as it has progressed.

" It is believed (or so confidently affirmed) that there was a large party in the Southern States devoted to the Union, whose presence and power would be manifested there as soon as the public force of the United States was present to sustain it. I need not say how fully the experience of the war has dispelled this delusion.

" Again, it was believed, and confidently relied on, that in the social structure of the Southern States there was a large population of the dominant race indifferent, if not hostile, to the basis on which that social structure rests, in which they were not interested, and who would be found the allies of those whose mission was supposed to be in some way to break it up; but the same experience has shown that the whole population of the South is united, as one people, in arms to resist the invader.

"Nothing remains, then, on which to rest any hope of conquest but a reliance on the superior numbers and the supposed greater resources of the Northern States. I think the results of the last (or pending) campaign have proved how idle such expectations were, against the advantages of a people fighting at home and bringing into a common stock of resistance, as a free-will offering, all that they possessed, whether of blood or treasure—a spectacle now historically before the world.

"It is in human experience that there must be those in the United States who cannot shut their eyes to such facts, and yet, in the despotic power now assumed by the Government, to give expression to any doubt would be to court the hospitalities of the dungeon.

"One word from the government of Her Majesty would encourage the people to speak, and the civilized world would respond to the truths they would utter, 'that for whatever purpose the war was begun, it was continued now in a vindictive and unreasoning spirit, shocking alike to humanity and civilization.' That potent word would be simply to announce a fact, which a frenzied mind could only dispute, that the Southern States, now in a separate Confederacy, had established before the world its competency to maintain the government of its adoption, and its determination to abide by it.

"To withhold it would not only seem in derogation of truth, but would be to encourage the continuance of a war, hopeless in its object, ruinous alike to the parties engaged in it, and to the prosperity and welfare of Europe.

"J. M. MASON."

"TO LORD JOHN RUSSELL."

"FOREIGN OFFICE, August 2, 1862.

"SIR: I have had the honor to receive your letters of July 24th and 1st instant, in which you repeat the considerations which in the opinion of the Government of the so-called Confederate States, entitled that Government to be recognized of right as a separate and independent power, and to be received as an equal in the great family of nations.

"In again urging the views you represent, as before, that the withdrawal of certain of the Confederates from the Union of the States of North America is not to be considered as a revolution, in the ordinary acceptation of that term, far less of an act of insurrection or rebellion, but as the termination of a Confederacy which had, during a long course of years, violated the terms of the Federal compact.

"I beg leave to say, in the outset, that upon this question of a right of withdrawal, as upon that of the previous conduct of the United States, Her Majesty's Government have never presumed to form a judgment. The interpretation of the Constitution of the United States, and the character of the proceedings of the President and Congress of the United States under that Constitution, must be determined, in the opinion of Her Majesty's Government, by the States and people in North America who have inherited, and until recently upheld, that Constitution. Her Majesty's Government decline altogether the responsibility of assuming to be judges in such a controversy.

"You state that the Confederacy has a population of twelve millions; that it has proved self-capable for eighteen months of successful defence against every attempt to subdue or destroy it; that in the judgment of the intelligence of all Europe the separation is final; and that, under no possible circumstances can the late Federal Union be restored.

"On the other hand, the Secretary of State of the United States had affirmed, in an official despatch, that a large portion of the once disaffected population has been restored to the Union, and now evinces its loyalty and firm adherence to the Government; that the white population now in insurrection is under five millions, and that the Southern Confederacy owes its main strength to the hope of assistance from Europe.

" In the face of the fluctuating events of the war; the alternations of victory and defeat ; the capture of New Orleans; the advance of the Federals to Corinth, to Memphis, and the banks of the Mississippi as far as Vicksburg; contrasted, on the other hand, with the failure of the attack on Charleston, and the retreat from before Richmond— placed, too, between allegations so contradictory on the part of the contending powers—Her Majesty's Government are still determined to wait.

" In order to be entitled to a place among the independent nations of the earth, a State ought to have not only strength and resources for a time, but afford promise of stability and permanence. Should the Confederate States of America win that place among nations, it might be right for other nations justly to acknowledge an independence achieved by victory, and maintained by a successful resistance to all attempts to overthrow it. That time, however, has not, in the judgment of Her Majesty's Government, yet arrived. Her Majesty's Government, therefore, can only hope that a peaceful termination of the present bloody and destructive contest may not be distant.

"I am, etc.,

"RUSSELL."

"TO JAMES M. MASON, ESQ."

Thus was foiled one of our sturdy old envoy's efforts to set his country's cause fairly before a people loving liberty, speaking the same language with us, and from whom we were descended within the memory of those then living. One bold and profound thinker among the English governing class, Lord Lowther, has written an admirable exposition of the dogma of State Rights, but though many other Englishmen understood its binding force, as nations cannot afford, as such, to indulge sympathy for those unable to maintain themselves against an oppressor, they "passed by on the other side."

Throughout all this unfair discrimination, with the world against him, environed by enemies on all sides, the President of the Confederate States, with admirable temper, pursued his steady efforts to establish relations with foreign Governments, though his maintenance of the strict truth under all circumstances was a disqualification he did not underrate. His despatches are dignified models of advocacy and remonstrance, and were the admiration of the diplomats of his time. His courage was as undaunted when he stood for the right against the world, as his dignity and honesty of purpose were impregnable, and his countrymen and his family do not now wish it had been otherwise. The just verdict of mankind cannot be rendered until all who had formed a preconceived opinion have passed away. Posterity is the just and generous judge to whom Confederates look to write his honored name high on the shining lists of brave and self-sacrificing heroes.

CHAPTER XXXI.

MEMPHIS, VICKSBURG, AND BATON ROUGE.

On June 7, 1862, a fleet of gun-boats steamed down the Tennessee River, flanking our positions on the Mississippi River, and a fleet moved down the Mississippi, bombarded Island No. 10, reduced it, bombarded Fort Pillow and reduced that fort, and then attacked Memphis and took possession, after a manful resistance with an inadequate force. After this disaster followed close the siege of Vicksburg, which was repelled by the assistance of our ram, the *Arkansas*, under Captain J. N. Brown. From the 15th to the 18th of June, the enemy endeavored to sink the *Arkansas* with heavy shells from their mortars, and an attempt was made to cut her out from under the batteries; but it failed, with the loss of one of their boats. On the 27th both Federal fleets retired, and the siege, which had lasted sixty-seven days, was ended. Two powerful fleets had been foiled, and a land force of from 4,000 to 5,000 men held at bay. Then followed the battle of Baton Rouge, and the destruction of the Ram *Arkansas* to save her from the enemy, and their return to New Orleans defeated.

CHAPTER XXXII.

CONFEDERATE CONGRESS.—THE PRESIDENT'S MES-
SAGE.—HORACE GREELEY.

In the absence of authorized reports of the debates in Congress which are unattainable, if they exist, I have from scrap books compiled excerpts to show the trend of public opinion, and appended Mr. Davis's message in which he treats of the recommendations made by that body, some of which are indicated by the subjoined extracts.

"CONFEDERATE CONGRESS, August 23, 1862.

"Resolution of thanks to General J. C. Breckinridge and command for gallant conduct at the battle of Baton Rouge; also resolution of thanks to General Earl Van Dorn and command, and citizens of Vicksburg, for their defence of that city."

"RICHMOND, August 18, 1862.

"Several resolutions were offered in the House looking to the doctrine of *lex talionis* and the enlargement of the conscription." It was clear that these two matters would occupy the attention of Congress before other business could be entertained.

"As to the conscription, the immediate extension of it to all persons capable of bearing arms between the ages of thirty-five and forty-five, is rendered absolutely necessary by the call for six hundred thousand troops by Lincoln. There can be little doubt that these six hundred thousand new men will be raised by the Yankee Government by October 15th, at the farthest."

"CONFEDERATE CONGRESS, August 18th.

"Mr. Foote, of Tennessee, offered a bill for retaliatory purposes. Referred to Committee on Military Affairs. (It recites that the enemy refused to treat our partisan soldiers as prisoners, and have also punished innocent private citizens for their acts. It provides that an officer who may have ordered such atrocities is to be put to death, if captured." An equal number of prisoners (officers to be preferred) taken from the enemy, to suffer the fate inflicted on our captured soldiers or citizens. Also a bill to regulate the treatment of prisoners. It provides that any officer or private captured by our army, who shall have committed any offence pronounced felonious by the laws of the Confederacy or any State, shall be delivered up for trial.

Also, a bill to punish negroes in arms. (It provides that Federal armies incongruously composed of white and black shall not be held entitled to the privileges of war, or to be held entitled to be taken prisoners. Of such as may be captured, the negroes shall be returned to their masters or publicly sold, and their commanders to be hung or shot, as may be most convenient.)

"Mr. Curry reported that the committee, of which he was chairman, had waited on the President, who said that he would communicate a message to the House immediately.

"Mr. Foote, resuming, also offered a bill to retaliate for the seizing of citizens by the enemy. (It provides that of the prisoners held by us, a number equal to that of the citizens seized shall be held as hostages for their safety, and subjected to like treatment; any officers, civil or military, concerned in their seizure, shall be imprisoned during the war.)"
—*President's Message*, August 18, 1862.

". . . The moneyed obligations of the Confederate Government are forged by citizens of the United States, and publicly advertised for sale in their cities, with a notoriety which sufficiently attests the knowledge of their Government; and its complicity in the crime is further evinced by the fact that the soldiers of the invading armies are found supplied with large quantities of these forged notes, as a means of despoiling the country people by fraud out of such portions of their property as armed violence may fail to reach. Two, at least, of the Generals of the United States are engaged, unchecked by their Government, in arming and training slaves for warfare against their masters, citizens of the Confederacy. Another has been found of instincts so brutal as to invite the violence of his soldiery against the women of a captured city.

". . . Retaliation in kind for many of them is impracticable, for I have had occasion to remark in a former message that,* *under no excess of provocation, could our noble-hearted defenders be driven to wreak vengeance on unarmed men, on women, or on children.* But stern and exemplary punishment can and will be meted out to the murderers and felons who, disgracing the profession of arms, seek to make public war the occasion for the commission of the most monstrous crimes.

". . . The report of the Secretary of the Treasury will exhibit in detail the operations of that department. It will be seen with satisfaction, that the credit of the Gov-

---

* The italics are mine.

ernment securities remains unimpaired, and
that this credit is fully justified by the comparatively small amount of accumulated debt
notwithstanding the augmentation of our mil·
itary operations.

"... Within a recent period we have
effected the object so long desired of an arrangement for an exchange of prisoners,
which is now being executed by delivery at
the points agreed upon, and which will, it is
hoped, speedily restore our brave and unfortunate countrymen to their places in the
ranks of the army, from which, by the fortunes of war, they have been for a time separated.   The details of the arrangement will
be communicated to you in a special report,
when further progress has been made in their
execution.

"The report of the Postmaster·General
discloses the embarrassments which resulted
in the postal service from the occupation by
the enemy of the Mississippi River and por·
tions of the territory of the different States.
The measures taken by the Department for
relieving these embarrassments as far as
practicable, are detailed in the report.   It is
a subject of congratulation, that during the
ten months that ended on March 3d last, the
expenses of the Department were largely decreased, while its revenue was augmented,

as compared with a corresponding period
ending on June 30, 1861, when the postal system was conducted under the authority delegated to the United States."

The London Index made the following comments on President Davis's message, 1862 :

"If any fault has been found with the late
message, save by those who cannot think
that the South can do any right or the North
any wrong, it is that it speaks almost too cold-
ly and indifferently of the glorious achievements of this summer's campaign—achievements which would have wrung an ample
meed of praise from the haughtiest and most
reserved of European statesmen. There is a
Roman, almost a stoical, sternness in the
manner in which the Confederate President
accepts, as matters of course, the victories
which have saved the capital; and the army might almost be disappointed did it not
know how thoroughly a ruler, himself a distinguished soldier, appreciates the exploits which
have signalized the soldiership of the South.
Never was anything further removed from
bombast or boastfulness than the language
in which Mr. Davis announces triumphs which
would have excited enthusiasm even in phleg-
matic England, and done honor to the veteran
armies of France.

"Mr. Davis's temper does not fail him,

even when he has to speak of the wanton barbarities suffered by the districts that have
been visited by the invaders, and of the un-
exampled outrages on the laws of civilized
warfare which reflect such signal infamy on
the Federal army and on the Federal Government. He speaks strongly, no doubt, but
in terms of just and measured reprobation,
of the crimes which have rendered a cause,
bad to begin with, utterly detestable in the
eyes of the civilized world."

CHAPTER XXXIII.

RETALIATION FOR OUTRAGES.

GENERAL POPE, commanding a new army in Northern Virginia, having issued the most brutal orders directed against peaceful citizens, the President wrote to General Lee as follows:

"RICHMOND, VA., July 31, 1862.

" GENERAL R. E. LEE, Commanding, etc.

" SIR : On the 22d of this month a cartel for the exchange of prisoners of war was signed between Major-General D. H. Hill, in behalf of the Confederate States, and Major-General John A. Dix, in behalf of the United States.

" By the terms of that cartel it is stipulated that all prisoners of war hereafter taken shall be discharged on parole till exchanged.

" Scarcely had the cartel been signed when the military authorities of the United States commenced a practice changing the character of the war from such as becomes civilized nations into a campaign of indiscriminate robbery and murder.

" The general order issued by the Secre-

tary of War of the United States in the city
of Washington, on the very day that the cartel was signed in Virginia, directs the military
commanders of the United States to take the
private property of our people for the convenience and use of their armies without compensation.

" The general order issued by General
Pope on July 23d, the day after the signing
of the cartel, directs the murder of our peaceful inhabitants as spies, if found quietly tilling their farms in his rear, even *outside of
his lines;* and one of his Brigadier-Generals, Steinwehr, has seized upon innocent and
peaceful inhabitants to be held as hostages, to
the end that they may be murdered in cold
blood if any of his soldiers are killed by some
unknown persons whom he designates as
" bushwhackers." *

" Under this state of facts, this Government
has issued the enclosed general order, recognizing General Pope and his commissioned
officers to be in the position which they have
chosen for themselves, that of robbers and
murderers, not that of public enemies, en-

---

* Major-General Pope, July 13, 1862, issued an order that if any
soldier should be fired upon on the march, the house nearest should
be razed to the ground ; and if any were injured where no house was
near, every household in the radius of five miles should be made to
pay such indemnity as was thought sufficient.

titled if captured to be considered as prisoners of war.

" We find ourselves driven, by our enemies, by steady progress toward a practice which we abhor, and which we are vainly struggling to avoid. Some of the military authorities of the United States seem to suppose that better success will attend a savage war, in which no quarter is to be given and no sex to be spared, than has hitherto been secured by such hostilities as are alone recognized to be lawful by civilized men in modern times.

" For the present we renounce our right of retaliation on the innocent, and shall continue to treat the private enlisted soldiers of General Pope's army as prisoners of war ; but if, after notice to the Government at Washington of our confining repressive measures to the punishment only of commissioned officers, who are willing participants in their crimes, these savage practices are continued, we shall reluctantly be forced to the last resort of accepting the war on the terms chosen by our foes, until the outraged voice of a common humanity forces respect for the recognized rules of war.

" While these facts would justify our refusal to execute the generous cartel by which we have consented to liberate an excess of thousands of prisoners held by us beyond the

number held by the enemy, a sacred regard
to plighted faith shrinking from the mere semblance of breaking a promise, prevents our
resort to this extremity. Nor do we desire
to extend to any other forces of the enemy
the punishment merited alone by General
Pope and such commissioned officers as
choose to participate in the execution of his
infamous orders.

" You are therefore instructed to communicate to the commander-in-chief of the armies
of the United States the contents of this letter, and a copy of the enclosed general order,
to the end that he may be notified of our intention not to consider any officers hereafter
captured from General Pope's army as prisoners of war.

" Very respectfully yours,
(Signed)   " JEFFERSON DAVIS."

" RICHMOND, August 1, 1862.

"SIR: On June 29th last, you were instructed by the Secretary of War to make inquiries of the General in command of the
United States forces, relative to alleged mur-
ders committed on our citizens by officers of
the United States army, and the case of William B. Mumford, reported to have been murdered at New Orleans by order of Major-
General B. F. Butler, and Colonel John Owen,
reported to have been murdered in the same

manner in Missouri, by order of Major-General Pope, were specially referred to.

" The inquiries thus made by you of Major-General McClellan were referred by that officer to his Government for reply, but no answer has yet been received.

"We have since been credibly informed that numerous other officers of the armies of the United States have, within the Confederacy, been guilty of felonies and capital offences which are punishable by all law human and divine.* A few of those best authenticated are brought to your notice.

" The newspapers received from the enemy's country announce as a fact that Major-General Hunter has armed slaves for the murder of their masters, and has thus done all in his power to inaugurate a servile war which is worse than that of the savage, inasmuch as it superadds other horrors to the indiscriminate slaughter of all ages, sexes, and conditions.

" Brigadier-General Phelps is reported to

---

* Notably NcNeil, a cruel and unscrupulous officer, shocked the moral sense of all soldierly men. By his order ten secessionists were shot at Palmyra, Mo., because an old gentleman (a Unionist) was missing, but who afterward turned up in Illinois. He approached General McKinstry in St. Louis, and offered his hand. The General said : "I don't shake hands with a murderer." McNeil afterward asked three gentlemen to drink with him in the Planters' House saloon. They turned on their heels and said : "We don't drink with a murderer." This was the reception he met with almost everywhere in St. Louis.

have imitated at New Orleans the example set by General Hunter on the coast of South Carolina.

"Brigadier-General G. N. Fitch is stated in the same journals to have murdered in cold blood two peaceful citizens, because one of his men, while invading our country, was killed by some unknown person defending his home.

"You are now instructed to repeat your inquiry relative to the cases of Mumford and Owen, and further to ask of the Commanding General of the enemy whether the statements in relation to the action of Generals Hunter, Phelps, and Fitch are admitted to be true, and whether the conduct of those Generals is sanctioned by their Government.

"You will further give notice that, in the event of our failure to receive a reply to these inquiries within fifteen days from the delivery of your letter, we shall assume that the alleged facts are true and are sanctioned by the Government of the United States.

"In such event, on that Government will rest the responsibility of the retributive or retaliatory measures which we shall adopt to put an end to the merciless atrocities which now characterize the war waged against us.

"Very respectfully yours, etc.,

    (Signed)   "JEFFERSON DAVIS."

"GENERAL R. E. LEE, Commanding," etc.

CHAPTER XXXIV.

CAMPAIGN AGAINST POPE.—SECOND MANASSAS.—
SHARPSBURG.—FREDERICKSBURG.

ALTHOUGH defeated, the army under General McClellan was still a formidable force, and might at any time threaten Richmond.

His camp at Westover was protected by his gun-boats, and the hills had been fortified to resist the Confederate forces.

General Lee, under the idea that a demonstration upon Washington would force McClellan's withdrawal for its protection, early in August, sent General Jackson in advance, to engage General Pope, who commanded a new army in Northern Virginia.

Immediately upon receiving information of this move, McClellan began to transfer troops to Washington, and Lee moved with the rest of his army to join General Jackson.

After several engagements the enemy was forced to withdraw, and the next morning Longstreet resumed his march to join Jackson.*

---

* At this time a Federal critic said : " The truth is, the rebel generals strip their armies for a march as a man strips to run a

Much desultory fighting took place on August 29th ; but on the 30th the enemy made a determined attack on Jackson's front, and Longstreet ordered his whole line forward to the charge, and defeated Pope's army.

The career of General Pope was as brief, boastful, and disastrous, as those of Generals Lee and Jackson were brilliant, audacious, and successful.

Immediately after the battle of Second Manassas, the army under Lee crossed the Potomac and entered Maryland.

While at Frederick City * General Lee

---

race.   Their men are ' destitute ' when they reach our lines, because they cannot cumber themselves with supplies.   They come to fight —not to eat.   They march to a battle-field, not to a dress parade. When shall our armies be found, for a like reason 'destitute in the presence of the enemy ? ' "

* Treatment of Confederate prisoners.

" There were 445 sick Confederate soldiers left in the hospital at Frederick, Maryland, before the fight of Sharpsburg, and these were 'captured' at a charge bayonet by the Yankees.   They were huddled together in the German Reform Church, with five crackers a day for rations, though the ladies of Frederick gave them what they could spare to eat.   They were then with prisoners, making a total of 1,400, marched six miles (to the Baltimore & Ohio Railroad, many of them falling on the way from illness), and sent to Baltimore ; the interruption on the trip being an attempt on the part of a sentinel to kill one of the prisoners who got off the cars to drink at a creek.

" In Baltimore they were placed in a prison crowded to suffocation.   The people of Baltimore, upon hearing of their arrival, carried them buckets of coffee and all sorts of eatables.   The next day they were marched out in charge of a Dutch captain, who, after parading them through the principal streets, put them on board the matured his plan of operations, and issued his order of battle.

Unfortunately for these plans of Lee, the battle order addressed to D. H. Hill was by some accident lost, and fell into the hands of McClellan, thus disclosing to him the movements of his adversary.* McClellan immediately pushed on to South Mountain Pass, where D. H. Hill had been left to guard the rear, while Jackson went to Har-

---

steamer *City of Norwich,* and they were soon (with the exception of six who died on the way) within the walls of Fort Delaware, made famous by the sufferings of our soldiers there. One of our men was stripped and whipped by a sergeant, who accused him of stealing. There were 2,700 prisoners there ; of this number 186 took the oath of allegiance, and 46 died. Out of the 2,700 there were 1,500 sick, and not 200 of them will be fit for service under a month.

"The Confederate officers were treated with consideration, but the privates experienced the most brutal usage. The prisoners who are alluded to returned yesterday by the flag of truce."—*Richmond Despatch,* 13th instant.

* General Robert Ransom, in his reminiscences of Mr. Davis, writes, in reference to General D. H. Hill and the lost order, as follows :

"In the early summer of '63, D. H. Hill was commanding at Richmond. He was sent thence to the army under Bragg. I happened to be present, a day or two after Hill had gone, when an intimate personal friend of Mr. Davis rather criticised the President for what he considered an unwise and too magnanimous act, remarking that the 'President certainly knew that Hill was no friend of his and was insubordinate, and had, by losing his order in '62, thwarted the plans of General Lee in Maryland.' Mr. Davis answered, 'Hill is a faithful soldier, General Bragg has asked for him, and it is not proven that he was to blame in reference to the lost order. Besides, men are not perfect, and I can have no personal resentment to true, brave men who are such fighters as all know

per's Ferry and Longstreet to Hagerstown.
Hill made a heroic defence, but being outflanked, fell back toward Sharpsburg during
the night.

On the morning of September 15th, General Lee stood at bay at Sharpsburg, with barely 18,000 men, and confronted McClellan's
whole army along Antietam Creek.

Colonel Walter Taylor, in his "Four
Years with Lee," says :

"The fighting was heaviest and most continuous on the Confederate left. It is established upon indisputable Federal evidence,
that the three corps of Hooker, Mansfield,
and Sumner were completely shattered in
the repeated but fruitless efforts to turn this
flank, and two of these corps were rendered
useless."

"These corps numbered an aggregate of
40,000, while the Confederates from first to
last had but barely 14,000 men."

The centre had been fiercely assailed, but
was held by Longstreet with Miller's guns of
the Washington Artillery,* and a thin gray

Hill to be, no matter what their feelings may be to me individually.'
Mr. Davis has been charged with visiting personal animosity upon
those in his power who were not his personal admirers.

"This is only one instance among many refuting the unjust
assertion. He was so much a man that jealousy and envy could
not live in his great soul."

* General Lee's report of the battle.

line of infantry, some of whom stood with unloaded guns without ammunition, but waving their colors to give semblance of support. This must be one of the severest tests to the bravery of troops, to stand as target without the means or the excitement of retaliating. All honor to them.

The battle was fought against great odds, and to have resisted this mass of men shows of what stuff our soldiers were made.

All the next day Lee remained on the battle-field, thinking McClellan would again attack, but he, not being so minded, the Confederate army recrossed the Potomac during the night into Virginia.

Late in October, 1862, General McClellan followed Lee into Virginia. Here he was relieved and succeeded by General Burnside.

On December 13th the battle of Fredericksburg was fought.

CHAPTER XXXV.

VISIT TO TENNESSEE.—BATTLE OF MURFREESBORO.

THE President became anxious about affairs in the West, and was importuned to make a tour of observation there. As soon as he could leave the seat of government he went, accompanied by one of his aids, and subsequently wrote to me the following letter:

From President to Mrs. Davis.

"CHATTANOOGA, TENN., December 15, 1862.

". . . We had a pleasant trip, and without an incident to relate, reached this place on the 11th, went to Murfreesboro on the 12th, and leave to-day for Mississippi. The troops at Murfreesboro were in fine spirits and well supplied. The enemy keep close in lines about Nashville, which place is too strongly fortified and garrisoned for attack by troops unprepared for regular approaches on fortifications. Much confidence was expressed in our ability to beat them if they advance. . . . Last night, on my arrival here, a telegram announced the attack made at Fredericksburg. You can imagine my anxiety. No answer to my inquiry for further information has yet arrived. If the necessity demands I will return to Richmond, though already there are indications of a strong desire for me to visit the further West, expressed in terms which render me unwilling to disappoint the expectation. . . . General Johnston will go directly to Mississippi, and reinforce General Pemberton. Joe * was quite excited at hearing of active operations behind us, and spoke of returning to his brigade. Many of the officers inquired for Colonel Johnston and felt as I did, regret at his absence."

The results of the campaigns of the army of the West have been better presented than I could tell them, even if space were granted me for the purpose; but my husband's life was so full of events that I must confine myself strictly to his personal history.

The moral effects of the campaign of 1862 were great. The disasters of the early part of the year had been redeemed. The whole world paid homage to the military prowess and genius that the Confederates had exhibited. They had raised the siege of Richmond, threatened the Federal Capital, and driven back the invaders of their territory to their starting-point. "Whatever may be the fate

---

* General Joseph R. Davis.

of the new nationality," said the London *Times*, "in its subsequent claims to the respect of mankind it will assuredly begin its career with a reputation for genius and valor which the most famous nations might envy."

CHAPTER XXXVI.

INTRODUCTION TO 1863.

THE year 1863 opened drearily for the President, but the Confederates generally seemed to have, for some unexplained cause, renewed hope of recognition by England and France, and with this they felt sure of a successful termination of the struggle.

Mr. Davis was oppressed by the fall of Donelson, Nashville, Corinth, Roanoke Island, New Orleans, Yorktown, Norfolk, Fort Pillow, Island No. 10, Memphis, General Bragg's defeat at Murfreesboro, the burning of the *Virginia* and the ram *Mississippi*, the sinking of the *Arkansas*, and other minor disasters. The victory at Fredericksburg was the one bright spot in all this dark picture.

Complaints from the people of the subjugated States came in daily. Women were set adrift across our borders with their children, penniless and separated from all they held dear. Their property was confiscated, the newspapers were suppressed, and the presses sold under the Confiscation act.

In Tennessee, county officers were nom-

inated, and an election held. Andrew Johnson, Governor of Tennessee, announced, " It
is not expected that the enemies of the
United States will propose to vote, nor is it
intended that they be permitted to vote, or
hold office ; " and an " iron-clad oath " was devised and forced upon all who desired any
position in the municipal or State Government, or even to engage in industrial pursuits. A convention was held to amend the
constitution of Tennessee, and the amendments were ratified by twenty-five thousand
majority, when in 1860 the State vote was
one hundred and forty thousand.

Peaceful and aged citizens, unresisting captives and non-combatants, were confined at
hard labor with ball and chain, others were
ironed for selling medicines to ill Confederates.

Prisoners of war were placed in close confinement, on bread and water. In fact, the
whole population were given the choice to
perjure themselves, or starve.

The slaves, after New Orleans was taken,
were driven from their homes, or if left undisturbed were forced to work under bayonet
guard on the plantations, the owners of which
received a small percentage of the gains if
they consented to share their property with
the General, his brother, or other officers.

Order 91 sequestrated all property west of
the Mississippi for confiscation, and officers
were assigned to the duty of gathering up
and burning all the personal effects except
such as the United States might require for
use, or intend to expose for sale at auction in
New Orleans.

Members of Congress were elected under
the military government of Louisiana. Mr.
Lincoln said, " The war power is now our
main reliance." An oath was required from
all residents of the conquered State to support the Constitution and the laws passed by
Congress " during the existing rebellion,"
unless they should be modified or declared
void by the Supreme Court. One-tenth of
any State so far subjugated could demand
and obtain admission as independent States
in the Union. Provisional judges were appointed to finally adjudicate all cases of equity, admiralty, and criminal law, with the power
to make all rules which might be needful for
their jurisdiction. Thus the military power
of the Government in relentless grasp held
Louisiana at its mercy.

The Constitution said : " The judicial power
of the United States shall be vested in one
Supreme Court and in such inferior courts as
the Congress may from time to time ordain
and establish."

Mr. Lincoln swore, in 1861, to sustain the
Constitution and the laws under it.   The con-
trast is sharp and significant of the progress
of a Northern revolution.   " Silent leges inter
arma." Under his rule the old landmarks
seemed to be blotted out.

The horrors of military rule and reconstruction were too numerous for particulari-
zation here.   I leave them to the historian.

"When the war closed, who were the victors? Perhaps it is too soon to answer that
question. Nevertheless, every day, as time
rolls on, we look with increasing pride upon
the struggle our people made for constitutional liberty. The war was one in which
fundamental principles were involved ; and,
as force decides no truth, hence the issue is
still undetermined, as has been already shown.
We have laid aside our swords; we have
ceased our hostility ; we have conceded the
physical strength of the Northern States.
But the question still lives, and all nations
and peoples that adopt a confederated agent
of government will become champions of our
cause. While contemplating the Northern
States—with their Federal Constitution gone,
ruthlessly destroyed under the tyrant's plea
of ' necessity,' their State sovereignty made a
byword, and their people absorbed in an ag-
gregated mass, no longer as their fathers left

them, protected by reserved rights against usurpation—the question naturally arises: On which side was the victory? Let the verdict of mankind decide."

The steady depletion of the Confederate forces and the consequent success of the enemy, increased the sufferings of our people; suffering made them querulous, and they looked about to find the person to blame for their misfortune. Some of them found the culprit in the President. The most hopeful man might be expected to lose heart under this heavy load, but Mr. Davis's faith in God's interposition to protect the right never faltered, and he steadily followed the dictates of his conscience, nothing daunted by our misfortunes. Now a formidable manifestation in the form of a bread riot occurred in Richmond.

"On April 2, 1863, Mr. Davis said that he received word in his office that a serious disturbance, which the Mayor and Governor Letcher, with the State forces under his command, were entirely unable to repress, was in progress on the streets. He at once proceeded to the scene of trouble in the lower portion of the city, whither the venerable Mayor had preceded him. He found a large crowd on Main Street, although the mass of the rioters were congregated on one of the side streets leading into that thoroughfare. They were headed by a tall, daring, Amazonian-looking woman, who had a white feather standing erect from her hat, and who was evidently directing the movement of the plunderers. The main avenue was blocked by a dray from which the horses had been taken, and which had been hauled across the street, and it was particularly noticeable that, though the mob claimed that they were starving and wanted bread, they had not confined their operations to food-supplies, but had passed by, without any effort to attack, several provision stores and bakeries, while they had completely emptied one jewelry store, and had also 'looted' some millinery and clothing shops in the vicinity. The fact was conclusive to the President's mind that it was not bread they wanted, but that they were bent on nothing but plunder and wholesale robbery.

"At the Confederate Armory in Richmond were engaged a number of armorers and artisans enrolled by General Gorgas, chief of ordnance, to work especially for the Government. These men had been organized into a military company under the command of a captain whose bearing was that of a trained, sturdy soldier accustomed to obey orders, and ready to do his duty unflinchingly, no matter what it might be. This company had been

promptly ordered to the scene of the riot and
arrived shortly after the President.

" Mr. Davis mounted the dray above mentioned and made a brief address to the formidable crowd of both sexes, urging them to
abstain from their lawless acts. He reminded
them of how they had taken jewelry and fin-
ery instead of supplying themselves with
bread, for the lack of which they claimed they
were suffering. He concluded by saying :
' You say you are hungry and have no
money. Here is all I have ; it is not much,
but take it.' He then, emptying his pockets,
threw all the money they contained among
the mob, after which he took out his watch
and said : ' We do not desire to injure anyone, but this lawlessness must stop. I will
give you five minutes to disperse, otherwise you will be fired on.' The order was
given the company to prepare for firing, and
the grim, resolute old Captain—who, Mr.
Davis says, was an old resident of Richmond,
but whose name he does not recall—gave his
men the command : ' Load ! ' The muskets
were then loaded with buck and ball cartridges, with strict observance of military
usage, and everyone could see that when
their stern commander received orders to fire
he intended to shoot to kill. The mob evidently fully realized this fact, and at once be-

gan to disperse, and before the five minutes had expired the trouble was over, and the famous misnamed bread riot was at an end."

This is a succinct and truthful account of this trouble, which created so much excitement at the time, and of the part which ex-President Davis bore therein. The subject having been recently revived and extensively discussed, and quite a variety of statements having been made in connection therewith, this account of Mr. Davis will be read with great interest, and all who personally remember the scenes and incidents of that memorable occasion will no doubt fully substantiate its correctness.

CHAPTER XXXVII.

CHANCELLORSVILLE.

IN the latter part of April, 1863, General Hooker crossed the Rappahannock, above Lee's position at Fredericksburg, with the intention of flanking and forcing him toward Richmond.

His army numbered, by his own report, 132,000 men, and upon reaching Chancellorsville he proceeded to throw up intrenchments.

Lee's army, in the absence of Longstreet's corps, numbered 57,000 of all arms.

General Jackson had not entirely recovered from an attack of diphtheria and was too weak to have been in the field, but he felt the importance of being present at the impending engagement. The Federals under General Hooker made a stand near Chancellorsville, and the west wing of Hooker's rested at Melzi Chancellor's farm, about two miles from Chancellorsville. General Jackson formed his corps into three columns for attack and, as he wrote in his last despatch to General Lee, trusted "That an ever-kind Providence will bless us with success." The Confederates rushed on

the earthworks of the enemy and took them
in reverse; here the 11,000 Germans, the mercenaries of General Howard, fled almost without resistance, carrying away with them the
troops sent to their support. They did not
even pause in General Hooker's intrenched
camp, but fled in a wild rout, without hats or
muskets, to the fords of the Rappahannock.
General Jackson's battle-cry was " Press on-
ward ! " At every success he raised his right
hand to heaven in prayer and thanksgiving.
Hooker was advancing a powerful body of
fresh troops to break General Jackson's cordon about the Federal rear. While General
Hooker pressed its front and the front of
General Jackson's right, a heavy line of infantry was being sent through the woods, preceded by a flag of truce to cover their advance. It was followed closely by their line
of battle, which poured a deadly fire into the
Confederates. General Jackson had advanced
a hundred yards beyond his line, expecting to
meet our skirmishers—a volley of musketry
from the enemy proclaimed their proximity,
and the General turned into the woods and
met General A. P. Hill with his staff coming
toward the party. General Jackson's officers
were mistaken for the enemy's cavalry and a
deadly fire poured in from our line of battle,
killing Captain Boswell outright and wound-

ing many others, and " woe worth the day,"
General Jackson. His right hand was penetrated by a ball, his left forearm was torn and
broken near to the shoulder, and the artery
severed. His horse dashed toward the enemy and lacerated the General's face and head
by dragging him under the boughs of trees ;
but he seized the rein with his right hand and
brought the animal back to our lines. He
tried to dismount, but, with an anxious look
over toward his troops, he fainted and fell
from his saddle. After some little delay he
was placed in a litter, but had only been there
a few minutes when one of his bearers was
shot down and the General fell, but Major
Leigh bore him up before he reached the
ground. Such a hurricane of shot and shell
was poured down the causeway that the rest
of the bearers fled and left Jackson on the litter, where he lay with his feet' to the foe.
Major Leigh and Lieutenant Smith lay down
beside their Commander and protected him
with their bodies until the firing ceased, then
the litter was borne toward our troops, when
the party met General Pender, who said he
feared he could not hold his ground. In a
feeble voice General Jackson gave his last
military order, " General Pender, you *must*
keep your men together and hold your
ground." The litter was carried through the

woods to avoid the enemy's fire, the boughs
of the brushwood tore the sufferer's face and
clothing, and at last the foot of one of the
bearers became entangled in a vine ; he fell
and the General was thrown heavily upon his
wounded side, which bruised the wounds
dreadfully and renewed the hemorrhage.

Next day, when Lee and Stuart, who had
succeeded Jackson in command, had joined
forces, they captured the works of the enemy.

General Sedgwick, after being delayed
twenty-four hours by Early at Fredericksburg, marched to the relief of Hooker, threatening thereby the Confederate rear. General
Lee turned with General McLaws's five
brigades (including Wilcox's, who had fallen
back from Fredericksburg), and General Anderson with three additional brigades, turned
upon Sedgwick.

General Early brought up his troops in the
afternoon of the 4th, and the corps of Sedgwick was broken and driven to the river, which
he crossed during the night.

On the 5th, General Lee concentrated for
another assault, but on the morning of the
6th he learned that Hooker "had sought
safety beyond the Rappahannock." *

When General Jackson arrived at the field

---

* General Lee's report.

hospital his arm was amputated, and he
seemed to rally somewhat, and was most anxious to get on by easy journeys to Lexington.
The proximity of the enemy made his removal
also desirable, and it was determined to remove him to Guinea Station. On the way
pneumonia set in, and all now felt this precious life hung on a thread. Mrs. Jackson
had been sent for, and came, bringing baby
Julia. When the baby was set on his bedside, her father caressed her with his wounded hand, murmuring in a faint voice, " Little
darling," from time to time. Now his darling
is " dead in her beauty," and it may be that
he is teaching her the song of the Redeemed
in the mansion prepared for her.

He rendered thanks for every service performed by those about him, and many times
reaffirmed his submission and trust in God,
begged his wife to speak aloud, because he
wanted to " hear every word" she said.
Mrs. Jackson, though racked by grief, joined
those about his bed in singing hymns which
seemed to quiet him. When at last he had
but a few moments to live, she announced it
to him. He answered, " I prefer it. I will
be an infinite gainer to be translated." When
his mind wandered, he called out, " A. P.
Hill, prepare for action," and several times,
" Tell Major Hawks to send forward provi-

sions for the men," even in his dying moments
being intent on ministering to them.

When General Lee heard of his extremity
he said, " Tell him I wrestled in prayer for
him last night as I never prayed, I believe,
for myself."

General Jackson died about three o'clock
in the afternoon.   His last words were, " Let
us pass over the river, and rest under the
shade of the trees."   All the evening before,
Mr. Davis, unable to think of anything but
the impending calamity, sat silent until twelve
or one o'clock.   When news came that the
General was sinking, the burthen of Mr.
Davis's regret was that he was helpless to
serve or comfort him in any way.   We kept a
servant at the telegraph office to bring the
latest news, and sent one to every train, where
other people in crowds were, on the same errand.   Before the engine slacked up in Broad
Street, the crowd shouted to the engineer,
" How is he?   Is he better?"   At eleven
o'clock the next morning the body was
brought down, wrapped in a handsome flag
Mr. Davis had sent for the purpose.   There
was not standing room in the broad street as
the cortege moved to the Governor's house.

There we went to take a last look at the
patriot saint, whose face still bore the marks
of the anguish he had suffered.   A tear

dropped on the face as Mr. Davis leant over the dead hero; and when a man came to the mansion and attempted to talk of some business matter to him, he remained silent for a while and then said, "You must excuse me. I am still staggering from a dreadful blow. I cannot think."

The body lay in state in the Capitol, where a constant procession of weeping mourners passed slowly by for three days and until late in the night. When at last the beloved form was taken to its last resting-place, the streets, the windows, and the house-tops were one palpitating mass of weeping women and men. The only other scene like it that I saw during the war was the crowd assembled when Mr. Davis was brought through Richmond to be bailed.

CHAPTER XXXVIII.

GETTYSBURG.

In the month of May, 1863, General R. E. Lee's army rested near Fredericksburg, while the Federal army under General Hooker occupied their old camps across the Rappahannock. Early in the month of June, finding that the Federal commander was not disposed again to cross swords with him, for the purpose of drawing him away from Virginia, so that her people might raise and gather their crops, Lee began a movement that culminated in the battle of Gettysburg.

Ewell's corps was sent on in advance, and at Winchester routed and put to flight the enemy under General Milroy, capturing 4,000 prisoners and their small-arms, 28 pieces of artillery, 300 wagons and their horses, and large amounts of ordnance, commissary, and quartermaster stores; then crossing the Potomac, he passed through Maryland and into Pennsylvania.*

---

* "HEADQUARTERS, ARMY OF NORTHERN VIRGINIA,
      "CHAMBERSBURG, Pa., June 27, 1863.
"General Orders, No. 73.
"The Commanding General has observed with marked satisfac-

General A. P. Hill with his three divisions followed in his rear.

General Longstreet covered these movements with his corps, then passing into the valley, he too crossed the Potomac.

To General Stuart was left the task of

---

tion the conduct of the troops on the march, and confidently anticipates results commensurate with the high spirit they have manifested.

"No troops could have displayed, or better performed, the arduous march of the past ten days.

" Their conduct in other respects has, with few exceptions, been in keeping with their character as soldiers.

" There have, however, been instances of forgetfulness on the part of some that they have in keeping the yet unsullied reputation of this army, and that the duties exacted of us by civilization and Christianity are not less obligatory in the country of the enemy than in our own.

"The Commanding General considers that no greater disgrace could befall the army, and through it our whole people, than the perpetration of the barbarous outrages upon the innocent and defenceless, and the wanton destruction of private property, that have marked the course of the enemy in our own country. Such proceedings not only disgrace the perpetrators and all connected with them, but are subversive of the discipline and efficiency of the army, and destructive to the ends of our present movement.

" It must be remembered that we make war only upon armed men, and that we cannot take vengeance for the wrongs our people have suffered without lowering ourselves in the eyes of all those whose abhorrence has been excited by the atrocities of our enemy, and offending against Him to whom vengeance belongeth, without whose favor and support our efforts must all prove in vain.

" The Commanding General therefore earnestly exhorts the troops to abstain with most scrupulous care from unnecessary or wanton injury to private property ; and he enjoins upon all officers to arrest and bring to summary punishment all who shall in any way offend against the orders on this subject.

" R. E. LEE, *General*,"

watching with his cavalry the movements of the enemy.

The Federal Commander had meanwhile disposed his force so as to cover Washington, and learning the movements of General Lee, he too crossed the Potomac.

On June 27th, General Lee was at Chambersburg, while Hill, Longstreet, and Ewell were within supporting distance.

Stuart with the cavalry was absent, and the lack of it prevented Lee from being apprised of the near approach of the enemy. It was an army without "eyes and ears."

Moving forward from Chambersburg, General Lee reached Cashtown on July 1st, where A. P. Hill was concentrating.

Here the Federal cavalry was first encountered, and as Hill's troops moved forward, they were met also by Reynolds's First Corps of the Federal infantry.

Stuart was still absent, but Lee, feeling in the dark, had encountered the Federal army.

Ewell's corps was called in, and a severe engagement ensued, which lasted until nightfall, when the Federals retreated through the town of Gettysburg, leaving in the hands of the Confederates over five thousand prisoners.

The Federal General Reynolds was killed. During the night, the Federals concen-

trated and fortified a ridge of high ground
from Cemetery Hill running back of the town
on the right, to Round Top on the left. Here
they confronted Lee on July 2d. At four
o'clock on July 2d, Longstreet's corps, except
Pickett, who had not yet arrived, assailed the
extreme left of the Federal line. Longstreet
gained ground up to the Emmettsburg road,
and captured artillery and colors. General
Hood was wounded, and Generals Barksdale
and Semmes were killed.

Ewell's divisions (at 8 P.M.) charged up
the Cemetery Hill, over the crest and the
stone walls, and met the enemy in a hand to
hand contest; the crest gained, they held it
until compelled to retire by the advance of
the enemy in overwhelming force.

On July 3d, General Lee, encouraged by
the successes of the two preceding days, determined to endeavor to break through the
enemy's centre, and for that purpose, Pickett's division, just arrived, and numbering
4,760 officers and men, with Heth's division
on its left, and Wilcox's brigade on its right,
and with Lane's and Scales's brigades under
General Trimble, as supports, were aligned
for the attack.

At 1.30 P.M., at a signal of two guns fired
in quick succession, from a position on the
Confederate right, on the Emmettsburg road,

137 guns opened fire on the Federal lines,
who replied with 80. Colonel Miller Owen,
an eye-witness, gives a spirited description
of the charge.

"For nearly two hours the dreadful din
continued, until the fire of the Federal batteries greatly decreased or was silenced; then
the Confederate divisions, numbering less
than 13,000 men, rose up and dressed their
ranks for the great charge on Cemetery Hill.

"It was a desperate undertaking, and the
men realized it, and were heard bidding each
other good-by from rank to rank.

"General Pickett galloped over to General Longstreet, and said, 'General, shall I
advance?' Receiving no reply, he saluted
and said, 'I am going to lead my division
forward, sir,' and galloped off to put it in
motion.

"Soon afterward the gray line emerged
from the trees skirting the Emmettsburg
road, Garnett's brigade on the left, Kemper's on the right, and Armistead's in the
rear of the centre. Garnett had been unwell
for several days, and in spite of the excessive heat of the weather, was buttoned up in
a heavy blue overcoat.

"Pickett's men went forward with great
steadiness, closing up their ranks as fast as
breaches were made by the Federal artillery,

which had again opened fire. The division of Heth, now commanded by Pettigrew, and numbering about 4,300 men, and the supporting brigades of North Carolinians of Lane and Scales under General Trimble, moved forward on his left flank, and Wilcox's Alabama brigade upon his right. Some of the artillery moved forward also, and fired over the heads of the advancing troops.

" The charge was watched with anxious interest by those of the Confederates not participating.

" Now Garnett, Kemper, and Armistead are close up to the stone wall, from behind which the enemy are lying and firing; they are over it, and fighting hand to hand over eleven captured cannon; the hillside is blue with the smoke of cannon and musketry, and all seems going well.

" Pettigrew has moved steadily forward on Pickett's left, Archer's Alabama and Tennessee brigade commanded by Colonel B. D. Fry on the right, Pettigrew's own North Carolina brigade, commanded by Colonel J. K. Marshal on the right centre, General J. Davis's Mississippi brigade on the left centre, and Brockenbrough's Virginia brigade on the left.

" These troops received the enemy's fire until they reached a post and rail fence be-

yond the Emmettsburg road. There they
were opened upon by a galling fire of cannister and shrapnel; still the line remained
steady and the advance continued.

" More fences were encountered, and the
alignment was disturbed; still on they
charged, keeping in line with Pickett.

" When within range of the enemy's line, a
heavy fire of musketry was delivered into
their ranks, yet there was no check.

" Archer's brigade reached the enemy first
in close contest, and the whole division gallantly dashed up to the stone wall behind
which the enemy was strongly posted.*

" Subject to a galling fire which reduced
their ranks, and finding further gallant effort
hopeless, the division fell back in some confusion.

" The brigades of Lane and Scales still
tenaciously hold the enemy's line that they
have crossed, and the close combat continues
in the little clump of trees on the ridge. Wilcox with his brigade charged on Pickett's
right flank up to the Federal line, but being
overwhelmed by numbers, withdrew.

" And now the Federals massed upon

* The fact that the right of Pettigrew's division touched Pickett's
left, is fixed in Lieutenant Finlay's (Fifty-sixth Virginia Infantry)
mind, by having shaken hands with one of Pettigrew's captains, who
exclaimed enthusiastically, " We will stand together at this wall."—
JOHN B. BATCHELDOR.

Pickett's and Trimble's front, and upon their flanks; Garnett and Armistead were both killed, and Kemper badly wounded. The men were falling fast, or yielding themselves to the overwhelming foe, the charge had failed, and the brave survivors of this grand assault recrossed the blood-stained field, and reformed their depleted ranks in the wood of Seminary Hill, from which they had lately advanced so gallantly to the charge.

"There they found General Lee, riding calmly up and down the lines, with only words of encouragement upon his lips. 'Never mind,' he said, as he urged them to form, 'we'll talk of this afterward; now, we want all good men to rally.' 'All will be well.'"

Mr. Davis thus writes of Gettysburg in his "Rise and Fall:"

"The battle of Gettysburg has been the subject of an unusual amount of discussion, and the enemy has made it a matter of extraordinary exultation. As an affair of arms it was marked by mighty feats of valor, to which both combatants may point with military pride. It was a graceful thing in President Lincoln if, as reported, when he was shown the steeps which the Northern men persistently held, he answered: 'I am proud to be the countryman of the men who assailed those heights.'"

CHAPTER XXXIX.

GENERAL LEE'S OFFER OF RESIGNATION.

THE President was a prey to the acutest anxiety during this period, and again and again said, "If I could take one wing and Lee the other, I think we could between us wrest a victory from those people." At another time he exclaimed, "With Jackson, Lee would be on his feet."

When General Lee had returned to Virginia after his repulse at Gettysburg, although he had withdrawn his army thoroughly organized, with confidence and pride unimpaired, and was in full possession of his legitimate line of defence, he was conscious that all had not been accomplished which the late advance was designed to compass.

The tone of the public press and the sentiment of the country indicated dissatisfaction with the result of the campaign, from which grander achievements had been expected than the number of troops and extent of our resources justified. General Lee could not remain entirely indifferent or unaffected by such expressions.

As he paced before his camp-fire on the night of July 4th, when his army was marching by on its way to the Potomac, he said to General Longstreet in the presence of other officers : " It is all my fault." So at Camp Orange, with manly dignity and generosity as remarkable as it is rare, denying no responsibility, indulging in no censures, he took upon himself alone the soul-depressing burden of the day, and wrote to the President the following touching and noble letter :

"CAMP ORANGE, August 8, 1863.

" MR. PRESIDENT : Your letters of July 28th and August 2d have been received, and I have waited for a leisure hour to reply, but I fear that will never come. I am extremely obliged to you for the attention given to the wants of this army, and the efforts made to supply them. Our absentees are returning, and I hope the earnest and beautiful appeal made to the country in your proclamation may stir up the whole people, and that they may see their duty and perform it. Nothing is wanted but that their fortitude should equal their bravery, to insure the success of our cause. We must expect reverses, even defeats. They are sent to teach us wisdom and prudence, to call forth greater energies, and to prevent our falling into greater disasters.

Our people have only to be true and united, to bear manfully the misfortunes incident to war, and all will come right in the end.

"I know how prone we are to censure, and how ready to blame others for the non-fulfilment of our expectations. This is unbecoming in a generous people, and I grieve to see its expression. The general remedy for the want of success in a military commander is his removal. This is natural, and in many instances proper. For, no matter what may be the ability of the officer, if he loses the confidence of his troops, disaster must sooner or later ensue.

"I have been prompted by these reflections more than once, since my return from Pennsylvania, to propose to your Excellency the propriety of selecting another commander for this army. I have seen and heard of expressions of discontent in the public journals at the result of the expedition. I do not know how far this feeling extends in the army. My brother officers have been too kind to report it, and so far the troops have been too generous to exhibit it. It is fair, however, to suppose that it does exist, and success is so necessary to us that nothing should be risked to secure it. I therefore, in all sincerity, request your Excellency to take measures to supply my place. I do this with the more earnest-

ness because no one is more aware than myself of my inability for the duties of my position. I cannot even accomplish what I myself
desire. How can I fulfil the expectations of
others? In addition, I sensibly feel the growing failure of my bodily strength. I have not
yet recovered from the attack I experienced the
past spring. I am becoming more and more
incapable of exertion, and am thus prevented
from making the personal examinations and
giving the personal supervision to the operations in the field which I feel to be necessary.
I am so dull that in making use of the eyes
of others I am frequently misled. Everything,
therefore, points to the advantages to be derived from a new commander, and I the more
anxiously urge the matter upon your Excellency, from my belief that a younger and abler
man than myself can readily be obtained. I
know that he will have as gallant and brave an
army as ever existed to second his efforts, and
it would be the happiest day of my life to see
at its head a worthy leader ; one that would
accomplish more than I could perform, and all
that I have wished. I hope your Excellency
will attribute my request to the true reason,
the desire to serve my country, and to do all
in my power to insure the success of her righteous cause.

"I have no complaints to make of anyone

but myself. I have received nothing but kindness from those above me, and the most considerate attention from my comrades and companions in arms. To your Excellency I am specially indebted for uniform kindness and consideration. You have done everything in your power to aid me in the work committed to my charge, without omitting anything to promote the general welfare. I pray that your efforts may at length be crowned with success, and that you may long live to enjoy the thanks of a grateful people.

"With sentiments of great esteem, I am very respectfully and truly yours,

"R. E. LEE, *General.*"

"To His Excellency JEFFERSON DAVIS,

"*President of the Confederate States.*"

The reply to this letter by President Davis so clearly illustrates the close and confidential relations existing between these two distinguished patriots, and is so honorable to both, that it is given in full.

"RICHMOND, VA., August 11, 1863.

"GENERAL R. E. LEE,

"Commanding Army of Northern Virginia.

"GENERAL: Yours of the 8th instant has been received. I am glad that you concur so entirely with me as to the wants of our country in this trying hour, and am happy to add that, after the first depression consequent upon our disasters in the West, indications have appeared that our people will exhibit that fortitude which we agree in believing is alone needful to secure ultimate success.

" It well became Sidney Johnston, when overwhelmed by a senseless clamor, to admit the rule that success is the test of merit, and yet there is nothing which I have found to require a greater effort of patience than to bear the criticisms of the ignorant, who pronounce everything a failure which does not equal their expectations or desires, and can see no good result which is not in the line of their own imaginings. I admit the propriety of your conclusions, that an officer who loses the confidence of his troops should have his position changed, whatever may be his ability; but when I read the sentence, I was not at all prepared for the application you were about to make. Expressions of discontent in the public journals furnish but little evidence of the sentiment of an army. I wish it were otherwise, even though all the abuse of myself should be accepted as the results of honest observation.

" Were you capable of stooping to it, you could easily surround yourself with those who would fill the press with your laudations and

seek to exalt you for what you have not done,
rather than detract from the achievements
which will make you and your army the subject of history, and object of the world's admiration for generations to come.

"I am truly sorry to know that you still
feel the effects of the illness you suffered last
spring, and can readily understand the embarrassments you experience in using the
eyes of others, having been so much accustomed to make your own reconnoissances.
Practice will, however, do much to relieve
that embarrassment, and the minute knowledge of the country which you have acquired
will render you less dependent for topographical information.

"But suppose, my dear friend, that I were
to admit, with all their implications, the points
which you present, where am I to find that
new commander who is to possess the greater ability which you believe to be required?
I do not doubt the readiness with which you
would give way to one who could accomplish
all that you have wished, and you will do me
the justice to believe that, if Providence
should kindly offer such a person for our use,
I would not hesitate to avail of his services.

"My sight is not sufficiently penetrating to
discover such hidden merit, if it exists, and I
have but used to you the language of sober

earnestness, when I have impressed upon you the propriety of avoiding all unnecessary exposure to danger, because I felt your country could not bear to lose you. To ask me to substitute you by someone in my judgment more fit to command, or who would possess more of the confidence of the army, or of reflecting men in the country, is to demand an impossibility.

" It only remains for me to hope that you will take all possible care of yourself, that your health and strength may be entirely restored, and that the Lord will preserve you for the important duties devolved upon you in the struggle of our suffering country for the independence of which we have engaged in war to maintain.

" As ever, very respectfully and truly,
(Signed) " JEFFERSON DAVIS."

CHAPTER XL.

As General Lee's army was marching through Pennsylvania it was thought by the Confederate Authorities that the time was auspicious for renewed efforts to adjust, with the Federal Government, the difficulties which prevented the execution of the cartel for the exchange of prisoners of war.

To promote these efforts, President Davis appointed Vice-President Stephens to proceed to Washington, and endeavor there to effect satisfactory arrangements.

The letter of instructions given by President Davis is herewith submitted:

"RICHMOND, VA., July 2, 1863.

"HONORABLE ALEXANDER H. STEPHENS,
Richmond, Va.

"SIR: Having accepted your patriotic offer to proceed as a military commissioner, under flag of truce, to Washington, you will herewith receive your letter of authority to the Commander-in-Chief of the Army and Navy of the United States.

OFFICERS OF THE CONFEDERATE ARMY AND NAVY.

"This letter is signed by me as Commander-in-Chief of the Confederate land and naval forces.

"You will perceive, from the terms of the letter, that it is so worded as to avoid any political difficulties in its reception. Intended exclusively as one of those communications between belligerents which public law recognizes as necessary and proper between hostile forces, care has been taken to give no pretext for refusing to receive it on the ground that it would involve a tacit recognition of the independence of the Confederacy.

"Your mission is simply one of humanity, and has no political aspect.

"If objection is made to receiving your letter on the ground that it is not addressed to Abraham Lincoln as *President*, instead of Commander-in-Chief, etc., then you will present the duplicate letter, which is addressed to him as President, and signed by me as President. To this letter objection may be made on the ground that I am not recognized to be President of the Confederacy. In this event, you will decline any further attempt to confer on the subject of your mission, as such conference is admissible only on a footing of perfect equality.

"My recent interviews with you have put you so fully in possession of my views, that

it is scarcely necessary to give you any detailed instructions, even were I at this moment well enough to attempt it.

"My whole purpose is, in one word, to
place this war on the footing of such as are
waged by civilized people in modern times,
and to divest it of the savage character which
has been impressed on it by our enemies, in
spite of all our efforts and protests. War is
full enough of unavoidable horrors, under all
its aspects, to justify, and even to demand, of
any Christian ruler who may unhappily engage in carrying it on, to seek to restrict its
calamities, and to divest it of all unnecessary
severities. You will endeavor to establish a
cartel for the exchange of prisoners on such a
basis as to avoid constant difficulties and complaints which arise, and to prevent for the future what we deem the unfair conduct of our
enemies, in evading the delivery of prisoners
who fall into their hands, in retarding it by
sending them on circuitous routes, and by de-
taining them sometimes for months in camps
and prisons, and in persisting in taking captive non-combatants.

"Your attention is also called to the un-
heard-of conduct of Federal officers, in driving
from their homes entire communities of women
and children, as well as of men, whom they
find in districts occupied by their troops, for no

other reason than because these unfortunates are faithful to the allegiance due to their States, and refuse to take an oath of fidelity to their enemies.

" The putting to death of unarmed prisoners has been a ground of just complaint in more than one instance, and the recent execution of officers of our army in Kentucky, for the sole cause that they were engaged in recruiting service in a State which is claimed as still one of the United States, but is also claimed by us as one of the Confederate States, must be repressed by retaliation if not unconditionally abandoned, because it would justify the like execution in every other State of the Confederacy, and the practice is barbarous, uselessly cruel, and can only lead to the slaughter of prisoners on both sides, a result too horrible to contemplate without making every effort to avoid it.

" On these and all kindred subjects you will consider your authority full and ample to make such arrangements as will temper the present cruel character of the contest, and full confidence is placed in your judgment, patriotism, and discretion that, while carrying out the objects of your mission, you will take care that the equal rights of the Confederacy be always preserved.   " Very respectfully,

" JEFFERSON DAVIS."

"HEADQUARTERS, RICHMOND, July 2, 1863.

" SIR : As Commander-in-Chief of the land
and naval forces now waging as against the
United States, I have the honor to address
this communication to you, as Commander-in-
Chief of their land and naval forces.

" Numerous difficulties and disputes have
arisen in relation to the execution of the cartel of exchange heretofore agreed on by the
belligerents, and the commissioners for the
exchange of prisoners have been unable to
adjust their differences.   Their action on the
subject of these differences is delayed and embarrassed by the necessity of referring each
subject as it arises to superior authority for
decision.   I believe that I have just grounds
for complaint against the officers and forces
under your command for breach of the terms
of the cartel, and, being myself ready to execute it at all times in good faith, I am not justified in doubting the existence of the same
disposition on your part.

" In addition to this matter, I have to complain of the conduct of your officers and troops
in many parts of the country, who violate all
the rules of war by carrying on hostilities, not
only against armed foes, but against non-combatants, aged men, women, and children ;
while others not only seize such property as
is required for the use of your forces, but de-

stroy all private property within their reach,
even agricultural implements; and openly
avow the purpose of seeking to subdue the
population of the districts where they are operating, by the starvation that must result
from the destruction of standing crops and
agricultural implements.

" Still, again, others of your officers in different districts have recently taken the lives
of prisoners who fell into their power, and
justify their act by asserting a right to treat
as spies the military officers and enlisted men
under my command who may penetrate for
hostile purposes into States claimed by me to
be engaged in the warfare now waged against
the United States, and claimed by the latter
as having refused to engage in such warfare.

" I have heretofore, on different occasions,
been forced to make complaint of these outrages, and to ask you that you should either
avow or disclaim having authorized them;
and have failed to obtain such answer as the
usages of civilized warfare require to be
given in such cases.

" These usages justify, and indeed require,
redress by retaliation, as the proper means of
repressing such cruelties as are not permitted
in warfare between Christian peoples. I have,
notwithstanding, refrained from the exercise
of such retaliation, because of its obvious ten-

dency to lead to a war of indiscriminate massacre on both sides, which would be a spectacle so shocking to humanity and so disgraceful
to the age in which we live and the religion
we profess, that I cannot contemplate it without a feeling of horror that I am disinclined to
doubt you would share.

"With the view, then, of making one last
solemn attempt to avert such calamities, and
to attest my earnest desire to prevent them,
if it be possible, I have selected the bearer
of this letter, the Honorable Alexander H.
Stephens, as a military commissioner to proceed to your headquarters under flag of truce,
there to confer and agree on the subjects
above mentioned ; and I do hereby authorize
the said Alexander H. Stephens to arrange
and settle all differences and disputes which
may have arisen or may arise in the execution of the cartel for exchange of prisoners of
war, heretofore agreed on between our respective land and naval forces ; also to agree
to any just modification that may be found necessary to prevent further misunderstandings
as to the terms of said cartel ; and finally, to
enter into such arrangement or understanding
about the mode of carrying on hostilities between the belligerents as shall confine the severities of the war within such limits as are
rightfully imposed, not only by modern civili-

zation, but by our common Christianity. I am, very respectfully, your obedient servant,

         " JEFFERSON DAVIS,

     " *Commander-in-Chief of the land and naval forces of the Confederate States.*

" TO ABRAHAM LINCOLN,

     " *Commander-in-Chief of the land and naval forces of the United States.*"

Mr. Stephens proceeded as far as Fortress Monroe under a flag of truce; but when he reached Newport News, the admiral of the Federal fleet arrested his further progress. The object of his mission, with a request for permission to go to Washington, was made known to that officer, who by telegraph communicated with the Government at Washington. The reply of that Government was:

" The request is inadmissible. The customary agents and channels are adequate for all needful military communications and conferences between the United States forces and the insurgents."

" This," subsequently wrote Mr. Davis, " was all the notice ever taken of our humane propositions. We were stigmatized as insurgents, and the door was shut in our faces. Does not this demonstrate an intent to subjugate our States?"

Mr. Stephens, after his return, wrote the following :

"RICHMOND, July 8, 1863.

" His Excellency, JEFFERSON DAVIS:

" SIR : Under the authority and instructions of your letter to me, on the 2d instant I proceeded on the mission therein assigned without delay. The steamer *Torpedo*, commanded by Lieutenant Hunter Davidson, of the navy, was put in readiness as soon as possible, by order of the Secretary of the Navy, and tendered for the service. At noon, on the 3d, she started down James River, hoisting and bearing a flag of truce after passing City Point. The next day (the 4th), at about one o'clock P.M., when within a few miles of Newport News, we were met by a small boat of the enemy, carrying two guns, which also raised a white flag before approaching us.

" The officer in command informed Lieutenant Davidson that he had orders from Admiral Lee, on board the United States flagship *Minnesota*, lying below and then in view, not to allow any boat or vessel to pass the point near which he was stationed, without his permission. By this officer I sent to Admiral Lee a note stating my objects and wishes, a copy of which is hereunto annexed, marked A. I also sent to the Admiral, to be forwarded, another in the same language, addressed to the officer in command of the United States forces at Fortress Monroe. The gun-boat proceeded immediately to the *Minnesota* with these despatches, while the *Torpedo* remained at anchor. Between three and four o'clock P.M., another boat came up to us, bearing the Admiral's answer, which is hereunto annexed, marked B.

"We remained at or about this point in the river until the 6th instant, when, having heard nothing further from the Admiral, at twelve o'clock M., on that day, I directed Lieutenant Davidson again to speak the gun-boat on guard, and to hand to the officer in command another note to the Admiral. This was done. A copy of the note is here appended, marked C. At half-past two o'clock P.M., two boats approached us from below, one bearing the answer from the Admiral to my note to him on the 4th. This answer is annexed, marked D.

"The other boat bore the answer of Lieutenant-Colonel W. H. Ludlow to my note of the 4th, addressed to the officer in command at Fortress Monroe. A copy of this is annexed, marked E. Lieutenant-Colonel Ludlow also came up in person in the boat that brought his answer to me, and conferred with Colonel Ould, on board the *Torpedo*, upon some matters he desired to see him about in

connection with the exchange of prisoners.
From the papers appended, embracing the
correspondence referred to, it will be seen
that the mission failed from the refusal of the
enemy to receive or entertain it, holding the
proposition of such conference ' inadmissible.'

"The influence and views that led to this
determination after so long a consideration on
the subject, must be left to conjecture. The
reason assigned for the refusal by the United
States Secretary of War, to wit: that ' the
customary agents and channels ' are considered adequate for all needful military ' communications and conferences,' to one acquainted
with the facts seems not only unsatisfactory,
but very singular and unaccountable; for it
is certainly known to him that these very
agents to whom he evidently alludes, heretofore agreed upon in a former conference in
reference to the exchange of prisoners (one
of the subjects embraced in your letter to me),
are now, and have been for some time, distinctly at issue on several important points.
The existing cartel, owing to these disagree-
ments, is virtually suspended, so far as the
exchange of officers on either side is concerned. Notices of retaliation have been
given on both sides.

"The effort, therefore, for the very many
and cogent reasons set forth in your letter of

instructions to me, to see if these differences
could not be removed, and if a clearer understanding between the parties as to the general conduct of the war could not be resorted
to by either party, was no less in accordance
with the dictates of humanity, than in strict
conformity with the uses of belligerents in
modern times. Deeply impressed as I was
with these views and feelings, in undertaking
the mission and asking the conference, I can
but express my profound regret at the result
of the effort made to obtain it, and I can but
entertain the belief that if the conference
sought had been granted, mutual good could
have been effected by it; and if this war, so
unnatural, so unjust, so unchristian, and so
inconsistent with every fundamental principle
of American constitutional liberty, 'must
needs' continue to be waged against us, that
at least some of the severer horrors, which
now so eminently threaten, might have been
avoided.

" Very respectfully,

"ALEXANDER H. STEPHENS."

CHAPTER XLI.

AFTER Gettysburg the non-combatants were fecund in expedients which would have compelled victory, had they been adopted. But unfortunately these military strategists agreed on but one point, viz., that the President and his cabinet were ignorant of the measures necessary to compel victory; these were in some inexplicable way very derelict. The *Examiner*, as the exponent of the critics, foretold every evil for the Confederacy, and thus discouraged the people, and weakened the power of the President to serve them.

Subsequent to the battle of Murfreesboro, in January, 1863, attention was concentrated upon a campaign in Mississippi with Vicksburg as the objective point. Of course, this section of country was very dear to the President, he knew every other family in it, and had a passionate desire to save them from the desolation that had fallen upon our only large city, New Orleans.

On December 28, 1862, General Sherman

made an offensive movement and was repulsed.

In January, 1863, General Grant landed at Young's Point on the Mississippi River, a few miles below, and opposite to Vicksburg, and soon after with his large army marched into the interior of Mississippi.

The destruction of valuable stores at Holly Springs by General Van Dorn frustrated Grant's plan of operations, and he retreated to Memphis.

Upon General Johnston's recovery from the wound received at Seven Pines, he had been assigned, on November 24, 1862, to the command of a Geographical Department including the States of Tennessee, Mississippi, Alabama, Georgia, and North Carolina. Mrs. Johnston and I were very intimate friends, and the day before his departure I went to see them. General Johnston seemed ill and dispirited. In answer to a hope expressed by me that he would have a brilliant campaign, he said, " I might if I had Lee's chances with the army of Northern Virginia ; " from which I inferred he was very averse to leaving Virginia.

When the events occurred that have been narrated, General Pemberton had felt severely the need of cavalry for observation and to keep open communications with our troops in Mississippi. As soon as General Johnston assumed command in person, General Pemberton renewed his strenuous efforts to procure it from him, hoping to check the invading army.

General Johnston arrived at Jackson on May 13, 1863, and telegraphed to James A. Seddon, Secretary of War, as follows:

" I arrived this evening, finding the enemy in force between this place and General Pemberton, cutting off communication. I am too late."

In the order assigning General Johnston to the Geographical Department of the West, he was directed to repair in person to any part of his command, whenever his presence might be deemed for the time necessary or desirable.

On May 9, 1863, General Johnston was ordered to " proceed at once to Mississippi and take chief command of the forces," and he telegraphed to General Pemberton from Tullahoma the same day, " Disposition of troops, as far as understood, judicious. Can be readily concentrated against Grant's army.

When he reached Jackson, learning that the enemy was between that place and the position occupied by General Pemberton's forces, about thirty miles distant, he halted there and opened correspondence with Pemberton, from which a confusion with conse-

quent disaster resulted, which might have
been avoided had he, with or without reinforcements, proceeded to Pemberton's headquarters in the field. What the confusion or
want of co-intelligence was, will best appear
from citing the important part of the despatches which passed between them.

On May 13th, General Johnston, then at
Jackson, sent the following despatch to General Pemberton, which was received on the
14th :

" I have lately arrived, and learn that Major-General Sherman is between us with four
divisions at Clinton. It is important to re-
establish communications, that you may be
reinforced, if practicable. I come up on his
rear at once. To beat such a detachment
would be of immense value. The troops
here could co-operate; all the strength you
can quickly assemble should be brought.
Time is all-important."

On the same day, the 14th, General Pemberton, then at Bovina, replied :

" I have the honor to acknowledge receipt
of your communication. I moved at once
with whole available force, about sixteen
thousand, leaving Vaughn's brigade, about
fifteen hundred, at Big Black Bridge ; Tilgh-
man's brigade, fifteen hundred, now at Baldwin's Ferry, I have ordered to bring up the

rear of my column ; he will be, however, fifteen or twenty miles behind it.

"Baldwin's Ferry will be left, necessarily, unprotected. To hold Vicksburg are Smith's and Forney's divisions, extending from Snyder's Mills to Warrenton, numbering effectives, seven thousand eight hundred men. . . . I do not think that you fully comprehend the position that Vicksburg will be left in, but I comply at once with your order."

On the same day General Pemberton, after his arrival at Edward's Depot, called a council of war of all the general officers present. He placed General Johnston's despatch before them, and stated his own views against the propriety of an advance, but expressed the opinion that the only possibility of success would be by a movement upon the enemy's communications.

A majority of the officers present expressed themselves favorable to the plan indicated by General Johnston. . . . General Pemberton then sent the following despatch to General Johnston :

"EDWARD'S DEPOT, May 14, 1863.

"I shall move as early to-morrow morning as practicable, with a column of seventeen thousand men, to Dillon's, situated on the main road leading from Raymond to Port

Gibson, seven and a half miles from Edward's Depot. The object is to cut the enemy's communications and to force him to attack me, as I do not consider my force sufficient to justify an attack on the enemy in position, or to attempt to cut my way to Jackson. At this point your nearest communication would be through Raymond."

The movement commenced at 1 P.M. on the 15th. General Pemberton states that the force at Clinton was an army corps, numerically greater than his whole available force in the field; that "the enemy had at least an equal force to the south, on my right flank, which would be nearer Vicksburg than myself in case I should make the movement proposed. I had, moreover, positive information that he was daily increasing his strength. I also learned, on reaching Edward's Depot, that one division of the enemy (A. J. Smith's) was at or near Dillon's."

On the morning of the 16th, about 6.30 o'clock, Colonel Wirt Adams, commanding the cavalry, reported to General Pemberton that his pickets were skirmishing with the enemy on the Raymond road, in our front. At the same moment a courier arrived and delivered the following despatch from General Johnston:

"Canton Road, ten miles from Jackson,
"May 15, 1863, 8.30 A.M.

" Our being compelled to leave Jackson makes your plan impracticable. The only mode by which we can unite is by your moving directly to Clinton and informing me, that we may move to that point with about six thousand."

Pemberton reversed his column to return to Edward's Depot and take the Brownsville road, so as to proceed toward Clinton, on the north side of the railroad, and sent a reply to General Johnston to notify him of the retrograde movement. Just as the reverse movement commenced, the enemy opened fire with artillery and attacked Pemberton at Big Black, defeated, and forced him to retire to Vicksburg.

On the morning of the 18th, the troops were, from right to left, on the defence, and 102 pieces of artillery, mostly field pieces, were placed in position. Grant's army appeared before the city on the 18th.

Pemberton relied upon the co-operation of a relieving army before any investment could be made, and had endeavored to secure supplies for the duration of an ordinary siege.

On May 25th, General Grant telegraphed General Halleck at Washington : " I can manage the force in Vicksburg and an attacking force of 30,000. My effective force is 50,000 ; " and General Johnston telegraphed to Richmond that the troops he had at his disposal against Grant amounted to 24,000, not including Jackson's cavalry command.

On May 18th, General Pemberton received by courier a communication from General Johnston containing these words : " If Hayne's Bluff is untenable, Vicksburg is of no value and cannot be held. If you are invested in Vicksburg you must ultimately surrender. Under these circumstances, instead of losing both troops and place, we must if possible save the troops. If it is not too late, evacuate Vicksburg and its dependences, and march to the northeast."

Relying upon his Government and General Johnston to raise the siege, General Pemberton called a council of war, laid Johnston's communication before them, and requested their opinion. It was unanimous that "it was impossible to withdraw the army from this position with such morale and matériel as to be of further service to the Confederacy." He then announced his decision to hold Vicksburg as long as possible.

On May 19th two assaults were made, on the left and centre. Both were repulsed and heavy loss inflicted ; the enemy then confined himself to gradual approaches and mining. Our loss was small.

How to dispose of the women and children during the siege was a problem which could be solved in only one way, viz., they must stay at home. Their fathers, husbands, brothers, or sons were many of them in the army of Northern Virginia, or in the West. The money left with their families was all exhausted; all industries were at a standstill. The interior of Mississippi had been desolated by fire and sword, and the women and children could not exist there unprotected and without food; so they grappled with the ills they knew, and remained at home. Caves were dug in the high clay hills, and there the non-combatants dwelt in darkness while the shells were flying. By the light of lamps they mended, patched, and darned for the soldiers, knitted them socks, and rendered every other service that brave and tender women learn to perform in the hour of danger. I saw one bright young bride, whose arm had been shattered by a piece of shell and afterward amputated; and a man who was there during the siege said, on July 26th : " We noticed one man with his wife in his arms—she having fainted with fright at the explosion of a shell within a few feet of her. A shell burst in the midst of several children who were making their way out of danger, and the dirt thrown up by the explosion knocked three of them down, but fortunately did no injury. The little ones picked themselves up as quick as possible, and wiping the dust from their eyes, hastened on."

The women nursed the sick and wounded, ate mule and horse meat, and bread made of spoiled flour, with parched corn boiled for coffee; but they listened to the whistling shells undaunted, nothing fearing except for the lives of those who were fighting far and near.

General Grant telegraphed to Washington, on June 8th, " Vicksburg is closely invested. I have a spare force of about 30,000 men with which to repel anything from the rear;" and on the 11th, General Johnston telegraphed to Richmond: "I have not at my disposal half the troops necessary. It is for the Government to determine what Department, if any, can furnish the reinforcements required. I cannot know here General Bragg's wants compared with mine. The Government can make such comparisons."

As already stated, General Johnston had been assigned to the command of a geographical department that included the State of Tennessee, and therefore General Bragg's command was subject to General Johnston's orders; but General Johnston seemed to regard it differently, and telegraphed the Secretary of War on June 12th: "I have not considered myself commanding in Tennessee since assignment here, and should not have felt authorized to take troops from that Department after having been informed by the Executive that no more could be spared. To take from Bragg a force which would make this army fit to oppose Grant, would involve yielding Tennessee. It is for the Government to decide between this State and Tennessee."

On the 15th he telegraphed, "I consider saving Vicksburg hopeless." To this last despatch the Secretary of War replied on the 16th: "Your telegram grieves and alarms us. Vicksburg must not be lost, at least without a struggle. The interest and honor of the Confederacy forbid it. I rely on you still to avert the loss. If better resource does not offer, you must hazard attack. It may be made in concert with the garrison, if practicable, but otherwise without. By day or night, as you think best." And again, on the 21st: "Only my convictions of almost imperative necessity for action induces the official despatch I have just sent you. On every ground I have great deference to your judgment and military genius, but I feel it right to share, if need be to take, the responsibility and leave you free to follow the most desperate course the occasion may demand. Rely upon it, the eyes and hopes of the whole Confederacy are upon you, with the full confidence that you will act, and with the sentiment that it *were better to fail nobly daring, than, through prudence even, to be inactive.* I look to attack in the last resort, but rely on your resources of generalship to suggest less desperate modes of relief. . . . I rely on you for all possible to save Vicksburg." On June 27th, General Grant telegraphed General Halleck: "Joe Johnston has postponed his attack until he can receive 10,000 reinforcements now on their way from Bragg's army. They are expected early next week. I feel strong enough against this increase, and do not despair of having Vicksburg before their arrival."

After being besieged for forty-seven days and nights, the brave troops, exposed to burning sun and drenching nights, confined to the narrow limits of the trench, with their limbs cramped and swollen, and growing weak and attenuated, felt and knew the end was near. They had repulsed the enemy's repeated assaults, and driven him discomfited from the trenches; they had taken five stand of colors as trophies of their prowess, but now the time had come when man could do no more. They were physically unable to make a sortie, and all hope of outside relief from Johnston was gone. General Pemberton therefore resolved to seek terms of capitulation, and the city surrendered to General Grant on July 4th.*

General Grant immediately telegraphed to Washington. " The enemy surrendered this morning. . . . General Sherman will face immediately on Johnston and drive him from the State."

On July 17th, General Johnston abandoned Jackson and retreated into the interior."†

---

* On May 9, 1864, General Pemberton resigned his commission and expressed his willingness to serve in the ranks ; the President conferred on him a lieutenant-colonelcy of artillery.

† " General Johnston is retreating on the east side of Pearl River, and I can only learn from him of such vague purposes as were unfolded when he held his army before Richmond."—Letter of President Davis to General Lee, July 21, 1863.

CHAPTER XLII.

PRESIDENT DAVIS'S LETTER TO GENERAL JOHN-
STON AFTER THE FALL OF VICKSBURG.

"RICHMOND, July 15, 1863.

" GENERAL J. E. JOHNSTON, Commanding,
etc.

" GENERAL : Your despatch of the 5th instant stating that you 'considered' your 'assignment to the immediate command in Mississippi' as giving you 'a new position' and
as 'limiting your authority,' being a repetition of a statement which you were informed
was a grave error, and being persisted in after your failure to point out, when requested,
the letter or despatch justifying you in such a
conclusion, rendered it necessary, as you were
informed in my despatch of the 8th instant,
that I should make a more extended reply
than could be given in a telegram. That
there may be no possible room for further
mistake in this matter, I am compelled to re-
capitulate the substance of all orders and instructions given to you, so far as they bear
on this question.

On November 24th last you were assigned,

by Special Order No. 275, to a defined geographical command. The description included a portion of Western North Carolina
and Northern Georgia, the States of Tennessee, Alabama, and Mississippi, and that portion of the State of Louisiana east of the
Mississippi River. The order concluded in
the following language : ' General Johnston
will, for the purpose of correspondence and reports, establish his headquarters at Chattanooga, or such other place as in his judgment
will best secure communication with the
troops within the limits of his command, and
will repair in person to any part of said command, whenever his presence may for the
time be necessary, or desirable.

"This command by its terms embraced the
armies under command of General Bragg in
Tennessee, of General Pemberton at Vicksburg, as well as those at Port Hudson, Mobile, and the forces in East Tennessee.

"This general order has never been
changed nor modified, so as to affect your
command, in a single particular, nor has your
control over it been interfered with. I have
as Commander-in-Chief given you some orders which will be hereafter noticed, not one
of them however indicating in any manner
that the general control confided to you was
restricted or impaired.

"You exercised this command by visiting in person the armies at Murfreesboro, Vicksburg, Mobile, and elsewhere, and on January 22d I wrote to you, directing that you should repair in person to the army at Tullahoma, on account of a reported want of harmony and confidence between General Bragg and his officers and troops. This letter closed with the following passages: 'As that army is part of your command, no order will be necessary to give you authority there, as, whether present or absent, you have a right to direct its operations, and to do whatever belongs to the General Commanding.'

"Language cannot be plainer than this, and although the different armies in your geographical district were ordered to report directly to Richmond as well as to yourself, this was done solely to avoid the evil that would result from reporting through you when your headquarters might be, and it was expected frequently would be, so located as to create delays injurious to the public interest.

"While at Tullahoma you did not hesitate to order troops from General Pemberton's army, and learning that you had ordered the division of cavalry from North Mississippi to Tennessee, I telegraphed to you that this order left Mississippi exposed to cavalry raids without means of checking them. *You did not*

change your orders,* and although I thought
them injudicious, I refrained from exercising
my authority in deference to your views.

" When I learned that prejudice and malignity had so undermined the confidence of the
troops at Vicksburg in their commander as to
threaten disaster, I deemed the circumstances
such as to present the case foreseen in Special Order No. 275, that you should ' repair in
person to any part of said command whenever
your presence might be for the time necessary
or desirable.'

" You were therefore ordered, on May 9th,
to ' proceed at once to Mississippi and take
chief command of the forces, giving to those in
the field, as far as practicable, the encouragement and benefit of your personal direction.'

" Some details were added about reinforcements, but not a word affecting in the remot-
est degree your authority to command your
geographical district.

" On June 4th you telegraphed to the
Secretary of War, in response to his inquiry,
saying : ' My only plan is to relieve Vicksburg ; my force is far too small for the purpose. Tell me if you can increase it, and
how much.' To which he answered on the
5th : ' I regret inability to promise more

---

* The italics are the author's.

troops, as we have drained resources, even to the danger of several points. You know best concerning General Bragg's army, but I fear to withdraw more. We are too far outnumbered in Virginia to spare any,' etc.

" On June 8th the Secretary was more explicit, if possible. He said : ' Do you advise more reinforcements from General Bragg ? You, as Commandant of the Department, have power so to order if you, in view of the whole case, so determine.'

" On June 10th you answered that it was for the Government to determine what department could furnish the reinforcements, that you could not know how General Bragg's wants compared with yours, and that the Government could make the comparison. Your statements that the Government in Richmond was better able to judge of the relative necessities of the armies under your command than you were, and the further statement that you could not know how General Bragg's wants compared with yours, were considered extraordinary ; but as they were accompanied by the remark that the Secretary's despatch had been imperfectly deciphered, no observation was made on them till the receipt of your telegram to the Secretary of the 12th instant, stating, ' I have not considered myself commanding in Tennessee

since assignment here, and should not have
felt authorized to take troops from that Department after having been informed by the
Executive that no more could be spared.'

" My surprise at these two statements was
extreme. You had never been ' assigned to
the Mississippi command.' You went there
under the circumstances and orders already
quoted, and no justification whatever is perceived for your abandonment of your duties
as Commanding General of the geographical
district to which you were assigned.

" Orders as explicit as those under which
you were sent to the West, and under which
you continued to act up to May 9th, when
you were directed to repair in person to
Mississippi, can only be impaired or set aside
by subsequent orders, equally explicit; and
your announcement that you had ceased to
consider yourself charged with the control of
affairs in Tennessee because ordered to repair in person to Mississippi, both places being within the command to which you were
assigned, was too grave to be overlooked;
and when to this was added the assertion that
you should not have felt authorized to draw
troops from that Department (Tennessee)
' after being informed by the Executive that
no more could be spared,' I was unable to
account for your language, being entirely con-

fident that I had never given you any such information.

"I shall now proceed to separate your two statements, and begin with that which relates to your 'not considering' yourself commanding in Tennessee, since assignment 'here,' *i.e.*, in Mississippi.

"When you received my telegram of June 15th, informing you that 'the order to go to Mississippi did not diminish your authority in Tennessee, both being in the country placed under your command in original assignment,' accompanied by an inquiry about the information said to have been derived from me, restricting your authority to transfer troops, your answer on June 16th was, 'I meant to tell the Secretary of War, that I considered the order directing me to command here as limiting my authority to this Department, especially when that order was accompanied by War Department orders transferring troops from Tennessee to Mississippi.'

"This is in substance a repetition of the previous statement without any reason being given for it. The fact of orders being sent to you to transfer some of the troops in your Department from one point to another to which you were proceeding in person, could give no possible ground for your 'considering' that Special Order, No. 275, was re-

scinded or modified. Your command of your
geographical district did not make you independent of my orders as your superior officer,
and when you were directed by me to take
troops with you to Mississippi, your control
over the district to which you were assigned
was in no way involved. But the statement
that troops were transferred from Tennessee
to Mississippi by order of the War Department, when you were directed to repair to
the latter State, gives but half the fact, for
although you were ordered to take with you
three thousand good troops, you were told to
replace them by a greater number, then on
their way to Mississippi, and whom you were
requested to divert to Tennessee, the purpose being to hasten reinforcements to Pemberton without weakening Bragg. This was
in deference to your own opinion, that Bragg
could not be safely weakened, nay, that he
ought even to be reinforced at Pemberton's
expense ; for you had just ordered troops from
Pemberton's command to reinforce Bragg. I
differed in opinion from you, and thought
Vicksburg far more exposed to danger than
Bragg, and was urging forward reinforcements to that point, both from Carolina and
Virginia, before you were directed·to assume
command in person in Mississippi.

" I find nothing then either in your despatch

of June 16th, nor in any subsequent communication from you, giving a justification for your saying, that you 'had not considered yourself commanding in Tennessee, since assignment here' (*i.e.*, in Mississippi). Your despatch of the 5th instant is again a substantial repetition of the same statement without a word of reason to justify it. You say, 'I considered my assignment to the immediate command in Mississippi as giving me a new position, and limiting my authority to this Department.' I have characterized this as a grave error, and in view of all the facts cannot otherwise regard it. I must add that a review of your correspondence shows a constant desire on your part, beginning early in January, that I should change the order placing Tennessee and Mississippi in one command under your direction, and a constant indication on my part, whenever I wrote on the subject, that in my judgment the public service required that the armies should be subject to your control.

"I now proceed to your second statement, in your telegram of June 12th, that 'you should not have felt authorized to take troops from that Department (Tennessee) after having been informed by the Executive that no more could be spared.'

"To my inquiry for the basis of this statement, you answered on the 16th, by what was in substance a reiteration of it.

" I again requested, on the 17th, that you should refer by date to any such communication as that alleged by you. You answered on June 20th, apologized for carelessness in your first reply, and referred me to a passage from my telegram to you of May 20th, and to one from the Secretary of War of June 5th, and then informed me that you considered ' Executive ' as including the Secretary of War.

" Your telegram of June 12th was addressed to the Secretary of War in the second person; it begins ' Your despatch,' and then speaks of the Executive in the third person, and on reading it, it was not supposed that the word ' Executive ' referred to anyone but myself; but of course, in a matter like this, your own explanation of your meaning is conclusive.

" The telegram of the Secretary of War of June 5th, followed by that of June 8th, conveyed unmistakably the very reverse of the meaning you attribute to them, and your reference to them as supporting your position is unintelligible. I revert therefore to my telegram of May 28th. That telegram was in answer to one from you in which you stated that, on the arrival of certain reinforcements, then on the way, you would have about 23,000; that Pemberton could be saved only by beating Grant; and you added, ' unless you can promise more troops we must try with that number. The odds against us will be very great. Can you add seven thousand ? '

" My reply was ' The reinforcements sent to you exceed by, say seven thousand, the estimate of your despatch of 27th instant. We have withheld nothing which it was practicable to give you. We cannot hope for numerical quantity, and time will probably increase the disparity.'

" It is on this language that you rely to support a statement that I informed you no more troops could be spared from Tennessee, and as restricting your right to draw troops from that Department. It bears no such construction. The reinforcements sent to you, with an exception presently to be noticed, were from points outside of your Department. You had, in telegrams of May 1st, 2d, and 7th, and others, made repeated applications to have troops withdrawn from other Departments to your aid; you were informed that we would give all the aid we possibly could. Of your right to order any change made in the distribution of troops in your own district, no doubt had ever been suggested by yourself, nor could occur to your superiors here, for they had given you the authority.

" The reinforcements which went with you from Tennessee were (as already explained and as was communicated to you at the time) a mere exchange for other troops sent from Virginia.

" The troops subsequently sent to you from Bragg were forwarded by him under the following despatch from me of May 22d : ' The vital issue of holding the Mississippi at Vicksburg is dependent on the success of General Johnston in an attack on the investing force. The intelligence from there is discouraging. Can you aid him ? If so, *and you are without orders from General Johnston,* act on your judgment.'

" The words that I now underscore suffice to show how thoroughly your right of command of the troops in Tennessee was recognized. I knew from your own orders that you thought it more advisable to draw troops from Mississippi to reinforce Bragg, than to send troops from the latter to Pemberton ; and one of the reasons which induced the instruction to you to proceed to Mississippi was the conviction that your views on the point would be changed on arrival in Mississippi. Still, although convinced myself that troops might be spared from Bragg's army without very great danger, and that Vicksburg was on the contrary in imminent peril, I was unwilling to

overrule your judgment of the distribution of
your troops while you were on the spot, and,
therefore, simply left to General Bragg the
power to aid you, if he could, and *if you had
not given contrary orders.*

"The cavalry sent to you from Tennessee
was sent on a similar despatch from the Secretary of War to General Bragg, informing
him of your earnest appeal for cavalry, and
asking him if he could spare any. Your request was for a regiment of cavalry to be sent
to you from Georgia. My despatch of May
18th pointed out to you the delay which a
compliance would involve, and suggested that
cavalry could be drawn from another part of
your Department, as had been previously indicated.

"In no manner, by no act, by no language,
either of myself or of the Secretary of War,
has your authority to draw troops from one
portion of your Department to another been
withdrawn, restricted, or modified.

"Now that Vicksburg has disastrously fallen, this subject would present no pressing demand for attention, and its examination would
have been postponed to a future period, had
not your despatch of the 5th instant, with its
persistent repetition of statements which I
had informed you were erroneous and without adducing a single fact to sustain them, in-

duced me to terminate the matter at once by
a review of all the facts.

" The original mistakes in your telegram of
June 12th, would gladly have been overlooked
as accidental, if acknowledged when pointed
out. The perseverance with which they have
been insisted on, has not permitted me to
pass them by as a mere oversight, or, by re-
fraining from an answer, to seem to admit the
justice of some of the statements.

" Respectfully, etc.,

(Signed)   " JEFFERSON DAVIS."

*Telegrams sent by General Johnston from Jackson, Miss., to
Richmond, Va.*

" May 28, 1863.

"TO PRESIDENT DAVIS : It is reported that the last infantry
coming leave Montgomery to-night.   When they arrive I shall have
about twenty-three thousand.

" Pemberton can be saved *only by beating Grant.*   Unless you
can promise more troops *we must try with that number.*

" The odds against us will be very great.   Can you add 7,000 ?
I asked for another Major-General, Wilcox, or whoever you may
prefer.   We want good General Officers quickly.   I have to organize an army and collect ammunition, provisions, and transportation."

"June 10, 1863.

" TO SECRETARY OF WAR : Your despatch of June 8th in cipher
received.   You do not give orders in regard to the recently appointed General Officers.   Please do it.

" I have not at my (disposal ? *) half the number of troops necessary.   It is for the Government to determine what Department, if
any, can furnish the reinforcements required.

---

* Word not legible in cipher despatch.

"I cannot know General Bragg's wants, compared with mine. The Government can make such comparisons."

"June 12, 1863.

"To THE SECRETARY OF WAR : Your despatch of 8th imperfectly deciphered and partially answered on the 10th. I have not considered myself commanding in Tennessee since assignment here, and should not have felt authorized to take troops from that Department, after having been informed by the Executive that no more could be spared. To take from Bragg a force which would make this army fit to oppose Grant would involve yielding Tennessee.

"It is for the Government to decide between this State and Tennessee."

"June 16, 1863.

"To THE PRESIDENT : Your despatch of 15th is received. I considered the order directing me to command here as limiting my authority to this Department. Especially when that order, accompanied by War Department orders transferring troops from Tennessee to Mississippi, and whether commanding there or not, that your reply to my application for more troops, that none could be spared, would have made it improper for me to order more from Tennessee.

"Permit me to repeat that an officer having a task like mine, far above his abilities, cannot in addition command other remote Departments. . . ."

"June 20, 1863.

"To THE PRESIDENT : I much regret the carelessness of my reply of the 16th, to your telegram of the 15th.

"In my despatch of 12th to the Secretary of War, I referred to the words, 'we withheld nothing which it was practicable to give.' In your telegram of May 28th, and the telegram of the Secretary of War to me of June 5th, except the last sentence, I considered 'Executive' as including the Secretary of War."

"CANDY CREEK CAMP, July 5th,
via JACKSON, July 7, 1863.

"To THE PRESIDENT : Your despatch of June 30th is received. I considered my assignment to the immediate command in Mississippi as giving me a new position and limiting my authority to this Department. The ordering of the War Department transferring

three separate bodies of troops from General Bragg's army to this—
two of them without my knowledge, and all of them without consulting me, would have convinced me, had I doubted these orders
of the War Department expressed its judgment of the number of
troops to be transferred from Tennessee.

"I could no more control this judgment by increasing the numbers than by forbidding the transfer.

"I regret very much that an impression which seemed to be
natural should be regarded as a strange error. I thank your Excellency for your approval of the several recommendations you mention."

CHAPTER XLIII.

MILITARY OPERATIONS AT CHARLESTON.

THE defence of Charleston against a demonstration by land and sea was the most noteworthy event of the summer of 1863. Foiled in their naval attack in April, the next effort was to occupy Morris Island and reduce Fort Sumter. Owing to the lack of diligence on the part of General Beauregard, General Gilmore secretly placed in battery 47 pieces of artillery in close vicinity to the Confederate pickets.

On July 10th, an assaulting column 2,500 strong crept up Folly River; the iron-clad fleet occupied the main ship channel off Morris Island. Axemen felled the interposing trees, and the concealed battery opened fire on the Confederate lines. The garrison was on the alert.

Just at break of day on the 11th, the Seventh Connecticut regiment charged the works, and went over the outer line, through a terrible fire from the Confederate rifles. The fort opened on them with three howitzers, and they were routed.

Although this assault on Fort Wagner was

repulsed, the neglect to make reconnoissances in time to prevent the battery on Folly Island from being established, compelled the evacuation of Morris Island, except Forts Wagner and Gregg.

General Beauregard subsequently used all his engineering skill, and for two months maintained a gallant struggle and kept the enemy at bay.

On July 18th, the Federal fleet poured a terrific fire into Fort Wagner, but without reducing it.

As the curtain of smoke, which had enveloped Wagner all day, slowly lifted, the enemy were seen debouching from their first parallel, and advancing over the narrow approach between it and the fort. The garrison of Wagner sallied forth from the bomb-proof and sand hills in the rear, to take their positions on the ramparts.

Colonel Robert G. Shaw, with his colored troops, led the attack. " They went forward at a ' double quick ' with great energy and resolution, but on approaching the ditch they broke ; the greater part of them followed their Colonel, mounted the parapet, and planted their flag upon the rampart, where Shaw was shot dead ; while the rest were seized with a furious panic, and acted like wild beasts let loose from a menagerie.

"They ran away like deer, some crawling on their hands and knees."* By this time the enemy was in full retreat, and the conflict was virtually ended.

The demoralization of the negro troops at the supreme moment threw the ranks of the Federals into disorder. The converging fire of artillery and infantry on the narrow approach prevented a rally. Few could move within the fatal area and live.

After the second successful defence of Wagner, the remainder of the month of July and the early part of August were employed in establishing batteries to bombard Sumter.

"At 1.30 P.M. on September 6th, an attempt was made to carry Battery Gregg. In five minutes the conflict was ended.

"Fort Wagner had now been held under a furious cannonade by land and sea, night and day, for fifty-seven days, and General Beauregard, who had been for some time considering the case, and to save the brave men forming the garrison of Wagner from the desperate chances of an assault, gave orders for its evacuation." †

On the night of September 6th the island was evacuated. The enemy had now undis-

---

* See Life Afloat and Ashore, Judge Cowley, page 93.
† Major Gilchrist on the Defence of Charleston.

puted possession of the entire island, including the works at Cumming's Point.

But over Sumter the Confederate flag floated, and the demand for its surrender was still rejected.*

Another effort to capture the fort was made by the Federals on the evening of September 8th, and they were again repulsed. After this repulse little more was done by the enemy for the rest of the year. The forts and the city were constantly bombarded, but the people ceased to be alarmed.

The activity of men of all classes was untiring. Under all this deadly hail they worked with indomitable spirit. The gun-boat, *Ashley* was built, finished, and launched under fire at Charleston.

A small earth-work near Sabine Pass, a place of great strategical importance, a few miles above the entrance to the Sabine River, was attacked by a fleet of twenty-three vessels. The Confederate force was 42 men and 2 lieutenants, and it drove the whole Federal fleet out of the Pass, captured two gun-boats, crippled a third, took 18 guns, killed 50, and took 150 prisoners. †

---

* On October 16, 1862, John Mitchell, the Irish patriot, arrived at Richmond. He had two sons in the Confederate army ; one, T. K. Mitchell, a captain, fell at his post when in command of Fort Sumter.

† For a full account, see The Rise and Fall of the Confederate Government, by Jefferson Davis.

CHAPTER XLIV.

LETTER TO HIS HOLINESS THE POPE.

Mr. Davis's early education had always inclined him to see in the Roman Catholics friends who could not be alienated from the oppressed. He addressed the following letter to His Holiness.

"Richmond, September 23, 1863.

" Very Venerable Sovereign Pontiff :

" The letters which you have written to the clergy of New Orleans and New York have been communicated to me, and I have read with emotion the deep grief therein expressed for the ruin and devastation caused by the war which is now being waged by the United States against the States and people which have selected me as their President, and your orders to your clergy to exhort the people to peace and charity. I am deeply sensible of the Christian charity which has impelled you to this reiterated appeal to the clergy. It is for this reason that I feel it my duty to express personally, and in the name of the Confederate States, our gratitude for such sentiments of Christian good feeling and love, and to assure Your Holiness that the people, threatened even on their own hearths with the most cruel oppression and terrible carnage, is desirous now, as it has always been, to see the end of this impious war; that we have ever addressed prayers to Heaven for that issue which Your Holiness now desires; that we desire none of our enemy's possessions, but that we fight merely to resist the devastation of our country and the shedding of our best blood, and to force them to let us live in peace under the protection of our own institutions, and under our laws, which not only insure to every one the enjoyment of his temporal rights, but also the free exercise of his religion. I pray Your Holiness to accept, on the part of myself and the people of the Confederate States, our sincere thanks for your efforts in favor of peace. May the Lord preserve the days of Your Holiness, and keep you under His divine protection.

(Signed)   " JEFFERSON DAVIS."

The Pope's Reply.

" ILLUSTRIOUS AND HONORABLE PRESIDENT, salutation :

" We have just received with all suitable welcome the persons sent by you to place in our hands your letter, dated 23d of September last. Not slight was the pleasure we experienced when we learned, from those persons and the letter, with what feelings of joy and gratitude you were animated, illustrious and honorable President, as soon as you were informed of our letters to our venerable brother John, Archbishop of New York, and John, Archbishop of New Orleans, dated the 18th of October of last year, and in which we have with all our strength excited and exhorted those venerable brothers that, in their episcopal piety and solicitude, they should endeavor, with the most ardent zeal, and in our name, to bring about the end of the fatal civil war which has broken out in those countries, in order that the American people may obtain peace and concord, and dwell charitably together. It is particularly agreeable to us to see that you, illustrious and honorable President, and your people, are animated with the same desires of peace and tranquillity which we have in our letters inculcated upon our venerable brothers. May it please God at the same time to make the other peoples of America and their rulers, reflecting seriously how terrible is civil war, and what calamities it engenders, listen to the inspirations of a calmer spirit, and adopt resolutely the part of peace. As for us, we shall not cease to offer up the most fervent prayers to God Almighty, that He may pour out upon all the people of America the spirit of peace and charity, and that He will stop the great evils which afflict them. We, at the same time, beseech the God of pity to shed abroad upon you the light of His grace, and attach you to us by a perfect friendship.

"Given at Rome, at St. Peter's, the 3d of December, 1863, of our Pontificate 18.

(Signed)   "·Pius IX."

During Mr. Davis's imprisonment, the Holy Father sent a likeness of himself, and wrote underneath it, with his own hand, attested by the seal of Cardinal Antonelli, " Come unto me, all ye who are weary and heavy laden, and I will give you rest." The dignitary and the man both illustrated the meek and lowly Lord of all, whose vice-gerent he was.

CHAPTER XLV.

CHICKAMAUGA AND MISSIONARY RIDGE.

On August 20th the bloody battle of Chickamauga was fought and our troops slept inside the intrenchments of the enemy. A month later Brigadier-General William Preston who was a gallant figure in the fight, was sent to Mexico, with authority to recognize and treat with the new Emperor Maximilian.

The defeat of Rosecrans's army at Chickamauga was complete, but the failure to promptly follow up the victory rendered it a barren one to the Confederates.

Bragg's army remained on the field of battle twenty-four hours, burying the dead and collecting arms, before the advance was begun, and then, moving slowly, found Rosecrans behind earthworks in and around Chattanooga.

Bragg immediately posted his army along Missionary Ridge and Lookout Mountain, and planned to drive Rosecrans out of Chattanooga, or to starve him into surrender.

In this situation, General Grant was assigned to the command in Tennessee. On October 23d he arrived at Chattanooga.

By his own report he found Rosecrans practically invested. Army supplies had to be hauled over almost impassable roads for sixty to seventy miles. The artillery horses and mules were starving.

Grant's first movement was to supply the army by a shorter route, and to that end he captured " Lookout Mountain."

The Confederate force, rendered weaker by detaching Longstreet to Knoxville, was overpowered by its multitudinous assailants, and after a bloody battle retreated during the night toward Tunnel Hill.

General Grant pursued but a short distance beyond Chattanooga.

This disaster depressed the hopes of the Confederates greatly ; misfortunes had of late crowded so thick upon them. General Bragg felt, like Sidney Johnston, that success should be in a measure the test of a military man's merit, and he asked to be relieved. The President knew that General Bragg was both an able general and a devoted patriot, and after granting the request he invited him to be his Chief of Staff, or, in citizen's phrase, military counsel at Richmond.

The President cast his eyes over the roster of gallant and educated soldiers, to get a successor for General Bragg, and found in General Hardee all the needful qualities for the command of the army of the West. His was a character, both moral and physical, which compelled the respect and won the affection of those he commanded, and both the President and General Bragg were much disappointed by General Hardee's declining the position. He said the responsibility was so great that he had no confidence in his being able to meet it as ably as some other man might. His declension was so positive that there was no appeal from it, and General Joseph E. Johnston, on December 16, 1863, was directed to personally take command.

CHAPTER XLVI.

THE dissatisfaction, which had been rather whispered than proclaimed, now began to be more pronounced, and the pernicious effects were noticed in the incendiary articles published in North Carolina, while her troops were bleeding on every field and performing prodigies of valor. The President wrote on this subject to the Governor of the State as follows :

President Davis to Governor Z. B. Vance.

Confidential.

"EXECUTIVE OFFICE,
"RICHMOND, VA., July 24, 1863.

" HIS EXCELLENCY Z. B. VANCE,
" Governor of the State of North Carolina.
" DEAR SIR : A letter has just been received by the Secretary of State, from one of the most distinguished citizens of your State, containing the following passage :
" ' I have just learned that the Union or

Reconstruction party propose holding meetings throughout the State. Trouble is fast brewing here, and I fear we shall soon have open resistance to the Government under the leadership of that reckless politician, Holden, Editor of the *Standard.*'

" This is not the first intimation I have received that Holden is engaged in the treasononable purpose of exciting the people of North Carolina to resistance against their Government, and co-operation with the enemy ; but I have never received any definite statement of facts as to his conduct beyond the assertion that his newspaper, which I do not read, is filled with articles recommending resistance to the constituted authorities.

" I know not whether his hostility and that of his accomplices is directed against the Confederate Government alone, or embraces that of his State ; nor am I aware whether he has gone so far as to render him liable to criminal prosecution.

" If, however, the facts stated in the extract of the letter which I have quoted be true (and the author is entitled to the greatest credit), the case is quite grave enough for me to consult with you on the subject, and to solicit from you such information and advice as you may be able to give me, for the purpose of such joint or separate action as may be

proper to defeat designs fraught with great
danger to our common country.

" I write you confidentially, because there
may be error or exaggeration in the reports
about this man, and I would be unwilling to
injure him by giving publicity to the charges,
if there be no foundation for them.

" Very respectfully and truly yours,

" JEFFERSON DAVIS."

" STATE OF NORTH CAROLINA, EXECUTIVE DEPARTMENT,
" RALEIGH, December 30, 1863.

" HIS EXCELLENCY PRESIDENT DAVIS.

" MY DEAR SIR : After a careful consideration of all the sources of discontent in North
Carolina, I have concluded that it will be impossible to remove it, except by making
some effort at negotiation with the enemy.
The recent action of the Federal House of
Representatives, though meaning very little,
has greatly excited the public hope that the
Northern mind is looking toward peace. I
am promised, by all men who advocate the
course, that if fair terms are rejected it will
tend greatly to strengthen and intensify the
war feeling, and will rally all classes to a more
cordial support of the Government. And, although our position is well known as demanding only to be let alone, yet it seems to
me that for the sake of humanity, without

having any weak or improper motives attributed to us, we might with propriety constantly tender negotiations. In doing so we could keep conspicuously before the world a disclaimer of our responsibility for the great slaughter of our race, and convince the humblest of our citizens—who sometimes forget the actual situation—that the Government is tender of their lives and happiness, and would not prolong their sufferings unnecessarily one moment. Though statesmen might regard this as useless, the people will not, and I think our cause will be strengthened thereby. I have not suggested the method of these negotiations or their terms. The effort to obtain peace is the principal matter.

" Allow me to beg your earnest consideration of these suggestions.

" Very respectfully yours,

" Z. B. VANCE."

"EXECUTIVE OFFICE, RICHMOND, VA.,
" January 8, 1864.

" DEAR SIR : I have received your letter of the 30th ult., containing suggestions of the measures to be adopted for the purpose of removing 'the sources of discontent' in North Carolina. The contents of the letter are substantially the same as those of the letter addressed by you to Senator Dorich, extracts

of which were by him read to me. I remarked
to Mr. Dorich that you were probably not
aware of the obstacles to the course you indicated, and without expressing an opinion on
the merits of the proposed policy, I desired
him, in answering your letter, to invite suggestions as to the method of opening negociations, and as to the terms which you thought
should be offered to the enemy. I felt persuaded you would appreciate the difficulties
as soon as your attention was called to the
necessity of considering the subject in its detail. As you have made no suggestions
touching the manner of overcoming the obstacles, I infer that you were not apprised by
Mr. Dorich of my remarks to him.

"Apart from insuperable objections to the
line of policy you propose (and to which I
will presently advert), I cannot see how the
more material obstacles are to be surmounted.
We have made three distinct efforts to communicate with the authorities at Washington,
and have been invariably unsuccessful. Commissioners were sent before hostilities were
begun, and the Washington Government refused to receive them or hear what they had
to say. A second time I sent a military officer, with a communication addressed by myself to President Lincoln. The letter was received by General Scott, who did not permit

the officer to see Mr. Lincoln, but promised
that an answer would be sent. No answer
has ever been received. The third time, a
few months ago, a gentleman was sent, whose
position, character, and reputation were such
as to insure his reception, if the enemy were
not determined to receive no proposals whatever from the Government. Vice-President
Stephens made a patriotic tender of his services in the hope of being able to promote the
cause of humanity, and although little belief
was entertained of his success, I cheerfully
yielded to his suggestion, that the experiment
should be tried. The enemy refused to let
him pass through their lines to hold any conference with them. He was stopped before
he ever reached Fortress Monroe on his way
to Washington. The attempt again (in the
face of these repeated rejections of all conferences with us) to send commissioners or
agents to propose peace, is to invite insult
and contumely, and to subject ourselves to
indignity without the slightest chance of being listened to.

"No true citizen, no man who has our
cause at heart, can desire this, and the good
people of North Carolina would be the last
to approve of such an attempt, if aware of all
the facts. So far from removing sources of
discontent, such a course would receive, as it

would merit, the condemnation of those true patriots who have given their blood and their treasure to maintain their freedom, equality, and independence which descended to them from the immortal heroes of King's Mountain and other battle-fields of the Revolution. If, then, these proposals cannot be made through envoys, because the enemy will not receive them, how is it possible to communicate our desire for peace otherwise than by the public announcements contained in almost every message I ever sent to Congress?

" I cannot recall at this time one instance in which I have failed to announce that our only desire was peace, and the only terms which formed a *sine qua non* were precisely those that you suggested, namely ' a demand only to be let alone.' But suppose it were practicable to obtain a conference through commissioners with the Government of President Lincoln, is it at this moment that we are to consider it desirable, or even at all admissible? Have we not just been apprised by that despot that we can only expect his gracious pardon by emancipating all our slaves, swearing allegiance and obedience to him and his proclamation, and becoming in point of fact the slaves of our own negroes? Can there be in North Carolina one citizen so fallen beneath the dignity of his ancestors as to accept, or to enter into conference on the basis of these terms ? That there are a few traitors in the State that would be willing to betray their fellow-citizens to such a degraded condition, in the hope of being rewarded for treachery by an escape from the common doom, may be true. But I do not believe that the vilest wretch would accept such terms for himself. I cannot conceive how the people of your State, of which none has sent nobler or more gallant soldiers to the field of battle (one of whom it is your honor to be), can have been deceived by anything to which you refer in ' the recent action in the Federal House of Representatives.' I have seen no action of that House that does not indicate a very decided majority, the purpose of the majority to refuse all terms of the South, except absolute, unconditional subjugation or extermination. But if it were otherwise, how are we to treat with the House of Representatives ?

"It is with Lincoln alone that we would confer, and his own partisans at the North avow unequivocally that his purpose, in his message and proclamation, was to shut out all hope that he could ever treat with us on any terms. If we break up our Government, dissolve the Confederacy, disband our armies, emancipate our slaves, take an oath of allegi-

ance binding ourselves to obedience to him
and disloyalty to our own States, he proposes to pardon us, and not to plunder us of
anything more than the property already
stolen from us, and such slaves as still remain. In order to render his proposals so
insulting as to secure their objection, he joins
to them a promise to support with his army
one-tenth of the people of any State who will
attempt to set up a Government over the
other nine-tenths, thus seeking to sow dis-
cord and suspicion among the people of the
several States, and to excite them to civil
war in furtherance of his ends. I know well
it would be impossible to get your people, if
they possessed full knowledge of these facts,
to consent that proposals should now be
made by us to those who control the Government at Washington. Your own well-known
devotion to the great cause of liberty and
independence, to which we have all committed whatever we have of earthly possessions, would induce you to take the lead in re-
pelling the bare thought of submission to the
enemy. Yet peace on other terms is impossible. To obtain the sole terms to which you
or I could listen, this struggle must continue
until the enemy is beaten out of his vain confidence in our subjugation. Then, and not
till then, will it be possible to treat of peace.

Till then, all tender of terms to the enemy will be received as proof that we are ready for submission, and will encourage him in the atrocious warfare which he is now waging.

"I have the honor to be, very respectfully, yours,

"JEFFERSON DAVIS.

"His Excellency Z. B. Vance,

"Governor of North Carolina."

CHAPTER XLVII.

THE MARYLAND LINE AND THE KILPATRICK AND DAHLGREN RAID.

In February, 1864, an expedition was organized in the Federal Army, of a force of three thousand picked cavalry, to make a dash on Richmond, release the prisoners, burn the city, and escape by way of the Peninsula to Old Point Comfort. On February 29th, it started one column of four hundred men under Colonel Ulric Dahlgren, to cross the James River in Goochland County, above Richmond, and the other, under Brigadier-General Judson Kilpatrick, to make a direct attack on the city, while Dahlgren attacked from the south side.

Crossing at Ely's Ford, after surprising and capturing the picket there, they passed in rear of General Lee's army (capturing " en route " a whole court martial of Confederate officers, but passing by a camp of sixty-eight pieces of artillery that was unprotected, and would have fallen an easy prey), until, under the guidance of a negro that had been sent by Secretary Stanton, they reached the James

River at Dover Mills, where a ford was supposed to be. Finding none, they accused the negro guide of treachery, and barbarously hung him to a tree with a leather strap.

In the winter of 1863-64, the Maryland line, consisting of the Second Infantry, First Cavalry, First, Second, and Third Maryland Artillery, were stationed at Hanover Junction to guard Lee's flank toward the Peninsula and the railroad bridges over the North and South Anna, on the preservation of which depended Lee's communications with Richmond.

This movement around Lee's flank was at once discovered, and Colonel Johnson was directed by General Lee to look out for it.

The Maryland line cavalry was extended in a picket line along the Pamunkey to New Kent Court House, leaving only seventy-five men in camp. With these, during the night, by his scouts, Johnson located Kilpatrick's column, and then started with sixty men and two pieces of artillery to close up on Kilpatrick.

Just before daylight of March 1st, the Marylanders struck one of Kilpatrick's flanking parties and drove them in on the main body. They followed the enemy through Ashland down to the outer defences of Richmond ; there Kilpatrick had dismounted his twenty-five hundred men and was making a regular attack on the works. General Wade Hampton heard that the Federal cavalry was approaching the city, and immediately moved out to attack him.

The Marylanders drew up on his rear picket just as, by a happy chance, an officer and five men bearing a despatch from Dahlgren galloped into their arms. The despatch informed Kilpatrick that Dahlgren would attack on the River Road at sunset, that Kilpatrick must attack at the same time, and together they would ride into Richmond. Colonel Johnson at once drove in Kilpatrick's picket, who, finding himself attacked in rear at once retreated toward the White House. The Marylanders followed him, never losing sight of his rear-guard, and driving it in ·on him whenever the ground allowed, until he got to Tunstall's, under the protection of infantry sent from Williamsburg or Yorktown for his rescue. The pursuers captured one hundred and forty prisoners and got off with an insignificant loss.*

Dahlgren, hearing the firing, concluded for reasons unknown to him, that Kilpatrick had attacked four hours before the appointed time, and kept under cover until dark, when he made an attack upon the north side of the

---

* Lieutenant R. Bartley, Signal Officer, U. S. A., accompanying Dahlgren.

city. Here, March 1st, he encountered the company of Richmond boys (under eighteen years of age) at the outer intrenchments, and their fire becoming " too hot, he sounded the retreat, leaving forty men on the field."

Continuing his retreat down the Peninsula, he was met by a few men of the Fifth and Ninth Virginia cavalry, and some home guards, all under command of Lieutenant James Pollard, Company H, Ninth Virginia cavalry, who, placing his men in ambush, waited until the Federals were close upon them, when a volley was fired, and Colonel Dahlgren, who had ridden forward and tried to discharge his pistol, fell dead, and his command were taken prisoners.

General Wade Hampton in his report said: " We captured upward of one hundred prisoners, representing five regiments, many horses, arms, etc. . . . and forced this body of the enemy to take a route which they had not proposed to follow, while the other force, under Dahlgren, was prevented from forming a junction with Kilpatrick by the interposing of my command between the two.

" This brought about the precipitate retreat of Dahlgren, and his ultimate death, with the destruction of his command."

He added: " I cannot close my report without expressing my appreciation of Colonel Bradley T. Johnson and his gallant command.

With a mere handful of men, he met the enemy at Beaver Dam, and never lost sight of him until he had passed Tunstall's Station, hanging on his rear, striking him constantly, and displaying throughout the very highest qualities of a soldier. He is admirably fitted for the cavalry service, and I trust it will not be deemed an interference on my part to urge, as emphatically as I can, his promotion." *

General G. W. C. Lee said: " A short distance beyond the fortifications I met the boy company, and some, or all, of the other companies of the Department battalion coming in; and was told, in answer to my inquiries, that the boy company had arrived first at the intermediate line of fortifications, and, not finding any troops there, had concluded that there was an outer line."

.   .   .   .

* General Hampton presented Colonel Johnson with a sabre in compliment for his having thus saved Richmond from capture, and General Elzey, who commanded the Department of Richmond, issued an order of which the following is an extract :

"HEADQUARTERS, DEPARTMENT OF RICHMOND,
"March 8, 1864.
"General Orders, No. 10.
"   .   .   .   To Colonel Eradley T. Johnson and the officers and soldiers under his command, the thanks of the Major-General are especially due for the prompt and vigorous manner in which they pursued the enemy from Beaver Dam to Richmond, and thence to Pamunkey, and down the Peninsula, making repeated charges, capturing many prisoners and horses, and thwarting any attempt of the enemy to charge them."

The "Department battalion" was composed of the clerks from *all the departments of the Government*, not from the Treasury Department alone—and of a company of Richmond boys under eighteen years of age, and it was this latter company that went by mistake to Green's farm, which was not far beyond the line of fortifications on the northern plank road to which the "Department battalion," and another (Armory Battalion?) were ordered; and *it was this company of boys which first became engaged with Dahlgren's column, and which had the most to do with checking it, and perhaps driving it off.*

The following special orders were discovered on the body of Colonel Dahlgren:

"Guides, pioneers (with oakum, turpentine, and torpedoes), Signal Officer, Quartermaster, Commissary; Scouts and pickets-men in rebel uniform. These will remain on the north bank and move down with the force on the south bank, not getting ahead of them; and if the communication can be kept up without giving an alarm, it must be done; but everything depends upon a surprise, and no one must be allowed to pass ahead of the column. Information must be gathered in regard to the crossings of the river, so that, should we be repulsed on the south side, we shall know where to recross at the nearest point. All

mills must be *burned*, and the *canal destroyed ;*
and also everything which can be used by the
rebels must be destroyed, including the boats
on the river. Should a ferry-boat be seized,
and can be worked, have it moved down.
Keep the force on the south side posted of
any important movement of the enemy, and
in case of danger some of the scouts must
swim the river and bring us information. As
we approach the city the party must take great
care that they do not get ahead of the other
party on the south side, and must conceal
themselves and watch our movements. We
will try and secure the bridge to the city (one
mile below Belle Isle) and release the prisoners at the same time. If we do not succeed,
they must then dash down, and we will try
and carry the bridge from each side. When
necessary, the men must be filed through the
woods and along the river bank. The bridges
once secured and the prisoners loose and over
the river, the bridges will be secured and the
city destroyed. The men must keep together
and well in hand, and once in the city, it must
be destroyed, and *Jeff Davis* and *Cabinet
killed*. Prisoners will go along with combus-
tible material. The officer must use his discretion about the time of assisting us. Horses
and cattle which we do not need immediately
must be shot rather than left. Everything on

the canal and elsewhere of service to the rebels must be destroyed. As General Custer may follow me, be careful not to give a false alarm. The signal officer must be prepared to communicate at night by rockets, and in other things pertaining to his department. The quartermasters and commissaries must be on the lookout for their departments, and see that there are no delays on their account. The engineer officer will follow to survey the road as we pass over it, etc. The pioneers must be prepared to construct a bridge or destroy one. They must have plenty of oakum and turpentine for burning, which will be rolled in soaked balls, and given to the men to burn when we get into the city. Torpedoes will only be used by the pioneers for destroying the main bridges, etc. They must be prepared to destroy railroads. Men will branch off to the right with a few pioneers, and destroy the bridges and railroads south of Richmond, and then join us at the city. They must be well prepared with torpedoes, etc. The line of Falling Creek is probably the best to work along, or, as they approach the city, Goode's Creek, so that no reinforcements can come upon any cars. No one must be allowed to pass ahead, for fear of communicating news. Rejoin the command in all haste, and, if cut off, cross the river above Richmond and join us. Men will stop at Bellona Arsenal and totally destroy it, and anything else but hospitals; then follow on and rejoin the command at Richmond in all haste, and if cut off, cross the river and join us. As General Custer may follow me, be careful and not give a false alarm."

General Fitzhugh Lee, in a letter to the *Historical Magazine* of New York, and published in the *Magazine* in 1870, says:

"Personally, as a man educated to be a soldier, I deplore Colonel Ulric Dahlgren's sad fate. He was a young man full of hope, of undoubted pluck, and inspired with hatred of 'rebels.'

"Fired by ambition, and longing to be at the head of 'the braves who swept through the city of Richmond,' his courage and enthusiasm overflowed, and his naturally generous feelings were drowned. His memoranda and address to his troops were probably based upon the general instructions to the whole command.

"The conception of the expedition, I have heard since the war, originated in General Kilpatrick's brain. It furnishes the best specimen of cavalry marching upon the Federal side; but it showed, upon the part of somebody, a most culpable want of knowledge of data upon which to base such a movement.

. . . . . .

"I have only to add in conclusion, that what appeared in the Richmond papers of that period as the 'Dahlgren papers,' was correctly taken from the papers I carried in person to Mr. Davis; and that those papers were not added to or changed in the minutest particular, before they came into my possession, as far as I know and believe; and that, from all the facts in my possession, I have every reason to believe they were taken from the body of Colonel Ulric Dahlgren, and came to me without alteration of any kind."

When Mr. Blair came to Richmond I mentioned Colonel Dahlgren's special orders, and he said, "Did you believe it?" I said that there had been no time for such a forgery, and that there was an itinerary in the same hand also. Upon Mr. Blair making some laughing remark of disbelief, I offered to send for the book, and said it had been photographed and sent to General Meade, who was then in our front—"with an inquiry as to whether such practices were authorized by his Government; and also to say that if any question was raised as to the copies, the original paper would be submitted." No such question was

then made, and the denial that Dahlgren's
conduct had been authorized was accepted.

Mr. Blair laughed again and said: "Now,
the fact is I do not want to believe it, and if you
could convince me I would rather not look at
it." I had felt much the same unwillingness,
having been intimate with his parents. Once
Commodore Dahlgren had brought the little
fair-haired boy to show me how pretty he
looked in his black velvet suit and Vandyke
collar, and I could not reconcile the two Ulrics.

The Maryland Line, commanded by Colonel Bradley T. Johnson, rendered noble service in the conduct of his force against the
Dahlgren raid.

Shortly after this, Colonel Johnson promised
me that the Maryland Line should capture
a flag for me.

In the following fall, September, 1864,
there was a sharp cavalry affair between
Early's cavalry, under Lomax, and Sheridan's,
under Custer and Wilson, at Bunker Hill, in
Buckley County, now West Virginia.

Charge and counter-charge succeeded each
other back and forth the turnpike, and in one
of them Captain George M. Emack, commanding Company B, First Maryland regiment, cut down the man carrying the guidon
of the opposing regiment, while he wrested
from his hand the guidon and brought it off.

Emack had the luck that some men have, of being hit almost every time he went under fire. He was the most reckless, daring soldier of that gallant command, and had received sixteen wounds in battle. In fighting for the guidon he received his seventeenth, which sent him to hospital for a week or two. Colonel Johnson directed him to deliver the captured guidon to me in person, as the performance of the pledge of the Maryland Line to me, with a letter announcing the fulfilment of the promise.

It was preserved as a souvenir of gallant service, and escaped the examination of my trunk when it was rifled at Fortress Monroe after the capture of President Davis. I have it now; but a fine Pennsylvania flag sent at another time was then taken from me, and possibly figures as one of the recaptured trophies of the Federal Armies.

CHAPTER XLVIII.

DIPLOMATIC CORRESPONDENCE.

Now that disasters threatened us from all sides, it was determined by Her Britannic Majesty's Government to take an open course of so-called neutrality toward us.

"H. B. M.'s LEGATION,
"WASHINGTON, D. C., April 1, 1864.

" MR. JEFFERSON DAVIS, etc., etc.,
    " Richmond, Va.

" SIR: I have been instructed by Earl Russell, Her Britannic Majesty's Secretary for Foreign Affairs, to convey to you the following extract of a despatch which has been forwarded to me by his Lordship. I have chosen the method which appeared to me to be the only available one, under the present unhappy circumstances in which the country is involved, and I trust that the absence of all recognized diplomatic or consular residents, or other agents of Her Majesty near Richmond, will be recognized as sufficient reason for its not being sent through usual channels. I need scarcely say that the bearer of this des-

JEFFERSON DAVIS, 1860-64.

VARINA ANNE DAVIS.

patch, whom you have consented to allow to visit Richmond, has been authorized by the Government of the United States to pass into your lines, on the flag of truce boat, for the purpose of delivering it, and will desire your permission to return to Washington by the same mode of conveyance.

" I have the honor to be, with high respect, your obedient, humble servant,

" LYONS."

Copy.

" You will also convey to Mr. Davis, at Richmond, through such channel as shall be available, and as you may in your discretion deem proper, the formal protest and remonstrance of Her Majesty's Government against the efforts of the authorities of the so-called Confederate States to build war vessels within Her Majesty's dominions, to be employed against the Government of the United States. Perhaps your Lordship might best accomplish this object by obtaining permission from the authorities of both belligerents to send a special messenger to Richmond with the necessary despatch, in which you will transmit this paragraph, or the substance of it, together with all that follows, to the close of this communication.

" Her Majesty's Government, in taking this course, desire Mr. Davis to rest assured that it is adopted entirely in that spirit of neutrality which has been declared the policy of this country with regard to the two belligerents now so lamentably desolating America, and which will continue to be pursued, with a careful and earnest desire to make it conducive to the most rigid impartiality and justice.

"After consulting with the law officers of the Crown, Her Majesty's Government have come to the decision that agents of the authorities of the so-called Confederate States have been engaged in building vessels which would be, at least, partially equipped for war purposes on leaving the ports of this country; that these war vessels would undoubtedly be used against the United States, a country with which this Government is at peace; that this would be a violation of the neutrality laws of the realm; and that the Government of the United States would have just ground for serious complaint against Her Majesty's Government, should they permit such an infraction of the amicable relations subsisting between the two countries.

"Her Majesty's Government confidently rely on the frankness, courtesy, and discernment which Mr. Davis has displayed in the difficult circumstances in which he has been placed during the past three years, for a recognition of the correctness of the position which Her Majesty's Government have taken upon this subject. No matter what might be the difficulty of proving in a court of law that the parties procuring the building of these vessels are agents of the so-called Confederate States, it is universally understood throughout the world that they are so, and Her Majesty's Government are satisfied that Mr. Davis would not deny that they are so. Constructed as 'rams,' as these vessels are, they would certainly be in a condition, on leaving port, to inflict the most serious damage on vessels belonging to the United States, as was shown by the destruction of the *Cumberland*, United States sloop of-war, by the 'ram' *Merrimac*, merely by the latter being run into collision with the *Cumberland*. Such vessels are, to all intents and purposes, equipped as war vessels of a certain power, although they be without a gun or any ammunition on board; nor can the frequent use of the word ' equip,' in the sense of ' to furnish with everything necessary for a voyage,' be held for a moment to limit its significance to the furnishing of a war vessel with everything upon her, or the ultimately putting of which on her might be contemplated. Such a construction cannot be entertained for an instant. It is clear that a hundred-and-twenty-gun ship might be equipped for war purposes

with any fraction of her armament on board,
although she might not be so powerful or so
efficient as she would be if she had the whole
of it.   A ram would be also equipped for war
purposes, although the absence of her ordnance and ammunition might render her less
effective than she would be with them.   This,
it is presumed by Her Majesty's Government,
will be conceded by Mr. Davis without further argument or illustration in support of it.

"This much being established to the perfect conviction of Her Majesty's Government
and the law officers of the Crown, and admitted, as they are convinced it must be, by
Mr. Davis, and by every other person of
sound and impartial judgment, there is not the
slightest room to doubt that it is purposed to
use the vessels in question against the United
States, a country with which this nation is at
peace and on terms of amity ; and that the permitting of them to leave the ports of Her
Majesty's dominions would be a violation of
the neutrality laws of the kingdom, and such
an injurious act toward the United States as
would justify the Government of that country
in seriously complaining of it as unfriendly and
offensive in the highest degree, even to the
imminent peril of rupturing the peaceful relations now existing between the two countries.

" Under these circumstances, Her Majesty's

Government protest and remonstrate against
any further efforts being made on the part of
the so-called Confederate States, or the authorities or agents thereof, to build or cause
to be built, or to purchase or to cause to be
purchased, any such vessels as those styled
rams, or any other vessels to be used for war
purposes against the United States, or against
any country with which the United Kingdom
is at peace or on terms of amity ; and Her
Majesty's Government further protest and remonstrate against all acts in violation of the
neutrality laws of the realm.

" I have the honor to be your Lordship's
obedient servant,   " RUSSELL."

The reply.

" RICHMOND, VA., C. S. A., April 6, 1864.
" To the RIGHT HONORABLE LORD LYONS,
C.B., & H. M.'s Minister to the Govern-
ment of the United States.

" MY LORD : I have been instructed by the
President to acknowledge the receipt of a despatch from your Lordship, enclosing a copy of
a portion of a despatch from Earl Russell, H.
B. M.'s Secretary of State for Foreign Affairs,
purporting to be a 'formal protest and remonstrance of Her Majesty's Government against
the efforts of the authorities of the so-called
Confederate States to build war vessels with-

in Her Majesty's dominions, to be employed against the Government of the United States.'

"The President desires me to say to your Lordship, that while he is not unwilling to waive, in existing circumstances, the transmission of such a document through other than the usual and proper channel, it would be inconsistent with the dignity of the position he fills, as Chief Magistrate of a nation comprising a population of more than twelve millions, occupying a territory many times larger than the United Kingdom, and possessing resources unsurpassed by those of any other country on the face of the globe—to allow the attempt of Earl Russell to ignore the actual existence of the Confederate States, and to contumeliously style them 'so-called,' to pass without a protest and a remonstrance. The President, therefore, does protest and remonstrate against this studied insult; and he instructs me to say, that in future any document in which it may be repeated will be returned unanswered and unnoticed.

"With respect to the subject of the extract from Earl Russell's despatch, the President desires me to state, that the plea of neutrality, which is used to sustain the sinister course of Her Majesty's present Government against the Government of the Confederate States, is so clearly contradicted by their actions, that it is regarded by the world, not even excepting the United States, as a mere cover for actual hostility, and the President cannot but feel that this is a just view of it. Were, indeed, Her Majesty's Government sincere in a desire and determination to maintain neutrality, the President could not but feel that they would neither be just nor gallant to allow the subjugation of a nation like the Confederate States by such a barbarous, despotic race as are now attempting it. He cannot but feel, with the history and traditions of the Anglo-Saxon race before him, that under a government faithfully representing the people of Great Britain, the whole weight and power of that nation would be unhesitatingly thrown into the scale in favor of the principles of free government, on which these States were originally formed, and for which alone the Confederate States are now struggling. He cannot but feel that with such a government, and with the plea of neutrality urged upon the people as it now is, no such pitiful spectacle could be witnessed as is now manifested by Her Majesty's present Government, in the persistent persecution of the Confederate States at the beck and bidding of officers of the United States; while a prime minister mocks and insults the intelligence of a House of Commons and of the world, by excusing the permission to allow British subjects to go

to the United States to fight against us, by
the paltry subterfuge that it was the great demand for labor and the high rate of wages
that were taking them thither. He cannot
but feel that a neutrality most cunningly, au-
daciously, fawningly, and insolently sought
and urged, begged and demanded by one
belligerent, and repudiated by the other, must
be seen by all impartial men to be a mere
pretext for aiding the cause of the one at the
expense of the other, while pretending to be
impartial; to be, in short, but a cover for
treacherous, malignant hostility.

"As for the specious arguments on the
subject of the rams, advanced by Earl Russell, the President desires me to state that he
is content to leave the world and history to
pronounce judgment upon this attempt to
heap injury upon insult, by declaring that
Her Majesty's Government and law officers
are satisfied of the questions involved, while
those questions are still before the highest
legal tribunal of the kingdom, composed of
members of the Government and the highest
law officers of the Crown, for their decision.
The President himself will not condescend to
notice them.

"I have the honor to be your Lordship's
obedient, humble servant

"BURTON N. HARRISON, *Private Secretary.*"

CHAPTER XLIX.

FORT PILLOW, OCEAN POND, AND MERIDIAN.

FORT PILLOW, situated on the east bank of the Mississippi River, was established by the State of Tennessee in 1861. It was afterward fortified by the Confederate States, and effectually prevented the passage of the Federal fleet. When the Confederates abandoned Corinth, Fort Pillow was necessarily evacuated also, and was immediately occupied by an inconsiderable Federal force.

On April 12, 1864, an attack was made upon the fort by two brigades of General N. B. Forrest's force, under Mississippi's gallant general, J. R. Chalmers.

The Confederates gained the outer works and drove the garrison to their main fortifications. About this time General Forrest arrived and reconnoitred the whole position, in doing which he had two horses shot under him and another wounded. He discovered a ravine leading up in the near vicinity to the southern face of the fort, which, if seized, would afford complete shelter for an attacking column.

Two ridges also gave the Confederate sharp-shooters complete command of the interior of the fort, and Forrest decided to send a formal demand for surrender. The command ing officer was notified that he was surrounded, and that, "if the demand was acceded to, the gallantry of the defence already made would entitle *all its* garrison to be treated as prisoners of war."

An answer, after considerable delay, was brought from the fort, written in pencil on a soiled scrap of paper, without envelope. "Your demand does not produce the desired effect." General Forrest read it and hastily exclaimed: "This will not do, send it back, and say to Major Booth that I must have an answer in plain English—yes or no."

Shortly the messenger returned with "no." Forrest immediately prepared to make the assault. The bugle sounded the "charge," and the Confederates, with a rush, cleared the parapet and swept with their fire every face of the work. General Forrest drove the enemy toward the river, leaving their flag fly-ing, but they turned and fired as they ran. The gun-boat failed them at the critical mo-ment, and stood out of range of the guns of the captured fort. Disappointed, and now thoroughly panic-stricken, many of the enemy threw themselves into the river and were drowned; others, with arms in their hands, endeavored to make good their escape in different directions, but were met by flanking parties of the Confederates and either killed or captured. Fortunately Forrest, riding into the fort, cut down the flag, and the firing instantly ceased.

On the Confederate side 14 officers and men were killed and 86 wounded. Under a flag of truce, a steamer came to the landing place, and parties were allowed to come ashore to look after their dead and wounded, to bury the former and remove the latter to the transport. Of the wounded, there were 61—34 whites and 27 colored, according to the reports of the Federal Surgeon at Mound City, Ill., Hospital. There were taken prisoners of war, 7 officers and 219 enlisted men (56 negroes, 163 whites) unwounded, which, with the wounded, make an aggregate of those who survived, exclusive of all who may have escaped, quite 300 souls, or fully fifty-five per cent. of all the garrison, while those who survived unhurt constituted forty per cent.* This was the so-called massacre of Fort Pillow.

The year 1864 opened auspiciously for the Confederates, and their hopes rose high after each victory.

Campaign of Lieutenant-General N. B. Forrest.

On February 20th Generals Finnegan and Colquitt, near Ocean Pond, Fla., with 5,000 men, achieved a victory over General Seymour's 7,000 troops that had just arrived from Charleston Harbor. This battle expelled the enemy from Florida.

On February 3d General Sherman, with 30,000 men, without opposition crossed the State of Mississippi to Meridian. The Federal cavalry started from Corinth and Holly Springs, and laid waste that fertile district on their way to join Sherman. Our great cavalry, leader, General Forrest, with 2,500 cavalry encountered, attacked, and defeated Grierson's and Smith's cavalry forces near West Point, and sent them back to Memphis. By this success General Forrest forced General Sherman to make a hurried retreat through one hundred and fifty miles of country that his soldiers had desolated and plundered.

General Banks now attempted to penetrate Central Texas, and destroy the Confederate lines of supplies which Texas still furnished plentifully, the transportation of them being the only difficulty. He was completely routed.*

---

* General R. Taylor : Destruction and Reconstruction.

CHAPTER L.

VIRGINIA CAMPAIGN, 1864.

GENERAL GRANT'S theory of war was, " to hammer continuously against the armed force of the enemy, until, by mere attrition, there should be nothing left."

Military genius, the arts of war, the skilful handling of troops, superior strategy, the devotion of an army, the noble self-denial of commanders, all must give way before the natural forces of "continuous hammering" by an army with unlimited reinforcements, and an inexhaustible treasury, a well-filled commissariat, and all directed by an unanimous people.

The work of the Federal War Department was based on the need for an army of a million of men. Vast stores were accumulated. Congress, with reckless prodigality, continued to pass the most extravagant appropriations for organizing armies, and for maintaining the countless forces which constituted an army of invasion so vast, that it was hoped it would be invincible.

Grant took command on March 17, 1864.

The Army of the Potomac, now massed on
the Rapidan, numbered 141,160 men. General Lee, to oppose this vast army, had 50,-
403 muskets. The cavalry divisions were
weak, neither of them being stronger than a
good brigade. His artillery was not as heavy,
nor was his ammunition as good in quality,
as that of the enemy. Lee's entire effective
strength did not exceed 64,000 men of all
arms, at the opening of the spring campaign
of 1864.

On May 4th General Grant began his
march.

It was doubtless expected that Lee would
retreat before this vast army, but he, on the
contrary, gave Grant such a blow in the Wilderness that he was compelled to halt and
deliver battle.

For two days the contest raged, and only
ceased from mutual exhaustion. It was during this battle that a notable event occurred :
" Heth and Wilcox, who had expected to be
relieved, and were not prepared for the enemy's assault, were overpowered and compelled to retire, just as the advance of Longstreet's column reached the ground. The
defeated divisions were in considerable disorder, and the condition of affairs was exceedingly critical. General Lee fully appreciated the impending crisis, and, dashing

amid the fugitives, called upon the men to
rally.   General Longstreet, taking in the situation at a glance, immediately caused his divisions to be deployed in line of battle, and
advanced to recover the lost ground.*

Lee, with his hat in his hand, spurred his
gray charger " Traveller " to the front of his
lines to lead them in person to the charge,
but the soldiers cried out with one voice :
" Go back, General Lee."   " Go back, Uncle
Robert."   " To the rear, General, to the
rear, and we'll fix everything all right," and
one tall Texan stepped to his horse's side,
and taking hold of the bridle, turned him
around and led him to the rear, while the
men, aroused to enthusiastic frenzy, gave
vent to loud yells, pushed the enemy before
them, and re-established the Confederate
lines.

Longstreet having the enemy much shaken,
now received the necessary orders to pursue ;
but at the moment when a turning movement
was being executed, and a complete success
was crowning his efforts, he and the officers
with him were mistaken, by a flanking party
of his own troops, for the enemy, and fired
into.   General Longstreet was seriously
wounded, and General Jenkins, who was

---

* Taylor's Four Years with Lee.

riding by his side, fell dead. The forward
movement was checked, and the enemy were
enabled to rally their forces and reform behind their intrenchments.

Grant's next move was to gain possession
of Spottsylvania Court House, but Lee com-
prehended his purpose and moved off in the
night. The heads of the opposing columns
arrived almost at the same time at their destination. Both armies then intrenched.

On the 12th, the enemy made a heavy assault on Ewell's front and broke through, but
were driven out with great loss. The on-
slaught was a complete surprise. A redoubt
on Ewell's front was stormed at the point of
the bayonet, nearly three thousand Confederates were taken prisoners, and eighteen
pieces of artillery fell into the hands of the
enemy.

General Lee, attributing this success to the
want of vigilance or courage of his men, instantly rode to the head of a Texas regiment.
Waving his hat in the air, he prepared to
lead it forward. Spurring rapidly to his side,
General Gordon seized hold of his horse's
rein, and exclaimed, " This, General Lee, is
no place for you ; these are men who never
failed you yet, and who will not fail now."

With unanimous voice the soldiers around
them refused to advance, unless General Lee

went to the rear, then charging with Gordon leading, the salient was recaptured.*

Although General Grant's army was still so strong that, after covering the Confederate front with double lines of battle, he still had a sufficient force with which to outflank his adversary and compel him to make a counter-move to prevent his getting between him and Richmond, he waited from the 13th to the 18th of May for reinforcements.

On the night of May 20th, General Grant again moved away in the direction of Hanover Junction. Here Lee again confronted him and offered battle, but Grant declined.

On May 26th he recrossed to the north side of the North Anna River and made a detour to the east. General Lee moved after him, and offered him battle again at Atlee's Station, and again it was declined. On June 3d, the two armies met on the blood-stained field of Cold Harbor. Here the Confederates threw up a light intrenchment of earth, which Grant assaulted all along the line. The assault was repulsed with extraordinary slaughter. In the short space of one hour 13,000 men were placed "hors de combat." Grant ordered a second assault in the after-

* In the Ordnance Museum, at Washington, is the stump of a large tree that had been cut down by bullets, so close and deadly was the musketry fire in the captured and recaptured salient.

noon. The men sullenly refused to advance.

After this battle General Grant gyrated toward the James River, below Richmond, crossed at City Point, and endeavored to surprise and capture Petersburg.

In this he was thwarted by Generals Beauregard and Wise, with the militia and homeguards. He then concentrated his army south of the Appomattox River and laid siege to the city.

"During the campaign reinforcements reached General Lee to the extent of 14,400 men, making 78,400 as the aggregate of all troops engaged under him from the Wilderness to Cold Harbor.

General Grant received 51,000 additional men during the same period, bringing his total up to 192,160 men employed by him from the Rapidan to the James.

"The Federal loss in the battles of the Wilderness, Spottsylvania, North Anna, and Cold Harbor is put at 'above 60,000 men' by Mr. Swinton, in his 'History of the Army of the Potomac.'"*

"The campaign of one month, from May 4th to June 4th, had cost the Federal commander 60,000 men and 3,000 officers, while

* Taylor's Four Years with Lee.

the loss of Lee did not exceed 18,000 men (of whom few were officers). The result would seem an unfavorable comment upon the choice of route made by General Grant. General McClellan, two years before, had reached Cold Harbor with trifling losses. To attain the same point had cost General Grant a frightful number of lives. Nor could it be said that he had any important success to offset this loss. He had not defeated his adversary in any of the battle-fields of the campaign, nor did it seem that he had stricken him any serious blow. The Army of Northern Virginia, not reinforced until it reached Hanover Junction, and then only by about 9,000 men, had repulsed every assault, and in the final trial of strength with a force vastly its superior, had inflicted upon the enemy, in about an hour, a loss of 13,000 men." *

When the army drew closer to Richmond, Mr. Davis's visits to General Lee, which had been previously made as often as his executive labor permitted, were paid every day, and the spirits in which the President returned were dependent on the General's account of the progress of the enemy; his temper always became more cheerful as affairs looked darker. Mr. Davis had a childlike faith in

---

* John Esten Cooke, in Eclectic Magazine, May, 1872.

the providential care of the Just Cause by Almighty God, and a doubt of its righteousness never entered his mind. Often I have
heard him in the night repeating to himself
with fervor his favorite hymn,

> " I'll strengthen thee, help thee, and cause thee to stand
> Upheld by my righteous, omnipotent hand."

When things grew darkest, he said, " We
can conquer a peace against the world in
arms, and keep the rights of freemen, if we
are worthy of the privilege. If he had de-
spaired of our cause he was too sincere to
have spoken words of hope to the soldiers.
After the army fell back to Petersburg, he
looked forward to personally taking command
in the West, and co-operating with General
Lee in one great battle which he hoped would
be decisive.

On one of the lonely rides he took to General Lee's headquarters, a very young soldier
joined him and went with him some distance
on the road. At last the President asked
him if he was not too far from camp, considering the close proximity of the enemy. Then
the boy told him, with a sheepish look, " I
joined you, sir, because you were so near
them, and I thought you ought not to be
alone. You ought to have a guard with you."
Mr. Davis noticed that he had on broken

shoes and proposed to change with him, but
the cheerful young patriot laughed and said
that was no matter, shook hands warmly, and
saying, " Now I think you are safe beyond
the enemy's scouts," bade good-by.

Our soldiers fought for the love they bore
to their country, but it was a desperate fight.
They had to contend against far more dreadful foes than the Federal army. They fought
cold, heat, starvation, and the knowledge that
their families were enduring the same priva-
tions. One poor fellow from Johnson's Island,
who was dying of the want endured there,
sent for me and asked me to write to his wife
of his last hours and give her his love. " I
have a letter from my wife," he said. " She
walked my little girl, who was just a month
old when I saw her last, up and down, up and
down, and tried willow-tea, and every other
remedy she could think of for the baby's
chills ; but the doctor said nothing but quinine could save her ; and Madam, my wife did
not have that, so my three years old baby
died, and now I am dying, and my poor,
starving wife will have nothing to comfort
her ; but," he panted out, " if our folks can
quit freemen, it is all right." This spirit of
devotion was manifested by the soldiers and
officers of the Confederacy everywhere, and
when their hearts failed them from brooding

over the needs of their helpless families, the
women choked back their tears, tried to forget their bare feet, their meagre fare, their
thousand alarms by night, and all the grinding
want that pressed them out of youth and life,
and wrote of the cheer our victories gave
them, of their prayers for success, and their
power to endure unto the end.

One noteworthy example of the self-sacrifice of our soldiers is remembered by me
with especial pride. On June 15 and 17,
1864, the women and children of Richmond
had been suffering for food, and the Thirtieth
Virginia sent them one day's rations of flour,
pork, bacon, and veal, not from their abundance, but by going without the day's rations
themselves. "Yet," said a journal of that
time, "despatches from General Lee show
that nearly every regiment in his army has
re-enlisted for the war."

On April 30th, when we were threatened
on every side, and encompassed so perfectly
that we could only hope by a miracle to overcome our foes, Mr. Davis's health declined
from loss of sleep so that he forgot to eat, and
I resumed the practice of carrying him something at one o'clock. I left my children quite
well, playing in my room, and had just uncovered my basket in his office, when a servant
came for me. The most beautiful and brightest

of my children, Joseph Emory, had, in play, climbed over the connecting angle of a bannister and fallen to the brick pavement below. He died a few minutes after we reached his side. This child was Mr. Davis's hope, and greatest joy in life. At intervals, he ejaculated, " Not mine, oh, Lord, but thine." A courier came with a despatch. He took it, held it open for some moments, and looked at me fixedly, saying, "Did you tell me what was in it?" I saw his mind was momentarily paralyzed by the blow, but at last he tried to write an answer, and then called out, in a heart-broken tone, "I must have this day with my little child." Somebody took the despatch to General Cooper and left us alone with our dead.

CHAPTER LI.

YELLOW TAVERN.—DEATH OF STUART.

ON the morning of May 13th, Mr. Davis came hurriedly in from the office for his pistols, and rode out to the front, where Generals Gracie and Ransom were disposing their skeleton brigades to repel General Sheridan's raiders, who had been hovering around for some days. At the Executive Mansion, the small-arms could be distinctly heard like the popping of fire-crackers. I summoned the children to prayer, and as my boy Jefferson knelt, he raised his little chubby face to me, and said, "You had better have my pony saddled, and let me go out to help father; we can pray afterward."

Wherever it was possible, the President went to the battle-field, and was present during the engagement, and at these times he bitterly regretted his executive office, and longed to engage actively in the fight.

A line of skirmishers had been formed near the Yellow Tavern, our forces were closely pressed, and seeing a brigade preparing to charge on the left, General J. E. B. Stuart dashed over there to form his troops and repel the charge. The Federals came thundering down, recognized Stuart, and fired twelve shots at him; he wheeled upon them and emptied his revolver, then checked his horse and rode for our lines, knowing he had been mortally wounded. His death-wound is said to have been dealt by a skulker concealed in a fence corner. A bullet struck him in the hip and passed through the abdomen. Like the Cid, he felt the menace to the foe his presence would be, and asked his staff to hold him upon the saddle, that the enemy might not see he was wounded. Thus supported, he rode into our lines to die, confident of having done his whole duty, at peace with God, and willing, if it was His will, to leave the struggle and the end to His good pleasure.

His wound was found to be necessarily mortal. His condition during Thursday, May 13, 1864, was very changeable, with occasional delirium and other unmistakable symptoms of dissolution. At these times his mind wandered, and like the immortal Jackson, in the lapse of reason his faculties were occupied with the details of his command. He reviewed, in broken sentences, all his glorious campaign around McClellan's rear on the Peninsula, beyond the Potomac, and upon the Rapidan, quoting from his own orders, with a last injunction "to make haste."

About noon, Thursday, President Davis visited his bedside and spent some fifteen minutes in the dying chamber of his young chieftain. The President, taking his hand, said, "General, how do you feel?" He replied, in his strong, cheery voice, "Easy, but willing to die, if God and my country think I have fulfilled my destiny and done my duty." Mr. Davis came home and knelt with me in a prayer in which he entreated that this "precious life might be spared to our needy country." As evening approached Stuart's delirium increased, and he wandered to the battle-fields over which he had fought, then to wife and children, and again to the front.

He held his family next only to his country. A notable instance was given once, when he was telegraphed that his first and only child was dying; this reply was sent with the tears raining over his cheeks: "I must leave my child in the hands of God, my country needs me here, I cannot come."

General Stuart was but thirty-one years old, yet he had attained a noble fame, and no one dissented from the praise bestowed upon "Beauty Stuart." He had lived void of offence toward his fellow-men, and life was for him one long feast of good-will toward them. From his boyhood, he had never sworn oaths or drunk spirituous liquors, or indeed indulged in any vice. With the simple faith of a child, he did what his conscience dictated. He sang, laughed, fought, and prayed throughout all the deprivations and hardships of the Confederate service, never daunted, never carping at the mistakes of others. When his young life was torn out of his stalwart body, and in the agonies of death he was told he could not live to see his young wife, as she could not reach him in the few hours left, he said gently, " I should have liked to have seen her, but God's will be done."

To the doctor, who sat holding his failing pulse, he remarked : " Doctor, I suppose I am going fast now. It will soon be over. But God's will be done. I hope I have fulfilled my duty to my country and my God."

At half-past seven o'clock it was evident to the physicians that death was very near, and they announced the fact, and asked him if he had any last messages to give. The General, with a mind entirely self-possessed, made disposition of his personal effects to his staff. To Mrs. R. E. Lee, he directed his golden spurs to be given as a dying memento of his love and esteem for her husband. To his

staff officers he gave his horses. So considerate was he in small things, even to his dying hour, that he said to one of his staff, who
was a very heavily built man, " You had better take the larger horse ; he will carry you
better." To his young son he left his glorious sword.

His worldly matters closed, he turned to
the contemplation of eternity, and asked the
Reverend Mr. Peterkin, of the Episcopal
Church, of which he was an exemplary member, to sing the hymn commencing,

> " Rock of ages, cleft for me,
> Let me hide myself in thee,"

and joined with all the voice his strength permitted. He then united in prayer with the
minister. To the doctor he again said, " I
am going fast now ; God's will be done."
Thus died General J. E. B. Stuart, the great
cavalry leader and exemplary Christian, at
peace with God and man.

His wife reached the house of death about
ten o'clock on the Thursday night, about one
hour and a half after his dissolution, and the
poor young creature was utterly desolate.
Her father was a Federal general in the regular army, and she was separated even from
her family in her hour of trial. General
Philip St. George Cooke, however, was an

honorable foe, and his old friends sorrowed with her for his sake also.

No military escort accompanied the procession, but our young hero was laid in his last resting-place on the hill-side, while the earth trembled with the roar of artillery and the noise of the deadly strife of two armies —the one bent upon desecrating and devastating his native land, and the other defiantly standing in the path, but invoking the blessing of Heaven upon their cause. They fought in better cheer for the memory of such sainted leaders as Stonewall Jackson and Beauty Stuart.

CHAPTER LII.

BOMBARDMENT OF CHARLESTON.

On August 21, 1863, a letter without signature was sent from Major-General Gilmore's headquarters, in front of Charleston, to General Beauregard, informing him that unless certain extraordinary conditions were complied with, or if no reply thereto was received within "*four hours*" after the delivery of the letter at Battery Wagner for transmission to Charleston, fire would be opened on the city from batteries already established. General Beauregard received that letter about eleven o'clock at night, and two hours later, when the city was in profound repose, Major-General Gilmore opened fire on it, and threw a number of the most destructive projectiles ever before used against the sleeping and unarmed population. If Major-General Gilmore only desired to go through the barren form of giving notice of his intentions without allowing the non-combatants time to withdraw, he would have accomplished that useless end, if, in his haste and eagerness to begin his work,

CONFEDERATE GENERALS.

he had not forgotten to sign so important a letter.

The time allowed was four hours from the delivery of the letter at Battery Wagner for transmission to General Beauregard's head-quarters, five miles distant. Major-General Gilmore knew very well that in the ordinary course of transmission, all the time allowed would elapse before he could receive a reply to his demand, and he knew quite as well that it was impossible, in the brief space of time allowed, to remove the non-combatants of a large and populous city. It is clear, therefore, that due time was not allowed, and that the object of the notification was not *that non-combatants might be removed.*

The object of the foe, according to Major-General Gilmore, was to enforce the surrender of an important fort which he could not re-duce, for after withstanding for nearly a year the most formidable bombardment from land and naval batteries ever before directed on one fort, the Confederate flag was still flying on Fort Sumter. Failing in that, his next ob-ject was to destroy the city to its very *heart*, or to make it uninhabitable by non-combatants.

Independently of the declaration of Major-General Gilmore that his purpose was to reach "the heart of the city," the manner in which the fire had been directed from the

commencement, showed beyond doubt that its
object was the destruction of the city itself,
and every part of it, and not, as assumed,
to destroy certain military and naval works in
and immediately around it.

Having failed to frighten the Confederate
commander into compliance with his unreasonable demand, Major-General Gilmore
threw a few more shells (twenty-seven in all)
into the city, for no conceivable object than to
frighten away and kill a few non-combatants,
to show how far he could throw his projectiles,
to gratify a spirit of malice, and then ceased.
From August 21st to October 27th, not a
shot or shell was thrown into the city.

He doubtless supposed that by that time
the non-combatants, whom he supposed had
been frightened away, had returned to the
city ; for he knew well that the mass of non-
combatant population of a large city situated
as Charleston, would not, and could not,
abandon their houses permanently and become homeless wanderers. He knew that
the climate of the country immediately around
Charleston was considered deadly at that
season of the year to white persons, and that
if any poor people, unable to secure residences
in the sparsely settled interior, had fled, on
the beginning of the fire, to the immediately
surrounding country to escape his shells,

they would naturally, after so long an intermission of fire, return to the city to escape the malaria, more deadly than his projectiles.

On October 27th, after an interval of more than two months, without a word of warning, he again opened fire and threw shells into the city, just enough to frighten, irritate, and kill a few non-combatants, but not enough to produce any military result, and then ceased firing for three weeks.

On November 17th, he again opened and continued a very slow fire. It was apparent that the fire was directed against churches during the hours of public worship, Christmas-day, 1863.

The Confederate prisoners in the hands of the enemy were held confined, under the fire of our batteries, to hinder our resistance.

CHAPTER LIII.

GRANT'S plan of campaign was, if he should be unable to defeat Lee, or fail to take Richmond, to cross the James River below Richmond, and possess himself of Petersburg, cut off the supplies from the Confederate Capital, and, reinforced by Butler with 30,000 men, attack it from the south.

Butler was ordered to concentrate his troops at City Point. From this base he was to destroy the railroad leading to Richmond. On May 7th he telegraphed he had " destroyed many miles of railroad, and got a position which, with proper supplies, we can hold against Lee's whole army."

On May 10th General Butler was badly beaten at Walthall Junction, and returned to his intrenched lines at Bermuda Hundreds.

The Confederate troops which had been ordered from Charleston under Beauregard, on May 14th reached the intrenched lines in the vicinity of Drury's Bluff. Butler moved forward again to confront them.

General Robert Ransom said, in a monograph upon this battle : " Beauregard, with headquarters at Charleston, had been urged to send up troops from his department, but none had arrived. Butler had moved up so as to cut the telegraph on the turnpike, and reach by a raiding party the railroad at Chester, during the first week in May. I was near Drury's Bluff with a battery of light guns and Barton's and Gracie's brigades, and our company of irregular cavalry. The President came to my camp, and finding out the state of affairs, asked if anything could be done to retard Butler's movements, stating that as Beauregard would not send troops, he had been peremptorily ordered to bring them, and that some were on the way. Knowing that audacity was my best arm, the next morning, with perfect leisure and with a front sufficient to cover an army of 50,000 men, I pushed upon Butler's advance, had a sharp skirmish, and came near capturing a brigade and battery, and Butler withdrew. Some of Beauregard's troops drove him from the railroad and turnpike, at Port Walthall. Upon Beauregard's arrival at Petersburg he was given command as far north as to include Drury's Bluff. While lying near Drury's Bluff on the night of May 9th, about ten o'clock, I got a despatch informing me of the fall of J. E. B. Stuart, mortally wounded, at Yellow Tavern, and that

Sheridan was expected to assault the outer works north of Richmond, at dawn the next day. Immediately my two movable brigades, Gracie's and Fry's, and a light battery were hastened to and through Richmond, and I arrived with them at the fortifications on Mechanicsville turnpike just in time, the morning of May 10th, to see a battery of artillery there, unsupported by anything, repulse the advance of Sheridan. During the night the clerks and citizens, under General Custis Lee, had spread a thin line along part of the fortifications toward the west, near the Brook and Meadow Bridge roads. Hunton's brigade was at Chafin's Bluff, it being impracticable to withdraw it from that position. As the day advanced Gracie's brigade was thrown in front of the works and pressed forward to feel Sheridan, but it was soon evident that we could make no real impression on him, and I regarded it as almost madness with two small brigades to engage in an open country five times my strength, thereby leaving Richmond entirely unprotected, except by the clerks and citizens. Sheridan withdrew, Gracie's and Fry's brigades returned to near Drury's Bluff.

During the week most all of Beauregard's troops had come up. In obedience to a despatch from him, at about 2 or 2.30 P.M., I met Beauregard at Major Drury's residence, about

a mile from the Bluff. He was surrounded by
a large staff, and clerks were busy. He accosted me with much gravity, almost solemnity, intimated to those present to withdraw, we were
alone, with perhaps the exception of two or
three persons. I remarked that I had got his
despatch and had come as quickly as possible.
He asked me if the President had told me
what I was wanted for, and to my replying
no, Beauregard said, in about these words :
' The President has ordered me to give Butler battle at once. It is against my judgment, and I have protested against it, but to
no avail. You make the fight to-morrow,
and you are to command the left wing.
Among other reasons given for not fighting
was that I am without officers to command,
and particularly those who know this country.
The President said you could be spared temporarily, and as you know the region, I have
given you the moving part of the army, and
you will take the initiative.' By this time the
room was again filled with officers and couriers, and a copy of the order of battle was
handed me. After reading it and finding that
Ransom's brigade formed part of the reserve,
I asked that it might be given to me in exchange for any I had had assigned to me,
stating that ' I had organized and commanded
it for more than a year, and that I knew it

and it knew me.' General Beauregard declined to make the change, saying, 'It is
the strongest brigade in my army, and I must
hold it in case of disaster.'

"My staff, couriers, and horses were in
Richmond, and were sent for;' there was not
a wagon to my division. Everything that I
could do was done to be ready. By sundown staff and horses had arrived, and by
10 P.M., or a little later, I was in position in
front of the breastworks on Drury's plantation. An independent regiment of cavalry
was to move between me and the river, for
information. At the first glimpse of daylight I moved to the south of Kingsland
Creek, and at once pushed upon the enemy.
A dense fog had suddenly enveloped everything. The skirmishers were quickly engaged, and immediately a general infantry
fire. The fighting was pressed to conclusion,
and by sunrise I had captured a brigade of
infantry and a battery of artillery, and swept
and occupied about three-quarters of a mile
of the enemy's temporary breastworks, which
were strengthened by wire interwoven among
the trees in their front; not however without
considerable loss and much confusion, owing
to the denseness of the fog. Requiring infantry cartridges, and knowing that delay
would mar the success gained, I sent instantly

to Beauregard reporting what had happened, and asked that Ransom's brigade might come to me at once to continue the pressure and make good the advantage already gained. Beauregard refused. The ammunition being still delayed, I again begged that Ransom's brigade be sent me, but instead of that there came two small regiments from Georgia. Just as they reported to me the fog lifted, the enemy made a dash on Hoke's left and broke Hagood's brigade ; but I threw these two Georgia regiments upon the advancing enemy, checked and repulsed him. After this I saw no more of the Georgia regiments, hearing however that by Beauregard's orders they had gone elsewhere. At this junction, and having been supplied ammunition, and while clearing away some trees that had luckily been felled by the enemy across the road, I got an order from Beauregard to advance by 'brigades in échelon, left in front.' This movement was begun, Gracie's brigade leading and I with it. After advancing some distance I heard firing to right and rear, and galloping in that direction to ascertain its cause, failed to find my two rearmost brigades where they ought to have been. The firing had ceased, and to my anxiety I found that a wide interval between my two left brigades and the other troops existed. Hastening on, I discovered my troops upon the line of our breastworks. Sending word to halt the forward brigades, and ordering the others to their positions, I galloped to Beauregard, then in sight and only two or three hundred yards off, I reported what had happened, and asked that nothing similar be permitted. He said, 'It is as well, I am hard pressed on the right, and we may have to withdraw to the breastworks, and most of our force come to the right; I fear my flank may be turned,' or words to that effect.

"I remained with Beauregard at his request for perhaps an hour. The firing did not indicate hard fighting on the right. There was no firing on my front. I heard, while with Beauregard, that the enemy was moving over the turnpike. This was reported to Beauregard direct. After being with Beauregard, I suppose an hour, I left for my command, awaiting his directions, as he had ordered me to remain stationary till he gave different instructions. Beauregard more than once, while I remained with him, remarked upon not hearing anything of Whiting, and seemed nervous about him. The day wore away, and I, becoming more than impatient, about 3 P.M., as I recall the time, went to seek Beauregard. I found him with many other gentlemen, the President, and Secretary Reagan, among others, in the turnpike just north of where the fortifications cross it. I heard no firing of any sort except an occasional shot from a field battery of the enemy, its shells were thrown directly up the turnpike. While we all stood in this locality a slight shower of rain fell, not enough to wet anyone in even thin clothing. A little before five o'clock, I think, Beauregard seemed to have determined upon some aggressive movement. I was directed to have my troops ready to move at an instant's notice, and to await orders. I galloped to my division and waited with impatience and disgust till after sundown, when the order came, ' Bivouac for the night.' About an hour or so after sunrise the next day, the 17th, we were ordered to move down the river road. Proceeding to some distance below the Howlett place, at about 4 P.M., not having come upon the enemy, I was relieved from command by a commendatory order. . . . Immediately I returned to my duties north of the James.

"Beauregard reluctantly came to the theatre of active war. He made verbal and written protests against giving battle to Butler. He courted defeat by expecting it. He showed repeatedly that he did not think victory possible. He refused me Ransom's brigade, anticipating ' disaster.' He held me by his side for an hour and delayed or stopped the movement of my division after 10 or 11 A.M. He looked for the turning of his flank, and was preparing for retreat to within intrenchments while the enemy was escaping, and not until Butler was safe at Bermuda Hundreds did Beauregard realize that victory complete and crushing ought, and could easily have been inflicted upon Butler. This, like other of his battles, was to be fought over on paper to establish Beauregard's record.

" The sequel to the battle of Drury's Bluff was in keeping with Beauregard's efforts to father upon the true and gallant Ewell, Beauregard's shortcomings at First Manassas, when, utterly failing, they were laid upon an unknown and nameless courier ; it is but another exemplification of that prolific incapacity which turned the rich fruit of the splendid genius of Sidney Johnston at Shiloh into bitter ashes."

Our troops were then withdrawn to an inner and shorter line, closer to the works at Drury's.

" On the afternoon of the 14th," wrote Mr. Davis, " I rode down to visit General Beauregard.*

---

* A letter from General Beauregard to General Bragg, dated Weldon, April 29th, gave the names of the Federal generals commanding forces on the Southern coast. The arrival, he said,

" My first question on meeting him was to learn why the intrenchments were abandoned. He answered that he thought it better to concentrate his troops. Upon my stating to him that there was nothing then to prevent Butler from turning his position, he said he would desire nothing better, as he would then fall upon him, cut off his base, etc.

" According to my uniform practice never to do more than make a suggestion to a general commanding in the field, the subject was pressed no further. We then passed to the consideration of the operations to be undertaken against Butler, who had already advanced from his base at Bermuda Hundreds. I offered, for the purpose of attacking Butler, to send General Ransom with the field force he had for the protection of Richmond. He

---

of any of these officers in Virginia would indicate the transfer of their troops thither, and concluded by saying that if it were desired he should operate on the north side of James River, maps ought to be prepared for him, and timbers, etc., for bridges ; and that he would serve with pleasure under the immediate command of General Lee, " aiding him to crush our enemies, and to achieve the independence of our country."

To-day the President sent it back endorsed as follows : "Maps of the country, with such additions as may from time to time be made, should be kept on hand in the Engineer Bureau, and furnished to officers in the field. Preparations of material for bridges, etc., will continue to be made as heretofore, and with such additional effort as circumstances require.

"I did not doubt the readiness of General Beauregard to serve under any general who ranks him. The right of General Lee to command would be derived from his superior rank. " JEFFERSON DAVIS."

reported to General Beauregard on the 15th, received his orders for the battle, which was to occur the next day, and about 10 P.M. was in position in front of the breastworks. A regiment of cavalry, not under Ransom's orders, was to guard the space between his left and the river, to give him information of any movement in that quarter.

General Whiting, with some force, was holding a defensive position at Petersburg. General Beauregard proposed that the main part of it should advance and unite with him in an attack upon Butler, wherever he should be found between Drury's and Petersburg. To this I offered distinct objection, because of the hazard, during a battle, of attempting to make a junction of troops moving from opposite sides of the enemy, and proposed that Whiting's command should move at night by the Chesterfield road, where they would not probably be observed by Butler's advance. This march I supposed they could make so as to arrive at Drury's soon after daylight. The next day being Sunday, they could rest, and all the troops being assigned to their positions, they could move to make a concerted attack at daylight on Monday.

" On Monday morning, I rode down to Drury's, where I found that the enemy had seized our line of intrenchments, it being unoccupied, and that a severe action had occurred, with a serious loss to us, before he could be dislodged. He had crossed the main road to the west, entering a dense wood, and our troops on the right had moved out and were closely engaged with him. We drove him back, frustrating the attempt to turn the extreme right of our line. The day was wearing away, a part of the force had been withdrawn to the intrenchments, and there was no sign of purpose to make any immediate movement. General Beauregard said he was waiting to hear Whiting's guns, and had been expecting him for some time to approach on the Petersburg road. Soon after this the foe, in a straggling, disorganized manner, commenced crossing the road, moving to the east, which indicated a retreat, perhaps a purpose to turn our left and attack Fort Drury in rear. He placed a battery in the main road and threw some shells at our intrenchments, probably to cover his retiring troops." *

One of the enemy's solid shot struck at the very feet of President Davis as he stood at the edge of the turnpike in conversation with General Beauregard. They, without apparently noticing the "close call," stepped slowly and deliberately out of range.

---

* Colonel W. Miller Owen : In Camp and Battle.

The enemy's guns soon limbered up and moved off, and Butler was in full retreat to Bermuda Hundreds.

On the next morning our troops moved down the river road as far as Howlett's, but saw no enemy.

General Beauregard, President Davis, and his aide, Colonel William Preston Johnston, were standing on the earthworks listening intently. Presently a single gun was heard in the distance. "Ah!" said Mr. Davis, "at last!" and a smile of satisfaction stole over his face.

But that solitary gun was all, and Butler retreated unmolested to his lines at Bermuda Hundreds.

"Soon after the affair at Drury's Bluff, General Beauregard addressed to me a communication, proposing that he should be heavily reinforced from General Lee's army, so as to enable him to crush Butler in his intrenchments, and then, with the main body of his own force, together with the detachment from General Lee's army, that he should join General Lee, crush Grant, and march to Washington." *

The following is the communication alluded to above.

---

* Mr. Davis, in Rise and Fall.

Richmond Va
12 Jany 65.

Mems. of a confidential conversation held this day with F.P. Blair of
Montgomery County Md.

———

Mr. Blair stated that not receiving
an answer to his application for permission to visit Richmond, which
had been sent from the Hd. Qrs. of
Genl Grants army, he returned to
Washington and there received the
reply which had been made to his
application, but by some means
had been withheld from him and
been forwarded after being been opened.

That he had originally obtained permission to visit Richmond from
Mr. Lincoln after stating to him that
he (Mr. B) had for many years held
friendly relations ~~with me then saying that with me~~
~~Mr. Lincoln, stopped him, the stated in application of his petition.~~ That with me
~~his feelings for me were unchanged~~
That he being a man of southern
blood felt very desirous to see the
War between the states terminated and
hoped by an interview with me to be
to able to effect something to that end.

That after receiving the pass which had been sent to him by my direction, he sought before returning, to have a conversation with Mr. Lincoln, had two appointments for that purpose but on each occasion was disappointed and from the circumstances concluded that Mr. Lincoln avoided the interview and therefore came not only without credentials but without such instructions from Mr. Lincoln as would have enabled him to speak for him. His views therefore were to be regarded merely as his own and said they were perhaps merely the dreams of an old man &c.

He said despairing of being able to see me he had determined to write to me and had the rough draft of a letter which he had prepared, and asked permission to read it. Soon after commencing to do so he said (pleasantly) that he found his style was marked by his old pursuit and that the paper appeared too much like an editorial. He omitted therefore portions of it reading what he considered the main points of his proposition. He had recognized the difference of our positions as not entitling him to a response from me, to to the arguments and suggestions which he desired to offer. I therefore allowed him to read without comment on my part. When he had finished I inquired as to his main proposition the cessation of hostilities, and the union of the military forces for the common purpose of maintaining the "Monroe doctrine" how that object was to be reached. He said that both the political parties of the U.S. asserted the Monroe doctrine as a cardinal point of their creed. That there was a general desire to apply it to the case of Mexico. For that purpose a secret treaty might be made as

I called his attention to my past efforts for negociation and my inability to see unless Mr. Lincoln's course in that regard should be changed, how we were to take the first step. He expressed the belief that Mr. Lincoln would now receive commissioners, but subsequently said he could not give any assurance on that point, and proposed to return to Washington to explain his project to Mr. Seward, and notify me if his hope proved well founded that Mr. Lincoln would now agree to a conference for the purpose of entering into negociations

She affirmed that Mr. Lincoln
did not sympathize with the radical
men who desired the devastation and
subjugation of the southern states; but
that he was unable to control the extreme
party which now had great power in
the Congress and would at the next
session have still more. Referred to the
existence of two parties in the Cabinet, to the
reluctant nomination of Mr. Chase to be
chief justice &c. &c. &c.

For himself avowed an earnest desire to
stop the further effusion of blood, as were every
drop of whose blood was southern he expressed
the hope that the pride the power and the
honor of the southern states should suffer no shock.
Looked to the extension of southern territory
even to the Isthmus of Darien, and hoped
if his views found favor that his wishes
would be realized. Reiterated the idea of
state sovereignty with illustrations and accepted the reference I made to explanation
given in the "Globe" when he edited it, of the
Proclamation of Presd. Jackson.

When his attention was called to the brutal
atrocities of their armies, especially the fiendish
cruelty shown to helpless women and children
as the cause of a deep seated hostility on the
part of our people and an insurmountable
obstacle to an early restoration of fraternal relations
he admitted the necessity for providing a new

channel for the better sorted, and another bond them that of former memories & interests this was supposed to be contained in the proposed common effort to maintain the "Monroe doctrine" on the American continent.

It was evident that he counted on the disintegration of the Confederate states if the war continued, and a that in any event he regarded the institution of slavery as doomed to extinction. I thought any remark by me on the first would lead to intimations in connection with public men which I preferred not more distinctly to know, than as manifested in his general remarks, on the latter point for the reason stated the inequality of his responsibility and mine I preferred to have no discussion.

The only difficulty which he spoke of as insurmountable, was that of existing engagements between European powers and the Confederate states. This point when referred to a second time as the decided obstacle to a short treaty which would terminate the war, was met by me with a statement that we had now no such complication. were free to act as we should seem best, and desired to keep state policy and institutions free from foreign control. throughout the conference Mr. Blair appeared to be animated by a sincere desire to promote a pacific solution of existing difficulty, but claimed no active power then that of serving as a medium of Communication between those who had thus far had no intercourse and were therefore without the conferences which might secure an adjustment of their controversy.

To his hopeful anticipation in regard to the restoration of fraternal relation between the sections by the means indicated, I replied that a cessation of hostilities was the first step towards the substitution of reason for passion, of sense of justice for a desire to injure, and that if the people were subsequently engaged together to maintain a principle recognized by both if together they should bear sacrifices share dangers and gather common renown, that new memories would take the place of those now planted by the events of this war, and might in the course of time restore the feelings which preexisted. But it was for us to deal with the problems before us and leave to posterity questions which they might solve though we could not. That in the struggle for independence ~~by the american~~ by our Colonial fathers had failure instead of success attended their effort, great Britain instead of a Commerce which has largely contributed to her prosperity, would have had the heavy expense of numerous garrisons to hold in subjection a people who deserved to be free and had resolved not to be subject.

Our conference ended with no other result than an agreement that he would learn whether Mr. Lincoln would, adopt his Mr. Blair's project and send to receive Commissioners to negociate for a peaceful solution of the questions at issue, that he would repeat to him my readiness to enter upon negociation and that I knew of no insurmountable obstacle to such a treaty of peace as would secure greater advantages to both parties than any result which arms could achieve.

4th Jany. 1865

The foregoing memorandum of conversation was this day read to Mr. Blair and ~~introduced and~~ altered in so far as he desired in ~~~~ respect to change the expressions employed.

Jeffer Davis.

"CONFEDERATE STATES, HEADQUARTERS DEPARTMENT
"NORTH AND SOUTH CAROLINA AND VIRGINIA,
"HANCOCK HOUSE, May 18, 1864, 9.30 P.M.

" Memorandum :

" The crisis demands prompt and decisive action. For this, the two armies are now too far apart, unless we consent to give up Petersburg, and place the capital in jeopardy. If General Lee will fall back behind the Chickahominy, engaging the enemy so as to draw him on, General Beauregard can bring up fifteen thousand men to unite with Breckenridge and fall upon the enemy's flank with over twenty thousand effectives—thus rendering Grant's defeat certain and decisive ; and in time to enable General Beauregard to return, with a reinforcement from General Lee, to drive Butler from before Petersburg, and from his present position. For three days, perhaps four, Petersburg and Richmond can be held by the forces left behind ; not longer.

" Without such concentration nothing decisive can be effected, and the picture presented is one of starvation. Without it General Lee must eventually fall back before Grant's heavy reinforcements, and the view presented merely anticipates this movement for offensive purposes. Meantime it is impossible to effectually protect our lines of

communication with North Carolina; and impossible to hold our present line in front of
Butler with a much reduced force. At present three thousand men can be spared with
safety. Day after to-morrow two thousand
more, perhaps, as our lines will probably be
stronger, if, as we expect, the forward line
can be occupied to-day.

(Signed)   " P. T. BEAUREGARD,
                " General Commanding."

.Endorsement on the above :

" GENERAL BRAGG, Commanding, etc., etc.

" This memorandum was handed to me
this day by Colonel Melton, A. & I. General's Department, and is referred to you for
attention. General Lee is best informed of
his situation, and his ability is too well established to incline me to adopt the opinion of
anyone at a distance as to the movements
which his army should make, either for its
preservation or the protection of its communications.

" If fifteen thousand men can be spared for
the flank movement proposed, certainly ten
thousand may be sent to reinforce General
Lee. If that be done *immediately*, General
Lee's correspondence warrants the belief that
he will defeat the enemy in Northern Virginia.

30th December 1864

Jefferson Davis
President &c &c
My dear Sir

The fact stated in
the enclosed note may serve to
answer enquiries as to the object
my visit, which, if ~~permitted~~
allowed by you I would not

communicate fully to any
one but yourself. The main
purpose I have in seeing you
is to confirm the views I entertain in reference to the state
of the affairs of our Country
and to submit to your consideration ideas, which in my opinion
you may turn to good account

2

and ~~some~~ properly, ~~conceived to~~
bring to practical results that
may, not only,
~~approve all~~ the ruin the
war has brought upon ~~this nation~~
but contribute to promote the
welfare
~~of all the~~ ~~the calamity of~~ ~~other nations~~ & others
that have suffered from it

In candor I must say
to you a Sir that I come
to you wholly unaccredited, except
in so far as I may be by having
permission to pass our lines &
offer to you my own suggestion.
Suggestions which I have submitted
to to no one in authority on this
side the lines & will not without
my conversation with you may
lead me to suppose they may ~~result~~
in something practical~~able~~ with the
hope of such result, if allowed,

well confidentially unknown to
have frankly & without reserve.
You will on your part, more
~~as~~ of course hold in reserve
all that is not proper to be said
to one coming as I merely as
a private citizen & addressing
one clothed with the highest
responsibilities;

unless the great interests
now at stake induce you to give
attribute more importance to
my application than it would
otherwise command, I could not
expect that you would invite
the intrusion — I confine known
to submit the matter to your judgment.

yours &c J.P. Blair

Washington, Jan. 18. 1865

F. P. Blair, Esq
Sir:
Your having shown
me Mr. Davis' letter to you of
the 12th Inst. you may say to
him that I have constantly been,
am now, and shall continue,
ready to receive any agent
whom he, or any other influence
that person now resisting the national authority, may informally
send to me, with the view of
securing peace to the people of
our one common country.

Yours &c
A. Lincoln.

" The advantage of that result of our success against a besieging army around Richmond is obvious.

(Signed) " JEFFERSON DAVIS."

"May 19, 1864."

Military courtesy required that the *memoranda* should be sent to General Lee, who, as soon as its purport was communicated to him, ordered General Beauregard to straighten his line, so as to reduce the number of men required to hold it, and *send* the *remainder to him.*

CHAPTER LIV.

THE LACK OF FOOD AND THE PRICES IN THE CON-FEDERACY.

To those who insist that the prisoners from the Northern army were maliciously starved, with murderous intent, I dedicate the following statistical compilation of the prices of provisions in Richmond and other places.

Our hapless soldiers starved and froze in the Northern prisons in the midst of plenty, but the benefit release would have been to them would not have been an increase in their comfort or in their bill of fare; the improvement in their state would have been induced by the sunshine and freedom. The sense of abject want would have been less insupportable in a community of deprivation and suffering with their comrades, as well as of active patriotic effort to serve the country.

Some quotations are taken from the diaries of private individuals, and also from my own domestic experience.

If, after reading these statistics, my readers

WADE HAMPTON

BRAXTON BRAGG

J. D. IMBODEN.

ALBERT SIDNEY JOHNSTON.

R. S. EWELL

JUBAL A. EARLY.

CONFEDERATE GENERALS.

will weigh the facts impartially, our vindication will be complete. Thousands of men were quartered upon us, at Andersonville and elsewhere, for whom we had neither food, clothes, nor medicine; the supplies in the country had been exhausted, the blockade prevented manufactured goods or medicines from being brought in to replenish our stores. The enemy had made medicines contraband of war, the food was not plentiful enough to feed our armies in the field, or the officers of the Government, much better than the prisoners; and the United States Government would not carry out the provisions of the cartel for fear of reinforcing our army by the return of the prisoners in their hands, and their prisoners and ours died of want and homesickness. To whom belonged the shame and the inhumanity of the needless sacrifice?

In July, 1862, both sections issued fractional notes in enormous quantities, and at first there was a sense of relief, and they fluttered from hand to hand "like leaves in wintry weather;" but gold rose in New York to ten per cent., and in Richmond to almost any per cent. the traders charged. By July 14th, it had advanced in New York to fifteen per cent.; the prices of provisions in the Confederacy on July 19, 1862, were:

Beef, pork, and mutton, 37½ cents per pound; shoat, 50 cents per pound; chickens, 57 cents to $1 apiece; ducks, $1 to $1.50 apiece; goslings, $2; pullets, $1 to $1.50 apiece; eggs, 75 cents to $1 per dozen; butter, 75 cents to $1 per pound.

Vegetables—beans, 50 cents per bunch: onions, 50 cents per quart (or one shilling apiece for the largest size); cymlings, $1 per dozen; cucumbers, $1 per dozen; string beans, $2 per peck; cabbage, 50 cents to 75 cents per head; Irish potatoes, $6 per bushel; tomatoes, $1.50 per dozen; blackberries, 25 cents per quart; whortleberries, 35 cents per quart; plums, 50 cents per quart; peaches, $1 per dozen.

Prices increased steadily for all varieties of food, as the supplies decreased and the value of Confederate money declined.

Ham was, on July 23, 1862, 75 cents per pound; small quarters of lamb from three to four dollars each; eggs, $1 per dozen; coffee, of poor quality, $2.50 per pound; butter, $1 and upward per pound; tea, $5 per pound; boots, $20 to $25 per pair; shoemakers' wages, $5 per diem.

November, 1862—coffee, which had in four months nearly doubled in price, $4 a pound; all good tea from $18 to $20 a pound; butter, $1.50 to $2 a pound; lard, 50 cents;

corn, $15 per barrel; wheat, $4.50 a bushel; muslin, $6 to $8 a yard; calico, $1.75 a yard; bleached cotton, $3.50 a yard; cotton, 50 cents a spool; soap, $1 a pound.

The price for coffee was now prohibitory to those who were not speculators.

The Confederate women made a substitute for coffee out of parched sweet potatoes and parched corn, and also of the grain of rye; for sugar they used sorghum syrup. They wove cotton cloth for blankets, and sewed up coverings for their feet out of old carpets, or rather such bits as were left after cutting them up for soldiers' blankets. They had only carpet or canvas soles. Blankets could not be had, and Bishop Meade sent his study carpet to the soldiers for blankets. One gentleman of Halifax County, in 1862, sent eight to be cut up for the same purpose.

" July—calico, $2.50 a yard at a bargain, and $3.50 and $4 a yard. The ladies paid, on January, 1863, for canvas boots made of old sails, cut out by the shoemaker but stitched and bound by the ladies, for sewing on the soles, $50. Last year he soled them for $10, and they were blacked with gun blacking." Shoes, $125 to $150. Ink was made of elderberries; flour cost $300 a barrel.

February 10, 1863.—General Lee wrote to the Secretary of War, on January 22d, that his army was not fed well enough to fit them for the exertions of the spring campaign, and recommended the discontinuance of the rule of the Commissary-General allowing officers at Richmond, Petersburg, and many other towns, to purchase government meat, etc., for the subsistence of their families, at schedule prices.

This letter was referred to the Commissary-General, who, after the usual delay, returned it with a long argument to show that General Lee was in "error," and that the practice was necessary, etc.

To this the Secretary responded by a peremptory order, restricting the *city officers* in the item of meat.

"Sugar is $20 per pound; new bacon, $8; and chickens, $12 per pair. Soon we look for a money panic, when a few hundred millions of paper money is funded, and as many more collected by the tax collectors. Congress struck the speculators a hard blow. One man, eager to invest his money, gave $100,000 for a house and lot, and he now pays $5,000 tax on it; the interest is $6,000 more; total $11,000."

Here is a notice from the livery stables in 1863:

ELLYSON.

A discount of Five per ct. on Bills for this paid AT THE OFFICE of the Chamberlain (before the hour of 3, P. M.) within five days after presentation.

To the Richmond City Gas Works,   No. 733

M_____ President Regis

Premises,

For Gas consumed from	1 July Mon	to	1 Oct June 1865.
State of Meter at this date,		316600	
Less do. at last settlement.		3,034 c	
Consumption,		13200	at $5 00 per thousand feet, $ 79.20
Less 5 per cent. discount for prompt payment of the bill within five days,			$

Presented June 13   Month

B. B. Howard Clk in Chf Office.

Recieved Payment,

By an Ordinance passed by the Council, May 6th, 1858, If any Bill remain unpaid for TEN DAYS next after that on which it is presented, the Auditor shall notify the Superintendent who shall stop the Gas from being used on the premises in respect to which the default exists; and, if not paid within fifteen days, 5 per cent, will be added to the original amount of the bill, and it shall be placed in the hands of the City Collector.

Richmond Gas to Richmond Arsenal,

1865 to seven cords J. wood @ $350 or $245.00

Received payment in full

Richmond
Feb. 14. 1865.

W. L. Brown
Lt. Col. Com

by J. W. Boards

"Notice—Owing to the heavy advance of feed, we are compelled to charge the following rates for boarding horses, on and after the first of March :

Board per month.....................$300
Board per day....................... 15
Single feed......................... 5

"Virginia Stables.   JAMES C. JOHNSON,
W. H. SUTHERLAND,
B. W. GREEN."

The family of the President had no perquisites, and bought their provender as they did their provisions, at the public marts and at the current prices. The President must have horses to perform his duty toward the army; but, after disposing of everything else available, Mr. Davis had sold every horse he could spare; and during his absence in the West, I sent my carriage and horses to be sold by a dealer. Some gentlemen of Richmond heard of it and bought the horses, and returned them to me. The note accompanying them was greatly prized, but how the horses, which of course could not be again sold, were to be fed, could not be foreseen.

Our deprivations were far less than those of persons not holding such high official positions, but they were many. A notice written by General R. Ransom, which is quoted in another part of this volume, gives an account of a breakfast at the Executive mansion, to the meagreness of which our necessities, not my will, consented.

"February 21st.—I saw a ham sell to-day for $350; it weighed fifty pounds, at $7 per pound. The fear is now, from a plethora of paper money, we shall soon be without a sufficiency for a circulating medium. There are $750,000,000 in circulation, and the tax bills, etc., will call in, it is estimated, $800,000,000."

"February 22d.—The offices are closed to-day, in honor of Washington's birthday. But it is a *fast* day; meal selling for $40 per bushel. Money will not be so abundant a month hence."

"To-day bacon is selling for $6 per pound, and all other things in proportion. A negro (for his master) asked me to-day $40 for an old, tough turkey gobbler. I passed on very briskly."

"It is rumored by blockade-runners that gold in the North is selling at from 200 to 500 per cent. premium. If this be true, our day of deliverance is not far distant."

"February 18, 1864.—Sugar has risen to $10 and $12 a pound."

"February 20th.—The price of turkey to-day is $60."

"March 12th.—Flour at $300 per barrel; meal, $50 per bushel; and even fresh fish at

$5 per pound. A market-woman asked $5 to-day for half a pint of snap beans to plant."

" Those having families may possibly live on their salaries ; but those who live at boarding-houses cannot, for board is now from $200 to $300 a month. Relief must come soon from some quarter, *else many in this community will famish.*"

" About noon to-day, a despatch came from Lieutenant-Colonel Cole, General Lee's principal commissary, at Orange Court House, dated 12th inst., saying the army was out of meat, and had but one day's rations of bread."

" March 18th.—I saw adamantine candles sell at auction to-day (box) at $10 per pound ; tallow, $6.50. Bacon brought $7.75 per pound by the 100 pounds."

" Flour selling in Columbus, Ga., 75 cents a pound, from wagons. Flour by the bushel, $5, meal $1, in 1864."

" March 25th.—Flour, $15 a barrel."

" March 29th.—Great crowds are funding their Treasury notes to-day; but prices of provisions are not diminished. White beans, such as I paid $60 a bushel for early this month, are now held at $75. What shall we do to subsist until the next harvest ? "

" April 1, 1864.—Tea, $22 ; coffee, $12 ; brown sugar, $10; flour, $125 a barrel; milk, $4 a quart."

Part of this diary is taken from the "Diary of a Southern Refugee."

"The following prices are now paid in this city: boots, $200; coats, $350; pants, $100; shoes, $125; flour, $275 per barrel; meal, $60 to $80 per bushel; bacon, $9 per pound; no beef in market; chickens, $30 per pair; shad, $20; potatoes, $25 per bushel; turnip greens, $4 per peck; white beans, $4 per quart; or $120 per bushel; butter, $15 per pound; lard, same; wood, $50 per cord. What a change a decisive victory—or defeat —would make!"

"April 7, 1864.—Sugar was $900 a barrel; bacon and lard fell to $8.25 a pound; corn, $12 a bushel; fodder, $12 a cwt. Breakfast, $10."

"In General Lee's tent meat was eaten twice a week. His bill of fare was a head of cabbage boiled in salt water, sweet potatoes, and a pone of corn-bread; when he invited an officer to dinner, he had to his astonishment four inches of middling—everyone refused from politeness, and the servant excused the smallness of the piece by saying it was borrowed."

"April 11th. — Potatoes sell at $1 per quart; chickens, $35 per pair; turnip greens, $4 per peck. An ounce of meat daily is the allowance to each member of my family, the cat and the parrot included. The pigeons of my neighbor have disappeared. Every day we have accounts of robberies, the preceding night, of cows, pigs, bacon, flour; and even the setting hens are taken from their nests."

"On July 21, 1864, wheat was $30 a bushel."

"July 2, 1864.—Tomatoes about the size of a walnut were $20 a dozen."

"Baby shoes, in 1864, cost $20, and for a fine cotton dress—what is now known as a French print cotton gown—unmade, $45. Boys' shoes, $100 a pair in the spring of 1865."

"February, 1865.—Gold, 60 for one. Early York cabbage seed, $10 an ounce; 230 defeated the Senate bill to put 200,000 negroes in the army. Virginia alone for specie could feed the army."

"An outbreak of the prisoners is apprehended; and if they were to rise, it is feared some of the inhabitants of the city would join them; they too have no meat—many of them —or bread either."

If a frank answer could be elicited from the men who sincerely believe our Government starved the prisoners in our hands, could they, after reading these extracts, reaffirm that opinion?

Travelling Expenses of an Officer of Artillery en route from Richmond, Va., to Augusta, Ga., March and April, 1865. *

March	11th, Meal on the road......	$20 00
"	17th, Cigars and bitters	60 00
"	20th, Hair-cutting and shave.................	10 00
"	" Pair of eye-glasses.....................	135 00
"	" Candles.............................	50 00
"	23d, Coat, vest, and pants..................	2,700 00
"	27th, One gallon whiskey....................	400 00
"	30th, One pair of pants	700 00
"	" One pair of cavalry boots...............	450 00
April	12th, Six yards of linen.....................	1,200 00
"	14th, One ounce sul. quinine.................	1,700 00
"	" Two weeks' board	700 00
"	" Bought $60, gold..........	6,000 00
"	24th, One dozen Catawba wine...............	900 00
"	" Shad and sundries......	75 00
"	" Matches.............................	25 00
"	" Penknife.............................	125 00
"	" Package brown Windsor................	50 00

Prices on Bill of Fare at the Oriental Restaurant, Richmond, January 17, 1864.

Soup, per plate.........	$1 50	*Wines, per Bottle.*	
Turkey, per plate.......	3 50	Champagne.	$50 00
Chicken, per plate......	3 50	Madeira	50 00
Rock fish, per plate	5 00	Port	25 00
Roast beef, per plate....	3 00	Claret................	20 00
Beefsteak, per dish	3 50	Sherry	35 00
Ham and eggs	3 50	*Liquors, per Drink.*	
Boiled eggs............	2 00		
Fried oysters...........	5 00	French brandy........	3 00
Raw oysters	3 00	Rye whiskey..........	2 00
Cabbage...............	1 00	Apple brandy.........	2 00
Potatoes...............	1 00	*Malt Liquors, per Bottle.*	
Pure coffee, per cup....	3 00		
Pure tea, per cup.......	2 00	Porter................	12 00
Fresh milk	2 00	Ale...................	12 00
Bread and butter.......	1 50	Ale, one-half bottle....	6 00
		Cigars.	
		Fine Havana..........	1 00

Game of all kinds in season.
Terrapins served up in every style.

* Colonel Miller Owen : In Camp and Battle with the Washington Artillery.

*Bill for a Dinner for Nine Poor Confederates at the " Oriental,"
January 17, 1864.*

Soup for nine........	$13 50	Brought forward......	$132 50
Venison steak........	31 50	Apples..............	12 00
Fried potatoes	9 00	5 bottles of Madeira..	250 00
Seven birds..........	24 00	6 bottles of claret.....	120 00
Baked potatoes.......	9 00	1 Urn cocktail	65 00
Celery	13 50	Jelly................	20 00
Bread and butter.....	14 00	Cake................	20 00
Coffee ....*...	18 00	1 dozen cigars........	12 00
	$132 50		$631 50

Approximate Value of Gold and Confederate Currency from January 1, 1862, to April 12, 1865.

Date.	Gold.	Currency.
January 1, 1862..........................	$100	$120
December 20, 1862........................	100	300
December 20, 1863........................	100	1,700
January 1, 1864..........................	100	1,800
December 20, 1864........................	100	2,800
January 1, 1865..........................	100	3,400
February 1, 1865..........................	100	5,000
March 1, 1865...............	100	4,700
April 10, 1865	100	5,500

CHAPTER LV.

EXCHANGE OF PRISONERS AND ANDERSONVILLE.

THE cause of all the sufferings of the men of the South who starved and froze on Johnson's Island and at Point Lookout, and those of the North who succumbed to the heat and exposure at Andersonville, and died for lack of proper medicines (made contraband by their own Government), was the violation of the cartel for the exchange of prisoners by the civil and military authorities of the United States Government.

The reasons for this violation are obvious.

The South, hemmed in on the land by a cordon of bayonets, and on the sea-coast by the enemy's fleet, had only the male population within its borders from which to recruit its armies; while the North, with the ports of the world open to her, could replace the immense losses incurred in battle and by capture, and find ample "food for powder" in every country and among all peoples; so their armies were easily augmented by large enlistments of foreigners and negro slaves captured in the South.

With this bountiful supply of material it seemed to matter little to her if a few thousands of such rank and file were, in violation of the cartel, detained in Southern "prison pens." The majority of these mercenaries had not even a common language in which to communicate their woes to the people for whom they were paid to fight or die.

It is undeniable that in the "pens" were many brave and patriotic men, who, imbued with the same devoted spirit that animated the people of the South, had been captured in the front line of battle bravely doing their duty ; but there were very many more of the kind of soldiers described by General Barlow in the New York *World* of August 11th. When he was borne off the field of Antietam badly wounded, he saw : "Stragglers who were amusing themselves in the rear of the troops who were fighting in the front. The country in the rear was filled with soldiers broken up and scattered from their commands, who were having 'picnics.' They were lying under trees, sleeping, cooking their coffee or other rations, and amusing themselves outside of the enemy's fire. This was by no means confined to the enlisted men, but I saw officers of various ranks, and men of high rank and of different corps and divisions, who had thus *deserted their commands at the front.*"

Dr. Mann, in the August *Century*, said in reference to the inmates of Andersonville :

"All classes and grades of society were represented within our prison. . . . Negro soldiers ; *Bowery roughs*, the worst class of all; mechanics, farmers, *gamblers*, etc. . . . Until about August 1st, there was absolutely no check to rascality of any kind, except our own individual physical strength . . . a class of *skulkers* and *gamblers*, from both the Eastern and Western armies, captured in the rear by the rebel raiders.

" An organized band of over two hundred members, selected from the most unprincipled and healthier prisoners, bound together by oaths, and armed with short, heavy clubs, overran the prison pen. They committed their depredations every night, and became a terror to us all. They finally grew so bold as to knock down and rob men during the day. The gang was known as the ' Raiders.' They had everything their own way for nearly three months, when it was discovered that several of our number had been murdered by them." A court composed of the prisoners themselves was organized, and " six of their number (Raiders) were found guilty of murder in the first degree and sentenced to be hung." They were executed by the prisoners, and " Wirz furnished material for a scaffold." An assemblage of this class of men in *a State* would destroy the welfare of the community, and render a bloody penal code a dreadful necessity. How great would be the misery of being cooped up with them under restrictions needful for their secure detention !

Keenly alive to the misery of friend or foe, and painfully anxious to assuage it, on July 6, 1861, hearing of the capture of the schooner *Savannah* with her crew, sailing under Con· federate orders, and that they had been put in irons and brought before the courts on charge of treason, President Davis wrote to President Lincoln :

" It is the desire of the Government so to conduct the war now existing as to mitigate its horrors as far as may be possible, and with this intent, its treatment of the prisoners captured by its forces has been marked by the greatest humanity and leniency consistent with public obligation. Some returned home on parole, others remained at large under similar conditions within the Confederacy, and all were furnished with rations for their subsistence, such as are allowed to our own troops. It was only after the severities to the prisoners taken on the *Savannah* that these indulgences were withdrawn and the prisoners were held in strict confinement.

" A just regard to humanity and the honor

of this Government, now requires me to state explicitly that, painful as will be the necessity, this Government will deal out to the prisoners held by it the same treatment and the same fate as shall be experienced by those captured on the *Savannah*, and if driven to the terrible necessity of retaliation by your execution of any of the officers or crew of the *Savannah*, that retaliation will be extended so far as shall be requisite to secure the abandonment of a practice unknown to the warfare of a civilized man, and so barbarous as to disgrace the nation which shall be guilty of encouraging it."

On July 20, 1862, the President, in secret session, recommended to Congress that all our prisoners who had been put on parole by the United States Government be released from the obligation of their parole. The recommendation was urged as a retaliation for the reckless breach of good faith on the part of the Northern Government with regard to the exchange of prisoners, and was accompanied by the exposure of this perfidy in a lengthy correspondence conducted by the War Department. The points of this interesting correspondence are here extracted.

" At the time permission was asked by the Northern Government for Messrs. Fish and Ames to visit their prisoners in the South, our

Government, while denying this permission, sought to improve the opportunity by concerting a settled plan for the exchange of prisoners. To execute this purpose our Government deputed Messrs. Conrad and Seddon as commissioners to meet those of the Northern Government under a flag of truce at Norfolk. Subsequently, a letter from General Wool informed General Huger that he, General Wool, had full authority to settle terms for the exchange of prisoners, and asked an interview on the subject. General Howell Cobb was then appointed by the Government to negotiate with General Wool, and to settle a permanent plan for the exchange of prisoners during the war. The adjustment was then considered to have been satisfactorily made.

"It was agreed that the prisoners of war in the hands of each Government should be exchanged, man for man, the officers being assimilated as to rank, etc.; that our privateersmen should be exchanged on the footing of prisoners of war; that any surplus remaining on either side after these exchanges, should be released, and that hereafter, during the whole continuance of the war, prisoners taken on either side should be paroled. In carrying out this agreement, our Government has released some three hundred prisoners above those exchanged by the North, the balance of the complete number of prisoners in the hands of the two Governments being so much in our favor. At the time, however, of sending North the hostages we had retained for our privateersmen, General Cobb had reason to suspect the good faith of the Northern Government, and telegraphed in time to intercept the release of a portion of these hostages (among them Colonel Corcoran) who were en route from points farther south than Richmond, to go North under the flag of truce at Norfolk. A number of these hostages, however, had already been discharged.

" It now appears that, in contravention to the solemn agreement of the Northern Government, not one of our privateersmen have been released, and the Fort Donelson prisoners, instead of being paroled, have been taken into the interior, where they are still confined.

" As a judgment upon this open and shameless perfidy of the North, it is proposed that our prisoners who have been paroled by the United States Government shall be released from their obligations. There is as little doubt of the honor of such a proposition, as there is of its justness as a retaliatory measure for an act of flagrant perfidy."

In pursuance of this view, the President

wrote substantially the following letter to General Lee.

"RICHMOND, VA., July 31, 1862.

"On the 23d of this month a cartel for a general exchange of prisoners was signed between Major-General D. H. Hill, in behalf of the Confederate States, and Major-General John A. Dix, in behalf of the United States. By the terms it is stipulated that all prisoners of war hereafter taken shall be discharged on parole till exchanged. Scarcely had the cartel been signed, when the military authorities of the United States changed the character of the war from that of civilized nations into a campaign of indiscriminate robbery and murder. The general order issued by the United States Secretary of War in Washington, on the very day that the cartel was signed in Virginia, directs the United States commanders to take the private property of our people for the convenience and use of their armies, without compensation.

"The General Order issued by Major-General Pope, on the day after the cartel was signed, directs the murder of our peaceful inhabitants as spies if found quietly tilling the farms in the rear, *even outside of his lines;* and Brigadier-General Steinwehr has seized upon peaceful inhabitants to be held as hostages, that they may be murdered in cold

blood if any of his soldiers are killed by some
unknown persons whom he designates as
' bush-whackers.'

" Under this state of facts Mr. Davis issued
a General Order, recognizing General Pope
and his commissioned officers to be robbers
and murderers, and not public enemies, entitled, if captured, to be considered prisoners
of war. We are driven by the enemy to a
course we abhor, and have vainly struggled
to avoid.

" For the present we shall not retaliate on
the innocent, and shall treat the enlisted soldiers of General Pope's army as prisoners of
war; but if these savage practices are continued after notice to the Government at
Washington, we shall reluctantly accept the
war on the terms chosen by our foes, until the
outraged voice of a common humanity forces
a respect for the recognized rules of war.

" We have consented to liberate an excess
of thousands of prisoners held by us beyond
the number held by the enemy, but would be
justified, by the facts, in refusing to execute
the generous cartel; yet we shrink from the
mere semblance of breaking faith, and do not
resort to this extremity.

" The punishment merited alone by General Pope and such commissioned officers as
choose to participate in the execution of his

infamous orders, will not be visited on other forces of the United States.

"Communicate this decision to the Commander-in-chief of the armies of the United States, and a copy of the enclosed general order.

"JEFFERSON DAVIS.

"To GENERAL R. E. LEE, Commanding, etc."

On July 4, 1863, the day after the battle of Gettysburg, General Lee, having taken 6,000 prisoners, wished to parole them on the spot, and 2,000 were released on parole, not to serve until properly exchanged. It was only after their release that the Federal Commander informed him that no exchanges would be made and no paroles respected. Therefore 4,000 Federal prisoners unnecessarily suffered the hardship of a march, under guard, from Gettysburg to Richmond. The following is General Meade's telegram to his superior officer :

"GETTYSBURG, July 4, 1863, 10 P.M.

"MAJOR-GENERAL HALLECK :

". . . A proposition made by General Lee under flag of truce, to exchange prisoners, was declined by me.

"GEORGE G. MEADE,

"*Major-General.*" *

---

* Rebellion Records, vol. xxvii.

His action was confirmed by his Government.

On October 1, 1864, when the number of prisoners was large on both sides, General Lee wrote to General Grant substantially as follows:

" To alleviate the sufferings of our soldiers, I propose the exchange of prisoners of war taken by the armies operating in Virginia, man for man, or upon the basis established by the cartel."

On the next day General Grant replied :

" I could not of right accept your proposition further than to exchange prisoners captured within the last three days, and who have not yet been delivered to the commanding general of prisoners.

" Among those lost by the armies operating against Richmond were a number of colored troops.   Before further negotiations can be had upon the subject, I would ask if you propose delivering these men the same as white soldiers."

General Lee said in rejoinder : " Deserters from our service, and negroes belonging to our citizens, are not considered subjects of exchange."

On October 20th, General Grant finally answered :

" I regard it my duty to protect all persons

received into the army of the United States, regardless of color or nationality; when acknowledged soldiers of the Government are captured, they must be treated as prisoners of war, or such treatment as they receive inflicted upon an equal number of prisoners held by us."

In a despatch from General Grant to General Butler, August 18, 1864, the former had said:

"*It is hard on our men held in Southern prisons not to exchange them, but it is humanity to those left in the ranks to fight our battles. At this particular time, to release all rebel prisoners North, would insure Sherman's defeat, and would compromise our safety here.*"

Later, two more proposals were made to the Federal authorities, but no answers were received to either of the letters; but General Sherman wrote from Atlanta, on September 29, 1864, to General Hood at Palmetto, acknowledged the receipt of General Hood's letter of September 27th, and very considerately promised to send to St. Louis for supplies of *combs, scissors, etc.*, and to send a train with these articles for the use of the United States prisoners of war held by Hood.

And again, Major-General Thomas, commanding Department of the Cumberland, on December 5, 1864, wrote to General Hood, acknowledged the receipt of General Hood's letter of same date, proposing the exchange of prisoners, and declined. General Thomas's assigned reason was : " Although I have had quite a large number of prisoners from your army, they have all been sent back North, and are consequently now beyond my control; I am therefore unable to make the exchange proposed by you."

" Finding," wrote Mr. Davis, " that exchanges could not be made, we offered their sick and wounded without any equivalents. Although the offer was made in the summer, the transportation did not arrive until November, and the most emaciated of the poor prisoners were then photographed and exhibited ' to fire the Northern heart.' "

One final effort was made to obtain an exchange. Mr. Davis sent a delegation from the prisoners at Andersonville to plead their cause at Washington. It was of no avail. They were refused an audience with President Lincoln, and returned to tell their fellow-prisoners there was no hope of relief.

In the official report of General B. F. Butler, he said :

" General Grant visited Fortress Monroe on April 1, 1864. To him the state of the negotiation as to exchange (Mr. Davis's proposition to exchange all white and free black soldiers, leaving the question as to slaves to be disposed of later) was verbally communicated, and most emphatic directions were received from the Lieutenant-General, *not to take any step by which another able-bodied man should be exchanged until further orders from him.*

"After conversation with General Grant in reply to the proposition of Mr. Ould to exchange all prisoners of war on either side held, man for man, officer for officer, I wrote an argument showing our right to our colored soldiers.

"This argument set forth our claims in the most *offensive form possible*, consistent with ordinary courtesy of language, for the purpose of carrying out the wishes of the Lieutenant-General, that *no prisoners should be exchanged.*"

Mr. Davis, a short time before his death, wrote a full account of the Andersonville Prison, the condition of affairs therein, and the causes of the mortality. This was published in *Belford's Magazine* for January and February, 1890.*

It should be a complete vindication of the Confederate authorities before all fair-minded men.

---

* And afterward in pamphlet form.

That the policy of humanity to prisoners was the fixed purpose of the Confederate Government, is evidenced by the treatment accorded to them as long as our necessities enabled us to minister to their comfort. In the second year of the war the *Herald's* correspondent wrote from Harrison's Landing, July 22, 1862 : "Several surgeons, left behind in care of our sick and wounded men in the hospitals, have arrived here, and report quite favorably their treatment by the Rebels.

". . . Father Hagan, Chaplain of the Excelsior Regiment, Sickles's brigade, visited the hospitals and found our wounded men receiving the same attention as their own. All the sick in Richmond—our prisoners with the others—are suffering from scarcity of medicines, and the Confederates complain bitterly of the action of our Government in declaring medicines contraband of war. Quinine is worth sixty dollars an ounce in Richmond, in New York five dollars or less."

Who, then, took the initiative? Did not the North do so in making quinine contraband of war? Was it not better that twenty so-called "traitors and rebels" should live than one Northern so-called "patriot" should be worn out on a bed of anguish for the lack of the drug needful to his recovery?

The frantic appeals made by the *Exam-*

iner of Richmond, to " hoist the black flag,"
"retaliate on the Yankee prisoners for the
starvation and abuse of our prisoners while in a
land teeming with plenty," inflamed many true
men against the President, because he would
not adopt that course; but throughout the
weary years of these pin-pricks, which annoyed and galled him greatly, he never re-
laxed his determined stand against this das-
tardly retributory policy. He answered hotly
to a member of Congress who was a pervert
to the *Examiner's* views, " I would not fight
with a rope around my neck, and I will not
ask brave men to do so. As to he torture of
prisoners, I can resign my office at the call
of the country, but no people have the right
to demand such a deed at my hands." The
Examiner was ably edited, and ingenious in
ways and means to make the President odious—but was unable at least to engraft an ig-
noble policy upon that of the Administration.

Mr. Davis, under date of February 12,
1876, wrote to his friend, General Crafts I.
Wright as follows:

" It would be impossible to frame an accusation against me more absolutely and unqualifiedly false, than that which imputes to me
cruelty to prisoners. A Richmond paper,
during the war, habitually assailed me for
undue clemency and care for them; and that

misnamed 'historian,' Pollard, in a book written after the war, accused me of having favored prisoners, in the hope that it might, in the event of our failure, serve to shield me."

The Confederate President, in a message of May 2, 1864, said : " On the subject of the exchange of prisoners, I greatly regret to be unable to give you satisfactory information. The Government of the United States, while persisting in failure to execute the terms of the cartel, make occasional deliveries of prisoners, and then suspend action without apparent cause. I confess my inability to comprehend their policy or purpose. The prisoners held by us, in spite of human care, are perishing from the inevitable effects of imprisonment and the home-sickness produced by their hopelessness of release from confinement. The spectacle of their suffering augments our desire to relieve from similar trials our own brave men, who have spent so many weary months in a cruel and useless imprisonment, endured with heroic constancy."

From a message delivered in 1865 to the Confederate Congress, I make the following extracts :

" I regret to inform you that the enemy have returned to the barbarous policy with which they inaugurated the war, and that the exchange of prisoners has been for some time suspended. The conduct of the authorities of the United States has been consistently perfidious on this subject."

When the United States had an excess of prisoners the agreement to exchange was repudiated by them, until the fortune of war gave us the largest number. A new cartel was made, and for many months we restored many thousands of prisoners in excess of those whom they held for exchange, and encampments of the surplus paroled prisoners, delivered by us, were established in the United States, where the men held constant communication with their homes.

" The prisoners taken at Gettysburg, however, remained in their hands, and should have been returned to our lines on parole, to await exchange." Instead of executing an exchange, pretexts were sought for keeping the Confederates in captivity. New constructions of an agreement which had not been disputed were promulgated, while we retained the advantage in the number of prisoners.

The enemy declared invalid the paroles of the prisoners captured by us, liberated on promise not to serve until exchanged, and those our soldiers gave under similar circumstances, as binding.

Their final proposal was to settle all dis-

putes under the cartel, that we should liberate
all prisoners held by us, without the promise
to release any of those held by them.

" A systematic effort was made to quiet the
relatives and friends of the prisoners in our
hands, by the assertion that we were the
parties who refused the cartel.

" The fact was that the rations of the prisoners were precisely the same, in quantity
and quality, as those served out to our own
gallant soldiers in the field,* and which had
supported them in their arduous campaigns.
The enemy did not pretend that they treated
prisoners by the same generous rule.

Here is a significant letter from General
Grant to Halleck.

"CITY POINT, VA., February 18, 1865.

" Your communication of the 15th inst., with
inclosure, calling my attention to the fact that
advantage is being taken by General Beall,
Confederate agent, of the recent agreement
between Judge Ould and myself, to supply
rebel prisoners with new uniforms and blank-

---

* A notice in one of the Richmond journals said : " There are
now in Richmond, and at the hospitals adjacent thereto, several
thousand of our wounded in the great battles on the Rapidan. They
are in great want of almost every necessary save a stout Southern
heart, a determined will and hand.   We know our citizens will supply them, to the extent of their ability, with fresh diet, clean linen,
and every appliance which their economy and frugality and general
domestic order may suggest."

ets, is received. The arrangement for the relief of prisoners of war was made at a time
when exchanges could not be made, and under it I see no way to *prevent* rebel prisoners
from being clothed. Having, however, a very
large excess of prisoners over the enemy, we
can, in making exchanges, select those who
*have not been furnished with new clothing or
blankets.* By this means but a very limited
number of rebel soldiers will be returned with
new uniforms. Should it become necessary,
prisoners for exchange can be required to
turn their blankets over to their comrades who
remain.

"Please give orders to General Hoffman
accordingly." *

Professor Dabney, of the University of Virginia, wrote as follows in answer to an article
of *The Nation* condemnatory of the Confederates for their abuse of prisoners.

" *To the Editor of The Nation.*

" SIR : As you state in your editorial of last
week that the diet at Johnson's Island was
'exceptionally abundant and varied,' I wish
to call the attention of your readers to certain
evidence to the contrary, which I have heard.

"After reading your article I went to a

---

* North American Review, March, 1886.

gentleman whose brother, a Confederate lieutenant, died, after leaving Johnson's Island,
from the effects of hardships suffered at that
place, and asked him whether his brother had
found the food 'exceptionally abundant and
varied.' Briefly stated, the lieutenant's account was as follows : The food, though usually satisfactory as to quality, was not always
so, as may be inferred from the fact that, in
order to have a better Christmas dinner than
was furnished him, he made soup out of some
fish-skins which he had raked out of a gutter.
As to the abundance, he heard the commandant of the prison, whom he praised highly for
his kindness, say that he was *well aware that
the prisoners did not have enough to eat*, but
that he was *under strict orders not to give
them any more.* Delicacies were sent him by
New York and Louisville ladies, but were
intercepted by the guards or other persons
and never reached him. Moreover, *in that
bitterly cold climate, he was not allowed a
blanket to cover himself at night until after
Christmas.*

"I am well acquainted with a Confederate
captain now living in Richmond, a perfect
Hercules in physique, who (if I remember
rightly) weighed fifty pounds less upon leaving Johnson's Island than when he entered its
prison walls.

"And now let me quote from 'Leute in den Vereinigten Staaten' (Leipzig, 1886), a work by Ernst Hohenwart (possibly a pseudonym), a German who spent nearly thirty years in the United States, and who fought as an officer in the Northern army. I shall italicize certain important phrases.

"'Much has been said of the cruel treatment of Northern soldiers in Southern prisons. Having myself been a prisoner in the South for more than thirteen months, and having been afterward stationed with my regiment at a place where more than twenty-five thousand Southern soldiers were confined, I think I have a right to an opinion as to the relative treatment of prisoners in the North and South.

"'It is true that the Southerners treated their prisoners much less well than the Northerners, *for the simple reason that they had not the means* to treat them better, and often, especially toward the end of the war, *themselves suffered from want.*

"'The South wished to permit the officers, according to European custom, to live in town on parole and half pay. I myself and other officers lived for some months in Raleigh, and were granted much freedom of movement, but *the North treated Southern officers like common soldiers*, and the South afterward did the same. *So long as they were able, they gave us good rations,* afterward very often spoilt bacon, cured with wood-ashes—they were short of salt *—or beef cured with saltpetre, or fresh horse meat; a pound of bread a day being added, and sometimes a handful of beans or rice. During the winter we were unable to buy anything additional, but, as soon as summer came, country people brought us provisions which we were permitted to buy. *The fare of our guards was not much better than our own.*

" ' *Of intentional cruelty I saw nothing,* but on the contrary, always found both officers and men very friendly and obliging, and most willing to alleviate our lot. When requested to bring us tobacco or other articles from town, they were always glad to do so, and *I never heard of a single instance in which such a request was refused.* . . .'

" Since writing the above I have seen another gentleman, who tells me that he knows a number of Confederates who ' varied ' their ' abundant ' diet at Johnson's Island with the flesh of rats, an article of food which was also enjoyed by the lieutenant whom I mentioned in the first part of my letter.

" R. H. DABNEY.

"UNIVERSITY OF VIRGINIA, February 2, 1890."

---

* Our salt had no preservative property.

In this connection Senator Daniel's opinion, expressed on January 25th, will be of interest. He said:

"He would have turned with loathing from misuse of a prisoner, for there was no characteristic of Jefferson Davis more marked than his regard for the weak, the helpless, and the captive. By act of the Confederate Congress and by general orders, the same rations served to the Confederates were issued to the prisoners, though taken from a starving army and people.

"Brutal and base was the effort to stigmatize him as a conspirator to maltreat prisoners, but better for him that it was made; for while he was himself yet in prison, the evidences of his humanity were so overwhelming that finally slander stood abashed and malignity recoiled.

"Even at Andersonville, where the hot summer sun was of course disastrous to men of the Northern clime, well nigh as many of their guard died as of them.

"With 60,000 more Federal prisoners in the South than there were Confederate prisoners in the North, 6,000 more Confederates than Federals died in prison. A cyclone of rhetoric cannot shake this mountain of fact, and these facts are alike immovable:

"1. Unable to get medicines in the Confederacy, an offer was made to buy them from the United States for the sole use of Federal prisoners. No answer was made.

" 2. Then an offer was made to deliver the sick and wounded without any equivalent in exchange. There was no reply for months.

" 3. Finally, and as soon as the United States would receive them, thousands of both sick and well were delivered without exchange.

" The record leaves no doubt as to the responsibility for refusal to exchange.

" Charles A. Dana, of the New York *Sun*, formerly Assistant Secretary of War, nobly vindicated President Davis while he lived, declared him 'altogether acquitted' of the charge, and said of him dead, 'A majestic soul has passed.'

" When General Lee congratulated his army on the victories of Richmond, he said to them: 'Your humanity to the wounded and the prisoners was the fit and crowning glory of your valor.' "

Here is an experience related by a responsible man.

A Story of Horror.

" Yesterday, in glancing over the *Century* for January, under the head of 'Shooting Into Libby;' I found two letters from Federal soldiers about Confederate guards shooting at Federal prisoners, while resting in the windows of Libby. They would make it appear that this was the amusement of the private soldier, with the knowledge and approval of Confederate authorities, saying: 'We never heard instructions that we might do this or not do that.'

"I cannot look on the Maxwell House without remembering as bloody and gratuitous a tragedy as ever stained the records of our civil war.

"In the winter of 1864 I was city editor of the *Daily Press ;* the Maxwell House, in an unfinished condition, was then used by the Federals as a prison for Confederate soldiers.

"One morning, as I came down-stairs and turned down Cherry toward Union, I saw a Federal guard taking his smoking gun from his shoulder, while people were standing around with expressions of horror on their faces. On asking a citizen what was the matter he answered, with indignation and subdued fear: 'Look! That Federal guard has murdered a Confederate soldier.'

"Looking to the fourth story of the Maxwell House, I saw a dead Confederate soldier with his head lying in a window and blood streaming from him down the walls and spattering the pavement below. The guard had orders to shoot any Confederate who

appeared at a window. He told the Confederate to go back or he would shoot. The
boy in gray, having no idea he would do so,
responded by playfully waving his hand at the
guard. In an instant a bullet went crashing
through his brain and he was a dead man.
The Confederate prisoners declared they had
received no intimation of any such order.

"Now, could we not, from this instance, as
truthfully declare the fact that Federal soldiers
amused themselves at Nashville by shooting
and killing Confederate prisoners?"

In a Yankee Prison.

Written for the *Nashville American.*

"It was the misfortune of the writer to be
captured on the memorable raid through
Indiana and Ohio, made by General John. H.
Morgan in July, 1863.

"I write of some of the unpublished events
occurring during an incarceration as a prisoner
of war, for twenty-two months, within *a five-
acre lot* on the shores of Lake Michigan, in a
place designated Camp Douglas. This prison
was for the safe-keeping of privates and non-
commissioned officers. It contained an area
of about five acres, laid off into main streets
of about thirty feet width, intersected at
regular intervals by cross streets about half
the width, perhaps. Barracks were erected

fronting the main avenues, intended to accommodate (?) about 180 men, and numbered one, two, three, etc., up to sixty odd. These were enclosed by a fence about twenty feet high, near the top of which was a plank walk for the Yankee guards. Each barrack had a rebel and Yankee sergeant, the former elected by the occupants, whose duty it was to call the morning roll, report the escapes, deaths, etc. My bunk was in the southeast corner of barrack No. 10, and my men honored me by electing me their sergeant, which unenviable position was held during the entire term of imprisonment. There were at one time 11,000 prisoners confined in this small enclosure.

"He who has never suffered the torture of continued hunger, knows nothing about the luxury of a full meal.

"I might tell of the ravages of the small-pox, of the inconveniences and discomforts of the itch and pediculus vestimenti, but these were mere bagatelles, little side-shows, compared to other performances going on within the big menagerie. Out of a mind replete with memories of this prison life of twenty-five years ago, I remember that on a cold December day, early in the morning, the entire Confederate camp was ordered to assemble in the Yankee square. This square was just across the fence from ours. 'What's up now?' was whispered from comrade to comrade. After being disposed in battle array, every ragged Rebel standing there with his coat-tails flapping in the breezes off Lake Michigan like the sails of some stranded schooner, the process was begun of divesting each and everyone of us of every rag of clothing that gave us the semblance of citizenship. Instead of the variegated costumes in which we were caparisoned, we were given a stiff, black cavalry hat, a brown-black coat and pants, the coat being divested of half its tail. In this unique garb we were marched back to our quarters. What disposition was ever made of the clothes we gave in exchange we never took the trouble to inquire. This was done to prevent escapes, which had grown to be monotonously frequent. But woe to the Reb who failed in the attempt, and was recaptured.

"By far the largest number of escapes from Camp Douglas were accomplished through the aid of one of the guards. He finally deserted with a batch of prisoners to Canada. He had no pity for us, but a slavish love for the $5 given him in advance by each escaping prisoner. A lot of prisoners trying to effect their escape one night were recaptured just outside the enclosure. Among them was a son of ex-Governor McGoffin,

of Kentucky. He, with the others, was suspended by the thumbs next morning for the
purpose of extorting the betrayal of his accomplices. They remained as dumb as oysters, although suspended *until the balls of
the thumbs absolutely burst open.*

"This thumb business was effected by a
twine string, making a noose and placed
over the thumb of each hand; the opposite
ends were thrown over a beam overhead. A
stout, heavy man then pulled upon the loose
ends until the victim's weight was almost entirely sustained by his thumbs and held thus
ad libitum.

"Another mode of punishment was called
'pointing for corn.' This consisted in standing stiff-legged, stooping over and touching
the ground with the index-finger of the right
hand. If you think this little manœuvre is
not difficult, assume the position for five or ten
minutes, and then report. I have seen a
hundred or more men in this ludicrous position at one time, and numbers faint and fall
down in line. Another mode of punishment
was to ride 'John Morgan's Mule.' This
mule was composed of six legs about twenty
feet long attached to a scantling 2+4 inches,
the narrow part of this horizontal piece being
placed upward, formed the back of this patient Bucephalus. I have seen his back so

full that there did not remain room for another rider. To say that this wooden horse was never without a rider, except at night, would be literally true.

" The last twelve months of our imprisonment was noted for scant rations. Hunger was the prevailing epidemic. I will relate the following actual occurrence as an illustration of the humiliating effects of long, continued hunger : At one end of our barracks was our kitchen, and by the door of the kitchen stood a barrel, into which was thrown the beef bones, slop, etc. Some of these starved creatures used to go to these barrels, fish out the bones, and appropriate what could be got off them to appease their terrible hunger. On one occasion a Yankee guard found a prisoner engaged in this business. He snatched the bone out of the prisoner's hand, cocked his pistol, presented it at the hungry prisoner, and ordered him down on his all-fours to bark like a dog for the bone he was holding above him, until his beastly inhumanity was satisfied. To say that we who witnessed this transaction were indignant is a poor description of what we felt.

" Each barrack was supplied with wooden spittoons placed along the aisle. A comrade from a neighbor barrack was visiting a friend in No. 10, and while sitting in an upper bunk attempted to spit into one of these spittoons, but missing it, spat upon the floor. The Yankee sergeant nosing around discovered the spit upon the floor, and demanded of me the name of the party who did it. Now, there was an unwritten law among us not to tell tales out of school, and it was kept inviolate in the presence of any torture that might be used to extort from us information that would subject a comrade to punishment. I informed him that I did not know who did it, but would not tell him if I knew. This, of course, infuriated him. He gave me two hours to find the person and divulge his name. If not done at the expiration of the time he would punish the 'hull d—d barracks.' The information not being forthcoming, we, to the number of one hundred or more, were ordered out into the street. Now, the snow lay on the ground to the depth of eighteen inches. Along the middle of the street was a pathway leading to the hydrant, and in this pathway we were drawn up in line. We were then ordered to right backward dress out into the snow up to our knees. We were then ordered to strip from the waist down. This command being executed, we were next ordered to sit down on the snow. This command was complied with, and if perchance some shivering prisoner had involuntarily pushed his shirt or blanket between himself and the dampness beneath, a detail was sent down the line in the rear and rudely snatched every remnant of clothing from beneath, so that there we sat with absolutely nothing intervening between us and the snow. These manœuvres were something new in military tactics, and doubtless never entered the brain of such sluggards as Hardee and Upton. How long we sat there, I do not know ; seconds seemed hours, minutes days. The outrage was reported to Colonel Sweet, the commandant, but no notice was taken of it.

"For the highest type of loyalty, that unselfish, generous, cheerful, unspotted kind, commend me to the Confederate prisoner of war, who for long months patiently endured the punishment and indignities heaped upon him by his inferiors. Day after day suffering the pangs of hunger. All this, and the privilege waiting him of taking the oath and going home any day he chose. There was simply no limit to his patient loyalty. There was nothing like it.   " J. B. WEST,

"Ex-O. S. Co. B., Second Ky. Cav., C. S. A.
NASHVILLE, TENN."

December 14, 1861.—John Hanson Thomas, William Harrison, Charles H. Pitts, and S. Teakle Wallis were, for their opinion's

sake, confined in a room darkened with vene-
tian shutters fastened outside with iron bars,
and there were only about twenty-two to
forty-four inches over the doors by which light
came into their rooms. They were never allowed out for a moment for two weeks, and
the impure air was stifling, though they used
disinfectants. They were after this sent to
Fort Lafayette, where they were turned into a
casemate with a brick floor, with no other furniture than guns and gun-carriages. They
were not allowed their trunks for seats. All
that night they walked their rooms ; the next
day they received their trunks, and then
spread their clothes upon the floor and laid
on them. The third day, loose straw was
given them. After ten days iron bedsteads
were furnished with straw beds, but no pillows or covering. They were subsequently
allowed the liberty of the Fort yard for stated
hours. I have not space for many testimon-
ials by men of undoubted veracity of the
cruelties inflicted on them in Northern prisons.

A letter from General I. R. Trimble said :

"I regret that a full statement of facts relating to our treatment on Johnson Island,
which I had prepared by a committee of officers, was left with the secretary and is now

beyond my reach. These facts would make
all fair-minded men blush with shame.

"More than $3,000 had been retained by
officials from remittances sent to prisoners by
relatives and friends, as all our letters were
opened.

"We were once three days and nights
without any fire in our room or kitchen, during the most inclement weather of 1864.

"WALNUT SPRINGS, LONDON, O.,
        "October 23, 1886."

Extracts from these letters are given that
our prisoners' side of the sufferings endured
in the North may be duly weighed by the
judgment of Northern people. No one book
would hold all the evidence which could be
adduced to prove the sufferings of our brave
men in Northern prisons. Ours was a country devastated by invaders who carried a
sword in one hand and a cord and torch in
the other. The North was bountifully supplied with everything needful for comfort and
luxury, but the Confederate prisoners expected only the bare necessaries of life, and these
were denied them. We shared our scanty
fare alike with those who came to destroy us
and were taken captive in the act, and with
the soldiers who were defending us and our
households. If it was not enough for the

prisoners, no more was it sufficient to sustain our soldiers in their herculean strife against a foe supplied with men and means *ad libitum.*

During the stringent period of our war I was obliged, through a tradeswoman, to sell my carriage and horses, my handsome articles of dress, jewelry, etc., to get the necessaries of life, and our nephew, commanding a brigade, came home from the front of Petersburg so much reduced in flesh that it was remarked. He gave as a reason that his negro servant could not bear starvation as well as he could, and he had, he supposed, given him too much of the rations intended for himself.

Though I recognize the reminiscence of our devoted friend, the brilliant soldier, and representative Southern patriot, General Robert Ransom, as the exact truth, we did not feel the deprivations of the war as onerous until hope was dead.

Comparative Mortality of Federal and Confederate Prisons.

A correspondent of the New York *Tribune* adduces the "logic of facts," in a very conclusive manner, in the following communication :

" The *Elmira Gazette* is authority for the following : In the four months of February, March, April, and May, 1865, out of 5,027 prisoners confined there, 1,311 died, showing a death - rate per month of $6\frac{1}{2}$ per cent., against less than three per cent. at Andersonville, or more than double at Elmira to that at Andersonville. Again, Mr. Keiley, in his journal of September, 1864, when confined there, kept a record of deaths for that month, and states them to be 386 out of 9,500 then there, or at a rate of four per cent. against three per cent. in Andersonville. It must also be taken into consideration that in the South our armies formed a barrier against the introduction of both food and medicine, while in our case there was abundance of everything.   " J. L. T."

The answer of the *Tribune* is a curiosity of lame, impotent evasion.   It says :

" We think Congress made a blunder in not opening the whole subject ; yet we cannot deem the above statistics either trustworthy or conclusive.   Many prisoners of war are diseased or wounded when captured ; inadequate or unwholesome food has brought many to the confines of the grave."

Disease and wounds, we presume, operated on both sides of the question.   Inadequate and unwholesome food—as the writer above had just shown—operated very unequally on the Southern side.

Federal prisoners in the South	270,000
Confederate prisoners in the North	220,000
Excess of Federal prisoners	50,000

Deaths in Prison.

Confederates in the North	26,436
Federals in the South	22,576
Excess of Confederates died	3,860

But if we make our calculations from the reports of the United States War Department, which show *sixty thousand* more Federal prisoners and *six thousand* more Confederate deaths, why, then, the per cent. is made even still greater in favor of Southern humanity.

Such salient points as these must ere long constitute a part of that faithful history which will be written as soon as passion subsides, and other men and other times can do us justice.

Mr. Davis was so painfully affected by the death-rate and suffering of the prisoners at Andersonville, that even in the few hours he spent at home their condition weighed dreadfully upon his spirits. He was quite feeble, but used to remain in his office from 10 A.M. until seven and sometimes eight o'clock in the

evening without food. If I sent luncheon to
him he forgot to eat it, and I fell into the
habit of going to his office daily for ten minutes to offer it to him. Whatever friend
chanced to be there partook of the refreshment with him. One day I found General
Lee there. Both were very grave, and the
subject of their conference was the want and
suffering at Andersonville, as portrayed by
General Winder's private letter to the President. Mr. Davis said, " If we could only get
them across the trans-Mississippi, there beef
and supplies of all kinds are abundant, but
what can we do for them here?" General
Lee answered quickly to this effect, " Our
men are in the same case, except that they
are free. Their sufferings are the result of
our necessities, not of our policy. Do not
distress yourself."

Disasters were reported from every quarter. Croakers vilified the President, and foretold evil results from every expedient tried by
the Administration. The army and many of
the Congressmen remained, if not confident,
at least willing to fight to the end.

CHAPTER LVI.

JOURNEY TO CHARLOTTE.

DARKNESS seemed now to close swiftly over the Confederacy, and about a week before the evacuation of Richmond, Mr. Davis came to me and gently, but decidedly, announced the necessity for our departure. He said for the future his headquarters must be in the field, and that our presence would only embarrass and grieve, instead of comforting him. Very averse to flight, and unwilling at all times to leave him, I argued the question with him and pleaded to be permitted to remain, until he said: "I have confidence in your capacity to take care of our babies, and understand your desire to assist and comfort me, but you can do this in but one way, and that is by going yourself and taking our children to a place of safety." He was very much affected and said, "If I live you can come to me when the struggle is ended, but I do not expect to survive the destruction of constitutional liberty."

He had a little gold, and reserving a five-dollar piece for himself, he gave it all to me, as well as all the Confederate money due to him.   He desired me not to request any of the citizens of Richmond to take care of my silver plate, of which we possessed a large quantity, for, said he, " They may be exposed to inconvenience or outrage by their effort to serve us."

All women like bric-à-brac, which sentimental people call their "household goods," but Mr. Davis called it "trumpery." I was not superior to the rest of my sex in this regard. However, everything which could not be readily transported was sent to a dealer for sale, and we received quite a large draft on a Richmond bank as the proceeds, but in the hurry of departure the check was not cashed, and I have it now.

Leaving the house as it was, and taking only our clothing, I made ready with my young sister and my four little children, the eldest only nine years old, to go forth into the unknown.   Mr. Burton N. Harrison, the President's private secretary, was to protect and see us safely settled in Charlotte, where we had hired a furnished house.   Mr. George A. Trenholm's lovely daughters were also to accompany us to remain with friends there.

I had bought several barrels of flour, and intended to take them with me, but Mr. Davis said, " You cannot remove anything in the shape of food from here, the people want it, and you must leave it here."

The deepest depression had settled upon the whole city; the streets were almost deserted.

The day before our departure Mr. Davis gave me a pistol and showed me how to load, aim, and fire it. He was very apprehensive of our falling into the hands of the disorganized bands of troops roving about the country, and said, " You can at least, if reduced to the last extremity, force your assailants to kill you, but I charge you solemnly to leave when you hear the enemy are approaching; and if you cannot remain undisturbed in our own country, make for the Florida coast and take a ship there for a foreign country."

With hearts bowed down by despair, we left Richmond. Mr. Davis almost gave way, when our little Jeff begged to remain with him, and Maggie clung to him convulsively, for it was evident he thought he was looking his last upon us.

In those days a special train was not contemplated, for the transportation was now very limited, and as we pulled out from the station and lost sight of Richmond, the worn-out engine broke down, and there we sat all night. There were no arrangements possible for sleeping, and at last, after twelve hours' delay, we reached Danville. A hospitable and wealthy citizen of that place invited me to rest with his family, but we gratefully declined and proceeded to Charlotte.

The baggage cars were all needing repairs and leaked badly. Our bedding was wet through by the constant rains that poured down in the week of uninterrupted travel which was consumed in reaching our destination. Universal consternation prevailed throughout the country, and we avoided seeing people for fear of compromising them with the enemy, should they overrun North Carolina. We found everything packed up in the house we had rented, but the agent, Mr. A. Weill, an Israelite, came to meet us there, and gave us every assistance in his power; and when he found there were no conveniences for cooking, he sent our meals from his own house for several days, refusing, with many cordial words, any offer to reimburse him for the expense incurred, and he offered money or any other service he could render. This acknowledgment of his kindness is, to some extent, a relief to my heart, which has borne his goodness in grateful memory for twenty-five years.

Mr. Harrison, after seeing us safely established in Charlotte, fearing he might be separated from Mr. Davis, and hoping to be of use, set out for Richmond to rejoin him.

CHAPTER LVII.

As hope died out in the breasts of the rank and file of the Confederate Army, the President's courage rose, and he was fertile in expedients to supply deficiencies, and calm in the contemplation of the destruction of his dearest hopes, and the violent death he expected to be his.

As late as April 1, 1865, he wrote to General Lee from Richmond, of the difficulty of finding iron enough to keep the Tredegar works employed, and said : " There is also difficulty in getting iron even for shot and shell, but I hope this may for the present be overcome by taking some from the Navy, which under the altered circumstances may be spared. . . . The question is often asked, ' will we hold Richmond,' to which my only answer is, if we can ; it is purely a question of military power. The distrust is increasing, and embarrasses in many ways."

Events now rapidly culminated in the overwhelming disaster he and our brave people had striven so energetically to avert. The gloom was impenetrable.

The siege of Petersburg was hotly pressed
by the enemy, and there were many splendid
instances of gallantry, but for want of space I
can only cite that of Battery Gregg, which
repulsed assault after assault—the Mississip-
pians, Georgians, North Carolinians, and
Louisianians, who had won honor on many
fields, fought this, their last battle, with most
terrible enthusiasm, as if feeling it to be for
them the last act in the great drama.

Two hundred against 5,000, the odds were
fearful, but they were animated by a noble
purpose and had no thought of abandoning
their post.

Fort Gregg fell, and but few of its brave
defenders survived, but those 200 men had
placed *hors de combat* 800 men of Gibbons's
corps.*

On the day it fell, General A. P. Hill, our
intrepid, skilful, handsome soldier, accompanied by a single courier, while endeavoring
to join his troops at Five Forks, ran across
two Federal soldiers. Upon demanding
their surrender, they shot him down and
then retreated. His body was brought back
to Petersburg by his faithful courier,† and the
country's mourning was proportionate to her
need of him, and her high estimate of his

---

* Colonel Miller Owen : In Camp and Battle.

† General Gibbons so informed General Wilcox at Appomattox.

skilful generalship. Our consolation was that he was saved the pang of Appomattox. General Lee now telegraphed President Davis, that he could no longer hold the lines of Petersburg, and would leave them at night, and that this would necessitate the evacuation of Richmond.

The enemy kept up an incessant fire upon the lines all day, and made many unsuccessful assaults, ceasing his efforts only at nightfall.

At twelve o'clock that night, the last man and the last gun of the brave army that had defended the lines of Petersburg for a twelve-month passed over the pontoon bridge and the retreat began that ended at Appomattox.

CHAPTER LVIII.

THE PRESIDENT'S ACCOUNT OF THE EVACUATION
OF RICHMOND.

I GIVE Mr. Davis's story of the evacuation of Richmond in his own words.

"On Sunday, April 2d, while I was in St. Paul's Church, General Lee's telegram announcing his speedy withdrawal from Petersburg and the consequent necessity for evacuating Richmond, was handed me. I quietly left the church. The occurrence probably attracted attention, but the people had been beleaguered, had known me too often to receive notice of threatened attacks, and the congregation of St. Paul's was too refined, to make a scene at anticipated danger. I went to my office and assembled the heads of departments and bureaus, as far as they could be found on a day when all the offices were closed, and gave the needful instruction for our removal that night, simultaneously with General Lee's from Petersburg. The event was foreseen, and some preparations had been made for it, though, as it came sooner than was expected, there was yet much to be done. The executive papers were arranged for removal.

"This occupied myself and staff until late in the afternoon. By this time the report that Richmond was to be evacuated had spread through the town, and many who saw me walking toward my residence left their houses to inquire whether the report was true. Upon my admission of the painful fact, qualified, however, by the expression of my hope that we should under better auspices again return, they all, the ladies especially, with generous sympathy and patriotic impulse responded, "If the success of the cause requires you to give up Richmond, we are content."

"The affection and confidence of this noble people in the hour of disaster were more distressing to me than complacent and unjust censure would have been. . . .

"Being alone in Richmond, a few arrangements needful for my personal wants were soon made after reaching home. Then leaving all else in the care of the house-keeper, I waited until notified of the time I would depart, and going to the station, started for Danville, whither I supposed General Lee would proceed with his army."

Here he promptly proceeded to put the town in a state of defence. Energetic efforts were made to collect supplies for General Lee's army.

Upon his arrival at Danville, President Davis wrote to Mrs. Davis as follows:

"DANVILLE, VA., April 5, 1865.

". . . I have in vain sought to get into communication with General Lee, and have postponed writing in the hope that I would soon be able to speak to you with some confidence of the future. On last Sunday I was called out of church to receive a telegram announcing that General Lee could not hold his position longer than till night, and warning me that we must leave Richmond, as his army would commence retiring that evening.

"I made the necessary arrangements and went to my office, and then to our house, to have the proper dispositions made there; nothing had been done after you left, and but little could be done in the few hours which remained before the train was to leave. . . . The people here have been very kind, and the Mayor and Council have offered assistance in the matter of quarters, and have very hand-somely declared their unabated confidence. I do not wish to leave Virginia, but cannot decide on my movements until those of the army are better developed."

From President Davis to Mrs. Davis.

"DANVILLE, VA., April 6, 1865.

" . . . In my letter of yesterday I gave you all of my prospects which could now be told, not having heard from General Lee, and having to conform my movements to the military necessities of the case. We are arranging an executive office where the current business may be transacted here, and do not propose at this time definitely to fix upon a point for a seat of government in the future. I am unwilling to leave Virginia, and do not know where, within her borders, the requisite houses for the departments could be found."

While employed in preparing for the defence of Danville, no trustworthy information in regard to Lee's army was received, until Lieutenant John Sargent Wise of Virginia, who declined to be paroled at Appomattox, arrived, from whom it was learned that when he left Lee's army, it was about to be surrendered. Other unofficial information soon followed, of such circumstantial character as to confirm these reports. How Mr. Davis bore defeat is best described by the following letter, written by Mr. Davis's faithful friend, M. H. Clarke, whose opportunities of knowing the President were better than those of another less intimately associated with him in a time of great trial.

"CLARKSVILLE, TENN., October 6, 1890.

"MY DEAR MRS. DAVIS : The history of his country is indissolubly woven with your honored husband, and therefore I offer my individual impressions of him in scenes which are yet unwritten. The sum of such impressions helps to give an idea of one phase of his many-sided individuality, both simple and grand, which rounded out the perfect man.

"I came out of Richmond with him, the chief and confidential clerk of the Executive Office, in charge of the office papers, a member of his military family, composed of his cabinet and staff; and I was close to his person, until he parted with me on May 6, 1865, near Sandersville, Ga., and sent me on, in charge of our wagon train, he leaving "everything on wheels' to join you.

"Thus daily and nightly he was under my eyes, which watched over him with affectionate and earnest solicitude.

"On that retreat (if so leisurely a retirement could be so called), when I saw an organized government disintegrate and fall to pieces little by little, until there was only left a single member of the cabinet, his private secretary, a few members of his staff, a few guides and servants, to represent what had been a powerful government, which had sustained itself against the soldiery of all nations of the earth; his great resources of mind and heart shone out most brilliantly. Still the head, he moved, calm, self-poised, giving way to no petulance of temper at discomfort, advising and consoling, laying aside all thought of self, planning and doing what was best, not only for our unhappy and despairing people, but uttering gentle, sweet words of consolation and wise advice to every family which he entered as guest; he filled my own distressed heart so full of emotions of love and admiration, that it could hardly contain them.

"To me he then appeared incomparably grander in the nobleness of his great heart and head, than when he reviewed victorious armies returning from well-won fields.

"I could give you many touching incidents of evenings around the fireside, or noon-day halts for rest and refreshment, of the little children taken on his knee, of tender and comforting answers to eager, breathless questions. He left every family sanctified by his blessed presence, adding his household words to their treasured memories. 'Here was where he sat; here he slept; he said this, and that.' Along the route, there were pleasant anecdotes and reminiscences to hearten up his following, and help the weary, anxious hours during those long days from April 2d to May 6th. Thoughtful of all details, he gave directions about the horses, how best to feed and care for them, remedies for the sick ones, how to cross the rivers, and was watchful of the comfort and health of all. He was the father and comforter, while still the leader and director of affairs.

"Through all these scenes, the real man shone out and dignified the mantle of his office. I thank God it was given to me to see him as I did, and to have embalmed in my heart such sweet and precious memories of our great chief.

"To me, the last Confederate officer on duty, he gave the great reward and honor of two personal visits to my roof-tree, knowing with his delicate perception how greatly I would value them, and the commendation that 'I gave true and faithful service to the last.'

"With profound regard, I am,

"Faithfully yours,

"M. H. CLARKE."

CHAPTER LIX.

SURRENDER OF LEE.

UPON crossing the Appomattox on the night of April 2d, Lee's army marched toward Amelia Court House. It had been his original intention to go to Danville, but being prevented from carrying out this purpose, he marched toward Lynchburg.

Encumbered by a large wagon train, his march was necessarily slow. His trains were attacked again and again by the enemy's cavalry, adding to the delay.

On April 4th Amelia Court House was reached and the army, being without rations, to appease hunger subsisted on young shoots just putting out upon the trees and parched corn.*

On the 5th the retreat was continued toward Danville; the intention was there to form a junction with Johnston's army, but the enemy had the shortest line, and at Jettersville headed him off, and the march was turned to Lynchburg, where Lee had expressed his

---

* The letter had been captured that asked for rations to be sent to that point.

belief, that he could carry on the war for twenty years.

On April 6th the rear-guard was attacked by a large force of the enemy, and Generals G. W. C. Lee, Ewell, and Anderson, and many others were captured.

General Rosser, of the cavalry, captured a body of 800 of the enemy, who had been sent by Grant, under General Read, to destroy the bridge at Farmville to impede Lee's march. Read was killed in single combat by General Dearing, who was himself mortally wounded.

On April 7th, Farmville was reached, and *here for the first time since leaving Petersburg provisions were issued to the army.* The enemy still pursuing, the quartermasters began to burn their wagons, and whatever they contained was destroyed.

The enemy followed closely, crossed the railroad bridge, and brought Lee to bay, attacked and were repulsed, and the retreat continued.

On the evening of the 8th, with his army wearied and diminished in numbers by men falling by the wayside who had never before abandoned their colors, but were now unable longer to keep up with the retreating column, General Lee decided, after conference with his corps commanders, that he would advance the next day beyond Appomattox Court House, and if the force reported there should be only Sheridan's cavalry, disperse it, and continue the march toward Lynchburg.

Gordon, whose corps had formed the rear-guard from Petersburg, and who had fought daily for the trains, was now transferred to the front. Next morning, April 9th, before daybreak, he, with Fitz Lee's cavalry, moved forward to the attack. He was confronted by Sheridan's cavalry, and he drove them steadily before him, and captured two pieces of artillery. All seemed going well, when Sheridan withdrew from the field, and then, like the lifting of a curtain, Gordon beheld the army of the James advancing through the trees with ten times his number. At the same time Longstreet, covering the rear, being threatened by Meade with a superior force, found it impossible to reinforce Gordon, who, stained with powder and exhausted by his recent battle, reared his knightly head and said, " Tell General Lee my corps is reduced to a frazzle."

Lee then said, " There is nothing left but for me to go and see General Grant." And a flag of truce was raised to suspend hostilities pending the interview between the commanders.

An eye-witness thus describes General

Lee's appearance when he rode off to see
Grant: " He was in full uniform, with handsome embroidered belt and dress-sword, tall
black army hat, and buff leather gauntlets.
His horse, 'old Traveller,' was finely groomed,
and his equipments, bridle-bit, etc., were pol-
ished until they shone like silver; he was accompanied by Colonels Marshall and Taylor,
of his staff." *

Generals Grant and Lee met at the farm-
house of Mr. McLean, a gentleman, who before and during the battle of Manassas, July
18, 1861, had resided at McLean's Ford, over
Bull Run, and moved thence to Appomattox to
be free from war's alarms.   Fate directed the
steps of both armies to his fancied secure and
quiet retreat, and there the end was to come.

A suitable room having been prepared, and
the two generals being seated, General Lee
opened the interview by saying: " General
Grant, I deem it due to proper candor and
frankness to say, at the very beginning of
this interview, that I am not willing even to
discuss any terms of surrender inconsistent
with the honor of my army, which I am determined to maintain to the last."   General
Grant replied, " I have no idea of proposing
dishonorable terms, General ; but I would be

* Colonel Miller Owen ; In Camp and Battle.

glad if you would state what you consider honorable terms."

General Lee then briefly stated the terms upon which he would be willing to surrender. General Grant expressed himself satisfied with them, and the propositions were reduced to writing.

General Lee read the propositions carefully, and copies were made of the paper by Colonel Marshall and General Grant's secretary.

While this was being done, Generals Grant and Lee exchanged a few words of civility, and the Federal generals who were present were introduced to General Lee, but nothing bearing upon the surrender was said.

General Grant having signed his note, General Lee conferred with Colonel Marshall, who wrote a brief note of acceptance of the terms of surrender offered which were as follows : " The officers to give their individual parole not to take arms against the Government of the United States until properly exchanged, and each company or regimental commander to sign a like parole for the men of their commands.

" The arms, artillery, and public property, to be parked and stacked, and turned over to the officers appointed to receive them.

" This will not embrace the side-arms of

the officers, nor their private horses or baggage.

"This done, each officer and man will be allowed to return to their homes, not to be disturbed by the United States authority so long as they observe their parole, and the laws in force where they may reside."

General Lee then rose to depart, and after bowing to the officers present, went out upon the porch, and beckoned to his orderly to lead up his horse. Descending the steps, he paused a moment and looked sadly out over the valley where his army lay, then mounted. General Grant, who had followed and descended a few steps, raised his hat in respectful salutation, as did those who stood upon the porch. Upon observing this courtesy, General Lee, removing his hat, bowed low upon his horse's neck and rode away.

" As soon as he was seen riding toward his army, whole lines of men rushed down to the roadside, and crowded around him to shake his hand. All tried to show him the veneration and esteem in which they held him. Filled with emotion he essayed to speak, but could only say, ' Men, we have fought through the war together. I have done the best I could for you. My heart is too full to say more.' We all knew the pathos of those simple words, of that slight tremble in his

voice, and it was no shame on our manhood
that ' something on a soldier's cheek washed
off the stain of powder ; ' that our tears answered to those of our grand old chieftain,
and that we could only grasp the hand of
' Uncle Robert' and pray ' God help you,
General.' " *

There were 7,892 men of the army of Northern Virginia who had arms in their hands at
the surrender. The total number, including
those who reported afterward, was between
26,000 and 27,000. Grant's army numbered
162,239.†

In connection with the evacuation of Richmond, the following incident is related by
General G. W. C. Lee :

" After I was taken prisoner at Sailor's
Creek, with the greater part of the commands
of General Ewell and General Dick Anderson, and was on my way to Petersburg with
the officers of the three commands, we met
the United States engineer brigade under
command of General Benham, whom I knew
prior to the breaking out of the war as one
of the captains of my own corps—engineers.

" He did not apparently recognize me, and
I did not make myself known to him ; but began talking to General Ewell, in a loud tone

---

* Colonel William Miller Owen : In Camp and Battle.
† Colonel Taylor : Four Years with Lee.

of voice which could be distinctly heard by
all around.

"I heard General Benham say, among
other things, that ' General Weitzel had found,
soon after his entrance into Richmond, a letter
from General Lee giving the condition of the
Army of Northern Virginia, and what he proposed to do should it become necessary to
withdraw from the lines before Richmond and
Petersburg, and that the letter was immediately sent to General Grant.' In answer to some
doubt expressed by General Ewell or someone
else, General Benham replied, ' Oh, there is
no doubt about the letter, for I saw it myself.'

"I received the impression at the time or
afterward, that this letter was a confidential
communication to the Secretary of War in
answer to a resolution of the Confederate
Congress asking for information in 1865.
When I mentioned this statement of General
Benham to General Lee, some time afterward, the latter said, ' This accounts for the
energy of the enemy's pursuit. The first day
after we left the lines he seemed to be entirely at sea with regard to our movements,
after that, though I never worked so hard in
my life to withdraw our armies in safety, he
displayed more energy, skill, and judgment in
his movements than I ever knew him to display before."

In requesting the above statement from General G. W. C. Lee, Major Walthall, then at Beauvoir with Mr. Davis, wrote him as follows :

" Besides its bearing in other respects, it may possibly throw some light upon the yet unexplained failure of General Lee's request for supplies at Amelia Court House, to reach the President or the War Department. . . . It seems to be certain that neither the President, Secretary of War, Quarter-Master - General, nor Commissary - General ever received the requisition.

" Colonels Taylor and Marshall (of General Lee's staff) both remember that it was well understood that such a requisition had been made, but cannot state with precision either the channels through which, or the functionary to whom, it was sent."

CHAPTER LX.

HONORABLE MENTION.

DID my space permit, I would pay special and glad homage to the men who fought and nobly sustained defeat, or now bear their wounds in cheerful poverty, or who fell, examples of all the noble qualities that exalt a nation. But the scope of these memoirs does not permit more than a glimpse of a few of the gallant figures that crowd the memory of every Confederate who looks backward on the field of war.

Louisiana gave us Richard Taylor, who fought under the eye of Stonewall Jackson in the Valley, and whose men charged and took Shields's batteries at Port Republic, and who in Louisiana hurled back in disorder the magnificent army of Banks.

Bishop General Polk, our saintly gallant veteran, whose death left our country, and especially the Church, mourning; Harry T. Hayes, Yorke, Nicholls, Gibson, Gladden, and Moulton, who charged with his men up the hill at Winchester into the fort deemed impregnable, and put Milroy's army to flight;

C. E. Fenner,* who, with his Batteries of " Donaldsonville," under Maurin and Prosper Landry, achieved distinction; the Louisiana Guard," under D'Aquin, Thompson, and Green, all gallant gentlemen whose renown their countrymen treasure above price.

From Georgia came Commander Tattnall, John B. Gordon, that gallant knight whose bravery and skill forced him through rank to rank to the highest command. Wounded in every battle, until at the last, at Appomattox, he beat back Sheridan's cavalry and captured artillery from him until within the last half-hour's life of the Army of Northern Virginia, when he reported his corps fought to a "frazzle." Then, and then only, was the emblem of truce displayed.

Joseph Wheeler, the young "Murat" of the cavalry, General Lawton and his no less distinguished brother-in-law, E. Porter Alexander, the skilful engineer and accomplished artillery officer, for gallantry promoted to be Brigadier-General and Chief of Artillery of Longstreet's Corps; and Hardee, the scientific dauntless soldier; Walker, David R. Jones, Young, Denning, Colquitt, and a shining list I have not space to name.

Mississippi gave her Ferguson, Barksdale, Martin, the two Adams, Featherston, Posey,

---

* Now Associate Justice of the Supreme Court of Louisiana.

and Fizer, who led an army on the ramparts
of Knoxville but left his arm there, and a host
of gallant men.

Alabama sent us Deas, Law, Gracie, and
James Longstreet, dubbed by Lee upon the
field of Sharpsburg his "old war horse," a
stubborn fighter, who held the centre there
with a scant force and a single battery of
artillery; the gallant Twenty-seventh regiment
of North Carolina troops, under Colonel
Cooke, stood as support, without ammunition,
but with flags waving to deceive the enemy.
Three times he repulsed the attacks of a
whole corps. When the cannoneers were
shot down, and help was needed at the guns,
his staff dismounted and took their places.

At Petersburg, when the end was near, and
Lee's lines were broken, he hurried with the
division of General Field to the breach, and
formed his troops across the line of the
enemy's victorious approach, held them at
arm's length until midnight, when the last
man and the last gun of Lee's army had
crossed the Appomattox, and he became like
Marshal Ney, the rear-guard of the once
"Grand Army;" and Rodes, ever in the front,
who laid down his life at Winchester while
led by the indomitable Early, he was fighting the overwhelming force of Sheridan.

"The gallant Pelham," the boy artillerist

who with one gun took position on the left flank of Burnside's army at Fredericksburg, and held his ground, annoyed, and threw into confusion the troops of the enemy advancing to charge Jackson's forces upon the hills at Hamilton's Crossing. Just after receiving his promotion as Lieutenant-Colonel of artillery, "for gallantry and skill," he met his death, leading a squadron in a charge. Shouting "Forward, boys! forward to victory and glory!" a fragment of shell penetrated his skull, and his brave spirit took its flight.

Tennessee gave us Forrest, the great leader of cavalry, Frazier, Cheatham, Jackson, Green, A. J. Vaughn, O. F. Strahl, Archer, and the last, but not least, on this very incomplete list, Cadmus Wilcox, who led his brigade at Gettysburg on July 2d, right into the enemy's lines, capturing prisoners and guns, and only failing in great results from lack of the support looked for.

Kentucky gave us John B. Hood, one of the bravest and most dashing division commanders in the army. Always in the front, he lost a limb at Chickamauga; John C. Breckinridge, "Charley" Field, S. B. Buckner, Morgan, Duke, and Preston; the latter with his fine brigades under Gracie, Trigg, and Kelly, gave the enemy the *coup de grâce* which terminated the battle of Chickamauga.

Missouri gave us Bowen, and Green, and Price, that grand old man, worshipped and followed to the death by his brave patriotic Missourians.

From Arkansas came the gallant Cleburne, McNair, McRea, and Finnegan, the hero of Olustee, Fla., and Ben McCullough, the old Indian fighter who yielded his life on the battle-field of Elkhorn.

From Maryland came brave Commander Buchanan, Generals Trimble, Elzey, Charles Winder, who laid down his life upon the field, and George Stewart, Bradley Johnson, who proved himself a very Bayard in feats of arms, and our Colonel of the Signal Corps, William Norris, who, by systematizing the signals which he displayed under the most furious fire, rendered inestimable service. To Maryland we owe also Snowdon Andrews, the brave and skilled artillery officer, who was so desperately wounded upon the field of Cedar Run that his surgeon reported " hardly enough of his body left to hold his soul."

South Carolina gave us Stephen Elliott, who remained in beleaguered Sumter, and when invited to take rest only did so because promoted and ordered elsewhere; the Hamptons, Kershaw, Hugers, Ramseur, M. C. Butler, Bee, Bonham, Bartow, Drayton, the Prestons, "Dick" Anderson, Jenkins, and Stephen

D. Lee, commander of artillery in Virginia and corps commander in the Army of Tennessee, a body of fine gentlemen who illustrated the proverbial daring of their class. She also gave Colonel Lucius B. Northrop, a gallant soldier of the old army, and one who, as Commissary General, possessed Mr. Davis's confidence unto the end of our struggle.

North Carolina sent Pettigrew, who commanded Heth's division in the charge at Gettysburg, wounded there, he lost his life before recrossing the Potomac; and D. H. Hill, Holmes, Hoke, Pender, Cooke, Ransom, Lane, Scales, Green, Daniel, and the roll of honor stretches out a shining list as I gaze into the past. "When shall their glory fade?"

Texas gave us Albert Sidney Johnston, and Gregg, Robertson, William "old tige" whom his soldiers loved Cabbell; it is easier to specify who was not a brilliant jewel in the gorgeous crown of glory than to name them all.

Florida gave Kirby Smith and Anderson and many other gallant and true men.

And "Old Virginia" gave us her Lees, Jackson, Early, Ewell, Pickett, Ed. Johnson, Archer, Heth, Lomax, Dearing, Ashby, Mumford, Rosser, the brothers Pegram; and the gallant men who fell on the heights of Gettysburg, Garnett, Kemper, and Armistead; and Dabney H. Maury, who with 7,600 in-

fantry and artillery held Mobile for eighteen
days against General Canby. Had our cause
succeeded, Virginia's gallant son would have
been promoted to be Lieutenant-General.

A. P. Hill, the fierce young fighter, who,
famous in many battles, came opportunely
from Harper's Ferry to Sharpsburg, beat back
Burnside, and saved the flank of Lee's army,
but fell at last on the field of Petersburg ; from
the first hour to his last not only doing his
best, but all that man could accomplish, to
serve his country.

Patriotic enthusiasm could present no
grander picture than that of General Wade
Hampton, a fit representative man of the much
ridiculed but *living* and beloved *chivalry* of
the South, who, while looking through his
glass during a cavalry battle near Petersburg,
saw his son Preston, who, possessed of great
personal beauty, much mind, and keen wit,
had just reached his twenty-first year, fall
dead on the field, and his brother Wade stoop
over him and fall across his beautiful young
brother's body. The bereaved father thought
them both slain, and unsheathing his sword,
rode straight, not to receive their dying words,
but for the hottest part of the battle, and
fought with all his might in a hand to hand
encounter, and himself came out—probably the
only division commander in the world to

whom a like incident has occurred—with a deep sabre cut which accentuates rather than mars the noble contour of his face.

Or what could be more touching than the meeting of General Lee with his young son Robert, on the bloody field of Fredericksburg, mounted on one of the artillery caissons of the battery in which he was serving as a private. He was so begrimed with smoke and powder that the General did not know his boy. Robert asked, "General, are you going to put us in again?" "Yes," said his father, "but my boy, who are you?" "Why, do you not know me, father? I am Robbie." "God defend you, my son," answered the General, "you must go in again."

CHAPTER LXI.

THE WASHINGTON ARTILLERY OF NEW ORLEANS.

THE Richmond people remember well the
Washington Artillery of New Orleans, their
fresh uniforms, and the splendid crimson and
gold standard with its silver cross cannon
under which, before they "smelt powder,"
they marched in review before the President
on Union Hill. These, and other New
Orleans companies, gave dinners, danced, and
sung, and "did the thing handsomely" wherever money was to be spent or amusement
was to be found during their brief visits from
the field; but while fighting their sixty battles
they performed prodigies of valor, "all that
was left of them."

But there was a different look in their eyes
after facing death so often; the lack of food
had reduced their physique, but the laugh was
as ready as ever, their well-brushed, threadbare uniforms were as natty and worn with as
jaunty a grace as when newly donned. Their
hospitality, albeit they could offer only potatoes or beans, was unstinted.

The Natchez troops marched out like the

B.F. CHEATHAM.

J.C. PEMBERTON

G.H. STEUART.

FITZ LEE.

JOHN H. MORGAN.

J.B. GORDON, OF GA.

E. KIRBY SMITH.

CONFEDERATE GENERALS.

Queen's Guards, a " Lah de dah " assemblage
of handsome young gentlemen born to wealth
and position, who recognized their duty to
bear their share of blows because it befitted
their birth. When the bloody work began,
however, they pushed in to the thickest of
the fight, and every woman and man in Mississippi thanked God for the place of their
nativity.

Barksdale's brigade, on December 11, 1862,
at Fredericksburg, prevented Burnside's army
of 100,000 men from building their pontoon
bridges, and, although bombarded by 150
pieces of artillery, held their position from 7
A.M. to 7 P.M. The same Brigade, composed of
the Thirteenth, Seventeenth, Eighteenth, and
Twenty-first Mississippi regiments, numbering
1,308 men, behind the stone wall at the foot
of Marye's Hill, repulsed Sedgwick's corps,
numbering 22,000. Under cover of a flag of
truce, the enemy charged again the " thin
gray line," and overran it through weight of
numbers, killing or capturing all the brave
defenders, with a loss to themselves of
nearly 5,000 men. The pride we felt in their
steady, dauntless courage cannot be expressed in words.

Captain John Taylor Wood, C. S. N., upheld the name and fame of his grandsire,
General Zachary Taylor. He is the son of

the late Surgeon-General R. C. Wood, U. S.
A., than whom a better and braver man never
lived. Commander Wood destroyed several
transports and vessels of the enemy, among
them the ship *Rappahannock*, of 1,200 tons ;
he assisted in preparing the *Virginia* (*Mer-
imac*) for service, took part in the fight between the *Virginia* and the *Congress, Cumberland, Wabash, Monitor,* and others, and
served efficiently during the enemy's attempt
to pass Drury's Bluff.

In the summer of 1863, Lieutenant Wood
succeeded in capturing in Chesapeake Bay
the United States gun-boats *Reliance, Satel-
lite,* and a number of other vessels, and was
promoted to be Commander in the Navy.

At Newbern, N. C., Commander Wood,
with his boat squadron, captured the United
States gun-boat *Underwriter* under the guns
of two of the enemy's forts. He destroyed
two gun-boats at Plymouth, N. C., when
General Hoke captured that place in 1864.

In August, 1864, the *Atlanta* cruised off
the north coast of the United States in the
neighborhood of New York and Boston, and
Commander Wood captured over thirty of
the enemy's vessels. For these services he
received the thanks of the Confederate Congress, and was promoted to be Post Captain.
Throughout all these hot encounters his piety

and gentle consideration for others was conspicuous on every field.

The gallant Captain Wilkinson's deeds pressed close upon those of his friend and brother-officer, and the world will not for· get Commanders Semmes, Maffitt, Pegram, Maury, Loyal, Jones, and other naval heroes who are too rich in fame to need my mite.

None fought more gallantly than Heros von Borcke, an Austrian officer of distinction, who came to offer his sword, and was assigned to J. E. B. Stuart's cavalry, and served with conspicuous bravery until severely wounded; he left the service with broken health. The President, loath to relinquish him, wrote to acknowledge the aid he had given, and sent him on a mission to England.

But Confederate women render their hearts' best homage to the gallant nameless dead, the " high privates " of our splendid army, and to those survivors who wear their " hodden gray " with proud memories of sacrifices made and duty faithfully performed, for no other reward than an approving conscience, who labor for their daily bread without a murmur, and are as ready now to affirm the justice of their cause as they are to fight for the United States. They do not say we believed we were right then, but they loudly proclaim we knew it then and know it now,

CHAPTER LXII.

As time wore on all the news we received was of that kind which is reputed to travel fast, but did not over the broken railways, and tangled and trailing telegraph wires. At last came the dreadful rumor that General Lee was retreating, and the President and his cabinet were coming to Charlotte to meet General Johnston and his army. I felt then that I must obey Mr. Davis's solemn charge, and also that I might embarrass him sadly by remaining there.

That night the treasure train of the Confederacy and that of the Richmond banks, escorted by the midshipmen under the accomplished and gallant Captain Parker, came through Charlotte ; and as among the escort were my brother Jefferson and Mr. Davis's grandnephew, and there seemed to be a panic imminent, I decided to go with my children and servants on the extra train provided for the treasure, which could only run as far as Chester, as the road was broken,

JEFFERSON DAVIS HOWELL.

We reached there in the morning and were met by Generals John S. Preston, Hood, and Chesnut. General Preston said, " We of this day have no future, but we can worthily bear defeat; anything that man can do I will for you or the President." General Hood said: " If I have lost my leg and also lost my freedom, I am miserable indeed." And General Chesnut bowed his dignified head and said: " Let me help you if I can, it is probably the last service I can render." And these three types of Southern gentlemen formed a noble picture as they stood calm in the expectation of our great woe.

With much trouble an ambulance was secured for my family and a wagon for our luggage, and after dark I started to follow the treasure train on the road to Abbeville. The ambulance was too heavily laden in the deep mud, and as my maid was too weak to walk and my nurse was unwilling, I walked five miles in the darkness in mud over my shoe tops, with my cheerful little baby in my arms. There were various alarms of " Yankees " at Frog Level and other places on the road, but about one o'clock we reached in safety a little church in which the treasure guardians had taken refuge. A little bride who had accompanied her husband, who was with the bank treasure, told me kindly, " We are lying on the floor, but have left the communion table for you out of respect, but the additional comfort of the table did not tempt one to commit sacrilege." After a weary night we moved on at daylight.

Captain Parker was exceedingly kind and attentive to us. We held no communications with the actual guardians of either the Confederate or bank treasury.

The price for provisions on the road, from the hostelries and even the private houses, was fifty cents or one dollar for a biscuit, and the same for a glass of milk. It was difficult to feed my children except when we reached the house of some devoted Confederate, and then I did not like to avail of their generosity.

Finally, when it seemed we had endured fatigue enough to have put a "girdle round the earth," more dead than alive, we reached Abbeville, where our welcome was as warm as though we had something to confer. The treasure trains, without halting, moved on to Washington, Ga.

Mr. Armistead Burt and his wife received us in their fine house with a generous, tender welcome, though fully expecting that, for having given us shelter, it would be burnt by the enemy. There we remained for a few days resting, and in painful expectation of worse news. It came, as we feared, all too soon.

The following letter was received, and a despatch announcing General Lee's surrender.

"AUGUSTA, April 21, 1865.

" MADAME : Herewith I send despatch just received, and which I hope will reach you promptly.

" I send you copy of despatch announcing the suspension of arms.

" I have the honor to be,
"Very respectfully,
" Your obedient servant,
"A. D. FRY."

A specimen of wild rumors is appended to show the cloud that covered us with thick darkness.

"COKESBURY DEPOT, Saturday Afternoon, 2.30 o'clock P.M.,
"April 22, 1865.

"MRS. DAVIS.

" MADAME : I have the honor, in compliance with my offer, to write from this place. I presume you heard the rumors of yesterday, viz., that an armistice of sixty days had been agreed upon, and General Grant had sent couriers to the different raiding parties to that effect ; that commissioners to negotiate terms had been appointed, consisting on our part of Generals Lee, Johnston, and Beauregard, and on the part of the Yankees of Grant, Sher-

man, and Thomas ; also that the French fleet
had attacked the Yankee gun-boats at New
Orleans, and had taken the city. One passenger said that President Davis left Ninety-
six Station by stage for Augusta, Ga.; another
that he had an escort of three hundred cavalry, and would come the route by Abbeville.
As all the above are reports, I know nothing
positive of their reliability. The Newbury
train is now one hour and a half behind time.
If it arrives in time for the Abbeville train, I
will add a postscript if there is anything new.
If I can do anything for you, you have but to
command me. . . . P.S. 3.30. The Newbury train is in. I saw Mr. Fleetwood, from
Columbia. He says he conversed with Colonel Urquhart, of the army, that the armistice
is positively so, and he had seen orders to
the Yankee raiders to that effect. He was
told that President Davis was escorted by
General Geary, and was on his way to Augusta, Ga.

> " Very truly your obedient servant,
>   " A. A. FRANKLIN HILL,
>   " *Major First Georgia Regulars.*"

A courier arrived with the news that General Johnston's army were engaged in the
preliminary arrangements for surrender. He
also informed me of Mr. Davis's arrival in

Charlotte, and of the announcement made to him there of the assassination of Mr. Lincoln. I burst into tears, the first I had shed, which flowed from the mingling of sorrow for the family of Mr. Lincoln, and a thorough realization of the inevitable results to the Confederates, now that they were at the mercy of the Federals.

I felt unwilling, if all was lost east of the Mississippi River, to hamper the Confederate President in his efforts to reach the trans-Mississippi, and there by resistance enforce better terms than our conquerors seemed willing to grant.

Our friend, Colonel Henry Leovy, kindly consented to meet him at the Saluda River with a note, to say that I would not wait his coming, but try to get out of the country as best I might, and meet him in Texas or elsewhere. This letter Mr. Leovy delivered, but Mr. Davis pushed on to Abbeville, hoping to see us before our departure. We had, however, left there for Washington, Ga., on the morning of the day he arrived.

Mr. Harrison arrived that day and brought me a telegram as follows, which he had received from Mr. Davis, who had asked him to join and take care of us.

"CHARLOTTE, N. C., April 24, 1865.

"B. N. HARRISON, Chester, S. C.

"The hostile Government reject the proposed settlement, and order active operations to be resumed in forty-eight hours from noon to-day.

"JEFFERSON DAVIS."

About half an hour's travel out of Abbeville, our wagons met the treasure of the Virginia banks returning. After a few words of greeting to the officer in command, the train moved on, and we continued our journey to Washington.

We found the whole town in a state of most depressing disorder. General and Mrs. Elzey called to see me, and said that when the news of the surrender was received there, the quartermasters' and commissaries' stores had been sacked, and Mrs. Elzey laughingly told me she had picked up a card of pearl buttons in the street which General Elzey insisted she should throw down again, as it was "undoubtedly public property." General Toombs called with many kind offers of hospitality, but I was anxious to get off before Mr. Davis could reach Washington, fearful that his uneasiness about our safety would cause him to keep near our train and of his being pursued by the enemy. My young brother Jefferson had been paroled at Augusta, and came at once to join and offer me his services.

Colonel Moody, a Mississippi lawyer who was going home, and Colonel Moran, of Louisiana, volunteered to accompany us and take charge of the party. Mr. Harrison, who had rejoined us at Abbeville, was travelling with us ; he had been an inmate of our house so long that we were mutually attached, and he rendered every service in his power. Added to these were Messrs. Hathaway, Messick, and Winder Monroe, all of Kentucky, and some paroled Confederate soldiers who drove the ambulance and wagons. We moved out on the afternoon of the same day that we reached Washington, and made ten miles that afternoon.

As soon as our tents were pitched, while we were trying to get our tea in the awkward manner of townspeople camping out, Mr. Davis's nephew-in-law, Mr. Richard Nugent, came up with a note from him bidding farewell and expressing his bitter regret at not seeing us at Washington for consultation, and offering a few words of counsel. Mr. Nugent took back an answer immediately, begging him not to seek an interview, and the ground felt very hard that night as I lay looking into the gloom and unable to pierce it even by conjectures. The next day we moved on and

met crowds of soldiers walking home, some
very foot-sore and depressed, but generally
cordial. I invited as many as would to take a
drive in one or the other of the wagons or the
ambulance.

On the third day one of our party found
we were to be halted by a number of disorganized mounted Confederates, to "have a
divide," as they thought we were quartermasters going off with treasure. After we halted
for the night the party came up to the camp
fire, and the commander of it recognized me
as having dressed his wounded arm in Richmond. After many protestations of regard,
they gave us a safe-conduct to pass by another
party whom we met on the cross roads. I
explained to them that in lieu of money I had
a few groceries, my clothes, and nothing more.
One of them said, "I am sorry it is not
money, you could have kept it." Now we
began to see branches of trees newly broken
lying in the road; evidently, from the number
of them, they indicated something, and it
gave the gentlemen in charge much uneasiness. Colonel Moody communicated his suspicions to me, that we were followed by some
enemy.

At last, after a long day's journey, we
halted about sundown, and my coachman went
into town for some milk. A party of men

met him, took the mule that he was riding, and told him that they would have all the mules and horses that night. Our dread was great of being left helpless in the woods without transportation. Upon hearing this circumstance the gentlemen parked the wagons and tied the horses and mules inside. They divided into watches so as to meet the robbers before they had made an assault.

Mr. Davis has related the rest of the journey better than another could.

CHAPTER LXIII.

THE JOURNEY TO GREENSBOROUGH.—THE SUR-RENDER OF JOHNSTON.

THE President and his party moved to Greensborough. The President telegraphed to General Johnston from Danville that Lee had surrendered, and on arriving at Greensborough, conditionally requested him to meet him there for conference, where General Beauregard had his headquarters. Mr. Davis wrote in substance of the meeting:

"In compliance with my request, General Johnston came to Greensborough, N. C., and with General Beauregard met me and most of my Cabinet there. Though sensible of the effect of the surrender of the Army of Northern Virginia, and the consequent discouragement which these two events would produce, I did not despair. We had effective armies in the field, and a rich and productive territory both east and west of the Mississippi, whose citizens had shown no desire to surrender. Ample supplies had been collected in the railroad depots, and much still remained to be placed at our disposal when needed.

" At the first conference of the members of the Cabinet and the generals, General Johnston expressed a desire to open a correspondence with General Sherman, with a view to suspend hostilities, and thereby to permit the civil authorities to enter into the needful arrangements to end the war. As long as we were able to keep the field, I had never contemplated a surrender, except upon the terms of a belligerent, and never expected a Confederate army to surrender while it was able either to fight or to retreat. Lee had surrendered only when it was impossible for him to do either, and had proudly rejected Grant's demand until he found himself surrounded and his line of retreat cut off. I was not hopeful of negotiations between the civil authorities of the United States and those of the Confederacy, believing that, even if Sherman should agree to such a proposition, his Government would not ratify it. After having distinctly announced my opinions, I yielded to the judgment of my constitutional advisers, and consented to permit Johnston to hold a conference with Sherman.

" Johnston left for his army headquarters, and I, expecting that he would soon take up his line of retreat, which his superiority in cavalry would protect from harassing pursuit, proceeded with my Cabinet and staff to Charlotte, N. C. On the way, a despatch was received from him, stating that Sherman had agreed to a conference, and asking that the Secretary of War, General Breckinridge, should return to co-operate in it.

" When we arrived at Charlotte, on April 18, 1865, we received a telegram announcing the assassination of President Lincoln. A vindictive policy was speedily substituted for his, which avowedly was to procure a surrender of our forces in the field upon any terms, to stop the further effusion of blood.

" On the same day, Sherman and Johnston united on a basis of agreement, which contained the following provisions :

" ' That both of the contending parties should maintain their *status quo* until either of the Commanding Generals should give notice of its termination, and allow reasonable time to his opponent.

" ' That the Confederate armies should be disbanded and conducted to the several State capitals, and deposit their arms and public property in the State arsenal; each officer and man to file an agreement to cease from acts of war, and abide by the action of the Federal and State authorities.

" ' That there should be recognition by the Executive of the United States of the several State Governments, on their officers and legislatures taking the oaths prescribed by the Constitution of the United States ; and where conflicting State Governments have resulted from the war, the legitimacy of all shall be submitted to the Supreme Court of the United States.

" ' That all Federal Courts should be re-established, in the several States, with powers as defined by the Constitution of the United States and of the States, respectively

" ' That the people and inhabitants of the States should be guaranteed, so far as the Executive can, their political rights and franchises, as well as their rights of person and property, as defined by the Constitution of the United States and of the States, respectively.

" ' That the Executive authority of the Government of the United States should not disturb any of the people by reason of the late war, so long as they live in peace and quiet, abstain from acts of armed hostility, and obey the laws.

" ' That, in general terms, war should cease; a general amnesty, so far as the Executive of the United States could command on condition of the disbandment of the Confederate armies, the distribution of arms, and the resumption of peaceful pursuits by the officers and men hitherto composing said armies, Not being fully empowered by our respective principals, to fulfil these terms, we individually and officially pledge ourselves to promptly obtain necessary authority, and to carry out the above programme.

    ' " W. T. SHERMAN, *Major-General,* etc.

    " ' J. E. JOHNSTON, *General,* etc.'

"I notified General Johnston that I approved of his last action, but in doing so doubted whether the agreement would be ratified by the United States Government. The opinion entertained in regard to President Johnson and Stanton, his venomous Secretary of War, did not permit me to expect that they would be less vindictive after a surrender of our army had been proposed than when it was regarded as a formidable body in the field. Whatever hope others entertained that the war was about to be peacefully ended, was soon dispelled by the rejection of the basis of the agreement by the Government of the United States, and a notice from Sherman of the termination of the armistice in forty-eight hours after noon of April 24th. On the 26th General Johnston again met General Sherman, who offered the same terms which had been made with General Lee. Johnston accepted the terms, and the surrender was made, his troops being paroled, and the officers being permitted to retain their side-arms, baggage, and private horses.

" The total number of prisoners thus paroled at Greensborough, N. C., as reported by General Schofield, was 36,817 ; in Georgia and Florida, as reported by General Wilson, 52,543 ; in all under General Johnston, 89,-360.

" General Lee had succumbed to the inevitable. Some persons, with probably a desire to pay a weak tribute to Lee's kind heart, or to rob Grant of his claims to magnanimity in the matter of the surrender, have said that General Lee had only surrendered to stop the effusion of blood.

" This is not true. He had no weaknesses where his plain duty was concerned. He surrendered to overwhelming force and insurmountable difficulties. In Grant's treatment of his prisoners, let him have all the credit that can attach to him. The surrender of Johnston was a different affair. Johnston's line of retreat, as chosen by himself through South Carolina, was open and had supplies placed upon it at various points. He had a large force, of which over 36,000 were paroled at Greensborough, N. C. We had other forces in the field, and we were certainly in a position to make serious resistance. This was all the more important, as such ability would have been of service in securing better terms in bringing the war to an end.

"It might have been possible to have made some arrangements that would have secured the political rights of the States, and their immunity from the terrible calamities that afterward fell upon them. General Johnston had these matters and the details of a plan for his proposed movement fully placed before him, with orders to execute it. He disobeyed the order and surrendered his army, and put every thing at the mercy of the conquerors, without making a movement to secure terms that might have availed to protect the political rights of the people and preserve their property from pillage when it was in his power."

Mr. Davis felt that General Johnston's failure to attempt what might have turned out to be his most valuable service to the people of the South, should have tempered the violence of his assaults upon some others who were exerting themselves in behalf of the South.

On May 8th, General Richard Taylor agreed with General Canby for the surrender of the land and naval forces in Mississippi and Alabama, on terms similar to those made between Johnston and Sherman.

On May 26th, the Chiefs of Staff of Gen-

erals Kirby Smith and General Canby arranged similar terms for the surrender of the
troops in the trans-Mississippi Department.

The total number thus paroled by General Canby in the Department of Alabama and
Mississippi was 42,293, to which may be added less than 150 of the navy; while the number surrendered by General Kirby Smith, of
the trans-Mississippi Department, was 17,-
686.

Extract from a letter written at this time :

". . . . It was at Salisbury where I
first encountered Mr. Davis during that sad
time, and I had found very pleasant quarters
at the home of the Episcopal clergyman, rector of that charge. About sunset, Mr. Davis,
General Cooper, Colonel William Preston
Johnston (I think), and one or two others of
the President's staff, came to the same house.

"At tea and after tea, Mr. Davis was cheerful, pleasant, and inclined to talk. I remember we sat upon the porch until about ten
o'clock, the President with an unlighted cigar
in his mouth, talking of the misfortune of General Lee's surrender.

"On the following morning, at breakfast,
Mr. Davis sat at the left hand of the host.
In the midst of the meal the clergyman's little
girl, a child of only seven or eight years, came
in crying and greatly disturbed. She ap-

proached the table just between the President and her father, and said :

"'Oh, papa, old Lincoln's coming and going to kill us all.'

"Mr. Davis at once laid down his knife and fork, and placing his right hand upon the child's head, turned her fearful face toward his own and said, with animation, 'Oh, no, my little lady, you need not fear that. Mr. Lincoln is not such a bad man, he does not want to kill anybody, and certainly not a little girl like you.'

"The child was soon pacified. I shall never forget the kindly expression of the President's face.

"At Charlotte, on the 18th, I saw him again, on the day following the assassination of Mr. Lincoln.

"The news had reached Charlotte, but was not credited. Somehow we learned that General Breckinridge would be on the train that afternoon, and with several other Kentuckians I went to the depot. His first desire was to see the President, so we went with him to Mr. Davis. We found him sitting in a chair in the door which opened on the sidewalk. After shaking hands with General Breckinridge, he asked immediately :

"'Is it true, General, that Mr. Lincoln was killed?' 'Yes, sir,' replied General Breckin-

ridge (who had just come from the front).
' General Sherman received a telegram this
morning that he was shot in Ford's theatre, at
Washington, last night.' Mr. Davis said
promptly, and with feeling, ' I am sorry to
learn it. Mr. Lincoln was a much better man
than his successor will be, and it will go harder
with our people. It is bad news for us.' "

The letter that follows shows General
Hampton's views of the surrender at the time,
and his loyal feeling to our cause, which, however, like Mr. Davis's, were never doubted.

"YORKVILLE, May 1, 1865.

" MY DEAR SIR: I left Hillsborough as soon
as I learned of the agreement made between
Generals Sherman and Johnston, and pushed
on rapidly to this point, where I arrived at
one this morning. A question arises as to
whether I was included in this convention, and
I have agreed to leave it to the Secretary of
War for his decision. The convention and
the subsequent order of General Johnston,
disbanded all the troops at once. I think you
will have to rely on a small body of picked
men to get you across the river. I will have
some such who will go on as soon as they arrive here, which they will do to-day or to-
morrow. My own movements will depend
on your orders and wishes. It will give me

great pleasure to assist you if I can do so, and you may rest assured that I shall stick to our flag as long as anyone can be found to uphold it.   I have given General Wheeler my views of this movement out West, and he will explain everything to you.   Should I not overtake you, I beg you to believe that you have my earnest good wishes and my prayers for your success.   On my return to Hillsborough on the 25th, I found to my great surprise, that a convention had settled terms between Generals Johnston and Sherman.   I told General Johnston that I did not consider myself as bound by his convention, but as he did consider me so bound, that the matter should be referred to you, and that I would abide your decision.

"I sent a despatch to you and I have come as rapidly as possible to this point, in hopes of hearing from you.   My plans will be determined by your decision and wishes.   Whereever and however I can best do service, there I wish to be.

"If I remain here I shall be most happy to render any service to Mrs. Davis.   That God may protect you and bring you back in safety and with success, is the prayer of

"Your sincere friend,

"WADE HAMPTON.

"To his Excellency, PRESIDENT DAVIS."

JEFFERSON DAVIS WHEN CAPTURED.

CHAPTER LXIV.

CAPTURE OF PRESIDENT DAVIS, AS WRITTEN BY HIMSELF.

"AFTER the expiration of the armistice I rode out of Charlotte, attended by all but two members of my cabinet, my personal staff, and the cavalry that had been concentrated from different fields of detached service. The number was about two thousand. They represented five brigade organizations. Though so much reduced in number, they were in a good state of efficiency, and among their officers were some of the best in our service.

"After two halts of half a day each, we reached the Savannah River.

"I crossed early in the morning of May 4th, with a company which had been detailed as my escort, and rode some miles to a farmhouse, where I halted to get breakfast and have our horses fed. Here I learned that a regiment of the enemy was moving upon Washington, Ga., which was one of our depots of supplies, and I sent back a courier with a pencil-note addressed to General Vaughan, or the officer commanding the advance, requesting him to come on and join me immediately. After waiting a considerable time I determined to move on with my escort, trusting that we should arrive in Washington in time to rally the citizens to its defence. When I reached there scouts were sent out on different roads, and my conclusion was that we had had a false alarm. The Secretary of State, Mr. Benjamin, being unaccustomed to travelling on horseback, parted from me at the house where we stopped to breakfast, to take another mode of conveyance and a different route from that which I was pursuing, with intent to join me in the trans-Mississippi Department. At Washington the Secretary of the Navy, Mr. Mallory, left me to place his family in safety.

The Secretary of War, Mr. Breckinridge, had remained with the cavalry at the crossing of the Savannah River. During the night after my arrival in Washington he sent in an application for authority to draw from the treasure, under the protection of the troops, enough to make to them a partial payment. I authorized the acting Secretary of the Treasury to meet the requisition by the use of the silver coin in the train. When the next day passed without the troops coming forward, I wrote to the Secretary of War to deprecate longer delay, having heard that Gen-

CAPTURE OF MR. DAVIS.

eral Upton had passed within a few miles of
the town, on his way to Augusta to receive
the surrender of the garrison and military
material at that place, in conformity with orders issued by General Johnston. This was
my first positive information of his surrender.

Not receiving an immediate reply to the
note addressed to General Breckinridge, I
explained to Captain Campbell, of Kentucky,
commanding my escort, that his company was
not strong enough to fight, and too large to
pass without observation, asked him to inquire if there were ten men who would volunteer to go with me without question wherever
I should choose. He brought back for answer that the whole company volunteered on
the terms proposed. I was gratified, but felt
to accept the offer would expose them to unnecessary hazard, and told him, in any manner he might think best, to form a party of ten
men. With these ten men and five of my
personal staff, I left Washington. Secretary
Reagan remained for a short time to transfer
to Mr. Semple and Mr. Tidball the treasure
in his hands, except a few thousand dollars.
Mr. Reagan overtook me in a few hours.

"I saw no more of General Breckinridge,
but learned subsequently that he followed our
route to overtake me, but heard of my capture, and, turned to the east and reached the

Florida coast unmolested. On the way he
met J. Taylor Wood, and, in an open boat
they crossed the straits to the West Indies.
The cavalry command left at the Savannah
River was paroled, on the condition of returning home and remaining unmolested, and
the troops inclined to accept those terms.
Had General Johnston obeyed the order sent
to him from Charlotte, and moved on the
route selected by himself, with all his cavalry,
so much of the infantry as could be mounted,
and the light artillery, he could not have been
successfully pursued by General Sherman.
His force, united to that I had assembled at
Charlotte, would have been sufficient to van-
quish any troops which the enemy had between us and the Mississippi River.

"Had the cavalry with which I left Charlotte been associated with a force large enough
to inspire hope for the future, instead of being discouraged by the surrender of their
rear, it would probably have gone on, and,
when united with the forces of Maury, Forrest, and Taylor, in Alabama and Mississippi,
have constituted an army large enough to attract stragglers, and revive the drooping spirits of the country. In the worst view of the
case it should have been able to cross to the
trans-Mississippi Department, and, there unit-
ing with the armies of E. K. Smith and Ma-

gruder, to form an army which, in the portion
of that country abounding in supplies and de-
ficient in rivers and railroads, could have continued the war until our enemy, foiled in the
purpose of subjugation, should have agreed,
on the basis of a return to the Union, to acknowledge the constitutional rights of the
States, and by a convention, or quasi-treaty,
to guarantee security of person and property.
To this hope I clung, and if our independence
could not be achieved, so much, at least, I
trusted might be gained.

" Those who have endured the horrors of
' reconstruction,' who have, under ' carpet-bag
rule,' borne insult, robbery, and imprisonment
without legal warrant, can appreciate the value
of even such a limited measure of success.

" When I left Washington, Ga., my object
was to go to the south far enough to pass
points occupied by Federal troops, and then
turn to the west, cross the Chattahoochie, and
meet the forces still supposed to be in the
field in Alabama.   If there should be no prospect of a successful resistance east of the
Mississippi, I intended to cross to the trans-
Mississippi Department, where I believed
Generals E. K. Smith and Magruder would
continue to uphold our cause.

" After leaving Washington I overtook a
commissary and quartermaster's train, having

public papers of value in charge, and finding
that they had no experienced woodman with
it, I gave them four of the men of my party,
and went on with the rest. On the second or
third day after leaving Washington I heard
that a band of marauders, supposed to be
stragglers and deserters from both armies,
were in pursuit of my family, whom I had not
seen since they left Richmond, but who, I
heard at Washington, had gone with my
private secretary and seven paroled men, who
generously offered their services as an escort,
to the Florida coast. I immediately changed
direction and rode rapidly east across the
country to overtake them.

" About nightfall the horses of my escort
gave out, but I pressed on with Secretary Reagan and my personal staff. It was a bright
moonlight night ; and just before day, as the
moon was sinking below the tree tops, I met a
party of men in the road, who answered my
questions by saying they belonged to an Alabama regiment ; that they were coming from
a village not far off, on their way homeward.
Upon inquiry being made, they told me they
had passed an encampment of wagons, with
women and children, and asked me if we belonged to that party. Upon being answered
in the affirmative, they took their leave.

" After a short time, I was hailed by a voice

which I recognized as that of my private secretary, Burton N. Harrison, who informed me
that the marauders had been hanging around
the camp, and that he and others were on
post around it, and were expecting an assault
as soon as the moon went down. A silly story
had got abroad that it was a treasure train,
and the *auri sacra fames* had probably in-
stigated these marauders, as it subsequently
stimulated General J. H. Wilson to send out
a large cavalry force to capture the same train.
I travelled with my family two or three days,
when, believing that they were out of the
region of marauders, I determined to leave
their encampment at nightfall to execute my
original purpose. My horse and those of my
party were saddled preparatory to a start,
when one of my staff, who had ridden into
the neighboring village, returned and told me
that he had heard that a marauding party
intended to attack the camp that night. This
decided me to wait long enough to see
whether there was any truth in the rumor,
which I supposed would be ascertained in a
few hours.* My horse remained saddled

---

* There was a proposition made to disembarrass us of our wagons,
to which I consented, and only asked time to get out a change of
clothes for my children ; but Colonel Moody objected to the time
necessary, and said it could be done next halt—and the next day we
were captured at daybreak,

and my pistols in the holsters, and I lay down
fully dressed to rest. Nothing occurred to
rouse me until just before dawn, when my
coachman, a free colored man who clung to
our fortunes, came and told me there was firing over the branch, just behind our encampment. I stepped out of my wife's tent and
saw some horsemen, whom I immediately
recognized as cavalry, deploying around the
encampment. I turned back and told my
wife these were not the expected marauders,
but regular troopers.* She implored me to
leave her at once. I hesitated, from unwillingness to do so, and lost a few precious
moments before yielding to her importunity.
My horse and arms were near the road on
which I expected to leave, and down which
the cavalry approached ; it was therefore
impracticable for me to reach them. As it
was quite dark in the tent, I picked up what
was supposed to be my "raglan," a waterproof light overcoat, without sleeves ; it was
subsequently found to be my wife's, so very
like my own as to be mistaken for it ; as I
started, my wife thoughtfully threw over my
head and shoulders a shawl. I had gone
perhaps fifteen or twenty yards when a trooper

---

* He had said as he first went out, "I hope I still have influence
enough with the Confederates to prevent your being robbed."

galloped up and ordered me to halt and surrender, to which I gave a defiant answer,
and, dropping the shawl and raglan from my
shoulders, advanced toward him ; he levelled
his carbine at me, but I expected, if he fired,
he would miss me, and my intention was in
that event to put my hand under his foot,
tumble him off on the other side, spring into
his saddle, and attempt to escape. My wife,
who had been watching, when she saw the
soldier aim his carbine at me, ran forward and
threw her arms around me. Success depended on instantaneous action, and recognizing
that the opportunity had been lost, I turned
back, and, the morning being damp and chilly,
passed on to a fire beyond the tent.

" Our pursuers had taken different roads,
and approached our camp from opposite directions ; they encountered each other and commenced firing, both supposing that they had
met our armed escort, and some casualties resulted from their conflict with an imaginary
body of Confederate troops. During the confusion, while attention was concentrated upon
myself, except by those who were engaged in
pillage, one of my aides, Colonel J. Taylor
Wood, with Lieutenant Barnwell, walked off
unobserved. His daring on the sea made him
an object of special hostility to the Federal
Government, and he properly availed himself

of the possible means of escape. Colonel
Pritchard went over to their battle-field, and I
did not see him for a long time, surely more
than an hour after my capture. He subsequently claimed credit, in a conversation with
me, for the forbearance shown by his men in
not shooting me when I refused to surrender.

" Many falsehoods have been uttered in regard to my capture, which have been exposed
in publications by persons there present—by
Secretary Reagan, by the members of my
personal staff, and by the colored coachman,
Jim Jones, which must have been convincing
to all who desired to know the truth. We
were, when prisoners, subjected to petty pillage, as described in the publications referred
to, and in others ; and to annoyances such as
military *gentlemen* never commit or permit.

" At this time quick firing was heard on the
side of the swamp. We afterward learned
that two Federal companies of our pursuers had met in the gray of the morning, and
each had mistaken the other for Confederate
troops.

" While the camp was being plundered,
which was done with great celerity, there was
a shriek dreadful to hear, and our servants told
us it came from a poor creature who, in prying
up the lid of a trunk with his loaded musket,
shot off his own hand. Out of this trunk the

hooped skirt was procured, which had never been worn but which they purported to have removed from Mr. Davis's person. No hooped skirt could have been worn on our journey, even by me, without great inconvenience, and I had none with me except the new one in the trunk. I have long since ceased to combat falsehood when it has been uttered and scattered broadcast, a much less distance than this one has been borne upon the wings of hate and vilification, and I now rest the case, though, could the tortures wantonly inflicted when he was a helpless prisoner, have been averted from my husband by any disguise, I should gladly have tried to persuade him to assume it; and who shall say the stratagem would not have been legitimate? I would have availed myself of a Scotch cap and cloak, or any other expedient to avert from him the awful consequences of his capture.

When we had travelled back a day's drive, as we were about to get in the wagons, a man galloped into camp waving over his head a printed slip of paper. One of our servants told us it was Mr. Johnson's proclamation of a reward for Mr. Davis's capture as the accessory to Mr. Lincoln's assassination. I was much shocked, but Mr. Davis was quite unconcerned, and said, " The miserable scoun-

drel who issued that proclamation knew better than these men that it was false. Of
course, such an accusation must fail at once;
it may, however, render these people willing
to assassinate me here." There was a perceptible change in the manner of the soldiers from
this time, and the jibes and insults heaped
upon us as they passed by, notwithstanding
Colonel Pritchard's efforts to suppress the
expression of their detestation, were hard to
bear. Bitterest among these was an officer
named Hudson. He informed me he intended to take our poor little negro protégé as his
own, and solicitude for the child troubled us
more than Hudson's insults.

Within a short distance of Macon we were
halted and the soldiers drawn up in line on
either side of the road. Our children crept
close to their father, especially little Maggie,
who put her arms about him and held him
tightly, while from time to time he comforted
her with tender words from the psalms of
David, which he repeated as calmly and cheerfully as if he were surrounded by friends. It
is needless to say that as the men stood at
ease, they expressed in words unfit for wom-
en's ears all that malice could suggest. In
about an hour, Colonel Pritchard returned, and
with him came a brigade, who testified their
belief in Mr. Davis's guilt in the same manner.

MARGARET HOWELL DAVIS.
(Now Mrs. J. H. Hayes.)

JEFFERSON HAYES DAVIS.

Men may be forgiven, who, actuated by prejudice, exhibit bitterness in the first hours of their triumph ; but what excuse can be offered for one who in cold blood, deliberately organizes tortures to be inflicted, and superintends for over a year their application to the quivering form of an emaciated, exhausted, helpless prisoner, who, the whole South proudly remembers, though reduced to death's door, unto the end neither recanted his faith, fawned upon his persecutor, nor pleaded for mercy.*

Mr. Davis described his entrance into captivity as follows :

"When we reached Macon, I was conducted to the hotel where General Wilson had his quarters. A strong guard was in front of the entrance, and when I passed in it opened ranks, facing inward and presented arms.

"A commodious room was assigned to myself and family.† After dinner I had an interview with General Wilson. After some conversation in regard to our common ac-

---

* See Appendix for further accounts of the capture and other matters appertaining to it.

† When dinner was brought, the negro brought in a tray covered with a cloth, and when that was lifted it disclosed a lovely bunch of flowers. With tears in his eyes he said, "I could not bear for you to eat without something pretty from the Confederates." I have one of the roses yet, and if he has gone to his reward, feel sure that this kind act was counted him for righteousness.

quaintance, he referred to the proclamation
offering a reward for my capture. I supposed
that any insignificant remark of mine would
be reported to his Government, and feared
that another opportunity to give my opinion
of A. Johnson might not be presented, and
told him there was one man in the United
States who knew that proclamation to be false.
He remarked that my expression indicated a
particular person. I answered yes, and that
person was the one who signed it, for he at
least knew that I preferred Lincoln to himself.

"Having several small children, one of
them an infant, I expressed a preference for
the easier route by water, supposing then, as
he seemed to do, that I was to go to Washington City. He manifested a courteous,
obliging temper. My preference as to the
route was accorded.* I told him that some
of the men with me were on parole, that they
were riding their own horses—private property—and I hoped they would be permitted
to retain them. I have a distinct recollection
that he promised me it should be done, but
have since learned that their horses were tak-
en ; and some who were on parole, viz., Major

---

* Colonel Pritchard, though evidently laboring under an invincible
prejudice, even an active sense of hate, tried to give us as little unnecessary pain as he could, but of the horrors and sufferings on that
journey it is difficult to speak.

Moran, Captain Moody, Lieutenant Hathaway, Midshipman Howell, and Private Messec,
who had not violated their obligation of parole, but were voluntarily travelling with my
family to protect them from marauders, were
prisoners of war, and all incarcerated in disregard of the protection promised when they
surrendered. At Augusta we were put on a
steamer, and there met Vice-President Stephens, Honorable C. C. Clay, General Wheeler, the distinguished cavalry officer, and his
adjutant, General Ralls.

" Burton N. Harrison, though they would
not allow him to go in the carriage with me,
resolved to follow my fortunes, as well from
sentiment as from the hope of being useful.
His fidelity was rewarded by a long and rigorous imprisonment. At Port Royal * we

---

* There a tug came out to us, bringing a number of jeering people
to see Mr. Davis, and they plied him with such insulting questions,
that he looked up at an axe fastened to the wall in the gangway ; the
look was observed, and the axe removed. From one of these people we learned that our old friend, General Saxton, was there, and
my husband thought we might ask the favor of him to look after our
little protégé Jim's education, in order that he might not fall under
the degrading influence of Captain Hudson. A note was written
to General Saxton, and the poor little boy was given to the officers
of the tug-boat for the General, who kindly took charge of him.
Believing that he was going on board to see something and return,
he quietly went, but as soon as he found he was to leave us he fought
like a little tiger, and was thus engaged the last we saw of him. I
hope he has been successful in the world, for he was a fine boy, notwithstanding all that had been done to mar his childhood. Some

were transferred to a sea-going vessel, which
instead of being sent to Washington City,
anchored at Hampton Roads.

---

years ago we saw in a Massachusetts paper that he would bear to
his grave the marks of the stripes inflicted upon him by us. We
felt sure he had not said this, for the affection was mutual between
us, and we had never punished him.

CHAPTER LXV.

THE SEPARATION AND IMPRISONMENT OF OUR PARTY.

BEFORE we were parted Mr. Davis told me if we should be separated by the authorities, to tell any of the Confederate agents I saw that they must use all the money they could get to pay the debts of the Confederacy. He also told me to request Mr. O'Conor to defend him; but in the meanwhile Mr. O'Conor had volunteered his services, and he was a tower of strength to us, to whom we owed more than can be expressed. He passed away before my husband, but his honored name still lives.

After lying at anchor a few days a tug came out, and my brother Jefferson, a paroled midshipman, without arms, and taken in no hostile act, came with a cheerful face, and throwing his arms around me, said, "They have come for me; good-by, do not be uneasy;" the cheery smile of the boy as he went over the side of the vessel to an unknown fate, haunts me yet. He and the other gentlemen of our travelling party were taken off together to their carefully concealed destination.

A second tug took Mr. Stephens, General Wheeler, our friends of the staff, and Mr. Davis's private secretary, who all preserved the same quiet demeanor. On the next day a tug with a company of German soldiers came up. Our little Jeff ran to us, pale with horror, and sobbed out, "They say they have come for father, beg them to let us go with him." Mr. Davis went forward, and returned with an officer, saying, "It is true, I must go at once." He whispered to me, "Try not to weep, they will gloat over your grief," and the desire to lessen his anguish enabled me to bid farewell quietly. Mrs. Clay preserved the same self-control. His parting from our children was a sacred sorrow, in which the people on deck participated so far as observation without sympathy would go. We parted in silence. As the tug bore him away from the ship, he stood with bared head between the files of undersized German and other foreign soldiers on either side of him, and as we looked, as we thought, our last upon his stately form and knightly bearing, he seemed a man of another and higher race, upon whom "shame would not dare to sit."

After a few hours Colonel Pritchard left us here, and asked me for my waterproof, which I thought would disprove the assertion that it was essentially a woman's cloak, and gave to him. Such provisions as we had were taken from us, and hard tack and soldier's fare was substituted. Captain Grant, of Maine, however, was a humane man, and did his best for us. The effort was made to get a physician for my sister, who was exceedingly ill, but Dr. Craven accounts for our inability to do so in his " Prison Life of Jefferson Davis," p. 77, by saying that the orders were to allow no communication with the ship. We were now visited by a raiding party, headed by Captain Hudson. They opened our trunks and abstracted everything they desired to have. Among these articles were nearly all my children's clothes. My boy Jeff seized his little uniform of Confederate gray, and ran up to me with it, and thus prevented its being taken as a trophy. A very handsome Pennsylvania flag, which had been captured by General Bradley Johnson in battle, was also taken out of my trunk. Then Captain Hudson valiantly came with a file of men to insist upon having my shawl, and said he would take everything I had if I did not yield it to him, though he offered to buy me another to replace it. It was relinquished, as anything else would have been to dispense with his presence.

We were anchored out a mile or two in the harbor, and little tugs full of mockers, male

and female, came out.   They steamed around
the ship, offering, when one of us met their
view, such insults as were transmissible at a
short distance.   Some United States officers
visited the ship, of whom I have no clear
memory, except of the " Roland " Mrs. Clay
gave them for the " Oliver " they offered.
Two or three of them looked into my sister's state-room, with whom Mrs. Clay was sitting.   She said, " Gentlemen, do not look in
here, it is a ladies' state-room."   One of them
threw the door open and said, " There are no
ladies here ; " to which Mrs. Clay responded,
" There certainly are no gentlemen there."
They retired swearing out their wrath.

The next day General Miles and some
other officers came on board, and summoned
Mrs. Clay and me.   He was quite young,
about, I should think, twenty-five, and
seemed to have newly acquired his elevated
position.   He was not respectful, but I
thought it was his ignorance of polite usage.
He declined to tell me anything of my husband, or about our own destination, and said
" Davis " had announced Mr. Lincoln's assassination the day before it happened, and
he guessed he knew all about it.

All newspapers were forbidden, and the
next day we sailed under sealed orders.   A
letter to Dr. Craven, but meant for my hus-

JEFFERSON DAVIS, JR.

band, quoted elsewhere, tells all that would interest anyone at this day. My first letter, which contained the same narrative, addressed to Mr. Davis, had been intercepted.

Mr. Davis wrote : " After some days' detention, Clay and myself were removed to Fortress Monroe, and there incarcerated in separate cells. Not knowing that the Government was at war with women and children, I asked that my family might be permitted to leave the ship and go to Richmond or Washington City, or some place where they had acquaintances; but this was refused. I then requested that they might be permitted to go abroad on one of the vessels lying at the Roads. This was also denied. Finally, I was informed that they must return to Savannah on the vessel by which they came. This was an old transport-ship, hardly seaworthy. My last attempt was to get them the privilege of stopping at Charleston, where they had many personal friends. This also was refused. My daily experience as a prisoner only served to intensify my extreme solicitude. Bitter tears have been shed by the gentle, and stern reproaches have been made by the magnanimous, on account of the heavy fetters riveted upon me while in a stone casemate and surrounded by a strong guard ; but these were less excruciating than the mental agony my

captors were able to inflict. It was long before I was permitted to hear from my wife and children, and this, and things like this, was the power which education added to savage cruelty."

CHAPTER LXVI.

CRUELTIES PRACTISED AT FORTRESS MONROE.

As the most conclusive evidence of General Miles's animus, and of the methods adopted toward Mr. Davis when he reached the fort, a statement of events in relation to putting fetters upon him at Fortress Monroe is given below, derived from a statement of the officer of the day, and verified by the prisoner and a witness, Captain J. Titlow, of the Third Pennsylvania Artillery.

"When Jefferson Davis was brought to Fortress Monroe he was confined in the gun-room of a casemate, the embrasure of which was closed with a heavy iron grating, and the two doors which communicated with the gunner's room were closed by heavy double shutters, fastened with cross-bars and padlocks. The side openings had been closed with fresh masonry,* the plastering of which was soft to the touch ; the rest of the four walls of solid masonry, the top being an arch to support the earth of the parapet. Two

---

* To this disregard of Mr. Davis's health was probably due his intense suffering from carbuncles and erysipelas afterward

sentinels, with muskets loaded and bayonets
fixed, paced to and fro across this small prison. Two other sentinels and a commissioned
officer occupied the gunner's-room, the door
and windows of which were strongly secured.
The officer of the day had the key of the outer
door, and sentinels were posted on the pavement in front of it. There were also sentinels
on the parapet overhead. The embrasure
looked out on a wet ditch, say, sixty feet
wide, the water in which was probably from
seven to ten feet deep ; scarp and counter-
scarp revetted with dressed masonry. Beyond the ditch on the glacis was a double
chain of sentinels, and in the casemate-rooms
on each side of his prison were quartered that
part of the guard which was not on post.
Worn down by privation, over-exertion, and
exposure, my husband was in no condition,
when thrown into prison, to resist exciting
causes of disease. The damp walls, the food
too coarse and bad to be eaten, the deprivation of sleep caused by the tramping of sentinels around the iron cot, the light of the lamp
which shone full upon it, the loud calling of the
roll when another relief was turned out, the
noise of unlocking the doors, the tramp of
the sentinels who came to relieve those on
the post, produced fever, and rapidly wasted
his strength. Without mechanical aid, even

though his efforts were not interrupted, no one man could have removed the grating from the embrasure. If that had been done, and he could have swum across the ditch and climbed up the revetment on the opposite side, which is doubtful, he would there have encountered the sentinels on the glacis. The circumstances, together with many manifestations indicating feeling toward him, led him to the conclusion that it was not the belief that these things were necessary to prevent his escape, but a purpose to inflict physical pain, and perhaps to deprive him of life.

On May 23, 1865, the officer of the day, Captain J. Titlow, of the Third Pennsylvania Artillery, came into his prison with two blacksmiths bearing a pair of heavy leg irons coupled together by a ponderous chain. Captain Titlow, in a manner fully sustaining his words, informed him that with great personal reluctance he came to execute an order to put irons upon him. Mr. Davis asked whether General Miles had given that order, and on being answered in the affirmative, said he wished to see General Miles. Captain Titlow replied that he had just left General Miles, who was leaving the fort. Mr. Davis then asked that the execution of the order should be postponed until General Miles returned. Captain Titlow said his orders would not permit that,

and that to an old soldier it was needless to say
that an officer was bound to execute such an order as it was given to him. Mr. Davis told
him that it was too obvious that there could be
no necessity for the use of such means to render his imprisonment secure, and on Captain
Titlow repeating that his duty was to execute
his orders, Mr. Davis said it was not such
an order as a soldier could give, or should receive, and he would not submit to it. That
it was evident the intention was to torture him
to death, that he would never tamely be subjected to indignities by which it was sought
in his own person to degrade the cause of
which he was a representative. The officer
of the day, with evident kind feeling, endeavored to dissuade him from resistance. .The
officer of the guard came in from the front
room, and united with the officer of the day
to induce him to yield. It was needless to
show, what was very apparent, that resistance
could not be successful, and Mr. Davis's answer was that he was a soldier and a gentleman, that he knew how to die, and, pointing
to the sentinel who stood ready, said, "Let
your men shoot me at once." He faced round
with his back to the wall and stood silently
waiting. His quiet manner led the officer of
the day to suppose that no resistance would
be made, and therefore the blacksmiths were

directed to do their work. As one of them stooped down to put on the fetter, Mr. Davis slung him off so violently as to throw him on the· floor. He recovered and raised his hammer to strike, but the officer of the day stopped him ; simultaneously one of the sentinels cocked and lowered his musket, advancing on the prisoner, who then encountered this assailant. But Captain Titlow now saw the new danger and promptly interposed, telling the sentinels they were not to fire; then ordered the officer of the guard to bring in four of the strongest men of the guard without firearms, for the purpose of overcoming by muscular strength the resistance which was threatened. Mr. Davis had nothing with which to defend himself, even his penknife having been previously taken from him. The contest was brief, which ended in his being thrown down, four men on his body and head. He could not see the blacksmiths when they approached to put on the irons, but feeling one he kicked him off from him. The smith recovered, and with the aid which the other men could give him, succeeded in the second attempt to rivet one fetter and secure the padlock which held the other. The object being effected, the officer of the day retired with the men he had brought in. Mr. Davis lay down on the cot, covered his ironed limbs with the blanket, and felt only a more intense contempt for the brutality with which he was treated than when a few minutes before he had announced his belief that he was to be tortured to death, and defied the power which attempted to de-grade him.

Of the dramatic account published in Dr. Craven's book,* he said it could not have been written by anyone who either knew the facts, or had such personal knowledge of him as to form a just idea of what his conduct would be under such circumstances. The fact, he added, was, that very little was said either by Captain Titlow or by himself, and that whatever was said was uttered in a very quiet, practical manner. For himself, he would say he was too resolved and too proudly conscious of his relation to a sacred, though unsuccessful cause, for such exclama-tion and manifestation as were imputed to him by Dr. Craven's informant, and given to the public in his book.

---

* The good doctor probably received the account from some un-reliable person. So revolting was the recital to all honorable and brave men, that General Birge, of whose kind heart I had several proofs, wrote to me not to be disturbed, the act could not have been perpetrated ; and there are certainly many persons in the North now who have not accepted it as a fact.

CHAPTER LXVII.

THE TORTURES INFLICTED BY GENERAL MILES.

THE following extracts from Dr. Craven's book will best present a feature of the tortures inflicted by General Miles:

" May 24, 1865. Calling upon the prisoner—the first time I had ever seen him closely —he presented a very miserable and afflicting aspect. Stretched upon his pallet and very much emaciated, Mr. Davis appeared a mere fascine of raw and tremulous nerves, his eyes restless and fevered, his head continually shifting from side to side for a cool spot on the pillow, and his case clearly one in which intense cerebral excitement was the first thing needing attention. He was extremely despondent, his pulse full and at ninety, tongue thickly coated, extremities cold, and his head troubled with a long-established neuralgic disorder. Complained of his thin camp mattress, and pillow stuffed with hair, adding that he was so emaciated that his skin chafed easily against the slats ; and, as these complaints were well founded, I ordered an additional hospital mattress and

softer pillow, for which he thanked me courteously."

"May 24, 1865. On quitting Mr. Davis,
at once wrote to Major Church, Assistant-
Adjutant-general, advising that the prisoner
be allowed tobacco—to the want of which,
after a lifetime of use, he had referred as one
of the probable partial causes of his illness—
though not complainingly, nor with any request that it be given."

After some days this request was granted.

"Complained that the footfalls of the two
sentries within his chamber made it difficult
for him to collect his thoughts ; but added
cheerfully, that with this (touching his pipe)
he hoped to become tranquil." *

"May 25th. I have a poor, frail body,"
he said, "and though in my youth and manhood, while soldiering, I have done some
rough camping and campaigning, there was
flesh then to cover my nerves and bones ;
and that makes an important difference."

"May 26th. Happening to notice that his
coffee stood cold and apparently untasted beside his bed in its tin cup, I remarked that
here was a contradiction of the assertion im-

---

* During this period Mr. Stanton is said to have gone down and
peered through the grating at the tortured man, and that General
Miles favored his friends with peeps at him when they were at all
curious.

plied in the old army question, ' Who ever
saw cold coffee in a tin cup ? ' referring to
the eagerness with which soldiers of all
classes, when campaigning, seek for and use
this beverage.*

" ' I cannot drink it,' he remarked, ' though
fond of coffee all my life. It is the poorest
article of the sort I have ever tasted ; and if
your government pays for such stuff as coffee,
the purchasing Quartermaster must be getting rich. It surprises me, too, for I thought
your soldiers must have the best; many of my
generals complaining of the difficulties they
encountered in seeking to prevent our people
from making volunteer truces with your soldiers whenever the lines ran near each other,
for the purpose of exchanging the tobacco we
had in abundance against your coffee and
sugar.'

" I told him to spend as little time in bed
as he could ; that exercise was the best medicine for dyspeptic patients. To this he answered by uncovering the blankets from his
feet and showing me his shackled ankles.

---

* This coffee was brought in the same cup, unwashed, in which
his soup had been served the day before, and whatever he tasted
cooked brought on intense pain. The bread brought to him was first
shredded through the hands of one of the soldiers, to see that it contained no " deadly weepons." Mr. Davis therefore decided to eat
no more than would barely sustain life, and found difficulty in doing this, the manner of its presentation was so revolting.

"'It is impossible for me, doctor; I cannot even stand erect. These shackles are very heavy; I know not, with the chain, how many pounds. If I try to move them they trip me, and have already abraded broad patches of skin from the parts they touch. Can you devise no means to pad or cushion them, so that when I try to drag them along they may not chafe me intolerably? My limbs have so little flesh on them, and that so weak, as to be easily lacerated.'

"That afternoon, at an interview sought with Major-General Miles, my opinion was given that the physical condition of State-prisoner Davis required the removal of his shackles until such time as his health should be established on some firmer basis. Exercise he absolutely needed, and also some alleviation of his abnormal nervous excitement. No drugs could aid a digestion naturally weak and so impaired, without exercise; nor could anything in the pharmacopœia quiet nerves so overwrought and shattered, while the continual friction of the fetters was counterpoising whatever medicines could be given.

"'You believe it, then, a medical necessity?' queried General Miles.

"'I do, most earnestly.'"

"May 27th. Mr. Davis said: 'My physical condition rendered it obvious that there

could be no idea that fetters were needful to
the security of my imprisonment. It was
clear, therefore, that the object was to offer an
indignity both to myself and the cause I represented—not the less sacred to me because
covered with the pall of a military disaster.
It was for this reason I resisted as a duty to
my faith, to my countrymen, and to myself.
It was for this reason I courted death from
the muskets of the guard. The officer of the
day prevented that result, and, indeed,' bowing to Captain Titlow, ' behaved like a man
of good feeling.' . . .

"Patriots in all ages, to whose memories
shrines are now built, have suffered as bad or
worse indignities."

He was uneasy lest my luggage should be
again searched and rifled, and indignities offered. Dr. Craven wrote :

" On my remarking, to soothe him, that no
such search was probable, he said it could
hardly be otherwise, as he had received a
suit of heavy clothes from the propeller ; and
General Miles, when informing him of the fact,
had mentioned that there were quite a number
of suits there.

" 'Now, I had none with me but such as my
wife placed in her own trunks when she left
Richmond, so that her trunks have probably
been opened ; and I suppose,' he added with

another grim smile, 'that the other clothes
to which General Miles referred, are now on
exhibition or preserved as " relics." My only
hope is that in taking my wardrobe they did
not also confiscate that of my wife and children ; but I realize that we are like him of old
who fell among a certain class of people and
was succored by the good Samaritan.' "

" May 29th. Complained of the dampness
of his cell, as one probable cause of his illness.
The sun could never dart its influence through
such masses of masonry. Surrounded as the
fort was with a ditch, in which the water rose
and fell from three to four feet with the tide,
it was impossible to keep such places free
from noxious vapors.

" Recurring to the subject of his family, Mr.
Davis asked me had I not been called upon
to attend Miss Howell, his wife's sister, who
had been very ill at the time of his quitting
the *Clyde.* Replied that Colonel James,
Chief Quartermaster, had called at my quarters and requested me to visit a sick lady on
board that vessel ; believed it was the lady he
referred to, but could not be sure of the name.
Had mentioned the matter to General Miles,
asking a pass to visit; but he objected, saying the orders were to allow no communication with the ship."

" June 1st. Except for the purpose of petty

torture, there could be no color of reason for withholding from him any books or papers dated prior to the war."

" June 8th. Was distracted, night and day, by the unceasing tread of the two sentinels in his room, and the murmur or gabble of the guards in the outside cell. He said his casemate was well formed for a torture-room of the Inquisition. Its arched roof made it a perfect whispering gallery, in which all sounds were jumbled and repeated. The torment of his head was so dreadful, he feared he must lose his mind. Already his memory, vision, and hearing were impaired. He had but the remains of one eye left, and the glaring whitewashed walls were rapidly destroying this. He pointed to a crevice in the wall where his bed had been, explaining that he had changed to the other side to avoid its mephitic vapors."

" June 10th. General Miles had taken charge of his clothing, and *seemed to think a change of linen twice a week enough.* It might be so in Massachusetts. But now even this wretched allowance was denied. The General might know nothing of the matter; but, if so, some member of his staff was negligent. It was pitiful they could not send his trunks to his cell, but must insist on thus doling out his clothes, as though he were a convict in some penitentiary. If the object were to degrade him, it must fail. None could be degraded by unmerited insult heaped on help-lessness but the perpetrators. The day would come when our people would be ashamed of his treatment. For himself, the sufferings he was undergoing would do him good with his people (the South). Even those who had opposed him would be kept silent, if not won over, by public sympathy. Whatever other opinions might be held, it was clear he was selected as chief victim, bearing the burden of Northern hatred which should be more equally distributed."

" June 14th. Would be glad to have a few volumes on the conchology, geology, or bot-any of the South, and was at a loss to think how such volumes could endanger his safe-keeping."

" June 18th. Mr. Davis said : ' One of the features of the proposition submitted by Gen-eral Sherman was a declaration of amnesty to all persons, both civil and military. Notice being called to the fact particularly, Sherman said, " I mean just that ; " and gave his reason that it was the only way to have perfect peace. *He had previously offered to furnish a vessel to take away any such persons as Mr. Davis might select, to be freighted with whatever personal property they might want to take with them, and to go wherever it pleased.'*

" June 24th. Called on Mr. Davis, accompanied by Captain Titlow, officer of the day. On entering, found the prisoner, for the first time, alone in his cell, the two guards having been removed from it in consequence of my report to Major-General Miles that their presence was counteracting every effort for quieting the nerves of the patient. Mr. Davis remarked that the change had done him good, his last night's sleep having been undisturbed."

" Representations in regard to the need Mr. Davis stood in of different pabulum, both for his eyes and mind, had been previously made by me to Major-General Miles, and had been confirmed, I rather believe, by Colonel Pineo, Medical Inspector of the department, who had visited Mr. Davis in my company on the 12th of the month, having a long and interesting conversation with the prisoner—a fact which should have been mentioned at an earlier date ; but as the conversation was one in which I took little part, the brief memorandum in my diary escaped my notice until revived by the fuller notes of this day's interview.

" While the State prisoner was yet speaking of the troubles of his sight, Major-General Miles entered, with the pleasant announcement that Mr. Davis was to be allowed to walk one hour each day upon the ramparts, and to have miscellaneous reading hereafter —books, newspapers, and such magazines as might be approved, after perusal at head-quarters—an improvement of condition, it must be needless to say, very pleasing to the prisoner."

" Mr. Davis was allowed to walk on the ramparts beside General Miles, and with two armed men behind him.

" I only noticed that Mr. Davis was arrayed in the same garb he had worn when entering the cell—*indeed General Miles had possession of all his other wardrobe*—and that while his carriage was proud and erect as ever, not losing a hair's breadth of his height from any stoop, his step had lost its elasticity, his gait was feeble in the extreme, and he had frequently to press his chest, panting in the pauses of exertion. The cortege promenaded along the ramparts of the south front, Mr. Davis often stopping and pointing out objects of interest, as if giving reminiscences of the past and making inquiries of the present. He was so weak, however, that the hour allowed proved nearly twice too much for him, and he had to be led back with only half his offered liberty enjoyed."

" June 25th. From this time, the prisoner received books and newspapers freely, chiefly reading of newspapers, [*] the New York *Herald* (only occasional numbers), and of books, histories—Mr. Bancroft appearing his favorite American author. I recommended him to be very moderate at first in his open-air exercise, gauging the amount of exercise to his strength ; and from time to time forward, Mr. Davis went out every day for an hour's exercise, the weather and his health permitting."

" July 11th. Found prisoner very desponding, the failure of his sight troubling him and his nights almost without sleep. His present treatment was killing him by inches, and he wished shorter work could be made of his torment. He had hoped long since for a trial which should be public, and therefore with some semblance of fairness ; but hope deferred was making his heart sick.

" Mr. Davis complained this sleeplessness was aggravated by the lamp kept burning in his room all night, so that he could be seen at all moments by the guard in the outer cell. If he happened to doze one feverish moment, the noise of relieving guard in the next room aroused him, and the lamp poured its full

---

* The newspapers allowed were of those the most hostile, and irregularly sent. The books sent were such as General Miles chose, though I sent a large box of books in English type, and these the express office showed by a receipt were delivered at the fort. Mr. Davis never received one, nor could I recover them afterward.

glare into his aching and throbbing eyes.
There must be a change in this, or he would
go crazy, or blind, or both.

" ' Doctor,' he said, ' had you ever the consciousness of being watched ? Of having an
eye fixed on you every moment, intently scrut-
inizing your most minute actions, and the
variations of your countenance and posture ?
The consciousness that the Omniscient Eye
rests upon us, in every situation, is the most
consoling and beautiful belief of religion. But
to have a human eye riveted on you in every
moment of waking or sleeping, sitting, walking, or lying down, is a refinement of torture
on anything the Camanches or Spanish Inquisition ever dreamed. . . . But the
human eye forever fixed upon you is the eye
of a spy, or enemy, gloating in the pain and
humiliation which itself creates. I have lived
too long in the woods to be frightened by an
owl, and have seen death too often to dread
any form of pain. But I confess this torture
of being watched begins to prey on my reason. The lamp burning in my room all night
would seem a torment devised by someone
who had intimate knowledge of my habits, my
custom having been through life never to sleep
except in total darkness.' "

" July 15th. Called on Mr. Davis accompanied by Captain Grill, Third Pennsylvania

Artillery, officer of the day. Found him extremely weak, growing more alarmed about his sight, which was failing rapidly. The phenomenon had occurred to him of seeing all objects double, due chiefly to his nervous debility and the over-taxation of constant reading."

"July 30th. Found Mr. Davis in a very critical state; his nervous debility extreme, his mind more despondent than ever heretofore, his appetite gone, complexion livid, and pulse denoting deep prostration of all physical energies. Was much alarmed, and realized with painful anxiety the responsibilities of my position. If he were to die in prison, and without trial, *subject to such severities as had been inflicted on his attenuated frame,* the world would form unjust conclusions, but conclusions with enough color to pass them into history." *

"Let me here remark that, despite a certain exterior cynicism of manner, no patient has ever crossed my path who, suffering so much himself, appeared to feel so warmly and tenderly for others. Sickness, as a general rule, is sadly selfish, its own pains and infirm-

---

* The italics are mine, but as we heard the book from which these excerpts are quoted was submitted to Mr. Stanton before it was published, and its details severely curtailed, suppose this significant passage crept in unawares.

ities occupying too much of its thoughts.
With Mr. Davis, however, the rule did not
work, or rather he was an exception calling
attention to its general truth."

When I obtained permission to write letters
to my husband, the only restriction imposed
by the Government was that the Attorney-
General should read those written and received, but General Miles also claimed their
perusal, and they "had to be sent open to
General Miles, and from him, he (Mr. Davis)
understood, similarly open to the Attorney-
General."

"There was no affectation of devoutness
or asceticism in my patient ; but every opportunity I had of seeing him, convinced me more
deeply of his sincere religious convictions.
He was fond of referring to passages of
Scripture, comparing text with text, dwelling
on the divine beauty of the imagery, and the
wonderful adaptation of the whole to every
conceivable phase and stage of human life.

"The Psalms were his favorite portion of
the Word, and had always been. Evidence
of their divine origin was inherent in their
text. Only an intelligence that held the life-
threads of the entire human family could have
thus pealed forth in a single cry every wish,
joy, fear, exultation, hope, passion, and sorrow of the human heart. There were mo-

ments, while speaking on religious subjects, in which Mr. Davis impressed me more than any professor of Christianity I had ever heard. There was a vital earnestness in his discourse, a clear, almost passionate, grasp in his faith; and the thought would frequently recur, that a belief capable of consoling such sorrows as his, possessed, and thereby evidenced, a reality—a substance—which no sophistry of the infidel could discredit.

" To this phase of the prisoner's character I have heretofore rather avoided calling attention for several reasons, prominent of which, though an unworthy one, was this: My knowledge that many, if not a majority, of my readers would approach the character of Mr. Davis with a preconception of dislike and distrust, and a consequent fear that an earlier forcing on their attention of this phase of his character, before their opinion had been modified by such glimpses as are herein given, might only challenge a base and false imputation of hypocrisy against one whom, in my judgment, no more devout exemplar of Christian faith, and its value as a consolation, now lives, whatever may have been his political crimes."

" July 24th. While walking on the ramparts in enforced companionship with General Miles, who, if he was seeking a subject that

would not offend the almost dying man, was
singularly unfortunate in his choice of a topic,
he observed, interrogatively, that it was reported John C. Calhoun had made much
money by speculations, or favoring the speculations of his friends, connected with this
work.

"In a moment Mr. Davis started to his
feet, betraying much indignation by his excited manner and flushed cheek. It was a
transfiguration of friendly emotion, the feeble
and wasted invalid and prisoner suddenly forgetting his bonds, forgetting his debility, and
ablaze with eloquent anger against this injustice to the memory of one whom he loved and
reverenced. Mr. Calhoun, he said, lived a
whole atmosphere above any sordid or dishonest thought—was of a nature to which
even a mean act was impossible. . . .

"Mr. Davis believed the hands of George
Washington not more free from the filthiness
of bribes than were those of the departed
statesman who had been thus libelled."

"August 16th. Prisoner suffering severely,
but in a less critical state, the erysipelas now
showing itself in his nose and forehead.
Found that a carbuncle was forming on his
left thigh, Mr. Davis urging this as a proof
of a malarial atmosphere in his cell, reiterating
his wish that, if the Government wanted to be

rid of him without trial, it might take some quicker process."

"August 20th. Called with Captain Evans, officer of the day. Mr. Davis suffering great prostration, a cloud of erysipelas covering his whole face and throat. The carbuncle much inflamed. Spirits exceedingly dejected, evinced by anxiety for his wife and children. That he should die without opportunity of rebutting in public trial the imputed conspiracy to assassinate Mr. Lincoln, was referred to frequently and painfully. That history would do him justice, and the criminal absurdity of the charge be its own refutation, he had cheerful confidence while in health ; but in his feebleness and despondency, with knowledge how powerful they were who wished to affix this stain, his alarm lest it might become a reproach to his children grew an increasing shadow."

"August 21st. Prostration increased, and the erysipelas spreading. Deemed it my duty to send a communication to Major-General Miles, reporting that I found the State prisoner, Davis, suffering severely from erysipelas in the face and head, accompanied by the usual prostration attending that disease. Also that he had a small carbuncle on his left thigh, his condition denoting a low state of the vital forces."

" August 23d. Said he concluded not to lose any more spoons for me, but would retain the one that morning sent with his breakfast. Unless things took a change he would not require it long."

(This was an allusion to the desire some of the guards had to secure trophies of anything Mr. Davis had touched. They had carried away his brier-wood pipe, and from time to time taken five of the spoons sent over with his meals from my quarters. . . . No knife or fork being allowed the prisoner, "lest he should commit suicide," his food had to be cut up before being sent over —a needless precaution, it always seemed to me, and more likely to produce than to prevent the act, by continually keeping the idea that it was expected before the prisoner's mind. It was in returning the trays from Mr. Davis to my quarters, that the spoons were taken—an annoyance obviated by his retaining one for use. This only changed the form of trophy, however; napkins that he had used being the next class of prizes seized and sent home to sweethearts by loyal warders at the gates.) *

---

* Everything he laid down was taken except his bible, and at last, when he had dropped asleep momentarily, a soldier felt in his night-gown to get a little medal I had persuaded him to wear about his neck.

"Errors, like all other men, he had committed; but stretched now on a bed from which he might never rise, and looking with the eyes of faith, which no walls could bar, up to the throne of Divine mercy, it was his comfort that no such crimes as men laid to his charge reproached him in the whispers of his conscience."

"August 24th. Visited Mr. Davis with Captain Titlow, officer of the day. Found him slightly better in mind and body.

"Observing me brush away with my foot some crumbs scattered near his bedside, Mr. Davis asked me to desist; they were for a mouse he was domesticating—the only living thing he had now power to benefit.

"Every conversation of this kind with Mr. Davis recalled the saying of some eminent writer, whose name has escaped me, that 'it is a noble thing to know how to take a country walk,' or words containing that idea, but more concisely and vividly expressed."

"August 25th. The captain gave me an order from General Miles, allowing State prisoner Davis to have a knife and fork with his meals hereafter. Mr. Davis was pleased, but said he had learned many new uses to which a spoon could be put when no other implement was accessible. In particular, it was the best peach peeler ever invented, and he illustrated as he spoke on a fruit that lay on his table. Denying him a knife and fork lest he should commit suicide, he said, was designed to represent him to the world as an atrocious criminal, so harrowed by remorse that the oblivion of death would be welcome. His early shackles had partly the same object, but still more to degrade his cause."

"September 1st. Was called at daylight by Captain Titlow, officer of the day, to see State prisoner Davis, who appeared rapidly sinking, and was believed to be in a critical condition. The carbuncle on his thigh was much inflamed, his pulse indicating extreme prostration of the vital forces. The erysipelas which had subsided now reappeared, and the febrile excitement ran very high. Prescribed such remedies, constitutional and topical, as were indicated; but always had much trouble to persuade him to use the stimulants so urgently needed by his condition.

" Mr. Davis renewed his complaints of the vitiated atmosphere of the casemate, declaring it to be noxious and pestilential from the causes before noticed. Mould gathered upon his shoes, showing the dampness of the place, and no animal life could prosper in an atmosphere that generated these hyphomycetous fungi. From the rising and falling of the tides in the loose foundations of the casemate, mephitic fungi emanated, the spores of which, floating in the air, were thrown off with such quantities, and such incessant repetitions of reproduction, as to thoroughly pervade the atmosphere, entering the lungs and blood with every breath, and redeveloping their poisonous qualities in the citadel of life. Peculiar classes of these fungi were characteristic of the atmosphere in which cholera and other forms of plague were most rankly generated, as had been established by the Reverend Mr. Osborne, in a long and interesting series of experimental researches with the achromatic microscope during the cholera visitation of 1854, in England. Men in robust health might defy these miasmatic influences, but to him, so physically reduced, the atmosphere that generated mould found no vital force sufficient to resist its poisonous inhalation.

"*Assured Mr. Davis that his opinion on the matter had for some time been my own, and that on several occasions I had called the attention of Major-General Miles to the subject.* Satisfied that the danger was now serious if he were longer continued in such an atmosphere, I would make an official report on the subject to the General Commanding, recommending a change of quarters.

"Mr. Davis again spoke of the wretchedness of being constantly watched, of feeling that a human eye, inquisitive and pitiless, was fixed upon all his movements, night and day. This was one of the torments imposed on the Marquis de Lafayette in the dungeons of Magdeburg and Olmutz. Indeed, the parallel between their prison lives, if not in some other respects, was remarkable. Lafayette was denied the use of knife or fork, lest he should commit self-destruction. He was confined in a casemate or dungeon of the two most powerful fortresses of Prussia first, and then Austria. While in Magdeburg, he found a friend in the humane physician, who repeatedly reported that the prisoner could not live unless allowed to breathe purer air than that of his cell ; and on this recommendation—the Governor at first answering that he 'was not ill enough yet'—the illustrious prisoner was at length allowed to take the air, sometimes on foot, at other times in a carriage, but always accompanied by an officer with drawn sword and two armed guards.

"Lafayette, however, in his second imprisonment was never shackled ; and though treated with the utmost cruelty, no indignities were offered to his person.

"It may be here remarked that the power of memory possessed by Mr. Davis appeared

almost miraculous—a single perusal of any
passage that interested him enabling him to
repeat it almost verbatim. This wonderful
gift of memorizing, and apparent universality
of knowledge, were remarked by every officer
of the day as well as myself, Mr. Davis having kindly relations with all, and conversation
suited to each visitor. As instances of this—
at which I was not present myself, but heard
related from the officers immediately after
their occurrence—let me mention two conversations.

"An officer of the day, very fond of dogs,
and believing himself well posted in all varieties of that animal, once entered the prisoner's
cell, followed by a bull-terrier or some other
breed of belligerent canine. Mr. Davis at
once commenced examining and criticising
the dog's points with all the minuteness of a
master, thence gliding into a general review
of the whole race of pointers, setters, and re-
trievers, terriers, bull-dogs, German poodles,
greyhounds, blood-hounds, and so forth; the
result of his conversation being best given in
the words of the dog-fancying officer: 'Well,
I thought I knew something about dogs, but
hang me if I won't get appointed officer of
the day as often as I can, and go to school
to Jeff Davis.'"

"OFFICE OF THE CHIEF MEDICAL OFFICER,
"FORT MONROE, VA., September 1, 1865.

"GENERAL: I have the honor to report prisoner Davis still suffering from the effects of a carbuncle. The erysipelas of the face had entirely subsided, but yesterday reappeared. His health is evidently rapidly declining.

"I remain, General, very respectfully,
"Your obedient servant,
"JOHN J. CRAVEN."

The routine report merely ran:

"I have the honor to report prisoner Davis's condition not perceivably different from that of yesterday: very feeble; no appetite."

"September 1st, Mr. Davis said: 'The women of the South had sent forth their sons, directing them to return with wounds disabling them for further service, or never to return at all. All they had flung into the contest—beauty, grace, passion, ornament; the exquisite frivolities so dear to the sex were cast aside; their songs, if they had any heart to sing, were patriotic; their trinkets were flung into the public crucible; the carpets from their floors were portioned out as blankets to the suffering soldiers of their cause; women bred to every refinement of luxury,

wore home-spuns made by their own hands ;
when materials for an army-balloon were
wanted, the richest silk dresses were sent in,
and there was only competition to secure
their acceptance. As nurses of the sick, as
encouragers and providers for the combatants,
as angels of charity and mercy, adopting as
their own all children made orphans in defence of their homes, as patient and beautiful
household deities, accepting every sacrifice
with unconcern, and lightening the burdens
of war by every art, blandishment, and labor
proper to their sphere, the dear women of his
people deserved to take rank with the highest heroines of the grandest days of the greatest countries.' "

"September 6th. As with the casemate,
there were to be two rooms used for the prisoner's confinement. In the outer one a lieutenant and two soldiers were constantly stationed on guard, having a view of the interior
chamber through a grated door. Opposite
this door was a fireplace. To its right when
facing the door, was a window heavily grated,
and with a sentinel continually on duty before
it, pacing up and down the piazza. Opposite
the window a door leading into the corridor,
but permanently fastened with heavy iron
clamps, and in this door a sliding panel in
which the face of a sentinel was continually

framed by night and day, ready to report to his officer the first sign of any attempt on the prisoner's part to shuffle off this mortal coil by any act of self-violence. It was of this face, with its unblinking eyes, that Mr. Davis so bitterly complained in after-days ; but this is anticipating. *The prisoner, as was said of Lafayette, is perhaps 'not sick enough yet,' and has to suffer some further weeks of exposure in his present casemate.*"

"September 22d. Called on Mr. Davis for the first time since returning from Richmond, accompanied by Captain Titlow, Third Pennsylvania Artillery, officer of the day. Found he had been inquiring for me several days, in consequence of suffering premonitory symptoms of a return of the erysipelas to his face. Reported his condition to Major-General Miles, respectfully asking permission to call in Colonel Pineo, Medical Inspector of the Department for consultation.

"Mentioned that General Terry, my old commander, had kindly placed the carriage of Mr. Davis at my disposal during the visit.

"Mr. Davis laughed about his carriage, and said that since some 'Yankee' had to ride in it, he would prefer my doing so to another."

"September 23d. Prisoner renewed his questions about the proposed change in his place of confinement, begging me, if I knew anything, even the worst—that he was to be kept as now until death put an end to his sufferings—not to conceal it from him any longer; that suspense was more injurious to him than could be the most painful certainty. Assured him that I had no further information. A place had been selected for his incarceration in Carroll Hall, the requisite changes in the rooms made, and I heard no reason for his non-transfer. If I did so, he should be informed immediately.*

"Mr. Davis renewed my attention to the steady deterioration of his health, which he regarded as chiefly due to the unfitness of his cell for human habitation. His head had a continued humming in it, like the whizzing of a wound watch when its main spring is suddenly broken. Little black motes slowly ascended and descended between his sight, and whatever page he was reading or object inspecting; and his memory likewise gave distinct indications of losing its elasticity. The carbuncle, however, was quite well, having left a deep-red cicatrix where it had been, precisely like the healed wound of a Minié bullet. Mr. Davis had not much flesh to lose on entering the fort, but believed he must

---

* The change was postponed as long as possible, as Dr. Craven evidently thought.

have lost what little of it could be spared while still preserving life."

" October 15th.   Colonel Pelouze called for a report of the health of the prisoner, with my opinion as to the advisability or necessity of a change in his place of confinement; visited the new quarters in Carroll Hall, and *directed* General Miles—being thereto empowered by his instructions—to remove Mr. Davis from the casemate to his new and more pleasant abode.

" Found Mr. Davis already looking much brighter, exclaiming as I entered, ' The world does move, after all.'   The panel in the side door opening into the corridor, in which a sentry's face was framed, gave him some annoyance, and he referred again to Lafayette in connection with the torture of a human eye constantly riveted on his movements.   If his wish were to commit suicide, such a precaution would prove wholly unavailing.   It looked rather as if the wish were to drive him to its commission."

" October 15th.   Ladies and other friends of persons in authority at the fort were let loose on the ramparts about the hour of his walk, to stare at him as though he were the caged monster of some travelling menagerie.*

* School-girls headed by their teachers came down to the fort and were allowed to intercept him in the restricted walks he took with General Miles for a companion !

He had endeavored to rebuke this during his last walk, when he saw a group of ladies waiting for his appearance, by turning short round and re-entering his cell. Dear and valuable as was the liberty of an hour's exercise in the open air, there were prices at which he could not consent to purchase it, and this was of the number. His general treatment Mr. Davis acknowledged to be good, though there were in it many annoyances of detail—such as the sentry's eye always fastened on his movements, and the supervision of his correspondence with his wife—unworthy of any country aspiring to magnanimity or greatness."

"October 25th. Mr. Davis had been for some time complaining that his light suit of gray tweed was too thin for the increasing cold of the days on the ramparts of the fortress, and finding that his measure was with a tailor in Washington, I requested a friend of mine to call there and order a good, heavy black pilot-cloth overcoat for the prisoner, and that the bill should be sent to me ; and also ordered from a store in New York some heavy flannels to make Mr. Davis comfortable for the winter.* These acts to me appearing

---

* I had also sent a box of like garments, but they had, General Miles said, never been received ; a subsequent one, however, was received,

innocent, and even laudable, cause great trouble, as may be seen by the following correspondence, finally leading to a peremptory order which almost altogether broke off the previously free relations I had exercised with Mr. Davis.

" Mr. Davis referred to the kindness of Captain Grisson, of the staff of General Miles, in regard to a little matter which, though trivial in itself, had given him much annoyance.   It arose in this manner : He had requested a barber to be sent to him, as his hair was growing too long.   Captain Grisson brought a hairdresser, but on the termination of the operation said it was the order of General Miles that the lopped hair should be carried to headquarters.   To this Mr. Davis objected, first from a horror of having such trophies or 'relics' paraded around the country, and secondly, because he wished to send it to Mrs. Davis ; this latter probably an excuse to avoid the former disagreeable alternative.   Captain Grisson replied that his orders were peremptory, but if Mr. Davis would fold the hair up in a newspaper, and leave it on a designated shelf in the casemate, the captain would step over to headquarters, report the prisoner's objections, and ask for further orders.   This was done, and Captain Grisson soon returned with the glad tidings that the desire to obtain possession of these 'interesting relics' had been abandoned.

"The change to Carroll Hall, as it was loftier, had been of the greatest benefit to the prisoner's health, the air being purer, his own room more cheerful, and only subject to the drawback that he had human eyes from three directions continually fixed upon him through the grated door entering his room, the window opening on the piazza at his left, and the door opposite the window, with an open panel in it, opposite which stood a sentry.

"November 1st.   Called with Brevet Captain Valentine H. Stone, Fifth United States Artillery, first officer of the day from the new regiment garrisoning the fort. . . . He appeared to scrutinize Captain Stone with great care, asking him all about his term of service, his early education, etc., as if anxious to find out everything ascertainable about the new men into whose hands he had fallen —an operation repeated with each new officer of the day who called to see him.   Indeed, his habit of analysis appeared universal with the prisoner.   It seemed as if he put into a crucible each fresh development of humanity that crossed his path, testing it therein for as long as the interview lasted, and then carefully inspecting the ingot which was left as the result.   That ingot, whether appearing to him

pure gold or baser metal, never lost its character to his mind from any subsequent acquaintance.

"Mr. Davis said it was scandalous that
Government should allow General Miles to
review his letters to his wife. They had to
pass through the hands of Attorney-General
Speed, who should be a quite competent
judge of offensive matter, or what was deemed
offensive. General Miles had returned to
him several pages of a letter written to Mrs.
Davis, containing only a description of his
new prison in answer to her inquiries, the
general declaring such description to be objectionable; perhaps suspecting that if told
where he was, Mrs. Davis would storm the
fort and rescue him *vi et armis.*

"'HEADQUARTERS MILITARY DISTRICT, FORT MONROE,
"'November 10, 1865.

"'SIR: The Major-General commanding
directs me to inquire of you if any orders have
been given by you, or through you, for an
overcoat for Jefferson Davis.

"'Such a report appeared in the papers.

"'Very respectfully,

"'A. V. HITCHCOCK,

"'*Captain and Provost Marshal.*'

"To which on the same date I returned the
following answer:

" 'Office of Post Surgeon,
" 'Fort Monroe, November 10th.

" ' Captain : I have received the communication dated November 10th, Headquarters
Military District, Fort Monroe, in which the
Major-General commanding directs you to
inquire if any orders have been given by me,
or through me, for an overcoat for Jefferson
Davis.

" ' In reply, I would respectfully state that
I did order a thick overcoat, woollen drawers,
and undershirts for Jefferson Davis. I found,
as the cold weather approached, he needed
thick garments, the prisoner being feeble in
health, and the winds of the coast cold and
piercing.

" ' I have the honor to be,
" ' Very respectfully your obedient servant,
(Signed) " ' John J. Craven,
" ' *Brevet Lieutenant-Colonel, Surgeon
United States Army.*

" ' Captain A. O. Hitchcock, A. D. C.'

" That objection to my action in the matter
should have been made, was about the last
thing I should have expected—the prisoner's
health being under my charge, and warm
clothing for cold weather being obviously one
of the first necessities to a patient in so feeble
a condition. Let me add, that Mr. Davis had

never asked for the warm clothing I deemed requisite, and that sending for it, and insisting upon its acceptance, had been with me a purely professional act.   In the valise belonging to Mr. Davis, which was kept at the headquarters of General Miles, no heavy clothing could be found, merely containing a few articles of apparel chiefly designed for the warm climate of the South.   General Miles, however, took a different view of my action, to judge from the following letter :

"'HEADQUARTERS MILITARY DISTRICT, FORT MONROE,
"'November 18, 1865.

"'COLONEL: The Major-General commanding directs that, in future, you give no orders for Jefferson Davis without first communicating with these head districts.

"Also, that in future, your conversations with him will be confined strictly to professional matters, and that you comply with the instructions regarding the meals to be furnished to prisoners Davis and Clay, and have them delivered more promptly.   Also, report the price paid for Mr. Davis's overcoat, and by whom paid.

"'A. O. HITCHCOCK,
"'*Captain and A. D. C.*
"'BREVET LIEUTENANT-COLONEL J. J. CRAVEN,
Post Surgeon.'

" This order I then regarded as cruel and unnecessary, nor has subsequent reflection changed my opinion. The meals for Mr. Davis I had sent at hours to suit his former habits and present desires—two meals a day at such time as he felt most appetite. I was now ordered to send his meals three times a day, and at hours which did not meet his wishes, and were very inconvenient to my family, his meals being invariably sent over at the same hour I had mine. The order to abstain from anything but professional conversation was a yet greater medical hardship, as to a man in the nervous condition of Mr. Davis, a friend with whom he feels free to converse is a valuable relief from the moodiness of silent reflection.

" ' CAPTAIN A. O. HITCHCOCK, A. D. C.

" ' CAPTAIN : I have the honor to acknowledge the receipt of your communication dated Headquarters Military District, Fort Monroe, Va., November 18, 1865 ; and in answer to your inquiry concerning the cost of the coat ordered by me for Mr. Davis, I would say :

" ' That I do not know the cost of the coat ; I have not yet received the bill. As soon as received, I will forward it to the Major-General commanding. I do not know that any

person paid for the coat, having directed that
the bill should be sent to me when ordering
it.

"'I remain, Captain, very respectfully,

"'JOHN J. CRAVEN,

"'*Brevet Lieutenant-Colonel and Post Surgeon and Chief Medical Officer, Military
District, Fort Monroe, Va.*'

"November 8th.   Major Charles P. Muhl-
enburgh, Captain S. A. Day, and many
others, displaying both generosity and consideration in their treatment of the distinguished captive.

"His self-control was the feature of his
character, knowing that his temper had been
high and proud, which most struck me during
my attendance.   His reticence was remarked
on subjects where he knew we must differ ;
and though occasionally speaking with freedom of slavery, it was as a philosopher rather
than as a politician—rather as a friend to the
negro, and one sorry for his inevitable fate in
the future, than with rancor or acrimony
against those opponents of the institution
whom he persisted in regarding as responsible for the war, with all its attendant horrors and sacrifices.

"Mr. Davis is remarkable for the kindli-
ness of his nature and fidelity to friends.   Of

none of God's creatures does he seem to wish or speak unkindly ; and the same fault found with Mr. Lincoln—unwillingness to sanction the military severities essential to maintain discipline—is the fault I have heard most strongly urged against Mr. Davis."

Dr. Craven concluded his diary, because his other visits were limited to mere medical examinations of the prisoner's condition. Shortly after Mr. Davis's removal to Carroll Hall, Dr. Craven was ordered away, and Dr. Cooper, a man equally kind-hearted and attentive, was stationed at the fort.

CHAPTER LXVIII.

HON. HUGH MacCULLOCH'S VISIT TO JEFFERSON DAVIS AT FORTRESS MONROE.

THE fact of the utter failure of Mr. Davis's health could no longer be concealed by General Miles's assurances of his comfort and the salubrity of his surroundings, and the Honorable Hugh MacCulloch, Secretary of the Treasury, determined to visit the prisoner at President Johnson's suggestion. In his "Men and Measures of Half a Century," published in 1889, he describes his interview with Mr. Davis at Fortress Monroe. I have taken the liberty of condensing his statement.

"The question what shall be done to the Confederate leader was referred to at Mr. Lincoln's last meeting with his Cabinet. Mr. Lincoln merely remarked in his humorous way: 'I am a good deal like the Irishman who had joined a temperance society, but thought he might take a drink now and then if he drank unbeknown to himself. A good many people think that all the big Confederates ought to be arrested and tried as traitors. Perhaps they ought to be, but I should be right glad if they would get out of the country unbeknown to me.'

"This question came up in the case of Jefferson Davis soon after Mr. Johnson became President. Some action must be taken in his case; what should it be? He was the most conspicuous of the enemies of the Government. By the people of the North he was regarded as the arch-traitor upon whose head vengeance should be visited. Should he be liberated, or should he be arraigned for treason? and, if arraigned, should he be tried by a military commission or a United States court? These were questions which required careful consideration both in their legal and political bearings.

"The legal question: 'Has Mr. Davis been guilty of such acts of treason that he can be successfully prosecuted?' was submitted to the Attorney-General, who, after a thorough examination of it and consultation with some of the ablest lawyers in the country, came to the conclusion that Mr. Davis could not be convicted of treason by any competent and independent tribunal, and that therefore he ought not to be tried. This conclusion was undoubtedly correct. It was a revolution, a general uprising of the South against the Government. The war in which they had been engaged was of such proportions that belli-

gerent rights had been accorded them by foreign governments.   Our Government, by exchange of prisoners and other acts, had
acknowledged the fact ; treason, therefore,
could not be charged, nor could one of their
number be legally convicted of the crime.   It
was clear that if Mr. Davis had been guilty of
treasonable acts, they were committed in the
Southern States, where conviction would be impossible.   The President was chagrined by the
decision, which was enforced upon the opinions
of the Attorney-General and other eminent
lawyers.   He was committed by his vindictive
speeches made at the commencement of his administration, but he saw the correctness of it,
and from that time he pushed his generosity
to those whom he had denounced as traitors
to an extreme.   Mr. Davis's position made
him the most conspicuous, but he was no more
guilty than many others against whom no
proceedings were contemplated.   There was
no evidence that he was responsible for the
horrors of Andersonville, or the general treatment to which Union soldiers were subjected
in Southern prisons.   He was, however, kept
in confinement until the spring of 1867, when
he was brought before the United States
Court at Richmond on the charge of treason,
and admitted to bail.   He was not tried,
although he expressed a desire to be, nor

was he among those who asked to be pardoned.

"When the question was pending, the President sent for me one day and said that he would like to have me go unofficially to Fortress Monroe, and ascertain whether or not the reports that had reached him about the treatment of Mr. Davis were true. . . .

"A few days after the request was made, I was able to comply with it.

"On my arrival at the fortress, Mr. Davis was walking upon the ramparts accompanied by a couple of soldiers. I was glad to notice that his gait was erect, his step elastic, and, when he came nearer, that he had not the appearance of one who was suffering in health by his imprisonment. I spent an hour or two in conversation with him.

"'I was,' he said, 'in the first two or three months of my imprisonment treated barbarously, but now I am permitted to have a daily walk, and my present quarters, as you perceive, are such as a prisoner charged with high treason ought not to complain of'—a cot, a small pine table, and two cane-bottomed chairs. The cot and chairs were hard, and of the plainest and cheapest kind, but the room was clean and well lighted. There was not much need of light, for the only book in the room was an old treatise upon military tactics

—a subject which was not then especially interesting to the prisoner. Newspapers were
forbidden to him. My interview was very
pleasant. There have been few men more
gifted than Mr. Davis, and few whose opportunities for intellectual culture have been
better improved. I had not known him
personally, but I knew what his standing was
among the able men of the country, and expected to meet in him an accomplished gentleman. To those who knew him well, it is not
necessary to say that I was not disappointed,
and that I was most favorably impressed with
his manner and conversation. I was his first
visitor, and he seemed to be pleased with my
visit and with the opportunity which it gave
to him for a free talk. He was indisposed to
say much about himself, and it was only by
direct questions that I learned the facts in
regard to the barbarous treatment to which
he had referred. ' I was,' he said, ' when
brought to the fortress, not only strictly confined to a casemate, which was little better
than a dungeon, but I was heavily ironed.
As I had been a submissive prisoner, and was
in a strong fortress, I thought that chains
were unnecessary, and that I ought not to be
subject to them. I resisted being shackled,
but resistance was vain. I was thrown violently upon the floor and heavily fettered.

This was not all. The casemate in which I
was confined was kept constantly and brilliantly lighted, and I was never relieved of the
presence of a couple of soldiers. My eyes
were weak and sensitive, I suffered keenly
from the light, and you may judge how my
sufferings were aggravated by my not being
permitted for months to have one moment to
myself.' I listened silently to this statement,
given substantially in his own language ; but
I felt as he did, that he had for a time been
barbarously treated. Chains were unnecessary, and the constant presence of the guards
in the casemate must have been to a sensitive
man worse than solitary confinement, which is
now regarded as being too inhuman to be inflicted upon the greatest criminals. I happened to know some of his personal friends
in the West, and he had a great deal to talk
about without saying much about himself.
He seemed to be neither depressed in spirits
nor soured in temper. He could not help
saying something about the war, but he said
nothing in the way of justification or defence.
He had the bearing of a brave and high-bred
gentleman, who, knowing that he would have
been highly honored if the Southern States
had achieved their independence, would not
and could not demean himself as a criminal
because they had not. The only anxiety he

expressed was in regard to his trial, not as to
the result, but the time. He thought the
delay was unnecessary and unjust. He was
kept in prison for two years before he was
arraigned and released on bail ; and, strangely
enough, Horace Greeley and Gerritt Smith,
the distinguished abolitionists, were among
the signers of his bond." *

---

* Men and Measures of Half a Century, page 408.

CHAPTER LXIX.

LETTERS FROM PRISON.

MR. DAVIS's letters will best express the cruelties of his duress, which may be read between the lines.

From Mr. Davis to Mrs. Davis.

"FORTRESS MONROE, August 21, 1865.

"I am now permitted to write to you under two conditions, viz., that I confine myself to family matters, and that my letter shall be examined by the United States Attorney-General before it is sent to you.

"This will sufficiently explain to you the omission of subjects on which you would desire me to write. I presume it is, however, permissible for me to relieve your disappointment in regard to my silence on the subject of future action toward me, by stating that of the purpose of the authorities I know nothing. . . . . . .

"I often think of 'old Uncle Bob,' and always with painful anxiety. If Sam has rejoined him he will do all in his power for the old man's comfort and safety.

"The Smith land had better be returned to

the heirs.* No deed was made, and the payments were for movable effects and for interest; their right to the land, which alone remains, clearly revives, since I am unable to
make the payment which is I *believe* due, and
shall be unable to fulfil the engagements
hereafter to mature; therefore, the sooner
the case is disposed of, the better. . . . I
have the prayer-book you sent, but the memorandum placed in it was withheld. . . .

". . . The confidence in the shield of
innocence with which I tried to quiet your apprehensions and to dry your tears at our parting, sustains me still.† If your fears have
proved more prophetic than my hopes, yet do
not despond. ' Tarry thou the Lord's leisure,
be strong, and He will comfort thy heart.'
Every day, twice or oftener, I repeat the
prayer of St. Chrysostom. . . . . .

" To the surgeon and regimental chaplain I
am under many obligations; the officers of the
guard and of the day have shown me increased
consideration, such as their orders would per-

---

* A plantation Mr. Davis bought during the war, and which the
State law would have permitted him to retain until able to pay for it,
but, keenly alive to the rights of others, he relinquished it.

† He leaned over me in bidding good-by on the ship, and whispered, "No matter what proof is adduced by the North, remember
that my dying testimony was to you that I had nothing to do with
assassination, or causing any other deed unworthy of a soldier, or of
our cause." With this assurance, he bade farewell.

mit. The unjust accusations which have been made against me in the newspapers of the day might well have created prejudices against me. I have had no opportunity to refute them by proof, . . . ; and can, therefore, only attribute the perceptible change to those good influences which are always at work to confound evil designs. . . . . . .

" Be not alarmed by speculative reports concerning my condition. You can rely on my fortitude, and God has given me much of resignation to His blessed will. . . . . .

" Men are apt to be verbose when they speak of themselves, and suffering has a rare power to develop selfishness, so I have wandered from the subject on which I proposed to write, and have dwelt upon a person whose company I have for some time past kept so exclusively that it must be strange if he has not become tiresome. . . . . . .

" It has been reported in the newspapers that you had applied for permission to visit me in my confinement; if you had been allowed to do so the visit would have caused you disappointment at the time, and bitter memories afterward. You would not have been allowed to hold private conversation with me. . . . . . .

" Remember how good the Lord has always been to me, how often He has wonder-

fully preserved me, and put your trust in
Him. . . .   " JEFFERSON DAVIS."

From Mr. Davis to Mrs. Davis.

" FORTRESS MONROE, VA., September 15, 1865.

" . . . As only an occasional newspaper
is given me, I cannot know whether any re-
plies are made to the fictions published in regard to myself; as their effect is not merely
to prejudice public opinion against myself,
but extends likewise to those who were polit-
ically associated with me, it would not seem
probable that even the timidity of this day
would keep silent all whose justification is the
truth. . . . . . .

" Tell me when you write whether your
personal property, seized by the command
which captured us, has been restored. I expected Generals Johnston and Sherman
would regard the expedition as contrary to
their agreements and take corresponding action, which would at least bear on the question of property claimed as the capture of
war. If they, or either of them, have done so,
the fact has not become known to me. General Sherman, however, I observe, indignant-
ly repels the idea of my having specie enough
to buy him, at the same time declining to
state his price. All I can say on the point is
that if he was to bring no more than Beadle

Bumble did, I could not have made the purchase."

From Mr. Davis to Mrs. Davis.

"FORTRESS MONROE, September 26, 1865.

". . . It is true that my strength has
greatly failed me, and the loss of sleep has
created a morbid excitability, but an unseen
hand has sustained me, and a peace the world
could not give and has not been able to destroy, will, I trust, uphold me to meet with
resignation whatever may befall me. . . .

"If one is to answer for all, upon him it
most naturally and properly falls. If I alone
could bear all the suffering of the country,
and relieve it from further calamity, I trust
our Heavenly father would give me strength
to be a willing sacrifice; and if, in a lower degree, some of those who called me (I being
then absent) to perform their behests, shall
throw on me the whole responsibility, let us
rejoice at least in their escape, expecting for
them a returning sense of justice when the
stumbling-blocks of fear and selfishness shall
have been removed from their paths. . . .

"The great mass, accepting the present
condition of affairs as the result of the war, and
directing their attention to the future issues
which are involved in the changes produced,
would bury the inevitable past with the sorrow which is unmingled with shame. . . .

CHAPTER LXX.

ACCOUNT OF JOURNEY TO SAVANNAH.

Letter to Dr. Craven.

I WROTE to Mr. Davis, hoping from the youth of General Miles some sympathetic impulse, and that he would read such parts of the letter to him as he might think unobjectionable; but the letter was suppressed, and I wrote another to Dr. Craven, intended for Mr. Davis's information, which gives enough of the details of our travels. After this time I wrote often to the good doctor.

MILL VIEW (NEAR AUGUSTA, GA.), October 10, 1865.

" COLONEL JOHN J. CRAVEN : . . . I dread paralysis for him, his nerves have been so highly strung for years without relief. If you can, and perhaps you may, prevail upon the authorities to let him sleep without a light. He is too feeble to escape, and could not bear a light in his room when in strong health. The sequel of these attacks has always been an attack of amaurosis, and in one of them he lost his eye. It first came on with an attack of acute neuralgia.

" When he was taken from me on the ship, the provost-guard and some women detectives came on board, and after the women searched our persons, the men searched our baggage.

" . . . They then told my servants that they could go ashore if they did not desire to go to Savannah. The husband of my faithful colored nurse forced her to go. I entreated to be permitted to debark at Charleston, as my sister, Miss Howell, still continued to be ill, and I feared to return on the ship with a drunken purser, who had previously required Colonel Pritchard's authority to keep him in order ; and going back, Mrs. Clay, my sister, and myself would be the only women on the ship—but this was refused. Acting as my own chambermaid and nurse, and the nurse also of my sister, we started for Savannah. We had a fearful gale, in which the upper decks once or twice dipped water, and no one could walk.

" God protected us from the fury of the elements ; but the soldiers now began to open and rob our trunks again. The crew, however, gave us some protection, and one of the officers in the engine-room gave up his cabin and locked everything we had left up in it. The Lieutenant of the Fourteenth Maine, Mr. Grant, though a plain man, had the heart of a gentleman, and took care of us with the greatest assiduity. Some of the soldiers and crew helped me to nurse, and saved me many an hour of wakefulness and fatigue.

"My little daughter Maggie was quite like an old woman ; she took her sister early every morning—for the nights were so rough I could not sleep, because it was necessary to hold the infant to avoid bruising it—and with the assistance of our faithful servant Robert, who held her still while she held her sister, she nursed her long enough for me to rest. Little Jeff and I did the housekeeping ; it was a fair division of labor, and not unpleasant, as it displayed the good hearts of my children.

"Arrived at Savannah, we trudged up to the hotel quite in emigrant fashion. My sister with the baby, and Robert with the baggage ; I, with my two little sons, little Maggie, in quite an old-fashioned manner, keeping all straight and acting as parcel-carrier ; for we could not procure any carriage and must walk until we reached the Pulaski House, where, after a day and night, we procured comfortable rooms.

"A black waiter, upon answering my bell, and being told to call my man-servant Robert, replied very impertinently that, 'if he should see Robert he would give the order, but did not expect to see him.' When Rob-

ert heard it, he waited till all the black servants had assembled at dinner, and then remarked that he should hate to believe there
was a colored man so low as to insult a distressed woman; but if so, though a peaceable
man, he should whip the first who did so.
The guilty man began to excuse himself,
whereupon Robert said: 'Oh, it was you,
was it? Well, you do look mean enough for
that or anything else.' From that time all
the greatest assiduity could do was done for
me, first from *esprit de corps*, and then from
kind feeling.

"The people of Savannah treated me with
the greatest tenderness. Had I been a sister
long absent and just returned to their home,
I could not have received more tender welcome. Houses were thrown open to me,
anything and everything was mine. My children had not much more than a change of
clothing after all the parties who had us in
charge had done lightening our baggage, so
they gave the baby dresses, and the other little ones enough to change until I could buy
or make more.

"Unfortunately for me, General ——, who,
I hear, was 'not to the manner born,' was in
command of the district at the time. I asked
permission to see him, and as I was so unwell
that I could not speak above my breath with

a cold, and suffered from fever constantly—
the result of exposure on the ship—I wrote to
beg that he would come to see me, for his
aide had told me the night before that I could
not be permitted to leave Savannah, and having been robbed of nearly all my means, I
could not afford to stay at the hotel. Besides,
as soon as I reached the hotel, detectives
were placed to watch both me and my visitors, so I did not feel at liberty, thus accompanied, to go to private houses.

"General ——'s aide, whose animus was
probably irreproachable, but whose orthogra-
phy was very bad, was directed to tell me
that, except under very extraordinary circumstances, he did not go out of his office, and
'all such' (which I afterward found to mean
myself) 'as desired to see him would call at
his office.' To which I answered, that I
thought illness and my circumstances constituted an extraordinary case ; but that I was
sorry to have asked anything which he 'felt
called upon so curtly to refuse.' On the following day I went, accompanied by General
Hugh Mercer. Need I say that General —— did himself justice, and verified my
preconceived opinion of him in our interview,
in which he told me he 'guessed I could not
telegraph to Washington, write to the heads
of departments there, or to anybody, except

through the regular channel approved;' and I could not write to my friends, 'except through the Provost-Marshal's office;' and that I was permitted to pay my expenses, but must remain within the limits of Savannah.

" With many thanks for this large liberty accorded so graciously, I bowed myself out, first having declined to get soldiers' rations by application for them to this Government.

" In this condition I remained for many weeks, until, fortunately for me, General Birge relieved him, but had it not in his power, however, to remove the restrictions any further than to take the detectives away, of whom I heard, but did not see. General Birge permitted me to write unrestrictedly to whom I pleased, and appeared anxious, in the true spirit of a gentleman, to offer all the courtesies he consistently could.

" My baby caught the whooping-cough, and was ill almost unto death for some days with the fever which precedes the cough; and then she slowly declined. I did what I could to give her fresh air; but the heat was so intense, the insects so annoying, and the two rooms such close quarters, that she and I suffered much more than I hope you or yours will ever know by experience.

" My most acute agony arose from the publication and republication, in the Savannah *Re-*

publican of the shackling scene in Mr. Davis's casemate, which to think of stops my heart's vibration. It was piteous to hear the little children pray at their grace, ' That the Lord would give father something which he could eat, and keep him strong, and bring him back to us with his good senses, to his little children, for Christ's sake ; ' and nearly every day, during the hardest and bitterest of his imprisonment, our little child Maggie had to quit the table to dry her tears after this grace, which was of her own composition.

" I believe I should have lost my senses if these severities had been persevered in, for I could neither eat nor sleep for a week; but the information of the change effected by your advice, relieved me ; and I have thanked God nightly for your brave humanity.

" Though I ate, slept, and lived in my room, rarely or never going out in the day, and only walking out late at night, with Robert for protection, I could not keep my little ones so closely confined. Little Jeff and Billy went out on the street to play, and there Jeff was constantly told that he was rich ; that his father had ' stolen eight millions,' etc. Little two-year-old Billy was taught to sing, ' We'll hang Jeff Davis on a sour apple-tree,' by giving him a reward when he did so. The little thing finally told me one day, ' You thinks

I'se somebody ; so is you ; so is father; but you is not; so is not any of us but me. I am a Yankee every time.' The rough soldiers, doubtless, meant to be kind, but such things wounded me to the quick. They took him and made him snatch apples off the stalls, if Robert lost sight of him for a moment.

"Finally, two women from Maine contemplated whipping him, because they found out that he was his father's son ; but a man took them off just in time to avoid a very painful scene to them as well as to me. These things went on in the street—I refer only to the street-teachings—as these women were, with one other, dishonorable exceptions to the ladies in the house. . . .

"Once, when our little boy Jeff had been most violently assailed by an officer's wife in the house, he came up with his face covered with tears after having stood silent during her abuse. I commended Jeff's gentlemanly conduct in making no reply; cautioned him against ever persecuting, or distressing a woman, or a fiend, if it took that shape, but made application the next day for permission to go away to Augusta; was refused, and then prepared the children to go where they would not see such people. . . .

"Hourly scenes of violence were going on in the streets, and not reported, between the

blacks and whites, and I felt that the children's
lives were not safe. During General ——'s
régime, a negro sentinel levelled his gun at
my little son to shoot him, for calling him
' uncle.'   I could mourn with hope if my children lived, but what was to become of me if I
was deprived of them ?   So I sent them off
with many prayers and tears, but confident of
the wisdom of the decision.   On the ship I
understood a man was very abusive in their
hearing of Mr. Davis, when my faithful servant Robert inquired with great interest,
' Then you tell me I am your equal ?   You
put me alongside of you in everything ? '   The
man said, ' Certainly.'   ' Then,' said Robert,
' take this from your equal,' and knocked him
down.   The captain was appealed to, and
upon a hearing of the case, justified Robert,
and required an apology of the levelled level-
ler.

   " . . . As soon as the dear children
were gone, I hoped with my little weak baby
(you see I am very honest with you) to make
my escape out of the country to them ; but
when, upon coming to Augusta—which General Steadman gave me leave to do immediately upon his accession to command,
through the very kind intercession of General
Brannen, who succeeded General Birge—I
was informed by a gentleman, who said he

had been told so authoritatively, that if I ever quitted the country for any possible object, I would—no matter what befell **Mr.** Davis— never be allowed to return ; and then abandoned the intention. . . .

" My baby has grown fat and rosy as the ' Glory of France,' a rose which Mr. Davis recollects near the gate of our house.

" Under the kind treatment I have received, the fine country air (five miles from Augusta), and the privacy, I have also grown much better; can sleep and eat, and begin to feel alive again with the frosty air, and loving words, and letters which meet me here as in Savannah.

" The whole Southern country teems with homes the doors of which open wide to receive me ; and the people are so loving, talk with such streaming eyes and broken voices of him who is so precious to them and to me, that I cannot realize I do not know them intimately. Mr. Davis should dismiss all fears for me. I only suffer for him. I do not meet a young man who fails to put himself at my disposal to go anywhere for me. I cannot pay a doctor's bill, or buy of an apothecary. ' All things are added unto me.'

" If I have written too long a letter, my dear sir, it is because I have not collected my facts, but sought ' quid scribam, non quem ad modum.'   " VARINA DAVIS."

"Fortress Monroe, Va., October 2, 1865.

". . . My days drag heavily on. To what, I have no means to direct, or to foresee. Having no communication with the outer world except with you, and in that restricted by the *judgment of the Commanding Officer as to what should be sent.* The example you give will illustrate. The 'new overcoat' I have not received, though, probably, when the statement was published on which you relied as telling at least one fact, it had reached this post. The matter being of such public importance as to have been followed in its progress through the tailor's shop, and down the Bay, the journals may give you the future history before it is known to me.

"My daily walks continue, the hour *dependent upon General Miles's engagements,** as I only go out when he can be present.

"Deprived of the opportunity to assemble with the members of the church, there is left to me the spirit communion with those I daily and nightly summon to meet together in His name, who is ever present, and thus I have read the morning service, including the lessons both of the Dominical and Calendar day.

---

* Sometimes General Miles said he forgot, sometimes was too busy, and often, very often, the walk was so late and so curtailed as to do the emaciated sufferer no good, but rather harm.

How full they are of Providences. Holy innocence closes the mouths of fiercest beasts and triumphs over the crafts and subtleties of wicked men; conscious sinfulness silences those who came to arraign a guilty mortal and entrap the righteous judge; repentance working deliverance to an oppressed and dispersed people; the prayers of the Church affecting the miraculous preservation of one apostle from the fate which had a short time before fallen upon another.

" I could not write daily as you wish, because I am not allowed to keep stationery. When it is specially granted it has to be accounted for, the whole being returned written or blank, as may be. . . . With you it is otherwise, and the Attorney-General will probably indulge us by forwarding your letters as often as you write. His past courtesy warrants such expectation. . . .

" William B. Reed, of Philadelphia, recently tendered to me his professional services in a very kind and handsome letter. Thomas J. Wharton, C. E. Hooker, and Fulton Anderson, are the Mississippi lawyers who offered their services and were recognized as counsel by the United States Secretary of State. I requested permission to acknowledge their kindness by a letter; it was not granted."

CHAPTER LXXI.

LETTERS FROM PRISON.

*From Mr. Davis to Mrs. Davis.**

"FORTRESS MONROE, VA., October 11, 1865.

". . . On the second of this month I was removed to a room on the second floor of a house built for officers' quarters. The dry air, good water, and a fire when requisite, have already improved my physical condition, and with increasing health all the disturbances due to a low vitality, it is to be expected, will disappear as rapidly as has been usual with me, after becoming convalescent. I am deeply indebted to my attending physician, who has been to me much more than that term usually conveys. In all my times of trouble, new evidences have been given me of God's merciful love.

". . . The *Herald* claims to give me regular information concerning my family, but if it did contain such news, as I only get occasionally a copy, the promise would be unfulfilled. . . . I have lately read the

---

* The intervening letters are simply records of suffering, deprivation, and fortitude under the trial.

' Suffering Saviour,' by the Reverend Dr. Krumacher, and was deeply impressed with the dignity, the sublime patience of the model of Christianity, as contrasted with the brutal vindictiveness of unregenerate man ; and with the similitude of the portrait given of the Jews to the fierce prosecutions which pursued the Revolutionists after the restoration of the Stuarts. One is led to ask, Did Sir Henry Vane and the Duke of Argyle imitate the more than human virtue of our Saviour, or was their conduct the inspiration of a conscience void of offence in that whereof they were accused ?

" Misfortune should not depress us, as it is only crime which can degrade. Beyond this world there is a sure retreat for the oppressed; and posterity justifies the memory of those who fall unjustly. To our own purblind view there is much which is wrong, but to deny what is right is to question the wisdom of Providence or the existence of the mediatorial government. . . .

" Every intelligent man knows that my office did not make me the custodian of public money, but such slanders impose on and serve to inflame the ignorant—the very ignorant—who don't know how public money was kept, and how drawn out of the hands of those who were responsible for it. My children, as they grow up and prove the pressure of poverty, must be taught the cause of it ; and I trust they will feel as I have, when remembering the fact that my father was impoverished by his losses in the war of the Revolution.

" Our injuries cease to be grievous in proportion as Christian charity enables us to for-give those who trespass against us, and to pray for our enemies. I rejoice in the sweet sensitive nature of our little Maggie, but I would she could have been spared the knowl-edge which inspired her 'grace,' and the tears which followed its utterance. As none could share my suffering, and as those who loved me were powerless to diminish it, I greatly preferred that they should not know of it. Separated from my friends of this world, my Heavenly Father has drawn nearer to me. His goodness and my unworthiness are more sensibly felt, but this does not press me back, for the atoning Mediator is the way, and His hand upholds me.*

" I hope the negroes' fidelity will be duly

---

*Little Maggie was told she might write to her father if she said nothing objectionable to the authorities. She thought long, and as she was then a very small girl, wrote with difficulty ; after days of labor she copied the 23d psalm " The Lord is my Shepherd, . . ." and with tearful eyes brought it to me, signed with her name, saying, " This letter will comfort father, and will not make the Yankees mad, will it?" The letter was suppressed.

rewarded, and regret that we are not in a situation to aid and protect them. There is, I observe, a controversy which I regret as to allowing negroes to testify in court. From brother Joe, many years ago, I derived the opinion that they should then be made competent witnesses, the jury judging of their credibility ; out of my opinion on that point, arose my difficulty with Mr. C——,* and any doubt which might have existed in my mind was removed at that time. The change of relation diminishing protection, must increase the necessity. Truth only is consistent, and they must be acute and well trained, who can so combine as to make falsehood appear like truth when closely examined.

"For, say, three months after I was imprisoned here, two hours consecutive sleep were never allowed me ; more recently it has not been so bad, but it is still only broken sleep which I get at night, and by day my attention is distracted by the passing of the sentinels who are kept around me as well by day as by night. I have not sunk under my trials, am better than a fortnight ago, and trust I shall be sustained under any affliction which it may be required me to bear. My

---

* An overseer who gave up his place with us, on account of the negroes being allowed a hearing in their own defence.

sight is affected, but less than I would have
supposed if it had been foretold that a light
was to be kept where I was to sleep, and
that I was at short intervals to be aroused,
and the expanded pupil thus frequently
subjected to the glare of a lamp. . . .
There is soon to be a change of the garrison
here. I will be sorry to part from many of
the officers, but as they are to go home I
should rejoice for such as are entitled to my
gratitude. *Au reste*, as I cannot control, so
I may hope for the best.

"I have not seen Jordan's * critique, and
am at a loss to know where that game was
played and was lost by my interference. If
the records are preserved they dispose summarily of his romances past, passing, and to
come. The events were of a public character,
and it is not possible for men to shift their
responsibility to another. Everyone who has
acted must have made mistakes, and the best
defence he can make to the public, and the
only one beneficial to his conscience, if he
has changed his theory, is to confess it;
let him whose opinions are unchanged conform his action to changed circumstances, and

---

* A publication made by General Jordan, in Harper's Monthly of
1865, calculated to inflame the minds of the North against Mr. Davis,
with a note appended by General Beauregard, scarcely less hostile
and offensive.

both classes may preserve their integrity and live and work in harmony. Our life is spent in choosing between evils, and he would be most unwise who would refuse the comparative good thus to be obtained. History is ever repeating itself, but the influence of Christianity and letters has softened its harsher features. The wail of destitute women and children who were left on the shore of Cork after the treaty of Limerick, still rings in the ears of all who love right and hate oppression ; but bad as was the treatment of the Irish then, those scenes of which you were reading not long before you left Richmond, enacted by Philip of Spain in the Low Countries, were worse. The unfortunate have always been deserted and betrayed ; but did ever man have less to complain of when he had lost power to serve? The critics are noisy—perhaps they hope to enhance their wares by loud crying. The multitudes are silent, why should they speak to save him who hears best the words most secretly uttered? My own heart tells me the sympathy exists, that the prayers from the family hearth have not been hushed. . . .

". . . John Mitchel has been released. He was permitted to take leave of me through the grates, and he offered to write to you. I have not seen our friend Clay for some time,

not having been out to walk lately on account
of a series of boils, or a carbuncle with a succession of points, which rose in my right armpit,
and has prevented me from putting on my coat
since the day I last wrote to you. I believe
the disease is now at an end, and but for the
rain I would have gone out to-day. I will
comply with your repeated request for a description of my room, and hope the reality
may be better than you have imagined the
case to be. The room is about 18×20 feet;
is situated at the corner in the second story
of a long two-story house which stands under
cover of the main parapet, and was built for
officers' quarters. In the centre of the end
wall, is a fireplace; in the centre of each of
the other walls is a door. The one opposite
to the fireplace opens into the room occupied
by the officer of the guard for the day, the one
on the south side looks out on a gallery which
runs along the building, and, beyond, is a
limited view of the interior of the fort; the
one on the north side connects with a passage
dividing the building. The doorway into the
officer's room is closed by an iron grating,
with locks on *his* side of it, and, turning on
hinge, affords the means of exit. The gallery
door is closed by a fixed iron grating with
glazed sash shutters outside. The passage
doorway is closed by iron grating, and a panel

shutter into which are inserted two panes of glass. Sentinels are no longer kept in the room I occupy. One sentinel only now walks back and forth along the gallery, one along the passage, and one in the officer's room, so as to give each of the three a view through his door of the interior of the room. They cause the broken sleep concerning which you ask. I have endeavored to overcome the distraction and annoyance this constant passing causes in the day, and to resist its disturbing effect at night; the success has not, however, been commensurate with the effort. Formerly the circumstances were much worse; and, before changes were made, a morbid condition had been produced so that wakefulness is continued by less than would have produced it. My bed stands in the corner of the walls of the gallery and officer's room; on the opposite corner is the water-bucket, basin and pitcher, and a folding screen which enables me to wash unobserved. On the gallery side of the chimney is a recess with a shelf for books, and pegs to hang up clothes. On the opposite side of the chimney, a closet. The bed is the common form of iron frame, two mattresses, sheets, blankets, and a cover with pillows and mosquito bar. Breakfast is sent to me about nine; dinner about four; and tea would be sent if I desired it. The food is

suited to my condition, and I have had no occasion to ask for change or addition. The
chair, though coarse, is so much better than
the one I had before it, as to be comparatively satisfactory ; a stand, such as is commonly
used in hospital wards, serves me as a table,
and for the present there is a stool which answers for a washstand. My clothes are not
with me, except those in immediate use. My
valise was taken charge of by General Miles.
I have not seen it since. I much regret that
you did not keep the things which had a value
from association, instead of leaving them in
the valise.

"FORTRESS MONROE, VA., November 3, 1865.

.   .   .   .

"I am sustained by a Power I know not
of. The Protector of the fatherless and the
widow, I am permitted to hope, hears your
prayer. Your trust that the Son of the
righteous will not be forsaken has also been
to me the suggestion of comfort. When
Franklin was brought before the privy council
of George III., and a time-serving courtier
heaped the grossest indignities upon him, he
bore them with composure, and afterward
attributed his ability to do so to the consciousness of innocence in the acts for which he was
reviled. .   .   . I have no means of com-

municating with any one but you, and, as I
understand the orders, all communications to
you must pass through Washington, and be
viséed.

". . . What, under Providence, may be
in store for us I have no ability to foresee.
I have tried to do my duty to my fellow-men,
and while my penitent prayers are offered to
our Heavenly Father for forgiveness of the
sins committed against Him, I have the sustaining belief that He is full of mercy ; and,
knowing my inmost heart, will acquit me
where man, blind man seeks to condemn.
From our mediating Saviour I humbly trust
to receive support, and, whatever may befall
me in this world, to have justice dictated by
Divine Wisdom and tempered with Divine
mercy in the next.

" Kiss dear little Winnie for me, and, as
she grows, teach her how her father loved
her when she was too young to remember.
Try to make my thanks to Mr. Schley and
the ladies equal to my gratitude. . . .
My faith tells me that our merciful Father
will give us whatever it is expedient we
should have. . . ."

"FORTRESS MONROE, November 21, 1865.

" To make the best of the existing condition
is alike required by patriotism and practical

sense. The negro is unquestionably to be at
last the victim; because, when brought into
conflict, the inferior race must be overborne;
but it is possible to defer the conflict and to
preserve a part of the kind relations heretofore existing between the races, when a life-
long common interest united them. The
object is worthy all the effort. To be successful, the policy must be as far removed from
the conservatism that rejects everything new,
as from the idealism which would retain
nothing which is old. If catch-words determine who shall mould the institutions and
administer the affairs of the Southern States
—the deluge. Though neither a spectator
nor an actor, a life spent more in the service
of my country than in that of my family, leaves
me now unable to disengage myself from the
consideration of the public interests. . . .
The best source of patience is the assurance
that the world is governed by infinite wisdom,
and that He who rules only permits injustice
for some counterbalancing good of which the
sufferer cannot judge.

"I yielded to your renewed request, and
wrote minute description of my room, its
furniture, the beats of the sentinels, etc.; that
part of my letter was objected to * and was

---

* By General Miles.

rewritten accordingly. Let me renew the caution against believing the statements of correspondents in regard to me. To calum-niate a state prisoner and thus either grat-ify or excite hatred against him, is an old device, and never was a fairer opportunity presented to do so without the fear of contra-diction than is offered in my case.

"November 22d. It is six months since we parted, and I know no more of the purpose in regard to me than I did then. Measured by painful anxiety for you and your helpless charge, these months are to me many, many years. From the anguish and doubly painful trial, because I could learn nothing of you, I have extracted the consolation of increased pride and fully sustained confidence. . . . I do take care of my health ; all the motives you enumerate are ever before me ; and others, of which you are less apt to think, furnish me the strongest inducements to de-sire life and strength to vindicate my conduct, at least to posterity, and for my family. Be hopeful—trust in "the faithful Promiser." Let us with faith and charity look out for a better morrow. . . . Shut out from the ever-changing world, I live in the past with a vividness only thus to be accounted for. . . ."

"FORTRESS MONROE, VA., December 7, 1865.

"I am deeply impressed by the kindness of the Bishop, and that of the priests who have so nobly shown their readiness to do their Master's work in relieving the afflicted and protecting the fatherless. They have sent thus the sweetest solace to one in the condition of Him, who went down from Jerusalem to Jericho. I feel with you, that God has been very good to us. . . .

"Reagan I knew to be a true-hearted, consistent man, and I never gave the least heed to the newspaper reports which attributed to him participation in censorious remarks against me during his confinement at Fort Warren. Some men I had to trust because of the confidence others had in them. When disaster fell upon me their desertion did not surprise me.

"I recently saw that Davis had been arrested; also, that a general petition for his release has been gotten up in North Carolina, which it was expected would be effectual. The proverb in relation to the desire of misery for companionship is not realized by me in this matter of imprisonment. I would that, like one of old, it were for me to say, I alone am left. To me—as it must to you—it is sometimes a puzzle to find the rule of discrimination. In such a situation Hume's balance

is peculiarly to be sought. . . . As natural rights belong only to those who can
maintain them, so natural affections and ex-
citements are only safe to those who are not
unnaturally restrained.

"I have been reading 'Thoughts on Personal Religion,' by Dr. Goulburn. His instructions as to prayer have impressed me particularly. How like is the experience of men. It
is no small encouragement to a sinner striving for a better state, to find that those who
have, at least in the world's estimation, won
the crown of glory, had passed through such
tribulation as he is beset with. Did it never
occur to you how much evil is done by the
use of a text startling in its terms, and so
iterated and reiterated that any explanation of
its meaning by reference to other texts bearing on the same subject is lost? It occurred
to me, after last writing to you, that something
of that kind might have happened to you in
regard to forgiveness; and I regretted not
having pointed out the illustration of his
meaning which our Saviour gave in the par-
able of the King who took an account of his
servants. When we shall pass into the future state of pure intelligence, so as to judge
not by external signs but by the inner motives,
how different men will appear to each other
from the estimates of their carnal life! May

it not be that we shall then find our most earnest efforts at self-examination brought us but to a poor knowledge of ourselves ?

" Though my prison life does not give me the quiet of solitude, its isolation as to intercourse affords abundant opportunity for turning the thoughts inward ; and, if my self-love, not to say sense of justice, would have resisted the reckless abuse of my enemies, I am humbled by your unmerited praise. It teaches me what I ought to be, and lifts my eyes to Him whose all-sufficient grace alone can raise me to your ideal standard. With the communion of the Church, I am not alone, nor without remembrance that the burthen is not permitted to exceed the strength. I live and hope.

" The ' heavy erasures ' concerning which you inquire, assuming that they were made by me, as the Attorney-General had politely informed you that he did not do it, were not by my choice. To your repeated requests to be informed as to my room, my clothes, and the change of garrison as affecting me, I replied in the letter to which you refer. Two leaves containing the answers to the two first questions were returned to me as matter which would not be forwarded, and they were rewritten omitting the answers described. Subsequently my attention was called to a sentence on another page, responding to your inquiry about the new garrison, and stating a consequent alteration in the matter of sentinels, which I was required to obliterate. I drew the pen through it and sent it back. General Miles afterward told me that it had still been legible as I left it, and added something not distinctly heard beyond the point of main interest, that the letter had been sent.

" My incarceration followed four years of terrible war. The North put forth its whole capacity on land and sea, by ball and bayonet, striving to retain the South in one Government with it; the South strained every nerve to maintain a separate existence. By the newspaper, to-day, I see that the North, as represented in Congress, stands quite united to keep the South *out* of the legislative halls of the Union, and the South, wistfully looking at the closed entrance, stands outside—and then she is told she has all the time been inside. . . .

"The ways of Him who doeth all things well are inscrutable to man. Let us learn to say, 'not mine but Thy will be done.' The bitterness which caused me to be so persistently slandered, has created a sentiment which will probably find vent in Congressional speeches, and test all your Christian fortitude. Remember that the end is not yet. A fair inquiry will show how ' false witnesses have risen up against me and laid to my charge things that I knew not of.' If you will recall the very early period when I was warned by letter that an emissary had been sent to Montgomery to assassinate me, you will see misconception of my position and a cruel desire for my destruction are not new-born. When the truth is revealed, the more honorable and manly of my enemies will recoil from further association with the others. Truth and the common sense of justice will generally protect the innocent, where the trial is according to the due course of law, and is sure to vindicate the memory of a victim. . . . There is an unseen hand which upholds me, save when my thoughts are concentrated on the objects of my dearest love and greatest solicitude. Perhaps He will give me that strength hereafter. In the many friends He has raised up for you, there is the promise of that peace to come. . . .

"December 8th. Another day has succeeded the night. The sun has risen bright, and the cold bracing air invites animal life to activity. To me there is the same monotonous round of prisoner's life in military confinement, such as is not known to the usages of war in cases like mine. I am, however, thankful for the power to bear, and trustful that the

power will be given me to bear in patience.
In a former letter I mentioned to you that the
trunk you had sent with clothes had arrived.
I notice that the shirts are new, *and it excites
the inquiry whether you have been robbed of
those which you took with your baggage when
you left me in Richmond.** . . . If the field
where the events of Jordan's intrigue occurred
was near to Drury's Bluff, Colonel Melton
knows how my designs were frustrated, and
how little the promise accorded with the action on the unwise plan substituted for mine.
A letter to Mr. Seddon put it beyond the power
of anyone to falsify that affair.   It was sent by
General Beauregard the day before he undertook the execution of his own plan, to account
for the change he made, and from which, when
it failed, he endeavored to escape by blaming
Whiting and Ransom. . . . . . .

After faithful self-examination it is permitted
to me to say, I have not done to others as
they do unto me.   There is no occasion, now,
to make Frankensteins.   Like ready-made
clothing, they wait in abundance for custom-
ers.   When Roberts grew angry with Byron,
you know he charged him with being miserable
because of a soul of which he could not get
rid.   The sentinel has stamped with such

---

* These were demanded from my trunk and given for his use to
the messenger sent for them from the fort,

noise, back and forth, in front of me, that, until another and more quiet walker comes on,
and I recover from the effect produced by the
attempt to write under such difficulty, I will
desist. . . .

"Somebody writing from Augusta to the
Boston Advertiser, makes an extraordinary
statement about a letter said to have been
written to someone in Columbus, by Mr. A.
H. Stephens, immediately after the Hampton
Roads conference—containing the assertion
that terms not humiliating to the South could
be obtained, but that I and my principal advisers did not want peace. Of course Mr. S.
could not have said anything of the sort, as
he had been twice employed to seek peace,
and, on the last occasion, made a report, written and oral, showing that no negotiation
would be entertained. *He was pressed to en-
large the written report by the addition of such
conclusions and impressions as the confidential
nature of a part of the conference would permit*, but though the two other commissioners
appeared willing to do so, Mr. S. strongly
objected, arguing that the bare recital of facts
was the best presentation of the case to the
public mind. Now, as it would have been
dishonest to conceal from me such an opportunity as is described, and treacherous to the
people to have given such an account as it

was thought would most certainly lead them
to the opposite conclusion, I take it that someone is slandering Mr. Stephens, and so publicly that even a philosopher might be moved
to correct it. . . . There has been certainly much zeal displayed in the planting
and cultivating of prejudice against me, but
many of the stories are so absurd that it required a morbid state of opinion to receive
them.

" ' Dobbin ' * always was sterling ; his father
and his mother were pure gold. Tell him how
gratefully I recognize his care for my children.
. . . On the whole, it must be more comfortable to be the deceived than the deceiver.
Sometimes I feel that there is a real compliment in the trust displayed by some of my
slanderers, to whom it must occur that, with a
single breath, I could topple over the miserable fabric. . . .

" In the time when nations were ruled by
arbitrary power, the Catholic priests stood
between the despots and their victims, sub-
limely defying the rage of one, and divinely
bending to raise the other. From time to
time the heroic spirit of that ancient line
has been called forth, and in plague, pesti-
lence, and famine, in the wilderness and on

---

* William Preston Johnston.

fields of blood, in the prison, on the scaffold, and among the deserted mourners, nobly have they maintained the glory of their order. . . .

"*I would write more freely if I knew that the Attorney-General only inspected my letters;* but, as I send them open and don't know how they are forwarded, and do know that objections have been made here to the contents of a letter enclosed to the Attorney-General, I conclude that they are read before they reach him, and may be stopped on the way."

CHAPTER LXXII.

LETTERS FROM FORTRESS MONROE.

From Mr. Davis to Mrs. Davis.

"FORTRESS MONROE, VA., January 16, 1866.

" I had feared that our negroes would be disturbed by the introduction of others among them, but could not have imagined that they would be driven away from their home by those pretending to be their especial advocates. What a beast he must have been who turned old Uncle Bob out of his house, to find where he could a shelter for the infirmities of more than a hundred winters. That claim was manifest. Of the truth, the fidelity, the piety which had so long secured him the respect of all who knew him, a stranger might plead ignorance. . . .

" 17th. I have been suffering from neuralgia in the head, and the usual effect upon the eyes causes me to write at intervals. Indeed, considering the circumstances, it is rather to be wondered at that I am not worse. Once a day it is still permitted to me to walk in the open air; and, though the time is brief, the result is beneficial. . . .

" 18th. The gifts with which men are divinely endowed are various, and the requirements of the Lord are never beyond the range of possibility; for He knows our infirmities and judges of our motives. These man cannot know, and is therefore forbidden to judge. We hope and pray for God's forgiveness on the ground of true repentance, and as we cannot tell, in the case of those who trespass against us, whether the repentance is true or feigned, we are bound to accept the seeming. This is possible, but is not easy for virtue far short of the God-like or saintly examples of the Redeemer, the first Christian Martyr. . . ."

From Mr. Davis to Mrs. Davis.

"FORTRESS MONROE, VA., January 24, 1866.

" Judge Campbell, I have been told, wrote a full account of the interview with Mr. Lincoln and Mr. Seward, and that it has been published in the Northern papers. Mr. Hunter promised me to write such a statement. The stories told of Mr. Stephens are improbable, because the meanest capacity must perceive *that my powers and duties rested on the organization made by the Southern States, and that it would have been treasonable usurpation to attempt to destroy the organization by the exercise of functions given to maintain it.*

When the Continental Congress sent Commissioners to meet Lord Howe, who had announced himself as empowered to treat for the adjustment of the controversy between the States and Great Britain, the Commissioners, on learning that the basis must be a return to allegiance, informed his Lordship that the Colonies having declared their independence, it was not competent for the Congress to return them to a state of dependence. In both cases, there was an obvious mode, but it was adopted in neither, viz., to suspend hostilities and submit propositions to be laid before the States. Judge Campbell made an inquiry which opened, and received an answer which closed, that view. *I suppose it is narrated in his statement.** Excluded from an opportunity to reply, slanders have worked without check, and have no doubt deceived many. Again, any dolt whose blunders necessitated frequent conviction, and whose vanity sought for someone on whom to lay the responsibility of his failures, could readily, and if mean enough would *now*, ascribe them to me. Things done against my known views, and of which explanations were written to me when success was expected to result from the change of

---

* It was not, but much was narrated which inflamed the public against the hapless prisoner.

plan, have lately been attributed to my orders.   Beauregard, Hood, Hardee, and
Cobb know of a case in point, memorable by
its consequences.   Generals Lee and Bragg
could give the history of the two largest armies. . . . I never sought to make up my
own record, intent on the discharge of my
duties in the various public positions I have
held.   If the question had occurred to me,
how will this be told hereafter? I would have
preferred to leave that task to others.   Nor
is the hazard great, for the dependence of the
parts of a whole will generally correct the
perversions of recital by interested narrators.

"That power to compare and sift testimony
is as necessary to a historian as to an attorney, and I hope the faculty will be put in
exercise proportionate to the field our time
has offered. . . .

"The New York paper containing an account of the interview between the South
Carolina committee and President Johnson,
was handed to me soon after its publication.
I did not credit the statement, because I was
sure you had not in such correspondence
given expression to your personal feelings.*

* Mr. Davis refers to a misstatement of President Johnson, that I
had written him offensive letters, when I had never written him but
one, and that was an application to be allowed to go to my husband,
and this was couched in respectful terms and handed to him by
Francis P. Blair, who would not have done anything to injure me

To all the trials, mental and physical, to which I am subjected I will oppose all the moral power I possess, that my life may be prolonged as far as such drains will permit, and my power to meet any future ordeal be as great as possible to me.

"Mr. Clay, like myself, no doubt, suffers from food unsuited to him, and to anyone in close confinement, even were it good, I think it would soon become so. . . .

"Bowed down by anxiety for my family, suffering from neuralgia and dyspepsia, covered by the dusky cloud of falsehood and injustice, I am supported by the conscious rectitude of my course, and humbly acknowledging my many and grievous sins against God, can confidently look to His righteous judgment for vindication in the matters whereof I am accused by man. . . ."

From Mr. Davis to Mrs. Davis.

"FORTRESS MONROE, January 28, 1866.

. . . .

"Did you ever hear that Colonel MacCree refused to dine with the Duke of Wellington? He, of course, gave no reason on that occasion, but it was well understood to be

or mine. President Johnson afterward acknowledged to the Honorable Reverdy Johnson, that he had made a misstatement in answer to my application for a copy of the putative letter.

on account of the treatment received by Napoleon after his surrender.

"It is not long since a newspaper paragraphist would have been rebuked by public opinion if he had attempted, by epithets and one-sided statements, to inflame the mind of his readers against a prisoner waiting a trial; but that would have been a small offence compared with that of a law-maker who would seek to produce the effect, and then, by retrospective legislation, to bring it to bear upon an anticipated trial by endowing such prejudiced minds with the power to judge. The minor objections growing out of the official character of the person, which, if alone, would be great, are hidden by the magnitude of the offence of uttering such libellous assertion under the circumstances which he knew surrounded me. That his authority was not called for, that he was not scoffed by the multitude as the home-bred sentiment of fair play demanded, shows you how deep-seated the disease has become.

"The same conclusion as to your course is reached by every line of thought. Trying as it may be, you will have to make the effort to leave me, for the present, out of all your plans; and may our Heavenly Father strengthen your heart for the difficult task of filling the place of both parents to our children. Tarry thou the Lord's pleasure, and let us always remember that all He does is right, and that hereafter it will be given to us to comprehend His ways and say all was well. . . .

"29th. . . . Oh, that the law-makers had facts instead of suggestions on which to base their action in regard to the Southern States. . . . Fear not what man can do, it is God disposes. Now I am shut up and slander runs riot to destroy my fair repute, but any investigation must redeem my character and leave it for an inheritance to my children, which in after-times they will not be the worse for possessing. The treatment I have received will be compared with my treatment of others, and it will be the reverse of the picture my enemies have drawn. Conscious rectitude is a great support to the sufferer, whatever may be the form or the end of the afflictions."

"FORTRESS MONROE, VA., February 3, 1866.

". . . Men turn to the judgment of posterity for the reversal of the decrees of their contemporaries, appealing with the self-sustaining hope of conscious rectitude, from 'Philip drunk to Philip sober.' . . .

"The newspapers will have informed you of the petition in my behalf by seven thousand

ladies of Richmond and vicinity. It was not
ineffectual, it refreshed my burdened heart as
the shower revives a parched field.

"I have just heard that Mr. Cass is dying,
and regret it as well on account of my kind
feeling for him and the respect which his ami-
able character commanded, as because he was
one of those on whom I felt I could rely to
vindicate my character from some of the accusations made against me.   After Mr. Crittenden, there was no one to whom I talked so
much and so freely concerning the sectional
troubles in 1860–61.   With Mr. Crittenden I
daily conferred when we served on the compromise committee in that winter, the record
of which shows who it was who opposed
every effort at accommodation.

"Like you, I feel sorry for the negroes.
What has been done would gradually and
measurably be corrected by the operation
of the ordinary laws governing the relation
of labor to capital, if they were let alone.
But interference by those who have a theory to maintain by the manufacture of facts,
must result in evil, evil only and continually. . . .

"At every renewal of the assertion that the
Southern people hate the negroes, my surprise is renewed ; but a hostility, not now or
heretofore existing, between the races may be

engendered by just such influences as are indicated. . . .

"On the night of the 13th I was sitting before the fire, because I could not sleep, and had a startling optical illusion, such you know as were common to me in fever; but to my vision, I saw little Pollie * walk across the floor and kneel down between me and the fire, in the attitude of prayer. I moved from consequent excitement and the sweet vision melted away. I have not called it a dream, because not conscious of being asleep, but sleep has many stages, and that only is perfect sleep which we call Death.

"To use your expressive phrase, I am hungry for the children's little faces, and have habitually to resist the power of tender feelings which may not be gratified. . . . To look only to those hopes of which man cannot deprive me, and to such relief as a record may afford, in the event to which my enemies refer as a means, not of learning the truth and doing justice, but of condemnation and punishment."

---

* The name of a sister he loved, and applied as an endearment to little Maggie.

From President Davis to Mrs. Davis.

"FORTRESS MONROE, VA., February 17, 1866.

. . . .

" 19th day. Mrs. Clay, after her return to Washington, sent me a coffee-pot, to enable me to make coffee for myself. Dr. Cooper came and gave me full instructions as to its use, making very good coffee as a part of the lecture. I have followed directions not with the best success; indeed, I am led to doubt whether cooking was designed to be my vocation.* . . . My eyes do not suffer much from inflammation; but the neuralgia of the head sometimes renders me almost blind during the paroxysm. I recollect Frederick Maginnis † very well; first met him at Manassas, and had a very favorable opinion of him.

" The 'Quadrilateral' was handed to me and I soon found, what was not told, that it had been sent by you. The writer has at-

---

* This little coffee-pot is now in my possession. In his first effort at cooking he wrenched off the soldered top instead of taking off the dripper, and he gently and apologetically explained, "I did not learn to cook early enough."

† A colored man who was a courteous, refined gentleman in his instincts. He offered his services to me gratuitously in Georgia, which were accepted on the usual terms of remuneration, and he was a second providence to us by his care of Mr. Davis after I was allowed to go to him. He afterward married my maid, who was as dear as she was faithful to me, and they both live now in Baltimore, respected by all who know them.

tempted the very difficult task of portraying the inconsistencies of human nature. Sir Walter Scott alone has succeeded in doing it. We have as much in real life as anyone can need, and in fiction we might be treated to pictures harmonized in coloring. The dis-closure of Ida's secret, *and the slaughter of prisoners who had laid down their arms, could not have been done by one as true and gen-erous and brave as the hero is represented.* The horse is the best character in the book, as I measure them. Do you recollect ' Old Duke ' the horse I rode in the Pawnee cam-paign? He might have stood for the por-trait, except that even in extreme age he was not gentle. . . ."

"FORTRESS MONROE, VA., March 13, 1866.

. . . .

" Your reception at Macon was such as I anticipated from my own experience, and it is so much the more valuable because those friends have little demonstrativeness and no insincerity. The kind manifestations men-tioned by you as made by the negro servants, are not less touching than those of more cul-tivated people. I liked them, and am grati-fied by their friendly remembrance. What-ever may be the result of the present experi-ment, the former relation of the races was one which could only incite to harshness a very brutal nature.

"I hope the reports of growing despondence, because of political action leading to organizations for expatriation, have been exaggerated. All cannot go, and those who must stay will need the help of all who can go away. *The night may seem long, but it is the part of fidelity to watch and wait for morning.*

"Warned by a sad experience against such calculations as would make hope sanguine and expectation swift, I will yet hope, though in patience, and strive to find adequate protection beneath the shield of the conviction that all things are ordered in wisdom and mercy and love, that I may fully feel, ' Even so, Father, for it is Thy will.'

" . . . . In all the affairs of life we are reduced to choosing between evils, every situation having its disadvantages. You recollect the instructive satire of Horace on the desire for change, etc.

"Remember me most affectionately to Ma. Tell her that the old one hit Le Roy at last, but that his faith held out and he never cried ' quarter.' . . .

"If my letter seems disjointed and obscure, do not infer any physical ill as the cause. The tramping and creaking of the sentinel's boots

disturb me so as to render it difficult to write
at all. . . ."

. . . .

" I am in the condition to give the highest
value to quiet, it being the thing never allowed to me by day or night. . . .

" The spring is slowly appearing and, as
well as the calendar, reminds me of the many
months during which I have been closely confined without any legal proceeding, or even
informal notice of the charges and evidence
on which I am held as a ' state prisoner.'
So I strive to possess my soul in patience, and
by every means attainable to preserve my
health against undermining circumstances.
The officers of the guard treat me with all the
consideration compatible with their position."

"FORTRESS MONROE, VA., April 8, 1866.

" . . . Next to the consciousness of
rectitude, it is to me the greatest of earthly
consolations to know that those for whom I
acted and suffer, approve and sympathize.
It is common in cases of public calamity for
those who feel the infliction, to seek for some
object on which to throw the blame, and rarely has it happened that the selection has been
justly or generously made. . . .

VOL. II.—48

" I feel deeply indebted to Dr. Craven and the ladies of his family for a benevolence which had much to suppress, and nothing selfish to excite, it, and but for which my captivity would soon have ended in death.

" The letter from my little Polly is a sweet, graceful image of her honest, affectionate heart. I am sure she will be a comfort and honor to her family in after-years. . . ."

"FORTRESS MONROE, April 21, 1866.

". . . The young soldier who saw you in the cars at Binghamton reported the interview, and described how bright and wide-awake little Winnie was. It was a great pleasure to me to hear an eye-witness.

" The weather is quite warm, the earth is clothed in her bright robes of promise, the birds sing joyously, and I will not, like the 'Bard of Avon,' complain that they are so tuneful while ' I so weary fu' o' care.' Though not the voice I long to hear, I draw from it the pleasure it was designed to give by the bounteous Creator, who did not mean that man's happiness should be at the mercy of man, and therefore formed him for companionship with nature, and endowed his soul with capacity to feed on hopes which live beyond this fleeting life. . . .

. . . Often has it occurred in the world's

history that fidelity has been treated as a crime, and true faith punished as treason. So it cannot be before the Judge to whom all hearts are open, from whom no secrets are hid. Dr. Cooper has just been here to visit me, he says all which is needful for me is air and exercise. It was the want which Cowper's bird had, and hardly had bird more usually sought for air and motion than I did when I had Byron's 'Heritage of Woe.' But I am not of Cato's creed, and do not hold that it is man's wisdom to equal the swallow, but man's dignity to bear up against trials under which the lower animals would sink. Resolution of will may not, according to Father Timon, prolong indefinitely our earthly existence, but it will do much to sustain the tottering machine beyond the observer's calculation. . . .

" 23d. You can imagine how one, shut out from all direct communication with his friends, dwells upon every shadow and longs for light.

" Yesterday my walk was extended to two hours, and I hope for the continuance of the extension, as the good doctor has urged the necessity for more air and exercise. . . ."

CHAPTER LXXIII.

PERMISSION to leave Georgia having been at
last obtained through General Stedman's in-
strumentality, Mr. Harrison kindly joined me,
and we left Georgia and went to Louisiana
and Mississippi, to find what had been left to
us.

In Vicksburg, where Mr. J. E. Davis was,
many of the negroes called with affectionate
expressions. A warm welcome was accorded
me everywhere, and especially in New Orleans. Here I saw our dashing cavalry officer, General Wheeler, serving in a hardware
store. Mr. J. U. Payne, Mr. Davis's life-long
friend, came with pressing offers of money and
service, which, when our need was greater, he
more urgently pressed upon us. It was with
difficulty that the milliners and merchants
could be persuaded to accept pay for the few
articles I could afford to buy to replenish my
wardrobe.

After a short stay which demonstrated
there was nothing to recover, Mr. Harrison,

my nurse and baby, and Frederick Maginnis, the good man mentioned in a foot-note appended to Mr. Davis's letters, and I, proceeded to New York City, where it had been intimated by President Johnson I should find permission to visit my husband. We remained in New York over ten days, but no permit came, and I rejoined my children after a year's absence from them.

A few days after our arrival, a rumor came to Montreal that Mr. Davis was dying. Upon hearing this I telegraphed the President : " Is it possible that you will keep me from my dying husband ? " He responded by a permission to go, subject to conditions to be stated at the fort, and sent a telegram from General Miles saying that Mr. Davis was in his usual health.

I left Montreal that night, and with my infant, her nurse, and Frederick went to Fortress Monroe, arriving there at four o'clock A.M. a cold, raw morning, on May 10, 1866, just a year from the surrender of the Confederacy. There was no hotel there then, and we sat in the little open waiting-room until half-past ten. The terror of what the parole would be, the anxiety about my husband's health, and the poor baby being detained in the raw weather without fire, made me very anxious for a messenger from the fort. At last he came in the person

of cheery, kind young Lieutenant Fessen-
den, who snapped his fingers at the baby and
made friends with her very soon—children
and animals are good judges of people, and
my baby saw in him a friendly sympathy that
quieted and drew her to him. He handed me
the parole not to take deadly weapons to my
husband, which I signed, and we went into the
casemate assigned to me.

Though covered by ten or fifteen feet of
earth and flanked by heavy masonry on one
side and earth and masonry on the other two,
the rooms were large and seemed to me a
great boon, since I could remain in them so
near my husband. I had not been there,
however, more than a week before a chill and
fever warned me they were not wholesome
residences.

In a little while General Miles came in and
assured me of "Davis's" good health. He
showed the same economy of titles in speaking of my husband from the time I went there
until our departure. Sometimes he varied his
nomenclature by calling him "Jeff Davis" or
"Jeff."

He asked me if I understood the terms to
be that I was to take no "deadly weepons"
into the prison, to which I answered in the
affirmative. After a little more delay an officer came and walked with me to Carroll Hall,

on the opposite side of the fort. There were three lines of sentries, which each required a pass-word of the officer, and at last we ascended a stairway, turned to the right, and entered the guard-room, where three young officers were sitting. Through the bars of the inner room I saw Mr. Davis's shrunken form and glassy eyes ; his cheek bones stood out like those of a skeleton. Merely crossing the room made his breath come in short gasps, and his voice was scarcely audible.

His room had a rough screen in one corner, a horse-bucket for water, a basin and pitcher that stood on a chair with the back sawn off for a washstand, and a hospital towel, a little iron bedstead with a hard mattress, one pillow, and a square wooden table, a wooden-seated chair that had one short leg and rocked from side to side unexpectedly, and a Boston rocker, which had been sent in a few weeks before. His table-cloth was a copy of the New York *Herald* spread on the little table. I was locked in with him and sent the baby home with Frederick.

The bed was so infested with insects as to give a perceptible odor to the room. He knew so little of such things that he could not imagine what annoyed him so at night, and insisted it was some cutaneous affection. His dinner was brought after a while by one

of the men, and was good enough, had it not
been slopped from one dish to another in the
carriage and covered by a gray hospital towel.
To a fastidious taste, rendered much more
so by illness, this was very offensive.   Mrs.
Cooper had, however, added oysters to the
menu that day, and he ate one and nothing
else, but his vitality was so low that even this
small amount gave him intense gastric pain.
The passing of the three sentinels by the
doors and window rendered me, though in
strong health, so nervous I could scarcely
keep my eyes still.

He was bitter at no earthly creature, but
expressed supreme contempt for the petty
insults inflicted hourly upon him by General
Miles, who, he said, had exhausted his ingenuity to find something more afflicting to
visit upon him.   Among other things, he told
me that General Miles never walked with him
on the ramparts, in enforced companionship,
without saying something so offensive and
irritating as to render the exercise a painful
effort.

Mr. Davis introduced to me the officers
that were in the guard-room—Captains Day
and Brewerton, both presentable men, with
gentlemanly manners ; and it was comforting to hear that our young friend, Colonel
Henry A. Dupont was on duty there, for of

him I expected every gentlemanly concession and observance consistent with his duty, and was not disappointed. These, and other gentlemen among the officers, were kind and courteous to us, and the friendly regard induced by their considerate conduct toward Mr. Davis has been a constant memory, and still survives through the long years that have intervened.

At first General Miles fixed the shortest period and certain hours for my stay with Mr. Davis. After many applications to spend the evenings with him, he at last consented, but if the General came over to the guard-room and found us cheerfully talking together, whether at seven, at eight, or at ten o'clock, he left the room and sent an order for me to go home. Once or twice he said personally that it was "shutting up time." I entreated him unavailingly to let me join Mr. Davis in his walks, as he was too weak to walk alone, and would avail himself of my arm, though he would not lean on General Miles.

One day the General sent his orderly for me to come to headquarters, and I went in fear and trembling, lest someone had accused me of carrying "deadly weepons." He received me civilly, and then said he had sent for me to see the orders under which he had shackled Mr. Davis. To say that my blood

ran cold is a faint expression of the thrill that
went through me.   He opened a large ledger-
book and showed me Mr. Stanton's order to
him, to adopt any means that would insure the
prisoner's safety.   I told him I did not see
his warrant in this order.   He said, "Mr.
Stanton knew I was going to do it, and I
thought it necessary."   This is quoted from
notes taken immediately after the conversation.

He said he had given Mr. Davis all that
a gentleman should require, and I suggested
to him that probably some gentlemen were
more exacting than those he knew.

Emboldened by his evident desire to explain,
I asked him why as much clean linen had not
been given as was requisite, and as many
changes of outer clothing as Mr. Davis required had not been sent to his cell; he said
he thought he had enough.   To an inquiry
why all reading matter had been forbidden
him, General Miles answered that at first he
was expected to deprive him of everything except his bible, and afterward, that he had been
directed to "give him mental ailment," which
he had done.   A proposition so stated I could
not dispute.   He went on to say that "Davis
would not beg, was a sullen prisoner, and when
he wanted any favor, if he asked for it, it would
be given to him."   I wanted to get a lighter

suit of clothes that had been worn but once, when my husband was taken prisoner. General Miles disclaimed any knowledge of them, and added : " I have not got them, and would have no use for them ; they would not fit me, you know." The interview had been so fruitless that I terminated it as soon as possible, and returned to the casemate.

Very soon after my arrival there General Burton called with his cheerful, affectionate wife, and they were, from the first day until the last, most kind and considerate to us, as was Mrs. William Hayes and the other officers' wives in the fort, of whom there were many and all disposed to be friendly.

Mrs. Hayes petted and loved our baby, who returned her affection fourfold. She kindly sent cream every day to Mr. Davis when permitted to do so, and Mrs. Cooper, one of our own dear people, did everything, and more than we could have wished, to comfort and cheer us in our misfortune, in which her kind husband co-operated with her cordially.

General Burton, as I accidentally learned, which statement was afterward verified by him, when deciding upon a casemate for me, was advised by General Miles to put me on the side of the fort occupied by the camp women ; he said there was an impropriety in associating me with the families of the officers ; but General Burton declined to offer me the indignity, and assigned me a casemate in the row with the officers' wives.

One day an orderly came for me to go to the prison; hitherto an officer had always accompanied me past the sentinels. I thought nothing of it, but when we reached the guard-room the captain on duty apologized for not coming in person, and told me General Miles had said a prisoner's wife had better come over with an orderly and unattended by an officer. It was a small matter to me, but these refined, kind-hearted gentlemen were unwilling to be misunderstood. General Miles, I heard, denied giving the order, and the officers signed a statement to the effect that he had verbally given it before several witnesses after guard-mounting. I think he made no further denial.

We excused much to General Miles, whose opportunities to learn the habits of refined people were said to have been few, and his sectional feeling was very bitter ; but that he should not have been moved at the age of twenty-six by the evident physical and mental anguish of his prisoner, and should have devised ingenious tortures for him, we could not understand.

Finally, after trying sincerely to propitiate him, my efforts ceased. On the occasion of a dressing-gown having been sent to Mr. Davis by some ladies in St. Louis, General Miles noticed the arrival of the package addressed to me, and the fact also that my man-servant carried white napkins, silver table furniture, and delicate viands of all kinds over to Carroll Hall, the number being limited only by my purse, to tempt my husband, who was slowly dying in my sight, General Miles said to me: " This fort shall not be made a depot for delicacies, such as oysters and luxuries for Jeff Davis. I shall have to open your packages, and see that this is not done."

I lost all my hard-earned patience and told him I was not his prisoner, and he would not find himself justified by the laws in infringing on my private rights. He looked at me a moment and said, " I guess I couldn't," and desisted.

A few days after this Mr. McCulloch came to the fort and visited Mr. Davis. I was not present at the interview, but obtained an audience with him at Dr. Cooper's house. General Miles remained in the room, and unwilling to leave the truth untold, or to annoy him, I asked a private audience, but General Miles said he felt he had a right to be present. Then, with an apology to him for plain speaking, emboldened by Mr. McCulloch's gentle, sympathetic manner, I laid the whole

case before him.   When the matter of General Miles's objection to Mr. Davis having
oysters was mentioned, Mr. McCulloch, with
a quizzical smile, said : " General, oysters are
hardly to be classed as luxuries on the sea-
coast, are they ? "   Enough of this sickening
retrospect, my memory does not furnish a record of the thousand little stabs he gave his
emaciated, gray-haired prisoner.   Suffice it to
say that he used his power to insult and annoy to the utmost, and in ways previously unknown and not to be anticipated by gentlefolk.

When he was to be promoted to a higher
grade, one of his friends wrote to Mr. Davis for an expression of his opinion about
General Miles's conduct to him, saying that,
from Mr. Davis not having characterized
it in his book, it was hoped he would say
there had been no unsoldierly persecution of
a helpless prisoner.   To this Mr. Davis sent
a most emphatic assertion of General Miles's
unmanly and cruel conduct, and also wrote a
letter to a Senator from Mississippi which
did not reach him, owing to his being out of
town when the confirmation occurred, else it
would have been read in the Senate.

Sir Hudson Lowe has received, in the years
that have elapsed since Napoleon's death, the
execration of all brave men for severities practised on him in St. Helena ; but these were

far less stringent, and the insults much less overt and degrading to England and to himself, than those inflicted by General Miles upon Mr. Davis. Mr. Davis's silence in his book was, because he did not choose to appeal to a public tribunal to characterize the wrongs he could not, in his old age and broken health, avenge.

One day General Miles came to the prison and said something not recalled with sufficient clearness for repetition, but of such an insulting character that Mr. Davis sprang at the bars, and as General Miles recoiled, he said, " But for these, you should answer to me, now."

My husband sank daily, until I feared he would not live through the month. There was unavoidable noise in changing guard during the night, which wakened him at each relief. His eyes had always been intensely sensitive to a light while sleeping, and the light burned brightly all night in his room, and the tramp of the sentinels was torture to him. In his nervous condition the shifting of the foot of an officer in the guard-room kept him awake. They did their best to be quiet, and he did his best to bear the noise, but it was a weary struggle for life and a slow sinking into death, which would have been welcome but for the charges he was waiting to rebut

before a lawful tribunal on earth. Dr. Cooper exhausted his skill to support the sinking
frame which had borne up so bravely, but
nothing seemed to give relief.

I went to Washington to gain a personal
interview with the President, with whom,
though we had been in the same city at intervals for fifteen years, I was not acquainted.
My object was to obtain from him permission
to take the lamp out of Mr. Davis's room, and
other little ameliorations of his sufferings.
Our old friend, Dr. Thomas Miller, invited
me to his house, and I asked by a respectful
note an audience from the President. He
sent me a verbal message of a discourteous
character, in which he suggested that I should
personally see the Republican Senators and
importune them as best I might. This course
was, however, not contemplated by me.

Mr. Reverdy Johnson, Mr. Voorhies, and
Mr. Saulsbury, always quick to espouse the
cause of the helpless, went to him and remonstrated rather sharply. Under this pressure he appointed an hour to see me. General Grant also set an hour for an audience,
but the President was so late in giving audience after my card was sent up that General
Grant, after waiting an hour, courteously left
his aide-de-camp to explain that he had an
engagement he must keep, but would be glad

if he could serve me in any way, and Mr. Davis never forgot the courtesy, nor did I. Senator Wilson called with kind words of sympathy also, as did my dear friends, Montgomery Blair and Mrs. Leigh. This was my first and last experience as a supplicant.

The President was civil, even friendly, and said, " We must wait, our hope is to mollify the public toward him." I told him that the public would not have required to be mollified but for his proclamation that Mr. Davis was accessory to assassination, and added, " I am sure that, whatever others believed, *you* did not credit it." He said he did not, but was in the hands of wildly excited people, and must take such measures as would show he was willing to sift the facts. I then responded that there was never the least intercourse between Mr. Davis and Booth, or an effort to establish it, and remarked that, " if Booth had left a card for Mr. Davis as he did for you, Mr. President, before the assassination, I fear my husband's life would have paid the forfeit;" to which the President bowed assent, and after a moment of silence remarked, now this was all over, and time was the only element lacking to Mr. Davis's release.

I remarked that, having made a proclamation predicated upon the perjury of base

men suborned for that purpose, I thought he
owed Mr. Davis a retraction as public as his
mistake.   To my astonishment, he said that
he was laboring under the enmity of many in
both houses of Congress, and if they could
find anything upon which to hinge an im-
peachment they would degrade him ; and with
apparent feeling he reiterated, " *I would if I
could, but I cannot.*"

While we were speaking, a Senator well-
known now, but of whom I had never heard,
insisted upon an audience and was admitted.
He was a lop-sided man who stood on one
leg by preference. He declined to sit, but
stood quite near me, with one leg twisted
around his stick, and threatened the President in such a manner as would have been
thought inadmissible to one of our servants. The President met his threats with
rising color but a stolid calm which was not
defiance, nor was it indignation. It was a
very painful sight to me, and I tried not to
hear.   At last the Senator left, and the President said, " I am glad you saw a little of the
difficulty under which I labor; trust me, everything I can do will be done to help Mr.
Davis—has he thought of asking pardon ? "
I answered " No, and I suppose you did not
expect this."   He said he did not, and added
" just now I *cannot* withdraw the proclama-

tion." He kindly hoped the pardon granted to J. E. Davis had covered our property also. I could not press him further. It was a new phase of humanity to me, I felt sorry for a man whose code of morals I could not understand. And so we parted, with kind words and courteous manner on his part, and much sympathy for his miserable state on mine.

Some weeks passed and Mr. Davis became gradually worse, he ate less, and slept little; he had never become accustomed to the unavoidable noise made by relieving guard during the night watches, and he had become so emaciated that the largest part of his thigh measured less than an ordinarily stout man's upper arm. I appealed to Dr. Cooper for a medical opinion, and he wrote the following letter:

"FORTRESS MONROE, VA., May 23, 1866.

"MADAM: I am in receipt of your communication of date, in which you ask of me 'how the health of your husband can be recruited, as you see him growing weaker and sinking daily.'

"I have done all in my power to keep his health up, but I must own I see him becoming more and more weak day by day. He has been well cared for in the matter of food; the tramp of the sentinels he no longer hears.

He has exercise one hour in the morning, and as much as he wishes for after four in the afternoon.

"Notwithstanding, he fails, and the only thing left is to give him mental and bodily rest, and exercise at will.

"This can only be by having the parole of the fort, with permission to remain with his family now residing there.

"He will probably recuperate.

"Your obedient servant,

"GEORGE E. COOPER,

"*Surgeon United States Army.*

"MRS. VARINA DAVIS,

"Fortress Monroe, Va."

This was sent to Washington—covered by a stronger letter written by Dr. Cooper, of a private nature, which we did not see.

General Miles was about this time relieved from Fortress Monroe, to which he had been sent apparently for the specific duty of jailor to Mr. Davis, and the relief was great to us. General Burton received permission, if he thought it consistent with Mr. Davis's safe keeping, to give him the parole of the fort by day—which the General gladly did.

As soon as our friends knew they could visit Mr. Davis, they came almost every day. Our great General Gordon, Preston John-

ston, and numbers of other friends came to dinner in the casemate, and chairs being scarce,
they sat on candle-boxes, and talked of their
and our past, and toasted in silence the glorious dead and less happy living heroes. But
the sufferer's improvement was almost im-
perceptible, and life came back slowly into
his exhausted, emaciated body. Leaning on
my arm, and sitting on the ramparts every
few minutes of his walk, he could not accomplish a hundred yards at first, but gradually
his muscles strengthened; but his sleep being
broken, his improvement was checked. He
now had every comfort that I could furnish
in his little prison, but still became more and
more wasted, and had not ceased to stagger
like a drunken man.

In a month or six weeks it was communicated to General Burton that if he
thought it was safe to offer his prisoner
the parole of the fort, he could do so. It
was not in General Burton's kindly, generous nature to hesitate, where he confided in
the honor of a man for the time subject to his
authority. The full parole of the fort was
granted, and then four rooms off the end of
Carroll Hall were set apart for us, with a kitchen at the back, and we were as comfortable
as people could be who could " not get out."

Excursion parties came to the fort still to

peer at Mr. Davis, and one day a vulgarian
inquired of Frederick the whereabouts of
"Jeff." He answered with a bow, "I am
sorry, madam, not to be able to tell you where
he is. I do not know such a person." She insisted that he did, saying, are you not his servant? " No, madam," he answered, " you are
quite mistaken, I have the honor to serve ex-
President Davis."

At another time, when I wanted him to ask
some of our special friends among the officers,
and notably General Burton, to see him wed
my maid, he said, " Please excuse me, I will
send them as much cake and wine as you
choose, but cannot receive people as guests
who hold Mr. Davis a prisoner." What this
judicious, capable, delicate-minded man did for
us could not be computed in money, or told in
words ; he and his gentle wife took the sting
out of many indignities offered to us in our
hours of misfortune. They were both objects
of affection and esteem to Mr. Davis as long
as he lived.

Our sister, Miss Howell, came to the fort
and remained with us, much to Mr. Davis's
delight. The Right Reverend Bishop Lynch,
Father O'Keefe, from Norfolk, the Rever-
ends William Brand, Barton, and Minnegerode, the latter our beloved pastor, came
often to see Mr. Davis, as well as charming

people from Baltimore, Richmond, Norfolk, and the surrounding country; they generally remained to dinner, and left in the evening boat; wine and delicacies of all kinds were pressed upon us by our friends. The Bishop of Montreal sent green chartreuse from his own stores, and to this powerful digestive stimulant the little Mr. Davis ate was due. He could only sleep when read to, and many times the day broke on me as he slept under the sound of my voice, with my hand on his pulse; at times it would stop, and then he was wakened and a glass of chartreuse given him, with one of half a dozen things kept ready for him to eat. Dr. Cooper said the walls of his heart were so weak, that a sound sleep might prove his death if too long continued; and so he came back slowly into life, though reduced to a walking skeleton. Never during this extreme torture and harrowing anxiety did his dignity give way, or his high bearing quail before the torment. He was too refined and dignified to be abusive, and too proud, in General Miles's delicate phrase, to "beg." He suffered as only men of his temperament can, but held aloft the standard of Confederate fealty and Christian virtue.

In the meanwhile, Mr. Charles O'Conor, with every effort in his power, pushed on the trial; and Mr. John Garrett, whose first impulse was sympathy with the sorrows of mankind, has most accurately related his efforts to secure my husband's release; and for both Mr. Davis has always since felt the most sincere gratitude and affection. Want of space has forced me unwillingly, in his case as in that of many others, to condense their statements, but I quote them as they are, only changing a few words.

" In May, 1866, an indictment was procured against the ex-chieftain, in the United States District Court of Virginia, held in Richmond. On June 11th, of the same year, on motion of Mr. Boutwell, the House of Representatives, by a vote of 105 yeas to 19 nays, resolved that Mr. Davis 'should be held in custody as a prisoner and subjected to a trial according to the laws of the land.' Mr. Davis, in the meantime, was exceedingly anxious to meet the questions arising on any indictment which might be presented. The Constitution of the United States guaranteed to every citizen a speedy trial, and he was anxious to receive the advantages and enjoy the rights of a just, equal, and fair trial. It was not written, however, that he should be tried for treason. Even President Johnson and General Grant saw the mistake of his capture, and Chief Justice Chase understood the impolicy of his trial. Little by little, as reason returned, Northern men like Greeley and Gerrit Smith came forward to do a great act of justice, looking toward his honorable liberation.

" In 1867, as the May term of the United States Circuit Court in Virginia approached, the counsel for Mr. Davis, encouraged by his devoted and faithful wife, determined to make one grand effort for his trial or unconditional discharge. The Chief Justice, the Attorney-General, and the Secretary of War were opposed to an early trial. Many efforts were then made with President Johnson to procure the pardon of Mr. Davis. He said, he made it an inflexible rule, ' never to grant a pardon on petition, unless it was accompanied by an application from the individual seeking the executive clemency.' Mr. Davis, on the other hand, always said, ' to ask for pardon was a confession of guilt,' and that such an application would prejudice his case.

" As soon as it was known that the Government would not try him, a movement was set on foot to secure his release on bond. Mrs. Jefferson Davis heard that Mr. John W. Garrett, then president of the Baltimore & Ohio Railroad, possessed great influence over Secretary Stanton, and determined, if possible, to obtain his aid in securing her husband's

release.   In this respect, she could not have
selected a more influential person to accomplish
her end.   Mr. Garrett and Mr. Stanton were
always warm personal friends.   President
Lincoln and Secretary Stanton expressed in
the warmest terms their appreciation of the
aid which he had often rendered them.

" Upon one occasion," Mr. Garrett said,
" Charles W. Russell, formerly of Wheeling,
Va., came to my office at Camden Station
and sent in his card.   Being at the moment
very much engaged, I detained him for an
hour, but hastened to see Mr. Russell as soon
as I could, and to my astonishment found him
accompanied with a lady who was closely
veiled, and who was the wife of Jefferson
Davis.   After assuring them that I had not
known any lady was waiting, I asked the occasion of Mrs. Davis's visit.   She replied
that she had just arrived from Fortress Monroe, where her husband was so closely confined that unless he could be quickly released
he would die ; that she had been informed
I possessed great influence with Mr. Stanton,
and had come to beg my active aid for the release of Mr. Davis.   She asked me to go to
Washington *with her*, but that, I assured her,
was impolitic ; I would go alone, ascertain
the prospect, and report to her.   She was
stopping with Mr. John S. Gittings.   During

our conversation Mrs. Davis said that she
had received a message from Mr. McCulloch,
on his way from Fortress Monroe, that she
could rely on his aid in the matter. I went
immediately to Washington, saw Mr. McCulloch, and told him that I had come to see
Stanton about the release of Mr. Davis.
Mr. McCulloch was thunderstruck, and said
it was useless to see Mr. Stanton, and that
Mr. Davis's release was impossible. I told
him what Mrs. Davis had said about his aid.
Finally we called in the Attorney-General,
Mr. Stansberry. Our errand was stated by
Mr. McCulloch, and the Attorney-General
remarked, after talking the matter over, that
he had seen stranger things than that done;
that he could see no objection to my making
the effort. I told them that, notwithstanding
their unfavorable opinion, I would see Stanton and make an effort for the release of Mr.
Davis. We learned at the office that the
Secretary of War was sick, and had refused
to see anyone; but, nevertheless, I asked my
colleagues to wait, until I returned from my
visit to Mr. Stanton. I immediately drove
to his house, sent up my card, and was
promptly admitted. He was lying on a
lounge, too ill to rise. I stated frankly the
matter that had brought me to disturb his repose. As I expected, Mr. Stanton exhibited

much anger, but I told him that two at least
of the cabinet were willing for the release ;
that the President only waited his order for
release ; that the country would approve such
action ; and lastly, Mr. Davis's health was failing, and that his death in prison would be
most embarrassing to the United States.
Our discussion was long, and often sharp, for
I was not to be set back by anything short of
a positive refusal, and that I should have
combated before the President.   At last he
remarked that he would raise no objection to
the Attorney-General arranging for the release.   With this answer I returned to Mr.
Stansberry ; the preliminaries were arranged,
and the name of Horace Greeley was suggested by me and accepted by Mr. Stansberry as one of Mr. Davis's bondsmen.   It
was decided that Mr. Charles O'Conor, one
of Mr. Davis's counsel, should come to Washington and arrange the terms.   Reporting the
result of my interview to Mrs. Davis, it was
arranged that William Prescott Smith should
go to New York for Mr. Greeley, and bring
him to my house, and thereupon the release
of Mr. Davis was arranged."

Mr. Shea wrote a letter, of which I give
the substance, which will more accurately
relate the circumstances of Mr. Davis's release than I could : " Mr. Horace Greeley

received a letter, dated June 22, 1865, from
Mrs. Davis, written at Savannah, Ga., where
she and her family were detained under
a sort of military restraint. Mr. Davis was
at Fortress Monroe; and the conspicuous
charge against him made by the 'Bureau of
Military Justice' was, of being accessory to
the assassination of President Lincoln. The
letter implored Mr. Greeley to insist upon a
speedy trial of her husband upon that charge,
and upon all other supposed cruelties that
were alleged he had inflicted. A public trial
was prayed, that the accusations might be publicly met, and her husband vindicated. To
this letter Mr. Greeley at once answered
Mrs. Davis, and directed it to the care of General Birge, at Savannah. The morning of the
next day Mr. Greeley came to my residence
and placed Mrs. Davis's letter in my hand,
saying that he could not believe the charge
true. He asked me to become professionally
interested in behalf of Mr. Davis. I told Mr.
Greeley that, *unless our Government was
willing to have it inferred that Wirz was
convicted and his sentence of death inflicted
unjustly, it could not now overlook the superior who was, at least popularly, regarded as
the moving cause of those wrongs.** I thought

---

* The italics are the author's.

that my services before a military tribunal
would be of little benefit. I consulted with
such friends, and Mr. Henry Wilson, Governor John A. Andrew, Mr. Thaddeus Stevens, and Mr. Gerrit Smith. The result was
that I undertook to do whatever became feasible. Mr. Charles O'Conor was, from the
first, esteemed the most valuable man to lead
for the defence by Mr. Greeley and Mr. Gerrit Smith. Public expectation looked to him,
and he had already volunteered his services
to Mr. Davis. Mr. O'Conor's personal honor
was without reproach; his courage without
fear; his learning, erudition, and propriety of
professional judgment conceded as pre-emin-
ent.

" *There was a general agreement among the
gentlemen of the Republican party whom I
have mentioned, that Mr. Davis did not by
thought or act participate in a conspiracy
against Mr. Lincoln; and none of those expressed that conviction more emphatically than
Mr. Thaddeus Stevens.* The single subject
on which light was desired by them was concerning the treatment of our soldiers while
in the hands of the enemy. *The Tribune* of
May 17, 1865, tells the real condition of feeling at that moment, and shows that it was
not favorable to Mr. Davis on this matter.
At the instance of Mr. Greeley, Mr. Wilson,

and, as I was given to understand, of Mr.
Stevens, I went to Canada the first week in
January, 1866, taking Boston on my route,
there to consult with Governor Andrew and
others. While at Montreal I had placed in
my possession the official archives of the
Government of the Confederate States, which
I read, especially all the messages and other
acts of the Executive sent to the Senate in
its secret sessions concerning the care and
exchange of prisoners. Individually, and
through their representatives at Richmond,
the people of the South pressed upon Mr.
Davis, as the Executive and as the Commander-in-chief of the Army and Navy, instant
recourse to active measures of retaliation, to
the end that the supposed cruelties to their
soldiers in prison might be stayed. Mr.
Davis's conduct, under such urgency, was a
circumstance all-important in determining the
justice of the charge against himself. It was
decisively manifest, from these sources of information, that Mr. Davis unflinchingly set
himself in opposition to such demands, and
declined to resort to any measure of violent
retaliation. *It impaired his personal influence, and brought much censure upon him
from many in the South, who sincerely believed the reports spread among the people to
be true.*

"The result of my examination was that
these gentlemen, and those others in sympathy
with them, changed their former suspicion to
a favorable opinion. They were from this
time kept informed of movements made to
liberate Mr. Davis or to compel a trial. All
this took place before anyone acting on his
behalf was allowed to communicate with or
see him.

"*The Tribune*, at once began a series of
leading editorials demanding that our Government proceed to a trial; and on January
16, 1867, Senator Howard, of Michigan, offered a joint resolution, aided by Mr. Sumner,
' recommending the trial of Jefferson Davis
and Clement C. Clay before a military tribunal or court-martial, for charges mentioned in
the report of the Secretary of War, of March
4, 1866.' I was then credibly informed that
Mr. Thaddeus Stevens had volunteered as
counsel for Mr. Clay.

"After it had become evident that there
was no immediate prospect of a trial, the counsel for Mr. Davis became anxious that their
client be liberated on bail, and one of them
consulted Mr. Greeley as to the feasibility of
procuring names of persons as bondsmen
who had conspicuously opposed the war of
secession. This was easy; and Mr. Gerrit
Smith and Commodore Vanderbilt were

selected, and Mr. Greeley, in case his name should be found necessary. This could not have been accomplished had not those gentlemen, and others in sympathy with them, been already convinced that the charges against Mr. Davis were unfounded. An application was made on June 11, 1866, to Justice Underwood, at Alexandria, Va., for a writ of habeas corpus, which, after argument, was denied, upon the ground that ' Jefferson Davis was arrested under a proclamation of the President charging him with complicity in the assassination of the late President Lincoln. He has been held,' says the decision, ' ever since, and is now held, as a military prisoner.' *The Washington Chronicle* of that date insisted that the ' case is one well entitled to a trial before a military tribunal ; the testimony before the Judiciary Committee of the House, all of it bearing directly, *if not conclusively*, on a certain intention to take the life of Mr. Lincoln, is a most important element in the case.' This was reported to be from the pen of Mr. John W. Forney himself, then Clerk of the Senate. The House of Representatives, on motion of Mr. Boutwell, of Massachusetts, the following day passed a resolution ' that it was the opinion of the House that Jefferson Davis should be held in custody as a prisoner, and subject to trial ac-

cording to the laws of the land.' It was
adopted by a vote of 105 to 19.

" It is very suggestive that, in the intermediate time, Mr. Clement C. Clay had been
discharged from imprisonment without being
tried on either of these charges, upon which
he had been arrested, and for which arrest the
$100,000 had been paid.

" This failure to liberate Mr. Davis induced
Mr. Greeley, and those friends who were acting
with him, to meet the issue promptly and to push
the Government to a trial, or to withdraw the
charge made by its Board of Military Justice.
Mr. Greeley hastened back to New York, and
The Tribune of June 12, 1866, contained, in a
leader from his pen, this unmistakable demand and protest :

"' How and when did Davis become a prisoner of war ?   He was not arrested as a public enemy, but as a felon officially charged, in
the face of the civilized world, with the foul-
est, most execrable guilt—that of having suborned assassins to murder President Lincoln,
a crime the basest and most cowardly known
to mankind.   It was for this that $100,000 was
offered and paid for his arrest.   And the proclamation of Andrew Johnson and William H.
Seward, offering this reward, says his complicity with Wilkes Booth & Co. is established
"by evidence now in the Bureau of Military

Justice." So there was no need of time to
hunt it up.

" ' It has been asserted that Davis is responsible for the death by exposure and famine of our captured soldiers ; and his official position gives plausibility to the charge.
Yet, while Henry Wirz was long ago arraigned, tried, convicted, sentenced, and
hanged for this crime—no charge has been
officially preferred against Davis. So we
presume none is to be.'

" *The Tribune* kept repeating this demand
during that year, and admonished the Government of the absurdity of its position, not
daring, seemingly, to prosecute a great criminal against whom it had officially declared it
was possessed of evidence to prove the
crime.

" The Government did not proceed with
the trial. Another year had passed since the
capture of Mr. Davis, and now another attempt to liberate him by bail was to be made.
The Government, *by its conduct, having
tacitly abandoned those special charges of inhumanity*, a petition for a writ was to be
presented by which the prisoner might be
tried by the civil authority to answer the indictment for treason. Mr. Wilson, Chairman
of the Committee of Military Affairs, offered
in the Senate, on March 18, 1867, a resolution

urging the Government to proceed with the
trial. The remarkable thoughts and language of that resolution were observed at the
time, and necessarily caused people to infer
that Mr. Wilson, at least, was not under the
delusion that the Government really had a
case on either of those two special charges
against Mr. Davis ; and a short time after
this Mr. Wilson went to Fortress Monroe to
see Mr. Davis. The visit was simply friendly,
and not for any purpose relating to his liberation.

" On May 14, 1867, Mr. Davis was delivered to the civil authority ; was at once admitted to bail, Mr. Greeley and Mr. Gerrit
Smith going personally to Richmond, in attestation of their belief that wrong had been
done to Mr. Davis in holding him so long
accused upon those charges, now abandoned.
Commodore Vanderbilt signed the bond
through Mr. Horace F. Clark, his son-in-law,
and Mr. Augustus Schell, his friend.

". . . Mr. Greeley's enormous sacrifice
to compel justice to be done to one man, and
he an enemy, should be written.

" Mr. Thaddeus Stevens, in May, 1866,
related to me how the Chief of this ' Military
Bureau' showed him ' the evidence' upon
which the proclamation was issued charging
Messrs. Davis and Clay with complicity in the

assassination of Mr. Lincoln. He said he refused to give the thing support, and that he said the evidence was insufficient and incredible. I am not likely ever to forget the earnest manner in which Mr. Stevens then said: 'Those men are no friends of mine. They are public enemies ; but I know these men, sir. They are gentlemen, and incapable of being assassins.'

" GEORGE SHEA.

"No. 205 WEST FORTY-SIXTH STREET,
"NEW YORK, January 15, 1876."

In accordance with the programme arranged between Mr. Garrett and the counsel for Mr. Davis on May 1st, petition to the United States Circuit Court was presented to Judge Underwood, at Alexandria, Va., to grant the writ of habeas corpus.

Judge Underwood issued the writ to Mr. Shea, who took it to Richmond and placed it in the hands of United States Marshal Underwood for service.

The writ was served on General Burton, the commander of Fortress Monroe, by Marshal Underwood and Deputy Marshal W. A. Duncan, on May 10th. General Burton had previously received the following orders from Washington :

"WAR DEPARTMENT, WASHINGTON, D. C.
May 8, 1867.

"BREVET BRIGADIER-GENERAL H. S. BUR-
TON, United States Army, or Commanding
Officer at Fortress Monroe.

"The President of the United States directs
that you surrender Jefferson Davis, now held
and confined under military authority at Fortress Monroe, to United States Marshal or
deputies, upon any process which may issue
from a Federal court in the State of Virginia.
You will report the action taken by you under
this order, and forward a copy of any process
served upon you to this office.

"By order of the President,

"E. D. TOWNSEND,
"*Assistant Adjutant-General.*"

General Burton, in the interview with the
Marshal, at first decided to deliver Mr. Davis
to him on the following morning, but afterward determined to obey the writ of habeas
corpus literally, requiring him to produce Mr.
Davis before the Richmond court.

*The Trial of Mr. Jefferson Davis, Rich-
mond, December 3, 1867.*

In the United States Court, Chief-Justice
Chase on the bench, the argument was com-

menced on the motion to quash the indictment against Jefferson Davis.

Robert Ould, counsel for Mr. Davis, argued that the fourteenth amendment punished Mr. Davis by disfranchisement, and this punishment was chosen by the voice of the American people as a merciful substitute for the penalties of death and confiscation contained in the Constitution of the United States ; that the punishment of Mr. Davis commenced upon the date of the adoption of the fourteenth article, and he therefore could not now be punished in any other way ; that the latest expression of the will of the people, in their Constitution, was the law, and repealed all former provision made for those who engaged in rebellion ; that the fourteenth article was that latest expression, intended expressly for and covering the cases of all engaged in the late rebellion ; and that no man could be punished twice for the same offence.

R. H. Dana, Esq., counsel for the United States, said that Mr. Ould's proposition was, in the nature of things, entirely new, and was unexpected to the Government counsel, and he expected also to the court.

Chief-Justice Chase said the argument of counsel was not unexpected to the court, it having supposed, after the announcement

of this motion to quash, that it was based on
the fourteenth article, that this line of argument would be pursued.

Time was given the Government counsel
to confer, and the Court took a recess at noon.

After reassembling, Governor H. H. Wells
and District Attorney Beach for the Government, replied, contending that the fourteenth
amendment merely created a disability, and
not a penalty, which is the subject of judicial
sentence, and was not inconsistent with the act
against treason.   The amendment was permanent and prospective, and could not be
reasonably construed to repeal existing pun-
ishments for past and future treasons.   The
Court then adjourned.   Dana closes to-morrow for the Government, and O'Conor for
Mr. Davis.

Mr. Charles O'Conor said :

" If the Confederate Government had
raised the black flag, and had not given
quarter, there would have been no objection
to resorting to extreme measures, and to
executing the leaders and commander-in-chief.
He referred to the case of Wirz, who had
been tried and executed for alleged inhumanity to prisoners.   It was a matter of notoriety
that civil war existed, and that Jefferson
Davis was the head and front of it.   What,
then, is the fact to be put on trial?   It would

be impossible to find an impartial jury to try the case, if it were put on trial. A conviction of Jefferson Davis could only be procured by a course so ignominious as packing a jury.

"The war was over, and the Government had in its hands half a dozen rebel belligerents, and it was ashamed to put them on trial. What was the mean office assigned to the judiciary in this matter? It was to require it to get a jury of twelve men to find a verdict of guilty against them. He called the attention of the court to the sixth amendment of the Constitution, which said, ' the accused shall enjoy a speedy trial by an impartial jury, in the vicinity where the crime was alleged to have been committed.'

"He referred to the execution of the parties tried for treason in England after the war in 1746, where the accused were carried to a distance from their homes and tried by a jury of strangers, and said it was with a knowledge of these atrocities fresh in their minds that our ancestors framed the constitutional provision quoted. They did not forbid indictments for treason in so many words, but they rendered them utterly impossible. In framing that Constitution they never intended that a territorial civil war should be followed by indictments for treason. In the view he

had presented he came back to the conclusion
with which he started, that the third section
was wise, just, and politic. He referred to
the amnesty of Charles II., which was not an
act of amnesty, but one of oblivion."

After hearing the argument the Court
stood: For quashing the indictment, Chief-
Justice Chase ; against it, John C. Underwood. The division was certified to the
Supreme Court, that the question may be considered and decided by it.

We left Fortress Monroe on Saturday
morning, May 4th, and at half-past five o'clock
in the afternoon the steamer reached the
wharf at Richmond. Mr. Davis said to me
on the way, "I feel like an unhappy ghost
visiting this much beloved city."

A great concourse of people had assembled.
From the wharf to the Spottswood Hotel there
was a sea of heads—room had to be made by
the mounted police for the carriages. The
windows were crowded, and even on to the
roofs people had climbed. Every head was
bared. The ladies were shedding tears,
many of them. Mr. James Lyons and his
beautiful wife had come for me, and Mr. Davis
accompanied General Burton. When he
reached the Spottswood Hotel, where rooms
had been provided for us, the crowd opened
and the beloved prisoner walked through ;

the people stood uncovered for at least a mile up and down Main Street. As he passed, one and another put out a hand and lightly touched his coat. As I left the carriage a low voice said : " Hats off, Virginians," and again every head was bared. This noble sympathy and clinging affection repaid us for many moments of bitter anguish. When Mr. Davis was released, one gentleman jumped up on the box and drove the carriage which brought him back to the hotel, and other gentlemen ran after him and shouted themselves hoarse. Our people poured into the hotel in a steady stream to congratulate, and many embraced him. Before our dear pastor, Mr. Minnegerode, left us, we united in a private thanksgiving to Almighty God, who had delivered Mr. Davis safely out of all the pitfalls set for his feet. We thought it best for us to leave Richmond that night and take the steamer to New York. When we reached the boat we bade an affectionate farewell to General Burton and to Captain Brewerton, with both of whom we were loath to part, and sailed for New York, reprieved, but not free.

CHAPTER LXXIV.

AFTER RELEASE IN 1867, TO 1870.

WHEN Mr. Davis was released, we were pecuniarily prostrate, our plantations had been laid waste and seized. The little money we had, had been sent by the Southern cities to me for my maintenance, and to give him com-forts in prison. Poor in purse but moderate in our wants, we turned our faces to the world and cast about for a way to maintain our little children, four in number, Margaret, Jefferson, William, and Varina.

Mr. Davis's fate hung upon the action of the United States Courts ; we knew that one effort had been made to suborn a witness,* but he was fortunately a Confederate, and died in preference to the infamy. My brothers were unable to trust themselves in the country ; Becket on account of the *Sumter* and *Alabama*, and Jefferson, whose causeless imprisonment had for a time invalided him. We had little, and my husband's health was apparently

---

* The unhappy and innocent victim of sectional rancor, Captain Wirz.

hopelessly gone. His emaciation was very great, and long imprisonment had left him with a lassitude very noticeable to those domesticated with him.

As soon as practicable we proceeded to Canada to rejoin our children, who had been under the care of my strong-hearted old mother and young sister. Great was the joy of our reunion, but the motion and life about us drove my husband wild with nervousness ; he said the voices of people sounded like trumpets in his ears. He and my mother sat together in loving accord and talked of old times, and the noisy ones remained with me ; but like Casper Hauser, long restriction had stiffened and impaired my powers, I could not think clearly or act promptly, difficulties seemed mountain high, the trees and flowers sheltered and bloomed for others, I knew they were fair, but they were not for me or mine. Our children, except the babies William and Varina, were at school in Montreal, and we concluded to remain there for the summer.

After Mr. Davis became somewhat stronger he went to Niagara and Toronto, to visit Mr. James M. Mason, and a number of other Confederates who had not yet returned home, and with cheerful intercourse among friends he slowly improved.

His friends desired to know something of

his life in prison, but he was always disinclined to speak of injuries inflicted upon himself, and had a nervous horror of appearing
to be a victim. Once, after a man had annoyed him dreadfully with questions about
his imprisonment, he said, " I imagine there
are no quidnuncs in heaven, else Lazarus
must have envied Dives the alienation of his
companions below."

He felt the pressing need there was, while
the events were fresh in his mind, to write a
history of the Confederacy, and I thought my
desire to assist him would overcome any patriotic memory. Mr. Davis sent for the letter and message books, which had been secretly taken from their place of concealment,
sent to Canada in the trunk of our sister, and
deposited in the Bank of Montreal. We
looked over them to mark, for copying, such
of the contents as would be of use, and I
was to copy and arrange them by dates. We
came very soon upon this telegram.

"DANVILLE, April 9, 1865.

" GENERAL R. E. LEE : You will realize the
reluctance I feel to leave the soil of Virginia,
and appreciate my anxiety to win success
north of the Roanoke. . . . I hope soon
to hear from you at this point, where offices
have been opened to keep up the current busi-

ness, until more definite knowledge would enable us to form more definite plans. May God sustain and guide you.

" JEFFERSON DAVIS."

All the anguish of that last great struggle came over us, we saw our gaunt, half-clothed, and half-starved men stand vibrating with courage to their finger-tips, their thin ranks a wall of fire about their homes; we saw them mowed down by a countless host of enemies, overcome, broken in health and fortune, moving along the highways to their desolated homes, sustained only by the memory of having vindicated their honor. He walked up and down distractedly, and then said, " Let us put them by for awhile, I cannot speak of my dead so soon."

Thus the history was deferred from year to year, to the day when greater calmness should enable him dispassionately to write the record of our people's glory.

One by one my brothers and sisters joined us in Montreal, and our mother rejoiced in having her children once more together. Her health had long been precarious, and after some months, much to Mr. Davis's regret, she went to a Southern friend in Bennington, Vt., for a visit.

In the meantime we had moved to Lenoxville, to be near Bishop's College for our little boys, as there was a good dame school attached. We were fairly comfortable at the hotel, notwithstanding that the servants about the table invariably condensed the menu of our good plain fare into the invitation, " Beef or beans ? "

My mother was seized with a severe illness in Bennington. I went there to bring her almost *in extremis* as far as Montreal, and in Bennington had additional proof of how far party and sectional rancor could carry people, and how pitiless they become. She was old, exceptionally weak, could not rally, and died at the house of Mr. John Lovell, whose family gave us every care and assistance that friendship could render.

In our mother Mr. Davis lost his dearest friend, and " as much of virtue as could die " perished with her. He mourned sincerely, and the sense of our loss deepened our gloom, but no despairing word was uttered by him, he looked forward hopefully to his vindication by a fair trial, and longed for the time to be set.

In the autumn of 1867 Mr. O'Conor, after incessant efforts, aided by men of all parties, succeeded in getting a time appointed for the decision of Mr. Davis's case, either for trial or a *nolle prosequi*, but both would have preferred the former as a test question. As winter drew on Mr. Davis was summoned to Richmond, but the *nolle prosequi* was filed.

It was a somewhat inglorious sequel to the threats of the United States Government "to make treason odious." A man who asked only a fair trial on the merits of his case, had been held on an accusation of treason and as-sassination, in close confinement, with circum-stances of unnecessary torture, for a year and a half, and constrained to remain in Fortress Monroe for two years, to the injury of his health and the total destruction of his inter-ests, not to dwell upon the separation from his family and home. He was denied a trial, while his captors vaunted their "clemency" in not executing their victim. These accusations were either true or false. He asked neither indulgence nor pardon, but urged a speedy trial, constantly expressing his ardent desire to meet it. He could not obtain one—yet the accusation of complicity in assassination was never withdrawn, and the epithet of "traitor" was hurled at his head by every so-called orator, patriot, or petty penny-a-liner in the North.

His deeds had not been done in a corner, he had openly avowed his principles before leaving the United States Senate. If he was the arch-conspirator who inspired and compelled the act of treason, why was he not arrested then and there, before he had accomplished the ruin of the Southern States and cost them and the United States millions of money and thousands of valuable and innocent lives? If, on the contrary, he was unwillingly borne to the position of chief Executive of eight millions of people of the South, who knew their rights and thought it incumbent upon them to maintain them, why was he, who was one of the last to yield to the dread necessity of strife, held more accountable than those whom he had tried to restrain?

Does anyone believe that if a warrant could have been found in the Constitution for the epithet of traitor, and if the fear of his entire justification by its provisions had not prevailed, that any feeling of mercy or pity would have saved the prisoner from execution, and his name from being one universally execrated both North and South? Instead, he was left to follow his course of dignified seclusion, "by all his country's honors blessed," among his own people, by whom, as well as by many at the North, he was beloved as much as he was esteemed. Might prevailed, but could not wrest from us the right of secession, or lawfully punish its assertion. "Dormitur aliquando jus moritur nunquam."

The Canadian winter proved too severe for Mr. Davis's enfeebled frame, and he was advised to spend it in the South.   After a pleasant visit to our dear friends, Mr. Charles Howard's family, in Baltimore, whose four brave sons had fought on the Confederate side with courage worthy of their ancestors, we sailed for New Orleans via Havana.   We reached Havana just before Christmas, and in time to see the flower-wreathed arches which had been erected in honor of the new Captain-General, who had been installed the day before.

There we were warmly welcomed by Mrs. Sarah Brewer.   She was a Southern woman of a respectable family, who owned and had successfully kept a hotel there for years.   Her liberality and kind offices to the Confederates had been the theme of many panegyrics by them, and we found her kindness had not been exaggerated.

It seemed strange to give our luggage in charge of Don Juan, a quiet little old Cuban, very unlike Lord Byron's hero.   The bright-colored houses which presented façades of green, pink, and blue, before which Moro Castle stood guard and glowed a soft rose color, seemed very strange, but were after a little while generally in harmony with the brilliant tropical foliage and flowers that peeped out everywhere throughout the city.

After a week spent there, during which we received many visits from Spanish gentlemen and ladies, who dumbly testified their good-will, we continued our journey to New Orleans.

The warmth of the welcome here no words can describe. One man finding that he could not penetrate into the St. Charles Hotel from below, climbed up the pillar that supported the balcony on which Mr. Davis stood, and seized him in his arms, the tears pouring over his face. As we proceeded to visit our family the most cordial manifestations of good feeling were made everywhere on the journey. One old Methodist minister stretched out his arms to Mr. Davis, and looking up reverently, said : " Now, Lord, let Thy servant depart in peace, since I have seen his salvation."

We found our property all destroyed, our friends impoverished, and our old brother very feeble, but cheery. As many of our negroes as could, came to see us, and Mr. Davis paid a few hours' visit to the rest at Brierfield and Hurricane, witnessed the destruction the enemy had worked, which had blotted out the labors of his life, and after a few weeks we returned to Lenoxville. Perhaps it was owing to the cumulative sorrow over the changes wrought in his life, but this journey did not work the expected improvement in his health, and his emaciation did not decrease. His physician feared entire nervous prostration would supervene. Our means were narrow, and we could not travel with our large family of little children without incurring great expense, and a general tour through Europe was under the circumstances impracticable. While vexed by every anxiety that could torture us, in coming down a long flight of steps with baby Winnie in his arms, Mr. Davis fell from the top to the bottom, breaking three of his ribs. His first question after he came out of the fainting fit into which he sank, was for the baby, and the next was a request that I should not see him die. He lay on the verge of eternity for many days, and then there was no question of the proper course for us. Our physician insisted on an entire change of climate and scene, and we decided to join our friends, the Rawsons, who were "going home" from Canada.

While in Lenoxville, we received notice that the father of a Federal spy who had been executed, had announced his intention of killing Mr. Davis. We remembered that "threatened men live long," and thought no more about it until an old man called to inquire about the spy, when my husband said, with a smile, "Then you are the man who has come to assassinate me?" But the creature disclaimed volubly, and then proceeded to un-

fold his business. His object was to get Mr.
Davis to certify that it was the son of our inglorious assassin who had been hanged, and
thus to secure to him "a nice, comfortable
pension that will about let me out of work."
When assured that the spy was a middle-aged
man, he could not reconcile himself to his
son's dereliction from duty in not being caught
and hanged; but, said he, "If you did not
look at him after he was dead, you might say
you thought it was him; only think of the
comfort to me."   War surely lowers the
moral standard of those who engage in
it, and "hardens a' within and petrifies the
feeling."

We sailed from Quebec with our friends,
who assisted Mr. Davis to the ship, as he was
still very weak from his accident. Our English friend who felt great sympathy with our
little Jeff in his extreme sea-sickness, gave him
some ginger-beer, from which the child soon
felt better. When we had all recovered somewhat and were on deck, the nine-year old boy
walked up to Mr. Rawson, and taking off his
little cap, said, with a courteous bow, "I have
to thank you, sir, for saving my life by ginger-
beer." The laughter this acknowledgment
provoked served not at all to discourage the
boy, his sense of obligation oppressed him
until he had offered thanks to his preserver.

When Ireland and the ivy-covered ruin of
Lord Lovell's castle met our eyes, we seemed
to have received a greeting from the peaceful
past and a welcome for the future. On our
arrival at Liverpool, the foreign land did not
look at all strange to us ; perhaps the atavism
of memories was unconsciously felt, and the
welcoming cheers of the people on the docks
gave Mr. Davis a comfortable sense of Anglo-
Saxon sympathy:

Much hospitality was tendered us by our
own dear people there, and by the English
residents, and had it been possible for us to
accept the many invitations extended to us,
we should have passed many happy hours
among our transatlantic friends ; but I had
young children, and would not leave or impose
them upon others who felt less interest in
them ; then again we represented no country,
and general visiting might have brought about
unpleasant contretemps. The Northern people were then, as now, the most numerous
class of travellers ; to them might be applied
the commentary on the Scotch, " Had Cain
been a Scot, God had altered his doom, not
forced him to wander but kept him at home."
It was quiet we sought, and I found it at Llan-
dudno, and Mr. Davis accepted an invitation
from Lord Shrewsbury to visit him at Alton
Towers, while with our dear friends the Nor-

man Walkers and the Westfeldts, I remained in Wales.

The quiet of my outing was broken by my little William being very ill with typhoid fever at Waterloo, where he and his brother were at school, and then I learned to love the English people and acquired a sense of home among them. Every kindness that good hearts and sound heads could devise was showered upon us during our long and dreary period of nursing and hopelessness. It is not too late to express sincere gratitude, for we never forgot to be thankful to our English cousins. The Confederates everywhere tried to serve us, and from that time we did not feel like strangers in a foreign country.

We lived in Leamington during the hunting season, and everywhere Mr. Davis attracted all who saw him. Many civilities were offered us there, and especially by Lord and Lady Leigh, of Stoneleigh Abbey. Under the influence of new scenes and cheerful company his health began to improve slowly, and by the winter, when we removed to London, he began to look less like a skeleton, and of his own choice to walk about and take more interest in affairs around him. Occasionally he went to the houses of Parliament, where he received many civilities. We gradually became more cheerful, and our medical man, in whom we found a friend, hoped that the walls of his heart would become normal again.

We went to Paris for a few weeks, and there the Emperor was attentive in a manner. He sent one of his staff to offer an audience to Mr. Davis, and the Empress kindly expressed her willingness to receive me. But Mr. Davis felt that the Emperor had not been sincere with our government. He did not wish to say anything uncivil, and could not meet him with the cordiality his Majesty's kindness warranted ; but reviews were held in his honor, and every attention was shown to him by the government. We had cards to the chapel, and there saw the Empress with the Emperor at mass, and kneeling by them was their beautiful boy, the little Prince Imperial. He was so like our own little William that we followed his course with interest, until, in the dawn of his discrowned manhood, he laid down his life in Africa, for a foreign country.

In Paris we had a happy reunion with Mr. and Mrs. Slidell, with the Honorable Ambrose Dudley Mann, and others we had known, and spent a few weeks happily there, but preferred to remain in London for several reasons. Even then the shadow of the bloody drama that was to end the dynasty of the Bonapartes hung over Paris, and the blue blouses talked treason in the Musée de Na-

poléon, and hissed out between their teeth
abuse of the army officers as they passed.

On our return to London we saw Mr. Benjamin quite often, and always with increasing pleasure. He had now become Queen's
Counsellor, and was very successful. He appeared happier than I had hitherto seen him,
but though he gave Mr. Davis one long
talk about Confederate matters, after that he
seemed averse to speaking of them. He was
too busy to spend much time anywhere, but
was sincerely cordial and always entertaining
and cheery. His success at the English bar
was exceptional, but did not astonish us. In
speaking of his grief over our defeat, he said
that his power of dismissing any painful memory had served him well after the fall of the
Confederacy.

Soon after our return from Paris, our skilful and wise physician, Dr. Maurice Davis,
discovered that Mr. Davis's heart trouble had
not decreased, and he ordered him up to Scotland, whither Dr. Mackay, the poet, kindly
consented to accompany him.

While visiting our friends, the Abingers,
and several gentlemen whose acquaintance
he made in Scotland, and during a more protracted visit to his friend, James Smith, of
Glasgow, who had given a fine battery to the
Confederates, and whose brother fell gallantly

fighting in the Confederacy, he recovered his
strength partially, but never again was robust.   His letters from Scotland were charming.   I regret that space is lacking to give
some of them.

In the course of the autumn Mr. Davis was
offered the presidency of a life insurance company and though something else would have
been preferable to him, our needs rendered
him unable to be a chooser, and he left me
in London and sailed for America.   After remaining some months in Memphis, where he
was received in the most enthusiastic manner, Mr. Davis came to London for me, to set
up our new home in Memphis.   On the eve
of our departure he heard by cable of the
death of his brother, Joseph E. Davis, and
his grief was great.

After a smooth voyage we reached Memphis, having left our two sons Jefferson and
William at school near Emmorton, Md., with
our well-beloved friend, the Reverend W.
Brand, and our daughter Margaret with a
governess in Liverpool, at the house of my
sister and adopted daughter, Madame Stoëss,
so baby Winnie was the only child with us.

The town looked very small after London,
and it was some time before the blessed
home air blew upon the weary wanderers and
brought with it rest.   At that time there were

many things to regret in the administration of the city.   The drainage was bad, and the police defective, but we learned to love the people and they loved us, and the memory of their cordiality, their sincerity, and ready sympathy will " hang round my heart forever."

There are so many men there liberal without ostentation, and there is so much originality, talent, and enterprise among them, and they are so full of the living interests of the present that, once there long enough to know the people, it is rarely that another home is desired, and the very name brings to us a "waking certainty" of blessed friendship which cannot suffer a change.   Memphis, the splendid Memphis of to-day, is, as it promised to be then, the " progressive city of the Southwest."

There the citizens offered Mr. Davis, as a gift, the handsomest residence to be procured. As an expression of their good-will the offer was acceptable; but he declined the house, preferring to support himself.

He soon mastered the mathematical problems of life insurance, and thought he would have made a success for the company; but, upon closer examination, he discovered that the policies had been issued regardless of the risks or of anything but numbers—the per cent. paid on renewals was enormous.   After

putting everything that he could command into the stock to save it, the company, he
found, must fail, as the yellow fever made the
Southern risks alone too great for profit.

He went North to sell the Carolina to a
sound Northern company that would save
those insured in that company ; but during his
absence some friends more affectionate toward
him than considerate of those who insured,
thinking to relieve him of his trouble and responsibility, just as he had completed his arrangement to transfer it, sold the Carolina out
to another company in Memphis. He was
deeply moved by the loss to those who had
insured in the Carolina, but could do nothing
but submit, and it was rather a comforting
memory to him that he had lost heavily by
the failure.

CHAPTER LXXV.

In 1874, three months before the failure
of the Carolina, our boy William Howell
died of diphtheria. All that sympathy and
kindness could do was tendered to us to alleviate our grief, but the death of one whose
character, talents, and personal beauty made
the joy of our lives, and promised to justify
the hope of our old age, was a blow which
must leave us mourning until the end. The
little boy used to go and sit with his father in
his office, silent and observant if his pen
dropped, or he wanted anything, and often
when I missed him, his father would say,
"You will not grudge me our grave little
gentleman's company when you know how I
enjoy his presence." Now we had but one
son left, Jefferson.

Worn with sorrow, but undaunted by failure and heavy pecuniary loss, Mr. Davis
looked about again for the means of making
a livelihood. His health was far from good,
and the people of Texas invited him to visit

them. After much urging he went, and received a royal welcome "all along the line." After his return, these dear generous people very much desired to give him a tract of land and stock enough to furnish and cultivate it, but we felt unwilling to accept so much, and the gift was affectionately declined.

He was engaged in a lawsuit to recover the Brierfield plantation, which had passed into other hands after the death of his brother, and hoped to live, even though the shrinkage in values would necessitate our living poorly, on the products of that plantation. While environed by these difficulties, Mr. Davis's health, which had been steadily declining, became worse, and he was ordered to take a long sea voyage. He sailed from New Orleans to Liverpool, and from there went to Paris to see his old friend, A. Dudley Mann, who was one of his dearest friends. He also saw his friends, Lord Campbell and Beresford Hope, with others who had been hospitable to him while temporarily a resident of England, and returned after three months time, much improved in health and strength.

CHAPTER LXXVI.

UNWILLINGNESS TO ASK PARDON.—MISSISSIPPI ANXIOUS TO SEND HIM TO THE SENATE.

THE policy of reconstruction devised by the victors of the North, was that the men of the Confederacy should pursue no vocation until a pardon had been asked of the President of the United States and granted by him. Our men considered it a form instituted merely for their humiliation, and as such complied with it as the means of feeding their helpless families, already spent with the hardships they had endured. *Necessitas non habet legem* is a maxim acceded to by mankind, and he felt that the men who asked pardon did it for a holy and legitimate end. My husband, even in his letters from prison, combated the idea of our people expatriating themselves, and since they could not en masse move out of the country, and the pillar of cloud compassed but did not lead them by day or night, they must do the only thing left for them, try to forget in toil and the care of their families the misery which had settled over them and their people.

Throughout all this period Mr. Davis had endeavored to preserve silence about everything political, though letters came by hundreds asking his opinions on all political subjects. As he had not asked pardon for an offence he had not committed, he was disfranchised, and as he could not be held responsible for acts in which he was forbidden by law to participate, his opinion, if given, would be perfunctory. He therefore either declined to answer at all, or gave this reason for not doing so. So far, however, from being wounded by his disfranchisement, he felt rather proud that Congress had testified to the steady faith he had kept with his own people. He had not changed his beliefs in the least degree, and had it been necessary, he would have taken the same course at any time of his life when his people had called him to cleave only unto them. He therefore could not honestly express the contrition he did not feel.

So to the end, he who had served his country in tented field, and in the halls of legislation, and merited and received the acclaim of soldiers and the esteem of statesmen and legislators throughout the United States, kept the dignified tenor of his way, unheeding the sectional clamor when his own conscience approved. His asking for pardon as the leader of the Confederacy would have been more significant than the petition of one who had held a less high position, and he would not sacrifice his convictions to expediency, even in seeming.

The people of Mississippi, kind and trusting as of old to the man they had honored with their confidence, wished Mr. Davis to allow his name to be used for the Senate. They said, "The franchise is yours here, and the Congress can but refuse you admission, and your exclusion will be a test question." Mr. Davis responded, "I remained in prison two years and hoped in vain for a trial, and now scenes of insult and violence, producing alienation between the sections, would be the only result of attempting another test. I am too old to serve you as I once did, and too much enfeebled by suffering to maintain your cause."

CHAPTER LXXVII.

THE WRECK OF THE PACIFIC.—THE MISSISSIPPI VALLEY SOCIETY.

IN 1875 Mr. Davis began to feel old age coming on apace, and wrote to invite Captain Jefferson Davis Howell, then captain of a passenger steamer on the Pacific coast, to come to us and ease his weary shoulders of their burthen. Our brother could not leave immediately, but bound to my husband by every tender tie, he promised to come as soon as he could. Just at this time one of my husband's crowning joys came through our brother, and "sorrow's crown of sorrows" settled on his head soon thereafter in the death of our well-beloved young hero, and pride in him and bitter grief contended in Mr. Davis's heart as long as he lived.

On February 20th Captain Howell, who was temporarily out of employment, embarked on the *Los Angeles* with a number of passengers for Victoria. The evening of the 23d, during a stiff gale, the machinery of the steamer became unmanageable, and the ship commenced drifting. Seeing all the danger,

Captain Howell asked for volunteers for desperate service, to relieve the ship. The second officer and four men stood forth and put off in a small boat under his command, and after two days and nights of strenuous effort, they reached Astoria, procured relief, and saved the ship.

The passengers passed resolutions, one of which was: "Whereas Captain Jeff. D. Howell, by noble deeds of daring, succeeded in reaching Astoria after we had supposed he had lost his own life in the vain endeavor to save us from a terrible death, we return our thanks to the Giver of all good for sparing the life of our noble benefactor."

One who was present told Mr. Davis, years afterward, of the enthusiasm the young fellow created in his breast as he stepped forward among the terror-stricken crew, calm and self-possessed, and called for volunteers to go with him to death for the sake of men he did not know, and to save the property of a company which had causelessly thrown him out of employment a few weeks before.

Attracted by his daring, he was taken into the service of the Goodall & Nelsons Steamship line and given the old *Pacific*, plying from Seattle to San Francisco, with the hope of commanding a fine steamer then on the stocks.

The North Pacific coast is at best a dangerous one, and in the last letter written before
his death he said : " This coast is dangerous,
and I am never thoroughly asleep until I
reach Seattle and leaving there, keep the same
watch to San Francisco again. I have not felt
robust this year, and in fact have not felt the
spring of youth since my imprisonment."

After she had cleared the harbor of Seattle,
Thursday, November 4, 1875, Captain Howell
went to sleep, but in a few minutes afterward
a sailing-vessel came too near the *Pacific*, and
seeing the danger, tacked first one way and
then another, and ran into the *Pacific*, wrecked
her, and was herself wrecked on the rocks
further on. The *Pacific* had three hundred
souls on board, many of them miners and
rough men, ladies, children, and helpless
people. The captain kept order, placed all
his passengers and crew on boats and rafts,
coming on deck stripped to his under-clothes
for swimming, and called to his mate on the
raft, " Chief, I will go down with her, after
you get away ; look around for me. If you
cannot see me, pray for me." He finally, however, gained the raft in company with an old
lady, who insisted upon clinging to him. The
exhaustion, the cold, the hunger of four nights
and three days of exposure, did not daunt
his great soul. During this time he did his

best to comfort the poor dying woman at his side, uttering never a complaint of his own suffering; but his strength failed, and he was swallowed up in the sea, which gave his body sepulture and freed the soul that had so long worshipped his Creator in spirit and in truth. Upon this gallant young hero, who had lived but twenty-eight years, one of the oldest captains of the Pacific Mail S. S. Company, with a burst of tears, delivered this simple eulogy:

" Jeff Howell was the best sailor and noblest gentleman that ever walked a quarter-deck." Another said, " The commander was the last to leave the ship, the young, noble, and chivalrous gentleman upon whose life and character no stain and no reproach had ever rested."

I make no apology for telling his story here, for it was written even to the hour of death upon the heart of his brother and benefactor.

Thus was torn every prop from the old age of one who had given his utmost aid, confidence, and love to the boy over whose education he had presided with a father's care, and in whose promise he had lived anew. Our son only was left to us now.

Sore-hearted, rooted up from the labors of his life, impoverished, repenting quickly for his sins against God, and conscious of wilfully wronging no man, my husband sought con-

stant occupation to still his grief; but to his
life's end our brother was cited as his model
of a Christian hero.

The prospect of directing the commerce of
the South American States to New Orleans
had always been a cherished hope of Mr.
Davis, and now he turned to it with the expectation of securing this object. He preferred that to all other cities, and believed its
decadence would be arrested and its prosperity assured by the great trade flowing from
her wharves over the whole United States.
There was simultaneously an English and a
Southern company organized, called the
Mississippi Valley Society, which he hoped
would co-operate together, and the interchange of commodities and products would be
inaugurated by ships built in England and
plying between New Orleans and South
American ports, until the channel of trade
was so worn that it would inevitably trend
that way. The defect in Mr. Davis's plan,
however, was that no immediate personal
profits inured to anyone, and an impersonal
interest is rarely pushed to the point of
success.

In 1877, immediately after the marriage of
our daughter Margaret to Mr. J. A. Hayes,
he went to England to confer with the
English company, and took our little daughter

Winnie and me with him, and with us the child of a dear friend, who was to be left at school in Germany.

The hedge-rows of old England were pranked out in their spring garments of pink May, and looked very lovely to us after our long absence. Though Mr. Davis seemed much better in health and his cheerfulness increased, a severe illness of several months and the unremitting attention he paid me, with the failure of his project of forming the company, reduced his newly acquired health.

Capital is too timid to embark in any scheme of which the profits are at the end of a long perspective. The ships to carry the trade were not promised and the effort failed. In the autumn Mr. Davis returned home alone, as I was too ill to bear the journey or leave the proximity of Dr. Maurice Davis, of London, our kind and skilful friend of years ago.

CHAPTER LXXVIII.

THE COMMENCEMENT AND COMPLETION OF THE
RISE AND FALL OF THE CONFEDERATE STATES
OF AMERICA.—THE DEATH OF JEFFERSON DA-
VIS, JR.—HONORS AWARDED BY MR. DAVIS'S COUN-
TRYMEN.

WHEN the affairs of the Mississippi Valley
Company were wound up, Mr. Davis looked
about for a place so quiet and secluded
that he could write his history uninterrupted.
This he found after inquiry in the neighborhood of Beauvoir Station, near which he
owned a tract of land, and of which he knew
something. Then there were only three or
four houses occupied there, and the isolation
seemed favorable to his purpose.

Beauvoir House was owned and occupied
by Mrs. Sarah A. Dorsey, an old schoolmate
of mine, and a literary woman of some note.
Several of her female relations and her young
brother lived with her. Mr. Davis rented
one of the cottages called the pavilion, to the
left of the main house, engaged board from
her for himself and family when they should be
with him, furnished it, put up shelves for his

books and papers, and with his servant settled himself there for the work, having written previously to an assistant to join him and
establish himself at some convenient distance
on the coast.   Mrs. Dorsey offered her clerical
services at stated hours during the day, and
thus a part of the first volume was written.

As soon as it was considered advisable, in
April of 1878, leaving my little girl in Carls-
ruhe, I returned home.   After a short time
spent with our daughter, Mrs. Hayes, and
our only remaining son Jefferson, now grown
a strong, sober, industrious, and witty young
man, who was exceedingly intimate with his
father, and loved him devotedly—indeed they
were like two young friends together—I joined
my husband at Beauvoir.

As Mr. Davis had lost all his papers, the
history of the Confederacy was unwritten save
by the deeds of its defenders, and he soon felt
he could not attempt to give anything worthy
of the name of history without reliable data ;
he therefore decided to give an account of his
administration of the government, and explain
his policy.   This he prefaced by his constitutional argument, setting forth the grounds of
his faith.   How he has done this, the approval of the lawyers and statesmen of the country
has declared better than I could.   Several
causes delayed the completion of the book.

In the course of this summer a virulent kind of yellow fever broke out in Memphis and in New Orleans, and from these two centres spread over the whole country, not alone in the towns but for miles in the interior. Our daughter Margaret had taken refuge from the heat of Memphis in the West, but as her husband could not leave his bank in Memphis, she, fearless of the consequences to herself, returned to the neighborhood of that place to be near him in case he should be ill. Our only son Jefferson was also in the bank, and insisted on remaining near his sister. We were environed by yellow fever on all sides at Beauvoir. Mr. Davis thought he could not leave on account of his literary labor to join our children, and I feared to leave him.

The long summer passed and autumn began while we were racked with the most acute anxiety. In October our son was taken with the fever very violently. I prepared at once to go to him, as his father was not physically able to make the journey; but he persuaded me to wait a day because the physicians would not let me see him, as even a pleasurable excitement would kill our boy, and if I should take the fever our heroic daughter would insist on nursing me and thus take the disease. I was taken very ill in two

days, and our son died after a short, sharp
illness in which he knew his danger and expressed his willingness to obey God's will.
He died as he lived, at peace with God
and man ; and tenderly mindful of those who
would have no strong young man to sustain
them when his noble spirit went to its rest.
The last of our sons, at the age of twenty-
one, was now taken from us, and we had but
two children left.

Mr. Davis was crushed by the blow and
could not rally. He ceased to labor on his
book and sat all day, silent in his wordless
grief. Occasionally he would say : " I do not
know why I suffer so much, it cannot be long
before I am reunited to my boy."

Mrs. Dorsey about this time felt the persistent advances of a fatal malady under which
she had been suffering for many years, and
concluded to seek the aid of an eminent surgeon in New Orleans, and while I was absent
in attendance upon my daughter, Mrs. Hayes,
who was quite ill, Mrs. Dorsey sold Beauvoir
House to Mr. Davis at a fair valuation, and
went to New Orleans. She seemed for a
while to recuperate, but eventually died from
the reappearance of her disease. Before her
death she extracted a promise from my husband to be her executor, to which he objected
on the score that he was old and could not

administer very well any trust; but upon her
showing persistence, he, believing the trust to
be one of an eleemosynary nature, consented
After her death he discovered that the property was devised to him, but in order that he
might not refuse it, the reversion was made to
our youngest daughter, then a minor. Mrs.
Dorsey's uniform kindness to him and deference to his wishes had endeared her to him,
and he felt her death very much. This again
interrupted the progress of the book.

After a few months Judge Tenney, a man
of just and cultivated mind, had been sent
down by the publishers to assist Mr. Davis
in compilation, and Mr. Davis derived much
aid from his labors, and comfort from the profound confidence he felt in his rectitude and
piety. I wrote to Mr. Davis's dictation, for
we knew nothing of typewriters then.

Finally, after three years from the commencement of the book, it was finished. It
was four o'clock, and I had been writing since
eight o'clock in the evening, when Mr. Davis
dictated: "In asserting the right of secession it has not been my wish to incite to its
exercise. I recognize the fact that the war
showed it to be impracticable, but this did
not prove it to be wrong; and now, that it
may not be again attempted, and the Union
may promote the general welfare, it is need-

ful that the truth, the whole truth, should be known, so that crimination and recrimination may forever cease, and then, on the basis of fraternity and faithful regard for the rights of the States, there may be written on the arch of the Union 'Esto perpetua.'" I looked up after a momentary silence to remind him that he had forgotten to continue, and he smilingly said, " I think I am done." And so was finished his life's work for his countrymen ; but a foot-note amusingly attests the strength of his convictions even about small things. " Note : The publishers are responsible for the authography of these volumes." He would not change his mode of spelling, and insisted that sabre and theatre were correct, and if the publishers insisted upon saber and theater, they must take the discredit of the innovation.

The expense of an assistant, and the price of the book, which placed it beyond the reach of poor Confederates, as well as the fact that an inadequate compensation to him had been agreed upon by his agent with the Messrs. Appleton, prevented the book from being pecuniarily remunerative to him ; but he said he had not undertaken it as a matter of profit, and therefore must be satisfied if the end was gained of setting the righteous motives of the South before the world.

As soon as "The Rise and Fall" was completed we embarked at New Orleans, and went to Liverpool, and from there to meet our young daughter, who had left Germany for the advantage of a few months in Paris before quitting school. We remained three months in Paris, and during this time Mr. Davis spent the greater part of his time with his old friend, A. Dudley Mann, at Chantilly. Mr. Benjamin came to us there, older, but the same cheerful buoyant person, and that proved to be our last farewell to him. We returned home in November of the same year, and took up our abode at Beauvoir.

The people of Alabama invited Mr. Davis to visit them the next year, and our daughter Varina, known as Winnie in the family, accompanied him. The enthusiasm with which he was received could not be described. All classes came to do him honor, and the journey was extended to Atlanta and Savannah, and at the former place Governor Gordon, our heroic paladin of the "long ago," presented Varina to an enthusiastic crowd as "The daughter of the Confederacy." She was adopted then by the rank and file of our veterans, and now values their suffrages more than any earthly privilege. Some years later, our whole family were urged to be present at the yearly agricultural fair at Macon. We were asked by, and accepted the kind invitation of Mr. and Mrs. Marsh Johnson, to remain with them during our stay. The enthusiasm baffled description, and on Veterans' Day, as it rained steadily, they were to march to Colonel Johnson's house to greet Mr. Davis; but they were too impatient to pursue the circuitous carriage route, but jumped over the fence and came running and shouting all the way to greet their old chief; the tattered battle flags were borne in the strong hands that saved them twenty years before from capture, and with tender words "they called him worthy to be loved," who looked his last at them through eyes shining with a pride in them too great for words; but the strong, brave heart that had not quailed under danger, imprisonment, and vilification, sunk under the weight of his people's love, and he was stricken with heart failure. After days of suffering and imminent danger, Dr. H. Mc-Hatton, his able physician, ordered him back to Beauvoir, and enjoined quiet upon him for the future.

Never defeated man had such a following, and never had people a leader who so loved them.

CHAPTER LXXIX.

GENERAL SHERMAN'S ACCUSATIONS.

THOUGH we lived in strict retirement, whenever a theme for abuse was wanted, one or the other of Mr. Davis's antagonists in the North assailed him.

At a meeting of the Frank P. Blair Post, Grand Army of the Republic, in St. Louis in 1884, General Sherman was reported to have made allegations, hereinafter quoted by Mr. Davis in a letter characterizing those statements.

General Sherman's remarks were published in the *Globe-Democrat* of St. Louis, and Mr. Davis wrote the following letter of denial:

"BEAUVOIR, MISS., November 6, 1884.

"*Editor St. Louis Republican*:

"DEAR SIR: I have to-night received the enclosed published account of remarks made by General W. T. Sherman, and ask the use of your columns to notice only so much as particularly refers to myself, and which is to be found in the following extract:

" The following is from the *Globe-Democrat's* report:

" ' Referring to the late war, he said, it was not, as was generally understood, a war of secession from the United States, but a conspiracy. " I have been behind the curtain," said he, " and I have seen letters that few others have seen and have heard conversations that cannot be repeated; and I tell you that Jeff Davis never was a secessionist. He was a conspirator. He did not care for division from the United States, his object was to get a fulcrum from which to operate against the Northern States, and if he had succeeded, he would to-day be the master spirit of the continent, and you would be slaves. I have seen a letter from Jefferson Davis to a man whose name I cannot mention, because he is a United States Senator. I know Davis's writing, and saw his signature, and in that letter he said he would turn Lee's army against any State that might attempt to secede from the Southern Confederacy." '

" This public assault, under the covert plea that it is based upon information which regard for a United States Senator does not permit him to present, will, to honorable minds, suggest the idea of irresponsible slander.

" It is thus devolved upon me to say that

the allegation of my ever having written such a letter as is described is unqualifiedly false; and the assertion that I had any purpose or wish to destroy the liberty and equal rights of any State, either North or South, is a reckless falsehood, especially, because it was generally known that for many years before, as well as during the war between the States, I was an earnest advocate of the strict construction State-rights theory of Mr. Jefferson. What motive other than personal malignity can be conceived for so gross a libel?

" If General Sherman has access to any letters purporting to have been written by me, which will sustain his accusations, let him produce them or wear the brand of a base slanderer. "Yours respectfully,

"JEFFERSON DAVIS."

In reply to the above letter, General Sherman is reported to have said:

" It was a matter between two gentlemen, and he would take his own time about replying to Mr. Davis. He would reply in time, and Mr. Davis would be accommodated with facts. He would not give the name of the United States Senator who had received that important letter from Mr. Davis."

He said later on, that the letter had been burned with others of his papers at Chicago.

Senator Vance being very positive that he could not have been the one referred to by General Sherman in his statement, authorized the following publication in the St. Louis *Globe-Democrat* :

" 'WASHINGTON, D. C., December 14th.

" ' Every letter ever written to me on a political topic by President Davis is to be found faithfully copied on the official letter-books of the Executive Department of North Carolina. Those letter-books were taken from me by General Sherman's troops at the closing of the war, and are now in possession of the War Department in this city. Aside from the letter-books, General Sherman never saw any letter addressed to me by President Davis. Although I have not seen those books and read their contents in almost twenty years, I am quite sure that no such letter can be found there. I could not have forgotten such a letter had it been received by me. The suggestion, therefore, that I am the person referred to in General Sherman's statements is entirely untrue. It is well-known by those acquainted with the history of those times that my differences with Mr. Davis were purely in regard to matters of detail, and that I supported him in his efforts to maintain the Confederacy with all the zeal that I could command and all the power of the State which I could bring to bear. This Mr. Davis's letters all show. To the letter of mine to Mr. Davis of October 25, 1862, the New York *Tribune* correspondent says no copy of any reply can be found, and suggests that probably the statement to which General Sherman refers is contained in it. Certainly no effort was made to find that letter. It is upon the letter-book, dated November 1, 1862. It has been widely published, and contains no such expression as a threat against the States attempting to secede from the Confederacy, but does contain this expression: " I feel grateful to you for the cordial manner in which you have sustained every proposition connected with the public defence." This much is due to the truth. Great as were the abilities, and high as were the courage and faithfulness of Mr. Davis, I had no disposition to load him with all the misfortunes of defeat.'

" *Mr. Davis to Governor Vance.*

" 'RALEIGH, N. C., December 14th.

" ' In reference to the recent controversy between General Sherman and Jefferson Davis, in which the former charges the latter with having threatened to force certain States to remain in the Confederacy, it has been stated

that Davis's letter, containing this threat, was
written to Governor Vance, now United
States Senator, in reply to his letter to President Davis of October 25, 1862. It has been
stated also that the letter of Davis had been
destroyed. This is a mistake ; the letter is
here, and is now in the possession of a gentleman of Raleigh. It is as follows :

" ' " RICHMOND, VA., November 11, 1862.

" ' " TO HIS EXCELLENCY GOVERNOR VANCE,
Raleigh, N. C.

" ' " DEAR SIR : I have the honor to acknowledge yours of the 25th ult., and regret
the disappointment to which some of the recruits of North Carolina have been subjected.
I concur with you as to the policy of allowing
the conscripts, as far as the state of the service will permit, to select the companies
and regiments in which they are to serve.
The right secured by law of a volunteer to select his own company was lost, it is true, by
enrollments ; but the policy was so obvious
of associating men together who would best
harmonize with each other, that it was my
purpose to continue the privilege beyond the
limit fixed by law. That, as you are aware,
it serves to check the discontent which resulted from retaining twelve-month men beyond the term of their original engagement,

and was fairly regarded as measure to equit-
ably distribute the burden of public defence.
I shall endeavor by a judicial decision to settle the question raised, and meantime I have
been cheered by the evidence of popular sentiment which supports any measure necessary
to protect our country and secure our political independence. Like yourself, I have hoped
that party distinctions which existed at a former time would be buried in the graves of the
gallant men who have fallen in defence of their
birthright, and that we should all as a band
of brothers strike for the inheritance our fathers left us. With sincere regard I am respectfully and truly,

" ' " (Signed.) JEFFERSON DAVIS." ' "

On January 16, 1885, Chester A. Arthur,
President of the United States, in answer to
a Senate resolution, January 13, 1885, sent
the copy of a letter to the Secretary of War,
from General W. T. Sherman, dated January 6, 1885.

In this letter to the secretary, that thus became of public record, General Sherman relates the incident of his having been present
at the meeting of the G. A. R. Post, in St.
Louis, and reiterates his remarks with slight
variation, " that he had seen papers which
convinced me (him) that the President of the

Southern Confederacy had, during the progress of the war, changed his States' rights doc-
trines, and had threatened to use force—even
Lee's army—should any State of the Confederacy attempt to secede from the Government."
He added : " Yet I shrink not from a just responsibility for every word uttered there or at
any time." The balance of his letter contains
only extraneous matter, having no reference
to the explicit charge made.

The following account of the presentation
of General Sherman's letter to the United
States Senate appeared in the public prints,
and one of the captions is quoted here :

*No Scapegoat Wanted. The South Re-
sponsible, not President Davis. Continua-
tion of the Debate in the United States Senate
on the Resolution to Print Senator Sherman's " Historical" Papers—Senators Vance
and Brown Stand by their Record—General
Sherman's Mendacity Thoroughly Exposed—
The Resolution Passed.*—WASHINGTON, January 13th.—In the Senate, at ten o'clock, on
motion of Senator Hawley, his resolution to
call upon the President for copies of the papers filed in the War Department by General
Sherman, as a reply to certain strictures of
Mr. Jefferson Davis, former President of the
Confederate States, was taken up.

Senator Vance said that as the Senate would probably pass this resolution and place on its record an unofficial paper by General William T. Sherman, which makes certain statements about persons, it was proper that all persons affected by those statements should be heard in the same form. He said that the newspapers stated General Sherman had been interviewed, who said that Vance was not the person alluded to as the Governor to whom the letter had been addressed. He thought that this denial at both ends of the line would conclude the matter, but it seemed he was mistaken.

General Sherman said: "At Raleigh a mass of public records had been carried off; yet a number were left behind at the State House and a mansion called the Palace, which we occupied as headquarters during our stay there, namely, from April 13 to April 29, 1860. These records and papers were overhauled by professional clerks, who delivered to Adjutant-General Sawyer such information as was material, and attention was only drawn to such as were deemed of sufficient importance. Among the books collected at the Palace in Raleigh was a clerk's or secretary's copy-book containing loose sheets and letters, among which was the particular letter of Davis, to which I referred in my St. Louis

speech. . . . It explained to me why
Governor Vance, after sending to me a commissioner to treat for his State particularly,
now awaited my answer. I am quite sure
that we generally thought it was the desire
of Governor Vance and of the officials to take
North Carolina out of the Confederacy, as I
have stated, but they were afraid of Jefferson
Davis, and wanted protection."

Concerning this statement, Senator Vance
remarked that he wished to say, first, that no
letters, documents, or public books of any
character were ever left at his residence or at
the Palace of the Governor while he was its
occupant; second, no clerk or secretary of
his ever kept, as reported, any copy-book for
correspondence, all official or public letters
being first copied in a letter-book which was
required by law to be kept in the executive
office, and then tied up into a bundle and
placed in files, where they still remain; third,
General Sherman did not find in the copy-
book the particular letter of Davis to which
he referred in his speech, for the simple reason
that there was no such letter there and no
such copy-books when Vance occupied the
house; fourth, he averred most positively, on
the honor of a gentleman and an American
Senator, that no letter containing such a
threat was ever received by him from Jeffer-

son Davis. All letters from President Davis
to him of any nature were to be found copied
in the letter-books of the Executive Department of North Carolina, which books were
now in the War Department.

The reasons given by General Sherman to
corroborate his statement were such, Senator Vance thought, as would scarcely commend themselves to a respectable lawyer.
General Sherman said he had paid little attention to the letter at the time, and did not
say that he ever saw it afterward. General
Sherman had said further: "Davis being
then himself a fugitive, his opinions were of
little importance." Senator Vance supposed
it was perhaps the little attention given to the
opinions of an unimportant man that enabled
General Sherman to remember so well the
contents of the letter after the lapse of nearly
twenty years. The suggestion as to the
probable fate of that mysterious letter, that it
was burned in the Chicago fire, was a mere
apology for its non-production, and contradicted the idea of its importance, for if it had
been such as General Sherman said it was, it
would have found its way into the public files.

But there was another matter averred by
General Sherman that more nearly concerned
Senator Vance, and to which he would ask
the attention of the Senate. "It may be,

sir," continued Senator Vance, "that Northern gentlemen who were on the victorious side during the Civil War cannot properly appreciate the feelings and sentiments of those who were on the side of misfortune and defeat. They seem to regard it as quite a sin and shame that we do not readily join in the denunciations that are heaped upon him who was the leader in that war, and hasten to condemn him on all occasions as the surest way of excusing our conduct and commending ourselves to the good opinion of our late opponents. Surely no man of even the slightest sense of honor in his composition would respect any Southern man who would thus debase himself. Surely the most flagrant and rampant trafficker in issues of sectional hatred would respect more an adversary who came to him walking upright on his feet than one crawling. If not, if a different sentiment is to prevail, what must we think of the manhood of men who should entertain it. Now, sir, be it known to you that those of us who pledged our faith to each other for the establishment of the Confederacy gave up all for which we contended when it failed, retaining to ourselves only one solitary satisfactory reflection, and that is that we had at least served our country faithfully, honestly, and devotedly as we understood it."

Senator Joseph Brown, of Georgia, also disclaimed ever receiving such a letter. General Sherman did not specify the other of the three ex-Governors who became senators as the person who received the apocryphal letter.

After this false charge three times disproved by the reputed actors in General Sherman's so-called conspiracy by Mr. Davis to intimidate the Governors, the Senate entered General Sherman's misrepresentations on the Journal of that body, and the consolation my husband had in looking at this crystallization of a slander, was that in the future an impartial seeker after truth will find and proclaim it. When the passions of the day have died out with the august figures that have passed, posterity will do justice.

Mr. Davis thus wrote to one of the Senators voting in the negative.

"BEAUVOIR, MISS., January 30, 1885.

"HONORABLE ———,

UNITED STATES SENATE.

"MY DEAR SIR: accept my thanks for your defence of me against slanderous accusations, and equally are they tendered for your vindication of our people against allegations alike unfounded and indefensible.

"General Sherman in a published address stated that he had seen letters and had conversations giving him information which few possessed and which showed that I was a conspirator whose object was by secession to get a fulcrum for the subjugation of the Southern States.

" As soon as the publication reached me, I pronounced this a reckless falsehood. He also states that he had seen a letter addressed to one now a United States Senator, which he knew to be in my handwriting and with my signature, in which letter I had declared my purpose to turn Lee's army against any State that might attempt to secede from the Southern Confederacy. I also denounced this assertion as false, and demanded that General Sherman should produce the evidence on which the accusations were founded, or wear the brand of a base slanderer.

" As he was reported in several newspapers to have said that it was a personal matter between him and myself, to which he would attend in due time and in his own manner, it was to have been expected that he would either retract allegations which he could not sustain, or produce the evidence on which he had made them. He has done neither, but in a wordy paper on extraneous matter has sought to obscure the true issue, as the cuttle-fish blackens the water to aid in its escape; he has thus virtually accepted the brand he had won by his wanton calumny, and I am content to leave him to his unenviable notoriety which he has thus, and twice before, acquired."

.   .   .   .

Through the influence of partisan hostility General Sherman has succeeded in having spread upon the records of the Senate his imaginary and false accusation without the refutation, and our consolation is that truth is the Excalibar of the innocent.

In defending the Confederates or himself against calumnies, Mr. Davis showed that age did not impair either his spirit or courage, and he asked no aid from his friends or coadjutors, his conscience was clear and he looked within and saw reflected only the aims of an unselfish, much-enduring patriot.

CHAPTER LXXX.

GENERAL JOSEPH E. JOHNSTON AND THE CONFEDERATE TREASURE.

THE quiet tenor of Mr. Davis's life flowed on ; in supervising his own affairs, and in receiving the visits of neighbors and friends, he rarely gave more than a glance at the political condition of the country, generally winding up his few gentle remarks of disapproval with the phrase " we are drifting fast." He seemed so averse to controversies that he neglected to read the " charges and specifications " put forth by Generals Johnston, Beauregard, and others. Some apocryphal histories came forth also in a kind of defamatory international leaflets, generally published at the North, and always inspired or attested by one or the other of the malcontent Confederate generals or their staff.

At this time General Johnston made himself conspicuous for a remarkable dual nature, partaking of the mistrustful St. Thomas and the faithful Abraham. In an interview with Colonel Frank Burr, of the *Press*, he expressed his doubt of the honesty of the President of

the Confederate States, and intimated that
he had made away with over two millions of
Confederate treasure ; and then the other
side of General Johnston's character asserted
itself, when, for his figures, he cited General
Beauregard's estimate, and declined to read
Colonel Burr's report of the conversation
before it was sent to the *Press* because, he
said, "that was not necessary; no man
ought to make a statement to a journalist
that he was not willing to stand by," * but
nevertheless he yet felt a profound confidence
that what he said would not be made public.

The history of the disposition of the Confederate treasure is given *in extenso* below,
and the case is rested on the evidence.   It is
not all quoted, because my memoir has been
extended much more than was anticipated,
and I am obliged to cut out very valuable
matter which will be found available to any
future biographer or historian in the rooms
of the Louisiana Historical building, at New
Orleans.

On April 15th Mr. Davis, being at Greensborough, S. C., issued the following order to
Mr. J. N. Hendren, Treasurer of the Confederate States :

"You will report to General Beauregard

---

* See letter of Colonel Burr to Mr. Davis given in this statement.

with the treasure in your possession, that he
may give it due protection, as a military
chest, to be moved with his army train. For
further instructions you will report to the
Secretary of the Treasury.

(Signed)   " JEFFERSON DAVIS.
Official.

(Signed)   " F. R. LUBBOCK, *Colonel and*
A. D. C."

General Johnston, in his " Narrative," page
408, says : " I arrived in Greensborough, near
which the Confederate troops were in bivouac,
before daybreak on April 19th.   Colonel
Archer Anderson, Adjutant-General of the
army, gave me two papers addressed to me
by the President.   The first directed me to
obtain from Mr. J. N. Hendren, treasury
agent, thirty-nine thousand dollars in silver,
which was in his hands, subject to my order,
and to use it as the military chest of the army.
The second, received subsequently by Colonel
Anderson, directed me to send this money to
the President, at Charlotte.   This order was
not obeyed, however.   As only the military
part of our Government had then any existence, I thought that a fair share of the fund
still left should be appropriated to the benefit
of the army, especially as the troops had received no pay for many months.   This sum

(except twelve hundred dollars which Mr. Hendren said that the Commissary-General had taken) was divided among the troops irrespective of rank, each individual receiving the same share.

" As there was reason to suppose that the Confederate Executive had a large sum in specie in its possession, I urged it earnestly, in writing, to apply a part of it to the payment of the army. This letter was entrusted to Lieutenant-Colonel Mason, who was instructed to wait for an answer. Its receipt was acknowledged by telegraph, and an answer promised. After waiting several days to no purpose, Colonel Mason returned without one."

When Mr. Davis was informed of the above statement by " one who had read the ' Narrative,' " he wrote to Colonel Anderson, referred to book and page, and inquired what letter from him as there described he had received. He responded as follows :

" RICHMOND, VA., December 21, 1880.
" TO THE HONORABLE JEFFERSON DAVIS,
    " Beauvoir, Miss.
" MY DEAR SIR : Your letter of the 17th instant was duly received. I am sorry to say that my memory does not enable me to give you any assistance in regard to the mat-

ter mentioned at page 408 of General Johnston's 'Narrative,' to which you direct my
attention. I do not remember anything connected with the subject, except that there
was a payment of silver coin to the army at
Greensborough, and I have no papers which
would afford information.

" Yours truly,
" ARCHER ANDERSON."

Mr. Davis wrote: " Not recollecting to
have met Colonel Mason at Charlotte, I
wrote him, asking what was the fact. Receiving no reply, I renewed the inquiry, but
though considerable time has elapsed, he has
not answered. It is possible that I might
have met the gentleman without recollecting
it, but not probable that I should have received such a letter and have forgotten it."

In 1878 Mr. Davis received a letter from
a former classmate at West Point, quoting
the statement of the United States Treasurer
as to the amount of treasure taken at the
surrender. Among the items was one that a
specified sum had been taken from " Jeff
Davis."

To this letter Mr. Davis replied:

"MISSISSIPPI CITY, February 4, 1878.
" The facts you state in regard to captured
treasure are new to me. It is probable that

most of it was the property of the Richmond banks. The item of money captured from ' Jeff Davis ' is unfounded, for the sufficient reason that I had no gold when captured, either private or public. Mr. Reagan, Secretary of the Treasury, had some gold, part of it his private property, more of it belonged to the C. S. treasury, which was seized in his saddle-bags; the amount does not, as my memory serves me, correspond with either item. It was probably appropriated by the drunken fellow Hudson, who was recognized as Adj. of the Michigan Regiment, and who Reagan told me got his saddle-bags.

" The rest of the C. S. treasury was in the possession of the treasurer and his assistant. They were in Washington, Ga., when I left there, and I have no knowledge of their future conduct.

" Colonel Pritchard told me that he had been sent in pursuit of the wagon train, and that he had no expectation of finding me with it. I will write to Mr. Reagan and ask him to answer your inquiries.

" The fact is, I staked all my property and reputation in the defence of State rights and constitutional liberty, as I understood them. The first I spent in the cause, except what was seized, appropriated, or destroyed by the enemy ; the last has been persistently assailed by all which falsehood could invent and malignity employ.

" I am ever affectionately yours,

" JEFFERSON DAVIS."

" C. J. WRIGHT, Chicago.

On December 18, 1881, there appeared in the Philadelphia *Press* the following extraordinary publication :

Confederate Gold Missing. General Johnston Calls Jefferson Davis to Account for over $2,000,000 in Specie.

PHILADELPHIA, December 17th.—The *Press* will publish to-morrow an interview with General Joseph E. Johnston, in which he charges that Jefferson Davis received a very large sum of money belonging to the Confederate Treasury at the evacuation of Richmond, for which he has never accounted. In the course of his remarks he says : "I had learned from General Beauregard that Mr. Davis had a large amount of specie in his possession, and I wrote urging that a portion of it be paid to the soldiers then in active service. My letter to Mr. Davis on this subject was quite urgent, and I entrusted it to Colonel Mason, of my staff, with instructions that he deliver it in person to Mr. Davis and bring a reply. Colonel Mason went to Charlotte, delivered the letter to Mr. Davis, but

beyond a telegraphic acknowledgment to me
that the letter was received, there has never
yet been a response to it.   Colonel Mason
waited some time and made several efforts to
get a reply from Mr. Davis, in obedience to
my instructions, but was obliged to return
without one."

"What became of the specie?"

"It followed or preceded the head of the
civil Government of the Confederacy to the
South about the time Mr. Davis went in that
direction."

'Have you any idea of the amount of specie
Mr. Davis carried South?"

"Colonel Paul, an eminent artillery officer
of the Confederacy, and now a prominent
lawyer of Richmond, a man of high character,
told me that he inspected the specie before its removal from Richmond, and after
it had been loaded ready for transportation.
He said that there was a car-load of it.   As
he only saw it boxed away ready for ship-
ment, he could, of course, give no information
as to the amount in dollars and cents.   General Beauregard, however, was in immediate
command at Greensborough while the President was there, and doubtless had an opportunity of knowing more accurately the amount
of money with the President than any one except the President's immediate political family.

He told me that he was convinced that the
President had $2,500,000 in specie at Greens-
borough. I have no doubt that General
Beauregard's estimate was within bounds.
After Mr. Davis left Charlotte and moved
South, a Confederate officer told me that,
while standing near a bridge crossing a creek,
a man rode up and inspected it. He said
that he was in charge of the President's
money train and wanted to see if the bridge
was safe or not. The man in charge told the
officer he had twenty wagon-loads of specie
in the train. This would be in perfect harmony with Colonel Paul's statement, that
there was a car-load when it left Richmond,
and with General Beauregard's, that there
was $2,500,000 at Greensborough."

" What became of the money ? "

" That I am unable to say. Mr. Davis has
never given any satisfactory account of it, and,
what is a strange thing to me, is the Southern
people here never held him to an account for
it. The $39,000 he left at Greensborough
the soldiers received. Major Moses, an attorney now living in Atlanta, has accounted
for $20,000 more. A short time before the
evacuation of Richmond the bankers of that
city placed in Mr. Davis's hands $360,000 in
specie for the defence of the city. There was
never any service rendered for this money, but

when Richmond was evacuated it was transported South with the specie belonging to the
Confederacy. A committee of Richmond
bankers were sent to receive it. At Washington, Ga., they succeeded in getting between
$110,000 and $120,000, but while transporting
it home it was captured by General Wilson's
cavalry and turned into the United States
Treasury. It is now there in litigation. The
Richmond bankers are suing for its recovery,
and it has never been decided to whom it belongs. Say $120,000 of it is there and $39,-
000 in the military chest left at Greensborough for the army, and $20,000 accounted for
by Major Moses. This would make $179,000
out of the $2,500,000 which General Beaure-
gard and other good authority estimate was
on hand."

This charge of General Johnston against
the integrity of Mr. Davis excited intense indignation all over the South. The friends of
General Johnston refused to believe he had
uttered the libel.

Statements made by officers and men of
the Confederate army, and from many in the
North, each reciting his personal knowledge
of the events as incorrectly related by General Johnston, burdened Mr. Davis's mail.

To the editor of the Philadelphia *Press*,
General Johnston, to stay the whirlwind he

had raised, sent the following so-called " disclaimer."

" *To the Editor of the Philadelphia Press.*
  " DEAR SIR: I was greatly annoyed by
reading the article in your paper of the 18th
inst., headed ' General Johnston's Narrative,'
and signed ' F. A. B.' This article is evidently based on a conversation which I did not
take to be an interview. In that conversation, therefore, a good deal was said which
nothing could induce me to say for publication, notably what relates to Confederate
treasure at Greensborough. Besides this, the
narrative is inaccurate, so much so that I will
not undertake to correct it, and it contains
letters which not only did not come from me,
but which have not been in my possession for
years. So I beg you to publish this to relieve
me of responsibility for the narrative.
              " Most respectfully yours,
                      " J. E. JOHNSTON.
  " WASHINGTON, December 20, 1881."

In this so-called " disclaimer," General
Johnston shelters himself under the plea that
he did not mean to make his slanderous accusation *publicly*, but he did not *deny* saying
that Mr. Davis appropriated to his own use
two millions and a half dollars of Confederate

treasure. He wrote "nothing could induce me to say *for publication*" what *he did say.*

That he did know that he was being interviewed by a representative of the *Press*, as he afterward acknowledged, the following letter from Colonel Frank Burr will show.

"PHILADELPHIA, August 20, 1885.

" HONORABLE JEFFERSON DAVIS.

" DEAR SIR : Your kind note of a recent date received, and I take great pleasure in furnishing you the following statement of facts in relation to my interview with General Joseph E. Johnston, published in the Philadelphia *Press* of some years ago (1881), to which you refer :

" Some month or six weeks before that publication was made I was on my way South, and on the train met General Johnston. When we reached Richmond we both took the same omnibus for the Exchange Hotel. . . . Later in the day I met him in the hotel, and we entered into conversation after dinner about general matters. I said to him I should very much like to get from him a good story of his surrender to Sherman, not the humdrum details that appeared in the books, but such a story of it as a man would naturally tell in conversation, giving all the

incidents, frivolous or otherwise. General
Johnston readily assented to my request, and
we went to his room. Soon after your book
on 'The Rise and Fall of the Confederate
Government' was issued, I started South to
review it, or allow prominent soldiers to
review it in a series of interviews. The first
man I visited upon this mission was General
Johnston, and I printed and published his
criticisms upon your work, covering some two
columns and a half of the *Press*. Once after
that interview, and before the time of which I
am writing, I met General Johnston again, so
that *before our accidental meeting on the cars
my character and occupation were thoroughly
fixed upon his mind.** Our conversation at
the first interview was directed solely to the
military operations between himself and General Sherman previous to the surrender.
Our conversation was interrupted by a business engagement which he had previously
made, and I left him with the understanding
that we were to meet again to finish the subject. My stenographer was travelling with
me, so immediately after our first conversation I went and dictated it while it was fresh
in my mind. The next day the conversation

---

* All the italics in this letter are the author's. The omissions are
simply unimportant words left out for want of space.

was renewed and continued for some time. When I left General Johnston I thanked him for the courtesy and said that, as this was an important matter and one which I hoped to make a feature of my trip, I should be glad to submit him the copy for revision before it was printed. He said no, that that was not necessary; that my former treatment of him and general correctness of expression were guarantee enough that I would not misrepresent him; and he added jocularly, that '*no man ought to make a statement to a journalist that he was not willing to stand by.*' After this at the table our conversation was renewed upon various matters, and we parted, he going south in one direction and I in the other. Immediately after my second conversation with him I dictated my impressions of it, as well as General Johnston's own statements, to my stenographer, so when I came to make up the article I had the expressions as given to me at the moment. But after I had written the article and recognized its importance, I wrote a letter to General Johnston, saying that I had finished the article and that it was subject to his order for revision, or any other purpose that to him might seem meet. I held the matter two weeks after this letter was mailed. I then gave the order for its publication. When it was printed and the

commotion came, the Washington correspondent of the New York *World* made General
Johnston say in an interview that he did not
know me, and that he was beguiled into the
conversation which I had reported. Without
any solicitation on my part, in a telegram to
the editor of the Philadelphia *Press*, General
Johnston denied the statement made by the
World's writer, and expressed his full understanding of my character and purpose. I do
not think that it is possible that, to anyone and
for any purpose, General Johnston has ever
said that he was not well acquainted with me,
and thoroughly understood the use I was to
make of what he said to me upon the occasion
to which I herein refer.

" I have been thus explicit, Mr. Davis, that
you may see how well I remember the small-
est detail. I can readily recall the words
that were spoken, the appearance of the room,
and everything in relation to that remarkable
interview. My memory is tenacious of all
matters of that character, and especially so as
to this one, which was severely impressed
upon my mind from the fact that there were
no other subjects intruded into my inquiry.
In the North here, where I am known, I think
it would be difficult for General Johnston or
any other person to make people believe that
I would either misrepresent or be guilty of a

breach of faith. I enclose you the letter
of our mutual friend, Senator Hill.
            "Very sincerely,
                "FRANK A. BURR."

The letter of Senator Hill is not needful to
Mr. Davis's vindication, and therefore I suppress it, though if desired at any time it can
be made public.

Having, by the letter of Colonel Burr, established the fact that General Johnston did
make the charge against Mr. Davis, knowing
Colonel Burr's position and connection with
the *Press*, I now give the *unsolicited* and
spontaneous testimony of men who were
eye-witnesses of the events connected with
the Confederate treasure, and with the separation of the armies and cabinet of the Confederacy.

The Honorable John H. Reagan, who was
the last Secretary of the Confederate Treasury, and who now represents Texas in the
United States Senate, wrote:

"Before we left Washington, Ga., the
money of the Richmond banks, which I understood had been under the protection of
the escort for the protection of the Confederate money, was placed under the exclusive
control of the agent of the banks, whose name
I do not remember. I do not know what

became of it. I understood from the verbal
statement of Mr. Trenholm, on his turring
over the business of the Treasury Department to me, that there was in the Confederate
Treasury some eighty-five thousand dollars
in gold coin and bullion; some thirty-five
thousand dollars in silver coin; about thirty-
six thousand dollars in silver bullion, and
some six or seven hundred thousand in Confederate Treasury notes; besides some sixteen or eighteen thousand pounds sterling, in
Liverpool acceptances.

"You will remember that the silver coin
and an amount of gold coin about equal to the
silver bullion, was paid out to the troops before they or the money reached Washington.
There I directed an acting treasurer to turn
over to two of our naval officers, whose
names I do not now remember, most of the
gold coin and bullion; with the understanding between us all, before you left Washington, that as soon as the excitement subsided
a little, they were to take this out to Bermuda or Liverpool, and turn it over to our
agents, that we might draw against it after we
should get across the Mississippi River. I
directed him to turn the silver bullion over to
Major Moses, as it was too bulky and heavy
to be managed by us in our then condition;
and I saw Moses putting it in a warehouse in

Washington before I left there. I also directed him to burn the Confederate notes in the presence of General Breckinridge and myself. The acceptances on Liverpool were turned over to me, and were taken by the Federal forces with my other papers when we were captured. You were not captured until several days after the disposition of all these funds, as above stated. These constitute, as I remember them, about all the material facts as to the public funds, and as to the money of the Richmond banks. . . .

" The slander that you had attempted to escape with a large amount of funds, was at first uttered as a means of bringing odium on your name, and on the Confederacy. But it has become stale and threadbare, and its falsity so generally understood, that I am persuaded a further denial of the charges would be regarded as useless."

As General Johnston mentioned in effect that General Beauregard was one of the parties who had knowledge of the alleged facts, General Beauregard stated to a reporter of the New Orleans *Picayune* the following :

" General Johnston is in error, for no report was ever made to me of the amount of Government treasure which accompanied or preceded the Government from Richmond,

and I have never known the amount. Just
before the surrender at Greensborough, we
received out of it $37,000 in silver, which was
paid out per capita to officers, soldiers, and
employees of the army, each one receiving
$1.15. I have preserved my share, intending
having a small medal made of it as a memento of the last days of the Confederacy. I
have no knowledge of what became of the
rest of the amount, whatever it may have
been, that the Government sent away or
brought away from Richmond."

The statement of Captain M. H. Clark, of
Clarksville, Tenn., who was acting treasurer
at the time of the surrender, is very full and
explicit. It was given in the *Courier-Jour-
nal*, Louisville, Friday, January 13, 1882, and
is as follows :

"CLARKSVILLE, TENN., January 10th.

"As the papers of late have been full of
communications from ex-Confederates in regard to the Confederate Treasury matters,
called out by a reported interview with General J. E. Johnston with a reporter of the Philadelphia *Press*, and as I have it in my power to
give a true history of the last days of the Confederate Treasury from the written documents
of that period still in my possession, I have
decided to prevent any further controversy,
and show what were the specie assets of the

Confederate States at the time of the dissolution of its Government.

" General surprise has been felt at General
Johnston's tardiness in disavowing his connection with the unworthy insinuations against
the Confederate President and Cabinet in the
article referred to.

" I will state as briefly as possible my connection with the Confederate Treasury.

" The President from Danville proceeded
to Charlotte, N. C. We arrived at Abbeville,
S. C., the morning of May 2d. At Abbeville,
S. C., the Treasury officers reported the train
at the depot, having been a part of the time under the escort of Admiral Raphael Semmes's
little naval force to protect it from the Federal cavalry, who were raiding on a parallel line
with our route, between us and the mountains.
Mr. G. A. Trenholm, the Secretary of the
Treasury, having been left quite ill near the
Catawba River, the President appointed the
Postmaster-General, Honorable John H. Reagan, acting Secretary of the Treasury, who
took charge of that Department, and placed
the coin under charge of the cavalry to con-
voy it to Washington, Ga. The party left
for Washington that night, and stopped for
breakfast a few miles from Washington. At
our breakfast halt, when the road was taken,
Mr. Benjamin came to me and said ' good-by,'

and turned off south from that point. Mr. Mallory left the party at Washington, Ga., going to a friend's in the neighborhood.

"Next morning Colonel William Preston Johnston informed me that Mr. Reagan had applied for me to act as Treasurer, to take charge of the Treasury matters, and I was ordered to report to him, and doing so, was handed my commission, which is now before me and reads as follows, viz. :

"'WASHINGTON, GA., May 4, 1865.

"' M. H. Clark, Esq., is hereby appointed Acting Treasurer of the Confederate States, and is authorized to act as such during the absence of the Treasurer.

"' JEFFERSON DAVIS.'

[This was the last official signature President Davis affixed to any paper.]

"Returning to my train to get some necessary articles, President Davis rode up with his party, when what I supposed were farewell words were passed between us, and my train, under charge of its Quartermaster, moved out. The Treasury train arrived shortly after President Davis's party left, and being reported at General Basil W. Duke's camp, about a mile from town, I went there with the proper authority, and he turned the whole of it over to me. Selecting the shade

of a large elm-tree as the ' Treasury Department,' I commenced my duties as ' Acting
Treasurer C. S.'

" Now for the specie of the Treasury.

" It must be remembered that a month or
more before the evacuation of Richmond,
Va., for the relief of the people, the Treasury
Department had opened its depositories and
had been selling silver coin, the rate being
fixed at $60 for $1 in coin. While at Danville, Va., the Treasury Department resumed
these sales, the rate there being $70 for $1.

" About $40,000 in silver, generally report-
ed (and no doubt correctly) at $39,000, was
left at Greensborough, N. C., as a military
chest for the forces there, under charge of the
Treasurer, Mr. John C. Hendren ; all of the
balance was turned into my hands, which
amounted, in gold and silver coin, gold and
silver bullion, to $288,022.90. Adding the
$39,000 left at Greensborough, N. C., the
Treasury contained in coin and bullion, when
it left Danville, Va., $327,022.90.

" If the Treasury at Richmond had contained $2,500,000 in coin, certainly the brave
men of our armies· would never have suffered
so severely from want of sufficient food and
clothing as they did during the winter of 1864-
65, for it had been demonstrated that gold
could draw food and raiment from without

the lines.   With the train at Washington, Ga., however, was the specie belonging to the Virginia banks, which *some time before had been ordered to be turned over to their officers*, who had accompanied *it out from Richmond*, and had never left it ; but the proper officer had not been present to make the transfer.   It had never been mixed with the Treasury funds, but kept apart and distinct, and when Acting Secretary Reagan ordered the transfer to be made, no handling of specie or counting was necessary, but merely permission for the cashiers and tellers to take control of their own matters.   I knew them all personally, but my impression is that it was about $230,000. General E. P. Alexander has already given in your columns the after-fate of this fund.

" While at Washington, Ga., communications were received from General John C. Breckinridge, that payments had been promised by him to the cavalry from the train. General Breckinridge's action was ratified, and President Davis gave some other directions before he left.   General Breckinridge arrived in Washington, Ga., an hour or so after President Davis left. · My recollection of his statement was that during the night of the 3d, en route from Abbeville, S. C., to Washington, Ga., he found the cavalry and train at a halt, resting.   Stopping, he learned from the officers that the men were dissatisfied at the position of affairs ; that they were guarding a train which could not be carried safely much farther ; the Federal cavalry were known to be in full force not a great distance off ; the destination and disposition of their own force was an uncertain one ; their paper money was worthless for their needs ; that they might never reach Washington, Ga., with it, etc. A crowd gathered around, when General Breckinridge made them a little speech, appealing to their honor as Confederate soldiers not to violate the trust reposed in them, but to remain Southern soldiers and gentlemen ; and that when they reached Washington with the train fair payments should be made.

" The men responded frankly, saying they proposed to violate no trust ; they would guard it, but expressed what they considered due to them in the matter ; and, as they would be paid some money in Washington, Ga., and no one could tell what would happen before they reached Washington, there was no good reason for delay.

" General Breckinridge replied that, if they wished an instant compliance with his promise, he would redeem it at once, and ordered up the train to the house at which he had stopped, and had the wagons unloaded ; the

quartermasters being ordered to make out
their pay-rolls, when a certain amount was
counted out and turned over to the proper
officers. The wagons were then reloaded,
and the route was taken up to Washington,
Ga. The boys told me they got about twenty-six dollars apiece ; enough, they hoped, to
take them through.

" It is this transaction which has produced
so many contradictory statements from men
and officers, many seeing nothing more, and
regarding it as the final disbursing of the Confederate specie. Proper receipts were given
and taken at the time, and I rated it as if
disbursed by myself, and covered it into the
Treasury accounts by the paper of which below is a copy :

" 'CONFEDERATE STATES OF AMERICA,
" 'WASHINGTON, GA., May 4, 1865.

" ' HONORABLE J. C. BRECKINRIDGE,
" ' *Secretary of War :*
" ' There is required for payment of troops
now on the march through Georgia, the sum
of one hundred and eight thousand three
hundred and twenty-two dollars and ninety
cents ($108,322.90), to be placed to the
credit of Major E. C. White, Quartermaster.
" ' A. R. LAWTON,
" ' *Quartermaster-General.'*
(Indorsed.)

" 'The Secretary of the Treasury will please issue as requested.

" 'JOHN C. BRECKINRIDGE,

" ' *Secretary of War.'*

(Indorsed.)

" ' M. H. Clark, Acting Treasurer, will turn over to Major E. C. White the amount named within, preserving the necessary vouchers, warrant hereafter to be drawn when settlement can be regularly made.

" 'JOHN H. REAGAN,

" ' *Acting Secretary of Treasury.'*

(Indorsed.)

" 'WASHINGTON, GA., May 4, 1865.

" ' Received of M. H. Clark, Acting Treasurer, C. S., the sum of one hundred and eight thousand three hundred and twenty-two dollars and ninety cents ($108,322.90) in specie, the amount called for by within paper.'

" I obtained permission from General Breckinridge and Mr. Reagan to burn a mass of currency and bonds, and burnt millions in their presence.

" Before reaching town I was halted by Major R. J. Moses, to turn over to him the specie which President Davis, before he left, had ordered to be placed at the disposal of

the Commissary Department, to feed the paroled soldiers and stragglers passing through,
to prevent their burdening a section already
stripped of supplies.   I turned over to Major
Moses the wagons and silver bullion, and all
of the escort except about ten men.

"In my statement of the specie assets of
the Treasury being $288,022.90, I counted the
payment to Major Moses as being $40,000.

"My last payment in Washington, Ga.,
was of eighty-six thousand dollars ($86,000)
in gold coin and gold bullion, to a trusted officer of the navy, taking his receipt for its transmission out of the Confederacy, to be held
for the Treasury Department.   .   .   .

"Judge Reagan and myself left Washington, Ga.

"I found the party, consisting of the President and staff, and a few others, Captain Given
Campbell and twelve of his men, near Sandersville, Ga.   There the President heard
disturbing reports from Mrs. Davis's party,
they fearing attempts to steal their horses by
stragglers, and decided next morning to take
his staff and join her party for a few days.   As
"everything on wheels" was to be abandoned
by him, I remained with my train, the chances
of the capture of which were steadily increasing.   I inquired as to the funds of the staff,
and found that they had only a small amount

of paper currency each, except, perhaps, Colonel F. R. Lubbock, A. D. C., who had, I believe, a little specie of his private funds. Colonel William Preston Johnston told me that the President's purse contained paper money only. I represented to them that they would need money for their supplies en route, and to buy boats in Florida, etc., and that I wished to pay over to them funds to be used for those purposes, and they consented. I paid, with the concurrence of Honorable John H. Reagan, the Acting Secretary of the Treasury, $1,500 in gold each to Colonel John Taylor Wood, A. D. C.; Colonel William Preston Johnston, A. D. C.; Colonel F. R. Lubbock, A. D. C., and Colonel C. E. Thorburn (a naval purchasing agent who was with the party), taking a receipt from each one; but as they were all of the same verbiage, I merely give one, as follows:

"'SANDERSVILLE, GA., May 6, 1865.

"'$1,500. Received of M. H. Clark, Acting Treasurer C. S., fifteen hundred dollars ($1,500) in gold coin, the property of the Confederate States, for transmission abroad, of the safe arrival of which due notice to be given the Secretary of the Treasury.'

"I also paid to each $10 in silver for small uses, from a little executive office fund, which

I had obtained in Danville, Va., by converting my paper when the Treasurer was selling silver there. For this I took no receipt, charging it in my office accounts. I also called up Captain Given Campbell and paid him, for himself and men, $300 in gold, taking the following receipt:

"'Received of M. H. Clark, Acting Treasurer C. S., three hundred dollars ($300) in gold, upon requisition of Colonel John Taylor Wood, A. D. C.

"'GIVEN CAMPBELL,
"'*Captain Company B., Second Kentucky Cavalry, Williams's Brigade.*'

"I then went to Judge Reagan with a bag containing thirty-five hundred dollars ($3,-500) in gold, and asked that he take it in his saddle-bags as an additional fund in case of accidents or separation. He resisted, saying that he was already weighted by some $2,-000 of his own personal funds, which he had brought out from Richmond, Va., in a belt around his person; but after some argument on my part he allowed me to put it in his saddle-bags. The party then were already on horse, and 'Good-by' was said.

"The President's party was captured a few days afterward, and upon their release from

prison several of the party told me that everyone was robbed of all they had, except Colonel F. R. Lubbock, who, after stout resistance and great risk, retained his money, upon
which the party subsisted during their long
imprisonment at Fort Delaware. No gold
was found on President Davis when captured,
for he had none. He could only have received it through me, and I paid him none.
The Treasury train was never with President
Davis's party. They found it at Abbeville,
S. C., rode away and left it there, and rode
away from Washington, Ga., shortly after its
arrival there, while it was being turned over
to me. It will have been noted that the receipts quoted are of two classes—payments
to troops and clerks for their own services;
but to officers of higher rank, like Generals
Bragg and Breckinridge, or to members of
the President's military family, they were for
transmission to a distance, to be afterward accounted for to the Treasury Department.

"The old Confederates brought nothing
out of the war, save honor; for God's sake,
and the precious memory of the dead, let us
preserve that untarnished, and defend it from
slanderous insinuations. To do my part, I
have spoken.   "M. H. CLARK,
              "*Ex-Captain P. A. C. S., and
               ex-Acting Treasurer C. S. A.*"

8 *JEFFERSON DAVIS.*

Although there are many more statements, letters, etc., in my possession respecting General Johnston's charge, and unfortunately lack of space has forced me to condense Colonel Clark's statement too closely, for the same reason I will present but one more, that of Colonel W. Preston Johnston, who was aide to the President, and with it submit the case.

"LOUISIANA STATE UNIVERSITY,
"BATON ROUGE, LA., January 6, 1882.

"GENERAL JOSEPH R. DAVIS, New Orleans, La.

"MY DEAR SIR: Your letter of December 29th, in relation to an alleged interview of General Joseph E. Johnston reflecting upon President Davis, has been received. I was greatly surprised when I first saw the report of the interview; but still more so when I found that General Johnston did not contradict it with an emphatic denial. If I had supposed that its insinuations required disproof, or that they would not be met by witnesses more fully informed than myself, I certainly should have promptly published such knowledge as I had. I rested so secure in the universal confidence of friend and foe in President Davis's integrity and patriotic self-abnegation, that I felt he might, in the future as in the past, oppose his unsullied record against a world of calumny. This unworthy charge has, as I anticipated, called forth detailed statements from a multitude of persons cognizant of the facts, whose concurrent testimony presents an irrefragable record. It has, furthermore, elicited even from partisans of General Johnston a response which evinces that President Davis's honor is as dear to each Southern heart as its own.

"I accompanied President Davis from Richmond till his capture. At Greensborough, N. C., I accepted a loan of $100 in gold, pressed upon me by a friend, as I had only Confederate money. I used this to pay the expenses of our military family. The sum was not quite exhausted when we were captured, as our incidental expenses were small. Having been an inmate of President Davis's house, as well as a member of his military family, I know that he came out of the war a poor man.

"I knew that $20 or $30 were distributed to each soldier. I was told by someone at Washington to draw that amount, but was too much engaged to do so.

"After leaving Washington, when President Davis determined to part company with the wagon train, Major Van Benthuysen, who had charge of it, handed me $1,200 to transport and took my receipt for it. I regarded it as a trust to be employed, if necessary, in getting our party to the Trans-Mississippi Department. I am of the opinion that our party received from Major Van Benthuysen some $5,000 or $6,000, but am not fully advised. This full sum of $1,200 was taken from my holsters by men of the Second Michigan Regiment when I was captured. I am quite sure that President Davis could not have carried much money about him, as he handed me his derringer to carry, being too feeble to endure its weight.

"But there is no ground for argument with any man who impugns the personal integrity of Jefferson Davis. The charge recoils upon the author. For twenty years, President Davis has breasted a storm of obloquy and calumny from every quarter. Yet, to-day, he stands unscathed, the representative man of the most glorious epoch of Southern history, so that in all our part of the Union it is hard to find a man who has done his duty by his country who would not prefer a word of approval from his lips to a crown of gold from the hand of the best of his detractors.

"Of course, no word from me can add anything to the lustre of President Davis's reputation in the eyes of those whose good opinion we chiefly value. But, as I am putting myself on record, I must permit myself to say

that, having stood so near him for four years
that no veil to his character was possible,
even if he had wished it, he has left upon my
mind an ineffaceable image of knightly purity,
of public rectitude, of undeviating patriotism,
and of moral grandeur which I shall forever
cherish as a consolation in adversity and defeat, and as a standard and ideal for myself
and my countrymen.

"I am, my dear sir, very sincerely yours,

"WILLIAM PRESTON JOHNSTON."

VOL. II.—56

CHAPTER LXXXI.

THE PROHIBITION ISSUE.

In 1887 the repose of Mr. Davis's life was grievously disturbed by the question of prohibition, which became a prominent issue in the politics of Texas. A constitutional amendment to prohibit the manufacture or the sale of any intoxicating liquors, including wine, ale, and beer, was to be submitted to popular vote. Scores of letters from Mr. Davis's friends in Texas besought an expression of opinion by him. Mr. Davis declined to answer, as he had no desire to come, even indirectly, before the public again. Finally, after a most urgent letter from his life-long and much-beloved friend, Colonel F. R. Lubbock, he consented to write a letter for publication.

It is as follows:

"Beauvoir, Miss., June 20, 1887.

" Colonel F. R. Lubbock.

" My Dear Friend. . . . My reason for not replying was an unwillingness to en-

ter into a controversy in which my friends in
Texas stood arrayed against each other.

" In departing from the rule heretofore observed, I trust that it will not be an unwar-
rantable intrusion.

" Reared in the creed of Democracy, my
faith in its tenets has grown with its growth,
and I adhere to the maxim that ' the world is
governed too much.'

" When our fathers achieved their independence, the corner-stone of the governments they constructed was individual liberty, and the social organizations they established were not for the surrender, but for the
protection, of natural rights. For this, governments were established deriving their just
powers from the consent of the governed.
This was not to subject themselves to the
will of the majority, as appears from the fact
that each community inserted in its fundamental law a bill of rights to guard the inalienable privileges of the individual.

" There was then a two-fold purpose
in Government: protection and prevention
against trespass by the strong upon the
weak, the many on the few.

" The world had long suffered from the op-
pressions of government under the pretext
of ruling by divine right, and excusing the
invasion into private and domestic affairs on

the plea of paternal care for the morals and good order of the people.

" Our sires rejected all such pretensions, their system being : Government by the people for the people, and resting on the basis of natural inalienable rights. Upon the basis of these general propositions I will briefly answer the inquiry in regard to the prohibition amendment at issue.

" ' Be ye temperate in all things,' was a wise injunction, and would apply to intolerance as well as to drunkenness. That the intemperate use of intoxicating liquors is an evil, few, if any, would deny.

" That it is the root of many social disorders is conceded, but then the question arises, what is the appropriate remedy, and what the present necessity ? To destroy individual liberty and moral responsibility would be to eradicate one evil by the substitution of another, which it is submitted would be more fatal than that for which it was offered as a remedy. The abuse, and not the use, of stimulants, it must be confessed, is the evil to be remedied. Then it clearly follows that action should clearly be directed against the abuse rather than the use. If drunkenness be the cause of disorder and crime, why not pronounce drunkenness itself to be a crime, and attach to it proper and adequate penalties ?

If it be objected that the penalties could not be enforced, that is an admission that popular opinion would be opposed to the law ; but if it be true that juries could not be impanelled who would convict so degraded a criminal as a drunkard, it necessarily follows that a statu tory prohibition against the sale and use of intoxicants would be a dead letter.

" The next branch of the inquiry is as to the present necessity.

" I might appeal to men not as old as my-self to sustain the assertion that the convivial use of intoxicants, and the occurrence of drunkenness, had become less frequent within the last twenty years than it was before. The refining influences of education and Christianity may be credited with this result. Why not allow these blessed handmaidens of virtue and morality to continue unembarrassed in their civilizing work. The parties to this discussion in your State have no doubt brought forward the statistical facts in regard to the effect produced in other States by this effort to control morals by legislation, and I will not encumber this letter by any reference to those facts.

" You have already provision for local pro-hibition. If it has proven the wooden horse in which a disguised enemy to State sover-eignty as the guardian of individual liberty was introduced, then let it be a warning that the progressive march would probably be from village to State, and from State to United States.

"A Governmental supervision and paternity, instead of the liberty the heroes of 1776 left as a legacy to their posterity. Impelled by the affection and gratitude I feel for the people of Texas, and the belief that a great question of American policy is involved in the issue you have before you, the silence I had hoped to observe has been broken. If the utterance shall avail anything for good, it will compensate me for the objurgations with which I shall doubtless be pursued by the followers of popularism of the day.

" I hope the many who have addressed me letters of inquiry on the same subject will accept this as an answer, though somewhat long delayed. Faithfully yours,

" JEFFERSON DAVIS."

" I certify that the foregoing is a true copy of the original received by me, and now in my possession. " F. R. LUBBOCK.

"July 23, 1887."

This letter, widely published, aroused the antagonism of the partisans of prohibition, who knew that it would probably result, as later it did, in their defeat at the polls.

Shortly after the letter was published, it was announced that Mr. Davis favored a pro-hibition policy, because at a camp meeting he had worn a temperance badge and compli-mented one of the lady orators!

In a letter to Reverend W. M. Leftwich, dated Beauvoir, August 24, 1887, Mr. Davis thus disposed of this absurd electioneering trick:

" Though we may disagree as to the best remedies against intemperance, we cannot differ as to the desirability of its suppression, and I would be least of all willing that you should attribute to me such laxity of opinion as would permit a change of position without anything to justify it.

" My letter to Governor Lubbock of July 20th, I must insist, is too plain to be of differ-ent construction. Four days after it was written I went to the sea-shore camp ground, and after the morning service was invited to dinner, and sat next to Mrs. Chapin at the table. She was to lecture in the afternoon, and very naturally led our conversation to the subject of which she is a zealous advo-cate. Agreeing as we did in regard to the evil of intemperance, we differed widely as to the proper and practicable remedies. At the close of the dinner I felt that I had been more

positive in my remarks to her than was needful, considering that my antagonist was a lady.
A friend who sat very near to us subsequently told me that I was rather hard. I could
only say that I did not mean to be discourteous, though anxious to be exactly understood.
In the afternoon I listened attentively to the
lecture ; it was an eloquent description of the
sufferings of women and children as a consequence of the drunkenness of husbands and
fathers. No specific remedy was. proposed,
and after she had closed her lecture and left
the pulpit, I congratulated her on her address,
and expressed my entire concurrence with the
sentiments she had uttered. My letter to
Governor Lubbock, written four days previously, was fresh in my mind ; it conveyed my
deliberate opinion, and I did not *then*, nor
do I *now*, see any conflict between the sentiments of that letter and those which Mrs.
Chapin had more forcibly expressed.

" Pleased at my congratulations, she asked
me to write my name in her book. Not
knowing what all this might imply, I declined. She offered me the badge she wore ;
this I declined also, because I did not know
the creed and canons of the order, and could
not accept its emblem—declining, however,
with a pleasant courtesy and deference which
is habitual with me to a lady.

" She had learned from Miss Willard the sympathy my wife felt with the efforts of the Woman's Christian Temperance Union, and proposed that I should take the badge to Mrs. Davis. I made no objection, and she transferred the badge she wore to the lapel of my coat. I wore it to my home and delivered it with the message to my wife, who acknowledged it in a personal letter to Mrs. Chapin, which she published.

" I saw no evil, and hoped much good, from the measure of local option by which public opinion and law would go hand in hand in a homogeneous group of people; but when it was proposed to extend such narrow sumptuary measures as were proposed in the Texas amendment, and instead of a village, town, or magistrate's beat, to embrace a whole State; and, further, when I heard that petitions were in circulation for prohibiting enactments by the Congress of the United States, there loomed up a gigantic monster before which the liberties our fathers left us could offer but a vain resistance. As it is, the law and the Federal Administration are bound to prefer Union soldiers in all selections for Federal office. First we were to have sumptuary legislation, dictated by the majority against us, a permanent minority in the Union; and, to enforce it, domiciliary visits by strangers to our people.

"You and all others who remember the events in the closing years of the war and the period of reconstruction, will require no words to enforce the horrors of a condition which should expose our people to spies, informers, and arbitrary power. The influence of science and religion have brought the fruit of increased morality, and in its train a temperance far exceeding that of any period historically recorded. Why not trust to these and like means for moral reform?

"Respectfully yours,

"JEFFERSON DAVIS."

Among the criticisms evoked by this letter was an address at Brookhaven, Miss., by a bishop of the Methodist Church South, which was reported by the *Times-Democrat* of New Orleans. Mr. Davis responded to this address in an open letter to the reverend orator, for which I have space for a few extracts only.

"You have expressed sorrow," Mr. Davis wrote, "because I answered the inquiry of a friend for my opinion on a political question, and employed many kind and complimentary expressions in regard to me ; but in view of your persistence in unjustified assailment, your compliments seem like the garlands with which, in the olden time, a sacrificial offering

was decorated. Now it is my turn to grieve, not for you personally, but that a dignitary of the Methodist Church South should have left the pulpit and the Bible to mount the political rostrum and plead the higher law of prohibition—the substitution of force for free will, moral responsibility, the obligation to do unto others as we would be done by, and the brotherly love taught by the meek and lowly Jesus whom we adore. In this I see the forbidden union of Church and State. My grief is real and relates to both.

"Disfranchised as I be, the love of my life for the Constitution and the liberties it was formed to secure, remains as ardent in age as it was in youth. 'The Methodist Church South' has been to me the object of admiration and grateful affection, because of its fidelity to principle despite the pressure of wealth and power, by the good of its underpaid ministers, who have gone along the highways to penetrate unfrequented regions, and there 'preach the gospel to the poor.' Often has my memory recalled the prophetic vision of Bishop Marvin. Will it be fulfilled by introducing politics into the organization of the Church he nobly illustrated? . . .

"Fanaticism looks through a reversed telescope, minimizing everything save its special object. What though one should point a prohibitionist to the civilizing, harmonizing, peace-securing, comfort-giving effects of commerce among the nations? If he thought it interfered with his peculiar 'ism,' would he not probably answer by irrelevant catchwords? The time was when sumptuary laws embraced what should be worn and eaten. If we begin the march of retrogression, where will it stop? If, as already proposed, there should be Federal laws to enforce the prohibition policy, your recollection of war and reconstruction days should enable you to anticipate the doings of an army of spies, informers, and deputy-marshals making domiciliary visits to insure the observance of the law. The moral decay which would inevitably result from such a condition, needs no portrayal. To me it seems the plain duty of every citizen who loves the liberty our sires bequeathed to us, to check the scheme before it acquires dangerous proportions. I hold it to be one of the natural rights of man to do as he pleases with his own, provided he inflicts no injury on another. To protect the use and prevent the abuse of that right is the necessity of social existence; to give adequate power, and yet efficiently to guard against the perversions of the grant, is the problem which the wisdom of ages has but partially solved. Hence the maxim, 'Eternal vigilance is the price of liberty.'

" There are surely better remedies for offence against the peace and good order of society than such a departure from our principles of constitutional liberty and community independence as would be Federal legislation to enforce a sumptuary policy. Father Mathew found reason and moral suasion such potent factors that his good work was not of a day, but lives after him in some who took the pledge, and others who have joined the temperance societies. These and other causes have so acted upon public opinion and social habits, as to give the prohibition movement the possibilities it now has, and could not have enjoyed in the not remote past. Why not trust to religion and education, to refinement and science, aided by the laws which have had the sanction of experience, to prevent the formation of habits of intemperance, rather than, at the sacrifice of personal liberty and moral responsibility, to undertake by coercive means the reformation of the drunkard? The former may be preachable; the latter, by such methods, is hopeless.

" In the letter to Governor Lubbock, I admitted intemperance to be a great evil; but is it the only one that afflicts society and calls for more active remedies? The opium habit is reported by statistics to be increasing, and, sad to relate, that its greatest ravages are

among the gentler and finer sex. Laws exist, but fail to prevent the abuse. In this,
prohibition does not prohibit. Are there not
other means? Is there no Peter to preach a
crusade for the redemption of woman, the
mother of Jesus? of woman, the last at the
cross, and first at the sepulchre? of woman,
the consoling friend in the hospitals, the leader in all the charities? Is there no St. George
to stay the hydra that is poisoning the salt of
the earth? I do not deprecate the effort to
abate the evil of intemperance, but here is an
evil more deleterious to mind and body, and
why, it is asked, is the field unoccupied to
which humanity and manhood are both calling for laborers?

"Atheism reviles, and free thought, namely
want of thought, denies the truth of revelation,
and in the broad day scoffs at the plan of salvation. The month in which you made your
address is reputed to have had an exceptionally large number of assassinations. The
newspapers have many notices of burglaries,
robberies, rapes, and infanticides. Divorces
are shamefully frequent. The war between
labor and capital gives cause for gravest apprehensions. The colossal wealth of the few
grows in geometrical proportions, while the
toiling millions plod on their weary way.
Are all these and other evils, crimes, and mis-

fortunes not enumerated due to one cause, or is the one idea a universal absorbent?"

As these excerpts clearly convey Mr. Davis's view of the issue involved, it does not seem necessary to give any further account of the controversy. It ended in the complete overthrow of the prohibitory movement in Texas, but the disturbance created by the abuse of him impaired his health, now quite feeble, and grieved him greatly. The Methodist bishop, followed by many of his clergy, attacked him, and some of them made him the theme of sermons. As he always admired the Methodists and worshipped with them when not at his own church, this added to his annoyance, not for the sake of the individuals who made the attack, but for the body of pious people before whom he felt himself wantonly misrepresented.

CHAPTER LXXXII.

THE EAST INDIA FLEET.

Of course, in the long years after the war, there were many recitations of Mr. Davis's shortcomings, given by one or other of those who thought a mistake had been made when he was asked to preside over the Confederate States. One of these is his alleged failure to purchase the E. I. fleet, which was revamped in 1889 and given to the journals of the day.

Judge Roman, in his book entitled " Military Operations of General Beauregard," states that :

" While journeying from Charleston to Montgomery, General Beauregard met Mr. W. L. Trenholm, whose father, George A. Trenholm, was a partner in the great firm of John Frazer & Co., of Charleston and Liverpool. This gentleman, as he informed General Beauregard, was the bearer of important propositions from the English branch of their house to the Confederate Government, for the purchase of ten large and powerful steamers, just built in England for the East Indian Company, which, no longer needing them,

Jefferson Davis on the Gallery of Beauvoir House

was desirous of finding a purchaser; the
ships were to be properly manned and fitted
out, and sent to the Confederate States,
thence to export enough cotton to pay for
them, and as much more as should be required to provide for the armament and equip-
ment of our forces. Such a plan, it was
thought by the Frazer house, could easily be
carried out. The United States Government
would require time to collect and rendezvous
its fleet, the inadequacy of which was well
known; and no fear need, therefore, be entertained of its ability, at that time, to enforce
a blockade of the Southern ports; an effective
blockade could be prevented. After a certain
number of voyages with large cargoes of cotton, for the purposes already mentioned,
these steamers might be converted into
cruisers, and employed to impede and destroy
Northern commerce."

General Beauregard, thoroughly impressed
with the incalculable benefits to be derived
from the adoption of such a project, promised
Mr. Trenholm to use his utmost endeavors in
furtherance of the measures that gentleman
was sent to advocate. In a letter to General
Beauregard, dated Charleston, September 18,
1878, Mr. Trenholm says: "This I remember well, that you warmly supported the proposition, and used your influence in aid of its

being brought before the Cabinet, which was
accomplished." But neither General Beauregard's earnest advice, nor the strong and cogent reasons given by Mr. Trenholm were of
any avail. The Confederate Government, under the erroneous belief that the war would
be a short one, declined entertaining the proposals made to it. "No discussion took
place in my presence," says Mr. Trenholm, in
the letter already alluded to, " but from questions put to me, I have always been under the
impression that few, if any, of those present"
(meaning the President and members of the
Cabinet) "realized at all the scope and importance of the measures laid before them."
Thus was closed upon the Confederacy a
door—then wide-open—through which might
have entered that material assistance, those
sinews of war, the want of which all the heroism of our troops and the endurance and
self-sacrifice of our people could not remedy.

The New York *Sun* of November 17, 1878,
contained what purported to be an interview
with General Beauregard, in which he said
he had gone with a messenger of Messrs.
Frazer & Co. to the Confederate Secretary of
War, and urged him to buy the fleet.

Mr. W. L. Trenholm wrote to Mr. Davis
December 18, 1878, of the alleged proposi-

tion made to the Confederate Government by
Mr. Trenholm.

Mr. Davis's Answer.

"One should speak with diffidence of
events which passed seventeen years ago, and
hence I should have preferred not being appealed to for my recollection of this matter.

"The first application was made to me in
February last. I enclose my reply to that
(copy) and also copy of my letter to General
Beauregard of September 18th. These letters have been read by Mr. Memminger, and
he tells me that only one matter was brought
before the Cabinet, viz., the proposition to
subsidize steamers, to keep open communication with the West Indies.

"Since the interview with Mr. Memminger, I have taxed my memory to recall what
passed, and it seems to me that, whether
it was before the Cabinet or not, the other
proposal, viz., to purchase certain steamers,
was spoken of at the cabinet meeting at which
I was present by invitation. I think I remember someone, possibly it was General Toombs,
making a remark that showed that he had
confused the two measures altogether, and
thought the proposition was for the Government to buy the steamers, and then subsidize

a company to manage them, or something of that sort.

"This is a vague and indistinct recollection, however, and I merely mention it because the same incidents may have made an impression upon the others.

"As well as I can remember, I spoke in favor of both measures. Mr. Memminger thinks otherwise, but subsequent effort has failed to elicit any other recollections on my part.

"Application having been made to others who were in a position to know all the circumstances of the alleged proposal to buy the fleet, so positively asserted by Judge Roman, the following answers were received. All show that their recollections are also 'vague and indistinct,' of events of such great importance that, had they been accomplished, the 'door,' as Roman says, 'would not have been closed upon the Confederacy, through which might have entered those sinews of war, the want of which proved fatal to the cause.'

"Honorable L. P. Walker, ex-Confederate Secretary of War, wrote:

"'I have read the article in the New York *Sun* which you enclosed me in your letter to me of the second instant. I do not remember the interview with me mentioned by General Beauregard, nor that any proposition was

submitted to the Confederate Government for
the sale to it of any steamers of the character
stated here. If any such proposition was
made, it has passed from my recollection.'

"To a like inquiry, addressed to Mr. Memminger, ex-Secretary of the Confederate
Treasury, he replied on November 27, 1878.

"'CHARLESTON, S. C., November 27, 1878.

"'HONORABLE JEFFERSON DAVIS,

"Beauvoir, Miss.

"'MY DEAR SIR: I have no recollection of
having heard of the proposition referred to by
General Beauregard. I remember my having
written to Mr. Trenholm, one of the firm of
Jno. Frazer & Co., to come on to Montgomery to present the advantages of establishing
a depot for cotton and munitions of war at
Bermuda, and some station in the West Indies, and that he came on and appeared before the Cabinet, warmly advocated this plan,
and that it met with my cordial approval; but
it was not approved by the Cabinet.

"'I remember nothing of any proposal to
purchase the steamers of the India Company.
Mr. William Trenholm remembers his appearance before the Cabinet in behalf of the
scheme above mentioned. His address was
confined to that scheme, but he says he made
the proposition to the Secretary of War and

to Mr. Mallory, the Secretary of the Navy, to purchase the steamers of the Oriental Company, but that they had many grounds of objection to the purchase, such as the great draught of water, which would prevent their entering Southern ports, their construction of iron, and the want of money. He has no recollection of ever having spoken to me or you on the subject, nor did it enter into the statement made before the Cabinet; and as to myself, I have no recollection of having been consulted by either Mr. Mallory or the Secretary of War.

> " ' Very truly yours,
> " ' C. G. MEMMINGER.' "

In a letter to Captain Bullock, C. S. N., written by Mr. Charles K. Prioleau, senior partner in the Liverpool firm of Frazer, Trenholm & Co., and dated Burges June 21, 1884, he says:

". . . . As regards the ten steamers, I thought you knew about them. They are a part of the East India Company's fleet, the *Golden Fleece, Jason, Hydaspes*, etc.; they were offered to me at the beginning of the war, before you came over, and before the Queen's proclamation. My idea was that, if they could have been armed and got out, they would have swept away every vestige of a Federal blockader then upon the water. Frazer, Trenholm & Co. had not then been appointed agents of the Government, and I did not offer these vessels to the Government, but I mentioned them in a private letter to Mr. G. A. Trenholm, leaving it to his discretion to put it before them.

" As a matter of fact, I never got any reply to this letter, and never knew that the ships had even been proposed to the Government till long after the war. No further inquiries were ever made me concerning them from any quarter. About nine or ten years (or perhaps not quite so much) ago, General Beauregard wrote me, saying that he was engaged upon his history, that he had heard about these steamers through William Trenholm, who had referred him to me for the particulars, and asked me if I would give him a statement, and allow him to mention my name as to my part of the transaction; to which I willingly consented, and gave him just the facts stated above. *Of course, I know now that the enterprise would have been impossible*, but we did not know anything for certain then ; and any opinion of mine would have been that of a layman, and on its face valueless ; therefore, when I heard no more I naturally concluded either that Mr. Tren-

holm had not thought it worth while to propose the undertaking, or that the Government
had been advised against it by their competent officers ; and there is no doubt now that
they were quite right not to risk so large a sum
of money on so doubtful an enterprise, even if
they could readily have raised it. It is, however, a little strange that, if the Government
knew of these ships at the time you left, they
did not instruct you to look at them. On the
whole, I am inclined to think that they were
never offered to the Government at all, but
William Trenholm knew of them from having
access to his father's correspondence. . . .
" Very truly." *

With this letter I dismiss the charge of
criminal neglect or supine disregard, on the
part of the President and his cabinet, of favorable opportunity or of our danger, as " vague
and indefinite."

The pain inflicted on Mr. Davis in his old
age and weak health by arraignments made
against him by his own people, was relieved
very much when he received an expression of
regard from either North or South. He was
gratified to learn, by a letter from a friend in
Maine, his name had not, as he had been informed, been expunged from the honorary

membership of Bowdoin College, in Maine. He appreciated gratefully the action of the officers of the college, and answered their kind letter only a few months before his death. He was also much pleased at being made a member of the Kappa Sigma Society, which was done in a particularly handsome manner. It was the society of which our son was a much-lamented and beloved brother.

CHAPTER LXXXIII.

GENERAL RANSOM'S REMINISCENCES OF MR. DAVIS.

GENERAL ROBERT RANSOM was invited to send a reminiscence of my husband, who admired him as a soldier and trusted him as a friend, and he responded as follows:

"On July 5, 1856, I first met Mr. Davis. He was then Secretary of War, and I a lieutenant of cavalry visiting Washington for the purpose of marrying my first wife, a young lady resident in that city and an intimate friend of Secretary and Mrs. Davis. I had been in the city a few days and had not paid my respects to the Secretary of War. On the evening of the 5th, the Secretary and Mrs. Davis held a reception, and I presented myself, and was, with the other company, received with the elegance and grace which characterized the host and hostess; but the Secretary remarked, with an air of playful reproof, 'Young gentleman, I expected to have seen you before.' Turning to Mrs. Davis, I said: 'Madam, do you think even the Secretary of War has a right to more than one visit from a young fellow on leave of absence, who is here to marry his sweetheart day after to-morrow, when she and I both hope to see you and receive your congratulations ? ' He instantly replied : ' Go to your sweetheart and tell her, with my love, I am her friend and shall be to her husband, if he be worthy of so noble a woman.' To the day of his death he was true to the voluntary promise made upon the eve of my marriage, more than thirty years before. One among innumerable instances of tenacious memory and inviolable good faith shown through a life as full of extreme vicissitude as falls to the lot of man.

"During the exciting period of ' Kansas Troubles,' in the autumn of 1856, I was again in Washington, and happened to be in company with Mr. Davis and other prominent men at a social gathering. The subject of the dispersion by Colonel E. V. Sumner, of the First Cavalry, of the ' Topeka Legislature,' was broached, and Sumner was criticised by someone for not taking some of his officers with him into the hall where it had assembled, as that fact had been noticed by the press of the country. I was with Colonel Sumner that day, July 4, 1856, at Topeka, and was his adjutant. I was asked by one of the persons present as to the correctness of the statement regarding Sumner's going alone into the hall, and I substantiated the fact. Mr. Davis, in answer to some adverse criticism upon Sumner, promptly replied : ' Brave and honest men are not suspicious, and Edwin Sumner is as brave as Cæsar and honest as Cato.' This illustrates Mr. Davis's fidelity to truth and justice, regardless of sectional birth or habitation. All knew Sumner was from Massachusetts. Mr. Davis appointed him senior colonel of the four new regiments which were added to the army in - March, 1855.

" Upon reaching Richmond, in the summer of 1861, after resigning the commission I held in the army, I delivered to President Davis a message from a young officer whom I had left upon the frontier. The young officer claimed Kentucky as his home. The message was to the effect that, if Mr. Davis would ask him to join the Confederacy, and give him high rank in the army, he, the young officer, would promptly repair to Richmond. Mr. Davis's response to me was prompt and emphatic, and to the effect: ' I know the young man well, and have long been his and his family's friend. If his State join the Confederacy, he will surely follow her fortunes ; if he voluntarily casts his lot with the Southern Confederacy, he shall have the recognition his character and ability deserve ; but I shall not make the least overture to him, as he ought to know from direct messages which I am aware he must have received from me.' The young man remained in the Federal army, but won no particular distinction. Mr. Davis has been traduced as a teacher of treason; this incident proves how far above the traitor he was by nature and arts.

"In October, 1861, I carried to Richmond the first full regiment of cavalry, the First North Carolina, which had reached that city. We were there a few days, and the regiment was reviewed by the President. It numbered about eight hundred present, was admirably mounted, and, for our facilities, well equipped. The appearance and drill were more than creditable for cavalry not three months in the ranks, and the President, at the close of the review, accompanied by Colonel Chilton and some other gentlemen, advanced to me, and after congratulations and compliments, said in words nearly as follows: 'If we had had this regiment at Manassas, Washington would have been ours.' It is well known that the Confederate army, at the battle of the first Manassas, was without cavalry, excepting an irregular company or two. Colonel Chilton afterward spoke of the remark of the President, as demonstrating the fact that Mr. Davis realized the demoralization which possessed the Federal army on the evening of the battle of the first Manassas. . . .

" In April, 1864, I was called from East Tennessee to Richmond by telegram, 'for other and distant service,' but a day or two after my arrival at Richmond was assigned to the command of the city and its outer defences, extending as far as Petersburg. It is needless to give the reasons for this change in the purposes of the President. For the next two months, hardly any forty-eight hours passed that I did not meet the President by appointment at his office or at his home; and often night and day, when upon the outer lines among and commanding troops Mr. Davis came to me to confer and always to encourage. It would run beyond the limit of my purpose, were I to detail all that memory and memoranda now supply of those many interviews; but that the world may know both the private life and public character of this singularly illustrious man, I shall narrate circumstantially some events that cannot fail to instruct and interest those who own truth. . . .

" The day after the combat at Yellow Tavern, near Richmond, when Stuart met Sheridan and received his mortal wound, I had hurried from the vicinity of Drury's Bluff to the defensive lines north of Richmond with two small brigades of infantry, and by sunrise, or before, confronted Sheridan, who had dispersed our cavalry. It was an hour to try every Confederate present. Mr. Davis was upon the field. No one could realize the situation more clearly than he. He never appeared to greater advantage. Calm, self-contained, cheerful, hopeful, determined, he was an inspiration to every soul who saw him. He did not once interfere, suggest, or order anything, but he was then demonstrating his readiness, and I have often thought his purpose, to assume control should the desperate moment arrive. He was kind enough to thank me then, and many times subsequently to refer most flatteringly to me for the operations of that day, and my service before Richmond during the spring and early summer of 1864.

"There was no individual who was more familiar with the topography of Richmond and its vicinity than Mr. Davis. He had made himself acquainted with every road and by-path, and with the streams and farms for twenty miles around. Fond of horseback exercise, he rode often and frequently late into the night. Sometimes till sunrise or later the next morning in going over the lines and getting personal knowledge of localities and facts which might prove useful.

"I recall very vividly the last visit he made me upon such an occasion. It was on the night

908

of June 11, 1864. I lay in bivouac a few
hundred yards from Bottom's Bridge, over
the Chickahominy, east of Richmond. Grant
was then moving down the east bank of that
stream for the purpose of making connection
with Butler across the James. About two or
three o'clock in the morning, I felt a light
hand on my shoulder as I lay asleep with my
head on my saddle, and started to rise. I recognized the voice of the President, in a low
tone. ' Do not rise,' said he. ' I know you
have but just fallen asleep, I give you an
early call. Grant will not attempt to cross
here, he is planning to do so below ; to-day
you will be relieved here. I have to send you
with Early to meet Hunter, who is devastating
the valley. Your task will be hard to organize the wild cavalry which has just been defeated at Rock Fish Gap, and that good soldier, but unhappy man, " Grumble Jones,"
killed. Make your arrangements. You will
get the order to-day.'

   " Mr. Davis was a very hospitable man, and
his home was a charming resort to those who
could appreciate the simple and unpretentious
cordiality which marked every member of his
family. Often I partook of that hospitality
while he was a resident of Richmond, and
since his return from Europe. The same
urbanity and gentleness prevailed at his home,

whether as President, Cabinet officer, in wealth or power, or as the private citizen having the burden of a nation's woes. That the world may learn it from the pen of one who has experienced his kindness under almost all circumstances, I take the liberty to invade the privacy of his home on the occasion of my last meal at his table while he was President of the Confederacy. In the fall of 1864, I was ordered to the command of Charleston and vicinity, and received my orders in Richmond. The President asked me to breakfast. I went to a somewhat late one, and found that I and a lady guest had to entertain ourselves for a few minutes waiting for the host, who had not retired, as Mrs. Davis told me, until sunrise. Soon Mrs. Davis led the way to the breakfast-room, seating me by her, while Mr. Davis placed the lady at his right. The grace was said as usual. Our breakfast was simple in the extreme, and there was anything but profusion. Mrs. Davis poured some hot Rio coffee, Java and Mocha were then only known from memory. Mr. Davis had before him a dish of rather fat bacon, cut very thin and fried crisp. The neat man-servant handed cold baker's bread, and brought in corn batter cakes, while a very small plate of butter, the gift of a lady friend, graced the centre of the table. Such was the breakfast of the President of the Confederacy. He possibly might have fared somewhat more sumptuously, for he was the recipient of some things from friends, but whatever of such supplies was received, or which he could procure, was sent to the soldiers in hospitals, whose needs he too well knew and never forgot. Mr. Davis could not have lived upon luxuries or enjoyed abundance when he knew his countrymen, standing as living walls between his home and a powerful enemy, were less well provided than himself.

"In personal appearance and traits he was very attractive. His figure was erect and graceful, though spare; his carriage easy, alert, and dignified; his voice singularly clear and gentle. He was very approachable. So many pictures of his features are preserved that they need no description. His faculties of observation, naturally very fine, were highly cultivated. He was an excellent swordsman. His success as a planter showed his practical capacity in ordinary matters. He was fond of domestic animals, and few men were better judges of all classes of them. He believed in the thorough-bred in a horse, though I do not know that he ever raised them to any extent. With the forest trees of the various regions of our country he was well acquainted, and was, perhaps, the equal of John Randolph as a geographer of his own country. Mr. Davis had not only read of the arts and sciences, of trades and commerce, and all that pertains to them, but was so conversant with such subjects that he was at home among experts in all branches. He must have been for the greater part of his life a hard student, and I think contracted the habit of 'burning midnight oil,' for he was a late riser. His memory was nearly infallible. A person whom he had met casually he could call by name years after, and convince the party he knew him by recalling instantly some incident of the meeting. He was a devout man, modest and humble in his relations to his Maker, without a tinge of the Pharisee.

"At his table he ' said grace,' or ' asked a blessing,' first seating himself, and then with bowed head, in silence making the invocation. When he lived in Memphis, I sometimes met at Mr. Davis's residence the venerable and Reverend Dr. Wheat, between whom and Mr. Davis there existed the sweetest relations. As together, on one occasion, we left his residence, Dr. Wheat said to me, ' If that man were a member of the Romish Church, he would be canonized as a saint, and his sufferings for our and the South's sake should forever enshrine him in our hearts as our vicarious sacrifice.'

" Of the relations which he established in his family in the position of husband and father, I am incompetent to write in the language befitting the parties concerned. Eulogy would be exhausted without exaggerating what seemed to the friend and guest the perfection of domestic existence. Knightly chivalry marked the tenderest attentions to wife and daughters, while with his sons he was a loving mentor and wise companion. An incident I witnessed will illustrate more than one characteristic. During one of my several visits to Memphis, when I was always a guest for longer or shorter periods, I was at dinner with the family. Just after being seated, and I think other company was present, an unusual commotion was heard in the passage leading to the dining-room, and almost instantly in rushed the bright, fair-haired Willie, his youngest son, a lad of eight or ten years, followed by half a dozen or more about his size and age, whom Willie had brought in to dinner. He rapidly told of some gardening or other work he had in hand, and which he wished finished at a certain time, and not being able to accomplish it so soon himself, he had gone into the streets and gathering his very promiscuous party of laborers, completed the task voluntarily assumed, and now wanted dinner for his co-workers.

I could easily discern the feelings of the father; with great cheerfulness and an expression of pride and satisfaction, Mr. Davis aided in preparing for his fine boy's guests, and with delicate tact and discriminating conversation soon had each little fellow as comfortable and unembarrassed as if on a picnic. The son had inherited from his parents high qualities and capacity, thus early indicated. The grave soon closed over the sons of the great father. To attempt to draw the veil from sacred griefs becomes not one who felt the agony such losses entailed, and who mourns the death of our South's greatest hero, and has wept with the sorrow of a bereaved son that the truest friend, the bravest soldier, the knightliest gentleman, and humblest Christian of our land no longer lives, the exemplar of all that makes men noble."

CHAPTER LXXXIV.

LIKE most people of keen perceptions, incisive wit, and high ideal standards, Mr. Davis was inclined to satire, and in his younger days indulged this propensity, never cruelly, but often to his own injury. His sense of the ludicrous was intense, his powers of observation were close, and his memory was phenomenal. He seldom forgot a face, name, or circumstance. If he travelled over a country once, he knew the topography of that part which he traversed, the trees that indicated the character of the soil, noted the grasses indigenous there, observed the kinds of domestic stock preferred, the general characteristics of the people, their occupations, their sources of wealth, and even their means of water-supply. With a mind ever alert and discriminating, he took to himself, never to be relinquished, all that nature and art spread out before him.

Always delicately soigné in his own person, he observed the lack of neatness in others, and was prone to see in it an indication of mental

characteristics. Once when describing a poor
man who came to him for a loan, he said, " He
was miserably poor, but his threadbare coat
was brushed and his copperas linsey trousers and his horny hands were clean, so I
gave him the money." Mr. Davis observed
the dress of ladies very closely, but could not
describe one which displeased him except by
saying, " It was very high-colored, outsetting,
and full of tags, and you could see her afar
off," by which he meant there were flying rib-
bons, and she had a " loud " expression.

There were few more shrewd judges of
character than he, but he was apt to be misled
by some of the qualities he admired and infer
the rest, and was thus sometimes mistaken in
his judgment. He was himself so consistent
that he could not understand the incongruities
of others. If he found a man sincere in one
thing, or the opposite, it was impossible for
him to believe that, swayed by a powerful motive, the reverse action could be adopted without all he attributed to him being forfeited ;
consequently, after every defection of a friend
he suffered keenly. Faithful in his lightest
profession of regard, and retentive of his
friendships, he was deeply wounded by the du-
plicity of those he had trusted—not expressed-
ly bitter, for pride and reticence, both of which
were unusually developed in him, prevented his

asking for sympathy by showing his wound—
but some keen satire, or general reflection
upon the faithlessness of men, would attest
his discovery, or the remark, " All men are
not built like martyrs," would show his contempt.

He noticed every shade of expression that
passed athwart the faces of those with whom
he held intercourse. Once, when a general
came to him to set forth his superior officer's
mistakes, and ended his long story with, " It
is only a matter of patriotic interest, of course
there is nothing personal to me involved,"
he was bowed out civilly and Mr. Davis said :
" He came to ask for General ——'s place."
On my expressing astonishment, he laughed
and answered, " I do not mean that he said so,
only he seemed to be too full of expedients to
gain a victory, and to suffer too much over the
General's neglect of his opportunities." In a
few days a newspaper contained the criticism
Mr. Davis had listened to, with a suggestion
of the name of the critic to fill the place not
likely to be vacant.

No young man ever came to him with a
tale of injustice, or sorrowful experience,
without finding a sympathetic listener and,
while he had the means, a liberal contributor
to necessities which had been implied or
stated.

It was a rule of his house that no one should be turned away hungry, however undeserving or unattractive. A child's cry of pain would make him quiver from head to foot. A tear on the cheek of one in his house, or a downcast look, caused him to inquire into the trouble, and sometimes his attempts to do justice were embarrassing enough.

On the following page will be found the back of a letter asking for assistance, the endorsement on which he never expected to meet any eye but his own.

Sometimes, when he was reading his mail I heard a groan and a muttered exclamation, "Poor creature, and my hands are tied!" It was always some appeal for help over which he was distressing himself.

He was excitable, but not petulant, easily persuaded where to yield did not involve a principle, and was more stern toward himself than to any other. His methods of showing sympathy were sometimes eccentric. Once in the street, a gentleman beggar asked him for the twentieth time for twenty-five cents. He took his arm and walked a square, remonstrating in this wise : " It mortifies me to see you lowered in this way. I will give you five dollars, and you can let me off with twenty applications, and feel more comfortable."

To his family he was niggardly in nothing,

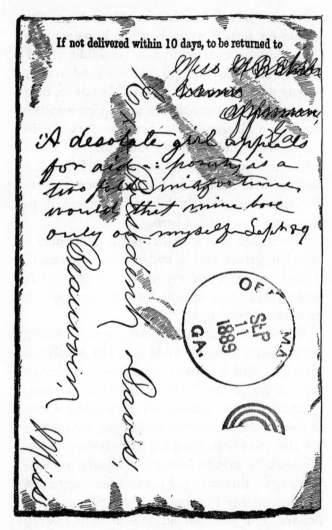

but his personal self-denial was unusual;
keenly alive to the pleasures of luxury, he

denied himself all that our love permitted him to relinquish.   He rarely made known a personal want.

His piety was of the kind that vaunts not itself, but was the rule of his life.   He forbore with those beneath him until patience ceased to be a virtue ; but with his equals he asserted and enforced his rights.   He was extremely reticent, always saying less than he thought, but was careful to convey the exact truth in the little he expressed.   He was courteous in the extreme to everyone, and his servants used commonly to express their appreciation of this by saying he was "a very fine gentleman."

In portraying the character of Mr. Davis it is difficult to place a just estimate upon his noble qualities without appearing rather as a panegyrist than a witness.

Forty-three years of intimate companionship, from the beginning of his political career until the end, left me with the profoundest respect for his unswerving mental and moral integrity, his stanch adherence to principle, his self-immolating devotion to duty, his calm, invincible courage, his wide sympathy with mankind, and his unfeigned reverence for his Creator.

In the greatest effort of his life, Mr. Davis failed from the predominance of some of these noble qualities.

Mrs. Mary A. Greer, of Mississippi, explained the causes of his failure in the following noble lines:

> " He failed because he was so great ; his duty
> Lay in Presidency, not Dictatorship.
> And he was one that would not enter Paradise
> By treachery, fraud, and usurpation.
> He held his lightest promise as a sacred thing,
> How much more his oath of office sworn.
> The law had circumscribed and set his bounds,
> The law he'd sworn to keep he would not break.
> He had within him strength to cope with all
> The fearful issues of the time, the stern volition,
> Steadfast purpose, and the ceaseless watch ;
> Strength to gather up the scattered slender means,
> To bind, to weld, to rivet firm in one,
> And name the force so formed success.
> All this within him lay, but power to do
> This was withheld, and power not freely
> Given he scorned to rudely seize.
> Patient sorrowing, much enduring soul,
> God strengthen thee ; in all his strength,
> Christ comfort thee ; in all his love,
> Angels tend thee ; in all thy ways
> Nobly thou hast wrought and overcome."

His foresight showed him the risks of secession, and his sincerity bade him proclaim them, while his courage urged him to attempt resistance to wrong against the world in arms, and his piety held out the hope that God would miraculously shield us. He cheerfully resigned everything and asserted a principle which, however it may now be derided, he knew was vital to the liberties of mankind.

No man doubted then that his election to the office of President of the United States would be the swift reward of his proving recreant to the interests of his own people ; but he sacrificed the labors and ambitions of his life to the maintenance of his faith. His family who survive him were engulfed in the common disaster and utter ruin, but are proud of his record, and hopefully await the verdict of posterity.

CHAPTER LXXXV.

THE END OF A NOBLE LIFE, AND A NATION'S SOR-
ROW OVER ITS LOSS.

MR. DAVIS's apparent feebleness had been accompanied by enough increase in weight to encourage my hopes of his health improving. He never stooped, but retained his fine soldierly carriage, and always walked with a light, firm step, and with apparent ease; his voice was sweet and sonorous as ever. A slight deafness was the only evidence of age. His eyes became so strong he frequently read without glasses. His mind was wonderfully alert, and he read and enjoyed newspapers, reviews, poetry, and fiction, and remembered what he read to a wonderful degree. He talked about the topics of the day with the fresh sympathy of a young man, and made many witty and wise comments upon them. He had an immense correspondence, the answers to which he dictated to me, and seemed, except on a few occasions, not to feel the labor.

He was always ready to hear any jest or story that was told him, or to offer sympathy

to those who needed it. His neighbors loved
him, and he enjoyed greatly their visits. One
of them especially, Major William H. Morgan,
used to come and talk over the war and the
news of the day, and Mr. Davis never tired
of his society.

One anxiety, however, preyed upon him
dreadfully, and this was his first debt. He
had never owed one he could not pay on demand, and was sixty-five years old before he
had a law-suit. He was a strict economist in
his own person, though lavish to his family—
never refusing us anything for which he
thought he could pay.

Two successive overflows of our plantation
on the Mississippi had plunged him deeply in
debt to his commission merchant, Mr. J. U.
Payne, a man inestimably dear to my husband, and one whose nobility of soul had prevented him from distressing his friend either
to give him security or payment. This generous consideration for Mr. Davis only en-
hanced his desire to pay the debt. Our good
son-in-law's health did not permit him to remain in a malarial country without imminent
risk, so that we could not avail ourselves of
his willingness to serve us, or of his powerful
aid to extricate the estate from debt, and
God had taken to himself all our sons and
all my brothers ; so that Mr. Davis, though

too feeble for the effort, went at intervals to Brierfield, which was inaccessible, and always reached at night by the steamboats, our only means of visiting the island.

He had been for a long time very weak and unable to bear exercise, but felt it his duty to attend to his affairs. Some members of his family were visiting us, and he preferred, as his stay would be short, that I should remain with them.

He arrived at the landing at night, but had been attacked on the boat with something which now appears to have been grippe, and was too ill to get off the boat, but went on to Vicksburg and returned the next day. He arrived again at night, and drove several miles home through the malarial atmosphere.

I received a telegram from a kind young man in Mr. Davis's employment, dated November 11th, saying my husband would not have a doctor, and was in bed, and I proceeded at once to take a boat for Brierfield. We met upon the river. Captain Leathers, whom we had known, as a boy, felt an intense interest in him, and had his father's boat hailed, and found out Mr. Davis was on board. He was asleep when I met him, but waked very soon and seemed better for meeting me. Two physicians whom we consulted at Bayou Sara declared that he had

acute bronchitis complicated with grave malarial trouble.

When we reached New Orleans, before
which he had suffered intensely, a cold rain
was falling. Our friend, Mr. Payne, with his
son-in-law, Justice C. E. Fenner, met us,
with Mr. Davis's physician and friend, Dr.
Chaillé, and our nephew and niece by marriage, Mr. Edgar H. Farrar and Mrs. Stamps.

It was evident we could not carry him to
Beauvoir where he longed to be, and we accepted Judge and Mrs. Fenner's kind invitation to go to them. An ambulance was sent
from the Charity Hospital, containing a soft
bed, spread by the hands of tender Mother
Agnes, who said it was her privilege, and accompanied by four young medical students,
whose fathers had all fought in our cause,
and who were full of reverence and sympathy
for our patient sufferer, he was borne to Judge
Fenner's house, apparently uninjured by the
transfer.

In alternating hope and discouragement,
surrounded by attentions lavished upon us by
the whole family, such as could not have been
exceeded by our own children, attended by our
dear friends, Dr. Chaillé and Dr. C. J. Bick-
ham, he made a brave struggle to overcome
the unseen forces to which he at last suddenly
succumbed. His fortitude and patience were

almost divine ; he tried not to give trouble to
his nurses, and offered thanks for everything.
Once, when Mrs. Fenner gave him some nour-
ishment and left the room, he remarked:
" She would be charming even without her
strict integrity and grace ; but I am giving
her trouble. When can we relieve her and
go to our dear home ? "

Neither of his two dutiful and devoted
daughters, who, he often said, had never disobeyed or given him pain, were with their
father, whose life they rendered happy by
their love. Our eldest daughter, Mrs. Margaret Hayes, was with her family in Colorado,
and the other had been ordered by our physician and urged by her father to take a sea
voyage for her health, and was in Paris ; I
entreated Mr. Davis to let me telegraph for
them, but he answered: " Let our darlings be
happy while they can ; I may get well." Margaret came, against our advice, rendered uneasy by the press reports ; but the poor child,
owing to an accident on the train, reached us
too late to see her father alive; at the risk of
his life her husband, a much-beloved son to
us, came from his sick-bed, with like result;
and our daughter Varina, buoyed up by encouraging reports of her father's improvement
was kept in ignorance of his condition until
his death. At his request she was forbidden

to return, as she was then pronounced by her physician too feeble for the journey.

I hoped, when this memoir was begun, to portray my husband's life even unto his peaceful bed of death, and to show how his people hung about him, eager to hear of his state, and treasure every word from his lips; how gladly they seized upon the slightest hope held out by his skilful and tender physicians; and how patiently he suffered acute pain, how thankfully he received every attention offered, and how bravely he tried to live through the long weeks of physical anguish, and how, when greatly discouraged, he gently said: " I have much to do, but if it is God's will, I must submit." My strength was miscalculated, and this meagre account must suffice.

Buoyed up by his wonderful constitution, which had never been impaired by excesses, he rallied several times, and on December 6th was considered convalescent. Waking from sleep at daylight on that morning, he said to me: " I want to tell you I am not afraid to die." I begged him not to speak of so dreadful a contingency, and he smiled and dropped asleep.

In the afternoon he awoke from a sound, quiet sleep, with a congestive chill. A moment before he lost consciousness he gently

declined the medicine that, urged by hope, I
pressed upon him, in these courteous words
which were his last : " Pray excuse me, I cannot take it." In three hours his brave, true
heart had ceased to beat.

Floral offerings came from all quarters of
our country. The orphan asylums, the col-
leges, the societies, drew upon their little
stores to deck his quiet resting-place. Many
thousands passed weeping by the bier where
he lay in state, in his suit of Confederate gray,
guarded by the men who had fought for the
cause he loved, and who revered his honest,
self-denying, devoted life. His old comrades
in arms came by thousands to mingle their
tears with ours. The Governors of nine
States came to bear him to his rest. The
clergy of all denominations came to pray
that his rest might be peaceful, and to testify
their respect for and faith in him. Fifty
thousand people lined the streets as the
catafalque passed. Few, if any, dry eyes
looked their last upon him who had given
them his life's service. The noble army of
the West and that of Northern Virginia escorted him for the last time, and the Washington Artillery, now gray-haired men, were
the guard of honor to his bier.* The elo-

* I have requested from the Committee who arranged the ceremonies permission to publish their likenesses, and have given them here.

quent Bishops of Louisiana and Mississippi,
and the clergy of all denominations, delivered
short eulogies upon him to weeping thousands, and the strains of " Rock of Ages "
once more bore up a great spirit in its flight
to Him who gave, sustained, and took it again
to Himself.

A few of the Grand Army of the North
followed him, with respectful sympathy for his
people's sorrow. Our old slaves sent the
following loving letter :

"BRIERFIELD, MISS., January 12, 1890.

" To MRS. JEFFERSON DAVIS,
    " Beauvoir, Miss.

" We, the old servants and tenants of our
beloved master, Honorable Jefferson Davis,
have cause to mingle our tears over his death,
who was always so kind and thoughtful of our
peace and happiness. We extend to you our
humble sympathy. Respectfully, your old
tenants and servants,

NED GATOR,	TOM McKINNEY,
GRANT McKINNEY,	MARY PENDLETON,
MARY ARCHER,	ELIJA MARTIN,
WILLIAM NERVIS,	ISABEL KITCHENS,
TEDDY EVERSON,	HENRY GARLAND,
LAURA NICK,	WILLIAM GREEN,

GUS WILLIAMS, and others."

Thornton Montgomery, now a man of
means, the successful son of Joseph E.
Davis's old servant, Ben Montgomery, sent
the following affectionate note of sympathy :

"CHRISTINE, NORTH DAKOTA, December 7, 1889

"MISS VARINA : I have watched with deep
interest and solicitude the illness of Mr. Davis at Brierfield, his trip down on the
steamer *Leathers*, and your meeting and returning with him to the residence of Mr.
Payne, in New Orleans ; and I had hoped that
with good nursing and superior medical skill,
together with his great will-power to sustain
him, he would recover. But, alas ! for human
endeavor, an over-ruling providence has
willed it otherwise. I appreciate your great
loss, and my heart goes out to you in this
hour of your deepest affliction.

"Would that I could help you bear the burden that is yours to-day. Since I am powerless to do so, I beg that you accept my tenderest sympathy and condolence.

"Your very obedient servant,
"THORNTON.
"To MRS. JEFFERSON DAVIS, Beauvoir, Miss."

Could there have been a surer testimony to
Mr. Davis's generous, just, and Christian spirit
than that these negroes have given ; certainly
none afforded me more comfort.

The New York *World*, published by an Union soldier, uttered a noble eulogium upon him. The New York *Sun* paid an eloquent tribute to him, and ended with these words: "A great soul has passed."

Mr. James Redpath, a life-long political opponent, thus eloquently expressed his admiration of him after having been for months domesticated with him.

"Before I had been with Mr. Davis three days, every preconceived idea of him utterly and forever disappeared. Nobody doubted Mr. Davis's intellectual capacity, but it was not his mental power that most impressed me. It was his goodness, first of all, and then his intellectual integrity. I never saw an old man whose face bore more emphatic evidences of a gentle, refined, and benignant character. He seemed to me the ideal embodiment of 'sweetness and light.' His conversation showed that he had 'charity for all and malice toward none.' I never heard him utter an unkind word of any man, and he spoke of nearly all his more famous opponents. His manner could best be described as gracious, so exquisitely refined, so courtly yet heart-warm. · The dignity of most of our public men often reminds one of the hod-carrier's 'store suit'—it is so evidently put on and ill-fitting. Mr. Davis's dignity was as natural and as charming as the perfume of a rose—the fitting expression of a serene, benign, and comely moral nature. However handsome he may have been when excited in battle or debate—and at such times, I was told, he seemed an incarnation of the most poetic conceptions of a valiant knight—it surely was in his own home, with his family and friends around him, that he was seen at his best; and that best was the highest point of grace and refinement that the Southern character has reached.

" Lest any foreigner should read this article, let me say for his benefit that there are two Jefferson Davises in American history—one is a conspirator, a rebel, a traitor, and the 'Fiend of Andersonville'—he is a myth evolved from the hell-smoke of cruel war—as purely imaginary a personage as Mephistopheles or the Hebrew Devil; the other was a statesman with clean hands and pure heart, who served his people faithfully from budding manhood to hoary age, without thought of self, with unbending integrity, and to the best of his great ability—he was a man of whom all his countrymen who knew him personally, without distinction of creed political, are proud, and proud that he was their countryman."

His own people poured out their sorrow in loving and eloquent words, and held meetings in his honor in every little hamlet in our Confederate country, and the great orator of the South, Senator Daniel, of Virginia, said of him, in an oration not inferior to any that ever was delivered :

" He swayed Senates and led the soldiers of the Union, stood accused of treasons in a court of justice. . . .

" He ruled millions and was put in chains. He created a nation, he followed its bier, and he died a disfranchised citizen.

" Though great in many things, he was greatest in that fortitude which, lifting him first to the loftiest height and casting him thence to the depth of disappointment, found him everywhere the erect and constant friend of truth. He conquered himself and forgave his enemies, but he bent to none but God. No public man was ever subjected to sterner ordeals of character and a closer scrutiny of conduct. He was in the public gaze for nearly half a century, and in the fate which at last overwhelmed the Southern Confederacy at its end, official records and private papers fell into the hands of his enemies. Wary eyes searched to see if he had overstepped the bounds which the laws of war have set to action, and could such evidence have been found, wrathful hearts would have cried for vengeance. But though every hiding-place was overhauled and a reward was ready for any who would betray the secrets of the captive chief whose armies were scattered, and whose hands were chained, though the sea gave up its dead in the convulsion of his country, there could be no guilty fact, and accusing tongues were silenced. Whatever record leaped to light, his home could not be shamed. . . .

"The people of the South knew Jefferson Davis. He mingled his daily life with those who had bound up with him all that life can cherish. To his hands they consigned their destinies. Ruin, wounds, and death became their portion. And yet they declare that Davis was an unselfish patriot and a noble gentleman; that as a trustee of the highest trust that man can place in man, he was clear and faithful; and that in his office he exhibited those grand, heroic attributes which were worthy of its dignity and their struggles for independence.

"Thus it was that when the news came that he was no more, there was no Southern home that did not pass under the shadow of affliction. Thus it was that the governors of commonwealths bore his body to the tomb, and that multitudes gathered from afar to bow in reverence. Thus it was that throughout the South scarred soldiers, widowed wives,

the kindred of those who had died in battle,
met to give utterance to their respect and
sorrow. Thus it is that the general assembly of Virginia is now convened to pay this
tribute. Completer testimony to human
worth was never given, and thus it will be
that the South will build a monument to record their verdict, that he was true to his
people, his conscience, and his God, and no
stone that covers the dead will be worthier of
the Roman legend, ' Clarus et vir fortis-
simus.' "

THE END.